HESPERIA: SUPPLEMENT XXVII

PROCEEDINGS OF THE

# INTERNATIONAL CONFERENCE

ON

## GREEK ARCHITECTURAL TERRACOTTAS OF THE CLASSICAL AND HELLENISTIC PERIODS

DECEMBER 12–15, 1991

EDITED BY

NANCY A. WINTER

THE AMERICAN SCHOOL OF CLASSICAL STUDIES AT ATHENS

PRINCETON, NEW JERSEY

1994

**Library of Congress Cataloguing-in-Publication Data**

International Conference on Greek Architectural Terracottas of the Classical and Hellenistic Periods (1991 : American School of Classical Studies at Athens)

    Proceedings of the International Conference on Greek Architectural Terracottas of the Classical and Hellenistic Periods : December 12–15, 1991 / edited by Nancy A. Winter.

    p.    cm. — (Hesperia. Supplement ; 27)

    Contributions in English, French, German, Greek, and Italian.

    Includes bibliographical references (p.   –   ).

    ISBN 0-87661-527-2

    1. Architectural terra-cotta—Greece—Congresses. 2. Architectural terra-cotta—Mediterranean Region—Congresses. 3. Architecture, Hellenistic—Greece—Congresses. 4. Architecture, Hellenistic—Mediterranean Region—Congresses. 5. Architecture, Classical—Greece—Congresses. 6. Architecture, Classical—Mediterranean Region—Congresses. I. Winter, Nancy A. II. American School of Classical Studies at Athens. III. Title. IV. Series: Hesperia (Princeton, N.J.). Supplement ; 27.

NA3551.A1I58 1991

729′.5—dc20                                                                   94-35502

CIP

© American School of Classical Studies at Athens 1994

TYPOGRAPHY BY THE AMERICAN SCHOOL OF CLASSICAL STUDIES PUBLICATIONS OFFICE
C/O INSTITUTE FOR ADVANCED STUDY, PRINCETON, NEW JERSEY
PLATES BY THE STINEHOUR PRESS, LUNENBURG, VERMONT
PRINTED IN THE UNITED STATES OF AMERICA
BY THE JOHN D. LUCAS PRINTING COMPANY, BALTIMORE, MARYLAND

# TABLE OF CONTENTS

Journal Abbreviations . . . . . . . . . . . . . . . . . . . . . . . . . . . . . . v
Glossary . . . . . . . . . . . . . . . . . . . . . . . . . . . . . . . . . . . . . vii
William D. E. Coulson: Opening Remarks . . . . . . . . . . . . . . . . . . . xiii

*General*
Marie-Françoise Billot: Terres cuites architecturales, peintures et mosaïques aux V$^e$ et IV$^e$ siècles . . . . . . . . . . . . . . . . . . . . . . . . . . . . . . . . . 1

*Mainland Greece: The Peloponnese*
Mary C. Roebuck: Architectural Terracottas from Classical and Hellenistic Corinth . 39
Charles K. Williams, II: Roof Tiles from Two Circular Buildings at Corinth . . . 53
Frederick P. Hemans: Greek Architectural Terracottas from the Sanctuary of Poseidon at Isthmia . . . . . . . . . . . . . . . . . . . . . . . . . . . . . . . . . . 61
Stephen G. Miller: Sosikles and the Fourth-Century Building Program in the Sanctuary of Zeus at Nemea . . . . . . . . . . . . . . . . . . . . . . . . . 85
Klaus Hoffelner: Die Dachterrakotten des Artemistempels vom Apollon-Heiligtum in Ägina . . . . . . . . . . . . . . . . . . . . . . . . . . . . . . . . . . . 99
Calliopi Krystalli-Votsi: Αρχιτεκτονικές Τερρακότες από την Αρχαία Σικυώνα 113
Doris Gneisz: Die Dachterrakotten von Aigeira . . . . . . . . . . . . . . . . . 125
Joachim Heiden: Klassische Dächer aus Olympia . . . . . . . . . . . . . . . . 135
Petros Themelis: Hellenistic Architectural Terracottas from Messene . . . . . . 141

*Northern Greece and Albania*
Gerhild Hübner: Die klassischen Tempeldächer von Kalapodi (Phokis) . . . . . 171
Amalia Vlachopoulou-Oikonomou: Τα Σφραγίσματα Κεραμίδων από το Ιερό της Δωδώνης . . . . . . . . . . . . . . . . . . . . . . . . . . . . . . . . . . . 181
Dhimosten Budina: Architectural Terracottas from the Towns of Kaonia: Antigonea and Buthrot . . . . . . . . . . . . . . . . . . . . . . . . . . . . . . . . . 217

*The Black Sea, Aegean Islands, and Asia Minor*
Konrad Zimmermann: Traufziegel mit Reliefmäander aus dem Schwarzmeergebiet 221
Volker Kästner: Kleinasien und Griechenland. Dachterrakotten nacharchaischer Zeit aus Pergamon . . . . . . . . . . . . . . . . . . . . . . . . . . . . . . 253
Stella G. Miller: Architectural Terracottas from Ilion . . . . . . . . . . . . . . 269

## TABLE OF CONTENTS

*South Italy and Sicily*

JOHN F. KENFIELD: High Classical and High Baroque in the Architectural Terracottas of Morgantina . . . . . . . . . . . . . . . . . . . . . . . . . . . . . . 275

GIOVANNA GRECO E MARIA JOSÉ STRAZZULLA: Le terrecotte architettoniche di Elea-Velia dall'età arcaica all'età ellenistica . . . . . . . . . . . . . . . 283

PETER DANNER: Ein architektonisches Terrakottafragment hellenistischer Zeit aus Reggio Calabria . . . . . . . . . . . . . . . . . . . . . . . . . . . . . 305

BERND BRANDES-DRUBA: Einige tarentiner Architekturterrakotten . . . . . . . . . 309

LUISA VIOLA: A Late Classical Sima from Heraclea in Lucania . . . . . . . . . . 327

# JOURNAL ABBREVIATIONS

*AA = Archäologischer Anzeiger*
*AAA = Αρχαιολογικά Ανάλεκτα εξ Αθηνών*
*AbhLeip = Abhandlungen der Sächsischen Akademie der Wissenschaften zu Leipzig, Philologisch-historische Klasse*
*AdI = Annali dell'Istituto di corrispondenza archeologica*
*AION = Annali del seminario di studi del mondo classico. Archeologia e storia antica*
*AJA = American Journal of Archaeology*
*AM = Mitteilungen des Deutschen Archäologischen Instituts, Athenische Abteilung*
*AnnPisa = Annali della scuola normale superiore di Pisa*
*AntK = Antike Kunst*
*Archaeology = Archaeology. An Official Publication of the Archaeological Institute of America*
*ArchCl = Archeologia classica*
*ΑρχΕφ = 'Αρχαιολογική 'Εφημερίς*
*Architectura = Architectura. Zeitschrift für Geschichte der Baukunst*
*ASAtene = Annuario della Scuola archeologica di Atene e delle Missioni italiane in Oriente*
*Athenaeum = Athenaeum. Studi periodici di letteratura e storia dell'antichità, Università di Pavia*
*AttiMGrecia = Atti e memorie della Società Magna Grecia*
*AuA = Antike und Abendland*
*BCH = Bulletin de correspondance hellénique*
*BdA = Bollettino d'arte*
*BICS = Bulletin of the Institute of Classical Studies of the University of London*
*Boreas = Boreas. Münstersche Beiträge zur Archäologie*
*BSA = Annual of the British School at Athens*
*BSR = Papers of the British School at Rome*
*BWPr = Winckelmannsprogramm der Archäologischen Gesellschaft zu Berlin*
*CR = Classical Review*
*CronCatania = Cronache di archeologia e di storia dell'arte, Università di Catania*
*Dacia = Dacia. Revue d'archéologie et d'histoire ancienne*
*Δελτ = Αρχαιολογικόν Δελτίον*
*DialArch = Dialoghi di archeologia*
*Ἔργον = Τὸ Ἔργον τῆς 'Αρχαιολογικῆς 'Εταιρείας*
*FA = Fasti archaeologici*
*FuB = Forschungen und Berichte. Staatliche Museen zu Berlin*
*GazArch = Gazette archéologique*
*GettyMusJ = The J. Paul Getty Museum Journal*
*Gnomon = Gnomon. Kritische Zeitschrift für die gesamte klassische Altertumswissenschaft*
*Gymnasium = Gymnasium. Zeitschrift für Kultur der Antike und humanistische Bildung*
*Hesperia = Hesperia. Journal of the American School of Classical Studies at Athens*
*IstMitt = Mitteilungen des Deutschen Archäologischen Instituts, Abteilung Istanbul*
*JbBerlMus = Jahrbuch der Berliner Museen*
*JdI = Jahrbuch des Deutschen Archäologischen Instituts*
*JFA = Journal of Field Archaeology*
*JHS = Journal of Hellenic Studies*
*JRS = Journal of Roman Studies*
*Klearchos = Klearchos. Bolletino dell'Associazione amici del Museo nazionale di Reggio Calabria*

*Klio* = *Klio. Beiträge zur alten Geschichte*
*Kokalos* = Κώκαλος. *Studi pubblicati dall'Istituto di storia antica dell'Università di Palermo*
*MarbWPr* = *Marburger Winckelmann-Programm*
*MEFRA* = *Mélanges de l'École française de Rome. Antiquité*
*MemLinc* = *Memorie. Atti della Accademia nazionale dei Lincei, Classe di scienze morali, storiche e filologiche*
*MM* = *Madrider Mitteilungen*
*MonAnt* = *Monumenti antichi*
*MüJb* = *Münchener Jahrbuch der bildenden Kunst*
*NSc* = *Notizie degli scavi di antichità*
*NumAntCl* = *Numismatica e antichità classiche. Quaderni ticinesi*
*ÖJh* = *Jahreshefte des Österreichischen Archäologischen Instituts in Wien*
*OpArch* = *Opuscula archaeologica*
*OpAth* = *Opuscula atheniensia*
*OpRom* = *Opuscula romana*
*PAAR* = *American Academy in Rome. Papers and Monographs*
*Pontica* = *Pontica. Studii si materiale de istorie, arheologie si muzeografie, Constanta*
*PP* = *La parola del passato*
Πρακτικά = Πρακτικά τῆς ἐν Ἀθήναις Ἀρχαιολογικῆς Ἑταιρείας
*QArchEtr* = *Quaderni del Centro di studio per l'archeologia etrusco-italica*
*RA* = *Revue archéologique*
*RendLinc* = *Atti dell'Accademia nazionale dei Lincei. Rendiconti*
*RendNap* = *Rendiconti dell'Accademia di archeologia, lettere e belle arti, Napoli*
*RivStCl* = *Rivista di Studi Classici*
*RM* = *Mitteilungen des Deutschen Archäologischen Instituts, Römische Abteilung*
*SicArch* = *Sicilia archeologica*
*StädelJb* = *Städel-Jahrbuch*
*Taras* = *Taras. Rivista di archeologia*

# GLOSSARY

Acanthus (Fr. acanthe, It. acanto, Germ. Akanthus, Gk. ἄκανθος). A plant with large, segmented, thistlelike leaves, used also on Corinthian capitals.
acrotère. *See* Akroterion.
αγελαία κεραμίς. *See* Plain tile.
Akanthusbüschel = a cluster of acanthus leaves.
Akanthuskelch = acanthus calyx.
ακροκέραμο. *See* Antefix.
ακροκέραμος κορυφαία. *See* Ridge palmette.
Akroterion (Fr. acrotère, It. acroterio, Germ. Akroter, Akroterion, Gk. ακρωτήριον). A decorative element, such as a statue or disc, placed at the edges of the roof, either at the corners of the pediment or along the ridge.
Akroterion base (Germ. Akroterkasten). The base provided for the akroterion.
Akroterkasten. *See* Akroterion base.
αμύγδαλο. *See* Ovolo.
ανάγλυπτα φύλλα. *See* Gadroon.
antefissa. *See* Antefix.
antefissa a testa femminile = female-head antefix.
antefissa nimbata/antefissa con nimbo = shell antefix.
Antefix (Fr. antéfix, It. antefissa, Germ. Stirnziegel, Gk. ακροκέραμο). The lowermost cover tile along the eaves, consisting of a cover-tile backer closed at the front with a plaque.
Antefixplatte = antefix plaque.
Anthemienkette = anthemion chain.
Anthemion (Fr. anthemion, Germ. Anthemion, Gk. ανθέμιο). A floral chain pattern.
anthemion à double file = double anthemion.
anthemion à file simple = single anthemion.
ανθέμιον φλογωτού ρυθμού. *See* Flame palmette.
ανθεμωτός πυρήνας. *See* Palmette heart.
ανθή φλογωτού ρυθμού. *See* Flame palmette.
Astragal. *See* Bead and reel.
astragale. *See* Bead and reel.
αστράγαλος. *See* Bead and reel.
Auge. *See* Volute eye.

baccellature. *See* Tongue pattern.
baguette. *See* Torus.
bandeau. *See* Fascia, Taenia.
bastoncino. *See* Torus.

Bead and reel (It. astragale, perle e astragali, Germ. Astragal, Perlstab, Gk. αστράγαλος, χάνδρα). A painted or molded pattern of alternating round or oval beads and double vertical bands of a spool.
bec de corbin. *See* Hawksbeak.
becco di civetta. *See* Hawksbeak.
βλαστόσπειρα = volute stems.
Blatt/Blätter = leaf/leaves.
Blattkern = palmette heart.
Blattstab. *See* Tongue pattern.
Blattstabmuster = tongue-pattern design
Blattstabsima. *See* Cavetto sima.
Blüte = flower, blossom.
Blütenkelch = calyx.
Blütenstengel = flower stalk.
Blütenstern = leaf star.
Buchstabe = letter.

canale di gronda. *See* Waterspout.
Cauliculus. The small stems of an acanthus.
cavet. *See* Cavetto.
Cavetto (Fr. cavet, It. gola, Germ. Kehle, Hohlkehle, Gk. κοίλωμα). A concave molding.
Cavetto sima (Fr. sima en cavet, Germ. Blattstabsima). A raking sima with cavetto profile, generally carrying the painted decoration of a tongue pattern above a single or double guilloche.
chaînette. *See* Guilloche.
χάνδρα. *See* Bead and reel.
clair sur sombre. *See* Light-on-dark decoration.
colmo. *See* Ridge.
Combination tile (Germ. Flach- und Deckziegel, Gk. κεραμίς επίζυγος). A tile that has the pan and cover elements manufactured in one piece.
coppo. *See* Cover tile.
Corinthian sima. *See* Ovolo sima.
couvre-joint. *See* Cover tile.
Cover tile (Fr. couvre-joint, It. coppo, Germ. Deckziegel, Kalypter, Gk. καλυπτήρας). The tile designed to cover the space between adjacent pan tiles, to protect the interstices and the wooden beam below; it sits on top of the two pan tiles.
Cyma recta. A molding with an upper concave and lower convex curve in profile.
Cyma reversa. A molding with an upper convex and lower concave curve in profile.

Cyma molding (Germ. Kymation). A molding having a partly concave and a partly convex curve in profile.

cymatium. *See* Cyma molding.

dachförmig = pitched.

Dachziegel. *See* Roof tile.

Dark-on-light decoration (Fr. sombre sur clair). A system of decoration in which the pattern is painted in dark colors against a light background, comparable to black-figured vase painting.

Deckziegel. *See* Cover tile.

decor vegetal = vegetal decoration.

doccione. *See* Waterspout.

doccione leonino = lion's head waterspout.

Doric leaf. *See* Tongue pattern.

Doric tongue. *See* Tongue pattern.

Dübel = dowel.

Dübellöcher = dowel holes.

Eaves (Fr. égout, rive, Germ. Traufe). The bottom edge of a sloped roof.

Eaves tile (Fr. tuile d'égout *or* de rive, It. tegola di gronda *or* di sponda, Germ. Traufziegel *or* Traufrand, Gk. στρωτήρας ηγεμών). The bottommost pan tile of each row of overlapping pan tiles running from the ridge down to the eaves.

écailles. *See* Scale pattern.

Egg and dart (It. kyma ionico, Germ. Eierstab, ionisches Kymation, Gk. ωά και λογχοειδή φύλλα). A painted or molded decoration of alternating egg-shaped elements separated by darts.

égout. *See* Eaves.

Eierstab. *See* Egg and dart.

έλικας. *See* Volute.

émissaire d'eau. *See* Waterspout.

engobe. *See* Slip.

Entenschnabel. *See* Hawksbeak.

επαετίς σίμη. *See* Raking sima.

επένδυση. *See* Revetment plaque.

επίχρισμα. *See* Slip.

Ersatzdach = replacement roof.

Ersatzstücke = replacement pieces.

faîte. *See* Ridge.

Falz. *See* Flange.

Fascia (Fr. bandeau, It. listello di base *or* di zoccolo, Germ. Plattenborte, Sockel, Gk. φάσα). The flat, vertical part of the plaque at the bottom of a sima.

fatto a stampo = moldmade.

feuille dorique. *See* Tongue pattern.

filet. *See* Taenia.

fiori di loto. *See* Lotus.

First. *See* Ridge.

Firstpalmette. *See* Ridge palmette.

Firstziegel. *See* Ridge tile.

Flach- und Deckziegel. *See* Combination tile.

Flachziegel. *See* Pan tile.

Flame palmette (Germ. Flammenpalmette, Gk. ανθή or ανθέμιον φλογωτού ρυθμού). A palmette with flame-shaped petals.

Flammenpalmette. *See* Flame palmette.

Flange (Fr. recourvrement, Germ. Falz). An undercut tongue projecting from one edge of a piece (pan tile, raking sima) to overlap and brace against the next lower piece on the slope.

Flechtband. *See* Guilloche.

fleurs de lotus. *See* Lotus.

Form. *See* Mold.

Frontleiste. *See* Taenia.

Fruchtstengel = vegetal scrolls.

Gadroon (Gk. ανάγλυπτα φύλλα). A tongue in convex relief.

gargouille. *See* Waterspout.

Geison tile (Germ. Geisonziegel). An eaves tile with a curved soffit forming a drip.

Geisonziegel. *See* Geison tile.

gewöhnlicher Ziegel. *See* Plain tile.

Giebelsima. *See* Raking sima.

gola. *See* Cavetto.

gronda. *See* Waterspout.

gronda leonina. *See* Lion's head waterspout.

Guilloche (Fr. chaînette, tresse, It. treccia, Germ. Flechtband, Gk. πλοχμός). A cable pattern.

Hakenmäander = hook meander.

Hakenkreuzmäander = swastika meander.

half-round. *See* Torus.

Halterungszapfen. *See* Tile spacer.

Hawksbeak (Fr. bec de corbin, It. becco di civetta, Germ. Entenschnabel, Überschlagskarnies, Gk. κουκουβάγια). A concave profile that resembles the beak of a hawk.

hell-auf-dunkel-Technik. *See* Light-on-dark decoration.

Hip roof (Fr. toit à croupe *or* à aretier, Germ. Walmdach, Gk. στέγη τρίριχτη). A double-sloped roof with a third slope at one short end in place of a pediment.

Hohlkehle. *See* Cavetto.

HOOK MEANDER (Germ. Hakenmäander). A key pattern formed of gamma-shaped hooks.
υδρορρόη. *See* Waterspout.
hypaethral (Germ. hypaithral) = unroofed.

ionisches Kymation. *See* Egg and dart.

καλούπι. *See* Mold.
Kalypter. *See* Cover tile.
καλυπτήρας. *See* Cover tile.
Kehle. *See* Cavetto.
Kelch = calyx.
Kelchblätter = sepal.
kelchförmig = calyx-shaped.
κεραμίς επαετίς. *See* Raking sima.
κεραμίς παραετίς. *See* Lateral sima.
κεραμίς επίζυγος. *See* Combination tile.
κεραμίς κορυφαία. *See* Ridge tile.
κεραμίς της στέγης. *See* Roof tile.
Knospe = bud.
κοίλωμα. *See* Cavetto.
κορυφή. *See* Ridge.
κουκουβάγια. *See* Hawksbeak.
κυμάτιο. *See* Molding.
kyma ionico. *See* Egg and dart.

languette. *See* Tongue pattern.
lastra. *See* Plaque.
lastra di rivestimento. *See* Revetment plaque.
lastre. *See* Plaque.
LATERAL SIMA (Fr. sima latérale, sima d'égout *or* de rive, It. sima laterale, Germ. Traufsima, Gk. παραετίς σίμη, κεραμίς παραετίς). The sima that runs along the sides of a roof at the bottom of the slope.
λεοντοκέφαλη υδρορρόη. *See* Lion's head waterspout.
LESBIAN LEAF. A painted or molded pattern showing a pointed leaf with central spine.
lesbisches Kymation = a molded Lesbian leaf.
LIGATURE. A character combining two or more letters.
LIGHT-ON-DARK DECORATION (Fr. clair sur sombre, Germ. hell-auf-dunkel-Technik). A system of decoration in which the pattern is painted in light colors against a dark background, comparable to red-figured vase painting.
Lilienblüte = fleur de lis.
linguetta. *See* Tongue pattern.

LION'S HEAD WATERSPOUT (Ital. doccione leonino *or* gronda leonina, Germ. Löwenkopf-Wasserspeier, Gk. λεοντοκέφαλη υδρορρόη). A sculptured lion's head covering the opening through a lateral sima or akroterion base at the eaves through whose mouth rain water is discharged.
listel. *See* Taenia.
listello di base. *See* Fascia.
listello di coronamento. *See* Taenia.
listello di zoccolo. *See* Fascia.
listello superiore. *See* Taenia.
Löwenkopf-Wasserspeier. *See* Lion's head waterspout.
Lorbeerzweig = laurel branch.
LOTUS (Fr. fleurs de lotus, Ital. fiori di loto, Germ. Lotos, Lotus). A flower represented with two leaves curving outward at the top.
λουρίδα. *See* Taenia.

Magerung = grog.
Magerungsteilchen = grog particles.
matrice. *See* Mold.
matrix. *See* Mold.
Matrize. *See* Mold.
MEANDER (Germ. Mäander, Gk. μαίανδρος). A maze or key pattern.
Medusa = Gorgon.
Megarian sima. *See* Ovolo sima.
μήτρα. *See* Mold.
MOLD (Fr. matrix, moule, It. matrice, Germ. Matrize, Form, Pressform, Gk. μήτρα, καλούπι). The form into which clay is pressed to manufacture multiple copies.
MOLDING (Fr. moulure, It. sagoma, Germ. Profilleiste, Gk. κυμάτιο). A contoured ornament on the visible face of a piece.
moule. *See* Mold.
moulure. *See* Molding.

nimbo = frame.
nimbo baccellato = shell frame.

ωά και λογχοειδή φύλλα. *See* Egg and dart.
οπτός πηλός. *See* Terracotta.
ove. *See* Ovolo.
OVOLO (Fr. ovolo, It. ovolo, ove, Germ. Wulst, Gk. αμύγδαλο). A convex molding forming almost one quarter of a circle.
OVOLO SIMA (also Corinthian *or* Megarian sima, Germ. Wellensima). A raking sima with an ovolo

profile above a fascia, over which is generally painted an anthemion.

palmetta dritta *or* ritta = upright palmette.
palmetta pendula = pendant palmette.
PALMETTE. A stylized palm leaf with fanned petals.
PALMETTE HEART (Germ. Blattkern, Palmettenkern, Gk. ανθεμωτός πυρήνας). The rounded base from which the palmette petals fan out.
Palmettenkern. *See* Palmette heart.
palmettes circonscrites = circumscribed palmettes.
PAN TILE (Fr. tuile courante, It. tegola, Germ. Flachziegel, Gk. στρωτήρας). The tile designed to carry rain water off a sloped roof.
παραετίς σίμη. *See* Lateral sima.
perle e astragali. *See* Bead and reel.
Perlstab. *See* Bead and reel.
PLAIN TILE (Germ. gewöhnlicher Ziegel, Gk. αγελαία κεραμίς). The ordinary tiles of the roof slope.
πλάκα. *See* Plaque.
PLAQUE (Fr. lastre, It. lastra, Germ. Platte, Gk. πλάκα). A vertical element that can be separate or attached to one end of a cover tile (forming an antefix) or a pan tile (forming a sima).
Platte. *See* Plaque.
Plattenborte. *See* Fascia.
πλοχμός. *See* Guilloche.
Pressform. *See* Mold.
Profilleiste. *See* Molding.

ραβδόγλυφο. *See* Torus.
RAKING SIMA (Fr. sima de rampant, sima rampante, It. sima di rampante, sima rampante, Germ. Giebelsima, Schrägsima, Gk. επαετίς σίμη, κεραμίς επαετίς). The sima that runs along the edge of the pediment (the rakes).
Ranken = scrolls, tendrils.
Rankensima = scroll sima.
Rautenziegel = diamond-shaped tile.
recouvrement. *See* Flange.
Reliefmäander = relief meander.
revêtement. *See* Revetment plaque.
REVETMENT PLAQUE (Fr. revêtement, It. rivestimento, Germ. Verkleidungsplatte, Gk. επένδυση). A plaque that is generally nailed to a wooden element to protect it.
RIDGE (Fr. faîte, It. colmo, Germ. First, Gk. κορυφή). The apex of a sloped roof, at the ridge beam.
RIDGE PALMETTE (Germ. Firstpalmette, Gk. ακροκέραμος κορυφαία). An upright plaque decorated with a palmette on both faces, attached to the ridge tile.
RIDGE TILE (Fr. tuile faîtière, Germ. Firstziegel, Gk. κεραμίς κορυφαία). The uppermost pan and/or cover tile that overlaps the ridge of a sloped roof.
rive. *See* Eaves.
rivestimento. *See* Revetment plaque.
roll. *See* Torus.
ROOF TILE (Fr. tuile, It. tegola, Germ. Dachziegel, Ziegel, Gk. κεραμίς της στέγης). A piece of fired clay, generally laid on the roof to overlap and be overlapped by another, to protect the building below.
Rundstab. *See* Torus.

sagoma. *See* Molding.
scaglie. *See* Scale pattern.
SCALE PATTERN (Fr. écailles, It. scaglie, Germ. Schuppenmuster, Gk. φύλλα φολιδωτά). A painted design resembling overlapping fish scales.
Schachbrett = checkerboard.
Schrägsima. *See* Raking sima.
Schuppenmuster. *See* Scale pattern.
scrolls. *See* Volute.
sigla. *See* Tile stamp.
SIMA (Gk. σίμη). A pan tile with a vertical plaque attached along one edge to divert rain water off the roof.
sima d'égout. *See* Lateral sima.
sima de rampant. *See* Raking sima.
sima de rive. *See* Lateral sima.
sima di gronda. *See* Lateral sima.
sima di rampante. *See* Raking sima.
sima en cavet. *See* Cavetto sima.
sima latérale. *See* Lateral sima.
sima "megarienne". *See* Ovolo sima.
sima rampante. *See* Raking sima.
σίμη. *See* Sima.
SLIP (Fr. engobe, Germ. Überzug, Gk. επίχρισμα). A thin layer of purified clay spread in liquified form across the surface of the piece before firing.
sockel. *See* Fascia.
SOFFIT (Germ. Unterseite). The underside of a piece.
Sonnenblume = sunflower.
spacer. *See* Tile spacer.
σφράγισμα κεραμίδων. *See* Tile stamp.
spiral. *See* Volute.
spirale. *See* Volute.
στέγη τρίριχτη. *See* Hip roof.
Stempel. *See* Tile stamp.

Stengelkannelierung = stem fluting.
Stirnleiste. *See* Taenia.
Stirnziegel. *See* Antefix.
Stroter. *See* Pan tile.
στρωτήρας. *See* Pan tile.
στρωτήρας ηγεμών. *See* Eaves tile.

Tänie = taenia.
TAENIA (Fr. bandeau, filet, listel, tainia, It. listello di coronamento, listello superiore, Germ. Stirnleiste, Frontleiste, Tänie, Gk. ταινία, λουρίδα). A flat band running across the top of a sima or the front edge of an eaves tile.
tainia. *See* Taenia.
ταινία. *See* Taenia.
tegola. *See* Pan tile, Roof tile, Tile.
tegola di gronda. *See* Eaves tile.
tegola di sponda. *See* Eaves tile.
TERRACOTTA (Fr. terre cuite, It. terra cotta, Germ. Terrakotta, Gk. οπτός πηλός). Fired clay.
terre cuite. *See* Terracotta.
tetto = roof.
tige = stem.
tile. *See* Roof tile.
TILE SPACER (Germ. Halterungszapfen). A tenon or prong projecting from the underside of an antefix, intended to fit between eaves tiles and brace against them.
TILE STAMP (It. sigla, Germ. Stempel, Gk. σφράγισμα κεραμίδων). Letters or figural representations stamped onto plain tiles before firing.
toit = roof.
toit à croupe *or* à aretier. *See* Hip roof.
tondino. *See* Torus.
TONGUE PATTERN (also Doric leaf *or* tongue, Fr. languette, feuille dorique, It. linguetta *or* baccellature, Germ. Blattstab, Zungenmuster, Gk. φύλλο). A row of panels with rounded ends at the top.
tore. *See* Torus.
TORUS (also half-round, roll, Fr. baguette, tore, It. bastoncino, tondino, Germ. Rundstab, Wulst, Gk. ραβδόγλυφο). A convex, half-round molding.
tralci = stems.
Traufantefix = Antefix.
Traufe. *See* Eaves.
Traufrand. *See* Eaves tile.
Traufsima. *See* Lateral sima.
Traufziegel. *See* Eaves tile.

treccia. *See* Guilloche.
tresse. *See* Guilloche.
tubo di gronda. *See* Waterspout.
tuile. *See* Roof tile.
tuile courante. *See* Pan tile.
tuile faîtière. *See* Ridge tile.
tuile d'égout. *See* Eaves tile.
tuile de rive. *See* Eaves tile.

Überschlagskarnies. *See* Hawksbeak.
Überzug. *See* Slip.

Verkleidungsplatte. *See* Revetment plaque.
voluta. *See* Volute.
VOLUTE (Fr. volute, It. spirale, voluta, Germ. Volute, Volutespirale, Gk. έλικας). A band that coils into a spiral.
VOLUTE EYE (Germ. Volutenaugen, Auge). The round center around which a volute coils.
VOLUTE STEMS (Germ. Volutenranken). The flat bands that coil into spirals at the ends.
Volutenauge. *See* Volute eye.
Volutenleier = volute bands formed into a lyre pattern.
Volutenranke. *See* Volute stems.
Volutenspirale. *See* Volute.

φάσα. *See* Fascia.
φύλλα φολιδωτά. *See* Scale pattern.
φύλλο. *See* Tongue pattern.

Walmdach. *See* Hip roof.
Wasserausguss. *See* Waterspout.
Wassernase = drip.
Wasserspeier. *See* Waterspout.
WATERSPOUT (Fr. émissaire d'eau, gargouille, It. canale, tubo di gronda, doccione, Germ. Wasserausguss, Wasserspeier, Gk. υδρορρόη). The opening through a lateral sima or akroterion base at the eaves through which rain water is discharged.
Wellensima. *See* Ovolo sima.
Wulst. *See* Ovolo, Torus.

Zapfen = tenon.
Ziegel. *See* Roof tile.
Zungenmuster. *See* Tongue pattern.
Zwickelpalmetten = filling palmettes.

# OPENING REMARKS

Ladies and Gentlemen,

On behalf of the American School of Classical Studies, I would like to welcome you to the School this morning to this international conference on Greek architectural terracottas. The conference is sponsored by the American School, and I thank you all for coming.

Many of you will remember the conference on Archaic Greek architectural terracottas that was held at the School three years ago, the proceedings of which were published in the first issue of *Hesperia* for 1990. I think you will agree that the publication is an excellent one and does much to further our knowledge of Greek terracottas. That conference three years ago was of great importance since it was the first international conference on Archaic Greek architectural terracottas to be held anywhere. It was also entitled the *first* international conference. I was asked at the time whether there would ever be a second conference; the fact that we are gathered together today is, of course, proof that we are having a second conference. The subject is so limitless that we may even have a third conference, or a fourth, and so on.

The subject of the first conference was Greek architectural terracottas of the Archaic period. This conference moves slightly forward in time to treat the architectural terracottas of the Classical and Hellenistic periods. The papers range widely and cover most of the ancient world from mainland Greece to the Black Sea, Asia Minor, and Southern Italy and Sicily. The concentration is, however, on the Peloponnese, and the first day is devoted to a discussion of the architectural terracottas from sites in the Peloponnese. The second day expands the geographical parameters to include sites in Albania, the Black Sea region, Asia Minor, and Sicily and Southern Italy. These last papers will be of the utmost importance in broadening our knowledge of the development of Greek architectural terracottas.

The two-day excursion that follows the conference has been planned so that sites where important new discoveries have been made can be visited: Corinth, Olympia, Messene, and Elis. It will be especially important to see this material, and on behalf of the School, I would like to thank the ephoreias of Prehistoric and Classical Antiquities at Nauplion and Olympia for their kindness in allowing our visits. I would also like to thank Nancy Bookidis for arranging the display at Corinth, Joachim Heiden for the display at Olympia, Nikos Yalouris for Elis, and Petros Themelis for Messene. A special opening of the exhibition of architectural terracottas from the Akropolis has been arranged to coincide with this conference. The exhibition is housed in the Akropolis Study Center at Makriyanni, and we are grateful to the Akropolis ephoreia and to Cornelia Hatziaslani for arranging the special opening of this important exhibition.

This conference could never have taken place without the initiative of the Librarian of our Blegen Library, Nancy Winter, and without the generosity of the anonymous donor who, as with the previous conference, has provided the funds for the conference. As you can imagine, the planning of this conference has entailed a lot of work, and on behalf of the School I would like to thank Nancy Winter for making everything happen so smoothly. Robert Bridges, the School Secretary, has supervised the audiovisual equipment, and Ioanna Driva, our Comptroller, has handled all the financial arrangements. Our principal receptionist, Christina Traitoraki, has done the translations of the abstracts found in your conference packets. The School's Administrative Assistant, Maria Pilali, and Cashier, Niamh Michalopoulou, helped with the planning. And two of our students, Sheila Dillon and Blanche Menadier, have also assisted. To all these and to the other staff of the School, whose names it would be impossible for me to mention individually, we are all very grateful.

The staff of the School joins me in wishing this conference every success.

WILLIAM D. E. COULSON
Director

AMERICAN SCHOOL OF CLASSICAL STUDIES
54 Souidias Street
GR-106 76 Athens
Greece
December 15, 1991

# TERRES CUITES ARCHITECTURALES, PEINTURES ET MOSAÏQUES AUX Vᴱ ET IVᴱ SIÈCLES

(Plates 1–8)

CES RÉFLEXIONS[1] pourraient aussi s'intituler «Remarques sur la constitution de quelques styles décoratifs de l'architecture». Indépendants et créateurs, les peintres sur terres cuites et marbres architecturaux et les mosaïstes restent néanmoins en étroite relation avec les peintres de vases, les bronziers, les orfèvres et les sculpteurs. Ils opèrent volontiers, dans les répertoires communs à plusieurs arts, quelques choix de motifs et d'interprétations. Je me propose d'analyser, d'un matériau architectural à l'autre—terre cuite, pierre et marbre, mosaïque—, la part des créations, des emprunts et des interprétations qui assurent la diversité ou l'unité du décor végétal ou abstrait des édifices sensiblement contemporains dans une même région. Une enquête complète ne saurait tenir dans les limites de cette étude. Les terres cuites architecturales seront le point d'ancrage d'une recherche dans deux secteurs géographiques différents, Athènes et le Péloponnèse, à deux époques différentes, le Vᵉ et le IVᵉ siècle.

## I. SITUATION DU PROBLEME

I.1. *Quelques exemples empruntés à l'archaïsme tardif introduiront plus efficacement ce propos* (Pl. 1 et 2).

I.1.1. Aux marges du groupe des simas dites «mégariennes»[2] (par ex. Pl. 1:b), fabriquées nombreuses à Corinthe et imitées ailleurs, caractérisées par leur profil et par leur anthémion

---

[1] Plusieurs conversations avec A.-M. Guimier-Sorbets sont à l'origine de cette étude. J'ai tiré grand profit de la lecture de trois volumes inédits qu' elle a consacrés à *La mosaïque dans le monde grec, des origines jusqu'à la fin de l'époque hellénistique*, qui décrivent la banque de données qu'elle a créée sur ces mosaïques: voir Guimier-Sorbets 1990, *passim*, et en particulier pp. 261–265. Il y a plusieurs années déjà, H. A. Thompson et W. B. Dinsmoor, Jr., m'ont accueillie à plusieurs reprises au Musée de l'Agora avec leur générosité légendaire et m' ont patiemment montré les terres cuites architecturales, les marbres peints, les dessins et les aquarelles qu'en avaient faits Piet de Jong, M. Welker et W. B. Dinsmoor, Jr. lui-même, qui m'aida à les photographier. A G. Dontas, naguère Ephore des Antiquités de l'Acropole, et à M. Brouskari, je dois d'avoir pu examiner à plusieurs reprises les terres cuites architecturales et plusieurs marbres peints de l'Acropole, notamment les caissons des Propylées, et de vérifier que les dessins de T. I. Willson étaient fiables. A. Jacques, Conservateur de la Bibliothèque de l' ENSBA (Paris), a bien voulu me permettre de publier des dessins inédits d'A. Paccard, dont M. Antilogus et J.-M. Lapèlerie m'ont fourni les photos. D'autres documents m'ont été aimablement communiqués par Ch. K. Williams, II, Directeur des Fouilles de Corinthe, et par N. Bookidis (Corinth Excavations), par J. McK. Camp, Directeur des Fouilles de l'Agora d'Athènes, et par J. Diamant-Jordan (Agora Excavations), par P. G. Kalligas, Ephore des Antiquités de l'Acropole, et par Ch. Vlassopoulou, par D. Salzmann qui a bien voulu mettre à ma disposition ses propres clichés, par J.-Cl. Hurteau (IRAA-CNRS) qui les a reproduits, par N. Lazaridou (Deutsches Archäologisches Institut, Athen), par K. Christofi, M. Sfakianoudi, L. Trouki et Ph. Collet (École Française d'Archéologie). Le dessin de la Figure 1 est dû à K. G. Kolokotsas, celui de la Figure 2, à C. Billot et Y. Rizakis. Que tous veuillent bien trouver ici l'expression de ma très amicale et profonde gratitude.

[2] D'après le type—profil et décor—de la sima du Trésor de Mégare à Olympie: Herrmann 1974, pp. 75–83, pl. 36–39, Beil. I; pour d'autres exemples, voir Le Roy 1967, pp. 96–113 et 121–127, pl. I, 33–39 et 43–45;

à double file en alternance,[3] se trouve celle de Toronè[4] (Pl. 1:a) : bien que respectant la même disposition de l'anthémion, elle emprunte la morphologie de ses lotus et leur liaison croisée à la céramique attique, aux vases d'Euphronios[5] dirait-on (par ex. Pl. 1:c), ce qui permet de la dater vers la fin du VIe siècle sans grande marge d'erreur. C'est peut-être l'exemple le plus frappant de la mobilité des répertoires que nous aurons souvent à constater : de Corinthe à Athènes, de la céramique à l'architecture.

I.1.2. Le décor des simas du Temple des Alcméonides de Delphes, malaisé à déchiffrer, a été plusieurs fois dessiné, notamment pour la publication.[6] Resté méconnu, un relevé inédit effectué par l'architecte H. Lacoste quelques années plus tard,[7] paraît plus fiable (Pl. 1:d). Il donne l'impression que le peintre a composé entre l'origine athénienne des commanditaires et la provenance parienne du marbre : de même que le profil, les palmettes très aérées relèvent du répertoire des céramiques et des marbres athéniens, notamment des simas du Télestérion d'Eleusis et du Temple d'Athéna des Pisistratides;[8] les lotus sont empruntés au répertoire cycladique alors bien représenté au Trésor de Siphnos[9] et peut-être déjà au Trésor

---

Heiden 1987, pp. 61–102, pl. 7–11, planches de profils 3–6; Roebuck 1990, pp. 55–59, fig. 2, pl. 6, 7. Par exemple ici Musée d'Argos C. 27517, Pl. 1:b.

[3] Vocabulaire architectural et décoratif emprunté à Ginouves et Martin 1985, pp. 178–179, pl. 61:7.

[4] Musée de Polygyros inv. 78.703: Cambitoglou 1978a, p. 28, fig. 31; Cambitoglou 1978b, p. 86, pl. 73:b; d'où Touchais 1979, pp. 587 et 589, fig. 149; Αρχαία Μακεδονία—Ancient Macedonia, n° 167, p. 224 avec fig. (fin du VIe siècle).

[5] *Euphronios*, fig. pp. 62, 68–69, 78–79, 90, 97, 110, 116–117, 119, 121, 129, 138. Bien que ce schéma de liaison se perpétue jusqu'aux environs de 470 (par ex. col de l'amphore du P. d'Oreithyie, Munich 2345, Arias et Hirmer 1960, fig. 158, 159), la sima étant traitée en figure noire, il n'y a pas de raison de la dater beaucoup plus tard que 500 av. J.-C. On remarquera sur les vases cités et sur bien d'autres que les palmettes s'opposent aux palmettes, les lotus aux lotus («anthémion à double file et à correspondance», cf. Ginouves et Martin 1985, pp. 178–179), comme très fréquemment sur la céramique attique depuis 570 env. et plus tard encore, ainsi que sur les simas attiques de la fin du VIe et du Ve siècle : Buschor 1929, simas n°s X/XI et XVI à XXI, fig. 20–23, 38–47 et 51, pl. 1 et 7–10; Vlassopoulou 1989, n°s 41–43 et 66; Vlassopoulou 1990, n°s 41–43, 63 et 65. La sima de Toronè est un intermédiaire sûrement attique entre, d'une part, les simas «mégariennes» corinthiennes ou corinthianisantes dont elle reprend le profil et l'anthémion à double file et à alternance, et d'autre part, la céramique attique pour la forme des lotus et l'articulation des deux files par des tiges entrelacées. Elle est aussi un intermédiaire contribuant à susciter, à Athènes même, d'autres essais authentiquement athéniens (simas X/XI à double file de palmettes correspondantes, Buschor 1929, fig. 20–23, pl. 1; Vlassopoulou 1989 et Vlassopoulou 1990, n°s 41–43) et des imitations corinthianisantes (simas XIII à XV et XXVII, Buschor 1929, fig. 31–33 et 37, pl. 3–6 et 11, avec anthémion à double file et à alternance; cf. Vlassopoulou 1990, n° 56).

[6] Courby 1927, pp. 102–103, pl. XIII. Ohnesorg 1993, pp. 38–40, pl. 83.

[7] Athènes, Ecole Française d'Archéologie, Planothèque, dessin n° 400; De La Coste-Messelière 1942–1943, p. 67, fig. 13 au centre et n. 2.

[8] Noack 1927, pp. 67–68, fig. 31; Shoe 1936, pl. XVIII, 10; Wiegand 1904, pp. 119–122 (fig. 118), et 124–126, pl. X, 1:a et b; De La Coste-Messelière 1942–1943, p. 67, fig. 13 au centre et n. 2. Ohnesorg 1993, pp. 41–44, frontispice, pl. 84, 85.

[9] Daux et Hansen 1987, encadrement de la porte: pp. 121–137, pl. 54–60; soffites de larmiers horizontaux: pp. 190–197, pl. 87–95; simas: pp. 215–221, pl. 101–103. On peut aussi rapprocher la fleur de lotus de celles de la frise de calcaire marneux: De La Coste-Messelière et De Miré 1957, p. 310, fig. 16.

de Marseille (*ca* 500 av. J.-C.).[10] Ainsi se crée une harmonie décorative entre le grand temple dorique et d'autres monuments du même sanctuaire.

I.1.3. A l'oeuvre dans le même temps ou quelques années plus tard, le peintre des épicranitis du Trésor des Athéniens[11] s'est formé dans les officines athéniennes de vases; il y a préparé ses cartons, deux anthémions différents de palmettes circonscrites pour la cella[12] (Pl. 2:b), un anthémion de palmettes circonscrites et de fleurs de lotus pour le pronaos[13] (Pl. 2:a). Ce transfert de la céramique à l'architecture—que les formes végétales rendent possible dès la dernière décennie du VI$^e$ siècle[14]—n'est pas simple copie, mais s'accompagne d'une création originale : on chercherait en vain sur les vases un anthémion qui alterne des palmettes circonscrites et cette forme de lotus que l'on ne rencontre, à la fin de l'archaïsme et au début de l'époque sévère, qu'isolée à l'extrémité d'une tige (par ex. Pl. 2:c).[15] Tenu à une lisibilité et à une symétrie parfaites, le peintre a soigneusement dessiné le calice de sépales à base doublement incurvée comme si elle épousait le tracé de deux volutes divergentes échappées de la tige. Ce type de calice à deux larges sépales concaves restera longtemps

---

[10] Larmier et simas du Trésor «de Marseille»: Daux 1923, pp. 68 et 78, fig. 69 et pl. XXIII. Les anthémions delphiques ont été utilement rapprochés par E. Langlotz dans le cadre d' une interprétation générale qui fait la part belle à Phocée: Langlotz 1975, pp. 47–48, pl. 7. Mais G. Gruben et son école revendiquent pour cycladiques l'architecture et le travail du marbre parien du Trésor de Marseille: Schuller 1991, pp. 88–112 *passim*. Et une fleur de lotus comparable est encore peinte dans le 2$^e$ quart du V$^e$ sur la sima, en marbre de Paros, du «Thesmophorion» de Délos: Vallois 1978, pp. 356–358; Bruneau et Ducat 1983, n° 48, pp. 159–160; Mertens-Horn 1988, pp. 58–59, pl. 14:c; Ohnesorg 1991, p. 176, fig. 9; Ohnesorg 1993, pp. 32–33, frontispice, pl. 32.

[11] Le débat sur la date de l'édifice oppose désormais trois thèses: 1) celle d'un édifice commémorant, d'après Pausanias (10, 11, 5), la victoire de Marathon, donc édifié peu après; 2) celle d'un édifice entièrement construit dans les dernières années du VI$^e$ siècle, vraisemblablement pour célébrer la réforme de Clisthène et l'avènement de la démocratie (état du débat et bibliographie principale de ces deux thèses par Kleine 1973, pp. 94–97, et Tölle-Kastenbein 1983, pp. 580–581; 3) celle d'un édifice construit en marbre de Paros à la même époque, peut-être donc pour les mêmes circonstances, jusqu'à la frise comprise, et achevé dans un autre matériau quelques années plus tard, a) nécessairement avant 490, et même avant l'achèvement du temple d'Aphaia à Egine disent les spécialistes plus sensibles aux caractères anciens non seulement de sa sculpture mais aussi de l'architecture des parties hautes de l'édifice (par ex. Bankel 1990, p. 410–412; Bankel 1993, pp. 157–172; Schuller 1991, pp. 107–111, b) après 490 disent ceux qui en retiennent au contraire les caractères les plus récents (par ex. Büsing 1979; Büsing 1988, pp. 29–32). Mon propos n'est pas d'alimenter par la date de ces décors peints le débat dont Dinsmoor 1946, pp. 86–121, et De La Coste-Messelière 1953, pp. 179–182 ont, chacun à leur manière, montré la vanité: il est vraisemblablement antérieur à 490 dans les hypothèses 2 et 3 a, postérieur à 490 dans les hypothèses 1 et 3 b. Mais je suis convaincue que ceux des épicranitis précèdent celui du linteau de la porte (*infra*, p. 25).

[12] Audiat 1933, pp. 45–46, pl. XXIII; effectué par A. Tournaire, le relevé inédit de l'anthémion du mur de refend (Planothèque de l'Ecole Française d' Archéologie, ici Pl. 2:b) paraît plus fiable que celui de la pl. XXIII.

[13] Audiat 1933, p. 45, pl. XXII.

[14] *Euphronios*, pp. 54–55, 155 et 159 pour les anthémions de palmettes, sans compter les compositions de surface, par ex. pp. 54–55, 110–111, 127, 133 et 239 (Smikros); pour les lotus à sépales renflés avec découpe inférieure en arc de cercle et à pétales latéraux individualisés en lame de faux, voir pp. 114, 169, 176 et 227 (Oltos), ou sur l'amphore nicosthénienne d'Oltos, Paris, Musée du Louvre G. 2, Arias et Hirmer 1960, fig. 99.

[15] Par ex. encore chez le P. de Pistoxénos: Boardman 1989, fig. 68.

commun aux vases et aux marbres; nous le retrouverons sur une sima en marbre de l'Acropole (ci-dessous I.1.4), plus tard au Parthénon et peut-être au Temple d'Athéna Niké.

I.1.4. A l'Acropole d'Athènes, la décoration des «Palmettensimen» d'un même toit résulte de transferts du même ordre : aux rampants, comme dans la cella du Trésor des Athéniens, des anthémions de palmettes circonscrites directement transcrits du répertoire des vases (Pl. 2:e); à l'égout, comme au pronaos du Trésor, un anthémion de palmettes et de lotus (Pl. 2:d);[16] on dirait les fleurs redevables à l'atelier de Douris,[17] avec la même codification du calice de sépales qu'au trésor delphique. Les palmettes, aérées, non circonscrites, sont communes aux vases comme aux marbres (voir la sima du Temple des Pisitratides). Les «Palmettensimen» sont associées à l'architecture E, datée de 490–480.

I.1.5. Revenons un instant à l'épicranitis du pronaos du Trésor des Athéniens, précisément aux lotus (Pl. 2:a). On peut les comparer à ceux des épicranitis du Temple d'Aphaia à Egine, si l'on en croit les dessins de Haller von Hallerstein[18] et de C. R. Cockerell[19] qui ont complété mutuellement leur documentation constituée lors de leur expédition commune à Egine en 1811.[20] Si l'on admet avec M. Schuller et H. Bankel que le Trésor des Athéniens est un peu antérieur au Temple d'Aphaia à Egine et que tous deux sont l'oeuvre d'une même «école d'architecture» attico-cycladique, la présence de lotus comparables dans le décor des deux édifice ne serait pas surprenante.

Le chapiteau d'ante du Temple d'Aphaia (Pl. 1:f) associe dans un même anthémion des palmettes circonscrites purement attiques et des lotus purement cycladiques.[21]

Enfin sur la sima, dans le dessin partiel que nous en a laissé Cockerell[22] (Pl. 1:e), le lotus de type cycladico-corinthien présente un détail emprunté à certaines simas corinthiennes

---

[16] Wiegand 1904, pp. 168–171 et 182, pl. X, 2:a et b et 3; Schuchhardt 1963, col. 812–819, fig. 15–17; Ohnesorg 1991, p. 176, fig. 8. Pour partie découverte en 1835 dans les fouilles profondes que L. Ross fait faire au Sud du Parthénon (Ross 1855, pp. 102–103 et n° 4), elle figure dans le très bel album de dessins de Poppe 1843–1845, pl. XVIII, fig. 1; elle est aussi dessinée par E. Landron pour Le Bas 1847, pl. II:5, II et III (reproduit dans *Paris-Rome-Athènes*, p. 96, fig. 58).

[17] Paris, B.N. inv. 542, coupe de Prométhée et d'Héra: Boardman 1975, fig. 295; Cleveland, Museum of Art, lécythe inv. 66.114: Kurtz 1975, pl. 11. Voir aussi un stamnos du P. de Syleus, Boardman 1975, fig. 195.

[18] H. Bankel, dans Bankel 1986, catalogue des dessins du Temple d'Aphaia conservés à la Bibliothèque Nationale Universitaire (BNU) de Strasbourg, p. 238, n° 2090 (BNU, Ms. 2724¹, 8, Aegina); Bankel 1993, pp. 61, 111, 158, 174 et 177, fig. 90, pl. 36:1, 38:1 et 48:1.

[19] Cockerell 1860, pl. IX, fig. 1, cf. pl. V, fig. 2.

[20] Cf. Furtwängler 1906, fig. 15, pl. 41, pp. 47–48: «Cockerell und Haller haben noch jenes prächtige, feinlinige Spiralband mit Lotosblüten auf den bekrönenden Gesimsen des Innen gesehen und gezeichnet, dessen Motiv wir hier in Abb. 15 wiedergeben. Uns Späteren war es nicht mehr vergönt auch Spuren davon zu entdecken». Voir aussi *Paris-Rome-Athènes*, pp. 104–105, fig. 68 et 70. Ce décor a été relevé aussi par Blouet et Poirot 1838, pl. 53 (relevé et restitution du détail, reporté ensuite comme décor sur la face antérieure du larmier dans la restitution; voir *Paris-Rome-Athènes*, p. 103, fig. 65).

[21] Bankel 1986, pp. 128–129, fig. 4:8 à 4:10; Bankel 1993, pp. 68–70, fig. 36–38, pl. 20, 21.

[22] Cockerell 1860, pl. XIII, fig. 3 et 4. Le décor est incomplet; L. Fenger en a proposé une restitution complète, symétrique par rapport à un axe horizontal, éventuellement possible pour le tracé des tiges végétales, mais très évidemment inspirée de la sima XVII de l'Acropole (Buschor 1929, fig. 41, pl. 7) : Fenger 1886, pl. VI, n° 6; intuition juste? Elle s'est trouvée au moins soutenue par la découverte de la sima du T. de Poséidon de Sounion, dont le profil archaïsant est très proche de celui de la sima du T. d'Aphaia: Dinsmoor, Jr. 1974b,

de terre cuite[23] (par ex. Pl. 1:b), l'extrémité commune des tiges jointives taillée en sifflet et donnant pratiquement naissance au pétale central; la forme de la palmette libre est aussi très corinthienne.

Ces quelques exemples d'ornements composites, aux emprunts clairement définis, qui font le style d'une pièce, d'un atelier d'architecture, d'une époque, d'une contrée, incitent à rechercher ce qui constitue la part spécifique des terres cuites, des marbres peints et des mosaïques des Ve et IVe siècles dans le décor architectural de leur époque et de leur région. Il s'agit de mettre en valeur les parentés et les différences qu'entretiennent, sur quelques caractères précis, les répertoires propres ou communs de ces arts qui, tous, relèvent du dessin et de la peinture.

I.2. *Les difficultés de méthode inhérentes à ce genre de recherches sont connues :*
- la polychromie—motifs décoratifs et couleurs—des architectures de marbre et de calcaire a largement disparu, le répertoire graphique s'est restreint, le contexte colorié s'est oblitéré, au profit de la teinte naturelle du calcaire et du marbre.
- Beaucoup d'éléments fonctionnels et décoratifs sont morcelés et éparpillés, à jamais séparés de leur édifice d'origine, de ses autres décors, de ses couleurs et du paysage architectural.
- La pénurie et l'incertitude des repères chronologiques, à l'origine de débats sans cesse renaissants, posent des problèmes accrus lorsque les travaux ont duré longtemps : faut-il dater un décor de l'époque où l'ouvrage a été sinon conçu, du moins commencé, de celle où les pièces ont été préparées au sol, de celle où elles ont été mises en place, ou des ultimes finitions avant que les échafaudages ne soient retirés? Toujours invoquées en la matière, les simas des temples d'Asclépios à Epidaure et d'Apollon à Delphes sont en fait chacune, dans un contexte différent, des cas d'espèce qui ne peuvent être généralisés à toutes les parties sculptées et/ou peintes de tous les édifices.
- Du reste, notre ignorance reste considérable du détail des projets, des précisions graphiques et orales qui accompagnaient ou non l'exécution d'une *syggraphè*, de la liberté laissée aux décorateurs et de la manière dont un chantier était conduit.

Toutefois, il semble que le matériel actuellement disponible pour l'Attique du Ve et pour certaines créations péloponnésiennes du IVe siècle favorise la reprise d'une réflexion de ce genre, tout comme nous l'avons vue possible pour le style décoratif attico-cycladique aux alentours de 500 av. J.-C.

## II. TERRES CUITES ET MARBRES ARCHITECTURAUX EN ATTIQUE AU Ve SIECLE

Aucune mosaïque ornementale n'étant connue en Attique au Ve ni au début du IVe siècle, ce qui nous reste du décor architectural polychrome de cette époque se partage entre les terres cuites et les marbres.

---

pp. 221–226, ill. 12–15, pl. 42. Bankel 1993, pp. 103–107, 112 et 158, fig. 61, 62 et 91:b, pl. 32:1–3 et pl. 53:2 (dessins de C. Haller von Hallerstein).

[23] Par ex. Corinthe FS 28: Roebuck 1990, pl. 7.

II.1. *Simas et antéfixes de terre cuite à décor végétal* (Pl. 3).

### II.1.1. Données archéologiques.

Cet ensemble très séduisant reste, en dépit de la publication rigoureuse d'E. Buschor, d'un abord délicat. Trop de ressemblances s'y mêlent, trop de formes identiques sous des compositions à peine diversifiées. Faute de différences très marquées, ni les profils, ni les décors n'esquissent de séquence assurée; aucune correspondance univoque ne peut s'établir entre eux.

Plusieurs fragments, que leur décor échelonne en réalité de la fin du VIe au milieu du Ve siècle, ont été trouvés dans les épaisses couches souvent cendreuses découvertes et fouillées dès le XIXe siècle au Sud du Parthénon, sous les déchets de taille du temple[24] : or la stratigraphie très profonde et difficile de cette région située entre l'édifice et le mur de Cimon, ainsi que la chronologie absolue (et parfois relative) des couches—stratigraphie et chronologie dont dépendent la date du Pré-Parthénon et la solution de nombreux autres problèmes— restent l'objet de complexes et vives controverses;[25] en particulier, contrairement à certaines convictions encore vivaces à l'époque où E. Buschor rédigea sa publication,[26] ce qui passa longtemps pour le «Perserschutt» ne contenant que les restes d'édifices antérieurs à 480 apparaît maintenant, en grande partie, comme une vaste zone de déblais constitués à partir de la reprise progressive des travaux sur l'Acropole[27] et susceptible d'inclure aussi des éléments architecturaux des années 479–447, voire, par endroits, plus récents.[28]

Enfin, aucune attribution certaine à un édifice précis ne justifie la moindre date.[29]

---

[24] Ross 1855, pp. 73, 102, 103–112 et 138–139; ses renvois à Poppe 1843–1845, pl. IV, X, XIV et XVIII permettent de situer la région où ont été trouvés certains fragments, mais n'indiquent rien sur l'aire de dispersion de la série à laquelle ils appartiennent, ni surtout la profondeur à laquelle ils ont été trouvés. Or la stratigraphie et la chronologie de cette région restent très controversées (voir note suivante), en dépit des fouilles effectuées entre 1885 et 1890 (Cavvadias et Kawerau 1906–1907), puis en 1896–1897. Historique des fouilles du XIXe siècle dans ce secteur: Carpenter 1970, p. 18.

[25] Après les travaux de W. Dörpfeld, d'A. Tschira, de R. Carpenter et de J. A. Bundgaard, état de la question et bibliographie très utiles par Drerup 1981, pp. 21–38, pl. 4 et 5. Plus brièvement Tölle-Kastenbein 1983, pp. 581–582. Des travaux récents dans le Parthénon ont montré que les blocs remployés du Pré-Parthénon ont subi les effets d'un violent incendie; il serait donc antérieur à 480, mais dans la seule mesure, toujours, où aucun autre incendie n'est connu par les textes que celui de 480/79 : Touchais 1988, p. 612.

[26] Buschor 1929, p. 24; suivi avec quelque imprudence par Vlassopoulou 1989, p. 8, et Vlassopoulou 1990, p. viii.

[27] Si l'on veut bien admettre que le «Serment de Platées» est un faux authentique.

[28] Voir par ex. Büsing 1969, pp. 1–30; Boersma 1970, pp. 42–64; Tölle-Kastenbein 1983, pp. 581–583. D'après les références données par L. Ross à l'album de Poppe 1843–1845, certains des fragments trouvés dans l'épaisse couche de débris située sous les déchets de taille du Parthénon sont effectivement d'époque archaïque, ainsi les simas X/XI; les autres appartiennent aux simas XII, XIII, XIV et XX/XXI, aux tuiles d'égout XIII, XIV, XV et aux antéfixes XII. Si la plupart de ces pièces peuvent être antérieures à 450, les tuiles d'égout XIII (Buschor 1933, pp. 14–15, fig. 17–18, pl. 7; Vlassopoulou 1990, n° 44) sont très probablement du milieu du siècle, car elles reproduisent une branche d'olivier à groupes de trois feuilles que l'on rencontre chez le P. des Satyres laineux et chez le P. des Niobides (Billot 1976, pp. 89–92; ajouter l'hydrie du P. des Niobides, British Museum E 198, *CVA, British Museum* 6, p. 4, pl. 87:3–4 et un cratère de son atelier: Epifanio 1982, pp. 347–356, pl. 85–89). Les simas XX/XXI restent à dater. Pour les simas X/XI, voir ci-dessous.

[29] En raison de l'angle aigu (K 103) formé par la sima XXII (Buschor 1929, pp. 44–45, pl. 11) et la tuile d'égout XXI (Buschor 1933, p. 19, fig. 27–28), cet ensemble avait été attribué par E. Buschor à la

II.1.2. Caractéristiques du repertoire.

Dans la perspective de cette étude, il nous faut ici souligner quelques caractéristiques de cet ensemble :

II.1.2.a. Dès la fin du VIe siècle, les simas, les antéfixes et les tuiles d'égout sont probablement façonnées et certainement peintes dans les officines de vases, sinon par les grands maîtres, du moins par les ouvriers chargés, dans leurs ateliers, des décors secondaires. Elles sont exécutées avec les mêmes vernis, les mêmes couleurs, et cuites suivant les mêmes techniques.[30] Bien que cette proximité des deux productions céramiques se distende à partir de la seconde moitié du Ve siècle avec l'apparition de nouveaux répertoires, elle ne disparaît pas avant le premier quart du IVe siècle.

Il en résulte des indications chronologiques précieuses, dont il faut faire un usage spécifique et prudent.

Il en résulte aussi que le conservatisme des ornements secondaires des vases se reflète sur les simas et sur les antéfixes :

• de même que l'anthémion à double file (par ex. Pl. 1:c) se perpétue au bas des cratères en cloche, sur la panse des hydries, sur le col des amphores et des cratères à volutes etc., de même, il s'impose sur les simas attiques au détriment de l'anthémion à file simple, réservé aux simas de faible hauteur[31] (sima XII, Pl. 3:b) et aux tuiles d'égout.[32]

• Ce phénomène est favorisé par le fait que sur les vases attiques, l'anthémion à double file oppose presque toujours, depuis le VIe siècle, les palmettes aux palmettes et les lotus aux lotus (anthémion à double file en correspondance); de même sur plusieurs simas.[33] Ainsi, l'anthémion à simple file de la sima XII de l'Acropole[34] (Pl. 3:b) apparaît en quelque sorte comme la moitié supérieure de l'anthémion de la sima XIX (Pl. 3:e) par exemple.[35]

• Les hydries du Peintre de Meidias[36] reproduisent encore vers 410 les anthémions de palmettes circonscrites, innombrables depuis la fin de l'archaïsme. De même, les schémas des simas attiques incluent volontiers la palmette circonscrite.[37] Sur les unes et les autres, l'élément complet se compose en pratique d'une palmette entourée d'une tige formant sous le coeur deux boucles adossées, à partir desquelles les deux extrémités alors divergentes poursuivent chacune un parcours en S. Cet élément structure indifféremment un anthémion à file simple de palmettes et de lotus (sima XII, Pl. 3:b), un anthémion à file double en alternance où les tiges assurent une liaison croisée dans l'interprétation attique des simas

---

Chalkothèque. Mais si l'édifice doit être restitué sur plan rectangulaire, cette attribution en est écartée : La Folette 1986, pp. 75–87, pl. 20–24.

[30] F. Gräber dans Dörpfeld 1881, pp. 14–16. Wiegand 1904, pp. 183–184.

[31] Buschor 1929, sima XII, pp. 24–27, fig. 26–29 et 35, pl. 2 (H = 10,2–10,5 cm.); Vlassopoulou 1989, n° 53, et Vlassopoulou 1990, n° 52. Une sima d'Eleusis (H = 8 cm.).

[32] Par ex. Agora A 1983 et A 821.

[33] Buschor 1929, simas X/XI, XVII à XXI. Musée de l'Agora inv. A 3886. Deux simas d'Eleusis. Une sima mise au jour au carrefour des rues Apellou, Eupolidos et Lycourgou: Alexandri 1968, p. 42, pl. 24:α, ici Pl. 3:f.

[34] Buschor 1929, pp. 24–27, fig. 26, pl. 2.

[35] Buschor 1929, pp. 40–41, fig. 45, pl. 8. Comparer, par exemple, avec l'anthémion à double file du cratère Palerme inv. G. 1283, du P. des Niobides : Arias et Hirmer 1960, fig. 176, 177.

[36] Par ex. Arias et Hirmer 1960, fig. 214 (British Museum inv. E. 214) et 216 (Florence, Museo Archeologico, inv. 81947).

[37] Par ex. Buschor 1929, simas X/XI, XII, XIII, XIV, XIX.

«mégariennes» (simas XIII [Pl. 3:c], XIV et XXII),[38] ou encore un anthémion à file double en correspondance où les tiges dessinent une lyre (sima XIX, Pl. 3:e).[39]

• A partir de 480 environ, le P. de Syleus et le P. de Pan (entre autres) réintroduisent, par exemple sur la célèbre pélikè d'Héraclès et de Busiris (Athènes, Mus. Nat. inv. 9683),[40] une fleur de lotus déjà archaïsante (voir Pl. 1:c et 2:f),[41] créant ainsi un type d'anthémion simple qui perdure sur les vases jusqu'aux environs de 430, et contribue, autant que les palmettes circonscrites qui en sont l'autre élément, à l'unité stylistique des simas XII à XIX (Pl. 3:b–e).

• Enfin, comme nous le verrons, la file de lyres opposées (simas XX/XXI, Pl. 3:h)[42] est acclimatée sur les vases depuis 490–480 (amphores et lécythes de Nole) et dure jusqu'à la fin du siècle. Sur les cols d'amphore, sur les épaules des lécythes, une superbe palmette ogivale, le plus souvent enfermée dans une lyre, se tient au centre de rinceaux souvent très développés et peuplés de palmettes : déployé, simplifié, le motif se retrouve pour longtemps sur les antéfixes.

II.1.2.b. En effet, ce conservatisme ornemental des vases se renforce d'un conservatisme propre aux terres cuites architecturales. Routine des fabrications, mode et, peut-être, souci de l'harmonie du paysage architectural suffisent à expliquer l'unité du corpus.

S'agissant des simas, cette unité tient beaucoup à l'adéquation réciproque des profils et de l'anthémion à double file. Le passage paraît assuré du profil «mégarien» (ci-dessus pp. 1–2), caractérisé par une rupture entre le bandeau inférieur plan et la courbure, et dont relève encore la sima du Télestérion d'Eleusis (*supra*, n. 8), au profil des simas en marbre de l'Hécatompédon, du Temple des Alcméonides et du «Thesmophorion» de Délos,[43] où la transition entre les deux parties produit un profil complet en *cyma reversa*. C'est à cette dernière famille que se rattachent la plupart des profils de simas de terre cuite; aucune évolution linéaire[44] ne s'y laisse discerner, mais seulement le profil très tendu des simas XVI et XIX. En tout état de cause, l'anthémion à double file convient particulièrement à ce type de profil en deux parties équilibrées et fondues.

Seule la sima XV (Pl. 3:d), par la césure de son profil, par ses palmettes libres et par ses tiges végétales en S indépendants se rapproche réellement des simas «mégariennes»,

---

[38] Buschor 1929, pp. 27–30 et 44–45, fig. 31–33, pl. 3, 4 et 11; Vlassopoulou 1990, n° 56.

[39] Buschor 1929, pp. 40–41, fig. 45, pl. 8.

[40] Beazley 1974, pl. 7–9. Pélikè du P. de Syleus (coll. Niarchos, Paris): *Münzen und Medaillen A.G., Kunstwerke der Antike, Auktion XVIII*, 29. Nov. 1958, n° 114, pl. 36, pp. 39–40; Boardman 1975, fig. 197.

[41] Fleur archaïsante, car elle remonte au moins à l'époque des simas de l'Hécatompédon, avec ses pétales latéraux en lame de faux incurvée pour épouser le tracé des tiges, son pétale ou pistil central en goutte ou larme, et ses deux groupes de trois étamines : Schuchhardt 1935/36, pp. 1–98, pl. 1–21. L'interprétation peinte en petit format qu'en donne par exemple l'atelier d'Euphronios, avec le pétale central losangé ou fusiforme (*Euphronios*, pp. 62, 68, 78, 90, 97, etc.), est reprise dans les années 480–470 et persiste sur les vases et sur les simas, avec une variante exceptionnelle sur la sima XV dont le lotus remonte aux sources plus anciennes (ci-dessous n. 46).

[42] Buschor 1929, pp. 41–44, fig. 46, 47, 50, 51, pl. 9, 10.

[43] De La Coste-Messelière 1942–1943, p. 67; Ohnesorg 1993, pl. 32, 83 et 84.

[44] Buschor 1929, fig. 35, 36.

notamment du groupe traité en «clair sur sombre»[45] (premier tiers du Ve siècle). En même temps, elle se situe dans la postérité directe de la sima de l'Hécatompédon par les détails de la facture du lotus au pétale central en forme de goutte et aux étamines distinctes, arrondies et groupées par trois[46] (Pl. 2:f). Elle assure donc pleinement la continuité avec le VIe siècle.

De manière plus triviale, les peintres de simas n'hésitent pas à exploiter toutes les possibilités des mêmes cartons, ainsi pour la sima trouvée au carrefour des rues Eupolidos, Apellou et Lycourgou (Pl. 3:f; *supra* n. 33) : les séries X/XI (Pl. 3:a) à anthémions doubles de palmettes correspondantes en sont le modèle premier; mais la liaison par arceaux verticaux est abandonnée au profit de lyres comme sur la série XIX (Pl. 3:e); la petite fleur de lis, à qui lotus et palmettes des simas XIX à XXI (Pl. 3:e et h) font généreusement place, se glisse ici à grand-peine entre des palmettes congénitalement trop rapprochées.

II.1.3. CHRONOLOGIE.

Dans ces conditions, et faute de trouvailles récentes stratifiées, nous ne pouvons qu'indiquer les quelques points sur lesquels la chronologie d'E. Buschor doit être abaissée.

II.1.3.a. Les simas X/XI (Pl. 3:a) restent les plus anciennes,[47] datées des années 520–500 par un unique argument d'ordre strictement stylistique[48] : en raison de leurs palmettes à multiples feuilles longues, minces et très serrées, elles ne peuvent avoir été conçues que dans l'orbite de Psiax,[49] d'Epiktètos,[50] d'Oltos surtout;[51] ces palmettes disparaissent dès la fin du VIe siècle du répertoire des vases, et ne subsistent que par copie dans celui des simas (par ex. Pl. 3:f) et des antéfixes. Deux traits de pure originalité, sans modèle connu sur les vases : l'alternance des palmettes à feuilles nombreuses et serrées avec les palmettes habituelles à feuilles peu nombreuses, larges et espacées, et l'arceau vertical qui relie les deux files de

---

[45] Buschor 1929, pp. 34–35, fig. 37, pl. 5. Pour les simas mégariennes en clair sur sombre, voir Le Roy 1967, pp. 121–127, pl. 43–45 et 102: Roebuck 1990, pp. 59–60, fig. 2, pl. 7. Ajouter une pièce trouvée à Sicyone et publiée ici même par K. Krystalli-Votsis; Krystalli-Votsis 1987, pl. 53:a.

[46] Cf. n. 41. A défaut de l'Hécatompédon, un autre édifice archaïque d'Athènes a pu fournir le modèle, ou même une stèle funéraire comme celle du New York Metropolitan Museum, inv. 17.230.6, où l'on note que les groupes de sépales sont liés par un bandeau: Richter 1961, pp. 19–20, fig. 73–76.

[47] Font partie des mêmes séries ou leur sont directement apparentés et proviennent du même atelier les fragments Louvre CA 1687 (Buschor 1929, p. 23) et CA 1689, qui proviennent de l'Acropole, deux fragments trouvés par N. Platon tombés au flanc Sud de l'Acropole à l'Asclépiéion (Platon 1963, p. 18, pl. 14:β et γ), un fragment conservé à la Johns Hopkins University (Reeder Williams 1984, n° 67, p. 99), le fragment d'angle Musée de Agora A 3885 et une sima d'Eleusis.

[48] Il est vrai que la plupart des nombreux fragments ont été trouvés à grande profondeur dès 1835, mêlés à des restes de charpente carbonisée et qu'ils portent eux-mêmes des traces d'incendie: Ross 1855, p. 102; Buschor 1929, p. 24. Sans aucun doute, l'édifice a été incendié. Mais en raison des incertitudes de la stratigraphie et de la chronologie, nous ne pouvons dire qu'il l'ait été en 480/79 (voir aussi *supra* n. 25).

[49] Boardman 1975, p. 17, fig. 12.

[50] Epiktètos: Boardman 1975, fig. 67; mais dans son oeuvre, les palmettes à feuilles très nombreuses sont généralement un peu plus aérées, par ex. Boardman 1975, fig. 66.

[51] Par ex. l'embouchure de la célèbre amphore nicosthénienne Louvre G. 2 : Charbonneaux, Martin et Villard 1968, fig. 364; et sur la plupart des coupes, de part et d'autre des anses : par ex. Boardman 1975, fig. 61; voir aussi une coupe de Pheidippos (Boardman 1975, fig. 79), une autre du P. de Délos (Boardman 1975, fig. 83), mais sur cette dernière, les feuilles sont déjà plus individualisées.

l'anthémion et qui, lui aussi, disparaît par la suite. Du reste, ces trois disparitions prouvent par la négative à quel point le style des simas attiques est soutenu par celui des vases. Ne subsistera qu'une nouveauté décorative, la branche de laurier sur le listel de couronnement; l'étroitesse des marges chronologiques ne permet pas de dire s'il s'agit, là encore, du transfert aux simas d'un motif inauguré dans le même temps sur les vases, ou si, bien plutôt, le peintre des simas en a donné l'idée à un atelier du début du V$^e$, d'Hermonax par exemple.[52]

A la fois têtes de liste et sans suite, les simas X/XI représentent encore maintenant, dans le contexte athénien, le premier transfert d'un profil du marbre à la terre cuite, et, avec la sima de Toronè, la première adaptation du répertoire des vases en architecture, sous l'influence des simas «mégariennes».

II.1.3.b. La sima XV (Pl. 3:d), les tuiles d'égout XVIII et les antéfixes XIV qui lui sont à peu près sûrement associées[53] représentent une autre forme de compromis entre l'influence corinthienne et le style athénien, entre le marbre et la terre cuite. Malheureusement, rien ne permet de préciser leur date dans le premier tiers du V$^e$ siècle.

II.1.3.c. Alors que Buschor pensait pouvoir situer les simas XII à XIV dans le premier quart ou tiers du V$^e$ siècle,[54] la facture de l'anthémion au lotus archaïsant ne les rend guère possibles avant 480 (voir ci-dessus).

L'apparition du motif de lyres horizontales garnies de palmettes vers 490, notamment sur les amphores de Nole (P. d'Eucharidès, de Pan, de Dutuit etc.) établit le *terminus a quo* des simas XVI à XXI,[55] ce qui n'impose évidemment pas que les plus anciennes d'entre elles, XVI et XVII, doivent être datées aussi tôt[56] : la file de lyres à palmettes dure au moins jusqu'à la fin du troisième quart du siècle et connaît son époque de gloire sur les cratères et les hydries de 465 à 430 environ.

La palmette à coeur remplacé par une palmette plus petite à feuilles multiples et serrées des simas XII à XVII et des antéfixes XII à XVI[57] est empruntée aux stèles pariennes du dernier quart du VI$^e$ et du début du V$^e$ siècle.[58]

En définitive, le *terminus a quo* des simas XII à XVII et des antéfixes XII à XVI se situe dans la décennie 480–470.

---

[52] Boardman 1975, pp. 193–194, fig. 352.
[53] Buschor 1933, pp. 17–18, fig. 25 et pp. 48–49, fig. 61–63, pl. 9; Vlassopoulou 1990, n$^{os}$ 58 à 60; ensemble daté entre 480 et 450 (Buschor 1929, p. 39).
[54] Buschor 1929, pp. 24–30.
[55] Jacobsthal 1927, pl. 51, 52, 74; Boardman 1975, fig. 164 (P. d'Eucharidès) et 339 (P. de Pan); Petit Palais G. 203 du P. de Dutuit : Kurtz 1975, pp. 14 et 125–126, pl. 55:3. Cratère trouvé à Agrigente, du groupe de Pezzino, 500–490 av. J.-C. : Schefold 1975, fig. 309.
[56] Buschor 1929, pp. 35–38, fig. 38–43, pl. 6 et 7; datées par E. Buschor, p. 39, entre 480 et 450, ce que n'autorise pas le soffite de la sima XVI, qui impose une date postérieure au milieu de siècle.
[57] Buschor 1933, pp. 45–50, fig. 59–64, pl. 7–10; Vlassopoulou 1989, n$^{os}$ 46–49; Vlassopoulou 1990, n$^{os}$ 46–49 et 59. Hübner 1973, pp. 73–77, fig. 1 et 2, pl. 57:1.
[58] Stèles sculptées à Paros et exportées vers Naxos, Théra, Amorgos, Egine, Thèbes, Samos, l'Eubée (Karystos) et Salamine. Certaines présentent une petite palmette superposée à la grande en guise de coeur: Buschor 1933a, pp. 43–46, Beil. XV und XVI; Karousos 1934, p. 61, fig. 46; Marangou 1986, pp. 124–125, pl. 49, 50. Déjà sur une palmette d'angle du geison horizontal du Trésor de Siphnos: Daux et Hansen 1987, pl. 87, 88.

Ainsi, les simas XII à XV, les antéfixes XII et des tuiles d'égout XIII (*ca* 450), XIV et XV, dont plusieurs fragments ont été trouvés sous la couche de déchets de marbre du Parthénon (ci-dessus n. 28), sont de nature à renforcer doutes et recherches sur le contenu et la date des couches en place et des remblais superposés entre le Parthénon et le mur Sud de l'Acropole, et sur les circonstances réelles dans lesquelles ils se sont progressivement accumulés. Elles confirment que l'on a recommencé à construire sur l'Acropole peu après Salamine et Platées.

### II.1.4. L'Architecture, domaine distinct.

Les simas constituent par ailleurs une production spécifique et destinée à des édifices où la lisibilité des décors est primordiale; aucun détail n'est donc laissé au hasard de l'exécution, même plus ou moins heureuse et soignée. Cette différence de nature et d'échelle avec les vases stimule la précision du détail, et suscite par exemple la création de calices de sépales (simas XVII [Pl. 3:g], XIX, cf. XX),[59] traditionnels pour les fleurs de lotus libres des vases de la fin de l'archaïsme et du style sévère,[60] mais inhabituels dans le type d'anthémion que reproduisent les simas XII, XIII, XIV et XV (Pl. 3:b–d).

### II.1.5. Reflexions sur le décor architectural peint à la fin du VIe et dans la première moitié du Ve siècle.

Nous venons d'observer l'ampleur des *transferts* de décor des vases aux simas et aux antéfixes de terre cuite.

Nous avions aussi noté deux exemples de transferts du répertoire des vases à celui des marbres, les épicranitis du Trésor des Athéniens (I.1.3, Pl. 2:a, b) et les «Palmettensimen» de l'Acropole (I.1.4, Pl. 2:d, e) : ils s'accompagnent d'une interprétation plus structurée des fleurs de lotus et de leur insertion dans des types d'anthémions qui, à même époque, ou bien ne comportent pas de fleur (comparer l'anthémion canonique, de palmettes seulement, de la cella du Trésor des Athéniens, à l'anthémion créé pour le pronaos), ou bien en offrent des formes différentes.

Nous avons par ailleurs constaté qu'à la fin du VIe et au premier tiers du Ve siècle, la peinture sur marbre atteste des liens tant avec la sculpture, notamment dans l'orbite des architectures cycladiques—sima du Temple des Alcméonides (Pl. 1:d), sima et chapiteau d'ante du Temple d'Aphaia (Pl. 1:e et f), sima du Thesmophorion de Délos—qu'avec le décor des vases (palmettes des simas du Télestérion d'Eleusis, du Temple d'Athéna des Pisistratides, du Temple des Alcméonides [Pl. 1:d], du chapiteau du Temple d'Aphaia [Pl. 1:f], épicranitis du Trésor des Athéniens [Pl. 2:a, b], «Palmettensimen» de l'Acropole [Pl. 2:d, e]). Le répertoire des simas et antéfixes de terre cuite, lui, ne s'inspire que de celui des vases; leurs anthémions archaïsants assurent du reste une tradition inattendue de la sima en marbre du Vieux Temple d'Athéna (*ca* 566, Pl. 2:f) aux simas XII et suivantes, notamment XV (Pl. 3:b–d), par l'intermédiaire des vases d'Euphronios, du P. de Pan et de beaucoup d'autres.

Toutefois, nous n'avons pas reconnu de liens privilégiés entre peintres sur marbre et peintres sur terre cuite. Du seul recours des uns et des autres aux décors de vases relèvent et les parentés stylistiques et les différences d'interprétation : empruntés à la même céramique à figure rouge de l'archaïsme récent, les lotus des simas XII à XIX d'une part, ceux de

---

[59] Buschor 1929, fig. 41 et 45, pl. 7–9; Vlassopoulou 1990, n° 63.
[60] Par ex. encore sur la coupe de Berlin F 2547, du P. du Mariage, 460–450 av. J.-C. : *CVA, Berlin* 3, pl. 109.

l'épicranitis du Trésor des Athéniens ou des «Palmettensimen» d'autre part, semblent, une fois parvenus dans le domaine architectural, intransmissibles de la terre cuite au marbre et *vice versa*.

A ce point de divergence, il nous faut poursuivre l'enquête sur les marbres peints du Ve siècle.

II.2. *Marbres peints à décor végétal* (Pl. 4 à 6).

Certains sont d'accès[61] ou de lecture difficile; sur la plupart, la polychromie a disparu, et les contours sont souvent évanides. En attendant que les investigations entreprises dans le cadre des restaurations l'Acropole livrent des documents supplémentaires, et que, partout, l'application de nouvelles techniques photographiques et des dessins d'interprétation complètent et renouvellent la documentation, l'étude doit souvent passer par un examen comparé et critique des dessins originaux qui ont été publiés depuis le XVIIIe siècle. Quelques inédits viendront ici les compléter.

Outre les anthémions, compositions linéaires, les marbres peints offrent aussi des compositions de surface sur plan carré ou rectangulaire, réservées au soffites de geisons d'angle et aux caissons des plafonds. Les structures des compositions apparaissant d'emblée comme l'un des termes de comparaison les plus immédiats entre les répertoires respectifs de la terre cuite et des marbres, nous les examinerons d'abord, avant de rappeler les formes des éléments (palmettes, fleurs) propres au décor des marbres.

II.2.1. LES COMPOSITIONS.

II.2.1.a. *Anthémions à file simple de palmettes circonscrites et de fleurs de lotus.*

• Athènes, Agora, portique, épicranitis naguère attibuée à la Stoa Poikilè[62] (Pl. 4:a, restitution aquarellée par M. Welker).

Thompson 1950, p. 327; Meritt 1970, pp. 236–237 et 250–251, pl. 62 (A 1710) et 64:b; *Agora* XIV, pp. 90–91.

Le lotus s'ouvre au bout d'une tigelle adventice.

La modénature de l'ensemble architectural auquel appartient cette épicranitis se laisse dater peu avant le milieu du Ve siècle, juste avant l'Héphaistéion.

• Athènes, Agora, linteau au lionnes peintes (Pl. 4:b, restitution aquarellée par Piet de Jong).

Stevens 1954, pp. 169–184, pl. A et 39–48, en particulier pl. 39, 41–46; *Agora* XIV, p. 31 n. 32.

Daté dans le 3e quart du Ve siècle. Parmi les emplois possibles, G. P. Stevens propose qu'il provienne d'une fenêtre ouverte dans le mur de refend qui sépare le pronaos et la cella de l'Héphaistéion.

• Athènes, Temple de l'Ilissos, architrave du pronaos, fasce supérieure (Pl. 4:d).

---

[61] On ne connaît le décor de l'épicranitis du grand temple d'Athéna Sounias que par une mention de Dinsmoor, Jr. s.d., p. 49: «The crowning course of the wall had a delicate lotus-and-palmette design».

[62] Depuis que la Stoa Poikilè a été effectivement mise au jour, cette attribution n'est plus rappelée, car elle mérite sans doute plus ample étude: Shear 1984, pp. 1–57, pl. 1–16; Camp 1986, pp. 68–72; Camp 1990, pp. 101–109.

Dessin de J. Stuart pour Stuart and Revett 1762, chap. II, p. 10, pl. VIII fig. 3 (cf. fig. 2A).[63]

Il est probable que ce décor faisait partie des finitions proches de la mise en place de la frise. Connue par la publication des Dilettanti, très proche de celle du Temple d'Athéna Niké, l'architecture du Temple de l'Ilissos a longtemps été attribuée au même architecte, Callicratès. B. Wesenberg, faisant la synthèse entre les données épigraphiques, archéologiques, architecturales et stylistiques, a récemment montré que le Temple d'Athéna Niké a été commencé dans les années 437–435, en tout cas en même temps que les travaux d'extension du Bastion et peu après le début de la construction des Propylées, sur un plan qui reproduit le temple archaïque et tient compte de l'environnement architectural, mais n'a pas de rapport organique avec celui du Temple de l'Ilissos.[64] Dans l'état actuel de la recherche, le sort des deux édifices semble donc devoir être disjoint, même si l'analyse des formes architecturales et des élévations les rapproche l'un de l'autre et des Propylées, et si l'attribution du Temple de l'Ilissos à Callicratès n'est pas sérieusement ébranlée.

La frise a longtemps opposé les tenants de la date haute proposée par F. Studniczka (années 448–445) à ceux d'une date basse; récemment, C. A. Picon et A. Krug[65] ont plaidé les années 425–420. Par ailleurs, selon B. Wesenberg, le style des bases laisserait supposer que l'édifice a été commencé lui aussi aux environs de 435, peu de temps après celui d'Athéna Niké; acceptant la date récente de la frise, il suppose pour cet édifice ce qu'il essaie de démontrer pour le Temple d'Athéna Niké (voir ci-dessous), une interruption des travaux par la guerre du Péloponnèse en 432/1 et une reprise en 425/4. Dans le même temps, M. M. Miles défend la thèse d'une construction menée à bien en très peu de temps dans les années 435–430, époque retenue par E. B. Harrison pour la frise.[66]

Quelques années plus tard, W. A. P. Childs défend à nouveau une date haute de l'édifice qui aurait été entièrement construit dans les années 445–440.[67] Mais il faut bien dire que l'argumentation qu'il développe à partir de l'analyse architecturale tendrait plutôt à soutenir celle de M. M. Miles et à dater l'édifice, au moins jusqu'à l'architrave, des années 437–432, car les parentés de son élévation avec celle des Propylées et du Temple d'Athéna Niké restent indéniables.

La date du décor oscille donc, provisoirement, entre 432 et 420 av. J.-C.

• Athènes, Parthénon, sima (Pl. 4:f, g).

Paccard 1845–1846 (Collection École des Beaux-Arts [EBA], prise en charge n° 2208) : 1) le dossier d'études préliminaires qui ne font pas partie de l'*Envoi* proprement dit contient un relevé sur calque inédit (ici Pl. 4:f) : au recto, à la mine de plomb (en clair sur la photographie), relevé effectué sur deux ou trois lotus à cinq pétales variant légèrement de largeur et de place par rapport à l'axe vertical de la fleur, et à deux sépales de hauteurs différentes d'une fleur à l'autre; au verso, au crayon gras pour permettre un report sur un dessin définitif,

---

[63] Redessiné dans l'édition française de C. P. Landon (Firmin Didot 1808), chap. II, pl. XII, fig. 3, et dans la deuxième édition anglaise de 1825, qui reproduit en fait l'édition française.
[64] Wesenberg 1981, pp. 28–54.
[65] Picon 1978, pp. 47–81; Krug 1979, pp. 7–21, pl. 1–9; Ridgway 1981, pp. 88–89.
[66] Miles 1980, pp. 309–325, pl. 91–96; bibliographie et état de la question pp. 309–310; Harrison 1981, p. 233.
[67] Childs 1985, pp. 207–251, pl. 43–45; état de la question pp. 207–211.

une «restitution» harmonisant les variations de l'entraxe du motif, complétant la palmette, réduisant la largeur de la tige périphérique, et supprimant les hypothèses d'un sépale médian et d'un losange sous le coeur de la palmette; A. Paccard retient les sépales les plus hauts; 2) dans l'*Envoi* (Paccard 1845–1846, sous le n° 18 [*Paris-Rome-Athènes*, pp. 162 et 170]), un relevé de la partie inférieure du motif (mine de plomb et encre de Chine sur papier) indiquant que la palmette comprend 11 feuilles à simple courbure.[68] Dessin de T. I. Willson pour Penrose 1851, p. 56, pl. I; palmettes complétées à 13 feuilles.[69] Dessin de L. et M. Magne pour Collignon 1912, pl. 21 et 41; palmettes et lotus abusivement restitués. Orlandos 1976–1978, pp. 556–557, fig. 386, fig. en couleur p. 643, pl. 74 (ici Pl. 4:g).

Pour les parties les plus difficiles à lire sur le marbre, l'accord se fait sur 11 feuilles de palmette à une seule courbure (A. Paccard dans ses relevés mais non dans sa restitution, L. et M. Magne, A. K. Orlandos); elles sont minces et espacées (A. Paccard, A. K. Orlandos). L'accord se fait aussi sur la fleur de lotus à deux sépales triangulaires, évasés, jointifs des tiges végétales, et à 5 pétales longs, minces et recourbés (A. Paccard, F. C. Penrose, A. K. Orlandos); le relevé de Paccard laisse penser que les pétales sont peut-être trop évasés sur d'autres reproductions, en tout cas trop courts sur celle d'A. K. Orlandos, et que les sépales sont jointifs à leur naissance, dans l'axe, entre les volutes. La restitution de A. K. Orlandos suit peut-être de trop près celle de T. I. Willson. Mais l'exécution a pu varier d'une pièce à l'autre de la sima.

La date du décor dépend du déroulement du chantier: sima peinte au sol[70] ou en place et posée au plus tard en 438, si l'édifice était complètement édifié lorsqu'il a été consacré? Sima peinte au sol avant 438 mais posée après l'installation des sculptures tympanales (l'édifice pouvait être hors d'eau sans que les simas soient posées)?[71] Sima peinte et posée (ou *vice versa*) immédiatement après l'installation des sculptures tympanales et des larmiers rampants? La fourchette théorique de réalisation se tient entre 440 env. et 432. Mais l'exécution des frontons laissait un temps suffisant à celle des simas. La dernière solution paraît donc la plus vraisemblable, et le décor serait des années 435–432.

• Athènes, Temple d'Athéna Niké, sima.

Le décor n'a été longtemps connu que par un seul fragment découvert lors des fouilles effectuées par L. Ross sur l'Acropole en 1836, peut-être lors des destuctions de la batterie et des murs byzantins sur la façade occidentale des Propylées : Ross 1855, p. 109 n. 1;

---

[68] Il est donc surprenant qu' A. Paccard restitue une palmette d' angle de 11 feuilles à double courbure sur Paccard 1845–1846, n° 9: *Paris-Rome-Athènes*, pp. 162 et 167. Ce dessin de la sima d'angle est malheureusement reproduit par De Laborde 1848, pl. 45; Michaelis 1871, p. 114, pl. II:9; Orlandos 1976–1978, fig. 384 et pl. 73:γ; Bühlmann 1872, p. 10, pl. VI F. 9, donne un dessin qui pourrait reposer sur un relevé original: la palmette est, comme toujours, complétée par erreur à 13 feuilles, mais elles sont à simple courbure et la fleur est identique à celle qu'A. Paccard a relevée.

[69] Reproduit par Michaelis 1871, p. 190, pl. VII:9; Orlandos 1976–1978, pl. 74, mais avec, p. 557, une critique incompréhensible: les fleurs de lotus ont été correctement relevées; ce sont les palmettes, restituées à 13 feuilles, qui sont fautives. La restitution de Lambert 1877, n° 1 (*Paris-Rome-Athènes*, pp. 252–253 et couverture) s'inspire de celle de F. C. Penrose.

[70] Sur la préparation en atelier de diverses pièces d'architecture, dont les caissons et les tuiles: Carpenter 1970, p. 117.

[71] Voir par ex. Wesenberg 1983, p. 76: «Spätestens 438/37 bei Vollendung der Parthenos muss der Tempel bis auf die Giebelskulpturen weitgehend fertiggestellt, muss zumindest die Cella unter Dach gewesen sein».

A. R. Rangabé en fait exécuter un dessin qu'il publie sur une planche de l' Ἀρχαιολογικὴ Ἐφημερίς de novembre 1837 (entre les pp. 36 et 37) et commente dans le fascicule de décembre 1837, p. 52. Poppe 1843–1845, pl. XIV, fig. 3. E. Landron pour Le Bas 1847, pl. 8, IV.[72] Dessin de Ricardo, *ca* 1844, reproduit par Lethaby 1908, fig. 157, p. 158. Orlandos 1947–1948, pp. 30–33, fig. 20–26, pl. II. Un nouveau fragment portant les traces d'une palmette a été retrouvé tout récemment : Büsing 1990, p. 74.

Comme l'a noté A. K. Orlandos, la palmette comporte 11 feuilles à courbure simple et non 13 à courbure double, ce qui écarte sur l'un et/ou l'autre point les dessins d'E. Landron et de Ricardo. La courbe des pétales latéraux est parallèle à celle de la tige (photographie, dessin commandé par A. R. Rangabé, dessins de C. Poppe, d'E. Landron et de Ricardo) : ils sont moins évasés que ne l'indique A. K. Orlandos. Sur ces quatre dessins exécutés indépendamment les uns des autres dans les années 1837–1844, le calice de sépales ressemble beaucoup à celui qu'A. Paccard dessine pour le décor du Parthénon, avec deux sépales en triangles longs et sinueux, bien individualisés mais jointifs à la naissance et incurvés suivant les volutes. Il se peut que A. K. Orlandos ait accusé l'évidente ressemblance de cette sima avec celle du Parthénon dans le sens de l'interprétation que T. I. Willson donne de cette dernière.

La date de la sima du Temple d'Athéna Niké dépend à nouveau de la durée et de la conduite du chantier. Frises et frontons sont désormais unanimement situés dans les années 425–420, aux alentours du décret *IG* I² 25 (= *IG* I³ 1, 36, 424/3) qui rend effective la rémunération d'une prêtresse et doit être contemporain de la consécration du temple.[73] B. Wesenberg[74] a montré qu'il n'y avait pas d'inconvénient 1) à laisser au décret *IG* I² 24 (= *IG* I³ 1, 35) une date relativement haute qu'impose sa graphie, 2) à admettre ce qu'impose l'archéologie, à savoir que la construction du temple n'a commencé que peu de temps après le début de celle des Propylées de Mnésiclès, voire simultanément, et que les deux édifices ainsi que l'extension et la surélévation du Bastion ont été menés de front, 3) à continuer à croire que le temple est bien l'oeuvre de Callicratès, du moins dans son premier état. Car entre ces débuts et l'élaboration de la frise, il y aurait eu interruption : elle intervient très probablement en 432, avec la guerre du Péloponnèse. L'édifice, colonnades incluses, s'élève alors jusqu'aux architraves comprises. Le tribut triplé en 425/4 permet la reprise des travaux, et d'abord une modification du plan : les piliers et leur architrave sont introduits entre les antes. Puis l'édifice s'achève rapidement.

L'hypothèse d'une interruption des travaux tend à justifier l'écart chronologique réel de dix à quinze ans entre le début du chantier et l'achèvement du temple. La coïncidence du changement de plan et d'élévation avec la reprise des travaux est l'autre hypothèse, majeure, de ce scénario qui n'est pas absolument convaincant.

En effet, puisque l'édifice était prêt à recevoir une frise lorsque les travaux ont été, selon B. Wesenberg, interrompus, il est surprenant que l'on n'ait pas trace d'une frise des années 435–430 : elle aurait dû être alors presque achevée. Par ailleurs, le changement de plan

---

[72] Reproduit par Bühlmann 1872, pl. 12 F. 9.

[73] Délivorrias 1974, pp. 50, 148–149, 182, 185–187 (état de la question); Despinis 1974, pp. 8–24, pl. 1–24; Ridgway 1981, pp. 40 et 89–93; Ehrhardt 1989, pp. 119–127, pl. 21–22; Brouskari 1989, pp. 115–118, pl. 20.

[74] Wesenberg 1981, pp. 28–54; état de la question pp. 28–31; rappel des données archéologiques sur la séquence des travaux à l'angle Sud-Ouest de l'Acropole pp. 42–46.

et l'élévation des piliers ont pu intervenir avant l'interruption supposée des travaux, ce qui expliquerait que l'exécution d'une frise ait été remise à plus tard. Enfin, pareille modification pourrait aussi expliquer que les travaux aient tout simplement duré, les circonstances aidant, sans être nécessairement interrompus.

Quoi qu'il en soit, l'anthémion qui décore la périphérie extérieure et intérieure de la cella, piliers compris, date probablement de l'époque des ultimes finitions (ci-dessous I.2.1.g). Que penser de la sima, qui ressemble tant à celle du Parthénon et que l'on dirait confiée par Callicratès au même atelier ? Si elle a été prévue, voire réalisée, dès avant la modification du plan et/ou l'éventuelle interruption des travaux, pour n'être finalement utilisée[75] que dans les dernières années 420, elle peut être contemporaine de celle du Parthénon. Sinon, il faut admettre qu'elle en est, quelque dix à quinze ans plus tard, la copie réduite.

II.2.1.b. *Compositions de surface de palmettes circonscrites, sans ou avec fleurs de lotus.*
• Athènes, Parthénon, un caisson de plafond du pronaos ou de l'opisthodome (Pl. 6:d) et le soffite du geison d'angle Sud-Ouest (Pl. 6:b).
\* Caisson de plafond du pronaos ou de l'opisthodome (Pl. 6:d).
Dinsmoor, Jr. 1974a, fond de caisson D 1, pp. 139 et 154, fig. 5, pl. 21.

Suivant que les caissons ont été peints au sol ou en place,[76] leur date oscille entre 442 env. et 432 si l'on admet que des travaux de finition ont pu durer jusqu'alors. Mais la réalisation en atelier paraît de beaucoup la plus facile et la plus économique, et la mise en place ne risquait pas vraiment d'endommager les pièces. Une date aux environs de 440 paraît donc vraisemblable.

\* Soffite du geison d'angle Sud-Ouest (Pl. 6:b).
Paccard 1845–1846, n° 18 (*Paris-Rome-Athènes*, pp. 162 et 170) où figure, en partie surimposée au relevé, une restitution :[77] «J'ai été assez heureux pour retrouver le bel ornement qui se trouvait aux quatre angles de l'édifice et qui décorait les plafonds compris entre les mutules d'angle; cet ornement, qu'aucun architecte encore n'avait dessiné, se trouve presque en entier à l'angle nord-ouest du Parthénon. J'ai été assez heureux également pour pouvoir en restaurer les parties effacées, en retrouvant un ornement presque entièrement semblable sur un vase grec» (*Mémoire* [EBA ms 241], p. 71 = *Paris-Rome-Athènes*, p. 365). Dessin de T. I. Willson pour Penrose 1851, pl. I, p. 56. Dessin de L. et M. Magne pour Collignon 1912, pl. 21.[78]

Les geisons d'angle ont été nécessairement posés avant 438. Le décor date *ca* 440 av. J.-C.

• Athènes, Propylées, deux séries de caissons de plafond (Pl. 6:a, en bas).
\* Un caisson carré appartenant au Portique Est, orné d'une palmette sur chaque face du carré et de lotus construits sur les diagonales, a fait l'objet de deux lectures : d'une part

---

[75] Si une première frise a reçu un début de réalisation, son style vieilli et des circonstances politiques nouvelles ont pu la faire écarter, au contraire d'une sima toujours réutilisable.

[76] Korres 1988, p. 107, qui a démontré que la frise de la cella avait été nécessairement sculptée en place, laisse ouverte la possibilité que les caissons aient été peints en atelier; ce paraît être de loin la solution la plus pratique.

[77] Reproduite par De Laborde 1848, pl. 45, par Michaelis 1871, p. 118, pl. II, fig. 24 et par Orlandos 1976–1978, p. 250, fig. 158 et pl. 35 à gauche.

[78] Reproduit par Orlandos 1976–1978, pl. 35 à droite.

le dessin d'E. Landron pour Le Bas 1847, pl. II, 6, n° I, avec une attribution erronée au Parthénon,[79] d'autre part le dessin de T. I. Willson pour Penrose 1851, pp. 59–60, pl. XXV, en haut à gauche (ici Pl. 6:a en bas à gauche).[80] Sur le premier, les tiges qui «encerclent» les palmettes se rejoignent pour donner naissance aux calices des fleurs : c'est, en quelque sorte, un anthémion de palmettes et de lotus inscrit dans un carré; sur l'autre, elles se referment au-dessus de la palmette et les fleurs, dépourvues de sépales, ne sont pas reliées aux palmettes. Cette deuxième lecture a été retenue par Bohn 1882, pp. 9–10 et 21, pl. XII, 4.

\* Un caisson rectangulaire appartenant au passage occidental, décoré de quatre palmettes circonscrites deux à deux opposées par le sommet: T. I. Willson pour Penrose 1851, pl. XXV, au milieu à gauche (ici Pl. 6:a en bas à droite). Bohn 1882, pp. 21–22, pl. XII:3. Peut-être Musée de l'Acropole inv. 8835, mais le décor est très effacé : voir *infra* II.2.1.d.

II.2.1.c. *Anthémions à file double de palmettes et de fleurs en correspondance, reliées par des tiges en S formant une file de lyres horizontales et deux à deux antithétiques.*

• Athènes, Agora, portique, chapiteau d'ante attribué naguère à la Stoa Poikilè (Pl. 5:a : restitution aquarellée par M. Welker).

Thompson 1950, pp. 327–328, pl. 103:a et b; Meritt 1970, pp. 236–237, 238–240 et 247–248, fig. 5, pl. 63:a et b et 64:a et c; *Agora* XIV, pp. 90–91, pl. 49:a et b.

Ensemble architectural dont provient l'épicranitis recensée ci-dessus en II.2.1.a. Peu avant 450 av. J.-C. d'après la modénature du chapiteau.

• Athènes, Héphaistéion, geison et épicranitis (Pl. 5:c, d).

\* Epicranitis-assise porte-caissons de la péristasis (Pl. 5:d) : Stuart et Revett 1794, chapitre I, vignette p. 1 (dessin de J. Stuart ou N. Revett, redessiné par W. Reveley),[81] pl. VII et VIII.[82] Selon toute vraisemblance, c'est ce décor que E. Schaubert a relevé en 1835 ou 1836 et dont H. Koch a publié le dessin,[83] malheureusement sans commentaire : Koch 1955, p. 194, fig. 83, ici Pl. 5:d.

\* Geison (Pl. 5:c): Paccard 1845–1846, n° 9 («Entablement restauré», *Paris-Rome-Athènes*, pp. 162 et 167), reporte sur la face antérieure du larmier du Parthénon un décor qu'il a relevé sur le larmier de l'Héphaistéion (Pl. 5:c) : «On voit donc qu'excepté l'ornement que j'ai mis dans la face du larmier, *lequel a le même dessin et les mêmes couleurs que celui qui existe encore dans le larmier de la corniche du temple de Thésée*, je n'ai presque rien à ajouter pour restaurer entièrement la décoration extérieure du Parthénon» (*Mémoire*, p. 71 = *Paris-Rome-Athènes*, p. 365). La rigueur de son travail préparatoire et l'utilisation de calques pour relever les motifs qu'il a reconnus (*Mémoire*, pp. 67–68 = *Paris-Rome-Athènes*, pp. 364–365; voir ci-dessus pour la sima) prêtent à ce dessin une grande fiabilité. Du reste, le décor est pratiquement

---

[79] Répétée par Reinach dans Le Bas 1888, p. 134. Reproduction dans *Paris-Rome-Athènes*, p. 97, fig. 59.

[80] Planche en couleur reproduite dans *Paris-Rome-Athènes*, p. 101, fig. 62.

[81] Reproduit dans *Paris-Rome-Athènes*, p. 64, fig. 34.

[82] Elles correspondent aux planches X et XI de l'édition française publiée chez Firmin Didot en 1812, et de la deuxième édition anglaise qui reproduit l'édition française.

[83] K. Iliakis semble avoir cru qu'il s'agissait du décor d'un chapiteau d'ante de l'Héphaistéion: Iliakis 1976, p. 256 et n. 55, avec renvoi à Koch 1955, pp. 99–100. Or H. Koch, réunissant les témoignages auxquels il joint le sien et l'analyse des dessins d'E. Schaubert, rappelle que la restitution d'un décor de ce genre sur le chapiteau d'ante a bien été proposée, mais par G. Semper, et qu'elle n'est nullement justifiée par les rares vestiges de couleur que l'on a observés ou cru observer autrefois.

identique à celui du chapiteau d'ante de portique de l'Agora, alors que la lecture de Paccard ne pouvait être guidée par la connaissance d'aucun décor de ce genre. Par ailleurs, des vestiges de couleurs, notamment de rouge sur la face verticale du larmier, ont été observés par E. Schaubert et H. Koch : Koch 1955, pp. 98–99. Enfin, la retenue dont Paccard fait preuve dans sa restauration, évitant toute copie abusive qu'il ne pourrait justifier, autorise à supposer qu'il ne s'est pas trompé de pièce d'architecture en rédigeant son mémoire et qu'il s'agit bien du larmier de la péristasis et non de l'assise porte-caissons. Il est donc très probable que nous disposons là d'un nouvel élément du décor polychrome de l'Héphaistéion.

Son étroite ressemblance avec celui du chapiteau d'ante de portique l'Agora—dont la modénature est, à son tour, proche de celle du chapiteau de l'Héphaistéion—invite à le situer aussi aux environs de 450, ce qui concorde avec la date des métopes, le plus souvent considérées comme antérieures à celles du Parthénon.[84]

Par ailleurs, une partie au moins des caissons de l'Héphaistéion, marqués de lettres d'assemblage datées d'environ 450 et même antérieures, était posée ou prête à l'être au milieu du siècle, ce qui ouvre la possibilité que les assises porte-caissons aient été déjà tout ou partie décorées.[85] Bien entendu, elles ont pu ne l'être que dans les années 425–420 après la mise en place des frises sculptées et juste avant que les plafonds fussent définitivement posés (voir *infra*, II.2.1.e et n. 92 à propos des simas) : le dessin de la publication des Dilettanti n'y contreviendrait pas. Mais à comparer ceux d'E. Schaubert et d'A. Paccard, on n'a pas l'impression que le style ait été très différent.

• Delphes, Marmaria, Trésor dorique, première assise courante de la cella (Pl. 5:b).
Daux 1923, pp. 86–87, fig. 89 et 94, pl. XXXI. Amandry 1984, pp. 191–194, fig. 14. Edifice daté vers 470 av. J.-C.

• Delphes, Trésor des Athéniens, linteau de la porte de la cella.
Büsing 1979, pp. 29–36, pl. V et VI:1. Sur un point précis, le dessin d'interprétation (pl. VI:1) n'est pas conforme à ce qui se lit sur le linteau (pl. V:3) où la pointe des sépales atteint le niveau de la deuxième feuille de la palmette à partir du bas, voire l'intervalle entre la deuxième et la troisième. La fleur ne se situe donc pas au même niveau que la palmette, mais un peu plus haut, comme au Trésor dorique. Par ailleurs, le tracé des tiges au contact des fleurs ne paraît pouvoir être déchiffré nulle part. En revanche, partout où il est lisible au voisinage des palmettes, il dessine des S assez plongeants pour relier une palmette à l'autre, et non à la fleur immédiatement suivante. Une restitution similaire à celle du chapiteau d'ante de l'Agora (Pl. 5:a) ou du geison de l'Héphaistéion (Pl. 5:c) ne serait donc pas exclue.

• Sounion, Temple de Poséidon, sima de rampant (Pl. 5:e).
Orlandos 1915, pp. 14–22, fig. 11–16; Orlandos 1953–1954, pp. 3–4, fig. 1–4; Dinsmoor, Jr. 1974b, pp. 221–226, ill. 12–15, pl. 42.

---

[84] Délivorrias 1974, pp. 48–49, 56 et 69; Harrison 1979, p. 220. En faveur de la même époque que les métopes du Parthénon, Ridgway 1981, pp. 26–30; mais l'auteur reconnaît des références thématiques aux époques archaïque et sévère, et invoque le Trésor des Athéniens pour certaines compositions (pp. 29–30); en tout état de cause, contrairement à sa suggestion, il paraît impossible de placer les métopes de l'Héphaistéion après celles du Parthénon.

[85] Wyatt et Edmonson 1984, pp. 135–167, pl. 28. Cette assise était interrompue par les poutres porte-caissons transversales; le décor se glisse sous le bec de corbin; déjà difficilement réalisable quand de surcroît l'assise était posée et sa face verticale, il a dû être peint au sol, en atelier.

Selon A. Délivorrias, la frise et l'unique pièce qui subsiste du fronton Est confirment l'époque de construction proposée par W. B. Dinsmoor (444–440 av. J.-C.), tandis que B. Sismondo Ridgway abaisserait volontiers la date des sculptures jusqu'aux environs de 420, mais sans développer grande argumentation.[86] Le profil archaïsant de la sima, proche de celui de la sima du Temple d'Aphaia, et l'acrotère, que son travail et son style pariens placent dans la descendance des acrotères d'Egine, sont antérieurs au Parthénon. *Ca* 440 av. J.-C.

Ce petit corpus comporte quatre variantes structurelles. L'une concerne le tracé des tiges, qui, sur la sima de Sounion comme sur la sima XVII de l'Acropole[87] se rejoignent sous le lotus, occultant le motif de lyre. Les deux autres concernent l'insertion de la fleur : au Trésor dorique de Marmaria et au Temple de Poséidon à Sounion, elle est «posée» dans l'axe des spirales, sans lien organique avec les tiges : l'anthémion répond très précisément à la définition donnée ci-dessus; sur le chapiteau de l'Agora d'Athènes et à l'Héphaistéion, la fleur s'ouvre à l'extrémité d'un tigelle adventice : il s'agit en fait d'un anthémion à file double de palmettes en correspondance, reliées par des tiges en S formant une file de lyres, avec fleurs en correspondance sur tigelles adventices (voir ci-dessous II.2.1.e). Le linteau du Trésor des Athéniens est trop peu lisible pour qu'on en puisse juger. Enfin, au Trésor dorique de Marmaria, comme sur les simas XVII et XX/XXI de l'Acropole, les lyres sont garnies de palmettes.

Mais en tout état de cause, il paraît improbable que cet ensemble, à lui seul, ne reflète pas l'existence de «cahiers de motifs», de répertoires, ce dont le groupe II.2.1.e nous donnera confirmation.

II.2.1.d. *Compositions de surface de palmettes, de fleurs et de lyres deux à deux antithétiques.*
• Athènes, Propylées, caissons rectangulaires (Pl. 6:a).

Musée de l'Acropole, inv. 8800, 8801 et peut-être 8835. Mais le décor de ce dernier est très effacé, de sorte qu'il pourrait relever du motif II.2.1.b (*supra*).

Dessin très fidèle de T. I. Willson pour Penrose 1851, pl. XXV, au milieu à droite (ici Pl. 6:a en haut à droite).

II.2.1.e. *Anthémions à file simple de palmettes reliées par des tiges en S avec fleurs sur tiges adventices.*
(Pour l'anthémion à file double, voir ci-dessus en II.2.1.c le chapiteau d'un portique de l'Agora et le geison de l'Héphaistéion.)
• Delphes, Pilier des Messéniens, couronnement peint.

Jacquemin et Laroche 1982, pp. 192–200, fig. 5.

Monument daté par le profil du couronnement, «proche des chapiteaux d'ante dorique des monuments attiques du troisième quart du V$^e$ siècle» (p. 194), en particulier de celui dit, encore en 1982, de la Stoa Poikilè (p. 204), recensé ci-dessus en II.2.1.c. Les circonstances politiques justifieraient son érection dans les années 450–440. Toutefois, pour autant qu'elles soient lisibles, les feuilles des palmettes à double courbure pourraient indiquer le dernier tiers ou quart du siècle.

• Athènes, Héphaistéion, simas d'égout et de rampant.

---

[86] Délivorrias 1969, pp. 127–142, pl. 57–75, Beil. 1; Délivorrias 1974, pp. 61–86; Ridgway 1981, p. 40 et n. 3 et pp. 84–85.
[87] Buschor 1929, pp. 36–38, fig. 41, pl. 7.

Dinsmoor 1940, pp. 32–37, fig. 11–14. Dinsmoor 1941, pp. 110–116, fig. 41 et 43. Dinsmoor, Jr. 1976, pp. 232–240, ill. 3, 4, 7, 9 et 10, pl. 39 et 40 (très importante n. 29). Dessin de E. Schaubert reproduit par Koch 1955, pp. 65–66 et 188, fig. 66–67. Les dessins d'E. Schaubert et de W. B. Dinsmoor, Jr. concordent : fleur à pétales minces peu évasés, palmette élancée de 13 feuilles à une courbe, assez raides. Sur les dessins publiés dans Dinsmoor 1940, p. 33 fig. 12 et dans Travlos 1971, fig. 344, les feuilles des palmettes ont un point d'inflexion.

Les simas sont contemporaines au plus tôt des frises, en tout cas des frontons (ou du plus récent des frontons). Mais les dates de ceux-ci, et leur composition même, sont très controversées.[88] Le débat engagé par E. B. Harrison sur la divinité du temple (Héphaistos et Athéna Héphaistéia? Artémis Eucléia?) ne permet pas de considérer 416/5, date d'achèvement du groupe d'Alcamène, comme un *terminus* assuré; or L. T. Shoe a daté le profil des simas de cette époque.[89] Les frises sont datées peu avant 431,[90] ou dans les années qui suivent,[91] mais en tout cas avant celle du Temple d'Athéna Niké. La seconde série de lettres qui marquent les caissons[92] peut être datée à partir de 430. Il paraît donc raisonnable de placer la sima dans les années 425–420, d'autant plus qu'elle est très proche de celle du Temple de Némésis à Rhamnonte.

• Rhamnonte, Temple de Némésis, simas d'égout et de rampant.

Iliakis 1976, pp. 245–247, fig. 1–2, pl. 51; Iliakis 1987, pp. 17–20, fig. 4–6, 8, 12.

L'architecture du temple indique qu'il a été construit dans la décennie 430–420, pendant que la statue de Némésis et sa base étaient élaborées.[93]

La sima, presque identique à celle de l'Héphaistéion, date donc de même vers 420 av. J.-C.

II.2.1.f. *Compositions de surface de palmettes et fleurs reliées par des tiges en* S.

• Sounion, Temple d'Athéna Sounias, caissons du plafond de la péristasis.

Dessins de N. D. Jôannitis pour Stais 1899–1900, col. 127–130, pl. 9 à droite.

Il s'agit à nouveau d'un anthémion inscrit dans un carré. L'édifice, dont une grande partie a été transférée vers la fin du Ier siècle ap. J.-C. pour être réédifiée au Sud-Est de l'Agora d'Athènes,[94] semble dater de la deuxième moitié du Ve siècle.[95]

• Athènes, Parthénon, caissons de la péristasis, types A (Nord et Sud) et B (Est et Ouest) (Pl. 6:c).

---

[88] Délivorrias 1974, pp. 16–60; en voir le compte rendu par Harrison 1976, pp. 209–210; Harrison 1979, p. 220; Ridgway 1981, p. 29, n. 29 et p. 40.

[89] Shoe 1936, p. 108.

[90] Délivorrias 1974, pp. 49–51; Ridgway 1981, pp. 85–88: «A date in the late 430's or shortly afterwards should not be wide of the mark».

[91] Von Bockelberg 1979, pp. 23–50, pl. 10–48; compte rendu par Harrison 1981, p. 233.

[92] Wyatt et Edmonson 1984, p. 161.

[93] Miles 1989, pp. 226–227, avec bibliographie antérieure. Compléter par Pétrakos 1987, pp. 277–282.

[94] En dernier lieu Dinsmoor, Jr. 1982, pp. 429–431; Camp 1990, pp. 147–150, fig. 96 et 97.

[95] Dinsmoor, Jr. s.d., pp. 40–49. L'auteur avait bien voulu me dire, il y a quelques années, que les caissons devaient être complètemment réétudiés, mais que la composition de leur décor, telle qu'elle avait été (fort mal) dessinée par N. D. Jôannitis, était fiable dans ses grandes lignes. H. A. Thompson et W. B. Dinsmoor, Jr. projetaient de republier le temple.

Züchner 1936, col. 319–320, fig. 6, 8 et 9; Orlandos 1976–1978, pp. 471–511, en particulier fig. 306, 313, 317–323, fig. en couleur p. 644, pl. 79–83 et 86. Les photographies de décors conservés incitent à préférer, pour la reproduction exacte de certaines fleurs, les dessins de Züchner 1936, fig. 6, et de Dinsmoor, Jr. 1974a, pl. 24 (ici Pl. 6:c).

*Ca* 440 av. J.-C.

II.2.1.g. *Anthémions de palmettes et fleurs reliées par des arceaux.*
• Athènes, Parthénon, *regulae* (Pl. 4:c).

Dessin de C. R. Cockerell, reproduit par Broendsted 1830, pl. XL. Paccard 1845–1846 : dans le dossier d'études préparatoires non jointes à l'envoi (voir ci-dessus en II.2.1.a pour la sima), relevé à la mine de plomb sur papier (Pl. 4:c) : «Quant à l'ornement qui se trouvait sur le listel de l'architrave, *ainsi que celui de la petite face qui est au-dessous des gouttes*, on le retrouve très bien conservé sur la façade de l'ouest» (*Mémoire*, p. 71 = *Paris-Rome-Athènes*, p. 365). Dessin de T. I. Willson pour Penrose 1851, p. 55, pl. 22.[96] Dessin de Orlandos 1976–1978, pp. 210–211, fig. 130, pl. 31.

Le dessin de Cockerell est fautif en ce qu'il relie fleurs et palmettes par des tiges en S. Celui d'A. K. Orlandos s'inspire beaucoup de celui de T. I. Willson : sur l'un et l'autre, les fleurs de lotus sont assez grêles. Une fois encore, le dessin d'A. Paccard présente beaucoup de garanties.

Les comptes mentionnent pour 443/2 des travaux à la colonnade, qui doivent être la réalisation des cannelures. La peinture des *regulae* est probablement de la même époque.

• Athènes, Temple d'Athéna Niké, anthémion périphérique décorant l'épicranitis à l'intérieur et à l'extérieur, les chapiteaux d'ante et les chapiteaux de piliers.

Ross, Schaubert et Hansen 1839, pl. IV, V, VI fig. 1, X fig. 1 et 3; p. 11 : «Die gemalten Ornamente der Architrave, Antencapitelle, Gesimse und Cassetten sind, so weit sich ihre Umrisse erkennen lassen, in den Kupfertafeln dargestellt (…). Die Farben liessen sich nicht mehr unterscheiden». Dessin de E. Landron pour Le Bas 1847, pl. 8:1.[97] Dessin de Ricardo (*ca* 1844) reproduit par Lethaby 1908, fig. 158. Büsing 1990.

Sur le dessin d'E. Schaubert, les découpes concaves à la base du calice sont moins accusées que sur le dessin d'E. Landron, et le calice comporte trois sépales jointifs. Sur le dessin de Ricardo, le calice a seulement la forme d'une capsule prolongée vers le haut. Quoi qu'il en soit de ce détail, sur les trois dessins, les pétales sont semblables et la palmette comporte 11 feuilles à un point d'inflexion. Les nouveautés morphologiques et syntactiques de cet anthémion en font une création manifestement plus récente que la sima.

Date : vers 420 av. J.-C.

II.2.1.h. *Files de lyres imbriquées et garnies de palmettes.*
• Rhamnonte, Temple de Némésis, chapiteau d'ante.

Iliakis 1976, pp. 253–256, fig. 8, pl. 57; l'anthémion proposé sur la fig. 9 paraît tout à fait hypothétique (*supra* n. 83).

Date : vers 420 av. J.-C.

---

[96] Reproduit par Michaelis 1871, p. 163, pl. 6:3.
[97] Reproduit dans *Le Bas* 1888, pl. 8:1, et, de là, par Hübner 1973, p. 122, fig. 17: les formes y perdent chaque fois en épaisseur et densité.

II.2.2. Caractéristiques morphologiques et syntactiques du répertoire des marbres.

Cette relecture impose une évidence : les peintres sur marbre ont la main plus légère que les peintres sur terre cuite. Cela tient moins à la syntaxe qu'à la morphologie des éléments végétaux.

### II.2.2.a. *Morphologie des fleurs.*[98]

• F 1 : dans la suite de l'épicranitis du Trésor des Athéniens (Pl. 2:a) et de la sima d'égout des «Palmettensimen» (Pl. 2:d) perdure un calice de deux sépales triangulaires, distincts ou jointifs dans l'axe, à côtés sinueux ou courbes, dont le côté inférieur concave, jointif ou supposé jointif de deux volutes : simas du Parthénon (Pl. 4:f, g) et du Temple d'Athéna Niké, un caisson carré des Propylées selon E. Landron (*supra* II.2.1.b), anthémion périphérique du Temple d'Athéna Niké. On observe la même persistance de ce type de calice dans la céramique, sous d'innombrables formes plus ou moins estompées ou articulées.

• F 2 : vers 440 apparaît une forme de calice à large base rectiligne ou à peine fléchie de part et d'autre de la tige qui porte la fleur; les sépales minces remontent le long des pétales dont ils cachent plus ou moins la naissance : sima du Temple de Poséidon à Sounion (Pl. 5:e), dont on peut rapprocher un caisson des Propylées (qui, par ailleurs, présente aussi une composition en lyre : Pl. 6:a en haut à droite); caissons A et B du Parthénon (Pl. 6:c); Pilier des Messéniens.

• F 3 : dans les années 480–470 si les décors du Trésor des Athéniens et du Trésor dorique de Marmaria ne sont pas plus récents, mais vers 450 seulement s'ils le sont, apparaît une fleur étroite à trois pétales minces et longs, dite souvent «fleur de lis», «Lilienblüte».

\* Elle peut se présenter sans sépales : geison de l'Héphaistéion (Pl. 5:c), *regulae* du Parthénon (Pl. 4:c), moulure du larmier rampant du Parthénon selon A. Paccard (Pl. 5:g),[99] caissons carrés des Propylées, les uns à fleurs sur les côtés et palmettes dans les angles[100] (Pl. 6:a en haut à gauche), les autres à palmettes sur les côtés et fleurs dans les angles selon la lecture de T. I. Willson (Pl. 6:a en bas à gauche), linteau aux lionnes peintes (Pl. 4:b), antéfixes en marbre des propylées du sanctuaire de Poséidon à Sounion (*ca* 420–410)[101] et antéfixes en terre cuite du Pompéion (*ca* 400),[102] caissons du Porche Nord de l'Erechthéion.[103]

\* Elle peut aussi présenter un calice de sépales, sorte de capsule mince ou épaisse prolongée latéralement par deux longs sépales : épicranitis et chapiteau d'ante d'un portique de l'Agora (Pl. 4:a et 5:a) où les sépales sont très minces; sima du temple de Poséidon à

---

[98] Par commodité, chaque caractéristique ou transformation morphologique des fleurs est ici désignée par la lettre F suivie d'un chiffre (F 1, F 2, F 3 etc.); de même pour les palmettes (P 1, P 2 etc.).

[99] Paccard 1845–1846, n° 16 = *Paris-Rome-Athènes*, pp. 162 et 170. Plusieurs relevés et dessins préliminaires de Paccard prouvent qu'il a vu, entre les «coeurs», une fleur à trois pétales, le pétale central losangé ayant été seul remarqué par les autres observateurs, dont Orlandos 1976–1978, fig. 386, pl. 74.

[100] Dessin de T. I. Willson pour Penrose 1851, p. 56, pl. XXV en haut à droite, ici Pl. 6:a en haut à gauche. R. Bohn de semble pas avoir reconnu ou retrouvé cette pièce.

[101] Orlandos 1953–1954, pp. 6–7, fig. 5–6. La découverte de la sima d'égout ayant exclu que ces antéfixes aient appartenu au temple, elles ont été rendues aux propylées du sanctuaire par Dinsmoor, Jr. 1974b, p. 224, n. 29, ill. 8 et 9, pl. 41, fig. 11, et Dinsmoor, Jr. s.d., p. 27, n. infrapaginale.

[102] Hübner 1973, pp. 78–79, pl. 58:2, Beil. 5:2.

[103] Stevens et Paton 1927, p. 89, fig. 57:B.

Sounion (Pl. 5:e) et Pilier des Messéniens où les sépales sont presque aussi épais que les pétales. Le calice peut aussi présenter trois sépales distincts (Trésor dorique de Marmaria, Pl. 5:b) ou plus ou moins jointifs (linteau du trésor des Athéniens, simas de l'Héphaistéion et du temple de Némésis à Rhamnonte)

• F 4 : vers 440 apparaît aussi une fleur à 5 pétales longs et effilés, deux filiformes et les trois autres plus larges (caissons A et B du Parthénon, Pl. 6:c; anthémion périphérique du Temple d'Athéna Niké), ou bien tous les cinq d'importance presque équivalente (simas du Parthénon [Pl. 4:f et g] et du Temple d'Athéna Niké). C'est, à plus grande échelle, l'interprétation d'un nouveau modèle de fleur créé dans les ateliers du P. d'Altamura et du P. des Niobides : sur leurs vases, plusieurs variantes (Pl. 4:e) coexistent avec l'ancien modèle archaïsant et le remplacent progressivement.[104]

II.2.2.b. *Morphologie des palmettes.*

• P 1 : comme sur les vases, la palmette ronde archaïsante, éventuellement circonscrite, aux larges feuilles à une seule courbure, persiste jusque vers 440 sur la sima du Temple de Poséidon à Sounion (Pl. 5:e), au soffite du geison d'angle (Pl. 6:b) et sur un caisson (Pl. 6:d) du Parthénon.

• P 2 : mais depuis 450 au moins, elle tend à être remplacée par une palmette ogivale plus élancée, plus aérée, à 9, 11 ou 13 feuilles plus courtes mais moins trapues et moins fléchies, la feuille centrale étant souvent plus longue que les autres et lancéolée. Cette évolution, amorcée sur les vases depuis les années 480, semble ne se manifester sur les marbres que vers 450. Encore peut-on distinguer entre les palmettes de type nouveau, relativement pointues et rigides, des anthémions (Pl. 4:a–d et 5:a–d) et celles des caissons du Parthénon et des Propylées ou du larmier d'angle du Parthénon (Pl. 6), directement transférées du décor des vases et tout imprégnées encore du style sévère qui s'y prolonge.

• P 3 : la feuille à un point d'inflexion apparaît vers 425–420, sur l'architrave du temple de l'Ilissos (Pl. 4:d) et à l'anthémion périphérique du Temple d'Athéna Niké, de conception plus récente que celui de la sima.

II.2.2.c. *Syntaxe.*
Ici encore se mêlent survivances, emprunts et nouveautés.

• S 1 : la palmette circonscrite perdure jusque vers 420, comme sur les vases et très probablement sur les simas de terre cuite (Pl. 3:f). Les tiges dessinent autour des palmettes des ogives plus ou moins étirées dont les exemples abondent aussi sur les vases; l'effet s'apparente à celui des compositions de lyres couchées garnies de palmettes. Ici encore, harmonies et correspondances se rencontrent d'une composition à l'autre et du domaine de la céramique à celui de l'architecture.

• S 2 : mais l'anthémion à palmettes circonscrites—épicranitis de l'Agora (Pl. 4:a), linteau aux lionnes peintes (Pl. 4:b), architrave du Temple de l'Ilissos (Pl. 4:d)—est toujours à simple file, contrairement à ce que l'on observe sur les simas de terre cuite.

---

[104] Par ex. Louvre G. 341, Arias et Hirmer 1960, fig. 173–181; Arias et Hirmer 1957, fig. 13, 37, 42, 43; Caskey et Beazley 1954, n° 108, cratère inv. 33.56, p. 77, pl. LVIII; *CVA, Bologna, Museo Civico* 4, III, 1, cratère en cloche Pell. 286, p. 13, pl. 75 (P. de Blenheim).

• S 3 : l'anthémion de palmettes seules n'a plus cours, alors qu'il est toujours en vigueur sur les vases : l'épicranitis de la cella du Trésor des Athéniens (Pl. 2:b) et les «Palmettensimen» (Pl. 2:e) restent sans postérité.

• S 4 : il n'y a pas, pour autant, rupture avec les compositions de palmettes qui s'offrent quotidiennement aux yeux de tous sous les anses de skyphoi, de stamnoi, d'hydries, de cratères : un caisson et le soffite du geison d'angle du Parthénon[105] ainsi que deux caissons des Propylées (Pl. 6:a, b et d) y ont leurs modèles trop évidents (cf. P 2), seulement contraints, ici, par le cadre quadrangulaire. Comme au Trésor des Athéniens et sur les «Palmettensimen», il s'agit de *transferts* directs du répertoire des vases à l'architecture.

• S 5 : le répertoire des marbres ignore l'anthémion à double file en alternance (palmettes opposées aux fleurs et *vice versa*).

• S 6 : la sima du Temple de Poséidon au Sounion (Pl. 5:e) est jusqu'à présent la seule sima de marbre à porter un anthémion à double file : son profil archaïsant, proche de celui de la sima du temple d'Aphaia (*supra* n. 22) et parent de ceux des simas de terre cuite, favorise peut-être l'emprunt de cette structure décorative particulièrement bien adaptée, nous l'avons vu (II.1.2.b), à ce genre de profils.

• S 7 : tous les autres anthémions à double file se développent sur des parties différentes, offrant des faces planes verticales : chapiteau d'ante de l'Agora (Pl. 5:a), geison et épicranitis de l'Héphaistéion (Pl. 5:c et d), assise décorée du Trésor dorique de Marmaria (Pl. 5:b), linteau du trésor des Athéniens. De la terre cuite au marbre, les lieux d'application d'un même schéma changent.

• S 8 : l'anthémion à double file en correspondance n'est jamais autrement conçu (voir S 2) que comme le redoublement, par effet de miroir, d'un anthémion simple relié par des S couchés; d'où le motif de lyre, garni (Trésor dorique de Marmaria, Pl. 5:b) ou non de palmettes.

H. Büsing considère que les décors du Trésor des Athéniens et du Trésor dorique sont contemporains des édifices, du moins de leur achèvement. C'est une hypothèse économique et vraisemblable, d'autant plus malaisée à discuter qu'il faut en bonne règle dater un décor par le contexte archéologique et non ce dernier par le style d'un décor.[106] Encore le cas est-il différent d'un grand édifice dont la polychromie ne saurait être complétée ou rafraîchie sans nouveaux et coûteux échafaudages, et d'un trésor toujours susceptible d'embellissements à peu de frais.

Une fois établi que la construction du Trésor des Athéniens a été interrompue (ci-dessus n. 11), le problème de la chronologie absolue, du début des travaux à l'achèvement de l'édifice, reste entier.

Etant donné que la file de lyres horizontales, deux à deux antithétiques et garnies de palmettes apparaît sur la céramique des années 480 (*supra* II.1.2.a et II.1.3.c), il n'y a pas

---

[105] La comparaison avec la céramique a été faite maintes fois, d'abord par Paccard (*Paris-Rome-Athènes*, p. 365), en dernier lieu par Orlandos 1976–1978, pp. 249–253, fig. 161.

[106] Büsing 1979 admet, ce que avons fait pour d'autres édifices, que la peinture du linteau relève des ultimes finitions; il montre que le décor ne peut, pour des raison stylistiques, dater qu'après 480. Dater des finitions superficielles ne permet pas de dater la construction du Trésor, le déroulement des travaux antérieurs, leur début avant ou après 490, ni même de l'achèvement de l'essentiel, pose des sculptures tympanales comprise, avant ou après 490.

contradiction à dater simultanément l'architecture, la sculpture et le décor peint du Trésor dorique aux environs de 470. Mais le succès du motif éclate un peu plus tard, dans les années 465–430, dans les ateliers—déjà cités à propos de la série XIII de tuiles de l'Acropole (*supra* n. 28) et de la sima du Parthénon—du P. d'Altamura, du P. des Niobides, du P. de Chicago, de Polygnotos etc.[107] : le motif de lyres s'enrichit alors de feuilles, tigelles et palmettes adventices, de croix et cercles dans l'interstice des quatre volutes, d'esquisses de palmettes entre les volutes divergentes. Tout se prête à ce qu'il soit complété par des palmettes et des fleurs verticales, pour un effet sensiblement comparable à celui de l'anthémion à double file élaboré sur le chapiteau d'ante de l'Agora (Pl. 5:a) ou sur le geison de l'Héphaistéion (Pl. 5:c). Vers 410–400, le P. de Cécrops pour le célèbre cratère inv. 77 d'Adolphseck, et plus tard encore, dans les années 390–380, le P. de Méléagre pour un cratère à volute dinoïde du Musée J. Paul Getty (inv. 87.AE.93) reprennent un anthémion à double file de palmettes et de lotus, avec lyres garnies de palmettes qui ne prolonge pas la tradition vasculaire de la file de lyres antithétiques mais recopie purement et simplement un décor d'architecture.[108] Les pirouettes losangées de l'astragale peint ne signent pas non plus une époque «ancienne». Le Trésor dorique serait-il de dix à vingt ans plus récent qu'on ne pense, ou son chantier aurait-il, lui aussi, duré ?

Je croirais plus volontiers que cette assise et le linteau du Trésor des Athéniens ont été décorés dans les années 450–430, voire plus tard, peut-être ensemble, mais pas nécessairement, au cours de travaux d'entretien financés par Athènes ou utilisant des peintres athéniens.[109] Peut-être faudrait-il mettre ces embellissements en rapport avec la décoration du Pilier des Messéniens.

• S 9 : en l'état actuel de notre documentation, le Pilier des Messéniens offrirait le plus ancien des trois anthémions à file simple relié par des tiges en S. S'y ajoutent les caissons de type A et B du Parthénon (Pl. 6:c), ceux du Temple d'Athéna Sounias et peut-être les caissons carrés des Propylées (Pl. 6:a) dont nous avons vu que les compositions de surface peuvent être en fait un anthémion enfermé dans un carré. L'anthémion à file simple n'apparaît donc pas plus tôt que l'anthémion à file double dans l'architcture de marbre.

• S 10 : dans quatre cas—linteau du Trésor des Athéniens d'après la restitution de H. Büsing, assise décorée du Trésor dorique de Marmaria, épicranitis de l'Héphaistéion d'après E. Schaubert (Pl. 5:d), linteau aux lionnes peintes—la fleur tient le même rang que la palmette. Ailleurs, le statut de la fleur est ambigu : la situation et la place qu'elle occupe dans la composition en font un élément de même rang, principal, que la palmette; elle est en réalité un élément secondaire puisque surgie à l'extrémité d'une tigelle adventice.

[107] Par ex. Arias et Hirmer 1957, fig. 34–36, 51, 54–58; Caskey et Beazley 1954, n° 108; Beazley 1963, n° 159, inv. 59.176, pp. 61–62, supplementary pl. 22, 23 (P. d'Altamura); *CVA, Bologna, Museo Civico* 4, III, 1, cratère Pell. PU 283, p. 8, pl. 56 (P. de Borée); cratère Pell. 279, p. 9, pl. 62; cratère Pell. 289, p. 13, pl. 72–74 (proche du P. de Penthésilée).

[108] *CVA Adolphseck, Schloss Fasanerie*, pp. 32–36, pl. 46–48. Burn 1991, fig. 1:a, c, d et 5:a; noter les formes très effilées de la fleur sur les autres anthémions.

[109] Comme les files de lyres garnies de palmettes sont beaucoup moins nombreuses sur les vases après 430, et que le P. de Cécrops et le P. de Méléagre reproduisent un décor d'architecture, 430 pourrait être, sous toutes réserves, le *terminus ante quem* approximatif du décor du Trésor dorique. Rien n'empêcherait que le linteau de Trésor des Athéniens ait été peint un peu plus tard encore, en même temps que les simas de l'Héphaistéion et du Temple de Némésis à Rhamnonte: on note que le calice de la fleur présente trois sépales jointifs.

• S 11 : Le décor du chapiteau d'ante du Temple de Némésis à Rhamnonte—une file de lyres imbriquées, orientées dans le même sens, garnies de palmettes à l'intérieur et de demi-palmettes dans les écoiçons—apparemment sans modèle immédiat dans la céramique attique, recompose des éléments banals, la file de lyres horizontales garnies de palmettes et la demi-palmette d'écoinçon.

Les marbres peints du Ve siècle restent donc très proches de la céramique contemporaine : elle soutient la continuité de leur répertoire (F 1, P 1, P 2, S 1, S 2) et propose de nouveaux modèles (F 4, P 2, S 4, S 8, S 11) dont le transfert à plus grande échelle est parfois assorti d'interprétations spécifiques (F 4, S 11).

Mais par ailleurs, d'authentiques créations (F 2, F 3, P 2, P 3, S 8, S 10), servies par une facture aérienne, assurent l'originalité des marbres par rapport aux vases et aux simas de terre cuite (S 5).

Réciproquement, le décor des vases vient à s'enrichir des créations de la peinture sur marbre à partir des années 420–410 : les Peintres du Dinos,[110] de Kadmos,[111] de Cécrops (voir ci-dessus), de Nicias s'emparent de leurs formes fines et élancées[112] et les substituent aux avatars du style sévère, allant jusqu'à recopier des anthémions complets comme nous venons de le voir sur le cratère inv. 77 d'Adolphseck et sur le cratère dinoïde du Musée J. Paul Getty, exemples célèbres, mais non isolés.[113] Incontestablement, des «cahiers de motifs», des cartons ont fini par circuler d'une corporation à l'autre : ils assuraient le succès et la durée des motifs ornementaux, pour le plus grand tourment des archéologues en quête de chronologie.

## II.3. *Regard synoptique sur les simas de terre cuite et sur les marbres peints du Ve siècle.*

Les parcours séparés du répertoire des simas et de celui des marbres, tous deux redevables aux peintres de vases, peuvent ainsi révéler, au-delà de leurs particularités, des structures et des formes communes. Ils invitent à une présentation synoptique, *qui ne vaut pas chronologie, ni relative, ni absolue,* mais qui met en évidence leur parenté originelle et, partant, des harmonies

---

[110] *CVA, Bologna, Museo Civico* 4, III, 1, inv. Pell. 300, pp. 16–17, pl. 86–87 (420–410): noter le contraste entre la zone supérieure, dont la formule remonte au dernier quart du VIe siècle, et la zone inférieure des anses où les tiges en S et surtout la fleur à calice de sépales reproduisent les motifs de la peinture sur marbre des années 450–420; détail dans Boardman 1989, fig. 179.

[111] Par ex. Beazley 1963, inv. 03.821, p. 81, pl. CII et suppl. 27; *CVA, Bologna, Museo Civico* 4, III, 1, inv. Pell. 301, p. 16, pl. 83–85.

[112] Hübner 1973, p. 119.

[113] *Anthémion à double file de palmettes, avec lyres garnies de palmettes et à fleurs sur tigelles adventices* sur le cratère Schloss Fasanerie inv. 77 (*CVA, Adolphseck, Schloss Fasanerie,* pp. 32–36, pl. 46–48) et sur le cratère dinoïde Musée J. Paul Getty inv. 87.AE.93. *Anthémion à simple file de palmettes, avec tiges en S et fleurs sur tigelles adventices* sur le cratère de Bologne, Museo Civico inv. Pell. 301 du P. de Cadmos (*CVA, Bologna, Museo Civico* 4, III, 1, p. 16, pl. 83–85); sur le cratère de l'Ermitage inv. St. 1807 du même peintre (Metzger 1951, pl. XXVII, cf. pl. XXV); sur l'hydrie du British Museum inv. E. 205, du P. de Nicias: *CVA, British Museum* 6, III, 1, p. 6, pl. 93:1a (cf. Hübner 1973, fig. 15). Ces échanges dans le strict domaine de la peinture ne sont qu'un aspect de la circulation des motifs, par des itinéraires divers, entre tous les arts qui, en dernier ressort, relèvent du dessin: le même anthémion simple, mais à palmette flammée, se rencontre sur une hydrie du P. de Modica (*CVA, Syracusa, R. Museo Nazionale,* inv. 38031, p. 12, pl. 26–28), sur un cratère récemment mis au jour à Corinthe (Williams et Zervos 1991, p. 6, n° 2, pl. 1), et naturellement sur le couronnement de la «Stèle au chat» (Athènes, Musée National inv. 715); il n'est pas (encore) attesté en architecture.

décoratives indépendantes des différences maintenues par la séparation des activités et des traditions artisanales.

C'est ainsi que pouvaient s'offrir simultanément aux regards, sans heurter le goût
- la sima XII de l'Acropole avec ses lotus très étroits (Pl. 3:b) et l'épicranitis d'un portique de l'Agora (Pl. 4:a);
- la sima XVII (Pl. 3:g), celle du temple de Poséidon à Sounion (Pl. 5:e) et les caissons A et B du Parthénon (Pl. 6:c),[114] tant pour la structure des anthémions que pour la forme et le détail des fleurs;
- la sima XXIII (Pl. 3:i) et l'anthémion périphérique du Temple d'Athéna Niké pour les arceaux, le calice des fleurs[115] et la liberté des palmettes;[116]
- les simas XIX et XX/XXI (Pl. 3:e et h), l'assise décorée du Trésor dorique de Marmaria (Pl. 5:b), les anthémions d'un portique de l'Agora (Pl. 4:a et 5:a), ceux de l'Héphaistéion (Pl. 5:c et d) et le chapiteau d'ante du temple de Némésis à Rhamnonte, pour les lyres garnies de palmettes. Les simas de terre cuite accusent le statut ambigu de la fleur sur tige adventice, statut associé du reste à la nouvelle forme de fleur étroite à trois pétales (F 3) : sur la sima XIX, cette «fleur de lis» est effectivement un élément surajouté qui se glisse en surnombre entre la palmette et la fleur de lotus canoniques[117] (de même entre les palmettes de la sima Pl. 3:f); sur la sima XX, elle occupe au contraire l'espace disponible entre deux palmettes et tient la place normalement dévolue à la fleur de lotus;[118] les panneaux de la sima XXI (Pl. 3:h)[119] constituent des unités isolées, à la manière des caissons rectangulaires des Propylées (Pl. 6:a) où les tigelles adventices divergent vers les angles; la séquence attendue de l'anthémion est rompue. De même que les sculpteurs des acrotères médians du Parthénon, le peintre de ces trois simas a osé un rendu en trois dimensions de la «fleur de lis». Il n'y a pas de raison objective de situer ces simas nécessairement dans la dépendance de l'Erechthéion,[120] ni de penser qu'elles soient postérieures à 430–420. Dès cette époque, comme plus tard, elles peuvent anticiper le décor floral des mosaïques du IVe siècle.[121]

II.4. *Copies et pastiches.*

Mais un moment vient où l'unité stylistique du décor architectural tient surtout à la copie et au pastiche.

---

[114] La sima XVII et la sima du Temple de Poséidon à Sounion ont été très tôt rapprochées: par ex. Buschor 1929, p. 38; Hübner 1973, p. 112. Les calices des fleurs de la sima XVII et des caissons du Parthénon sont remarquablement proches. La sima de Sounion et les caissons du Parthénon sont par ailleurs contemporains, *ca* 440 av. J.-C.

[115] Sur Buschor 1929, pl. 12, les sépales sont séparés et tourmentés à l'excès. E. Buschor propose de dater cette sima du début du IVe siècle, ce qui paraît trop tard.

[116] Il paraît du reste indéniable que le peintre de la sima XXIII fréquentait les décorateurs de vases à l'époque des P. de Cadmos et de Cécrops.

[117] Buschor 1929, pp. 40–41, fig. 45, pl. 8.

[118] Buschor 1929, p. 41, fig. 46, pl. 9.

[119] Buschor 1929, pp. 41–44, fig. 47, 50 et 51, pl. 10. Vlassopoulou 1989, n° 66; Vlassopoulou 1990, n° 65.

[120] Le relief utilise la troisième dimension, mais n'a pas le monopole de son rendu. Les fleurs sur tiges adventices qui enrichissent plusieurs anthémions de l'Erechthéion peuvent dériver de créations peintes.

[121] Par ex. Salzmann 1982, Sikyon 3, n° 118, pl. 20 et 21:3; Pella 12, n° 105, pl. 38:4; Vergina 1, n° 130, pl. 40:3.

Elle est évidemment parfaite lorsque, par exception, la morphologie spécifique des éléments, palmettes et lotus, passe d'un support à l'autre. Ainsi, la sima IX de l'Acropole[122] ne s'interprète que comme un pastiche de sima en marbre, peinte en sombre sur le ton du matériau, comme les «Palmettensimen» de rampant et d'égout (ci-dessus I.1.4, Pl. 2:e); la file de coeurs anticipe sans doute le décor du larmier au fronton du Parthénon[123] (Pl. 4:g et 5:g). De même, plusieurs simas de terre cuite à décor d'oves,[124] dont celle du petit distyle *in antis* du sanctuaire d'Athéna Sounias,[125] imitent très évidemment la sima à oves sculptés à jour des Propylées de l'Acropole.[126] Et l'on observe encore à la fin du Ve siècle et au début du IVe d'autres transferts de décors complets du marbre à la terre cuite, ainsi l'anthémion de palmettes circonscrites et de «fleurs de lis» au soffite de tuiles d'égout d'Eleusis.[127]

En sens inverse, les antéfixes en marbre des propylées du sanctuaire de Sounion (ci-dessus et n. 101) reproduisent les modèles contemporains en terre cuite, attestés par exemple au Pompéion (ci-dessus et n. 102).

Issus des mêmes origines céramiques, arrivés au terme de parcours distincts mais proches, les répertoires du marbre et de la terre cuite fusionnent et s'usent. Les sculpteurs de l'Erechthéion viennent d'inventer un style nouveau.

Pour prolonger ces observations, il faut souligner que le répertoire des marbres peints athéniens a eu la vertu d'aider les ateliers corinthiens et corinthianisants à s'affranchir du style sévère, non seulement en proposant des compositions à reproduire, ainsi par la sima d'Olympie dite «du type de l'Héphaistéion»,[128] mais en allégeant et en redressant les formes, notamment en créant cette fleur à trois pétales (F 3) qui allait transformer, pour la durée du IVe siècle, l'apparence de toutes les «fleurs de lotus» (voir Pl. 5:f) : un ou plusieurs ateliers corinthiens ont su s'en inspirer, qui ont produit dans les années 425–380 la sima du Ptoion,[129] celle du temple d'Apollon à Tegyra,[130] deux simas inédites d'Elatée, plusieurs simas d'Argos (voir Pl. 7:b) et celle du Temple d'Apollon Maléatas à Epidaure.[131]

## III. TERRES CUITES ET MOSAÏQUES DANS LE PELOPONNESE AU IVe SIECLE

La situation s'annonce différente au IVe siècle; du moins nous est-elle imposée différente par l'état de la documentation : peu ou pas de marbres peints, les stucs se sont le plus souvent détachés du calcaire et du poros, la mosaïque décorative demeure, attestant un essor considérable (Pl. 7 et 8).

---

[122] Buschor 1929, pp. 18–19, fig. 16 et 19.
[123] Orlandos 1976–1978, pl. 74.
[124] Musée de l'Agora A 574, A 577, A 941, A 1993, A 2323, inédits. A 105 + A 418 publiés par Rotroff 1983, pp. 273 et 291, n° 70, pl. 57. Une sima à oves couvrait le tombeau IV dans la nécropole découverte au carrefour des rues Eupolidos, Apellou et Lycourgou: Alexandri 1968, p. 42.
[125] Orlandos dans Stais 1917, col. 185–186, fig. L–N; Dinsmoor, Jr. s.d. pp. 50–51.
[126] Bohn 1882, pl. XIV.
[127] Hübner 1973, pp. 87–94 *passim*, fig. 4 et 6:3, pl. 60:3.
[128] *OlForsch* V, pp. 115 et 125, fig. 39, pl. 42–43; Hübner 1973, pp. 120–121, fig. 16, pl. 69:2.
[129] Le Roy 1967, p. 145, pl. 36.
[130] Lauffer 1971, pp. 239–240, pl. 212.
[131] Billot 1991, p. 206, fig. 7.

III.1. Il est cependant frappant de voir à nouveau la céramique attique exercer son influence sur ce nouvel art de la peinture[132] qu'est la mosaïque, par des *transferts* très précis des zones secondaires des vases aux bordures et bandes des tapis :

• à Olynthe, sur la mosaïque de la Centauromachie,[133] un *rais-de-coeurs* comme il s'en trouve non seulement sur les kymations lesbiques de l'architecture[134] mais aussi en bordure des grands cratères à volutes de Polion, des Peintres de Cadmos, de Pronomos, de Talos;[135]

• à Olynthe encore, dans l'andrôn de la Villa de la Bonne Fortune, à la périphérie de la mosaïque de Dionysos et de la mosaïque de seuil aux deux Pans, *un anthémion de palmettes opposées obliques reliées par des tiges en S obliques*,[136] innombrable sur les vases;

• à Olynthe toujours, sur la mosaïque aux doubles sphinges où l'on retrouve des palmettes opposées dans les angles,[137] et sur la mosaïque de la Centauromachie,[138] un *rameau de laurier*, qui appellerait lui aussi trop de références, ne serait-ce que le cratère de Pronomos déjà cité pour le rais-de-coeurs;

• à Erétrie, dans la Maison aux mosaïques, en bordure de la mosaïque de seuil aux sphinges et panthères, un *anthémion de palmettes circonscrites et de lotus*;[139] ceux-ci présentent un large calice de deux sépales contigus, à base doublement concave, et deux grands pétales évasés. Dans le panneau circulaire de la mosaïque aux Arimaspes, un *anthémion de palmettes et de lotus reliés par des tiges en S*;[140] les pétales des lotus sont séparés par des points. Pour le type du calice, il nous faut remonter aux simas XVII et XIX de l'Acropole, mais de semblables formes vieillies persistent dans la céramique, avec l'anthémion de palmettes circonscrites, jusqu'au début du IVe siècle.[141]

• à Athènes même, le rinceau de palmettes de la mosaïque circulaire de la rue Ménandre ne peut se réclamer que des décors foisonnants de la fin du Ve et du premier quart ou tiers du IVe siècle,[142] ce qui serait éventuellement un argument décisif en faveur d'une datation de la mosaïque à même époque.[143]

Traitant ci-dessus (II) des décors architecturaux athéniens sur terre cuite et marbre au Ve siècle, nous n'avions pas dû chercher leurs origines ailleurs que dans la céramique attique. En vertu des mêmes références directes,[144] le décor secondaire des mosaïques d'Athènes,

---

[132] L'iconographie sort du cadre de nos investigations.
[133] Salzmann 1982, Olynth 4, n° 79, pp. 11, 23 et 99–100, pl. 15:2.
[134] Salzmann 1982, p. 23.
[135] Boardman 1989, fig. 306, 310, 323, 324.
[136] Salzmann 1982, Olynth 12, n° 87, pp. 11, 24 et 102, pl. 14:2 et 15:1.
[137] Salzmann 1982, Olynth 9, n° 84, pp. 11, 22–23 et 101, pl. 12:3.
[138] Salzmann 1982, pl. 15:2.
[139] Salzmann 1982, Eretria 3, n° 38, pp. 12, 27 et 91, pl. 27:3 et 4; Ducrey, Metzger et Reber 1993, p. 86, fig. 45, 96 et 97, pl. I:5, 6.
[140] Salzmann 1982, Eretria 2, n° 37, pp. 12, 27 et 90–91, pl. 26; Ducrey, Metzger et Reber 1993, p. 88, fig. 45, 101 et 102, pl. II:1 et III:1, 2.
[141] Par ex. sur la pyxide Universität Heidelberg Inv. 69/5: Hampe 1971, n° 80, p. 50.
[142] Jacobsthal 1927, pl. 110–117; Boardman 1989, fig. 244, 245, 289, 291, 292, 337, 340 etc.
[143] Salzmann 1982, Athen 5, n° 22, pp. 30–31 et 87, pl. 42:2–4 et 43:3.
[144] Sur cette question en général, Salzmann 1982, pp. 56–57. Toutefois, l'origine des motifs décoratifs ne permet pas de régler la question fondamentale de la signification de la mosaïque, succédané de tapis ou

d'Erétrie et même d'Olynthe est pure création athénienne, à verser au dossier de l'unité ou de l'hétérogénéité ornementale de l'architecture d'Athènes dans le premier tiers du IVe siècle.

III.2. Mais nos perspectives se diversifient lorsque certaines compositions se révèlent transférées non plus de la céramique, mais de l'architecture elle-même. D. Salzmann a montré qu'entre autres pavements à panneau circulaire inscrit dans un carré, la mosaïque aux Arimaspes d'Erétrie, avec ses oiseaux vus de dessous, «reflète», au sens figuré sinon propre du terme, une peinture de plafond[145] et n'est pas la seule de ce genre ni à Erétrie ni en Grèce. Dépourvues d'indices optiques, d'autres compositions s'annoncent cependant du même ordre; ainsi les deux panneaux carrés de la mosaïque au gorgonéion d'Erétrie, à décor végétal centré, reflètent-ils certainement des caissons de plafond[146] comparables à ceux du Parthénon et des Propylées. Sans épuiser la question, très vaste,[147] l'exemple d'Erétrie, justement relatif au répertoire végétal qui retient ici notre attention, a le mérite de mettre l'accent sur la circulation *directe* des motifs décoratifs d'une partie à l'autre, d'un matériau à l'autre de l'architecture d'une même région ou de régions différentes. Exemple d'autant plus éloquent que les fleurs de l'un des panneaux suscitent un rapprochement immédiat avec celles de la «sima pâle» d'Olympie, qui échappe tout à fait aux styles péloponnésiens.[148]

III.3. Dans le Péloponnèse, riche de terres cuites architecturales—à la fois parce qu'il en produisait beaucoup et que les circonstances ont permis d'en découvrir un certain nombre—, riche aussi de mosaïques, et singulièrement dans le Nord-Est, plusieurs cas s'imposent de comparaisons très précises entre les deux productions.

III.3.1. Sur l'une des mosaïques les plus anciennes de Sicyone, la mosaïque au gorgonéion (Pl. 7:c et 8:c),[149] les lotus de la bordure circulaire du tapis suscitent des réminiscences immédiates[150] : une sima de Delphes (Pl. 7:a) et une autre, à anthémion identique, de Némée[151] pour la forme générale de la fleur et du pétale central, et pour les sépales très minces et remontants. L'une et l'autre ont été fabriquées à Corinthe ou par des artisans corinthiens. La sima de Delphes a été datée de 460–450, la mosaïque *ca* 400 ou du premier quart du IVe siècle, indépendamment l'une de l'autre et sur appréciation stylistique. La durée d'un motif peut expliquer l'écart chronologique; la vraisemblance inviterait à le réduire, d'autant plus que les palmettes de la mosaïque n'affichent aucune caractéristique

---

pavement polychrome perçu comme tel : la nature et l'itinérance des décors sont indépendantes de la fonction des objets ou succédanés d'objets qu'ils viennent orner.

[145] Salzmann 1982, p. 57, Eretria 2, n° 37, pl. 26; Ducrey, Metzger et Reber 1993, p. 88, fig. 45, 101 et 102, pl. II:1 et III:1–5.

[146] Salzmann 1982, Eretria 1, n° 36, pp. 12, 27, et 90, pl. 27:2; Ducrey, Metzger et Reber 1993, pp. 85–86, fig. 44 et 95, pl. I:1–4.

[147] Guimier-Sorbets et Barbet 1994; Salzmann 1982, p. 58.

[148] *OlForsch* V, pp. 114, 124 et 131, fig. 38, pl. 41:c.

[149] Votsis 1976, pp. 575–581, fig. 1–7. Salzmann 1982, Sikyon 4, n° 119, pp. 11, 22 et 112, pl. 10:1 et 2; 11:1 et 4.

[150] En particulier Pl. 8:c au fond à droite.

[151] Le Roy 1967, toit 59, pp. 134–135, pl. 49-50. Némée, AT 55 et AT 75, 2: Miller 1978, pp. 83–84, fig. 4 et pl. 26:c et d; Miller 1979, pp. 89–90, pl. 32:a.

du IV$^e$ siècle. Nous retrouvons ici tous les délicats problèmes d'estimation que posent l'assise décorée du Trésor dorique de Marmaria et le linteau du Trésor des Athéniens, au sein d'un corpus pourtant plus nombreux. Ici, les trois documents ne se rapprochent que par un seul élément, la fleur intégrée dans deux schémas d'anthémions différents, à tiges en S jointives sur les deux simas, à arceaux sur la mosaïque. De surcroît, la mise en oeuvre de l'anthémion est très différente sur les deux simas, la mouluration de celle de Némée étant exceptionnellement complexe. On peut affirmer seulement que la fleur a été créée puis copiée deux fois, ou copiée trois fois, dans un ordre très incertain.

III.3.2. La mosaïque aux tritons du pronaos du Temple de Zeus à Olympie (Pl. 7:d)[152] a été datée du milieu ou de la seconde moitié du III$^e$ siècle av. J.-C. par les monnaies trouvées dans le support. La restitution dessinée par A. Blouet pour l'*Expédition scientifique de Morée* I, pl. 63–64,[153] à une époque où la mosaïque était moins délabrée, et les vestiges de bordures des panneaux laissent envisager, au moins pour les bordures, une époque plus ancienne, soutenue par une sima d'Argos (Pl. 7:b) datée vers 400 av. J.-C.

III.3.3. La composition végétale qui occupe les écoinçons de la mosaïque aux centaures de Sicyone[154] (Pl. 7:g) utilise deux petits fleurons qui figurent aussi sur les antéfixes du Temple d'Apollon Maléatas (Fig. 1),[155] vers 390–380. Sur mosaïque et antéfixes, la même palmette s'élance, étroite aux feuilles raides. On a proposé pour la mosaïque le deuxième tiers du IV$^e$ siècle, sans argument précis.

III.3.4. La fouille du «Building IV» sous la Stoa Sud de Corinthe a révélé un fragment de mosaïque (Pl. 8:d) du IV$^e$ siècle, nécessairement antérieure à 300 av. J.-C., mais sans *terminus post quem*.[156] Nous y retrouvons le même petit fleuron, mais allégé, tel qu'il se rencontre au soffite des simas d'égout du bâtiment de scène du Théâtre d'Argos dans le premier quart du III$^e$ siècle (Pl. 8:e et Fig. 2).

III.3.5. La mosaïque circulaire trouvée dans le Quartier du Théâtre de Corinthe[157] recense presque tout le répertoire des simas (voir Pl. 5:f et 7:e, f) et des antéfixes de 370 environ à la fin du siècle, dont la grande et la petite sima aux acanthes d'Olympie (voir ici même la communication de J. Heiden) et toutes les antéfixes du type de la Stoa Sud[158] ou qui lui sont apparentées,[159] et dont la production commence au milieu du siècle. Cet anthémion inscrit dans un tapis circulaire résume, jusqu'aux enjolivures, la morphologie et la syntaxe

---

[152] Salzmann 1982, Olympia 2, n° 138, pp. 63 et 117–118, pl. 71:5 et 6, 72 et 102:4.
[153] Salzmann 1982, pl. 72:1.
[154] Votsis 1976, pp. 582–583, fig. 8; Salzmann 1982, Sikyon 2, n° 117, pp. 11, 25–26, 111–112, pl. 22:1.
[155] Lambrinoudakis 1978, p. 120, pl. 96:δ; la série 69 de Delphes, également fabriquée à Corinthe, est identique: Le Roy 1967, p. 140, pl. 53 et 127 (restitution erronée).
[156] Williams 1980, pp. 114–116, pl. 18:b et 19:a. Salzmann 1982, p. 128. On prendra garde cependant que la disparition d'un ou deux galets à mi-hauteur du pétale central ne doit pas faire croire à l'existence d'un sépale, comme sur les simas d'Argos.
[157] Williams et Fisher 1976, p. 114, pl. 24; Williams et Zervos 1983, pp. 18–19, pl. 6:c; Salzmann 1982, Korinth 2, n° 64, pp. 26 et 95, pl. 23.
[158] *Corinth* I, iv, pp. 86–87, pl. 20:1 et 21:1.
[159] Epidaure (dont une série plus ancienne), Pérachora, Dodone etc.

Fig. 1. Epidaure, Temple d'Apollon Maléatas, antéfixe

d'une grande partie de la production corinthienne et corinthianisante du Péloponnèse au IVe siècle.

III.3.6. Sur l'angle de la sima d'Olympie dite «du Mètrôon» (Pl. 8:a) mais attribuée par A. Mallwitz au bâtiment central de l'aile Ouest du Léonidaion,[160] et de ce fait datée de 340 environ, une fleur lobée[161] déploie ses pétales au-dessus de feuilles d'acanthe que nous retrouvons parfaitement identiques sur la mosaïque à décor floral de Sicyone (Pl. 8:b);[162]

[160] *OlForsch* V, pp. 126–131, fig. 42–43 et pl. 52; Mallwitz 1972, pp. 251–252, fig. 200.
[161] J'emprunte cet adjectif à la terminologie proposée par A.-M. Guimier-Sorbets 1990 pour la description des mosaïques.
[162] Salzmann 1982, Sikyon 3, n° 118, pp. 11, 18, 25–26 et 112, pl. 20 et 21.

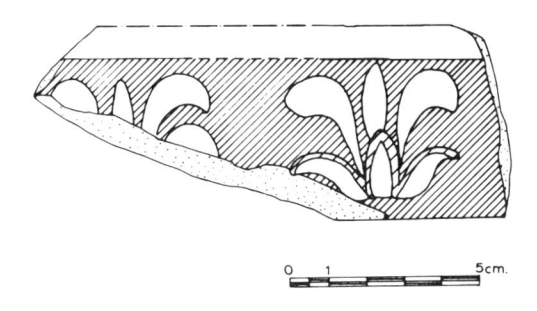

FIG. 2. Argos, Théâtre, bâtiment de scène, sima C. 23841

notons que la technique de la mosaïque n'impose pas nécessairement que le contour des feuilles d'acanthe soit plus exactement «crénelé» que denté, car le mosaïste a su réaliser aussi des feuilles d'acanthe dentées à contour lisse,[163] et qu'il s'agit, sur la mosaïque comme sur la sima, d'un choix de dessinateur et de peintre, à l'origine du carton de l'une et de l'autre.

Ce sont là trop de coïncidences très différentes pour que le style du décor architectural à Corinthe et dans son orbite, au cours du IVe siècle, ne résulte pas du choix délibéré de plusieurs modèles similaires ou identiques, traités dans les diverses techniques qui relèvent du dessin et de la peinture. Comme nous l'avions reconnu à propos des marbres et des vases d'Athènes, il est certain que des «cahiers de motifs» non seulement existaient, mais circulaient d'une corporation à l'autre.

## BIBLIOGRAPHIE

*Agora* XIV = H. A. Thompson et R. E. Wycherley, *The Agora of Athens* (*Agora* XIV), Princeton 1972

Alexandri, O. 1968. «Χρονικὰ τῶν ἀνασκαφῶν. Γ' Ἐφορεία Κλασσικῶν Ἀρχαιοτήτων Ἀθηνῶν», Δελτ 23, 1968, Β'1 [1969], pp. 39–42

Amandry, P. 1984. «Notes de topographie et d'architecture delphiques», *BCH* 108, pp. 177–198

Αρχαία Μακεδονία—*Ancient Macedonia* = Αρχαία Μακεδονία—*Ancient Macedonia* (*Cat. d'exposition tenue au Museum of Victoria, Melbourne / Queensland Museum, Brisbane / Australian Museum, Sydney 1989*), Athènes 1988

Arias, P., et M. Hirmer. 1957. *Spina*, Munich

———. 1960. *Tausend Jahre griechische Vasenkunst*, Munich

Audiat, J. 1933. *Le Trésor des Athéniens* (*Fouilles de Delphes*, II, *Le Sanctuaire d'Apollon*), Paris

Bankel, H. 1986. *Haller von Hallerstein in Griechenland, 1810–1817, Architekt-Zeichner-Bauforscher*, H. Bankel, éd., Berlin

———. 1990. «The Athenian Treasury as Dated by Its Architecture», dans *Akten des XIII. Internationalen Kongresses für klassische Archäologie, Berlin 1988*, Mainz, pp. 410–412

———. 1993. *Der spätarchaische Tempel der Aphaia auf Aegina* (*Denkmäler antiker Architektur* 19), Berlin/New York

Beazley, J. D. 1963. *Attic Vase Painting in the Museum of Fine Arts, Boston* III, Boston

———. 1974. *Der Pan Maler*, 3[eme] éd., Mayence

---

[163] Salzmann 1982, Sikyon 3, n° 118, pp. 11, 18, 25–26 et 112, pl. 20 et 21, feuilles dentées et feuilles «crénelées» sur pl. 21:5; comparer les 4 feuilles lobées à contour continu (pl. 20 et 21:1), semblables à celles de la sima, aux 4 feuilles lobées à contour «crénelé» des angles (pl. 20 et 21:4).

Billot, M.-F. 1976. «Terres cuites architecturales du Musée Épigraphique», Δελτ 31, 1976, A' [1980], pp. 87–135
———. 1991. «Terres cuites architecturales d'Argolide», *RA*, pp. 199–209
Blouet, A., A. Raviosié, et A. Poirot. 1831. *Expédition de Morée* I, Paris
———. 1838. *Expédition de Morée* III, Paris
Boardman, J. 1975. *Athenian Red Figure Vases. The Archaic Period*, Londres
———. 1989. *Athenian Red Figure Vases. The Classical Period*, Londres
Boersma, S. J. 1970. *Athenian Building Policy from 561/60 to 405/4*, Groningue
Bohn, R. 1882. *Die Propyläen der Akropolis zu Athen*, Berlin
Broendsted, P. O. 1830. *Voyages dans la Grèce accompagnés de recherches archéologiques* II, éd. française Firmin Didot, Paris
Brouskari, M. 1989. «Aus dem Giebelschmuck des Athena-Nike Tempels», dans *Beiträge zur Ikonographie und Hermeneutik, Festschrift für Nikolaus Himmelmann*, H. U. Cain, H. Gabelmann, et D. Salzmann, éd., Mayence, pp. 115–118
Bruneau, Ph., et J. Ducat. 1983. *Guide de Délos*, 3ème éd., Athènes
Bühlmann, J. 1872. *Die Architektur des klassischen Altertums und der Renaissance*, Stuttgart
Büsing, H. H. 1969. «Vermutungen über die Akropolis in Athen», *MarbWPr*, pp. 1–30
———. 1979. «Ein Anthemion in Delphi», dans *Studies in Classical Art and Archaeology. A Tribute to P. Heinrich von Blanckenhagen*, G. Kopcke et M. B. Moore, éd., Locust Valley, N.Y., pp. 29–36
———. 1988. «Athener Schatzhaus und Parthenon», dans Πρακτικά του XII Διεθνούς Συνεδρίου Κλασικής Αρχαιολογίας, Αθήνα, 4–10 Σεπτεμβρίου 1983, IV, Athènes, pp. 29–32
———. 1990. «Zur Bemalung des Nike-Tempels», *AA* [*JdI* 105], pp. 71–76
Burn, L. 1991. «A Dinoid Volute-krater by the Meleager Painter: An Attic Vase in the South Italian Manner», *Greek Vases in the J. Paul Getty Museum* 5, Malibu, pp. 107–163
Buschor, E. 1929. *Die Tondächer der Akropolis*, I, *Simen*, Berlin/Leipzig
———. 1933. *Die Tondächer der Akropolis*, II, *Stirnziegel*, Berlin/Leipzig
———. 1933a. «Altsamische Grabstelen», *AM* 58, pp. 22–46
Cambitoglou, A. 1978a. «Τορώνη», Ἔργον 1978 [1979], pp. 26–30
———. 1978b. «Ἀνασκαφὴ Τορώνης», Πρακτικά 1978 [1980], pp. 80–92
Camp, J. M. 1986. *The Athenian Agora. Excavations in the Heart of Athens*, Londres
———. 1990. *The Athenian Agora. A Guide to the Excavations and Museum*, 4ème éd., Athènes
Carpenter, R. 1970. *Die Erbauer des Parthenon*, Munich
Caskey, J. D., et J. D. Beazley. 1954. *Attic Vase Painting in the Museum of Fine Arts, Boston* II, Oxford/Boston
Cavvadias, P., et G. Kawerau. 1906–1907. *Die Ausgrabung der Akropolis vom Jahre 1885 bis zum Jahre 1890*, Berlin
Charbonneaux, J., R. Martin, et F. Villard. 1968. *Grèce archaïque*, Athènes
Childs, W. A. P. 1985. «In Defense of an Early Date for the Frieze of the Temple on the Ilissos», *AM* 100, pp. 207–251
Cockerell, C. R. 1860. *The Temples of Jupiter Panhellenius at Aegina and of Apollo Epicurius at Bassae near Phigalia in Arcadia*, Londres
Collignon, M. 1912. *Le Parthénon*, Paris
*Corinth* I, iv = O. Broneer, *The South Stoa and Its Roman Successors* (*Corinth* I, iv), Princeton 1954
Courby, F. 1927. *La terrasse du temple* (*Fouilles de Delphes*, II, *Le sanctuaire d'Apollon*), Paris
Daux, G. 1923. *Les deux trésors* (*Fouilles de Delphes*, II, *Le sanctuaire d'Athéna Pronaia*), Paris
Daux, G., et E. Hansen. 1987. *Le trésor de Siphnos* (*Fouilles de Delphes*, II, *Le sanctuaire d'Apollon*), Paris
De La Coste-Messelière, P. 1942–1943. «Geison et sima au temple des Alcméonides», *BCH* 66–67, pp. 66–67
———. 1953. «Trois notules delphiques. (…) Trésor des Athéniens: les palmettes», *BCH* 77, pp. 179–182
De La Coste-Messelière, P., et G. De Miré. 1957. *Delphes*, Paris
De Laborde, L. 1848. *Le Parthénon. Documents pour servir à une restauration*, Paris

Délivorrias, A. 1969. «Poseidontempel auf Kap Sunion. Neue Fragmente der Friesdekoration», *AM* 84, pp. 127–142

———. 1974. *Attische Giebelskulpturen und Akrotere des fünften Jahrhunderts* (*Tübinger Studien zur Archäologie und Kunstgeschichte* 1), Tübingen

Despinis, G. 1974. «Τὰ γλυπτὰ τῶν ἀετωμάτων τοῦ ναοῦ τῆς 'Αθηνᾶς Νίκης», Δελτ 29, 1974, Α' [1977], pp. 8–24

Dinsmoor, W. B. 1940. «The Temple of Ares at Athens», *Hesperia* 9, pp. 1–52

———. 1941. *Observations on the Hephaisteion* (*Hesperia* Supplement 5), Princeton

———. 1946. «The Athenian Treasury as Dated by Its Ornament», *AJA* 50, pp. 86–121

Dinsmoor, W. B., Jr. s.d. *Sounion* (*Keramos Guides*), Athènes

———. 1974a. «New Fragments of the Parthenon in the Athenian Agora», *Hesperia* 43, pp. 132–155

———. 1974b. «The Temple of Poseidon: A Missing Sima and Other Matters», *AJA* 78, pp. 212–238

———. 1976. «The Roof of the Hephaisteion», *AJA* 80, pp. 223–246

———. 1982. «Anchoring Two Floating Temples», *Hesperia* 51, pp. 410–452

Dörpfeld, W. 1881. «Über die Verwendung von Terrakotten am Geison und Dach griechischer Bauwerke», *BWPr* 41, Berlin

Drerup, H. 1981. «Parthenon und Vorparthenon. Zum Stand der Kontroverse», *AntK* 24, pp. 21–38

Ducrey, P., T. R. Metzger, et K. Reber. 1993. *Le Quartier de la Maison aux mosaïques* (*Eretria, fouilles et recherches* VIII), Lausanne

Ehrhardt, W. 1989. «Der Torso Wien I 328 und der Westgiebel des Athena-Nike-Tempels auf der Akropolis in Athen», dans *Beiträge zur Ikonographie und Hermeneutik, Festschrift für Nikolaus Himmelmann*, H. U. Cain, H. Gabelmann et D. Salzmann, éd., Mayence, pp. 119–127

Epifanio, E. 1982. «Un cratere imerese dell'officina del Pittore dei Niobidi», dans *Aparchai, Nuove ricerche e studi sulla Magna Grecia e la Sicilia antica in onore di P. E. Arias*, Pisa, pp. 347–356

*Euphronios* = *Euphronios, peintre à Athènes au VI$^e$ siècle av. J.-C. Exposition Musée du Louvre, Paris, 18 septembre–31 décembre 1990*, Paris 1990

Fenger, L. 1886. *Die dorische Polychromie*, Berlin

Furtwängler, A. 1906. *Aegina. Das Heiligtum der Aphaia* I, Munich

Ginouves, R., et R. Martin. 1985. *Dictionnaire méthodique de l'architecture grecque et romaine*, I, *Matériaux, techniques de construction, techniques et formes du décor*, Athènes/Rome

Guimier-Sorbets, A.-M. 1990. *Les bases de données en archéologie. Conception et mise en oeuvre*, Paris

Guimier-Sorbets, A.-M., et A. Barbet. 1994. «Le motif de caisson dans la mosaïque, du IVe siècle av. J.-C. à la fin de la République romaine: ses rapports avec l'architecture, le stuc et la peinture», dans *IV. Internationales Mosaikkolloquium, Trier, 8–12 August 1984*, Paris, à paraître

Hampe, R., éd. 1971. *Katalog der Sammlung antiker Kleinkunst des archäologischen Instituts der Universität Heidelberg*, II, *Neuerwerbungen 1958–1970*, Mayence

Harrison, E. B. 1976. Recension de Délivorrias 1974, dans *AJA* 80, pp. 209–210

———. 1979. «The Architectural Sculpture of the So-called Theseum», dans *Greece and Italy in the Classical World, Acta of the XI International Congress of Classical Archaeology, London, 3–9 September 1978*, Londres, p. 220

———. 1981. Recension de *AntP* 18, 1979, dans *AJA* 85, pp. 232–234

Heiden, J. 1987. *Korinthische Dachziegel. Zur Entwicklung der korinthischen Dächer*, Frankfort/Berne/New York/Paris

Herrmann, K. 1974. «Die Giebelrekonstruktion des Schatzhauses von Megara», *AM* 89, pp. 75–83

*Hesperia* 59 = *Proceedings of the First International Conference on Archaic Greek Architectural Terracottas, Athens, December 2–4, 1988* (*Hesperia* 59, 1990), N. A. Winter, éd.

Hübner, G. 1973. «Dachterrakotten aus dem Kerameikos von Athen», *AM* 88, pp. 67–143

Iliakis, K. 1976. «Η Ζωγραφική αρχιτεκτονική διακόσμηση του ναού της Νέμεσης στο Ραμνούντα», Δελτ 31, 1976, Α' [1980], pp. 244–259

———. 1987. «Η στέγη του ναού της Νέμεσης στο Ραμνούντα ή μια απόπειρα αναπάραστασής της», Αναστήλωση-Συντήρηση-Προστασία Μνημείων και Συνόλων 2, pp. 11–29

Jacobsthal, P. 1927. *Ornamente griechischer Vasen*, Munich
Jacquemin, A., et D. Laroche. 1982. «Notes sur trois piliers delphiques», *BCH* 106, pp. 191–212
Karousos, Ch. 1934. Τὸ Μουσεῖο τῆς Θῆβας, Athènes
Kleine, J. 1973. *Untersuchungen zur Chronologie der attischen Kunst von Peisistratos bis Themistokles (Istanbuler Mitteilungen. Beiheft* 8), Tübingen
Koch, H. 1955. *Studien zum Theseustempel in Athen (AbhLeip* 47:2), Leipzig
Korres, M. 1988. «Πῶς καὶ γιατί ἡ ζωφόρος τοῦ Παρθενῶνος λαξεύθηκε ἐπάνω στο κτήριο», dans Πρακτικά του XII Διεθνοῦς Συνεδρίου Κλασικῆς Αρχαιολογίας, Ἀθήνα, 4–10 Σεπτεμβρίου 1983, IV, Athènes, pp. 104–107
Krug, A. 1979. «Der Fries des Tempels am Ilissos», *AntP* 18, pp. 7–21
Krystalli-Votsis, K. 1987. «'Ανασκαφὴ Σικυῶνος», Πρακτικά 1987 [1990], pp. 65–68
Kurtz, D. C. 1975. *Athenian White Lekythoi*, Oxford
La Follette, L. 1986. «The Chalkotheke on the Athenian Akropolis», *Hesperia* 55, pp. 75–87
Lambert, M. 1877. *Envoi de Rome 1877, L'Acropole d'Athènes*, Paris
Lambrinoudakis, V. K. 1978. «'Ανασκαφὴ στὸ ἱερὸ τοῦ 'Απόλλωνος Μαλεάτα», Πρακτικά 1978 [1980], pp. 111–121
Langlotz, E. 1975. *Studien zur Nordostgriechischen Kunst*, Mainz
Lauffer, S. 1971. «Topographische Untersuchungen im Kopaisgebiet, 1970», Δελτ 26, 1971, B'1 [1974], pp. 239–245
Le Bas, Ph. 1847. *Voyage archéologique en Grèce et en Asie Mineure fait par ordre du Gouvernement Français (1842–1844), avec la coopération d'E. Landron, Architecture*, 5ᵉ livraison, *Atlas*, Paris
———. 1888. *Voyage archéologique en Grèce et en Asie Mineure, Planches de topographie, de sculpture et d'architecture gravées d'après les dessins de E. Landron, publiées et commentées par S. Reinach*, Paris
Le Roy, Ch. 1967. *Les terres cuites architecturales (Fouilles de Delphes* II), Paris
Lethaby, W. R. 1908. *Greek Buildings Represented by Fragments in the British Museum*, Londres
Mallwitz, A. 1972. *Olympia und seine Bauten*, Munich
Marangou, L. 1986. «Γλυπτά ἀρχαϊκῶν καὶ κλασικῶν χρόνων στὴν Αμοργό», dans *Archaische und klassische griechische Plastik, Akten des Internationalen Kolloquiums vom 22.–25. April 1985 in Athen* I, Mayence, pp. 119–128
*Mémoire* = A. Paccard, *Envoi de Rome 1845–1846. Le Parthénon. Mémoire* (EBA ms 241), Paris
Meritt, L. S. 1970. «The Stoa Poikile», *Hesperia* 39, pp. 233–264
Mertens-Horn, M. 1988. *Die Löwenkopfwasserspeier des griechischen Westens im 6. und 5. Jahrhundert v. Chr. (Mitteilungen des Deutschen Archäologischen Instituts, Römische Abteilung. Ergänzungsheft* 28), Mainz
Metzger, H. 1951. *Les représentations dans la céramique attique du IVe siècle*, Paris
Michaelis, A. 1871. *Der Parthenon*, Leipzig
Miles, M. M. 1980. «The Date of the Temple on the Ilissos River», *Hesperia* 49, pp. 309–325
———. 1989. «A Reconstruction of the Temple of Nemesis at Rhamnous», *Hesperia* 58, pp. 131–240
Miller, Stephen G. 1978. «Excavations at Nemea, 1977», *Hesperia* 47, pp. 58–88
———. 1979. «Excavations at Nemea, 1978», *Hesperia* 48, pp. 73–103
Noack, F. 1927. *Eleusis. Die baugeschichtliche Entwicklung des Heiligtumes*, Berlin
Ohnesorg, A. 1991. «Herstellung und Bemalung von Marmordächern des 6. Jhs. v. Chr.», dans *Bautechnik der Antike. Diskussionen zur archäologischen Bauforschung* 5, pp. 172–177
———. 1993. *Inselionische Marmordächer (Denkmäler antiker Architektur* 18:2), Berlin/New York
*OlForsch* V = A. Mallwitz et W. Schiering, *Die Werkstatt des Pheidias in Olympia (Olympische Forschungen* V), Berlin 1964
Orlandos, A. K. 1915. «Τὸ ἀέτωμα του ἐν Σουνίῳ ναοῦ τοῦ Ποσειδῶνος», Δελτ 1, 1915 [1916], pp. 1–17
———. 1947–1948. «La construction du Temple d'Athéna Niké», *BCH* 71–72, pp. 1–38
———. 1953–1954. «Ἡ γραπτὴ ἀρχιτεκτονικὴ διακόσμησις τοῦ ἐν Σουνίῳ ναοῦ τοῦ Ποσειδῶνος», ΑρχΕφ Τ. Γ', pp. 1–18
———. 1976–1978. Ἡ ἀρχιτεκτονικὴ τοῦ Παρθενῶνος, Α'–Γ', Athènes
Paccard, A. 1845–1846. *Envoi de Rome 1845–1846. Le Parthénon* (Collection EBA, prise en charge n° 2208), Paris

*Paris-Rome-Athènes* = *Paris-Rome-Athènes. Le voyage en Grèce des architectes françaises aux XIX<sup>e</sup> et XX<sup>e</sup> siècles*, Paris 1982
Penrose, F. C. 1851. *An Investigation of the Principles of Athenian Architecture*, Londres
Pétrakos, V. Ch. 1987. «Οἱ ἀνασκαφὲς τοῦ Ραμνοῦντος (1813-1987)», ΑρχΕφ 1987, pp. 267-297
Picon, C. A. 1978. «The Ilissos Temple Reconsidered», *AJA* 82, pp. 47-81
Platon, N. 1963. «'Εργασίαι διαμορφώσεως 'Ασκληπιείου», Δελτ 18, 1963, Β'1 [1965], pp. 18-22
Poppe, C. 1843-1845. *Sammlung von Ornamenten und Fragmenten antiker Architektur, Sculptur u. s. w.*, Berlin
Reeder Williams, E. 1984. *The Archaeological Collection of the Johns Hopkins University*, Baltimore/Londres
Richter, G. M. A. 1961. *The Archaic Gravestones of Attica*, Londres
Ridgway, B. S. 1981. *Fifth Century Styles in Greek Sculpture*, Princeton
Roebuck, M. C. 1990. «Archaic Architectural Terracottas from Corinth», dans *Hesperia* 59, pp. 47-63
Ross, L. 1855. *Archäologische Aufsätze* I, Leipzig
Ross, L., E. Schaubert, et Ch. Hansen. 1839. *Die Akropolis von Athen nach den neuesten Ausgrabungen* I. Abt.: *Der Tempel der Nike Apteros*, Berlin
Rotroff, S. 1983. «Three Cistern Systems on the Kolonos Agoraios», *Hesperia* 52, pp. 257-297
Salzmann, D. 1982. *Untersuchungen zu den antiken Kieselmosaiken, von den Anfängen bis zum Beginn der Tesseratechnik (Archäologische Forschungen 10)*, Berlin
Schefold, K. 1975. *Götter- und Heldensagen der Griechen in der spätarchaischen Kunst*, Munich
Schuchhardt, W. H. 1935/36. «Die Sima des Alten Athenatempels der Akropolis», *AM* 60/61, pp. 1-98
———. 1963. «Archaische Bauten auf der Akropolis von Athen», *AA* [*JdI* 78], col. 797-824
Schuller, M. 1991. *Der Artemistempel im Delion von Paros (Denkmäler antiker Architektur 18:1)*, Berlin/New York
Shear, T. L., Jr. 1984. «The Athenian Agora: Excavations of 1980-1982», *Hesperia* 53, pp. 1-57
Shoe, L. T. 1936. *Profiles of Greek Mouldings*, Cambridge, Mass.
Stais, V. 1899-1900. «'Ανασκαφαὶ ἐν Σουνίῳ», ΑρχΕφ, col. 113-150
———. 1917. «Σουνίου ἀνασκαφαί», ΑρχΕφ, col. 168-213
Stevens, G. P. 1954. «Lintel with the Painted Lioness», *Hesperia* 23, pp. 169-184
Stevens, G. P., et J. M. Paton. 1927. *The Erechtheum*, Cambridge, Mass.
Stuart, J., et N. Revett. 1762. *The Antiquities of Athens* I, Londres
———. 1794. *The Antiquities of Athens* III, Londres
Thompson, H. A. 1950. «Excavations in the Athenian Agora: 1949», *Hesperia* 19, pp. 317-337
Tölle-Kastenbein, R. 1983. «Bemerkungen zur absoluten Chronologie spätarchaischer und frühklassischer Denkmäler Athens», *AA* [*JdI* 98], pp. 580-582
Touchais, G. 1979. «Chronique de fouilles», *BCH* 103, pp. 527-615
———. 1988. «Chronique de fouilles», *BCH* 112, pp. 611-696
Travlos, J. 1971. *Bildlexikon zur Topographie des antiken Athen*, Tübingen
Vallois, R. 1978. *L'architecture hellénique et hellénistique à Délos*, II, *Grammaire historique de l'architecture délienne (Deuxième livraison)*, Athènes
Vlassopoulou, Ch. 1989. Πήλινες διακοσμημένες κεραμώσεις ἀπὸ τὴν ἀθηναϊκὴ Ἀκρόπολη. Κατάλογος ἐκθέσης, Κέντρο Μελετῶν Ἀκροπόλεως, Athènes
———. 1990. «Decorated Architectural Terracottas from the Athenian Acropolis. Catalogue of Exhibition», dans *Hesperia* 59, pp. i-xxxii
Von Bockelberg, S. 1979. «Die Friese des Hephaisteion», *AntP* 18, pp. 23-50
Votsis, K. 1976. «Nouvelle mosaïque de Sicyone», *BCH* 100, pp. 575-588
Wesenberg, B. 1981. «Zur Baugeschichte des Niketempels», *JdI* 96, pp. 28-54
———. 1983. «Parthenongebälk und Südmetopenproblem», *JdI* 98, pp. 57-86
Wiegand, Th. 1904. *Die archaische Porosarchitektur der Akropolis zu Athen*, Leipzig/Cassel
Williams, C. K., II. 1980. «Corinth Excavations, 1979», *Hesperia* 49, pp. 107-134
Williams, C. K., II, et J. E. Fisher. 1976. «Corinth 1975: Forum Southwest», *Hesperia* 45, pp. 99-162
Williams, C. K., II, et O. H. Zervos. 1983. «Corinth 1982: East of the Theater», *Hesperia* 52, pp. 1-47
———. 1991. «Corinth 1990: Southeast Corner of Temenos E», *Hesperia* 60, pp. 1-58
Wyatt, W. F., et C. N. Edmonson. 1984. «The Ceiling of the Hephaisteion», *AJA* 88, pp. 135-167
Züchner, W. 1936. «Fragmente auf der Akropolis und im Asklepieion zu Athen», *AA* [*JdI* 51], col. 305-334

Crédit d'illustrations

PLATE 1:a. Cl. M.-F. B. d'après *BCH* 103, 1979, p. 590, fig. 149 (reproduit avec la permission de Torone Excavations) b. Cl. EFA; c. Cl. M.-F. B. d'après *Euphronios*, n° 5, p. 90; d. Cl. EFA, Ph. Collet; e. Cl. ENSBA d'après Cockerell 1860, pl. XIII, fig. 3 et 4; f. Cl. M.-F. B. d'après Bankel 1986, p. 130, fig. 4:10 (reproduit avec la permission de l'auteur).

PLATE 2:a. Cl. M.-F. B. d'après Audiat 1933, pl. XXII; b. Cl. EFA, Ph. Collet; c. Cl. M.-F. B. d'après *Euphronios*, n° 12, p. 114 (reproduit avec la permission de Metropolitan Museum of Art); d. Cl. DAI Athen, AKR 1959; e. Cl. DAI Athen, AKR 1968; f. Cl. M.-F. B. d'après Travlos 1971, fig. 331.

PLATE 3:a, b, c. Cl. Première Ephorie, Acropole; d. Cl. DAI Athen, AKR 951; e. Cl. DAI Athen, AKR 936; f. Cl. Troisième Ephorie n° 1151; g. Cl. Première Ephorie, Acropole; h. Cl. DAI Athen, AKR 938 i. Cl. DAI Athen, AKR 942.

PLATE 4:a, b. Cl. Agora Excavations; c. Cl. ENSBA; d. Cl. ENSBA, d'après Stuart et Revett 1762, chap. II, p. 10, pl. VIII fig. 3; e. Cl. M.-F. B. d'après Arias et Hirmer 1960, fig. 173; f. Cl. ENSBA; g. Cl. EFA, Ph. Collet, d'après Orlandos 1978, pl. 74.

PLATE 5:a. Cl. Agora Excavations; b. Cl. EFA; c. Cl. ENSBA; d. Cl. EFA d'après Koch 1955, fig. 83; e. Cl. M.-F. B. d'après Orlandos 1953–1954; f. Cl. EFA, Ph. Collet; g. Cl. ENSBA.

PLATE 6:a. Cl. EFA, Ph. Collet d'après Penrose 1851, pl. XXV; b. Cl. ENSBA; c, d. Agora Excavations d'après Dinsmoor, Jr. 1974a, pl. 24 et fig. 5.

PLATE 7:a, b. Cl. EFA, Ph. Collet; c. Cl. Quatrième Ephorie, Nauplie; d. Cl. D. Salzmann; e. Cl. Corinth Excavations; f. Cl. EFA; g. Cl. DAI Athen, 78/429.

PLATE 8:a. Cl. DAI Athen, Ol. 5393; b. Cl. D. Salzmann; c. Cl. Quatrième Ephorie, Nauplie; d. Cl. Corinth Excavations; e. Cl. EFA.

FIGURE 1: EFA, Planothèque, n° 8442.

FIGURE 2: EFA, Planothèque, n° 5318.

MARIE-FRANÇOISE BILLOT
CNRS-IRAA

Adresse personnelle:
38, rue Lacépède
75005 Paris, France

# ARCHITECTURAL TERRACOTTAS FROM CLASSICAL AND HELLENISTIC CORINTH

(PLATES 9–19)

THE MANUFACTURE of architectural terracottas continued on a large scale at Corinth without interruption throughout the Classical period. The tile makers maintained the same high quality as in the Archaic period, producing both for home consumption and for export. In addition they set up workshops for important construction projects at other sites such as Olympia. In a paper of this length it is hardly possible to cover the large amount of 5th- and 4th-century material found at Corinth. I propose, therefore, to show only representative and unusual pieces of successive periods and to indicate the high quality of the tiles produced.

Various significant innovations appear in the Classical and Hellenistic periods. The first change, one important for the whole appearance of the roof, is the use of the cyma reversa profile on the raking sima and light-on-dark decoration. Toward the end of the 5th century the tile painters often made minor changes in the decoration as well, apparently to provide variety. During the 4th century the lateral sima using plastic decoration was developed. In some instances, too, we can detect archaizing tendencies in the painting of the raking sima. Finally, in the Hellenistic period, designs that had been used over several centuries were revitalized. Good examples have been found on sima pieces excavated to the north of Temple Hill. They had belonged to the important buildings in the area, destroyed in 146 B.C.

For the most part we cannot connect tiles with individual buildings, but there are a few datable landmarks that give useful information for the dating of the tiles and the development of their decoration. The Tile Works has provided many tiles from the latter part of the 5th century. From them much can be learned about the styles of that period. The South Stoa and the Asklepieion in their turn do the same for the end of the 4th century. Together these three groups of tiles make possible significant comparisons.

At first the principal difference from the Archaic period was the use of light-on-dark decoration with a single lotus and palmette band on the raking sima, rather than the double alternating and reversed lotus and palmette band of the Archaic period. A meander was also substituted for the guilloche on the fascia at the bottom and on the face of the eaves tile. At the same time the profile of the raking sima was changing from the sharp divisions of the torus molding and fascia to the smoother curve of the cyma reversa. In the first quarter of the 5th century there was considerable variety in the combinations used, but by the second quarter the changes were well advanced.

The quality of tile production in the second quarter of the 5th century is illustrated by a group of combination eaves tiles with palmette antefixes[1] (FA 125, Pl. 9:a) from north of

---

[1] *Corinth* IV, i, FA 2, pp. 12–13, fig. 5:c, p. 47; also a series of unpublished antefixes, FA 125–FA 140, FA 142, with the exception of FA 129, FA 135, and FA 136, which are a little larger. Other similar pieces are also noted by Ida Thallon-Hill.

Temple Hill. The regular leaves of the palmette of the antefix forming a nearly circular arc are clearly an extension of the shape used in the Late Archaic period. The lower part below the palmette is more elongated than before and less stiff. An extra leaf has now been added on either side between the spiral and the lotus calyx. On the face of the eaves tile is a meander. The narrow space between the black border of the center square and the meander border is characteristic of the 5th century. The antefixes resemble those from Roof 56, the Lesche of the Cnidians at Delphi, dated 475–460 B.C.,[2] and those of the Classical temple at Kalapodi.[3] The Corinth tiles are perhaps a little later than those from Delphi but still date to the first half of the 5th century.

Another antefix fragment[4] (FA 417, Pl. 9:b) of equally good quality, which preserves most of the palmette, is probably somewhat later. Its leaves are more attenuated and its spade-shaped center longer and narrower. This piece was built into the wall of the later kiln at the Tile Works.

Two sets of tiles from raking simas also belong to the second quarter or middle of the 5th century. Some of these were published by Hill. Additional pieces were later discovered in the area to the north of Temple Hill. These simas are on a smaller scale than the combination tiles already discussed and cannot be from the same building. Nonetheless, the meander preserved on the bottom fascia of one set[5] (FS 5, FS 6 [Pl. 9:c], FS 425) is very similar to that used on the combination tiles. The upper molding of these sima pieces is decorated with a bead and reel above a Lesbian leaf. The cymatium has a typical alternating eleven-leafed palmette and three-petaled lotus. The lotus and palmettes are connected below by tendrils ending in down-curving spirals under the palmettes and looping up under the calyx of the lotus. This is a pattern found throughout the Classical period. The outer petals of the lotus flower curve over the top of the palmette as in Roofs 55 and 56 at Delphi, dated about 480 B.C. and 475–460 B.C. respectively.[6] This form of lotus is also found in the sima from Ptoion dated toward 450 B.C. or mid-5th century.[7]

The second set of tiles[8] (FS 9, FS 428 [Pl. 9:d]) resembles the first except for the lotus whose outer petals do not extend over the palmette. In this characteristic this set recalls those tiles from Roof 58 at Delphi, dated 460–450 B.C.[9] Otherwise the two sets are virtually identical. This is also true of their profiles (Fig. 1, profile nos. 1 and 2). Both still have a fairly strong curve and project out some distance at the top. The cyma reversa is still in the process of development. These tiles should be dated about the middle of the 5th century. The Delphi roofs they resemble are also of Corinthian workmanship.

---

[2] Le Roy 1967, pp. 128–132, 137–139; A 186, p. 130, pl. 48:17; p. 139 for the date.
[3] Hübner 1990, p. 167, pl. 15:a.
[4] Unpublished.
[5] For FS 5 and FS 6, see *Corinth* IV, i, p. 66 and pl. V; Heiden 1987, pp. 117–118; also Van Buren 1926, p. 97, no. 104, and Shoe 1936, I, p. 78, II, pl. 33:9. The date of the end of the 5th century given by Van Buren and by Shoe is too late. FS 425, found in the area north of Temple Hill, is unpublished.
[6] Le Roy 1967, pp. 127–128, 139, pls. 45, 103 for Roof 55; pp. 128–132, 139, pls. 46, 103, 110 for Roof 56.
[7] Le Roy 1967, p. 145 and pl. 56; Heiden 1987, p. 118.
[8] For FS 9, see *Corinth* IV, i, p. 67; FS 428, found to the north of Temple Hill, is unpublished.
[9] Le Roy 1967, S 44, pp. 133–134, 139, pl. 48.

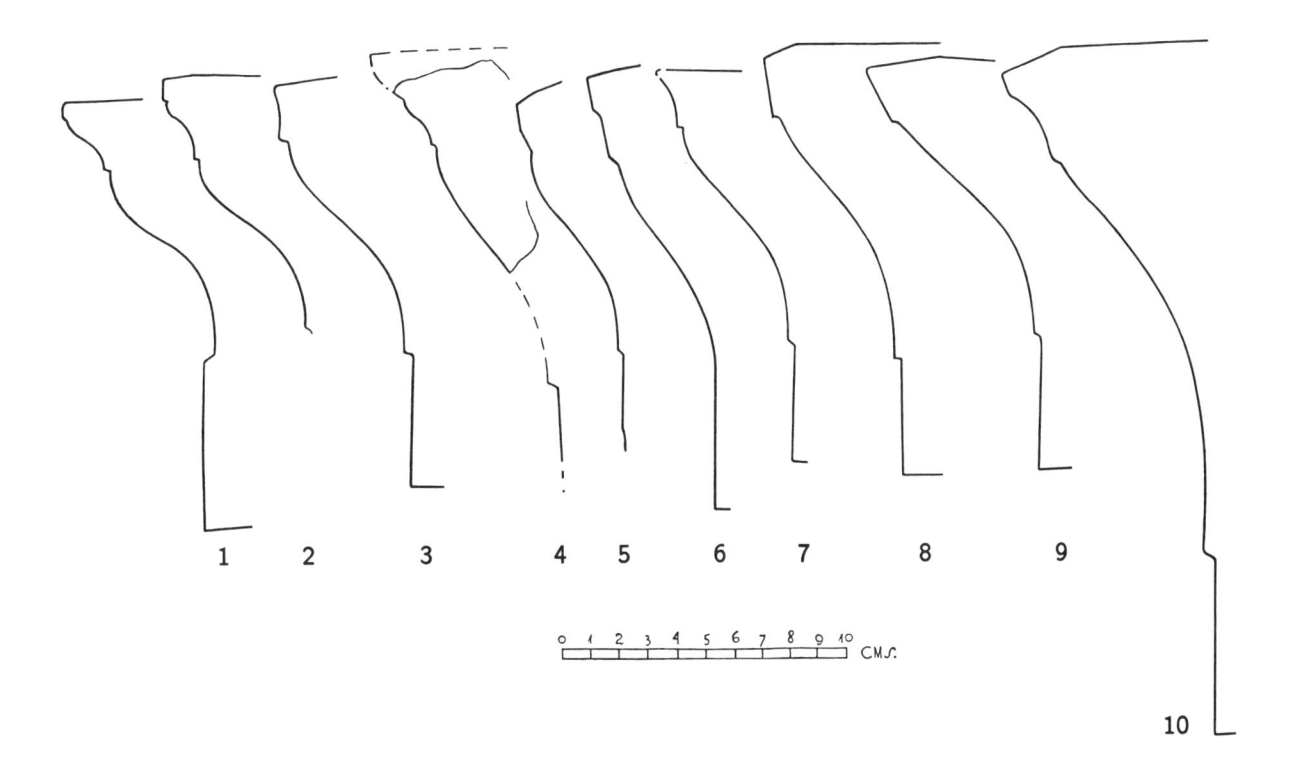

Fig. 1. (1) FS 6; (2) FS 9, FS 428; (3) FS 900; (4) FS 885; (5) FS 876; (6) FS 865; (7) FS 860; (8) FS 867; (9) FS 875; (10) FS 877

The Tile Works at Corinth has provided us with a wealth of material, but we are concerned here only with the roof tiles. The greater part of the architectural terracottas date to the period around 430–420 B.C. There were two kilns. The earlier dates to the Archaic period and on into the 5th century. A cistern (formerly designated Well C) appears to have been filled when this kiln went out of use. The material in it dates from the late 6th century and first half of the 5th century, with some pieces as late as 460–420 B.C.[10] The second kiln was largely built of tile pieces of various sorts. Some forty-six pieces, mostly simas, from the wall of the kiln were inventoried. Other tiles were also found in fill in the area, some of which evidently washed in when the Tile Works went out of use. Presumably the pieces built into the wall of this kiln were left lying around when the first kiln was abandoned. There is no evidence of a third kiln that might have produced other material. Probably the second kiln was built soon after the first ceased to be used. While there is an occasional Archaic piece in the wall, most of the material is generally homogeneous, from about the end of the third quarter of the 5th century, providing a good source of information for this period.

[10] Merker 1988, p. 193 and note 3, p. 198 and note 10; Weinberg 1954, p. 130, fig. 2:c and note 132 and pp. 132–133; Weinberg 1957, pp. 290, 292 and note 22; Corinth VII, iii, p. 205, deposit 26 (Well C Tile Works).

One tile[11] (FA 415, Pl. 9:e) built into the wall of the second kiln very possibly was intended to be used as an akroterion. Only one side is painted and the surface is flat, not molded. The scale is rather large. It is unlikely that it was meant to be an antefix. The design consists of a palmette with a diamond-shaped heart, below which are the upper parts of two large spirals held together by a dark red band. The leaves of the palmette are quite straight and stiff, except for the lowest ones, which curve somewhat to conform to the line of the spirals. The decoration resembles that of the ridge palmettes of the Archaic period. This piece may still belong to the first half of the 5th century.

Two antefixes give an idea of the variations found in the second half of the 5th century. One[12] (FA 425, Pl. 9:f) comes from the Tile Works cistern. It should not, therefore, be later in date than 420 B.C. Its design differs from that of the earlier antefixes of the first half of the 5th century in several respects. The lowest leaves project out as far as those above. It is this that results in the altered profile. The design of the lower part of the antefix under the palmette also is unlike that used earlier. The lotus of the earlier pieces is replaced by down-curving spirals. Their tendrils follow the line of the sides, then curve upward once more to form double spirals along the edge of the tile. Below the center spirals is a seven-leaved palmette suspended from a diamond-shaped heart.

A second antefix[13] (FA 200, Pl. 10:a) from the Potters' Quarter shows the same delicacy of treatment found in FA 425. At the top is the usual palmette. The lower part, however, represents another variation. The central pattern is the same as before, but the tendrils end in single rather than double spirals. In the center below the spirals is a lotus flower, but unlike that of the earlier antefixes the calyx of the lotus is curved rather than angular, giving quite a different appearance. There are eyes in the spirals and half palmettes between the tendrils and the lotus. Both FA 425 and FA 200 show some affinity to the antefixes from Delphi of Series 63 and 69, the latter dated between 450 and 420 B.C.[14]

Many raking sima pieces were built into the Tile Works kiln wall and thus are discards. The quality of the painting varies, being very good in some, quite sketchy in others. One excellent piece, from a Tile Works well rather than the kiln, although only a small fragment of the upper part of the sima[15] (FS 885, Pl. 10:b), might be said to represent the next stage in sima development after FS 9 and FS 428 (Pl. 9:d). The moldings at the top, decorated with a bead and reel and a Lesbian leaf below, while not identical to the earlier pieces, are very similar. The lotus is of the same type, but the outer petals flare less. The palmette, however, is quite different. Its leaves are fewer and more widely spaced, resembling some of the Delphi pieces. The profile (Fig. 1, profile no. 4), as far as it is preserved, has a definite curve, although this is not as pronounced as in FS 9 and FS 428. FS 885 appears to be intermediate between them and the next group of simas.

The workmen who painted the raking simas seem to have relieved the monotony of the typical design at this time by minor variations. A few examples will serve to illustrate

[11] FA 415 is unpublished.
[12] FA 425 is unpublished.
[13] *Corinth* XV, ii, pp. 272, 281, pl. 58, no. 63.
[14] Le Roy 1967, series 63: p. 136, A 57 and A 58, pl. 51; series 69: pp. 141, 148, A 95, A 109, and A 110, pl. 53.
[15] FS 885, unpublished, comes from a 4th-century well in the Tile Works.

this effort. Certain elements remain fairly constant, such as the upper molding or moldings with egg and dart or bead and reel or both and the meander on the fascia at the bottom. The palmettes, too, are fairly standard, eleven leaves with tendrils below ending in down-curving spirals below them and a loop under the lotus. There is an occasional difference in the treatment of the palmette center. The variations come mainly in the form of the lotus. In FS 900[16] (Pl. 10:c) the calyx has a teardrop-shaped center flanked on either side by a pointed leaf curving downward. Above these latter are tall rectangular boxes, probably intended as leaves. The flower is made up of three petals. FS 876[17] (Pl. 10:d) is basically the same, but instead of straight-sided rectangles it has curved leaves of white lined in dark red. FS 865[18] (Pl. 10:e) varies this same design by giving the lotus flower five petals, the lower two of which are thin and narrow and curve outward. The upper side petals also spread out more. FS 860[19] (Pl. 11:a) has a different version. Here the space in the loop of the tendrils under the lotus is filled with a teardrop or dagger. The two side leaves of the calyx are smaller and more widely spaced but still lined with red. The lower two petals, also more widely spaced, curve out and down. The heart of the palmette, unlike the others, is reserved and has a small dart. The palmette leaves of all these vary somewhat from tile to tile, FS 900 and FS 865 having more of a tendency toward a double curve than the others. As far as the profiles (Fig. 1) are concerned, FS 900, which is not from the Tile Works, has a stronger curve with greater projection than the others. It is much flatter, however, than those of the middle of the 5th century. The others, all from the Tile Works, one (FS 865) from the kiln wall, are similar and resemble the profile of Mallwitz's "Blütensima" from the Pheidias Workshop, dated *ca.* 430 B.C.[20] For palmettes with the slight double curve, compare those from the Temple of Ares.[21]

A different treatment of the cymatium occurs in some other pieces of raking sima, also built into the wall of the Tile Works kiln. In these the lotus calyx is made up of three tulip-shaped leaves. In one example[22] (FS 867, Pl. 11:b) the lotus flower has five petals. They are not unlike those of FS 860, though less widely spaced. Each spiral under the palmette has an additional tendril at the side. The palmette leaves are thicker and rounder at the ends than those in the previous group of simas.

A much larger sima[23] (FS 877, Pl. 11:c) again differs in design. The calyx is made up of the same three tulip-shaped leaves and is carefully outlined. There are three petals in

---

[16] FS 900, unpublished, is from the Asklepieion area.

[17] FS 876, unpublished, comes from the first accumulation of fill that washed in after the Tile Works went out of use.

[18] FS 865, unpublished, was built into the wall of the second kiln of the Tile Works.

[19] FS 860, unpublished, came from a Byzantine well in the Tile Works.

[20] *OlForsch* V, pp. 112–113, 121, 124–125, 131–132, pls. 15, 38, 39, 40:1; Heiden 1987, pp. 109, 119, 123, profile 7:5; Shoe 1936, I, pp. 78–79; II, pl. 33:5; Mallwitz 1980, no. 41, p. 150, pl. 102:4.

[21] Dinsmoor 1940, p. 33, fig. 12 and p. 51 for date of erection, between 440 and 436 B.C.; Hübner 1973, p. 117, fig. 13.

[22] FS 867 was built into the wall of the second kiln of the Tile Works. It is unpublished. For others with a tripartite lotus calyx, see *Corinth* IV, i, pp. 25, 78, fig. 25, for FS 128, and pp. 78–79 for FS 129; Roof 80 at Delphi (Le Roy 1967, pp. 154, 168, S 48 and 49, pls. 59:1, 2 and 104) probably should be put here rather than with the late 4th-century roofs of the South Stoa type.

[23] FS 877, unpublished, was built into the wall of the second kiln at the Tile Works.

the flower, very like the upper three of FS 867. Beneath the lotus calyx is a small triangle. Because of the height of the sima, both the lotus and the palmette are elongated and the spade-shaped palmette center is very tall. The palmette leaves show a slight tendency toward a double curve. Running under the lotus and palmette band are S-shaped spirals that turn upward under the lotus, downward under the palmette. The palmettes resemble those on the Hephaisteion-type sima at Olympia, dated around 430–420 B.C.[24] This sima is from a Corinthian workshop (the Pheidias Workshop). It does, however, show some Athenian influence in the decoration. The spirals are used in the same way as those on the frieze of the South Hall of the Erechtheion.[25] The profiles of FS 867 and FS 877 (Fig. 1, profile nos. 8 and 10) are flatter than the others we have discussed. In FS 877 there is virtually no curve; it is almost concave. The palmette is very similar to that of Roof 70 at Delphi, dated by Le Roy between 420 and 400 B.C.[26] Again the palmettes and lotus flowers of Roof 70 are somewhat elongated.

The same designs used on the cymatia of the raking simas were often reproduced on the soffits of the eaves tiles. A few illustrative examples come not from the Tile Works but from other parts of the excavation. The tripartite lotus calyx with five flower petals and a regularly shaped palmette is found on FT 277[27] (Pl. 11:d); it can be compared with FS 867 (Pl. 11:b). Another type is found on FT 158[28] (Pl. 12:a, b), whose palmettes resemble those of FS 865 (Pl. 10:e) and FS 876 (Pl. 10:d). While the lotus is not exactly the same, all have side leaves of much the same type. FT 168[29] (Pl. 12:c, d) presents another version of this design. A final example[30] (FT 156, Pl. 13:a, b) is interesting because of the acanthus leaves on either side of the calyx center. Such leaves occur on the South East Building[31] and the Hephaisteion-type sima,[32] but they turn upward in the Corinth piece and downward on the Olympia simas and the palmettes are not the same. The meander of the face of these eaves tiles is typical of the 5th century.

Two other pieces built into the kiln wall, a raking sima fragment[33] (FS 875, Pl. 13:c) and an eaves tile[34] (FT 170, Pl. 13:e), do not seem to fit with the others. At first glance their thick, rather blunt palmette and lotus leaves and the straight sides of the palmettes suggest a later date. The calyx of the lotus of FS 875 is rather sketchy and careless, but a close examination shows that the side leaves are of the same basic type as on other simas. The meander, too, is very poorly painted and has a wide border around the square such as is found later. It is difficult to place this piece, but because it is a discard and is so poorly

---

[24] *OlForsch* V, p. 115, fig. 39, pp. 132–133, pls. 42, 43; Heiden 1987, pp. 119, 121, pl. 15:2.

[25] Hübner 1973, pp. 120–121, pl. 69:1.

[26] Le Roy 1967, Roof 70, pp. 141–144, 148, pls. 54, 103.

[27] FT 277, unpublished, was found in a well with Roman Arretine ware in the Lerna section of the Asklepieion.

[28] FT 158, unpublished, from the South Stoa area. FT 26, *Corinth* IV, i, p. 103, belongs to the sames series.

[29] FT 168 is from the Asklepieion area; *Corinth* XIV, p. 89 and pl. 22:6, from the bottom of the Northeast manhole of the Lerna plateia drain. The date given in the text is too late.

[30] FT 156, unpublished, was found in Well IV of the South Stoa. For the well, see *Corinth* VII, iii, p. 226.

[31] Heiden 1987, pp. 127–131, 160, pl. 16:2; Mallwitz 1980, no. 42, pp. 150–151, pl. 102:4; Mallwitz 1972, pp. 202–203, figs. 163–164.

[32] Heiden 1987, p. 119, pl. 15:2; Hübner 1973, p. 120, fig. 16, pl. 69:2.

[33] FS 875 is unpublished.

[34] FT 170 is unpublished.

executed, while its profile (Fig. 1, profile no. 9) fits in with others of the late 5th century, it seems likely that it is a careless or trial piece. Much the same can be said of the fragment of eaves tile, whose workmanship is also very poor. This type of careless painting occurs in another sima piece built into the kiln wall[35] (FS 871, Pl. 13:d). The meander is fairly neat and well done, but the leaves of the palmette, only nine in number, are thin and widely spaced. The outline of one side of the palmette is straight, the other curved. The calyx of the lotus also is crudely drawn.

Other pieces of interest were built into the kiln wall. One, an antefix[36] (FA 414, Pl. 14:a), is important because it is the prototype of that used in the South Stoa and other late 4th-century buildings. The palmette leaves, eleven in number, are quite regular with a slight double curve. The center leaf is angular at the top. The palmette is rather tall and less rounded than those from north of Temple Hill of the earlier 5th century. The center of the palmette is spade-shaped as before. On the lower part of the antefix, just below the center of the palmette, are grooved spirals with eyes. These turn inward. They curve downward and outward to the bottom, then turn upward again along the sides, ending in a double spiral. In the space between the two is a small diamond-shaped dart. Below the central spirals hangs a lotus, the outer petals of which extend well out to the side. On either side of the lotus is a half palmette. The lower part of FA 414 did not take the mold as sharply as it should have. The lower part of an antefix of the same type[37] (FA 440, Pl. 14:b) shows how it should look. The quality of this piece is quite fine. It has been suggested that it belonged to the 4th-century temple of Asklepios,[38] but this fragment was a surface find in the later excavations of 1946–1947 and cannot be connected with the temple. As we shall see, the antefixes of the South Stoa and the Asklepios temple differ from these in several ways (pp. 48–49 below). The palmette leaves are thicker and blunter at the ends and the lotus petals do not spread out as much.

From the kiln wall also comes a small lateral sima or perhaps a crowning molding[39] (FS 1077, Pl. 14:c) only 0.10 m. high. One side and part of the center where a spout was attached are preserved. The decoration is raised and consists of an S-shaped spiral on its side. Between the spirals, at the bottom, is a lotus flower; between them, above, is a heart-shaped flower. In the center of each spiral is an eye. The upper edge is cut out to follow the line of the design. Is this perhaps a forerunner of the plastic lateral simas? The work is quite delicate. The tendrils and spirals are round in section. One is reminded of the workmanship on the antefix from the cistern in the Tile Works (FA 425, p. 42 above, Pl. 9:f) and some of the antefixes at Delphi.[40] Part of a finial[41] (FM 38, Pl. 15:a, b), also from the kiln wall, is important because of the questions it raises about the first use of plastic decoration on lateral simas. It is decorated on both faces with fluted plastic tendrils with small acanthus leaves

---

[35] FS 871 is unpublished.
[36] FA 414 is unpublished.
[37] FA 440 is a surface find from the Asklepieion area.
[38] Coulton 1964, pp. 128–129, fig. 13.
[39] FS 1077 (formerly FM 46), from the collapsed section of the wall of the second kiln at the Tile Works, is unpublished.
[40] As, for example, series 63 and 69, note 14 above.
[41] FM 38, unpublished, was built into the west wall of the second kiln at the Tile Works.

along the stems. These stems in some cases divide into grooved spirals. At the end of some of the tendrils is what appears to be the open end of a bell-shaped flower. This piece is on a large scale; the preserved height is 0.32 m., comparable in size to a large lateral sima. Comparison with pieces of a lateral sima[42] (FS 104, FS 105, FS 776, FS 1047, Pl. 14:d, e) shows similarities in design and treatment. The fluted tendrils, grooved spirals, and acanthus leaves all occur in the sima in a better-executed form. Even the bell-shaped flower is there in a different form. In the finial we seem to have the same component parts as in the sima. The upper molding of the sima is decorated with a Lesbian leaf, the fascia at the bottom with a meander of the type normally found in the 5th century. The workmanship is very fine, like that of the South East Building at Olympia, a product of a Corinthian workshop.[43] If, as Heiden argues,[44] the first lateral simas with plastic decoration come after the construction of the South East Building, this sima from Corinth must belong at the very beginning of the series. Could it be earlier than the Olympia building? One piece, FS 776, is from the Potters' Quarter at Corinth.

An eaves tile[45] (FT 172, Pl. 16:a, b) from a Tile Works well is an unusual piece, interesting because of the use of a regular pan tile as an eaves tile. The wide groove on the soffit indicates that this pan tile was substituted for a normal eaves tile. On the face is an ivy pattern, on the soffit what resembles a wave pattern. There are other examples of this usage at Corinth. One comes from the Gymnasium[46] and is decorated with a similar ivy pattern. A sima piece in the Nauplia Museum[47] also has an ivy design. A date in the latter half of the 5th century is indicated for the Corinthian pieces. The sima seems to be earlier.

Another 5th-century piece[48] (FM 27, Pl. 16:c) is a fragmentary corner, from either a sima or a molding. On one side is painted a large spiral from which extend two smaller spirals bordering the edge. On the other side there is a meander on the lower part that is set off from the rest. Above is a group of tendrils ending in spirals. The tile curves upward and inward at the corner. The meander indicates a 5th-century date.

---

[42] *Corinth* IV, i, p. 29, note 4, p. 31, fig. 34 and p. 75; Heiden 1987, pp. 165–166, pl. 23:1. On the trip that followed the conference Dr. Petros Themelis discovered a join between FS 105 and the lion's head spout, FS 1047 (formerly in the National Museum in Athens). This now gives us a fine nearly complete sima for further study. The current suggested date is the first half of the 4th century.

[43] See note 31 above.

[44] Heiden 1987, pp. 127–131.

[45] FT 172 was found in Well A, a 4th-century well at the Tile Works; Weinberg 1954, p. 133, note 138a; *Corinth* VII, iii, no. 27, p. 205.

[46] Wiseman 1969, pp. 99–101, FA 519, FA 520, fig. 17, pl. 31:f. This piece is from an eaves tile. For the ivy pattern, see Weinberg 1954, pp. 132–133, fig. 3, citing a lebes with ivy pattern found in the Tile Works; Talcott 1935, no. 8, pp. 500–501, fig. 19, a black-glazed kantharos with an ivy pattern. The well (Talcott 1935, p. 497) was flourishing around 440 B.C. and abandoned around 430 B.C. Other 5th-century pottery with ivy decoration comes from the North Cemetery at Corinth: *Corinth* XIII, pp. 121, 164–165, white-ground lekythoi with ivy pattern, dating to the middle and early third quarter of the 5th century. The ivy on the roof tile seems more like the 5th-century examples than those of the later 4th century.

[47] Hübner 1975, sima no. 17352, pp. 127–128, pl. 67:4–6, fig. 6; dated by Hübner *ca.* 460 B.C.

[48] FM 27, unpublished, has no context.

A fine antefix[49] (FA 420, FA 423, Pl. 16:d) from the Tile Works is an elaborate example of the flame type. On the lower part of the antefix at the bottom are two rows of acanthus leaves. In the center, above them, are two tendrils that rise upward in a lyre shape. These curve around at the top into further tendrils and two small spirals. From the tendrils on each side hangs a small bell-shaped flower. Directly above the acanthus leaves at the center is a small round object with a mushroom-shaped cap. The lyre-shaped arrangement of tendrils with spirals also occurs on Attic antefixes and on some antefixes from Delphi, as on Roof 70.[50] The flame-type palmettes of the mid-4th century and later are usually heavier and bear little resemblance to the Corinth piece. I suggest a date in the early 4th century for the one from the Tile Works.

In the 4th century the best-known group of tiles comes from the South Stoa. Represented are raking and lateral simas; antefixes for the covers behind the lateral sima as well as antefixes and eaves tiles for the rear of the stoa, which did not have a gutter; ridge tiles with palmettes; and many ordinary pan and cover tiles. Evidence of repairs is to be seen in a later set of ridge tiles and in a number of pan and cover tiles.

Leaving aside the question of the exact date of the South Stoa (whether it was built in the 330's or at the very end of the 4th century), the style represented had a widespread influence on the decoration of many of the buildings of the latter part of the 4th century and into the 3rd century. Workshops were set up in a number of places such as Olympia and even Athens[51] to produce these tiles.

The basic design on the raking sima[52] (Pl. 16:e) is the lotus and palmette band, which endured all through the Classical period. But where the trend had been toward taller palmettes with narrower, wider-spaced leaves, now they are once again more rounded with broader leaves. The antefixes[53] (Pl. 17:a), as has already been mentioned, find their prototype in one from the Tile Works (FA 414, p. 45 above, with note 36, Pl. 14:a). The outer petals of the lotus flower, however, do not spread out as much but rather curve up at the ends. The upper leaves of the palmette are broader with rounder ends. The ridge palmettes, too, show similarities with the earlier ones. There are two types of these palmettes[54] (Pl. 17:b), one of which (FR 65) has a rounder profile than the other (FR 62). There are also Hellenistic

---

[49] FA 420 is possibly from the first accumulation of fill washed in after the Tile Works went out of use. FA 423 comes from Late Roman fill.

[50] Le Roy 1967, Roof 70, pp. 141–144, A 97 + A 174, A 98, A 99, pl. 55:18–20; also series 69, note 14 above.

[51] For information on workshops, see Heiden 1987, pp. 108–109, 135, 153–169, 196–199; *OlForsch* V, pp. 133–134.

[52] For a general account of the roof of the South Stoa, see *Corinth* I, iv, pp. 83–88, pls. 19–22. For the raking sima, *ibid.*, pp. 85–86, pl. 20:3. Some twenty-nine pieces were inventoried, too numerous to be listed here. For the lateral sima, pp. 84–85, pl. 20:1 and 2 with twenty-five pieces inventoried.

[53] *Corinth* I, iv, pp. 86–87, pls. 19:1, 20:1, 21:1a. The following antefixes were inventoried: for eaves tiles, FA 247, FA 248, FA 346–FA 360; for simas, FA 212, FA 249, FA 345, FA 361.

[54] *Corinth* I, iv, p. 86, pl. 21:1b and c, pl. 21:3, right. Inventoried: rounder type, FR 54, FR 56–FR 58, FR 60, FR 61, FR 63–FR 65, FR 67, FR 69, FR 70, FR 73, FR 83; second type, FR 55, FR 59, FR 62, FR 72.

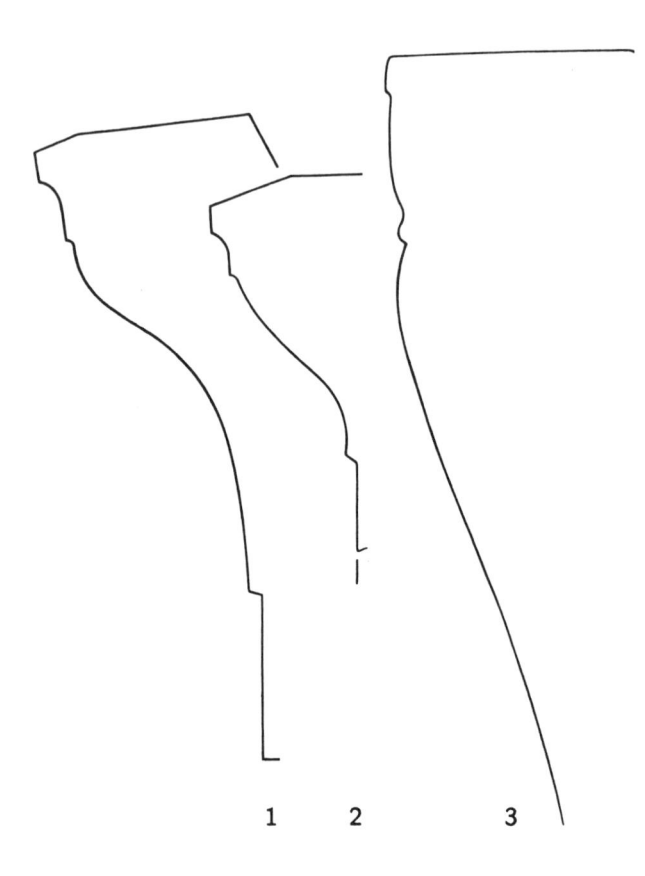

FIG. 2. (1) South Stoa; (2) FS 442; (3) FS 50

repairs[55] (FR 66, FR 68, Pl. 17:c). It seems that the tile makers for the South Stoa copied the earlier tiles to some extent and that there is an archaizing tendency here, revealed by comparison with a sima from the Tile Works[56] (FS 867b, Pl. 18:a). In the profiles of the raking simas of the South Stoa and FS 442 from the Asklepieion (Fig. 2, profile nos. 1 and 2) we also see a return to the earlier form, rounder and projecting out more.

One group of tiles from the Asklepieion, belonging either to the temple or to some other building of similar date, is very like those of the South Stoa. Pieces of the raking sima[57] (FS 442, Pl. 18:b), the lateral sima[58] (FS 433, Pl. 18:e), and the antefixes[59] (FA 184 and FA 434, Pl. 18:c, d) have all been recovered. The leaves of the palmettes of the raking sima

[55] *Corinth* I, iv, p. 88, pl. 21:3a and b; inventoried: FR 66, FR 68, FR 71.
[56] FS 867b, unpublished, was built into the wall of the second kiln of the Tile Works. The palmette has more regularly rounded leaves than others such as FS 860 and FS 865 (pp. 42–43 above, Pls. 10:e, 11:a). Both types occur built into the kiln wall and are of approximately the same date.
[57] FS 442, unpublished. Another possible set for the temple is made up of FS 439, FS 440, FS 444.
[58] *Corinth* XIV, p. 36, pl. 11:5; Heiden 1987, p. 155. Inventoried: FS 433–FS 436.
[59] FA 184 and FA 434 are unpublished. Other antefixes inventoried are FA 143, FA 144, FA 146, FA 181–FA 188, FA 192, FA 577.

are less rounded than those of the South Stoa and tend to have a double curve again, while the acanthus leaf on the fluted stem of the lateral sima does not curve upward.

An entirely different group of simas from the 4th century has also been found at Corinth as well as at other sites such as Olympia, Delphi, and some smaller sanctuaries.[60] These are raking simas with a painted egg-and-dart band on the cymatium. Several have been found at Corinth.[61] I show one here[62] (FS 10, Pl. 18:f). There is some variation in style and date, but they seem to fit in the middle to the end of the 4th century, this being one of the latest examples, perhaps even 3rd century.

In conclusion, I mention a few pieces from the Hellenistic period to complete the picture of Greek Corinth. In them one sees a return to greater vitality and imagination in the treatment of the designs used over several centuries.

The area to the north of Temple Hill contained a series of stoas in the Greek period. This part of the excavation was uncovered in 1930.[63] In the most recent of the stoas and at the north side of a street that bordered it were found many architectural terracottas. Among them were two fine complete simas, one a corner piece, the other a lateral sima. The excavator has suggested that after the destruction of 146 B.C. some Sikyonians cleared part of the area of the blocks and any other material of use to them. Presumably the tiles would have fallen on the blocks so they were moved aside and stacked separately alongside the piers of the basement. The two sima pieces were placed beside Pier 17. It is presumed that the tiles formed the roofing of the buildings in the area at the time of the destruction of the city by Mummius.

The corner sima piece[64] (FS 382, Pl. 19:a, b) is particularly interesting because of the way in which the tile makers made the transition from the plastic decoration on the lateral side to the painted decoration of the raking sima. On one side of the lion's head spout are the customary plastic tendrils with an acanthus leaf from which grow two spirals. In the fork of the spirals is a bud. On the bottom projecting molding is a painted meander pattern. At the top is a torus molding with a painted egg and dart. The lion's head is very highly modeled, with a deep groove down the center of the forehead and wild locks of hair. On the other side of the spout the upper molding is plain at the top with a Lesbian leaf below. On the cymatium, next to the spout, is half of a painted palmette. At the corner is a flower with five petals which extends across to the raking sima side. On this side the upper border continues unchanged, but the meander at the bottom continues on a recessed fascia. The cymatium has an alternating eleven-leafed palmette and a nine-petaled flower with notched ends, giving a flame effect. The palmette has a diamond-shaped center, the flower a bell-shaped center. Between the two of them at the bottom is an S-shaped spiral.

[60] Le Roy 1967, pp. 153–154, 168, series 78–79, pls. 58 and 104; Heiden 1987, pp. 175–177; Bommelaer 1978, pp. 173–197; Mallwitz 1980, pp. 149–150, no. 45, pl. 102:4.

[61] *Corinth* IV, i, pp. 67–68, 70, 73–74, 76, FS 10, FS 12, FS 19, FS 38, FS 53, FS 59, FS 106–FS 108; also FS 902, FS 1024, and FS 1070, all unpublished.

[62] FS 10, *Corinth* IV, i, p. 67.

[63] De Waele 1931, pp. 410–411, 416–418.

[64] De Waele 1931, p. 417, fig. 10; with this also go FS 414 and FS 1014 as well as raking sima pieces FS 40 and FS 51 (*Corinth* IV, i, pp. 71, 73) and unpublished pieces FS 384, FS 429, and FS 903. See also *OlForsch* IV, pp. 84, 127, pl. 94.

This sima measures 0.28 m. in height and 0.69 m. in length for the lateral sima and 0.76 m. in length for the raking sima; overall it is not quite as large as the tiles of the South Stoa. Probably it belonged to the roof of the stoa in which it was found.

The other sima piece[65] (FS 381, Pl. 19:c) is a complete section of a lateral sima. The design is basically that used in the 4th century, but it shows some differences from the South Stoa. The upper molding is decorated with a Lesbian leaf pattern. The meander on the base molding is raised rather than painted. The acanthus and spiral design on either side of the lion's head has an acanthus leaf alongside the spout, not found on the South Stoa but found on some other 4th-century simas. There is a small spiral added to the top of the end spiral, as well as a bud. In the fork of the spirals below is another bud. The hair of the lion is rather more formalized than in the other sima. With this sima can be connected a number of pieces of raking sima[66] (FS 50, Pl. 19:d) found both to the north and to the south of Temple Hill. The upper molding is the same and the meander is also raised, not painted. The principal decoration is similar to that on the raking sima of the corner piece, but the palmette has fewer and narrower leaves and there is a Mycenaean-type lily between the palmette and the flower. The profile (Fig. 2, profile no. 3) once more is fairly flat. With these should be put some very large ridge tiles with palmettes[67] (FR 39, FR 41, Pl. 19:e) found in the same area. These pieces are all on a large scale. The lateral sima measures 0.39 m. in height and 1.13 m. in length while the preserved height of FS 50 is 0.36 m. and the height of the ridge palmette is 0.31 m. Tiles of this size, found in this area, can only belong to one building, the Temple of Apollo. I think we can safely say that the temple and the stoa below were roofed with these impressive tiles at the time of the destruction of the city in 146 B.C.

## BIBLIOGRAPHY

Bommelaer, J.-F. 1978. "Simas et gargouilles classiques de Delphes," *BCH* 102, pp. 173–197

*Corinth* I, iv = O. Broneer, *The South Stoa and Its Roman Successors* (*Corinth* I, iv), Princeton 1954

*Corinth* IV, i = I. Thallon-Hill and L. S. King, *Decorated Architectural Terracottas* (*Corinth* IV, i), Cambridge, Mass. 1929

*Corinth* VII, iii = G. R. Edwards, *Corinthian Hellenistic Pottery* (*Corinth* VII, iii), Princeton 1975

*Corinth* XIII = C. W. Blegen, H. Palmer, and R. S. Young, *The North Cemetery* (*Corinth* XIII), Princeton 1964

*Corinth* XIV = C. Roebuck, *The Asklepieion and Lerna* (*Corinth* XIV), Princeton 1951

*Corinth* XV, ii = A. N. Stillwell, *The Potters' Quarter: The Terracottas* (*Corinth* XV, ii), Princeton 1952

Coulton, J. J. 1964. "The Stoa by the Harbor at Perachora," *BSA* 59, pp. 100–131

De Waele, F. J. 1931. "The Greek Stoa North of the Temple at Corinth," *AJA* 35, pp. 399–423

Dinsmoor, W. B. 1940. "The Temple of Ares at Athens," *Hesperia* 9, pp. 1–52

Heiden, J. 1987. *Korinthische Dachziegel. Zur Entwicklung der korinthischen Dächer*, Frankfurt am Main/Bern/New York/Paris

[65] FS 381, De Waele 1931, pp. 416–417, fig. 9; Heiden 1987, p. 155 and note 713; *OlForsch* IV, pp. 83–86, pl. 79, Willemsen evidently misread De Waele. His date of the 1st century B.C. for the two simas (pp. 84, 86, 127) is incorrect. Others of the same series are FS 141–FS 143, FS 250 (*Corinth* IV, i, pp. 80, 89) and the unpublished pieces FS 417, FS 421, FS 422.

[66] FS 50, *Corinth* IV, i, pp. 72–73, fig. 30, p. 28 and note 6. Others belonging to this series are FS 49 (p. 72), FS 58 (p. 73), and the unpublished pieces FS 819, FS 915, FS 916.

[67] The ridge tiles FR 39–FR 43 are unpublished.

Hübner, G. 1973. "Dachterrakotten aus dem Kerameikos von Athen," *AM* 88, pp. 67–143
———. 1990. "Die Dachterrakotten der archaischen Tempel von Kalapodi (Phokis)," in *Proceedings of the First International Conference on Archaic Greek Architectural Terracottas, Athens, December 2–4, 1988* (*Hesperia* 59, 1990), N. A. Winter, ed., pp. 167–174
———. 1975. "Dachterrakotten im Magazin des Museums von Nauplia," in *Tiryns. Forschungen und Berichte* VIII, Mainz, pp. 117–136
Le Roy, Ch. 1967. *Les terres cuites architecturales* (*Fouilles de Delphes* II), Paris
Mallwitz, A. 1972. *Olympia und seine Bauten*, Munich
———. 1980. *Die Funde aus Olympia*, Athens
Merker, G. S. 1988. "Fragments of Architectural Terracotta Hydras in Corinth," *Hesperia* 57, pp. 193–202
*OlForsch* IV = F. Willemsen, *Die Löwenkopfwasserspeier vom Dach des Zeustempels* (*Olympische Forschungen* IV), Berlin 1959
*OlForsch* V = A. Mallwitz and W. Schiering, *Die Werkstatt des Pheidias in Olympia* (*Olympische Forschungen* V), Berlin 1964
Shoe, L. T. 1936. *Profiles of Greek Mouldings*, Cambridge, Mass.
Talcott, L. 1935. "Attic Black-glazed Stamped Ware and Other Pottery from a Fifth Century Well," *Hesperia* 4, pp. 476–523
Van Buren, E. D. 1926. *Greek Fictile Revetments in the Archaic Period*, London
Weinberg, S. 1954. "Corinthian Relief Ware, Pre-Hellenistic Period," *Hesperia* 23, pp. 110–137
———. 1957. "Terracotta Sculpture at Corinth," *Hesperia* 26, pp. 289–319
Wiseman, J. 1969. "Excavations in Corinth, the Gymnasium Area, 1967–1968," *Hesperia* 38, pp. 64–106

MARY C. ROEBUCK

P.O. Box 65
Eastsound, WA 98245

# ROOF TILES FROM TWO CIRCULAR BUILDINGS AT CORINTH

SOME EVIDENCE, although minimal, exists at Corinth for at least two round structures in the Classical past. One building is represented by three, or perhaps four, fragmentary hexagonal tiles; this building apparently was large in size. The second structure, attested by seven fragments of scalloped roof tile, definitely was a smaller building. These eleven pieces at the moment exist in total isolation; no foundation or superstructure has yet been found with which either building can be associated.[1]

The first group of tiles discussed here[2] is six-sided, designed to have one point at the apex, a second angle at the bottom of the tile. It is clear which end of any fragment is preserved, for the undersurface of the lower half of this type of tile has a channel along its edges, similar to that found on all normal interlocking Corinthian pan tiles, where the channel is used to achieve a water-resistant joint. The upper half of the tile has on its top surface a raised edge also designed as a precaution against water seepage.

No tile of the first group is preserved whole. Two are half preserved; the other two are much more fragmentary. Three fragments are from the lower half of a tile, of which the undersurface preserves a channel 0.075–0.08 m. wide. The tiles of the Tholos in the Athenian Agora also have a channel in this position, but it is of a slightly different shape.[3]

The fragmentary upper half of tile FM 21 has no such channel running along the edge of its undersurface, for this surface would have rested directly on the supporting wood structure for the roof and thus could not have interlocked with another tile.

These hexagonal tiles are, in reality, diamond-shaped with the diagonal edges spreading at an angle of 65 degrees from the longitudinal axis. Where the diagonals meet at the side of the tile, the angle is cut back to make a very short lateral edge. These lateral edges do

---

[1] Two antefixes from circular or faceted roofs are preserved in the Corinth inventory. One, FA 199, is published in *Corinth* XV, ii, no. 62, pp. 272, 281. There it is dated to the late 6th–early 5th century. The first half of the 5th century probably now is a better chronological position for this piece. FA 202, which is unpublished and has only a small part of its antefix preserved, is from the central part of the Forum. I thank Dr. Mary C. Roebuck for pointing out to me these two antefixes.

[2] FM 20. Large fragment of diamond-shaped pan tile, bottom third preserved, with a channel along the edges of its undersurface.

FM 21. Large fragment of diamond-shaped pan tile; fragment preserves upper half, except apex, with raised lip along edges of top surface.

FM 22. Large fragment of diamond-shaped pan tile; large part of lower half preserved, with a channel along the edges of the undersurface.

FM 56. Small fragment of diamond-shaped pan tile preserving bottom angle, undersurface with meeting point of two edge channels.

[3] Miller 1988, pp. 134–139, pl. 45:3. For a tile of similar design and with the very same type of channel on its undersurface, see Touchais 1979, p. 565, fig. 96. The style of the anthemion on the antefix, however, may argue for a difference in date. I thank Dr. Nancy Winter for this last reference.

not deform the visual effect of the overall diamond pattern of the roof once the tiles are in place and overlapped. Indeed, the dimensions of the lateral edges are not only small but may vary by tile. Moreover, the lateral edges are not cut parallel to one another. Rather, they were angled 2 degrees from the longitudinal axis of the tile. If the lateral edges were extended upward, they would meet at the apex of the roof. Assuming that all lateral edges angled 2 degrees off the longitudinal axis (as they do in the preserved edge of FM 21) and assuming that all tiles at the level in the roof in which this tile lay had their lateral edges abutting, a maximum of 90 tiles could be restored at this ring. Tile FM 21 is *ca.* 0.54 m. thick at its midpoint. If all tiles of this one ring were similar, then the ring of roof tiles would have a circumference of *ca.* 48.60 m.

The finished downside vertical edges of the tile are about 9 degrees off the vertical when the tile is laid horizontal. The 9 degrees probably can be considered an approximate indication of the general slope of the roof.

All these tiles are made of a Corinthian buff to tan clay, going pink at the core. All have liberal amounts of mudstone in the mix. Except that the tiles were designed for a conical roof, they are typical products of the Corinthian roof-tile industry. Unfortunately no decorated eaves tiles have been discovered to go with the building for which the tiles were designed.

With this evidence at hand, one can restore this specific Corinth roof with every tile having the same angle on all four of its diagonal sides. If all tiles should ever prove to have equal corner angles, the roof could be restored with small, relatively square tiles at the apex of the roof with a resultant awkwardness of design there and larger tiles of the same shape at the eaves. The more satisfactory conclusion, but not yet attested as the correct one, is that the roof tiles graded from a long narrow hexagon at the top to broader and, in proportion, shorter hexagonal tiles as the horizontal rows of diamond tiles approached the eaves. This latter solution, as restored on the roof of the Tholos of the Athenian Agora, is also suggested as the better solution for this Corinthian roof.[4]

Seven rather unassuming fragments of fictile roof tile attest the existence of a second round building at Classical Corinth. No sima fragments or roof palmettes were found with the fragments. All the tiles found had been dumped onto bedrock under Building 5 of East Theater Street, apparently as part of an Early Roman cleanup by the new Corinthian colonists.

Despite the paucity of fictile evidence, a number of interesting principles can be established about the design of these tiles and roof. The fragments are all small; none has a length of more than 0.22 m. or a width of more than 0.24 m. The single most important fragment, FM 134, is a flat, thick (0.04 m.) tile that preserves part of both lateral edges, the top edge of the tile, and a hole for nailing or pegging the tile to the roof timber. The top and side surfaces are slipped; the bearing undersurface is not only not slipped but is quite rough, although flat. This tile reveals a number of different facts about the roofing system of the specific building it covered.

First, the tile has sides that flare outward from a flat top edge that is 0.146 m. wide (Fig. 1). The flare is *ca.* 9 degrees to a side and indicates that the roof from which it came was

[4] Miller 1988, pl. 48:1, 2.

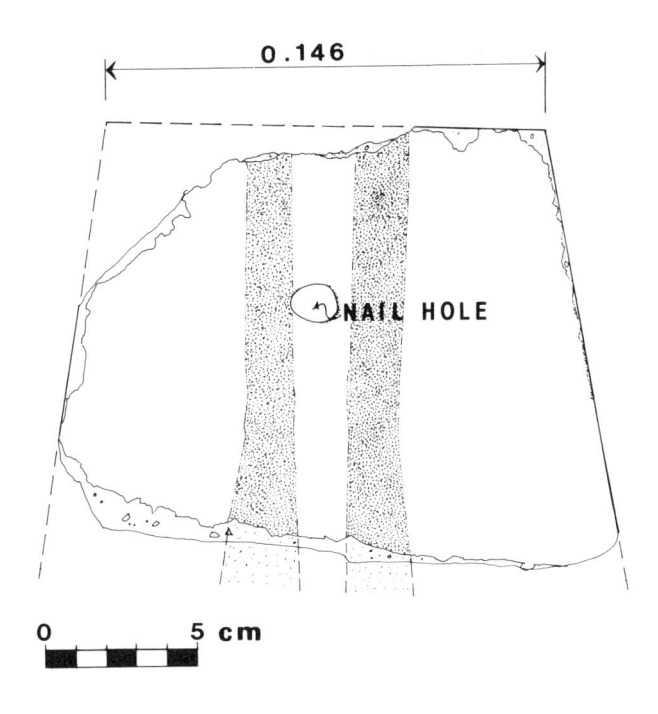

Fig. 1. FM 134

either conical or multifaceted. Twenty such tiles ([9 + 9] x 20 = 360 degrees) would be needed, laid side to side, to complete the tile ring at this level of the roof.

Second, a reserved band (0.018–0.020 m. wide) is defined along the longitudinal axis of the top surface of the tile by two parallel black-glazed lines, each between 0.015 and 0.017 m. wide. A distinct broadening of the glazing starts just above the break at the lower end of the tile. This type of decoration, at this moment unique to these fragments, and the findspot strongly suggest that all pieces came from a single roof.

Third, the top surface of the tile is totally flat and has neither lip nor channel along any preserved edge, such as are to be found on all normal Corinthian pan tiles. A design without such lips could allow leakage at the overlap, a fact that was apparently of no concern to the designer of this circular building.

Fourth, a hole 0.013 m. in diameter has been drilled into the tile after firing. This hole, on the longitudinal axis of the tile and at *ca.* 0.05 m. from its top edge, apparently was once used to peg the tile to the wood substructure.

Five other fragments, FM 127, FM 129, FM 136, FM 137, and FM 138 (Fig. 2:a–e), add one more fact. Of the group only FM 136 does not preserve any part of a lateral edge. One sees a number of generic characteristics within this group. As with the first tile, FM 134, the top slipped surface of all the fragments has a reserved central band between glazed lines or areas running along its longitudinal axis. These two glazed bands widen as they progress to the bottom edge of the tile. Where the four tiles preserve part of a lateral edge, that edge flares at *ca.* 11–12 degrees from the central reserved band of the tile.

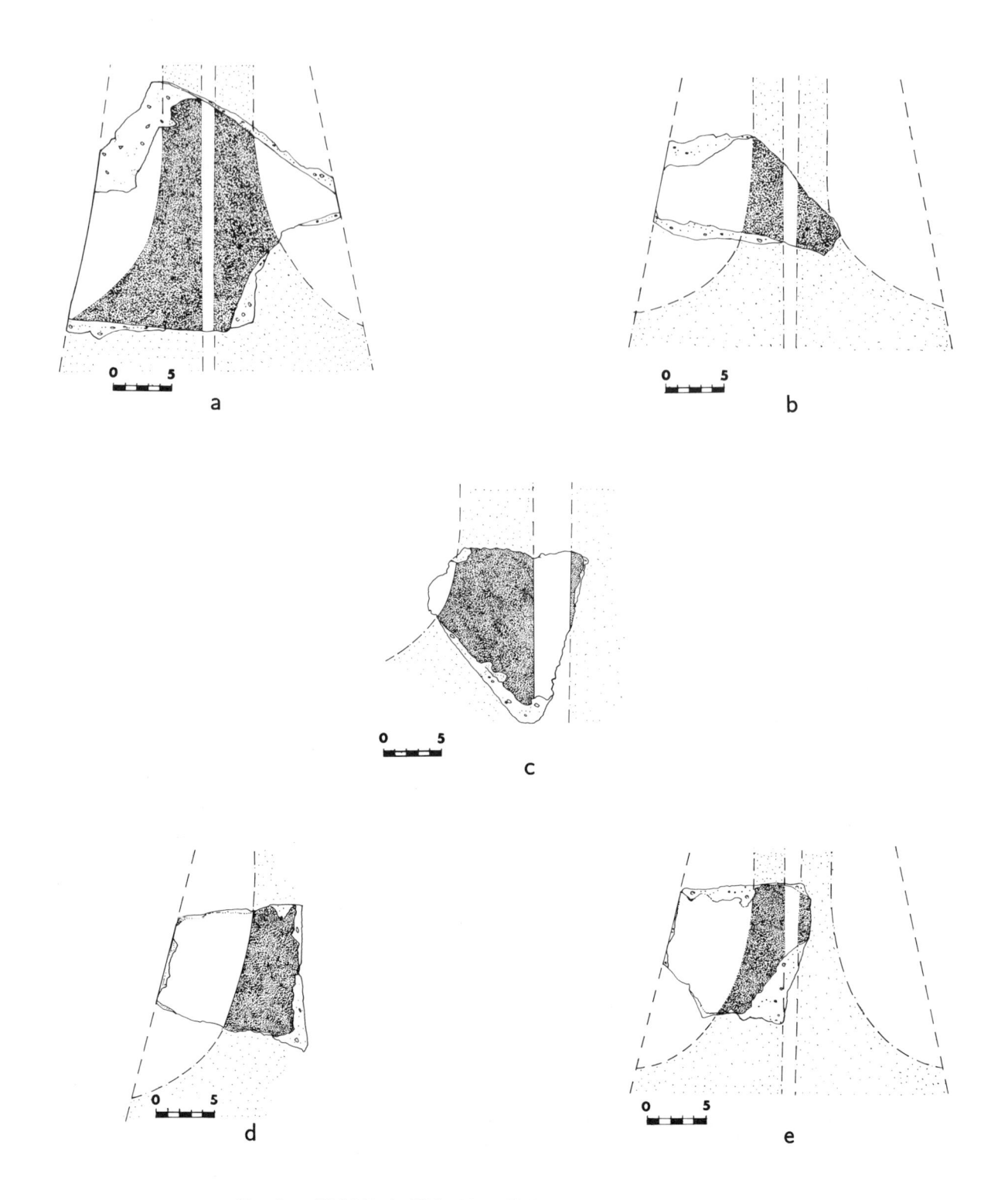

FIG. 2. a. FM 127, b. FM 129, c. FM 136, d. FM 137, e. FM 138

FM 127 (Fig. 2:a) adds two facts. First, it preserves two lateral edges, but those edges do not have the conventional raised lip found on the usual Corinthian pan tile. The flare of the lateral edges is *ca.* 26 degrees between the sides. The glazed bands that flank the central reserved strip here are broad, *ca.* 0.032 m. wide, and curve out to the lateral edges of the tile. On one preserved side (left, when looking down on the top of the tile) one can see that the glaze is continued from the top surface down the vertical side edge. If two such tiles were fitted together side by side, the resultant reserved area would define a pointed scallop or scale.

The bearing surface, or underside, of this tile adds still more information to the understanding of this special roofing system. Although the undersurface is rough, as on all the tiles of the series, the surface is articulated by two parallel channels cut into the clay, apparently while the clay was wet or damp. There are also signs that the ends of the channels were enlarged thereafter, perhaps on the job. The channels are 0.06 m. wide, almost 0.02 m. deep, running lengthwise, and about 0.05 m. apart. The heads of the channels start at *ca.* 0.045 m. above the point where the painted top surface goes down the lateral face of the tile.

From the evidence of this tile, then, we have the following information. The painted design of the top surface produced pointed scales or scallops. In addition, certain roof tiles of the overall roofing system did have raised lips on their lateral edges, at least at some point or points where certain scale tiles overlapped other tiles. The lower series was laid with a 0.05 m. space between adjacent lateral edges, attested by the channels described above. One could then restore at least one row of lip-edged tiles under the series of scalloped tiles represented by FM 127.

Pan tile FM 128 (Fig. 3) has no original side edge preserved. Its top surface as preserved is solidly glazed except for the customary vertical reserved line along the axis of the tile, here 0.015–0.017 m. wide. The upper left-hand corner of the top surface may possibly present a small area of reserved scale. If not, a brush stroke in the glaze at this point indicates that the reserved scallop area of the upper portion of the tile was just beyond the preserved break.

It is the bottom surface of this fragment that offers the important information. The undersurface preserves two lines scratched into the rough clay, crossing each other at right angles, as well as the top end of a channel that was meant to receive the lipped side edge of an underlying tile. The cutting is *ca.* 0.095 m. from the incised line that demarks the longitudinal center of the tile. The cutting here is not only positioned more to the side of the center of the tile than are either of the cuttings on FM 127 but also appears to be lower (closer to the front of the scalloped tile by a good 0.15 m.) than are the channels in the undersurface of FM 127.

The clay of all fragments of this group is greenish cream with a pinkish core. The clay is comparable to that used in a large series of Classical Corinthian roof tiles and also close to the fabric of the roof tiles of the South Stoa but with more grit than is usually found in Hellenistic tiles manufactured at Corinth. It has a heavy admixture of large-sized fragments of mudstone. The surface is covered with a fine clay slip.

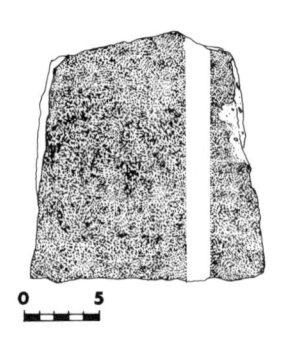

FIG. 3. FM 128

The above information permits a proposed restoration of the roof following certain design principles. A roof with scalloped terracotta tiles (Fig. 4) apparently follows the rules of design governing the representation of feathers in terracotta sculpture and pottery.[5]

According to these rules, once the pattern is adopted, each superimposed row of tiles must overlap so that the axis of each tile of any overlapping ring is on axis not with that of the tile immediately below or above it but with the tile two rows below or above, that is, in every other ring. This means that axis lines descend from the apex to the eaves both along the central axis of each tile in the first ring below the apex and from the joint between tiles of that ring. The joint axes would, of course, descend in a line that runs along the axis of each tile in the second ring below the apex. Since the roof is a cone, these axis lines flare as they descend to the eaves.

Two inconveniences arise from such a design. One is the increasing size of the tiles in every ring as they approach the eaves. The tiles of every ring must be larger than those that overlap them. Such a design allows only limited scope for mass production. Second, for a roof that is designed to cover a building of large diameter, the tiles as they descend can become out of scale with the other architectural elements and impossible to manufacture or lay. At the bottom edge of the roof the large scale of the tiles could easily become inappropriate to the scale of the sima. This problem was avoided in the Lysikrates Monument by the addition of a secondary sima ring close to the edge of the roof at the point where the rings of tiles would have become so large as to become a design handicap; below this point the tiles could be started once more in reduced size. The result is that tiles of reasonable size could be continued from there to the eaves, with the terminal ring of tiles relating directly to

[5] The influence of feathers on the design of scalloped roof tiles can be seen in the marble roof of the Late Classical Lysikrates Monument and in Roman structures such as the Babbius Monument at Corinth (*Corinth* I, iii, pl. 12:2) and a circular building immediately west of the Odeum (*Corinth* X, p. 109, fig. 100). A circular foundation that lies immediately west of the Odeum, discovered after the publication of the Odeum itself, is of a size and date that are appropriate for this roof slab. The two small monopteroi of the Nympheum of Herodes Atticus at Olympia use the feather-patterned roof but with a creased central axis, not a rib. See *OlForsch* I, p. 75, fig. 15. The terracotta roof from Corinth under discussion in this paper should be equated with the designs in marble, except that here the central reserved line represents the central quill of a natural feather. Domed roofs have been excluded from this list.

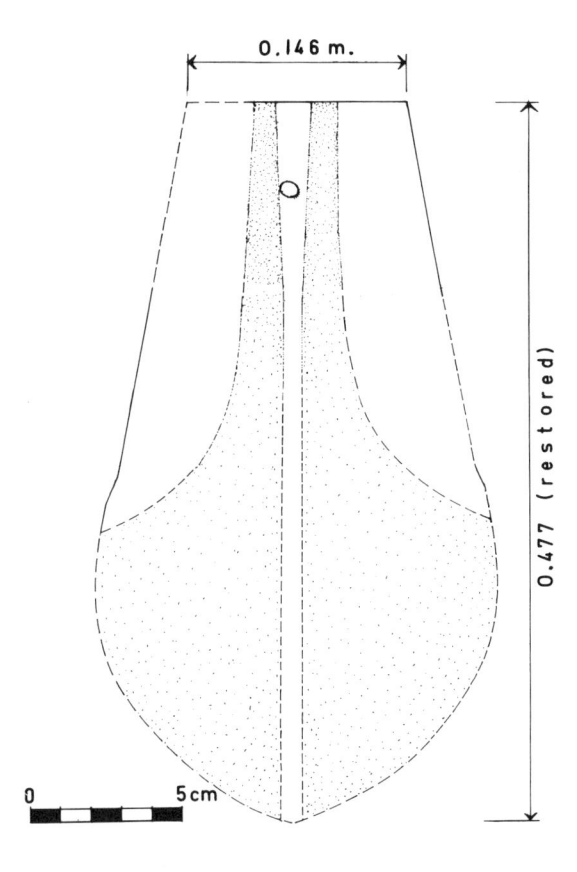

FIG. 4. Hypothetical reconstruction of a tile

the sima tiles, which in turn would be related to the scale of the façade. The solution of a secondary sima near the bottom of the scalloped roof may not have been needed on the Corinth roof if the building was small enough. We do know, however, from the cuttings in the undersurface of FM 128 and FM 127 that the width of the row of tiles at the eaves got out of synchronization with the scale-patterned tiles. This row probably was of sima tiles with a more or less conventional Corinthian pan-tile design, with a raised lip on the side edges.

Another disadvantage of this roof design arises from the lack of interlocking lip-and-channel joints. In the Athenian Tholos and the first-mentioned Corinthian circular building the tiles have interlocking joints. In this second example, however, the builder(s) apparently hoped that a generous overlap without interlocks would protect the monument from leakage and water damage. Perhaps the amount of calculation necessary for designing accurate lip-and-channel jointing was too much effort for the project, whatever the intended use of the building.

In any case the scale-patterned roof appears to have been a success for small buildings, for the design was used into the Roman period, although such roofs in Corinth were then executed in marble, not terracotta. The Babbius Monument and at least one other such monument attest to the use of this form into the 1st century after Christ. Such marble roofs, however, resolve the problems posed by this design. Leakage between large numbers of small tiles is avoided and the tiles need not be specially manufactured in small groups; the whole terracotta design is simply carved onto large, wedge-shaped marble slabs.

## BIBLIOGRAPHY

*Corinth* I, iii = R. Scranton, *Monuments in the Lower Agora and North of the Archaic Temple* (*Corinth* I, iii), Princeton 1951
*Corinth* X = O. Broneer, *The Odeum* (*Corinth* X), Cambridge, Mass. 1932
*Corinth* XV, ii = A. N. Stillwell, *The Potters' Quarter: The Terracottas* (*Corinth* XV, ii), Princeton 1952
Miller, Stephen G. 1988. "Circular Roofing Systems and the Athenian Tholos," in Πρακτικά του XII Διεθνούς Συνεδρίου Κλασικής Αρχαιολογίας, Αθήνα, 4–10 Σεπτεμβρίου 1983, IV, Athens, pp. 134–139
*OlForsch* I = H. Schleif and H. Weber, "Das Nymphaeum des Herodes Attikos," in *Olympische Forschungen* I, E. Kunze and H. Schlief, eds., Berlin 1944, pp. 53–82
Touchais, G. 1979. "Chronique des fouilles," *BCH* 103, pp. 527–615

Charles K. Williams, II

Corinth Excavations
American School of Classical Studies
54 Souidias Street
GR-106 76 Athens
Greece

# GREEK ARCHITECTURAL TERRACOTTAS FROM THE SANCTUARY OF POSEIDON AT ISTHMIA

(PLATES 20–22)

OSCAR BRONEER discovered the Temple of Poseidon in 1952 and continued excavation until 1967, by which time he had uncovered substantial portions of the sanctuary (Fig. 1).[1] The current project has continued the work of Professor Broneer, concentrating its efforts on understanding the development of the sanctuary through studies of the stratigraphy, topography, architecture, and artifacts.[2] Although much of the temenos, and most of the larger sanctuary, remains to be excavated, about a hundred fragments of Greek painted roof tiles have been recovered that help to fill gaps in our information about the architectural monuments at Isthmia. These tiles come from the roofs of at least nine small-scale buildings, ranging in date from the second quarter of the 6th century to the 3rd century B.C.[3] Although none can with certainty be associated with a particular foundation, some idea of the chronology and topographic setting of the buildings can be derived from the stratigraphy of the site, from small-scale poros architectural fragments, and from the tiles themselves.[4]

## ARCHAIC TILES

Figure 2 is the reconstructed plan of the temenos for the period 575–550 B.C., soon after the inauguration of Panhellenic games at Isthmia. Of particular importance is the shape of the temenos plateau and the surrounding gullies, which are oriented from southwest

---

[1] For a summary of the Isthmian sanctuary at the end of Broneer's excavations, see Broneer 1976. Broneer's description and interpretation of the remains, exclusive of the Temple of Poseidon, are described in *Isthmia* II. Additional work was done in the Roman bath and the Late Antique wall and fortress by Paul Clement (1967–1976). Elizabeth Gebhard succeeded Broneer as Director in 1976, and Timothy Gregory followed Clement in 1986.

[2] Cf. Gebhard and Hemans 1992, pp. 1–77. The reader should refer to this source for a description of the stratigraphy and the new interpretations of the chronology of the temenos up to the destruction of the Temple of Poseidon, *ca.* 470 B.C. The next report will describe the sanctuary from *ca.* 470 to the 3rd century after Christ.

[3] I would like to thank all my colleagues for their continued assistance in my studies at Isthmia, in particular the Director of the project, Elizabeth Gebhard of the University of Illinois at Chicago. I would also like to thank Nancy Winter for her invitation to take part in this conference as well as for her observations on the Isthmia material made during the summer of 1991. Recent work at Isthmia has been made possible by a three-year grant from the National Endowment for the Humanities (#RO-21847-89). See Gebhard and Hemans 1992, p. 1, note 3, for a list of staff members in the current project.

[4] The amount of material from buildings other than the Archaic and Classical Temples of Poseidon is relatively small. Thus, we are more in a position at the present stage of the excavations to benefit from previous scholarship than to contribute a great deal of new information on the subject of Corinthian roof tiles. The exception is the roof of the Archaic Temple of Poseidon, from which thousands of fragments have been recovered. See Hemans 1989.

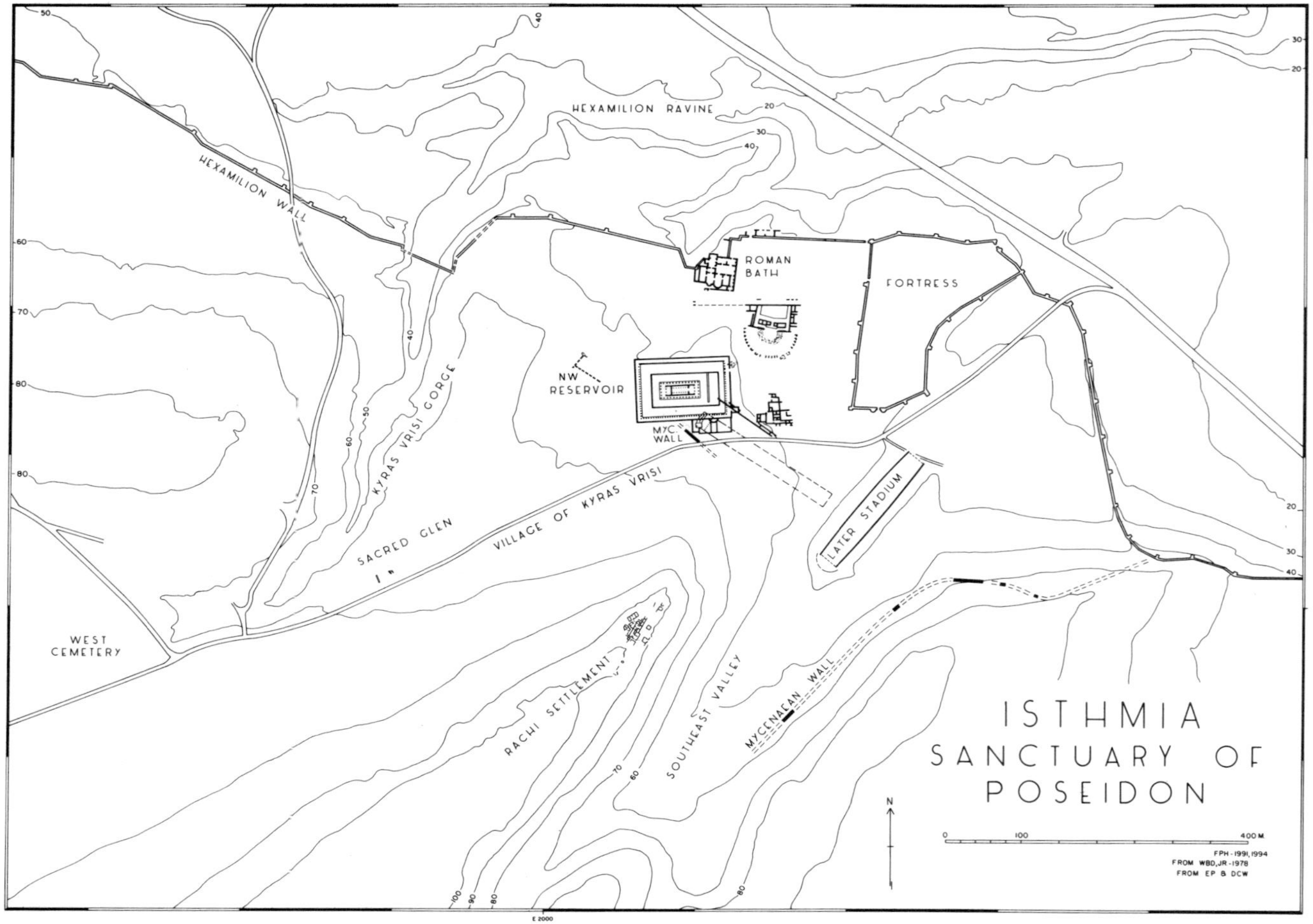

FIG. 1. Excavated monuments of the Sanctuary of Poseidon at Isthmia

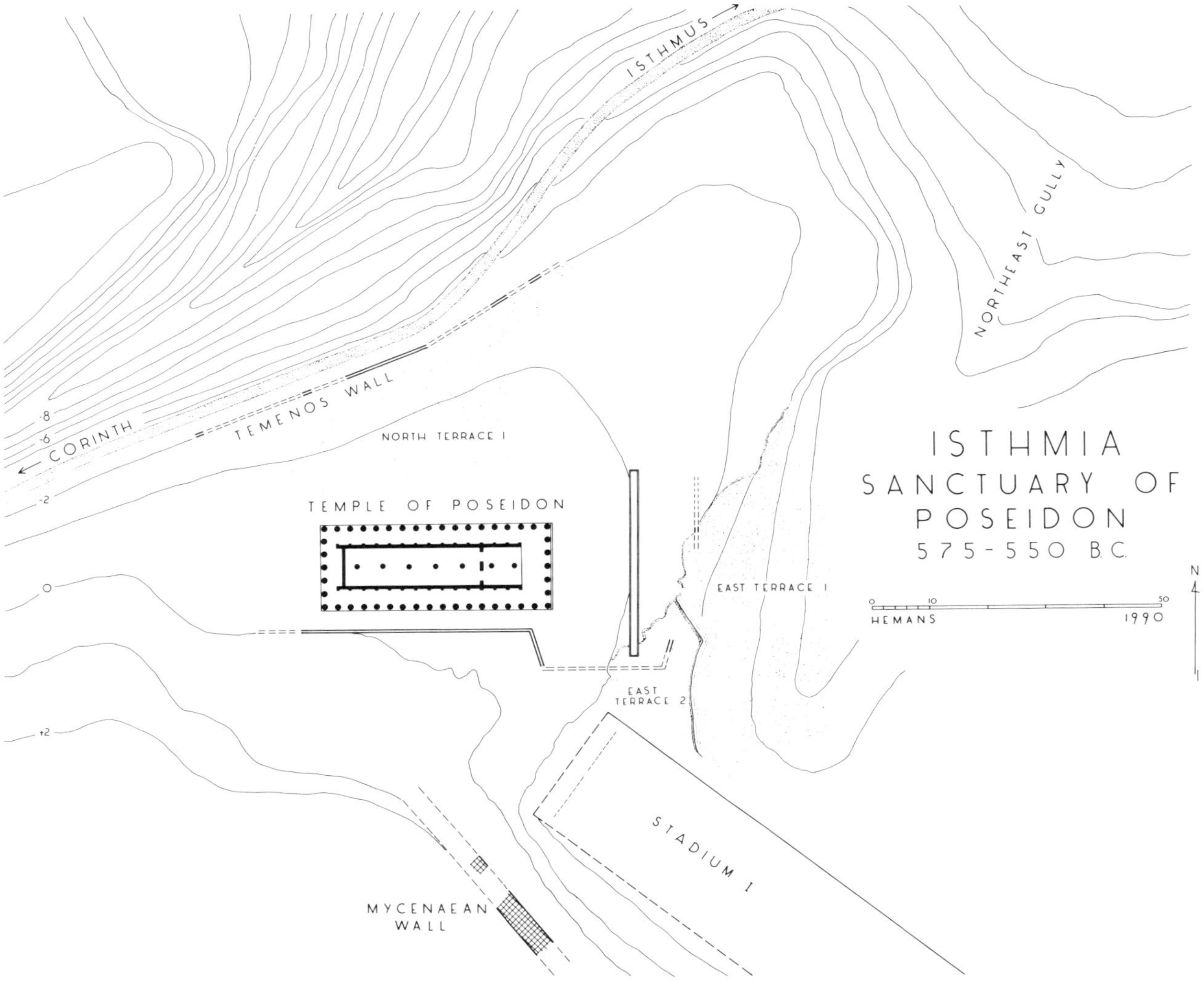

Fig. 2. Partially restored topographic map of the central sanctuary at Isthmia, 575–550 B.C.

to northeast. With the exception of the Temple of Poseidon, the topography determined the orientation of all the Greek buildings. Not until Roman times was the temenos made rectangular to follow cardinal directions (Fig. 1). The earliest well-preserved features are the Archaic Temple (completed *ca.* 650 B.C.) and the temenos wall, which defines limits that were retained until the 5th century.[5] The eastern part of the temenos, surrounding the Long Altar, served as the place of sacrifice throughout the history of the sanctuary; to the southeast lay the early stadium that was the center of the celebration of the games.[6] Along the northern edge of the plateau was a highway that carried traffic between Corinth and the Isthmus. Although the position of the road appears to intrude awkwardly into the space surrounding the temple, no other place in the vicinity presented a gradient shallow enough to allow construction of an alternative route at a greater distance from the temple. Thus, the road was always an important feature of the site.

At the present stage of the project, a large area within the temenos, at the northeast corner of the plateau, has not been excavated, and the areas immediately surrounding the temenos remain largely unexplored. Of the Archaic tiles that have an excavated context, most were discovered in the Northwest Reservoir, suggesting that buildings may once have lined the road which led from Corinth.[7] The small scale of the terracottas indicates that these were treasuries (oikoi), small stoas, or propylaia.

The earliest painted tiles at Isthmia are fragments of two types of pentagonal antefixes and a raking sima. These are late examples of their types and can be dated stylistically to the second quarter of the 6th century, suggesting that at least two buildings were constructed soon after the traditional foundation date of the Isthmian games in 582 or 580 B.C. (**1–5**).[8] No architectural fragments or building foundations of comparable date have yet been recognized, but excavation in 1989 has provided evidence that there were extensive additions to the sanctuary during this period. At the southeast corner of the temenos the first stadium track was created as well as a walkway that linked the track to the temenos.[9] Across the north half of the temenos the terrace between the temenos wall and temple was resurfaced. It seems likely that the buildings represented by the terracottas formed part of the same building program.

During the latter half of the 6th century, the stadium was expanded by the addition of a spectator embankment on its north side. Another, larger terrace was laid over the eastern side of the temenos, which soon afterward, during the last quarter of the century, was paved with sea pebbles to provide a durable surface. During the same period formal gateways were added to the temenos at the north and east. The north propylon is the better preserved

---

[5] Gebhard and Hemans 1992, pp. 39 and 47.

[6] Gebhard and Hemans 1992, pp. 15–16 and 57–61.

[7] The Northwest Reservoir is located *ca.* 100 meters northwest of the Temple of Poseidon and appears to have been in use until the destruction of the sanctuary in the early 2nd century B.C. *Isthmia* II, pp. 28–29.

[8] Arguments for dating the architectural terracottas are given in the catalogue. For the most part the evidence is stylistic; none of the terracottas described here have been found in contexts earlier than the 2nd century B.C.

[9] Very little material has been recovered to provide a date for the construction of the first stadium track. There is better evidence to date an expansion of the stadium and a terrace associated with it to the 3rd quarter of the 6th century; thus the first track was built before *ca.* 550 B.C. Gebhard and Hemans 1992, pp. 57–63.

of the two foundations. Professor Broneer had proposed that this foundation was Classical in date, but excavation in 1989 demonstrated that it was built in relation to the early terraces on the north and joined with the Archaic temenos wall.[10] The remains of the propylon at the east were completely removed in the late 4th or early 3rd century, but, based on the size and shape of the bedding, it was comparable to the one on the north.

Three roofs are represented by "Megarian"-type simas of the late 6th century (**7**, **9**, and IA 545 described under **9**). All were probably made during the last quarter of the 6th century, a date that coincides with the renovations mentioned above. Like the earlier pieces, the fragments cannot be assigned to specific buildings, but the propylaia added to the temenos are likely candidates for two of the roofs. By the end of the 6th century a total of at least five small buildings seems to have been located within or near the temenos, including the two built in the earlier part of the century. In addition to the two gates, Isthmia, like the other Panhellenic sanctuaries, seems to have had treasury-sized buildings.

With one possible exception (**3**), all the painted tiles found at Isthmia are Corinthian. There are, however, a number of small unpainted fragments of Laconian-type tiles with a deep red slip and fabric that were recovered from the late 6th-century terrace. These may be an indication that Greek states other than Corinth may have contributed buildings to the sanctuary, but the number of possible non-Corinthian buildings could not be more than one or two.

None of these Late Archaic buildings appears to have survived through the 5th century, and they may in fact have been destroyed at the same time as the Archaic Temple, *ca.* 470 B.C. Most of the tiles show signs of burning, while the debris from the destruction of the sanctuary in the 2nd century shows no sign of burning. The extremely small number of Archaic tiles, and the absence of such among the well-defined 2nd-century destruction deposits excavated in 1989, seems to support this hypothesis.[11]

## CLASSICAL AND HELLENISTIC TILES

Much larger numbers of Classical and Hellenistic tiles have been recovered than Archaic ones, but the vast majority come from only three roofs. Thirty of a total of 33 antefix fragments are from these three roofs: 3 from Roof 1, 13 from Roof 2, and 14 from Roof 3.[12] The eaves tiles show a similar distribution (Roof 1, **13** and **14**; Roof 2, **19**; Roof 3, **21**). Other types of tiles are present in very small quantities, often single examples from a roof, and the buildings they represent were probably located at some distance from the center of the sanctuary: for example, the theater, located below the temenos to the northeast.

After the Archaic Temple burned *ca.* 470 B.C., the layout of the temenos was significantly altered (Fig. 3). The temenos wall was dismantled across most of the north and east sides of the sanctuary; by the end of the century a new bedding for the road to the isthmus was laid

---

[10] *Isthmia* II, pp. 10–11. For the date of the North Propylon in the 6th century, its relationship to the Archaic temenos wall, and the identification of the East Propylon, see Gebhard and Hemans 1992, pp. 47–51, 73–74.

[11] Deposits after 470 B.C. will be described in the next report (see note 2 above).

[12] The catalogue includes only Classical/Hellenistic tiles for which more than one example has been found. Thus, of the 33 Classical/Hellenistic examples of antefixes, only 30 are listed in the catalogue, under Roofs 1–3.

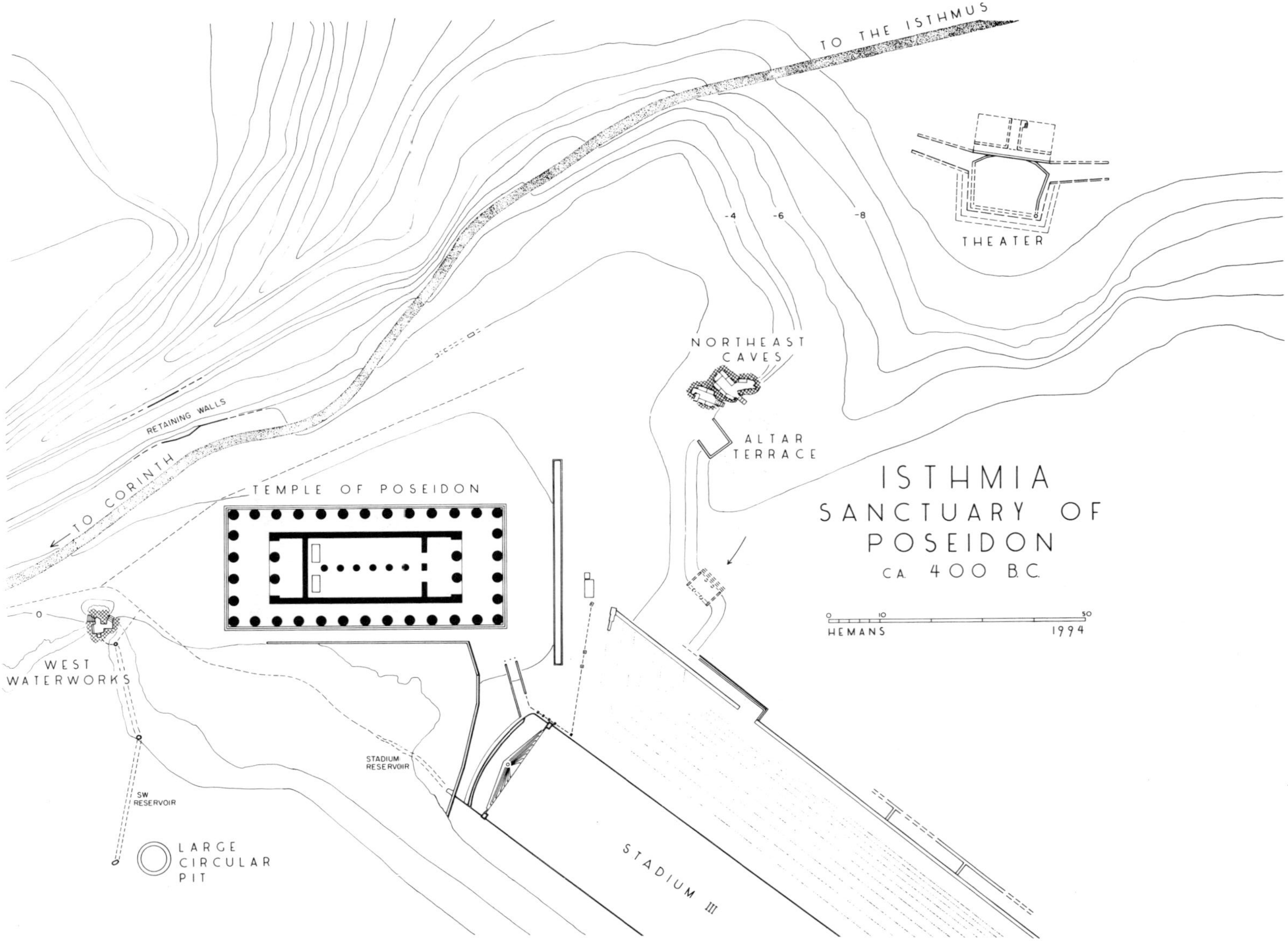

Fig. 3. Partially restored topographic map of the central sanctuary at Isthmia, *ca.* 400 B.C.

along the north side of the plateau and the stadium had been completely rebuilt. One of the new buildings constructed at this time is represented by a group of three finely executed antefix fragments and six eaves tiles (Roof 1, **12–14**). The style of the antefixes is comparable to examples from Delphi (Groups 67–70) that Christian Le Roy dates to the second half of the 5th century. The most closely dated examples of the style are from Olympia, recovered from Pheidias' workshop, and are dated by Alfred Mallwitz to *ca.* 430 B.C. All are characterized by volutes in shallow relief with a very smooth contour and fine painted detail. The Isthmia type, however, has a simpler design than those found either at Olympia or Delphi and is probably somewhat earlier. A cornice block and triglyph-metope block found on the slope of the Northwest Gully date to approximately the same time period and might also be associated with the same building.[13] Both blocks are in good condition with fine work, including a painted meander on the fascia at the bottom of the cornice block.

Two unusual fragments of combination pan/cover tiles made of poros stone probably also date to the 5th century (**10** and **11**). Unfortunately, neither is well enough preserved for us to be certain of all the characteristics of the roof or even to know whether they both came from the same building. The larger piece (**10**) preserves nearly the full width of the cover and a small portion of the pan. Although this is a combination tile, the lack of undercutting beneath the cover suggests that the tile was used at the edge of the roof. A stucco coating is preserved across much of the top surface.

The smaller piece (**11**) preserves part of one side of a cover rising from a finished edge. Part of the cover has been cut away from the vertical edge of the tile at an angle of *ca.* 20 degrees. On the underside, toward the front of the tile, a cutting was made at a right angle to the preserved finished edge, either to overlap the tile beneath it or the edge of the roof. Behind this cutting a sufficient portion of the underside of the tile remains to show that the cover overlapped the adjacent pan tile. The excavation context of the pieces, from deposits of Late Hellenistic and Early Roman date, suggests they were made after the destruction of the Archaic Temple, *ca.* 470 B.C.[14]

Between the second half of the 5th century and the latter half of the 4th century there appears to have been little construction activity at Isthmia. The next group of tiles (Roof 2, **15–19**) dates to the end of the 4th century, based on their similarities to those from the South Stoa at Corinth.[15] Antefixes, ridge palmettes, and a raking sima (**17, 18,** and **15** respectively) all have the same designs and workmanship as the South Stoa types and must be close in date. In addition, the eaves tiles of the roof (**19**) have been identified based on the similarity of the workmanship of the meander design with that of the raking sima.

Another type of 4th-century sima with a large egg-and-dart motif on the cymatium can also be assigned to the same building (**16**). The attribution is made because the meander

[13] *Isthmia* II, nos. 117 and 118, p. 131.

[14] Only Classical and Hellenistic types have been found in the debris from the early 2nd-century destruction of the sanctuary.

[15] A well-preserved lion's head corner sima with the same design on the cymatium as IA 707 (**15**) was found in the debris of the Rachi settlement, located on the ridge south of the sanctuary. The fine condition of the sima is anomalous in comparison with material from the sanctuary. If this sima was used on the same roof as the fragments found in the sanctuary, and then reused on the Rachi, it must have been removed from the sanctuary before the destruction of the Rachi (*ca.* 200 B.C.) in order to account for its presence in the settlement.

pattern on the lower fascia and the bead and reel on its soffit have the same workmanship as those on the sima and eaves tiles. If a greater number of roofs were represented in the tiles that have been recovered at Isthmia, this attribution would seem less likely. The fact that so few roofs are represented makes their shared characteristics seem a stronger reason to relate them to the same building.

Fragments from Roof 2 were found in every section of the temenos (**17** and **19**), but most were found outside the temenos, with a concentration to the south and southeast. This distribution suggests that Roof 2 represents a building located outside the southeast corner of the temenos. Since the tiles are similar to those used on the South Stoa at Corinth, one might speculate that a stoa was erected adjacent to the stadium.

The remaining tiles, grouped under Roof 3 (**20–22**), do not share common features. The meander pattern of the sima is quite different in both color and draftsmanship from the eaves tile. Nor can any feature of the antefix be directly associated with the eaves or sima. All these tiles, however, are stylistically later than the pieces from Roof 2. The sima, in particular, is carelessly made in comparison with the earlier roof. While it is possible these pieces do not belong to the same roof, all are roughly contemporary and represented in large numbers. It may be the case that by the 3rd century carefully matching the designs of different components of a roof was no longer of any great concern. Another possibility is that the various elements of the roof were not designed for a specific building but rather the roof was created from pieces taken from an inventory.

There are several poros architectural fragments that belonged to small buildings constructed in the late 4th and early 3rd centuries. Four small Doric capitals have been found in the temenos and two outside it; they were dated by Broneer to the 4th century and assigned to three separate buildings.[16] Four large fragments of Doric cornices of the same date were also recovered by Broneer in the temenos area; three of these belonged to the same structure.[17] Although none of these poros architectural fragments can be assigned to specific building foundations, they confirm the picture represented in the tiles that at least two small buildings were erected near the temenos during the late 4th or early 3rd century.

## CONCLUSIONS

Building activity at Isthmia appears to have been concentrated within relatively discrete periods of time. The dates suggested for the tiles on stylistic grounds correspond to the periods of construction at the sanctuary which have been documented by deposits cleared in the old and new excavations. This correspondence suggests that the smaller buildings were conceived as part of larger building programs that encompassed the entire sanctuary.

---

[16] *Isthmia* II, nos. 100–102 and 104, p. 130, were found within the temenos. The two found outside the temenos belonged to the same buildings; no. 99 is comparable to 100, and 103 (found in the Rachi settlement) is comparable to 104.

[17] *Isthmia* II, nos. 120–122, p. 132, from one building. No. 126 was from a second building. An additional cornice, no. 123, found in the Northwest Reservoir, was thought by Broneer to be from a third building. Three other fragments from other buildings were found at greater distances from the temenos. Nos. 124 and 125 were found in the Sacred Glen, and no. 127 was found in the later (Hellenistic) Stadium.

During the first period in the second quarter of the 6th century, small buildings were completed following the inauguration of the games. The second period falls near the end of the 6th century when at least three additional small structures were added. Remains from each of these building programs, however, are few and the only foundations yet identified are the propylaia located on the north and east sides of the temenos.

After the fire of the 470's B.C., during the third quarter of the 5th century, the north temenos wall was dismantled and the boundary moved closer to the Temple of Poseidon. At least one small building was added within or near the temenos at about the same time as the new temple was being constructed. The last major building period represented by the tiles occurs during the late 4th and early 3rd centuries, when at least two small buildings were constructed near the temenos.

## CATALOGUE[18]

All measurements are in meters unless otherwise indicated.

### ARCHAIC TILES

**1.** IT 160   Pentagonal antefix   Fig. 4, Pl. 20:a
H. 0.13, W. 0.077, Depth 0.066.
Fabric 2.5Y 8/2, slip 10YR 7/4, brown 10R 3/2, red 10R 4/4.

Pentagonal antefix of Corinthian clay, which is porous with small to large inclusions. Only a portion of the right side with the upper and lower edges is preserved; the left and right sides are broken. The antefix was originally attached to a combination eaves/cover tile at the left.

At the bottom is the right-hand side of an inverted lotus that occupied the center of the antefix. A tendril passes over the top of the lotus at the upper right. The relief is deep, and small bits of brown and red color are preserved on the edges of the tendril and lotus respectively. At the top center of the tile there would have been a small palmette.

The height of the tile, the angle of the preserved upper edge, and the slope of the tendril indicate that the tendrils would have turned upward to connect with a small lotus at each side of the tile, that is, there would have been too much space at each side of the tile for the tendril to have ended in a simple volute. The use of a small lotus at each side of the antefix is characteristic of this type of pentagonal antefix, a type that was among the last made before the outside profile of the tile began to follow the contour of the decoration.[19]

Several examples are known from Didyma and Miletos, and it was once believed that the type developed in Ionia. Le Roy concluded that the origin was Corinth, based on a comparison of the style of the lotus with decoration on Corinthian pottery.[20] Two of the three examples Le Roy published from Delphi are described as having Corinthian fabric.[21] The more

---

[18] The tiles included in the catalogue were selected for their good state of preservation, except for the Archaic examples which are all included. With the possible exception of IT 20 (**3**), the tiles are of Corinthian manufacture. Context, listed at the end of each entry, includes the field notebook (NB) reference, the trench number (Tr.), and the lot number. Trenches can be located from the trench plans published in Gebhard and Hemans 1992, figs. 2 and 3, pp. 10–11. Lots are the units of excavation and storage for ceramics and other materials.

[19] Nancy Cooper, in her description of the development of the antefix, places the group in phase IV of the attached antefixes; Cooper 1989, pp. 59–60, pl. 20. See also Billot 1990, pp. 110, 123.

[20] Le Roy 1967, pp. 87–89.

[21] Le Roy 1967, pp. 87–89, pls. 30 and 123, series 33 and 34. Series 33, antefixes A.2 and A.8 are of Corinthian fabric. Antefix A.1, in series 34, is not Corinthian. See also Van Buren 1926, p. 133 (no. 45), pl. 89.

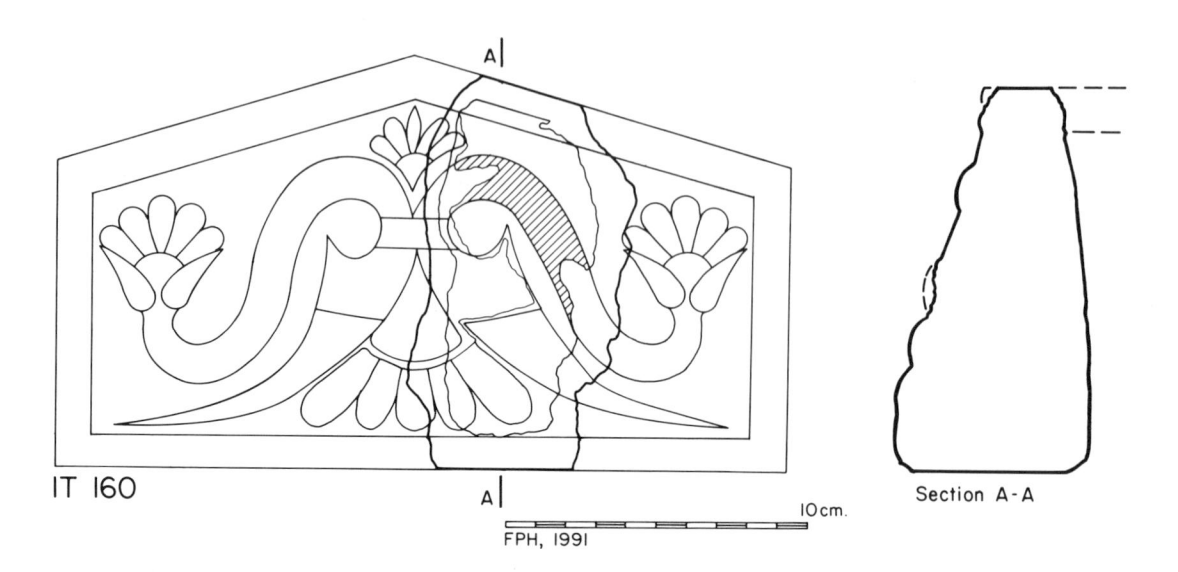

Fig. 4. Restored drawing of pentagonal antefix IT 160 (**1**), based in part on IT 732 (**2**). On this and the other restored drawings, diagonal hatched lines indicate areas on the tile where paint is preserved or where it can be restored from fragments of paint. Closely spaced lines indicate shades of dark brown, black, or dark red; less closely spaced lines indicate lighter shades of brown or red. The outline surrounding the areas where paint is indicated shows the extent of the preserved surface of the tile.

recent recognition of an example from Corinth by Marie-Françoise Billot as well as this example from Isthmia supports Le Roy's conclusion.[22]

Le Roy dates the Delphi series to 570–560. A date for IT 160 in the second quarter of the 6th century, perhaps as early as the 570's, seems likely (see p. 64 above).

Date: second quarter of the 6th cent.
Context: NB 11 (1956) p. 4, Early Stadium Tr. 7; associated finds are Roman.

**2.** IT 732    Pentagonal antefix    Fig. 4

H. 0.08, W. 0.113, Th. 0.068.
Fabric 2.5Y 8/2, slip 10YR 7/4, brown 10R 3/2, red 10R 4/2.

Pentagonal antefix of Corinthian clay, of the same type as **1**. Only a part of the bottom center of the tile is preserved, and contains a large portion of the inverted lotus and a small piece of the left tendril in deep relief. The surface is abraded but small bits of brown/red and red/purple are preserved in the crevices of the relief. The back of the tile shows paring marks.

Date: second quarter of the 6th cent.
Context: none.

**3.** IT 20    Pentagonal antefix    Fig. 5, Pl. 20:b

H. 0.098, W. 0.105, Depth 0.04.
Fabric 10YR 7/4 (burned), slip 10YR 8/3, purple/red 10R 4/3, red 2.5YR 4/6.

Pentagonal antefix, possibly Argive. Clay is homogeneous, with small to medium inclusions, not Corinthian in appearance. The red appearance of the fabric may be a result of later burning of the tile. Most of the left half of the antefix is preserved, with a red inverted lotus at the center and a purple/red volute at the left in deep relief. The figures are surrounded by a thin relief line, possibly an Argive feature.[23] The

---

[22] Billot (1990, p. 110, note 68) identifies a piece from Isthmia as a member of the same group, citing Isthmia inventory number IT 20 (**3**). This is probably a confusion of inventory numbers since IT 160 (**1**) is clearly the tile that belongs in the group. The Corinth piece is identified by Billot as FA 555.

[23] Nancy Winter, personal communication.

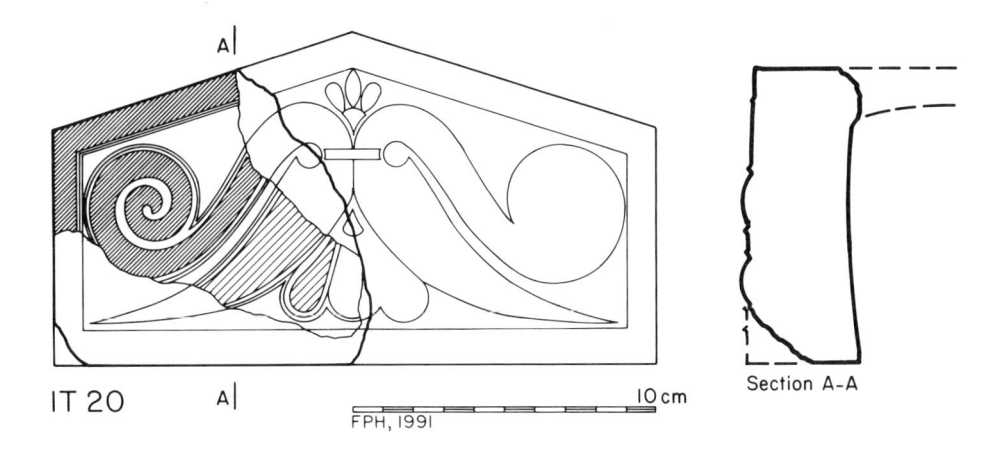

FIG. 5. Restored drawing of pentagonal antefix IT 20 (**3**)

purple/red border is preserved on three sides. The tile was burned after it was broken.

The straight sloping upper edges and the horizontal lower edge of the tile indicate that this piece is a late example of the pentagonal type and should be dated to the second quarter of the 6th century, perhaps close to 550 B.C.

Date: second quarter of the 6th cent.

Context: NB 6 (1954) p. 108, from outside the excavations.

**4.** IA 663   Cavetto raking sima   Fig. 6, Pl. 20:c

H. 0.118, L. 0.131, W. 0.061, slope 1:12.[24]

Fabric 10YR 8/3, slip 10YR 8/4, dark red 10R 4/3, black/brown 10YR 4/1.

Corinthian raking sima with cavetto profile from the left side of the gable. Broken and worn on both sides and bottom. The lower edge was thin, overlapping the edge of the roof member underneath it, as shown by a small preserved portion of the inside surface (see section, Fig. 6).

The fascia has a tongue pattern above a single-braid guilloche, with tips of tongues on the top molding. Tongues are dark red with a vertical band in reserve at the center. The pattern repeats at an interval of *ca.* 0.041. Surrounding the tongues are a reserve band, which is in turn surrounded by black.

The guilloche is poorly preserved. Black/brown circles at the center are surrounded by an alternating red and black braid, bands in reserve, and a black frame. The pattern repeats at intervals of *ca.* 0.025. Circles were incised to guide the painting of the guilloche.

The cavetto profile does not closely resemble any of the examples from Delphi published by Le Roy. It is closest to examples late in his typology (type b, series 19 and 23).[25] Draftsmanship on IA 663, however, is better than the examples Le Roy places at the end of the Delphi series, and the Isthmia piece makes extensive use of incised lines to guide the painting.

Date: second quarter of the 6th cent.

Context: NB 20 (1959) p. 356, Northwest Reservoir, Tr. GW 2; associated finds are 1st century after Christ.

**5.** IT 1075   Cavetto raking sima

H. 0.097, L. 0.092, Th. 0.059.

Fabric 10YR 8/2, slip 5YR 8/2 (burned), reddish brown 5YR 3/2 (burned).

Corinthian raking sima fragment with cavetto profile, same type as **4**. Broken and worn on both sides and

[24] The slope measurements for the simas are for the sloping rear surface with respect to the top and bottom edges of the tile. The actual slope of the roof would have been greater.

[25] Le Roy 1967, pp. 57–59, pls. 98–100. IA 663 (**4**) has a ratio of upper fascia to the depth of the cavetto of *ca.* 1:1.3, closest to S.202.

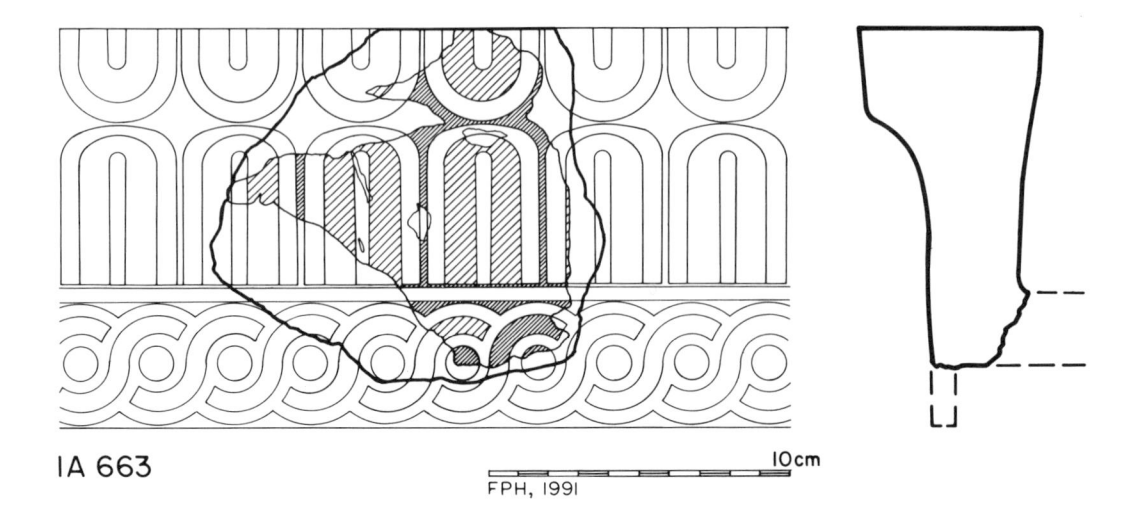

FIG. 6. Restored drawing of cavetto raking sima IA 663 (**4**)

bottom. Decoration is like that of **4**, but colors are different as the result of burning after it was broken.
Date: second quarter of the 6th cent.
Context: none.

**6.** IA 4063   Eaves tile         Fig. 7:a, Pl. 20:d
H. 0.0545, L. 0.115, W. 0.155.
Fabric 2.5Y 8/2, slip 2.5Y 7/4, red 2.5Y 4/4 (burned to olive brown), black/brown 10YR 3/1.

Corinthian eaves tile with single-braid guilloche. Smooth and slipped on top and fascia. Rough and unfinished on bottom, showing impressions from having been dried on matting or ground but somewhat smoother for *ca.* 0.04 toward front edge. Surfaces and broken edges are charred.

Incised outlines and compass points at center of circles. Pattern repeats at interval of 0.033. Braid alternates black and red within circle diameter of 0.042. Red braid has been charred to olive-brown color.

The single-braid guilloche is typical of Corinthian eaves tiles from the late 7th century to approximately the last quarter of the 6th.[26]
Date: probably second quarter of the 6th cent.
Context: none, found in tile pile, 1989.

**7.** IA 689   Raking sima         Fig. 8, Pl. 20:e
H. 0.116; L. 0.159, W. 0.11, slope 1:20.
Fabric 10YR 8/3, slip 10YR 8/3, red 10R 5/8, black 10YR 3/1.

Corinthian raking sima, "Megarian" type, from right side of gable, broken at both sides. Vertical dowel hole at rear, probably for the attachment of an acroterion at the corner of the gable (see section, Fig. 8).[27]

Double chain of lotus flowers and seven-leaved palmettes in red and black on fascia and ovolo. Upper molding broken away. Pattern repeats at interval of

---

[26] An early example is Corinth FA 101, 101a, with a guilloche on the eaves; *Corinth* IV, i, pp. 11, 57–58, fig. 1. A date in the last quarter of the 7th century is proposed by Roebuck (1990, p. 51) based on comparison of the antefix to examples from the pre-Peisistratid Telestereion at Eleusis, dated *ca.* 610 B.C. A date in the third quarter of the 7th century is proposed by Williams (1978, pp. 347–348, note 13) based on the comparison made between the decoration of Protocorinthian pottery and the roof tiles by Payne (1931, p. 252) and the lower chronology of Protocorinthian pottery. The use of the guilloche gives way to the meander in the last quarter of the 6th century as, for example, in the Treasury of the Megarians at Olympia, *ca.* 510 B.C.

[27] Acroterion attachment identified by Nancy Winter.

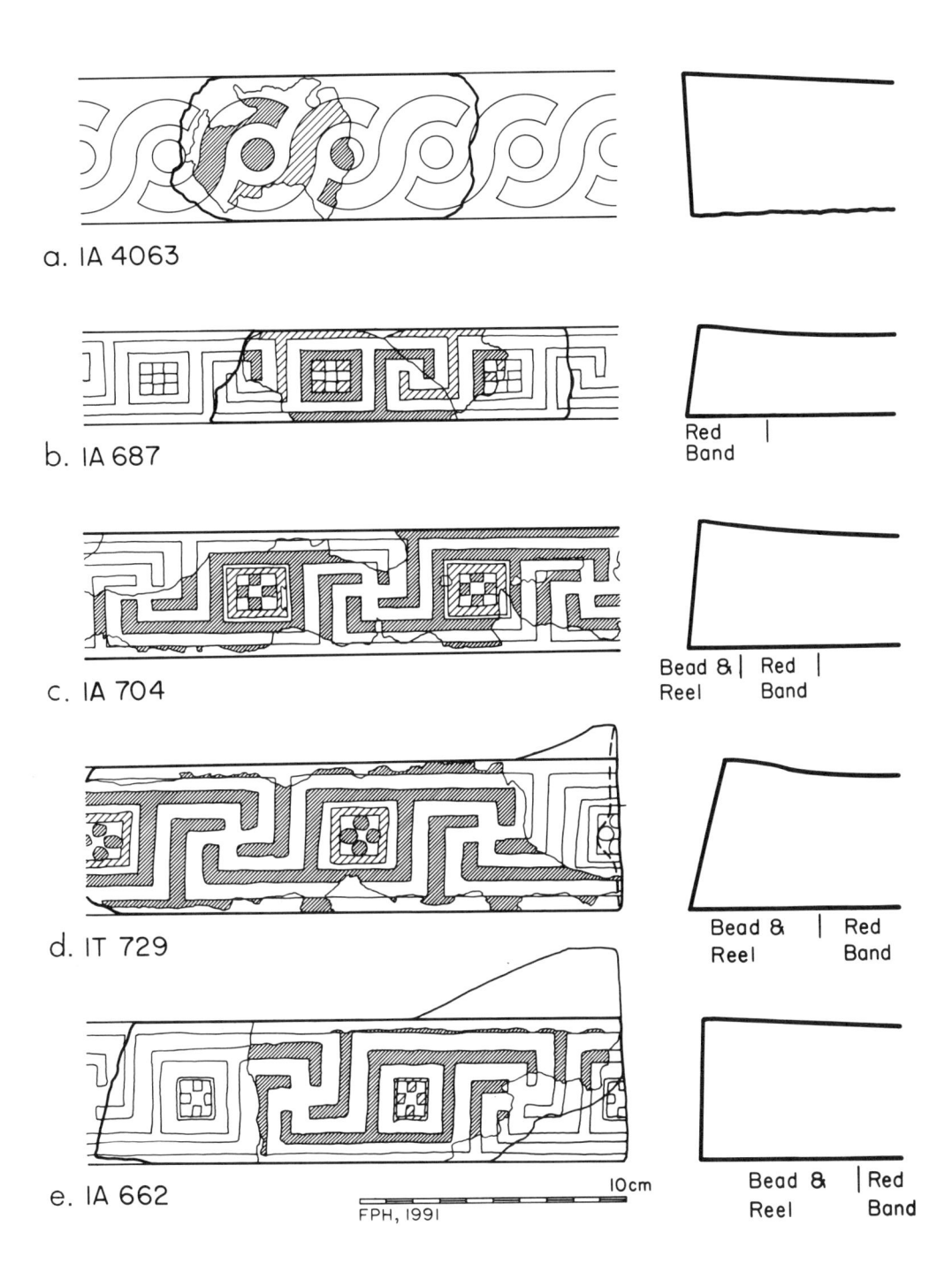

FIG. 7. Restored drawings of eaves tiles in chronological order: a. IA 4063 (**6**); b. IA 687 (**8**); c. IA 704 (**13**); d. IT 729 (**19**); e. IA 662 (**21**)

*ca.* 0.093. There is a red band 0.014 wide at front edge of the soffit.

The curve of the torus is pronounced, more so than most simas found at Corinth.[28] The Isthmia piece is also very short, and yet the overall depth of the piece from face to rear is comparable to examples of greater height.[29] The date is based on the comparison with the Treasury of the Megarians at Olympia.

Date: last quarter 6th cent.

Context: NB 20 (1959) p. 360, Northwest Reservoir, Tr. GW 2. Found with IA 687 (**8**). Ceramic context is 1st century after Christ.

**8.** IA 687   Eaves tile           Fig. 7:b, Pl. 20:f

H. 0.035, L. 0.136, W. 0.097.

Fabric 2.5YR 8/2, slip 2.5Y 8/2, red 5YR 5/6, black 10YR 4/1.

The earliest meander-patterned eaves tile at Isthmia and the only tile with such a small height. Single-stopped meander, with red used for the top horizontal line and hook and black at the bottom. Border of checkerboard is black, and interior squares are red. Ground is painted white.

The meander repeats at an interval of *ca.* 0.065. Both horizontal and vertical guide lines are visible, and the painting is precise within those lines. Checkerboard outline is 0.023 wide and 0.019 high. On the soffit there is a plain red band *ca.* 0.03 wide.

Date: last quarter 6th cent.

Context: Found with IA 689 (**7**).

**9.** IT 173   Raking sima          Fig. 9, Pl. 20:g

H. 0.144, L. 0.26, W. 0.083, slope 1:29.

Fabric 10YR 8/2, slip 10YR 7/4, red 10R 4/4, black 10YR 3/1

Corinthian raking sima, "Megarian" type, from left side of gable, broken at right edge. Five-leaved palmette and lotus in red and black on fascia and torus, with pattern repeating at interval of 0.13. Upper molding not preserved. Incised lines surround lotus leaves.

Similar to Corinth FS 1010 but with single petal at center of lotus and a more rounded torus profile.[30] Similar in design to Delphi Roof 45 but smaller in size.[31] Isthmia pieces IA 719 and IA 545 also belong to the end of the dark-on-light series. IA 719 is from the same building as IT 173. IA 545 is smaller in scale and from another building. The profile of IT 173 is quite close to Corinth FS 28, a light-on-dark sima,[32] indicating a late date for the Isthmia piece, *ca.* 500 B.C.

Date: *ca.* 500 B.C.

Context: none, from outside excavations.

## CLASSICAL AND HELLENISTIC TYPES

### Poros Combination Tiles

**10.** IA 4086   Poros combination tile        Fig. 10

H. 0.113, W. 0.194, L. 0.204.

Poros combination tile preserving nearly the full width of the cover and part of the attached pan, broken on all edges and along the bottom. The original width of the cover was *ca.* 0.174. Lack of undercutting beneath cover suggests it was used at the eaves. Stucco coating preserved across much of the cover. Front edge of the cover is dark from exposure to weather.

Date: probably mid-5th cent. (see p. 67 above).

Context: Lot 89-460, NB 70 (1989) p. 66, east temenos, ceramic context is late 3rd or early 2nd cent. B.C.

**11.** IA 3642   Poros combination tile        Fig. 11

H. 0.095, W. 0.102, L. 0.119.

Poros tile preserving one edge with part of the cover rising above it. Rear edge of the cover has been cut away at an angle of *ca.* 20 degrees. Bottom front edge has cutting to overlap the edge of the roof or the tile below it. Right half of the underside (away from the preserved edge) has been cut away beneath the cover.

Date: probably mid-5th cent. (see p. 67 above).

---

[28] Roebuck 1990, fig. 2, p. 57.

[29] Le Roy (1990, pp. 37–38) has suggested that the profile was made with the aid of a template ("gabarit"). This method of manufacture would have created more variation in the profile than had been previously assumed.

[30] Roebuck 1990, p. 59, fig. 2, pl. 7, with further references p. 59, note 68.

[31] Le Roy 1967, S.28, S.29, and S.211, pp. 101–102, 109, pls. 38, 102, 109. Series 45 is dated *ca.* 500 B.C.

[32] Roebuck 1990, pp. 59–60, fig. 2, pl. 7.

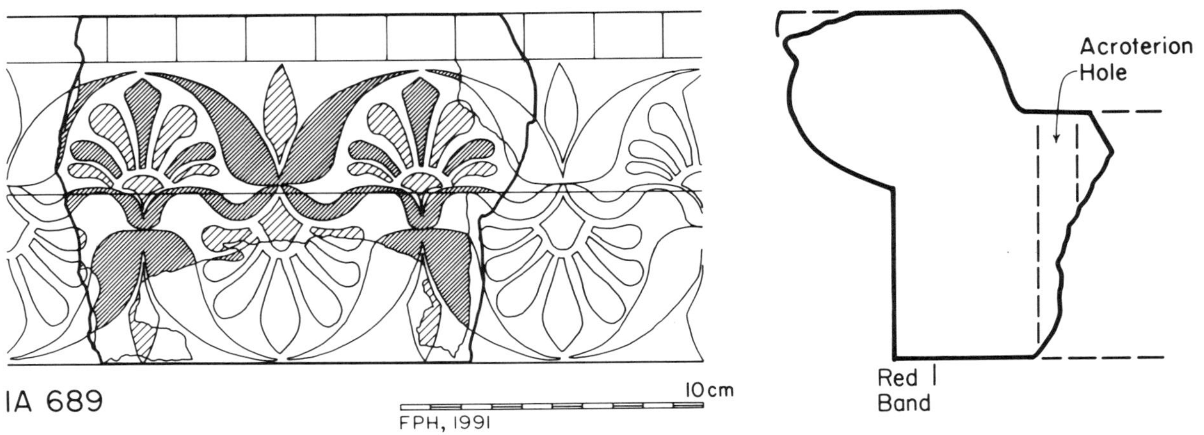

Fig. 8. Restored drawing of raking sima IA 689 (**7**)

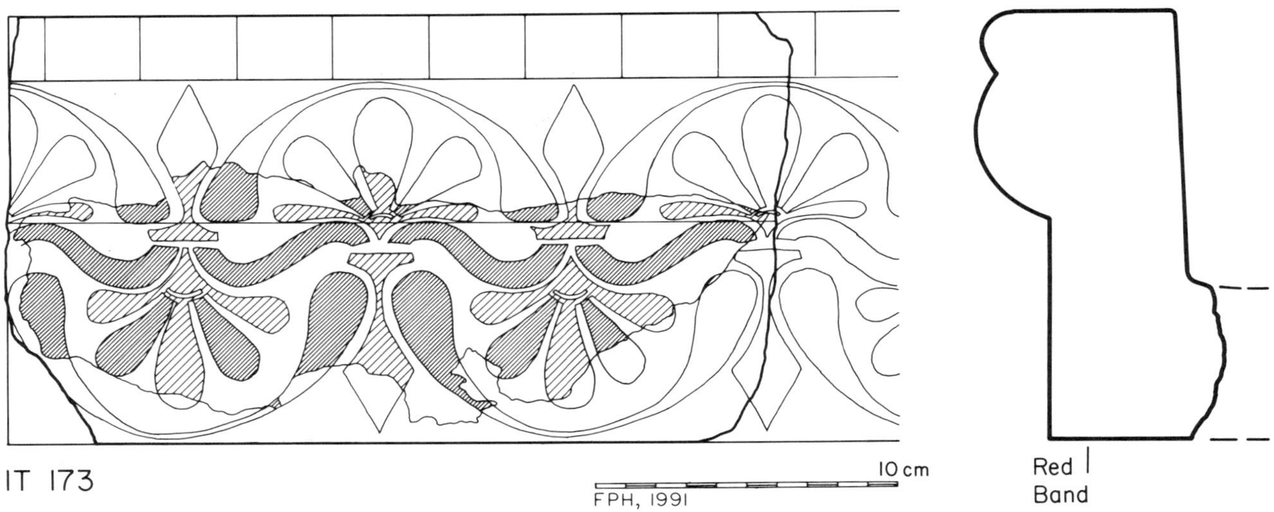

Fig. 9. Restored drawing of raking sima IT 173 (**9**)

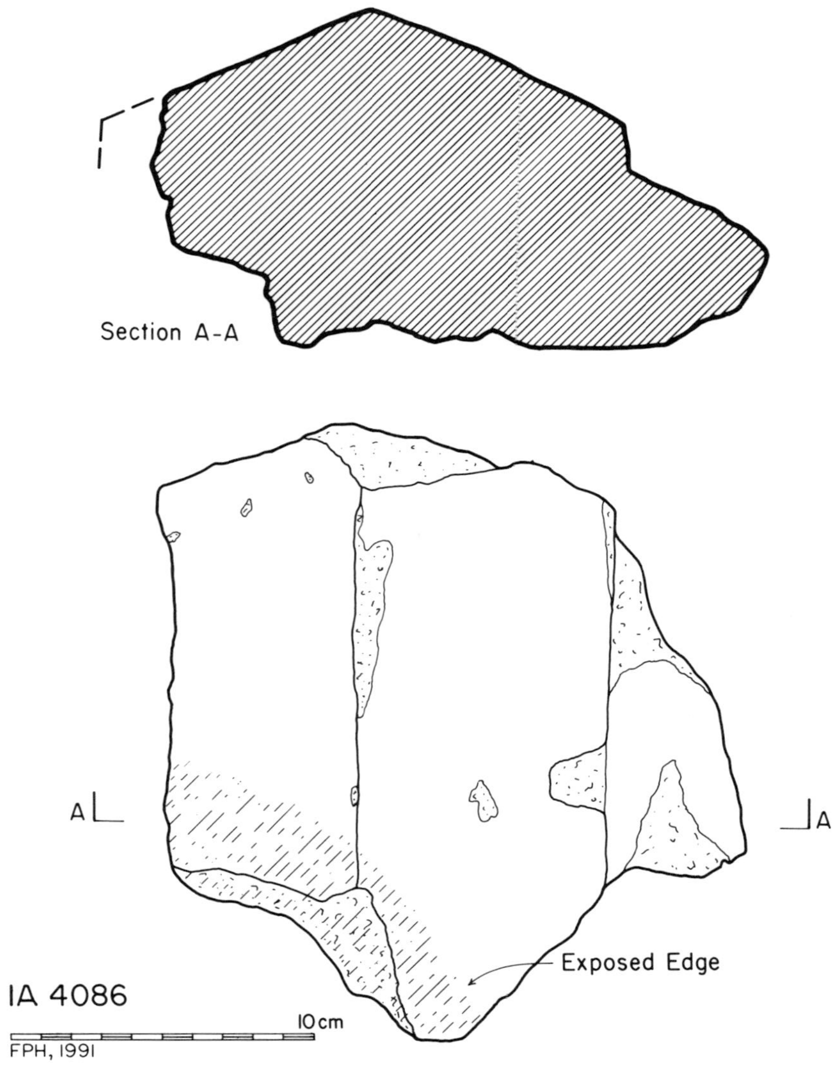

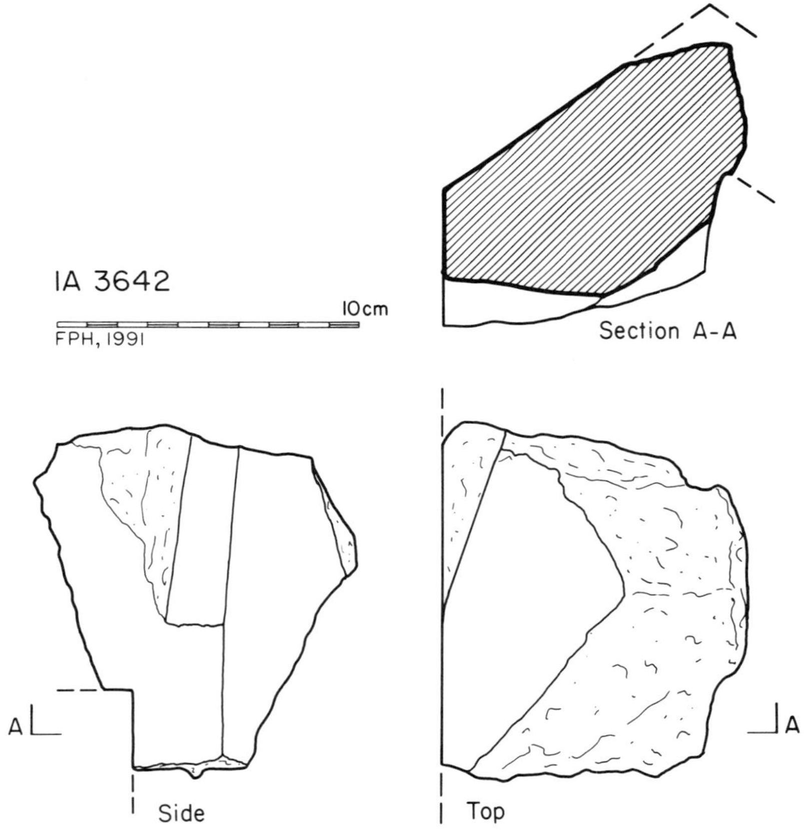

Fig. 11. Poros combination pan/cover tile IA 3642 (**11**)

Fig. 10. Poros combination pan/cover tile IA 4086 (**10**)

Context: Lot 89-555, NB 80 (1989) p. 61, northeast temenos, ceramic context is 1st century after Christ.

*Roof 1*

The types of tiles described hereafter have been recovered in larger numbers and are grouped by roofs. Three types of palmette antefixes have been recovered, and while the decorative motifs cannot be compared directly with the simas and eaves tiles, the quality of the draftsmanship provides a good indication for matching these to the appropriate roofs. Thus the Roof 1 antefixes and eaves tiles have been assigned to the same building based on their exceptionally fine workmanship. No sima from this roof has been identified. Roof 1 eaves tiles display careful line work in the meander and checkerboard patterns, with incised lines visible. The checkerboard is particularly distinctive, with a fairly wide, purple border surrounding carefully made squares. The soffit has a narrow bead-and-reel design, a feature that appears to have chronological significance. On Roof 1 the design is *ca.* 0.02 wide, on Roof 2 *ca.* 0.05, and on Roof 3, *ca.* 0.06 (Fig. 7:c–e). The greatest number of fragments from Roof 1 come from the north and northeast part of the temenos, in contexts of the early 2nd century B.C. and 1st century after Christ.

**12.** IA 3094  Palmette antefix, Roof 1  Pl. 21:a

H. 0.183, W. 0.161, Depth 0.057.
Fabric 5YR 8/4, slip 10YR 8/4, red 2.5YR 6/4, purple 10R 3/3, black 2.5YR 3/0.

Nearly complete, missing portions at upper and lower left. Cover behind antefix was *ca.* 0.165 wide, with sides *ca.* 0.05 high rising to *ca.* 0.08 at center.

Eleven-leaved palmette with spade-shaped heart. S-shaped vine tendrils below the palmette enclose eyes at each end. At the outside center of each tendril is a small three-petaled lotus. At the bottom center there is a palmette with nine or eleven leaves, but the bottom edge is broken away. Right of center at bottom is an acorn. Relief is shallow.

The fine details are extremely well executed. Red/purple is applied around the heart, at the center of the heart, and in a row of dots along the edge of heart. Fine red dots and lines on lotus, lower half of acorn, and on eyes within tendrils. Outside edges are orange/red.

IA 3094 is similar in workmanship and style, but simpler, to a group of terracottas from the workshop of Pheidias at Olympia dated to 430 B.C.[33] The use of elaborate floral relief on the Olympia pieces does not appear in the Isthmia pieces. Thus a somewhat earlier date, toward the middle of the century, is likely. Two smaller fragments of the same type are IS 262 and IT 29.

Date: third quarter of the 5th cent.

Context: Lot 89-138, NB 68 (1989) p. 96, Tr. 89-19, north temenos, part of the sanctuary destruction debris that was deposited as road fill along the south edge of the Classical/Hellenistic road during the first quarter of the 2nd century B.C.

**13.** IA 704  Eaves tile, Roof 1  Fig. 7:c, Pl. 21:b

H. 0.048, L. 0.315, W. 0.216.
Fabric 5YR 7/4, slip 2.5Y 8/4, red (soffit) 2.5YR 5/6, purple (fascia) 10R 3/6, brown 10YR 4/3.

Meander repeats at intervals of 0.084, lines 0.005–0.006 wide; checkerboard has purple outline 0.0225 wide and 0.0195 high with lines 0.003 wide. Bead and reel on the soffit is 0.019 wide and repeats at intervals of 0.037; beads are *ca.* 0.019 wide and *ca.* 0.014 high; red band is 0.03 high.

IT 4061 has the same workmanship, but the bottom has no bead-and-reel design.

Locations of fragments: north and northwest temenos IT 309, IT 704, IT 1025, IA 4061; northeast temenos IT 522.

Context for IA 704: NB 31 (1960) p. 744, northwest temenos, Tr. NW c.

**14.** IA 705  Eaves tile, Roof 1  Pl. 21:c

H. 0.0445, L. 0.11, W. 0.11.

Eaves tile like IA 704 (**13**) but with lotus and palmette on the soffit. Total depth of band on underside is 0.096 with lotus and palmette 0.07 high at the front edge followed by narrow bead and reel and purple band. Lotus and nine-leaved palmette on brown/black ground with purple outline of leaves on lotus; pattern repeats at intervals of 0.101.

Context: NB 31 (1960) p. 662, Northwest Reservoir, Tr. GW 5; associated finds are Roman.

---

[33] *Olympia* II, p. 198, pl. 122, dated early 5th century; *OlForsch* V, pp. 116–117, pls. 17, 18, 44, 45, dated to *ca.* 430 B.C.; Hübner 1973, p. 123, pl. 70:2–4.

*Roof 2*

The eaves tiles of Roof 2 can be matched with the raking simas based on a comparison between the meander patterns. The characteristics of the meander also provide the link between the two simas that have a different design on the cymatium. The designs on the tiles of Roof 2 are very similar to those from the South Stoa at Corinth; antefix and ridge-palmette tiles are matched to the simas and eaves tiles on that basis.

**15.** IA 707   Raking sima, Roof 2   Fig. 12, Pl. 21:d

H. 0.165, L. 0.30, W. 0.19, preserving left end of tile and full profile.

Upper taenia, 0.02 high, is red. Cymatium is 0.088 high with alternating lotus and palmette with a half lotus on left side at join. Red is employed in the heart of the palmette and on the upper edges of lotus leaves at the center. Vertical incised lines are located at the center of each figure: spacing from the left edge is 0.072, 0.082, 0.074. Lower profile is typical meander with checkerboard pattern that repeats at intervals of 0.086 and 0.091.

The bead and reel on the soffit is *ca.* 0.04 deep and repeats at intervals of *ca.* 0.063; red band is *ca.* 0.027 high.

Based on its similarities to the roof tiles of the South Stoa at Corinth, this is the most closely datable of all the Classical/Hellenistic examples from Isthmia.[34] Differences between the two roofs can be attributed to the smaller scale of the Isthmia roof; as a result, there are fewer motifs. The South Stoa sima has a height of *ca.* 0.215 and proportionately larger spacing of the painted motifs.

Another fragment is IT 260, found in the southwest temenos.

Date: fourth quarter of the 4th cent., based on the South Stoa at Corinth.

Context: none, from outside excavations, 1960.

**16.** IA 4040/4041   Raking sima, Roof 2   Fig. 13, Pl. 21:e

H. 0.159, L. 0.23, W. 0.11.
Fabric 10YR 7/4, slip 2.5Y 7/4, red 2.5YR 4/6, black 2.5YR 3/0.

Two joining pieces of raking sima with cyma reversa profile. Taenia at top is not preserved. Cyma has egg and dart with black outlines on a brick red background. Pattern repeats at an interval of 0.105. Lower fascia is recessed with a double black meander framing a black cross in a red frame; the pattern repeats at an interval of 0.085.

Soffit has a bead and reel *ca.* 0.041 deep repeating at an interval of *ca.* 0.075. Compass holes are visible at the centers of the two preserved circles; diameter 0.04. A small portion of a red band is preserved at the inside edge of the bead and reel. Slip 10YR 8/2, brick red 2.5YR 5/4, black 2.5YR 4/0.

Van Buren cites examples of egg-and-dart simas from Corinth, Elateia, Epidauros, Gonnos, and Apollonia in Thrace, all dated to the 4th century.[35]

A piece from Lusoi is dated to the Hellenistic period, based on the poorly painted checkerboard in the meander.[36] Series 78 and 79 from Delphi are dated to the 4th century by Le Roy.[37]

The draftsmanship and profile of the Isthmia piece is closer to two pieces from Delphi with lion's head spouts. Jean-François Bommelaer, based on an analysis of the style of the lions and the chronology of the monument, places them in the first quarter of the 4th century, possibly as early as 400 B.C.[38]

The meander and soffit design and the overall draftsmanship of IT 4040/4041 matches that of IT 707 (**15**). On that basis the two fragments are assigned to the same roof, where they could have decorated opposite pediments.

IT 422 is another fragment from the same egg-and-dart sima, but the meander is more widely spaced, at an interval of 0.099.

---

[34] *Corinth* I, iv, 83–88, pls. 19–21. The date of the South Stoa has been the subject of much recent discussion, and the importance of the date to the chronology of Classical and Hellenistic roof tiles has been emphasized by Le Roy 1990, pp. 38–39, note 29. Broneer (*Corinth* I, iv, pp. 156–157) places the construction date soon after the battle of Chaironeia (338 B.C.).

[35] Van Buren 1926, pp. 99–100, raking cornices 117–123, nos. 201–207.

[36] Van Buren 1926, p. 47, no. 206.

[37] Le Roy 1967, pp. 153–154, 165–166, pls. 58 and 104 (S.34–38, 99, 108, 169, 170).

[38] Bommelaer 1978, pp. 173–197.

Fig. 12. Restored drawing of raking sima IA 707 (**15**)

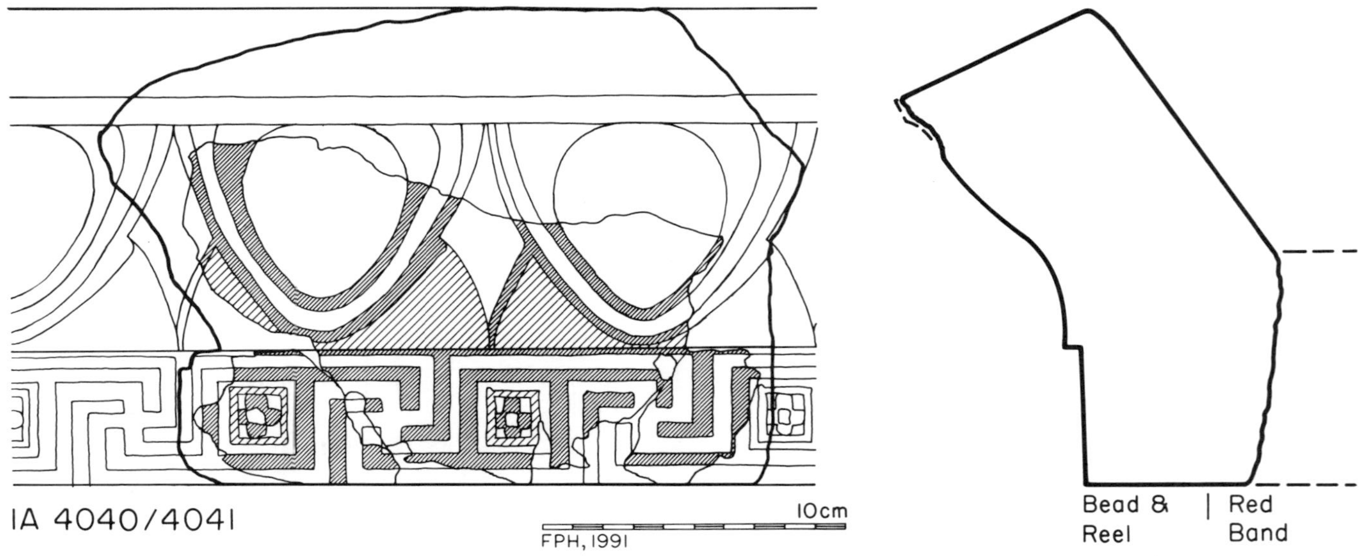

Fig. 13. Restored drawing of raking sima IA 4040/4041 (**16**)

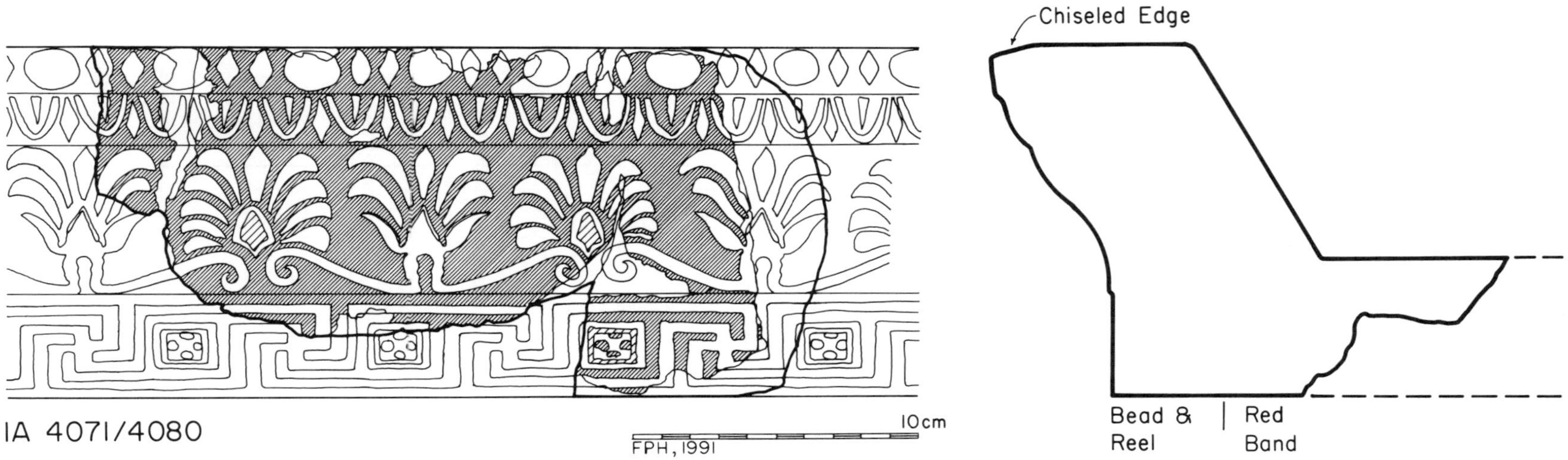

IA 4040/4041

Fig. 14. Restored drawing of raking sima IA 4071/4080 (**22**)

IA 4071/4080

Date: fourth quarter of the 4th cent.

Context: Lot 89-358, NB 76 (1989) p. 46, Tr. 89-39, north temenos, part of the sanctuary destruction debris that was deposited as road fill along the south edge of the Classical/Hellenistic road during the first quarter of the 2nd century B.C.

**17.** IT 168/234   Palmette antefix, Roof 2   Pl. 22:a

H. 0.225, W. 0.17, Th. 0.065.

Fabric 10YR 7/4, slip 10YR 8/2, red (outside edges) 10R 4/4, red (face) 2.5YR 5/4, black 10YR 3/1.

Complete except for chip off the top. Cover behind antefix has sides 0.048 high, sloping to 0.08 at center.

Eleven-leaved palmette with spade-shaped heart. Below are vine tendrils flanking three inverted lotus leaves on the center axis. Five smaller leaves hang from tendrils to each side of central lotus. Tendrils have raised edges. Black ground with relief in buff reserve; red applied to heart, between lower leaves, at centers of upper tendrils, and on outside edges.

Locations of fragments: north temenos IT 249; northeast temenos IT 481, IT 482; southwest temenos IT 304; outside central sanctuary or no context IT 23, IT 25, IT 26, IT 27, IT 169, IT 168/234 (**17**), IT 735, IT 834, IT 980.

Date: fourth quarter of the 4th cent., based on South Stoa at Corinth.

Context: fragments are concentrated outside the central sanctuary toward the south and southeast, associated ceramics are Roman.

**18.** IT 269/278   Ridge palmette, Roof 2   Pl. 22:b

H. 0.20, W. 0.16, Th. 0.105.

Fabric 5YR 8/3, slip 10YR 8/4, red/purple 10R 4/4, black 5YR 3/1.

Ridge palmette, broken at center, top, and bottom. Nine-leaved palmette has red on the spade-shaped heart and on the outside edges.

Another fragment, IT 248, is from the north temenos.

Context: IT 269 and 278, both from outside the excavations, 1958.

**19.** IT 729   Eaves tile, Roof 2   Fig. 7:d, Pl. 22:c

H. 0.054, max. H. 0.074 at right, L. 0.213, W. 0.238.

Fabric 7.5YR 8/4, slip 2.5Y 8/4, red (soffit) 2.5YR 4/6, black 5R 3/1.

Lower right corner of eaves tile. Meander repeats at an interval of 0.097. Horizontal incised guidelines. The two preserved checkerboards are 0.024 and 0.021 wide. Bead and reel on the soffit is *ca.* 0.05 deep and repeats at intervals of *ca.* 0.091; beads are roughly circular, *ca.* 0.045 in diameter; purple/red band is *ca.* 0.04 high.

Another fragment, IT 350, has lotus and eleven-leaved palmette decoration on the soffit which repeats at an interval of *ca.* 0.125. Purple is used for the heart of the palmette and the center of the lotus.

The painting on the eaves tiles from Roof 2 is much more carelessly done than on Roof 1. The meander on the front face is generally more widely spaced but varies from an interval of 0.085 to 0.103. Round dots or irregular blobs are often found in the checkerboard rather than squares. Vertical guidelines are generally not used and the vertical painted lines of the meander are often not perpendicular to the horizontal. Several fragments have relatively deep claw-chisel and flat-chisel marks on the bottom side beyond the painted pattern.

Locations of fragments: north temenos IA 3095; northeast temenos IT 350; southwest temenos IT 287; south temenos IT 270; southeast temenos IT 272; outside central sanctuary or no context IA 4079, IT 1029, IT 1030.

Date: fourth quarter of the 4th cent.

Context: NB 19 (1961) p. 67, Theater, channel trench.

*Roof 3*

The workmanship of the tiles grouped together as Roof 3 is markedly inferior to that of Roof 1 and 2. As described in the text, the tiles assigned to Roof 3 have no features that link them to a single building and are grouped together on the basis of their date.

**20.** IA 4033   Palmette antefix, Type 3   Pl. 22:d

H. 0.268, W. 0.194, Th. 0.072.

Fabric 5YR 7/3 to 10YR 8/3, slip 10YR 8/3, red (outside edges) 2.5YR 4/4, red (face) 10R 4/4, black 10YR 3/1.

Cover tile with antefix, complete. Cover behind antefix has sides 0.068 high, sloping to 0.09 high at center.

Nine-leaved palmette with diamond-shaped heart. Below are vine tendrils flanking inverted lotus with three leaves on center axis. Five smaller leaves hang from tendrils to each side of central lotus. Relief is higher than on Roofs 1 and 2. Tendrils are in flat relief. Brown/black ground with relief in buff reserve; red applied to heart, lotus, at centers of the upper tendrils, on upper side of hanging leaves, and on outside edges.

Locations of fragments: north temenos IT 28, IT 233, IT 4033 (**20**); northeast temenos IT 483, IT 484, IT 485; southwest temenos IT 24; temple IT 17, IT 34; outside central sanctuary or no context IT 21, IT 104, IT 148, IT 285, IT 819.

Date: probably first half of the 3rd cent., based on the comparison with Roof 2 antefixes.

Context for IT 4033: Lot 89-154, NB 68 (1989) p. 182, north temenos, Tr. 68; joining piece from outside the excavation.

**21.** IA 662   Eaves tile, Roof 3   Fig. 7:e, Pl. 22:e

H. 0.053, H. right edge 0.079, L. 0.204, W. 0.16. Fabric 5YR 8/3, slip 5YR 8/3, red 2.5YR 5/6, black 5YR 3/1.

Meander repeats at interval of *ca.* 0.08, lines *ca.* 0.0045 wide; checkerboard outline 0.013 wide and 0.016 high, entirely in red with lines *ca.* 0.001 wide. Bead and reel on soffit 0.06 high and repeats at interval of *ca.* 0.09 with circular beads *ca.* 0.057 in diameter; red band is *ca.* 0.043 high.

Eaves tiles from Roof 3 are carelessly made. They are distinguished from Roof 2 tiles by the painted red checkerboard outline and by the difference in size between the diameters of the beads on the soffits.

Locations of fragments: north temenos IT 11, IT 247, IT 51/161; northeast temenos IT 411; northwest IT 662 (**21**); Palaimonion area IT 172, IT 271; no context IT 240, IT 1028.

Date: first half of the 3rd cent.

Context: NB 20 (1959) p. 334, Northwest Reservoir, Tr. GW.

**22.** IA 4071/4080   Raking sima   Fig. 14, Pl. 22:f

H. 0.123, W. 0.268, Th. 0.18, three joining fragments.

Upper taenia 0.015 high with bead and reel, reserve on black ground, repeats at intervals of 0.043; reels are diamond shaped, beads 0.02 wide. Molding below upper taenia has egg and dart on purple ground *ca.* 0.015 high; darts are diamond shaped, pattern repeats at intervals of 0.0225.

Lotus-and-palmette frieze 0.054 high on cymatium with purple highlights at heart of palmette and along central edges of lotus leaves. Incised lines spaced 0.117 at middles of palmettes.

Meander frieze on lower fascia repeats at intervals of 0.075, checkerboard outline is 0.017 wide and 0.013 high, with round blobs for squares.

Soffit has bead and reel 0.038 deep, with circles 0.033 in diameter. Purple band is preserved 0.029 wide but is broken away.

Other fragments: IA 4039 from the north temenos; IT 808 from the later stadium; IT 425 from the theater.

Context: Lot 89-345, NB 76 (1989) pp. 51, 54, north temenos, Trs. 89-39 and 89-41; Lot 89-358, NB 81 (1989) p. 21, north temenos, Tr. 89-40; Lot 89-343, NB 75 (1989) p. 75, Tr. 89-37.

## BIBLIOGRAPHY

Billot, M.-F. 1990. "Terres cuites architecturales d'Argos et d'Épidaure. Notes de typologie et d'histoire," in *Hesperia* 59, pp. 95–139

Bommelaer, J.-F. 1978. "Simas et gargouilles classiques de Delphes," *BCH* 102, pp. 173–197

Broneer, O. 1976. "The Isthmian Sanctuary of Poseidon," in *Neue Forschungen in griechischen Heiligtümern*, U. Jantzen, ed., Tübingen, pp. 39–62

Cooper, N. K. 1989. *The Development of Roof Revetment in the Peloponnese (Studies in Mediterranean Archaeology. Pocketbook* 88), Jonsered

*Corinth* I, iv = O. Broneer, *The South Stoa (Corinth* I, iv), Princeton 1954

*Corinth* IV, i = I. Thallon-Hill and L. S. King, *Decorated Architectural Terracottas (Corinth* IV, i), Cambridge, Mass. 1929

Gebhard, E. R., and F. P. Hemans. 1992. "University of Chicago Excavations at Isthmia, 1989: I," *Hesperia* 61, pp. 1–77

Hemans, F. P. 1989. "The Archaic Roof Tiles at Isthmia: A Re-examination," *Hesperia* 58, pp. 251–266

*Hesperia* 59 = *Proceedings of the First International Conference on Archaic Greek Architectural Terracottas, Athens, December 2–4, 1988 (Hesperia* 59, 1990), N. A. Winter, ed.

Hübner, G. 1973. "Dachterrakotten aus dem Kerameikos von Athen," *AM* 88, pp. 67–143

*Isthmia* II = O. Broneer, *Topography and Architecture (Isthmia* II), Princeton 1973

Le Roy, Ch. 1967. *Les terres cuites architecturales (Fouilles de Delphes* II), Paris
———. 1990. "Les terres cuites architecturales de Delphes vingt ans après la publication," in *Hesperia* 59, pp. 33–39
*OlForsch* V = A. Mallwitz and W. Schiering, *Die Werkstatt des Pheidias in Olympia (Olympische Forschungen* V), Berlin 1964
*Olympia* II = W. Dörpfeld and R. Bormann, *Die Baudenkmäler (Olympia, Ergebnisse der von dem deutschen Reich veranstalteten Ausgrabungen* II), Berlin 1892
Payne, H. 1931. *Necrocorinthia*, Oxford
Roebuck, M. C. 1990. "Archaic Architectural Terracottas from Corinth," in *Hesperia* 59, pp. 47–63
Van Buren, E. D. 1926. *Greek Fictile Revetments in the Archaic Period*, London
Williams, C. K., II. 1978. "Demaratus and Early Corinthian Roofs," in Στήλη. Τόμος ἐις μνήμην Νικολάου Κοντολέοντος, Athens, pp. 345–350

FREDERICK P. HEMANS

WICHITA STATE UNIVERSITY
School of Art and Design
1845 Fairmount
Wichita, KS 67260

# SOSIKLES AND THE FOURTH-CENTURY BUILDING PROGRAM IN THE SANCTUARY OF ZEUS AT NEMEA

(Plates 23–27)

EXCAVATIONS during the past two decades at the Panhellenic sanctuary of Zeus at Nemea have revealed that following a violent destruction in the late 5th century B.C. the site was abandoned for the next three-quarters of a century or more. Further, when the games were returned to Nemea in the 330's B.C., a large-scale building program was needed to refurbish the old sanctuary; this involved repairs to old buildings but especially the construction of many new structures. These new structures included the extant Temple of Zeus, the Xenon, the Bath, an unidentified Rectangular Building on the east side of the sanctuary, the Stadium with its entrance tunnel, and a newly discovered structure outside the Stadium.[1] It is this last building and its place within the larger program which will be the immediate focus of this presentation.

Excavations with the goal of removing a modern highway from the ancient stadium resulted not only in the unification of the track and viewing areas but also in the discovery of a building at the west, or sanctuary, end of the stadium entrance tunnel.[2] The building is located at the end of a putative but necessary road that tied the sanctuary to the Stadium and is situated between two projecting ridges of native rock which forced athletes and judges through the building in order that they might enter the tunnel and then the Stadium (Pl. 23:a). This is not the place to argue the identification of the building, but I propose to call it, nonetheless, an *apodyterion*.[3]

The *apodyterion* is a rectangular building, about 13.00 × 15.75 m., with its entrance on the north (long) side and a small door leading to the Stadium tunnel near the eastern end

---

[1] For the late 4th-century building program, see Stephen G. Miller 1990, pp. 65–67; see also pp. 23, 43, and 61–62.

[2] Although official excavations by the University of California at Berkeley have not taken place for some years, a variety of work in removing roads through the archaeological zone has continued. The last and largest of these took place in 1989 and 1990 when the Ministry of Public Works officially closed the highway that had bisected the ancient stadium and the Ministry of Culture asked that we undertake the task of completing the work in the stadium and providing for drainage to protect the antiquities. To be thanked particularly for support of this effort are the Ephoreia of Antiquities in Nauplion and especially Fani Pachyianne (Ephor), Elsi Spathari, and Zoe Aslamatzidou. It was the legal advice of Georgios Pachyiannes which resulted in the formula allowing this road to be closed after fifteen years of discussion and futile attempts. I dedicate this study to him.

[3] Similar structures, although not heretofore identified as such, exist at Epidauros and Olympia and probably elsewhere. For the building at Epidauros, see Kavvadias 1902, p. 83 and pl. A, Building Δ, and Tomlinson 1983, p. 42, fig. 5, building no. 18. For the situation at Olympia, see *OlForsch* XIV, p. 84, where the court behind the Echo Stoa is recognized in a most tentative way as possibly "der Wasch-, Umkleide-, und Warteplatz für die Athleten. . . ."

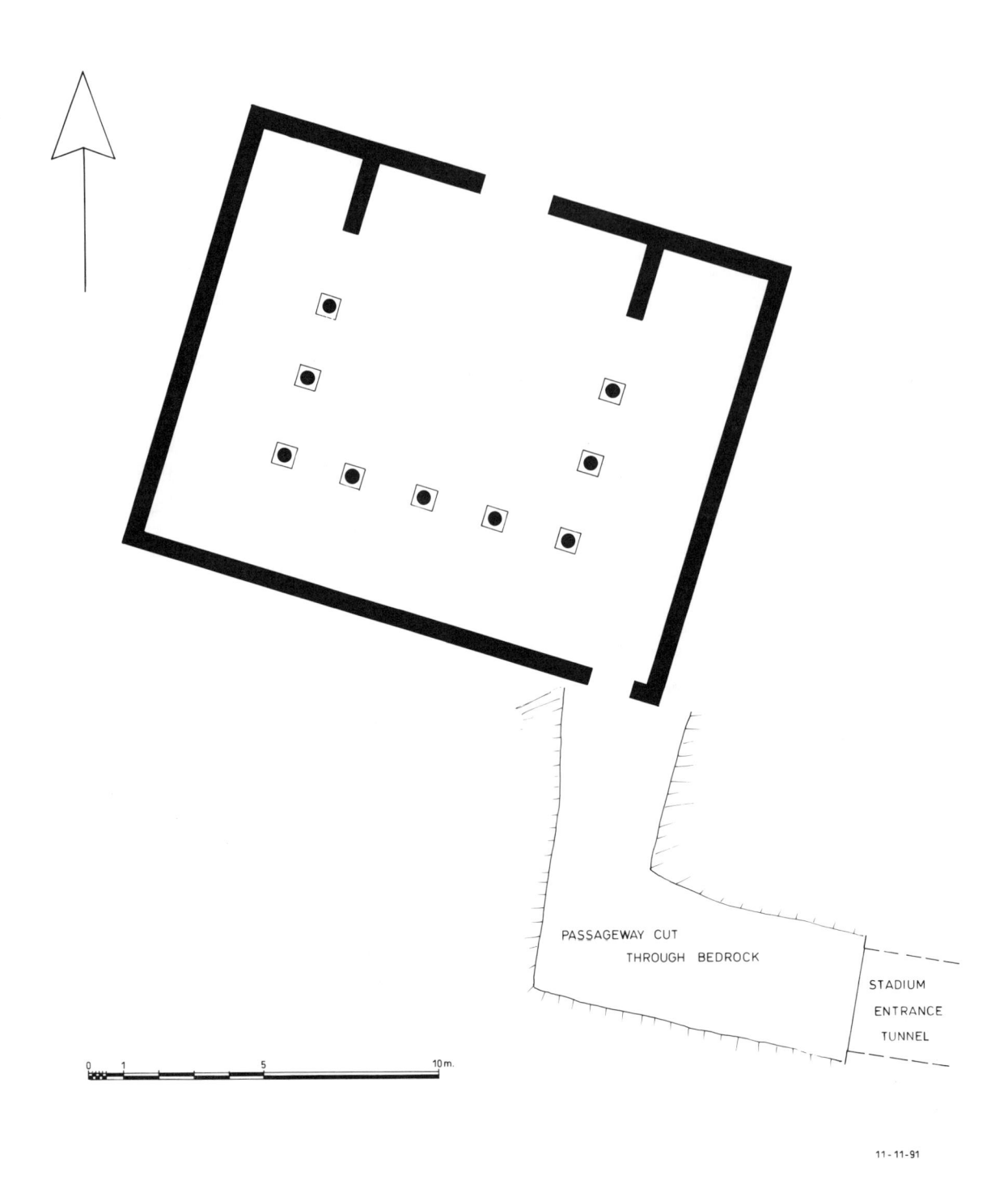

Fig. 1. Restored ground plan of the *apodyterion*

of its south side (Fig. 1).[4] The central area of the building was hypaethral and was surrounded by Doric columns on three sides. These colonnades supported a roof, from which a great number of tiles have been recovered.

Unlike most of Nemea, where Early Christian farming has dug through and disturbed the more ancient material,[5] the destruction debris of the *apodyterion* was essentially undisturbed, and many tiles were found smashed where they had fallen. It was thus possible to reconstruct several of them and to make specific observations about these tiles as a group. The tiles are all Laconian,[6] specifically, Laconian pan tiles that work in the typical way, the wider end at the top with a groove and a thickened edge on the concave upper surface serving to prevent water from running under the next tile. The upper, or weather, surface is noticeably smoother than the convex lower surface and always bears traces of a thin wash. As in the example chosen (Fig. 2 and Pl. 23:b, c),[7] they are all about 0.96 m. in length with a width at the upper end of about 0.49 m. and at the lower of about 0.42 m. They average about 15 kilograms in weight, although the variation is as much as a full kilogram above or below that average.

At this point a slight digression is necessary to make two points observed during the excavations. First, very few traces of carbon and only two iron nails were found in the destruction debris. Since metallic objects are generally well preserved by the soil of Nemea, this must mean that much of or all the wood of the building had been removed. This is not particularly surprising since we know that such removal of wood from a building occurred and could even be a recognized part of a lease.[8] Nonetheless, it is striking to document such activity in the archaeological record, especially since we can estimate that the quantity of wood involved was about 13 cubic meters.[9] A restored drawing of the timbering necessary indicates the minimum amount of wood in the building (Fig. 3).

---

[4] The precise location and nature of the doorways cannot be established because the walls of the building have been completely robbed out in these areas.

[5] For some particular instances of such disturbance, see *Nemea* I, pp. 5–6, 19–20, 23 (note 60), 25, 33, 53, 57, 70, 79, 83, 87, 91, 93, 95, 192, 220, 228, 232 (note 639), 234, 236, 239–243 (esp. note 661), 250, 257, 301–302.

[6] Although some fragments of Corinthian tiles were scattered around the area, the actual destruction debris of the building produced only about two dozen Corinthian pieces, which may well have been used in the building for some purpose other than the roof.

[7] AT 316. The variations in size are slight, although the texture and color of the clay have wide variations that are, however, of no apparent significance. These range from a friable greenish white clay (2.5Y 8/2 on the Munsell scale) to a hard light-red clay (10R 8/3 on the Munsell scale), always with heavy inclusions. The wash on the weather surface also varies from reddish brown to nearly black, again without any seeming correlation to differences in stamps.

[8] For example, in *IG* II² 2499 of 306/5 B.C. the shrine of Egretes is to be leased to Diognetos, who at the end of his ten-year lease is to be allowed to take with him the woodwork (τὰ ξύλα), the tiling (τὸ κέραμον), and the doors and windows with their frames (τὰ θυρώματα) if he fulfills the terms of his lease; if he fails to fulfill the lease, these items are forfeited.

[9] The following calculations must be recognized as highly theoretical, except for those of the weight of the tiling. Since the weight of the pan tile averages 15 kilograms and the weight of a cover tile can be estimated at about 11 kilograms, the weight per square meter of the tiling can be estimated at about 58 kilograms when dry and potentially at about 72 or 73 kilograms when wet.

The nature of the roof-timber system cannot be established so firmly, however, except for the existence of a wood epistyle directly on top of the columns and measuring about 0.30 m. in width (seen most clearly from

The second observation is related to the first. A conservative reckoning shows that about half of the pan tiles of the *apodyterion* roof have been recovered.[10] This is an extraordinary amount that can be contrasted, for example, with the distinctive tiles of the Tholos in the Athenian Agora, of which less than 1 percent of the original total has been preserved.[11] Yet not a single complete cover tile of the Nemea *apodyterion* has been recovered, and the total number of fragments of cover tiles represents much less than 1 percent of the original total.[12] It thus seems likely that the cover tiles were systematically removed as was the wooden timbering of the roof (see note 8 above).

The construction date of the *apodyterion*, and therefore presumably of these tiles, is secure in the last quarter of the 4th century B.C. Such a date is not only logical given the connections of the building to the Stadium and its tunnel but is supported clearly by the pottery associated with its construction fill.[13] The pottery from the destruction debris makes it equally clear that the *apodyterion* had already collapsed in the first half of the 3rd century B.C.[14] The history of this building thus closely parallels the history of Nemea with its late 4th-century building program and its abandonment when the games were transferred to Argos in the second quarter of the 3rd century B.C.[15]

The greatest interest of these pan tiles from the *apodyterion* is the stamps many of them bear. There are two basic types, one of which exhibits two variants. Type 1 bears in relief the word ΣΩΣΙΚΛΕΟΣ, that is, the genitive of the name Sosikles. One of the variants of this type (1a) has an impression within an impression, both of which frame the word but the lower and smaller of which has little ivy-leaf-shaped tabs at the ends (Fig. 4:a and Pl. 24:a). The other variant of the first type (1b) has a single impression, the surface of which is slightly convex on the long axis (Fig. 4:b and Pl. 24:b). That these are two distinct stamps and not one a recutting of the other is clear from the variations in the forms of the letters, especially

---

the burnt area on the top of the Doric capital, A 374). I have restored a square (in section) beam for this element. Clearly sleeper beams were needed on the top of the walls to accept rafters. I have restored these as about 0.22 m. on a side because the mud brick of the walls was of that height and twice that width. Rafters have been restored 0.50 m. apart on center and serve both to mark the joint between pan tiles and to support them. Using an average weight-bearing wood strength, rafters 0.10 m. wide and 0.15 m. high would be sufficient to support the wet weight of the tiles plus a meter of snow. I have, however, restored 0.15 m. square rafters, partly because it is clear that the load-bearing strength of wood was frequently underestimated in antiquity and partly in order to provide a sufficient resting surface for the tiles. I thank Georgios Stephanopoulos for his help in calculating the load-bearing capabilities of the proposed roof system.

[10] The coverage of the pan tile is about 0.45 m. sq. and the total area to be roofed in the *apodyterion* is about 154 m. sq. This should mean that some 342 pan tiles were needed to cover the building. (An actual count based on the restored drawing, Figure 3, results in a total of 340 pan tiles.) The total weight of the pan tiles on the building would then have been about 5,130 kg. or, when wet, perhaps about 6,500 kg. The total of all the pan tiles that have actually been recovered from the building was 3,131 kg.; they were weighed after a rain when they were still partially wet.

[11] See Stephen G. Miller 1988a, p. 138.

[12] The total original weight of the cover tiles for the whole building can be estimated at about 3,322 kg. The total weight of all cover-tile fragments recovered is about 25 kg.

[13] Pottery lots SACWAY 56–59.

[14] Pottery lots SACWAY 44, 45, 62, 53, 60–65, 69, 74–76, and 79.

[15] For the transfer of the games to Argos in the 3rd century, see Stephen G. Miller 1990, p. 57.

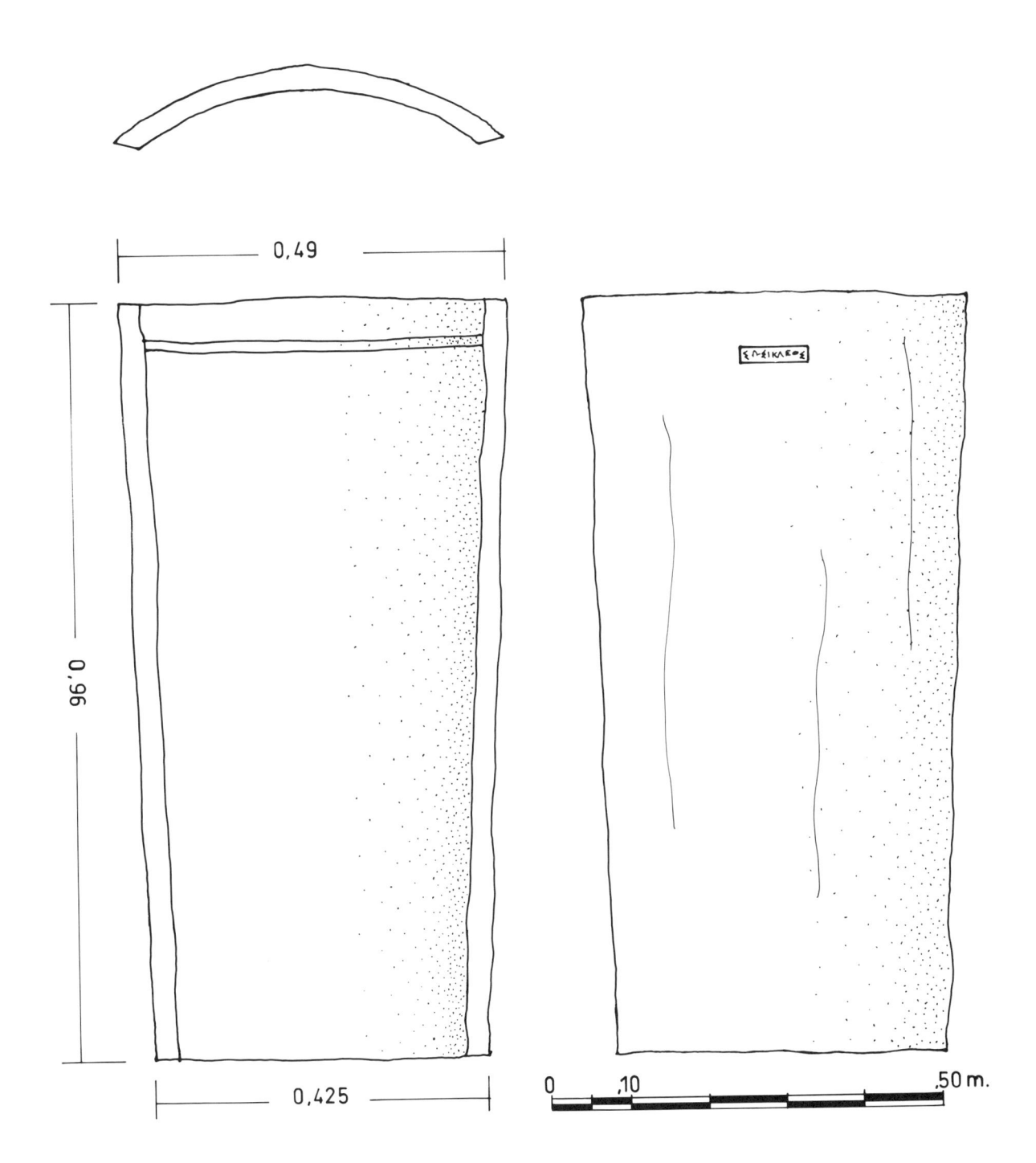

Fig. 2. Laconian pan tile, AT 316, drawing

CROSS SECTION A-A WITH TILES RESTORED

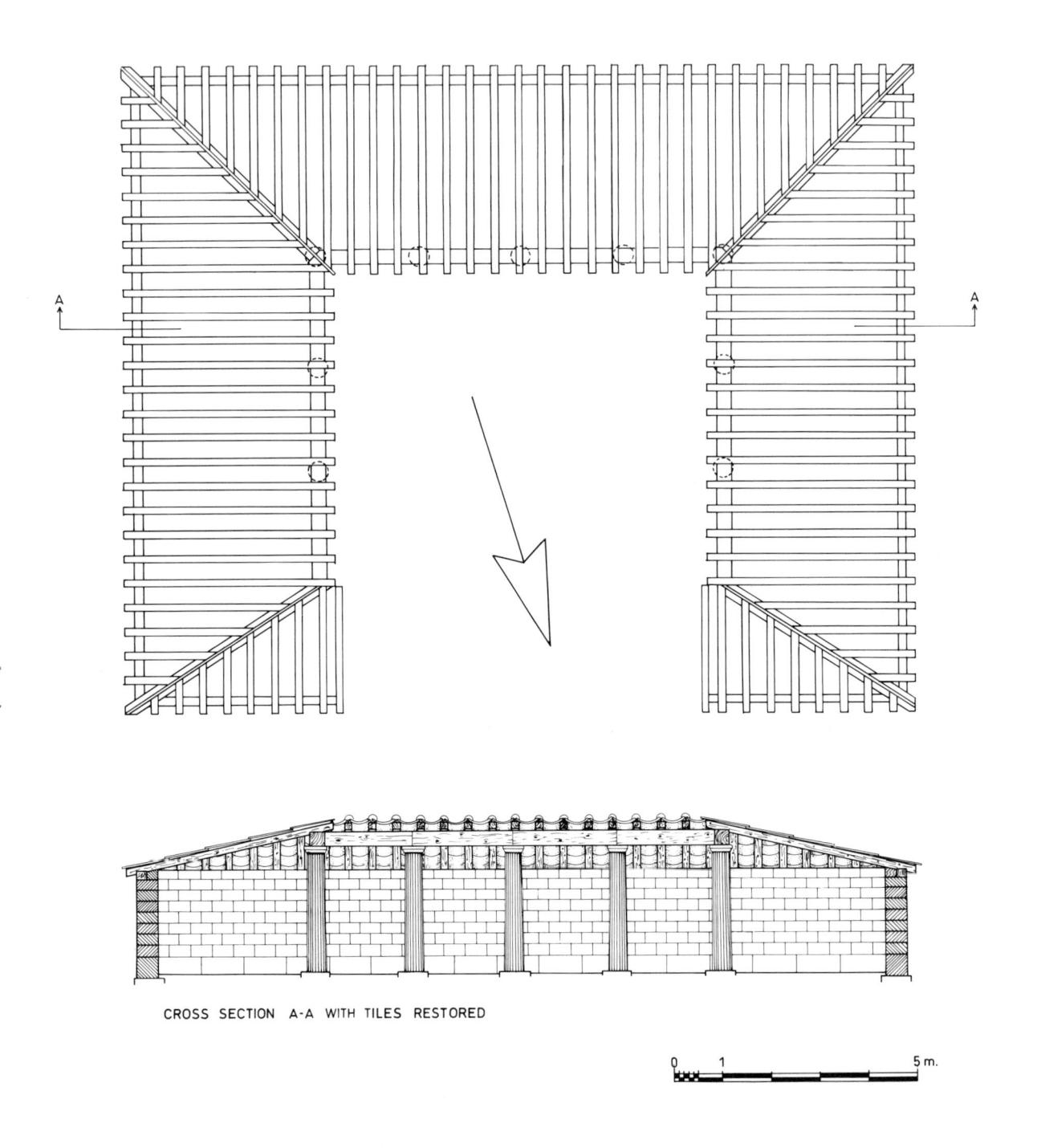

Fig. 3. Theoretically restored roof-timbering system for the *apodyterion*

SOSIKLES AND THE 4TH-CENTURY BUILDING PROGRAM 91

a. AT 324

b. AT 346 + 325

c. AT 284

d. AT 258

e. AT 66 + 174

f. AT 178

Fig. 4. Tile stamps from Nemea

the omegas.[16] There are preserved 12 different stamps of the first variant and 44 of the second, or a total of 56 for this type.[17]

Stamp Type 2 (Fig. 4:c and Pl. 24:c) is much larger than the first and bears in relief the word ΣΩΚΛΕΙΟΣ, that is, the genitive of Sokles. Despite the difference in name, we are not dealing with a different person, for Sokles is generally accepted to be a shortened form or a pet name or nickname for Sosikles, which must be the full proper name of our man.[18] The debris of the *apodyterion* at Nemea has produced 40 different examples of this type (see note 17 above).

In addition there are 2 extremely fragmentary stamps that cannot be identified by type, for a total of 98 stamps that may represent nearly a third of all the pan tiles originally on the roof. Not all the tiles were provided with stamps, for several complete examples lack them. These exhibit a groove sweeping across the convex underside of the tile and executed by a finger while the clay was wet (Pl. 24:d). There is also one example of a cat's paw imprint along the side of the concave weather surface, but this is perhaps due to an accident while the tile was being made (Pl. 24:e).

All the Sosikles-Sokles stamps are located on the convex undersurface near the upper, wider end. They were thus not exposed to the weather and would have been visible only from below once they were in place.[19] The same is true of modern tiles, the stamps of which

[16] I have been unable to find any good parallels for this type of omega with the horizontal bars up on the sides rather than at the base of the letter. Of course, most extant examples are in stone.

[17] Some of the stamps are represented by very small fragments, some of which might have come from the same tile. Therefore, the total number may be misleadingly high, but the proportions of the types must be about the same, regardless of the absolute numbers.

[18] See, for example, G. E. Benseler's revised edition of Pape 1875, p. 1469: Σωκλῆς, έους, m. = Σωσικλῆς, Wehrenbrecht (d.i. in der Abwehr od. dem Schüssen glänzend); see also Richardson 1902, p. 219: "The name Socles, a 'Koseform' for Sosicles, is common enough, and affords no particular interest."

We should note, however, that both forms appear for different men on the same inscription from Thespiai, *SEG* XXIII 271, lines 28 and 76. Presumably, the individual could chose which form he wanted used for his name.

[19] This is unlike both the other Nemean stamps and the normal practice that appear on the weather surface; cf. Felsch 1990, p. 301: "... tiles of Hellenistic and later date, which are always stamped on the upper face." Since it is the upper face of the tile that is pressed into the mold, Richardson (1902, p. 221) suggested that the stamp was affixed to the mold so that the tile was shaped and impressed in a single operation. As Richardson noted, there are problems with such an interpretation because the stamps are not all in the same position on the tiles; note, for example, the two Nemean stamps cited below, AT 66 and AT 174 (Pl. 25:b), which are not at the same distance from the upper edge of the tile. Richardson supposed that the stamp might have been slightly loose on the mold. One might also suppose that several molds, each with its own stamp, were used during production. In any event, and if such an interpretation is correct, the Sosikles-Sokles tiles might have already been in the process of manufacture before the stamps were prepared and the latter had to be pressed on the back side of the tile while it was still in the mold.

One should mention at this point the debate about the meaning of the phrase τύπον ξύλινον κεραμίδων, which appears in Delian inscriptions *ID* 442B.172 and 457.22. The τύπος has been understood as a wooden mold for the manufacture of tiles by, among others, Richardson 1902, p. 221; Grace 1935, p. 427, note 4; Bundgaard 1957, p. 219, note 14; and the undersigned. The τύπος has been understood as a wooden stamp used to produce impressions (or, in the present case, inscriptions) in the wet clay of tiles by, among others, Wace 1906–1907, p. 17, note 3; Orlandos 1955, p. 113; and Hübner 1973, pp. 86–87. Perhaps the most curious reference is that in Orlandos and Travlos 1986, p. 255, where τύπος is defined as a stamp for roof tiles but also as a mold for bricks.

commonly have the name and telephone number of the manufacturer on the underside. Depending on the nature of the roof construction, the modern examples are frequently not visible, nor were the ancient ones at Nemea.

These considerations take us to the question of the nature of the Sosikles-Sokles stamps and the identity of Sosikles himself. There are at Nemea three other types of stamps that can be associated with the late 4th-century building program; all are from the Sanctuary of Zeus and none from the Stadium. The first of these is represented by six fragments, all broken at some point along the right side and all on the concave or weather side of the tile.[20] The inscription reads ΔAMOIO—, which is to be understood as a form of *damosios* (Fig. 4:d and Pl. 25:a).[21] Clearly these tiles are marked as public property and stand in apparent marked contrast to the personal name attested on the Sosikles-Sokles examples.

The second type of stamp is represented by two examples, both broken along the left side and each found in a well south of the Temple of Zeus (Fig. 4:e and Pl. 25:b).[22] They bear the genitive adjectival form NEMEIOY with a ligature at the right end of the stamp. It takes little imagination to restore [Διὸς] Νεμείου and to see these tiles also as public or official property of the sanctuary.[23] In contrast to the Sosikles-Sokles series, these stamps are on the concave weather surface of Laconian pan tiles, as should be expected (see note 19 above).

The final type of stamp is represented by a single example discovered in 1962 above the Xenon on the south side of the Sanctuary of Zeus (Fig. 4:f and Pl. 25:c).[24] The impression is on the weather side of a Laconian pan tile and preserves only the first three letters NEM—. Again, this is clearly a statement of official property of the sanctuary.

Thus, at first glance, the Sosikles-Sokles series appears to fail to correspond with other stamps at Nemea in its lack of an official status. One explanation might be that the tiles for the *apodyterion* were not official because that structure, at some remove from the Sanctuary of Zeus, was itself of a status different from that of buildings in the sanctuary. This explanation cannot hold, however, because three examples of the Sosikles series have been found in the Sanctuary of Zeus itself.[25] Rather, the question of the purpose of the stamps needs to be

---

For a modern example of what I take to be a τύπος ξύλινος κεραμίδων, see Rostoker and Gebhard 1981, pp. 220–222.

[20] AT 17, AT 195, AT 196, AT 248, AT 252, AT 258. The first was discovered long ago and no record of its provenience has been preserved, but the last five were clustered in Sections P 14 and P 15 near the Rectangular Building east of the Temple of Zeus. See Stella G. Miller 1984, pp. 185 and 190.

[21] By analogy with the examples from the Argive Heraion given below (see note 34 below), we should perhaps understand δαμόσιο[ι Διὸς Νεμείου], but in the absence of the ending of the word on the Nemean tiles, such a suggestion cannot be pressed.

[22] See *Nemea* I, p. 303.

[23] The significance of the ligature is not so immediately apparent, even though it clearly consists of at least a pi, a chi, and a rho.

[24] See *Nemea* I, p. 285.

[25] AT 157 (type 1b), and AT 188 and AT 189 (type 1a); see Stella G. Miller 1984, p. 185, where the reading of the inscription should be corrected to ΣΩΣΙΚΛΕΟΣ. These three tiles come from precisely the same area as do the *damosios*-type tiles mentioned above, and while the fragments of the one type cannot come from the same tile as the fragments of the other because of the differences in fabric, both types might have been used on the same building. For the significance of this possibility, see below on the tiles from the Argive Heraion.

raised. It might be suggested that such stamps give the manufacturer's name,[26] a common interpretation and certainly the initial feeling about the Nemean examples. But the genitive of possession in the other, official Nemean stamps ought to alert us to the possibility that Sosikles (whose name is also given in the genitive) is not the manufacturer but in some sense the owner of these tiles. Such a possibility becomes a certainty when we consider the identity of Sosikles.

The name Sosikles or Sokles is not particularly rare (see note 18 above). Indeed, we know of one Sokles who held a contract for painting ceiling coffers and moldings on the Temple of Asklepios at Epidauros.[27] Closer to our Sosikles-Sokles in time and place, and surely to be identified with him, is the Sokles who worked at the Argive Heraion. The American excavators there discovered at least eight fragments of tile stamps bearing some part of the inscription ΣΩΚΛΗΣΑΡΧΙΤΕΚΤΩΝ (Pl. 25:d).[28] Yet another example preserving the inscription —ΛΗΣΑΡΧΙΤΕΚΤΩΝ was found in an intrusive pit in a Mycenaean tholos about a kilometer west of the Heraion.[29] But a complete example of the same series was found by Heinrich Schliemann on March 2, 1874, in the village of Chonikas about one and a half kilometers south of the Argive Heraion and apparently in a reused situation.[30] This Laconian pan tile is 1.00 m. long and 0.51 m. wide at the top, 0.44 m. at the bottom (Pl. 26:a, b).[31] Unlike the examples from Nemea, it is 0.035 m. thick over its whole length;[32] rather than a raised lip or edge at the top end, a thin groove (0.005 m. wide and 0.002 m. deep) sags down from the corners to a maximum distance of 0.033 m. from the top edge at the

[26] Such would be the interpretation based on the opinion of Orlandos 1955, pp. 115–116 and note 1, who presents a series of personal names, mostly in the genitive, as the *ergostasiarchoi* responsible for the manufacture of the tiles upon which the names appear. The same interpretation is to be found in Martin 1965, pp. 84–86. This interpretation is accepted by Hübner 1973, p. 86, and Hübner 1976, p. 180, note 29. Such an interpretation seems either to be ignored or not accepted by Felsch 1990, p. 301, who regards stamps of Hellenistic and later date as serving exclusively "to facilitate checking by the client or as protection against theft of the finished tiles." Felsch thus anticipates a part of the conclusion of this discussion.

[27] *IG* IV² 102, BI.76–78; cf. Roux 1961, p. 429, and Burford 1969, p. 215.

[28] Richardson 1902, p. 217 gives seven different fragments, but the fragment pictured in Plate 25:d here, which cannot be any of those he listed, clearly belongs to the same series and has several lines of penciled English on its back side. Most is illegible, but the final two lines read: Seems [... *ca.* 9 ...] of building / east of Stoa.

I would like to thank warmly Olga Alexandre for help in studying this fragment and the full tile described below and for permission to publish. She and the staff of the National Museum, especially Viki Prokopiou and Elisabeth Stasinopoulou, have been most gracious and helpful, as was Theodora Kakarouga, who prepared the drawings shown as Plates 26:a and 27:a.

[29] Stamatakes 1878, pp. 285–286; cf. Wace 1921–1923, p. 337, no. 82. Although Richardson (1902, p. 217) states that this is in the "Central Museum", by which he perhaps means the National Museum; it has not been possible to locate it yet.

[30] Diary 1874 A 15, Schliemann Archives, Gennadius Library, American School of Classical Studies. Schliemann (who must have misheard the name because he calls the village Phonikas) in a single sentence mentions the tile ("une immense brique courbe") with its dimensions and the two stamps; there can be no doubt of its identity. I thank Christina Varda for her assistance in locating the Schliemann reference.

[31] National Museum inv. no. 10736; *IG* IV 541–542; cf. Richardson 1902, p. 217.

[32] This greater overall thickness (and therefore greater mass) explains the much greater weight of this tile than that of the Nemean examples. It has not been possible to weigh the Heraion tile, but its weight must be more than 20 kg., to judge by lifting it.

center. The purpose of this groove is clearly to prevent water from running up under the overlapping tile above.

On its concave, or weather, surface, again unlike the Nemea examples, are two stamps. One is near the top of the tile, 0.044 m. from the edge on the right end, 0.040 m. on the left (Pl. 27:a, b).[33] It measures 0.022 by 0.170 m. and bears the relief letters: ΣΩΚΛΗΣΑΡΧΙΤΕΚΤΩΝ. The other stamp is near the bottom of the tile, 0.065 m. from the edge and measuring 0.022 by 0.162 m. (Pl. 27:a, c). It bears in relief the letters: ΔΑΜΟΙΟΗΡΑΣ. As pointed out long ago by Richardson,[34] this stands for δαμόσιοι (κέραμοι) Ἥρας. We should note that the tiles are not merely public property, nor merely the property of Hera (that is, of the sanctuary), but the public property of Hera. In other words, the tiles belong to Argos, which controls the sanctuary, and they are intended to be used specifically for the sanctuary. This means, in turn, that Sokles is acting as architect in an official capacity on behalf of the city as well as the sanctuary. The letter forms of the stamps indicated to Richardson that the date of the tile should be well along in the 4th century.[35] A comparison of the omega of the stamp with dated Attic inscriptions suggests that Richardson was essentially correct.[36]

Is the architect Sokles of the Argive Heraion to be identified with the Sosikles-Sokles of Nemea? I believe so, even though absolute proof is not possible. Certainly, two different men stamping the same name on tiles at two sites so close as Nemea and the Argive Heraion at the same date would be an extraordinary coincidence. Such a coincidence becomes even more incredible when one remembers that both sites were under the control of Argos and were closely linked in that city's administration. For example, many *theorodokoi* were appointed both for the festival of Nemean Zeus and for that of Hera Argeia.[37] The same individual frequently served as the *agonothetes* for both festivals.[38] And the same men were *Hellanodikai* for both festivals.[39] The date when this close linkage began is not known, but it was certainly in place by 323 B.C.[40] It would then hardly be surprising if the same man, Sosikles-Sokles, were the official *architekton* of the two festival sites.

Sosikles-Sokles is, I believe, something like the "city architect" envisioned by J. J. Coulton as a development of the Hellenistic period, although Coulton sees the practice beginning in

---

[33] But note that this stamp was almost certainly covered by the next tile above when in place on the roof. So both at Nemea and at the Heraion the personal name was not easily visible, if visible at all, on the building.

[34] Richardson 1902, p. 217.

[35] Richardson 1902, p. 219.

[36] Such evidence for dating is, of course, extremely tenuous but does give a general range. The closest parallel seems to me to be the decree dated to 307/6 B.C. and presented in Kirchner 1935, no. 67.

[37] For a list of examples, see Amandry 1980, p. 245, note 80; to this add Piérart and Thalmann 1980, p. 256; see also Charneaux 1983, p. 266, who notes that only one of all the conferrals by Argos of *theorodokia* on an individual was not for both festivals; see also Stephen G. Miller 1988b, pp. 147–163.

[38] As, for example, Philip V of Macedon in 209 B.C. (Livy 27.30–31).

[39] As seen in a decree in honor of Alexander of Sikyon, Argos Museum inv. E 125, lines 16–18. First published by Vollgraff 1916, pp. 64–71. For the various dates proposed for this decree, see Amandry 1980, p. 226, note 30.

Once the Nemean Games moved to Argos, both they and the festivals of Hera were celebrated in the same place perhaps already in the 3rd century B.C. but certainly by the time of Pausanias (see 2.24.2).

[40] This is the date of the list of *theorodokoi* from Nemea; see Stephen G. Miller 1988b, p. 162.

Athens by 337/6 B.C. at the latest.[41] Among the many examples cited by Coulton, we might note Diognetos who was employed by Rhodes in the late 4th century B.C. on an annual retainer until he lost his position to a rival, Kallias of Arados.[42] Perhaps even closer to the position of Sosikles at Argos is the Athenian "architect in charge of the sanctuaries" of the same period.[43] Indeed, it seems likely that such an official existed within the Argive administrative system even as at Athens and that it was Sosikles who filled this position for a time. This official architect emerges from our new knowledge of Sosikles and from a fragment of a stamped tile discovered in the area of the West Baths in Argos itself giving one Menon as architect.[44] The impression on this tile is from the same stamp as one found more than eighty years ago at the Sanctuary of Pythian Apollo at Argos.[45] These two stamps indicate that Menon, like Sosikles, was responsible for official city work and was a successor of Sosikles-Sokles as the "city architect" of Argos. This position apparently had responsibility for all projects of the city or at least for all projects concerning sanctuaries, not only for the sanctuaries of Zeus and of Hera. The extent to which these "city architects" were concerned with problems of design is not clear, but that they were directly responsible for execution of buildings and other programs of construction and maintenance is clear. The modern equivalent might be something like "Director of Public Works".[46]

Once we have so identified Sosikles, we can understand that the stamps on the Nemean tiles with his name are analogous to and not different from those with the official stamp of Nemea. In his official capacity as architect for part of the building program at Nemea, Sosikles ordered tiles which were given identifying labels at the factory.[47] The stamps set the

[41] Coulton 1977, p. 29.

[42] Vitruvius 10.16.3–8. For one of the duties of the Rhodian architect, see $SIG^3$ 581.97–98, a treaty between Rhodes and Hierapytna dated to the period 200–197 B.C., the inscribing of which falls within the architect's realm.

[43] $IG$ II$^2$ 840.13–14; 841.14–15; 842.2. These references correct those given by Coulton 1977, p. 165, note 90. Another similar official architect who was part of the city administration is perhaps to be understood in "the architect elected by the Demos" who was responsible for supervision of the repairs to walls of Athens and Piraeus in 307/6 B.C., as attested by $IG$ II$^2$ 463.6. To Coulton's references to official architects should be added those in Shear 1978, pp. 54–56 and in Bousquet 1985, p. 717 and note 6.

[44] This tile, which reads ΜΕΝΩΝΑΡΧΙΤΕ[ΚΤΩ(Ν)], was discovered by Pierre Robert in an apparently very late or even modern context. I am grateful to him and to Pierre Aupert for permission to mention it here and to Marie-Françoise Billot for generously sharing this information with me.

[45] Vollgraff 1909, p. 448, no. 12. It reads Α]ΡΧΙΤΕΚΤΩ(Ν); the final nu seems to have been left off the stamp or the stamp was not fully impressed in the damp clay. This stamp (on both tiles mentioned) bears some affinities with those from the Argive Heraion in size and form of letters and should be close to them in date, but the broken cross-bar of the alpha suggests a later date for it and for Menon.

Although no direct connection can be established between the "city architect", the stamped tiles just mentioned, and the Sanctuary of Apollo, we might note that it was during the second half of the 4th century B.C. that repairs and remodeling of the sanctuary are epigraphically recorded; Vollgraff 1956, p. 110. Therefore a "city architect" or an "architect in charge of the sanctuaries" was certainly needed by the Argives at this period.

[46] It must be remembered that, although I believe that the man is the same, the form of the stamps from the Argive Heraion and from Argos and that of the stamps from Nemea is different. Different interpretations are possible, such as supposing that Sosikles undertook his work at Nemea at some point in his career when he was not the official architect of Argos, but none are capable of proof.

[47] Close analysis, which has not yet been possible, might show that the tiles of Sosikles were made in the complex of three kilns in the Sanctuary of Zeus. Three kilns have been recovered, but there was probably

tiles apart, at the factory and on the construction site, for the work of Sosikles and enabled him to maintain some sort of inventory control. Even if our knowledge of Sosikles is still quite limited, he can at least take his place in the all too short list of ancient architects known to us.[48] Indeed, it might even be possible to credit him with the design of the *apodyterion*.

Finally, we may now ask, even if I cannot provide an answer, whether every tile that bears the name of a man in the genitive (and these become increasingly common in the later Hellenistic and Roman periods[49]) does not give us the name of the ancient *architekton* of the building from which the tile came.

## BIBLIOGRAPHY

Amandry, P. 1980. "Sur les concours argiens," *BCH* Supplement 4, pp. 211–253

Bousquet, J. 1985. "L'Hoplothèque de Delphes," *BCH* 109, pp. 717–726

Bundgaard, J. A. 1957. *Mnesicles*, Copenhagen/Stockholm/Oslo

Burford, A. 1969. *Greek Temple Builders at Epidauros*, Liverpool

Camp, J. McK. 1989. "The Philosophical Schools of Roman Athens," in *The Greek Renaissance in the Roman Empire: Papers from the Tenth British Museum Classical Colloquium* (*Bulletin of the Institute of Classical Studies of the University of London* Supplement 55), S. Walker and A. Cameron, eds., London, pp. 50–55

Charneaux, P. 1983. "Sur quelques inscriptions d'Argos," *BCH* 107, pp. 215–267

Coulton, J. J. 1977. *Greek Architects at Work*, London

Felsch, R. C. S. 1990. "Further Stamped Roof Tiles from Central Greece, Attica, and the Peloponnese," in *Hesperia* 59, pp. 301–323

Grace, V. R. 1935. "The Die Used for Amphora Stamps," *Hesperia* 4, pp. 421–429

*Hesperia* 59 = *Proceedings of the First International Conference on Archaic Greek Architectural Terracottas, Athens, December 2–4, 1988* (*Hesperia* 59, 1990), N. A. Winter, ed.

Hill, B. H. 1966. *The Temple of Zeus at Nemea*, Princeton

Hübner, G. 1973. "Dachterrakotten aus dem Kerameikos von Athen," *AM* 88, pp. 67–143

———. 1976. "Antefixa Deorum Athenarum," *AM* 91, pp. 175–183

*ID* = *Inscriptions de Délos* I–VII (various eds.), Paris 1926–1972

---

a fourth that was destroyed in the 1920's by a well constructed at that time. Two of the kilns were rectangular in plan, the third circular, and one supposes that they were for the manufacture of Corinthian and Laconian tiles, respectively, with the shape of the tile in section reflected in the plan of the kiln where it was made; see Perreault 1990, p. 208, note 13. Although one of the rectangular kilns was put out of operation by the construction of the Xenon in the last third of the 4th century B.C., the circular kiln continued in operation after the construction of the Xenon and apparently into the early part of the 3rd century. It might well have been the spot of manufacture of Sosikles' tiles and was certainly an important part of the building program of the period.

For the kilns, see Hill 1966, pp. 20 and 46; Stephen G. Miller 1975, pp. 162–165; Stephen G. Miller 1976, pp. 186–189; Stephen G. Miller 1978, pp. 80–81.

[48] Although I cannot prove, or even suggest, that the same man is involved, attention should be called to the funeral stele of a Sosikles found at Phlious, a scant four kilometers from Nemea, and dated by its publisher to the 3rd century B.C. See Scranton 1936, p. 246, no. 16.

[49] See Orlandos 1955, pp. 115–116 for a list that Hübner (1976, p. 180, note 29) has updated with more recent discoveries. Note also the interpretation by Camp (1989, p. 51) of the ligature AP or APX as architect rather than as archon in association with names in the genitive (Dionysios and Diodoros) on roof tiles of the Odeion in the Athenian Agora of the 2nd century after Christ.

One other type of individual is documented as putting his name on tiles, at least sometimes in the genitive. This is the *ergones*, who seems to be a kind of subcontractor responsible to the *architekton* for some specific task in the construction project. See Orlandos and Travlos 1986, pp. 117–118. It seems, however, that the name is usually accompanied by the word *ergones* as a specifier, perhaps to distinguish him from the *architekton*. See Orlandos 1955, p. 115, note 10.

*IG* II² = *Inscriptiones Atticae Euclidis anno posteriores*, II–III, *Editio minor*, ed. J. Kirchner, Berlin 1913–1940 (in 4 parts)
*IG* IV = *Inscriptiones Graecae, IV, Argolidis*, ed. M. Fraenkel, Berlin 1902
*IG* IV² = *Inscriptiones Graecae, IV, Editio minor, Epidauri*, ed. F. Hiller von Gaertringen, Berlin 1929
Kavvadias, P. 1902. «'Ανασκαφαὶ ἐν Ἐπιδαύρῳ», Πρακτικά 1902 [1903], pp. 78–92
Kirchner, J. 1935. *Imagines Inscriptionum Atticarum*, Berlin
Martin, R. 1965. *Manuel d'architecture grecque* I, Paris
Miller, Stella G. 1984. "Excavations at Nemea, 1983," *Hesperia* 53, pp. 171–192
Miller, Stephen G. 1975. "Excavations at Nemea 1973–1974," *Hesperia* 44, pp. 143–172
———. 1976. "Excavations at Nemea, 1975," *Hesperia* 45, pp. 174–202
———. 1978. "Excavations at Nemea, 1977," *Hesperia* 47, pp. 58–88
———. 1988a. "Circular Roofing Systems and the Athenian Tholos," in Πρακτικά του XII Διεθνούς Συνεδρίου Κλασικής Αρχαιολογίας, Αθήνα, 4–10 Σεπτεμβρίου 1983, IV, Athens, pp. 134–139
———. 1988b. "The Theorodokoi of the Nemean Games," *Hesperia* 57, pp. 147–163
———, ed. 1990. *Nemea: A Guide to the Site and Museum*, Berkeley
*Nemea* I = D. E. Birge, L. H. Kraynak, and Stephen G. Miller, *Topographical and Architectural Studies: The Sacred Square, the Xenon, and the Bath* (*Excavations at Nemea* I), Berkeley 1992
*OlForsch* XIV = W. Koenigs, *Die Echohalle* (*Olympische Forschungen* XIV), Berlin 1984
Orlandos, A. K. 1955. ΤΑ ΥΛΙΚΑ ΤΩΝ ΑΡΧΑΙΩΝ ΕΛΛΗΝΩΝ I, Athens
Orlandos, A. K., and I. N. Travlos. 1986. ΛΕΞΙΚΟΝ ΑΡΧΑΙΩΝ ΑΡΧΙΤΕΚΤΟΝΙΚΩΝ ΟΡΩΝ, Athens
Pape, W. 1875. *Wörterbuch der griechischen Eingenname*, 3rd ed., revised by G. E. Benseler, Braunschweig
Perreault, J. Y. 1990. "L'atelier de potier archaïque de Phari (Thasos): La production de tuiles," in *Hesperia* 59, pp. 201–209
Piérart, M., and J. P. Thalmann. 1980. "Nouvelles inscriptions argiennes (I) (Fouilles d l'Agora)," *BCH* Supplement 6, pp. 255–278
Richardson, R. B. 1902. "Stamped Tiles from the Argive Heraeum," in C. Waldstein, *The Argive Heraeum* I, Cambridge, Mass., pp. 216–224
Rostoker, W., and E. Gebhard. 1981. "The Reproduction of Rooftiles for the Archaic Temple of Poseidon at Isthmia," *JFA* 8, pp. 211–227
Roux, G. 1961. *L'architecture de l'Argolide aux IVᵉ et IIIᵉ siècles avant J.-C.*, Paris
Scranton, R. L. 1936. "Inscriptions from Phlius," *Hesperia* 5, pp. 235–246
*SEG* = *Supplementum Epigraphicum Graecum*
Shear, T. L., Jr. 1978. *Kallias of Sphettos and the Revolt of Athens in 286 B.C.* (*Hesperia* Supplement 17), Princeton
*SIG* = *Sylloge Inscriptionum Graecarum*
Stamatakes, P. 1878. «Περὶ τοῦ παρὰ τὸ Ἡραῖον καθαριθέντος τάφου», *AM* 3, pp. 271–286
Tomlinson, R. A. 1983. *Epidauros*, London
Vollgraff, W. 1909. "Inscriptions d'Argos," *BCH* 33, pp. 445–466
———. 1916. "Novae inscriptiones argivae," *Mnemosyne* 44, pp. 46–71
———. 1956. *Le sanctuaire d'Apollon Pythéen à Argos* (*Études péloponnésiennes* I), Paris
Wace, A. J. B. 1906–1907. "Excavations at Sparta, 1907. The Stamped Tiles," *BSA* 13, pp. 17–43
———. 1921–1923. "Excavations at Mycenae. The Tholos Tombs," *BSA* 25, pp. 283–407

STEPHEN G. MILLER

UNIVERSITY OF CALIFORNIA AT BERKELEY
Department of Classics
Berkeley, CA 94720

# DIE DACHTERRAKOTTEN DES ARTEMISTEMPELS VOM APOLLON-HEILIGTUM IN ÄGINA

(Plates 28, 29)

NACH PAUSANIAS (2,30,1) gab es in der Stadt Ägina—im Bereich des sog. Kolonnahügels, benannt nach der einzigen heute noch aufrechtstehenden Säule—drei nahe beieinanderstehende Tempel des Apollon, der Artemis und des Dionysos; und bisher kannte man nur die genaue Lage des Apollontempels. Da die alten Grabungen nur einen Teil des Heiligtums östlich vor dem Apollontempel erfaßt hatten,[1] war zu hoffen, daß von den bei Pausanias genannten Tempeln im unausgegrabenen Abschnitt noch Reste zu finden wären. Zu Beginn der Grabungen unter H. Walter kam südöstlich vom Apollontempel, noch innerhalb der Temenosmauer, ein in zwei Teile zerfallenes Fundament zum Vorschein (Fig. 1 punktiert). Später erst wurde östlich davon ein dritter Fundamentteil aufgedeckt (Fig. 1 strichliert), der über die Situation in diesem Bereich des Heiligtums aufklären half:[2] Nicht ganz so hoch erhalten wie die beiden anderen Teile, dafür wesentlich tiefer in den Boden gesetzt, folgt das Fundament hier dem nach Osten zunehmend abfallenden Gelände. Mit der Ecke eines in Streifenform verlegten Unterbaus wurde jetzt der Grundriß eines kleinen, rechteckigen Gebäudes erkennbar. Es gibt gute Gründe in ihm den Tempel der Artemis zu erkennen, liegt es doch nahe, ihr Zuhause in der Nähe des Brudertempels zu suchen, gleichwie der Standort des Dionysostempels nahe beim Theater, das dem Heiligtum im Osten gegenüberlag, zu finden sein sollte. Inzwischen ist das Heiligtum östlich vom Apollontempel auch soweit ergraben, daß hier die Existenz eines weiteren Tempels innerhalb der Temenosmauern mit großer Wahrscheinlichkeit ausgeschlossen werden kann. Die Reihenfolge, in der Pausanias die Tempel und seine Inhaber aufzählt, würde sich damit bestätigen.

Die Fundamentreste umschreiben ein Rechteck von *ca.* 7,6 × 14,8 m, seine Längsachse ist um *ca.* 26° nach Süden abgedreht. Es spricht manches dafür, daß der Tempel nicht wie üblich von Osten, sondern von Westen her zu betreten war. Auch die Tempelform ist nicht eindeutig festzulegen. In Frage kommen ein Tempel *in antis*, ein Prostylos, aber auch ein einfacher Oikosbau ohne Säulenstellung wäre denkbar, wenngleich auch unwahrscheinlich. Doch soll weiter nicht die Rede sein vom Fundament oder zuweisbaren Architekturgliedern, allein das Dach mit seinen verzierten Tonziegeln steht hier zur Diskussion.

Bei der Zuweisung der einzelnen Terrakottafragmente zum Artemistempel gaben zwei Gründe den Ausschlag: mehrere Teile der Ziegel, Simen und Antefixe wurden direkt beim Fundament oder in dessen näherem Umfeld gefunden, und, nach dem Ausweis der Fundamentreste sowie der Untersuchung aller im Heiligtum aufgefundenen Bauglieder und Ziegel auf mögliche Zugehörigkeit, wurde dieser Tempel erst in klassischer Zeit errichtet.

---

[1] Wolters 1925b, S. 2–12; Wolters 1925a, S. 46–49; Welter 1925, S. 317–321; Welter 1938b, S. 1–33; Welter 1938c, S. 480–538; Welter 1938a, S. 49–63.

[2] Walter 1993, S. 34–53, Abb. 24.

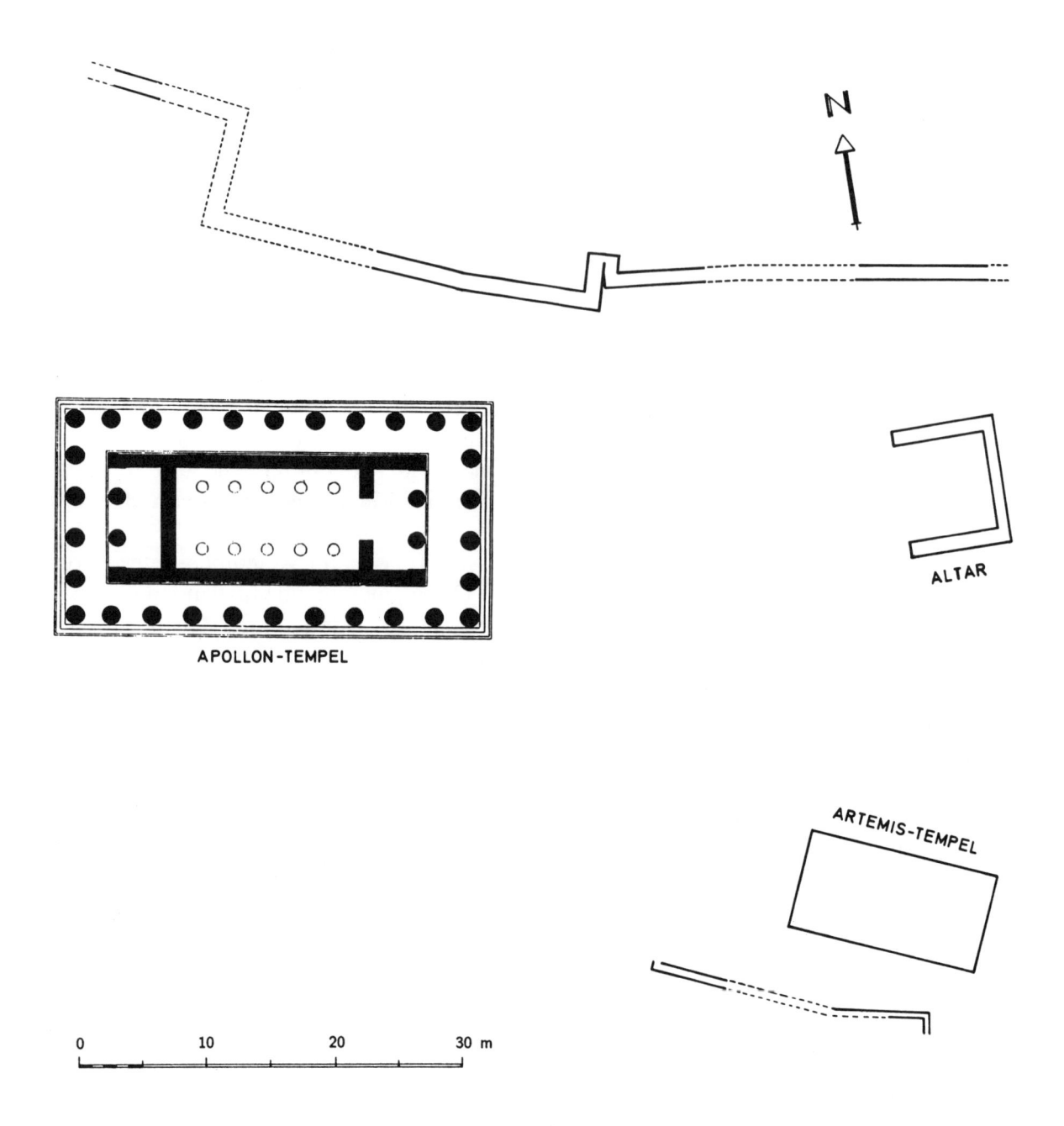

FIG. 1. Das Apollon-Heiligtum in frühklassischer Zeit

Es ist das einzige sicher nachweisbare Gebäude im Heiligtum zwischen Vollendung des spätarchaischen Apollontempels und der Niederlage gegen die Athener 459/8 v. Chr.

Das Dach des Artemistempels wurde mit korinthischen Ziegeln eingedeckt, Strotere und Kalyptere dabei als selbständige Ziegelteile hergestellt. Der verwendete Ton gleicht dem korinthischen, ist gelbgrün bis braun und stammt wahrscheinlich aus den in Ägina und direkt

FIG. 2. Rekonstruktion Antefix

beim Apollon-Heiligtum anstehenden Tongründen. Man magerte ihn mit zerriebenem Vulkangestein und etwas Ziegelsplitt, überzog die Außenhaut mit einem feinen, dünnen, gelbgrünen Schlämmer und glättete diesen nach dem Trocknen. Die nicht sichtbaren Ziegelpartien wurden glatt abgestrichen.

Vom ursprünglichen Dachschmuck blieben erhalten: zwei Stirnziegelfragmente der Traufseite, zwei Bruchstücke der Firstpalmetten, zwei zusammenpassende Teile der Giebelsima und ein kleines Fragment ihrer Sockelleiste (Pl. 28). Naturgemäß ist die Zuweisung von normalen, unverzierten Dachziegeln schwierig und unsicher, wenn diese erst aus einer großen Menge zumeist nur bruchstückhafter Ziegeln—mehreren Dächern angehörig und in der Konsistenz des Tones optisch nur schwer voneinander zu scheiden—gleichsam herausgefiltert werden müssen. Ist, wie hier, auf der Rückseite der Traufantefixe noch die Verbindung zum Kalypter erhalten bzw. erkennbar, ist anhand seiner Sattelneigung wenigstens die Zuordnung unverzierter Deckziegel möglich. Da mit Ausnahme der Kalypterbreite keine ganzen Ziegelmaße erhalten sind, ist die Suche nach den Flachziegeln, den Stroteren, ohne sonstige Anhaltspunkte ein fast aussichtsloses Unternehmen.

DAS ANTEFIX (Pl. 28:a, b; Fig. 2)

Glücklicherweise sind die beiden Bruchstücke (Z1, Z45) derart erhalten geblieben, daß sie sich gegenseitig ergänzen und so eine Rekonstruktion der gesamten Stirnziegelfront

FIG. 3. Rekonstruktion Firstpalmette

ermöglichen (Fig. 2). Das Ornament wurde in einer Preßform hergestellt und blieb als leicht erhabenes Relief stehen. Der Preßdruck erreichte auch den Kern des Stirnziegels, wie die Blattkonturen selbst im 2 cm tiefer liegeden Bruch bei Z45 (Pl. 28:b) deutlich erkennen lassen. Das Ornament besteht im unteren Teil aus zwei antithetisch gestellten S-Ranken, deren Mittelpartie waagrecht zu liegen kommt, sich oben berühren und nach auswärts einrollen, während sie unten weit auseinanderstehen und sich nach innen kehren. Die Spiralen enden in kreisrunden Volutenaugen. Der Zwischenraum unten wird von einer kleinen, hängenden, fünfblättrigen Palmette über Blattkern ausgefüllt. Jeweils ein Blättchen schiebt sich links und rechts in den Zwickel der auswärts fahrenden Rankenvoluten. Im Zwickel darüber öffnet sich auf einem Blattkern eine weitgefächerte, siebenblättrige Palmette. Das Ornament selbst ist tongrundig gelbgrün, der Hintergrund schwarz gefirnißt, Volutenaugen und Blattkerne wurden rot bemalt, wie gleichfalls die Seitenränder der Stirnziegelfront. Ergänzt man die Vorderseite, erhält man als Breite 19,3 cm, als Höhe *ca.* 22 cm. Bei beiden Fragmenten ist rückwärts der Übergang zum Deckziegel noch teilweise erhalten. Die Unterseite ist ovalrund und rauhflächig.

DIE FIRSTPALMETTE (Pl. 28:c, d; Fig. 3)

Von den Stirnziegeln des Dachfirstes fand man bisher nur zwei kleine Bruchstücke (Z36, Z143). Ton- und Oberflächenbeschaffenheit sind dieselbe wie bei den Traufantefixen, mit dem Unterschied, daß das Ornament hier nicht in einer Form gepreßt, sondern nur aufgemalt wurde. Auch die Maltechnik ist entsprechend: das Ornament tongrundig auf schwarz gefirnißtem Grund, rot sind Blattkern und Seitenränder.

Wenigstens die obere Stirnziegelhälfte läßt sich ergänzen (Fig. 3): Über dem Blattkern sitzt eine neunblättrige Palmette, die, verglichen mit den Traufziegeln, von gestreckter Form ist, die Firstpalmette insgesamt daher etwas höher als das Traufantefix gewesen sein wird. Vom Rankengewinde der unteren Hälfte sind nur noch die oberen, nach außen sich einrollenden und spitz auslaufenden Volutenenden zu sehen. Im Zwickel darunter noch eine kleine, hängende Raute.

DIE GIEBELSIMA (Pl. 28:e, f; Fig. 4)

Zwei zusammenpassende Fragmente (Z35/Z35a; Pl. 28:e) vermitteln Form und Dekor der Giebelsima (Fig. 4). Die Hauptzone der Sima, ein kräftig geschwungenes Profil (cyma reversa), ist bemalt mit einem Anthemion aus sich abwechselnden, stehenden Lotosblüten und Palmetten. Aus dem Kelch des Lotos wächst in der Mitte und in Geborgenheit zweier sich weit öffnender Kelchblätter, der Blütenstempel senkrecht empor. Vom Kelchboden laufen zwei Ranken abwärts, rollen sich beidseitig nach einem bogenförmigen Schwung volutenförmig ein und bilden den Sitz der elfblättrigen Palmette. Von den Voluten wächst jeweils ein kurzer, schwungvoll gestalteter Seitentrieb heraus. Die gestreckte Form der Palmetten erinnert an den gleichfalls gestreckten Blattfächer der Firstpalmette. Die Maltechnik entspricht den Trauf- und Firstziegeln, Rot verwendete man für Blütenkelchränder (begleitet von Ritzkonturen), Kelchblattfüllung, Blattkerne und Stempelnarbe.

Oben geht die Profilkurve (Fig. 4) in einen nur schwach ausgebildeten Rundstab über, verziert mit einem ionischen Blattstab—Blattfüllung schwarz, tongrundig umrahmt auf rotem Hintergrund, Rautenblatt dazwischen tongrundig—und endet in einem noch schmaleren, glatten Kopfband. Wegen der beschädigten Oberfläche kann nicht mehr festgestellt werden, ob seine Stirnpartie bemalt war. Der Simahals fehlt zwar an diesem Stück, ist aber in einem weiteren Fragment (Z109, Pl. 28:f) belegt. Demnach war er mit einem Mäanderband, unterbrochen von rot umrahmten Schachbrettfenstern, bemalt. Die Simaziegel ragten etwas über das Geison hinaus, da vorne auf ihrer Unterseite ein *ca.* 4 cm breiter Streifen mit einem Astragal verziert wurde. Der noch erhaltene Teil im Anschluß an den Astragal ist flächig rot bemalt.

DATIERUNG

Ornamentform, Ausführung in tongrundiger Technik und das Wellenprofil der Sima sichern die Entstehung der Dachterrakotten des Artemistempels von Ägina in klassischer Zeit, genauer, der ersten Hälfte des 5. Jh. v. Chr. Eine Stirnziegelserie von Delphi[3] soll am Anfang der Betrachtung stehen. Über ihre bloße motivische Ähnlichkeit hinaus steht bei beiden Antefixen der Dekor, verglichen mit älteren Beispielen, in einem vollkommen neuen Verhältnis zum Bildgrund—ein Hauptanliegen vor allem auch des Vasenmalers der Wendezeit von der Archaik zur Klassik. Nicht mehr das bloße Füllen einer vorgegebenen Fläche interessierte den Maler zuerst, sondern die Bezugnahme von Dekor und Malgrund stellte er sich zur Aufgabe. Die Suche nach dem ausgewogenen Verhältnis läßt ein neues Verständnis

---

[3] Le Roy 1967, S. 122–123, Taf. 43, 44 (A.42, A.49, A.39), Rek. Taf. 125.

FIG. 4. Rekonstruktion Giebelsima (Z35/Z35a), Profil

in der dekorativen Malerei deutlich werden. Trotzdem gibt es auch Unterschiede: Beim delphischen Antefix sitzt das Ornament noch unruhig und unsicher im Bildrahmen, beinahe verständlich, daß die Ranken durch ein Halsband zusammengehalten werden müssen. Die Palmette wieder bezeugt archaisches Erbe: nur die beiden untersten Blätter fallen leicht über, die restlichen verharren noch etwas steif in der Fläche. Demgegenüber sind die Ornamentteile des äginetischen Stirnziegels bereits fest in den Rahmen gefügt und streng durchstrukturiert. Das Gewicht der Palmette wird spürbar und, von den Rankenvoluten federnd aufgefangen, im Gleichgewicht gehalten. Die Blätter fallen gleichförmig und ausgewogen in den Fächer. Kein Wunder, daß die hängende Lotosblüte, in archaischer Zeit beliebtes Motiv in der unteren Stirnziegelpartie, zurückgedrängt und die Ranke fortan bodenstämmiger Träger der Palmette wird. Überspitzt formuliert: Das pflanzliche Ornament gewinnt, über die gleichmäßig pulsierende Kraft archaischer Auffassung hinaus, an Vegetabilität und Verbundenheit zum Boden hinzu.

Die attischen Stirnziegel des strengen Stils von der Akropolis[4] lassen sich den äginetischen nur schwer gegenüberstellen, am besten vielleicht noch die Stirnziegeln der Agora-Tholos,[5] die trotz aller motivischen Unterschiede dasselbe strenge Formgerüst aufweisen. Ein Stirnziegel aus Olympia,[6] in dem sich Altes mit Neuem verbindet, ist zeitlich vor dem äginetischen zu reihen. Das archaisch-Flächige haftet ihm aber noch stark an. Die Trennlinie zwischen spätarchaischer und frühklassischer Auffassung von Dekor und Malgrund zeigt sich wohl am deutlichsten in den Firstpalmetten des jüngeren Aphaiatempels von Ägina.[7] Rein motivisch gesehen sind sie mit den Traufantefixen aus dem Apollon-Heiligtum und von Delphi sehr ähnlich. Die Unterschiede in Ausführung und Auffassung sind groß. Ungewöhnlich allein ist schon, daß Rankenpartie und Zwickelpalmetten im tongrundigen Stil, die Blattkrone aber in schwarzfiguriger Technik bemalt wurden. Zwei überaus kräftige Rankenstränge werden durch ein ebenso kräftiges Halsband zusammengehalten. Die seitlichen Zwickelpalmetten füllen die Fläche nicht nur, sondern sprengen sogar den vorgegebenen Rahmen. Die dazwischen herabhängende Palmette allein reichte dem Maler offenbar nicht aus, zusätzliche Blättchen in den Seitenzwickeln der Rankenvoluten schienen seiner Vorstellung angepaßter. Der abwechselnd rot und schwarz bemalte Blattfächer verrät dann seine archaische Herkunft. Die vorhandene Fläche zu füllen galt dem vorrangigen Anliegen des Malers, ein Verhältnis von Dekor und Malgrund wurde erst gar nicht gesucht. Für Veränderungen offen stand er nur dem Motiv gegenüber und bedingt zur neuen Maltechnik. Die Anthemien der marmornen Traufantefixe[8] dagegen bezeugen fortschrittlicheres Gestalten. Das Ornament wurde auf den vorgegebenen Rahmen abgestimmt und kann sich darin entfalten. Der Weg von hier zu den Stirnziegeln des Artemistempels ist nicht mehr allzuweit.

---

[4] Buschor 1933, S. 45–54 bes. die Stirnziegel XVII und XVIII, S. 51–52, Abb. 68, 69. Vgl. dazu einen Stirnziegelfund aus dem Kerameikos, Hübner 1973, S. 73–77, Abb. 2 und von Delphi die Serie 66, Le Roy 1967, Taf. 52 (A.94, A.182), Rek. Taf. 125.
[5] Thompson 1940, S. 65–73, Abb. 54, Farbtafel.
[6] *Olympia* II, Taf. 122:1.
[7] Furtwängler 1906, S. 41, Taf. 48:3–3a; Van Buren 1926, S. 4, 162–163, Taf. 3, 5 (r.o.).
[8] Furtwängler 1906, Taf. 47.

Allein über das Profil (Fig. 4) ist eine genauere zeitliche Einordnung der Sima (Pl. 28:e, f) nur bedingt möglich. Die Kymakurve ist schwungvoll durchgezogen, zieht sich oben und unten nicht ein, sondern läuft gerade aus. Das Wellenprofil entstand wahrscheinlich aus der Zusammenziehung der ursprünglich abgesetzten, torusartigen Profilierung archaischer Simen. Die Sima vom Dach 52 aus Delphi[9] könnte dabei das Übergangsstadium markieren:[10] Der obere gebauchte Profilteil geht in einem nur mehr schwach akzentuierten Knick in die bereits schräg und glatt abfallende untere Hälfte über. Die Kurven der nur wenig jüngeren Simen von Knidier Lesche und Dach 55[11] haben den durchgehenden Schwung bereits vollzogen. Der Simakopf hängt auch jetzt noch weit über, die für die archaische Zeit so typische, stark konvexe Ausbuchtung wandelte sich aber zunächst in eine nur schwach ausgebildete S-Kurvung, die in der Folgezeit noch an Ausprägung gewinnt. Im Vergleich dazu wäre das stärker geschwungene Profil der äginetischen Sima eher nach jenen der delphischen Beispiele anzuordnen und in die Nähe etwa einer Korinther Sima,[12] einer Schatzhaussima bzw. jener der Pheidias-Werkstatt von Olympia[13] zu stellen.

Aufschlußreichere Datierungskriterien findet man im Anthemionornament. Es besteht aus stehenden Palmetten und Lotosblüten, die auf bogenförmigen Ranken sitzen, welche im Blütenkelch gerade ansetzen und sich unter dem Blattfächer zu Voluten einrollen. Die hochgewachsenen Blüten und Blätter, ihr vegetabilischer Charakter insgesamt, vor allem aber die differenziert gestalteten Lotosblüten rücken das Anthemion näher zu denen hochklassischer Simen, etwa der Phidias-Werkstatt, dem Dach 70 von Delphi[14] oder der olympischen Sima vom sog. Hephaisteion-Typus,[15] als zu den frühklassischen Simen von Delphi und Olympia,[16] deren Ornamentformen sich noch deutlich an überkommenen Vorbildern orientieren. Wie ich meine, der Schein trügt. Die Bauweise des Ornaments hält sich an strenge Prinzipien, deren frühe Wurzeln noch zu spüren sind. Die Palmetten werden von Kelchblättern und Bogenranken ganz nach alter Manier eingefaßt. Blattfächer und Lotosblüte hingegen stehen in einem beziehungsreichen Verhältnis, "atmen" dieselbe Luft. Dies zuallererst bewirkt den vegetabilischen Eindruck, das Ornament selbst, rein motivisch gesehen, ist durchaus in schlichter Form gehalten. Zutaten beschränken sich auf kleine Ableger, die von den Spiralenden herauswachsen oder einfache Rotakzentuierungen. Zwickelfüllungen oder Akanthisierung, wie in den motivisch verwandten und jüngeren Simen, fehlen.

Eine im Detail derart ausführlich gestaltete Lotosblüte, wie sie die äginetische Sima zeigt, war auf korinthischen Terrakottasimen der ersten Hälfte des 5. Jh. bislang nicht

---

[9] Le Roy 1967, S. 123–124, Taf. 44, 102.

[10] Vgl. Heiden 1987, S. 122.

[11] Dach 56 der Knidier-Lesche: Le Roy 1967, S. 128–129, Taf. 46, 103, Rek. Taf. 126; Dach 55: Le Roy 1967, S. 127–128, Taf. 45, 103.

[12] *Corinth* IV, i, Taf. 5.

[13] *Olympia* II, S. 196–197, Taf. 121:2; *OlForsch* V, S. 112–113, Taf. 14–16; Heiden 1987, S. 107–113, Taf. 12:2, 13.

[14] Dach 70: Le Roy 1967, S. 141–142, Taf. 54, 103.

[15] *OlForsch* V, S. 115, Abb. 39, Taf. 42, 43.

[16] Delphi: neben Dach 56, Le Roy 1967, S. 128–129, Taf. 46, 103, noch die Dächer 50, 52, 57–59, Le Roy 1967, S. 122, Taf. 43, S. 123–124, Taf. 44, S. 133–134, Taf. 48–50; Olympia: *Olympia* II, Taf. 121:1.

anzutreffen. Motivisch verwandte Beispiele sind aber in der Architekturmalerei und auf marmornen Simen durchaus bekannt. So z.B. in einem Anthemion auf dem Türsturz des Athener-Schatzhauses.[17] Die Lotosblüte sitzt auf dem aufgesprungenen Blütenkelch, die steil und rund auseinanderfallenden Kelchblätter rahmen die Palmette ein. Dazwischen wächst das Mittelblatt senkrecht empor. Geringfügig älter als das Anthemion des Athener-Schatzhauses scheint mir die Bemalung einer marmornen Traufsima von der Akropolis[18] zu sein, dessen Kelchform schon viel früher im Traufleistenornament des peisistratidischen Athenatempels[19] zu finden ist, ebenfalls auf Marmorgrund gesetzt. Vielleicht ging mehr von diesem Gestaltungszweig die Anregung aus, Lotosblüten auch auf Terrakottasimen im Detail vielfältiger und "lebensnaher" darzustellen. Sind aber im Athener-Schatzhaus Palmette und Lotos durchaus noch archaisch eng aneinandergereiht und umschlungen, vermittelt das äginetische Anthemion ein anderes, offeneres Verhältnis zwischen diesen Elementen. Die Umfassung der Palmette ist freier und erfolgt distanzierter. Ausgehend von hier setzt sich die Reihe fort über einen gemalten Anthemion-Wandfries am sog. Dorischen Schatzhaus im Pronaia-Heiligtum von Delphi[20] um etwa 470/460 v. Chr., über den Anthemionfries auf dem Hals des Antenkapitells der "Stoa poikile",[21] bis hin zu den bemalten Marmorsimen des Poseidontempels von Sunion und Hephaistostempels von der Agora, dessen eigenwillige Lotosdarstellung auf einer korinthischen Tonsima aus Olympia am Ende des Jahrhunderts wiederkehrt[22] und danach benannt wurde. Dazwischen markiert eine Sima aus dem Ptoion[23] ungefähr die Jahrhundertmitte. Motivisch am nächsten steht ihr freilich das Anthemionband einer delphischen Sima,[24] formal gesehen ist es aber eine Weiterentwicklung: Die Lotosblüte dort erscheint als eine organische Ganzheit, Einzelformen wie Fruchtknoten, Kelch und Kelchblätter sind zugunsten der Gesamtform zurückgenommen. Darauf vor allem beruht die vertikale Bestimmtheit der Lotosblüte und die Umschlingung der Palmette durch die seitlichen Kelchblätter verliert deutlich an Prägnanz, wogegen die Blüten der äginetischen Sima viel stärker noch von der Einzelform getragen sind. Damit gewinnt man als zeitlichen Ansatz das Jahrzehnt 470–460 v. Chr. Der ausgeprägtere pflanzliche Charakter und die strengere Fassung setzt sie von der Sima der Knidier-Lesche ab, bescheinigt der äginetischen eine etwas jüngere Entwicklungsstufe und weist schon auf die hochklassischen Simen von Olympia und Delphi voraus.

Die Sockelzone wurde mit einem Hakenkreuzmäander bemalt (Pl. 28:e). Zwischen Profilwelle und glattem Kopfband, dessen Bemalung (vermutlich ein Astragal) verloren ging, ist ein schwach ausgeprägter Rundstab, verziert mit ionischem Blattstabmuster, eingeschoben

---

[17] Büsing 1979, S. 29–36, Taf. 4, 5. Nach ihm entstand das Anthemion in strengklassischer Zeit, noch vor Errichtung des "Dorischen" Schatzhauses im Athena-Pronaia-Heiligtum, das allgemein zwischen 475–460 v. Chr. angesetzt wird.
[18] Schuchhardt 1963, S. 797–823, Abb. 16; Schede 1909, Taf. 4:23.
[19] Schede 1909, Taf. 2:13.
[20] Daux 1925, S. 86–87, Abb. 89, 94, Taf. 31.
[21] Thompson 1950, S. 327–329, Taf. 103:a.
[22] Orlandos 1953–1954, S. 3–4, Abb. 1, 2; zum Hephaistostempel, Koch 1955, S. 65–66, 188, Abb. 67; zur "Hephaisteionsima" von Olympia, *OlForsch* V, S. 112–113, Taf. 14–16.
[23] Le Roy 1967, S. 145, Taf. 56.
[24] Le Roy 1967, S. 141–142, Taf. 54, 103.

(Fig. 4). Schachbrettmäander, ionischer Blattstab[25] und Astragalzone auf der Unterseite sind jedoch wenig aufschlußreich für die Entstehungszeit der Sima.

Zuletzt seien noch historische Gründe angeführt, die die Dachterrakotten des Artemistempels auch von dieser Sicht in das 2. Viertel des 5. Jh. v. Chr. datieren: Es ist anzunehmen, daß die Ägineten mit der Besetzung ihrer Insel durch die Athener 459/8 v. Chr. und den ihnen auferlegten hohen Tributzahlungen (30 Talente), bishin zu ihrer Vertreibung von der Insel 431 v. Chr., kaum mehr in der Lage waren, ein umfangreicheres Bauvorhaben, welches ein Tempel immer darstellte, in Auftrag geben und finanzieren zu können. So überrascht es auch nicht, daß im Apollon-Heiligtum Architekturfunde der hochklassischen Zeit bisher weitgehendst ausblieben und die keramischen Befunde und Kleinfunde,[26] im Vergleich zur Zeit davor, quantitativ wie qualitativ ein eher bescheidenes Bild vermitteln.

## DAS ERSATZDACH

Eine Gruppe von dekorierten und unverzierten Ziegeln belegt ein Dach aus dem frühen 4. Jh. (Pl. 29). Weil für ein Gebäude dieser Zeit im Apollon-Heiligtum weder Fundamente noch Architekturteile nachzuweisen sind, mehrere Stücke im Bereich des Artemistempels gefunden wurden und die Höhe der erhaltenen Sima auf einen kleinen Bau schließen läßt, dürften diese Teile von einer Neueindeckung des Tempeldaches herrühren.

Gründe, warum das erste Dach später ersetzt wurde, sind nicht sicher zu benennen. Weil die beiden Firstziegelfragmente Z36 und Z143 (Pl. 28:c, d) Brandspuren aufweisen, könnte das Dach durch ein Feuer beschädigt worden sein. Schäden könnten aber auch durch Witterungsunbilden oder aufgrund mangelnder Pflege der Bauwerke, vor allem in der Zeit nach der Vertreibung der Ägineten von der Insel 431 v. Chr. bis zu ihrer Rückkehr 405 v. Chr., entstanden sein.

Das wenige Erhaltene gibt eine Vorstellung über Form und Bemalung der Giebelsima, sowie von der Gestaltung der traufseitigen Stroterstirnen. Das Traufantefix ist nur in zwei kleinen Bruchstücken überliefert. Die Farbschattierung des Tons reicht von hellgelb bis leicht grünlich bzw. ocker und unterscheidet sich deutlich von den ursprünglichen Dachziegeln. Man versetzte ihn mit dunklem Vulkangesteinssplitt und überzog die Außenhaut mit einer dünnen Schlämmschicht, die gut geglättet wurde.

### Die Giebelsima (Pl. 29:a, b; Fig. 5)

Anhand der zwei gefundenen Bruchstücke Z19, Z139 läßt sich die Giebelsima im Profil und Dekor fast lückenlos ergänzen (Fig. 5). Der Aufbau ist dreiteilig: glatte Halsfascie, stark überhängendes Wellenprofil, davon abgesetzt, das leicht schräg geschnittene, glatte Kopfband. Ein Perlstab schmückt das Kopfband, ein einfaches Anthemion aus stehenden Lotosblüten und Palmetten das Wellenprofil und ein Hakenkreuzmäander mit Schachbrettfenstern die Halszeile. Hinzu kommt ein weiterer Streifen mit Perlstabverzierung auf der das Dach vorkragenden Unterseite, dem ein ungefähr gleichbreiter, flächig rot bemalter Streifen

---

[25] Ionische Blattstabbemalung auf der Abschlussleiste galt bisher als Zeichen eines eher jüngeren Entstehungsdatums; dazu *OlForsch* V, S. 126–127 und Heiden 1987, S. 177–179.

[26] *Alt-Ägina* II, iii.

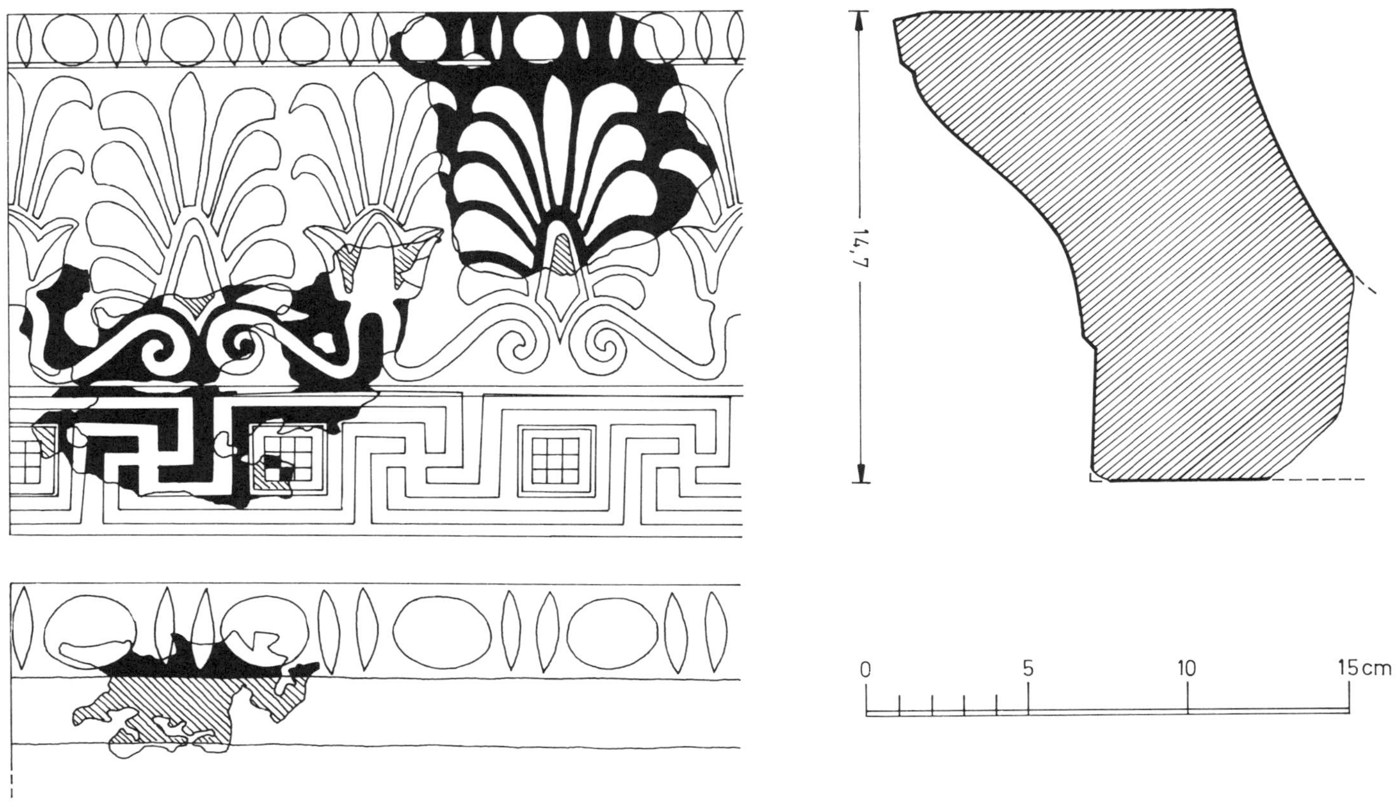

Fig. 5. Rekonstruktion Giebelsima (Z19, Z139), Profil

folgt. Rot verwendete man weiters für Blattkerne, Kelchränder und Schachbrettumrahmung. Die elfblättrige Palmette sitzt über den Spiralenden des Rankengewächses, die Lotosblüten auf kurvig geschwungenen Windungen dazwischen. Am größeren Stück Z19 ist linksseitig die Stoßfläche erhalten. Der Überlappungsteil zum nächsten Ziegel ist zwar ausgebrochen, im Bruch aber noch erkennbar. Die Stoßfuge verläuft in der Mitte der Lotosblüte.

Das Mäanderband auf der Sockelzone setzte sich über die Traufseiten des Daches fort, schmückte dort die Stirnseiten der Flachziegel und auch der Astragal auf der Unterseite lief weiter. Am einzigen vom Dachrand erhaltenen Stroterfragment (Z121, Pl. 29:c) wurde die seitliche Anathyrose fein säuberlich abgeschlagen. Die Oberseite ist zum Rand hin stark aufgewölbt, die Ziegelunterseite im undekorierten Bereich rillenförmig vergröbert, um ein Abgleiten vom Gesimse möglichst zu unterbinden. Zwei schwarz aufgemalte Buchstaben des griechischen Alphabets (ΣΩ) werden Versatzmarken darstellen.

## Das Antefix (Pl. 29:d, e)

Von den Stirnziegeln der Traufseiten sind nur zwei kleine Bruchstücke, jeweils von ihrer rechten unteren Ecke, erhalten. Wie bei Traufantefixen üblich, wurde das Ornament über eine Form in den Ton gepreßt, sodaß es sich leicht reliefiert abhebt. Leider ist bei beiden Bruchstücken vom Dekor nur noch das Ende einer sich nach außen einrollenden Ranke zu sehen. Obwohl im Unterschied zu Z29 (Pl. 29:e) das Fragment Z18 (Pl. 29:d) zusätzlich noch einen roten Basisstreifen besitzt, ist ihre Zusammengehörigkeit nicht anzuzweifeln. Eine formale Beurteilung ist schwierig.

## Datierung

Da im Mäanderband der Sockelzone und abschließenden Astragal kaum Kriterien für eine genauere zeitliche Einordnung des Ersatzdaches zu finden sind, ist diese allein anhand der Anthemionbemalung der Giebelsima zu versuchen, wird aber durch den Mangel an Vergleichsbeispielen aus dem korinthischen Raum vom späten 5. Jh. und der ersten Hälfte des 4. Jh. v. Chr. erschwert. Hinzu kommt die bruchstückhafte Erhaltung, wodurch der Gesamteindruck nur in einer zeichnerischen Rekonstruktion (Fig. 5) beurteilt werden kann.

Die äußerst malerischen und dekorativen Simen XXII und XXIII von der Akropolis,[27] beide etwa um 400 v. Chr. entstanden, unterscheiden sich zu stark in der Auffassung des Motivs und in der Qualität der Ausführung, um zeitliche Unterschiede oder Gemeinsamkeiten herauslesen zu können. Schon besser lassen sich die Simenfunde von Olympia danebenstellen: etwa die Giebelsima vom "Hephaisteion"-Typus aus dem späten 5. Jh. v. Chr., die Traufsima vom Südost-Bau aus dem frühen zweiten Viertel und die Giebelsima des Leonidaions aus dem dritten Viertel des 4. Jh. v. Chr.[28] Allen drei gemeinsam ist die in der zweiten Hälfte des 5. Jh. v. Chr. aufkommende Übernahme von Akanthusformen in den Ornamentschatz, worin auch gleichzeitig der deutlichste Unterschied zum äginetischen Simadekor gegeben ist. Trotz der nur bruchstückhaft erhaltenen Lotosblüte (Fig. 5) war der Blütenkelch hier sicher nicht akanthisiert, lediglich seine Ränder wurden mit rotem

---

[27] Buschor 1929, S. 44–46, Abb. 52, Taf. 11, 12.
[28] "Hephaisteionsima": *OlForsch* V, S. 115, Taf. 43; Südost-Bau: *Olympia* II, S. 197–198, Taf. 121:4; Heiden 1987, S. 127–131, Taf. 16:2; Leonidaion: *OlForsch* V, S. 129–131, Abb. 42, 43; Heiden 1987, S. 131–140, Taf. 17, 18.

Pinselstrich nachgezogen. Davon abgesehen fehlt dem Anthemion sowohl die Präzision in der Ausführung, als auch die Lebendigkeit im Motivischen vor allem im Vergleich zur Sima vom "Hephaisteion"-Typus. Unterschiede in der Anzahl der seitlichen Kelchblätter der Lotosblüten oder die stärkere Flächigkeit können aber nicht über strukturelle und formale Ähnlichkeiten zur Südostbau-Sima hinwegtäuschen. Bereits ein gutes Stück davon entfernt ist die Leonidaion-Sima mit ihren archaisierenden Lotosblüten entstanden. Von der merkbar hastigen und routiniert schablonenhaften Malweise ist im äginetischen Simadekor noch wenig zu spüren.

Motivisch, weil Akanthusformen weitgehendst fehlen, und handwerkstechnisch am besten vergleichbar sind Simen von Korinth, Tiryns und Delphi.[29] Sie sind sich untereinander sehr ähnlich und dürften fast alle dem letzten Viertel des 4. Jh. v. Chr. zuzuordnen sein. Die letztmögliche Ausdrucksform dieses Anthemiontyps verkörpert unter ihnen wohl am besten die Giebelsima der Südstoa von Korinth.[30] Der flüchtig hingeworfene und sorglose Malstil, nur mehr darauf bedacht die Fläche zu überziehen, die erstarrten Gebilde schematisierter Palmetten und Lotosblüten mit deutlichen Auflösungs- und Zerfallserscheinungen, sowie die verlorengegangene Vegetabilität und Lebendigkeit früherer Simabemalungen kennzeichnen dieses Jahrhundertviertel. Die Palmetten und Lotosblüten der äginetischen Sima dagegen besitzen ein klares und festes Formgerüst. Wenig noch ist erkennbar von ungehaltener Bewegtheit, überdehnten S-Ranken, um Blüten und Blättern mehr Luftraum zu geben und den damit einkehrenden Auflösungserscheinungen.

Allgemein stellt man fest, daß das Anthemion im Laufe des 4. Jh. v. Chr. in der schematisierten Darstellungsweise zusehends erstarrt, "verwildert" und auseinanderfällt. An einer von den Ausgräbern an das Ende des 5. Jh. v. Chr. datierten Sima aus Olympia[31] ist noch nichts davon zu spüren. Nicht lange nach ihr wird die äginetische Sima entstanden sein. Eine Datierung in das erste Viertel des 4. Jh. liegt daher nahe und läßt vermuten, daß das Dach des Artemistempels bald nach der Rückkehr der äginetischen Bevölkerung 405 v. Chr. neu eingedeckt worden ist.

## BIBLIOGRAPHIE

*Alt-Ägina* II, iii = I. Margreiter, *Die Kleinfunde aus dem Apollon Heiligtum* (*Alt-Ägina* II, iii), Mainz 1988

Büsing, H. H. 1979. "Ein Anthemion in Delphi," in *Studies in Classical Art and Archaeology. A Tribute to P. Heinrich von Blanckenhagen*, G. Kopcke und M. B. Moore, Hrsg., Locust Valley, N.Y., S. 29–36

Buschor, E. 1929. *Die Tondächer der Akropolis*, I, *Simen*, Berlin/Leipzig

———. 1933. *Die Tondächer der Akropolis*, II, *Stirnziegel*, Berlin/Leipzig

*Corinth* I, iv = O. Broneer, *The South Stoa and Its Roman Successors* (*Corinth* I, iv), Princeton 1954

*Corinth* IV, i = I. Thallon-Hill und L. S. King, *Decorated Architectural Terracottas* (*Corinth* IV, i), Cambridge, Mass. 1929

Daux, G. 1925. *Le sanctuaire d'Athèna Pronaia* 1 (*Fouilles de Delphes* II), Paris

Furtwängler, A., E. R. Fiechter, und H. Thiersch. 1906. *Aegina, das Heiligtum der Aphaia*, Munich

---

[29] Z.B. die Simen S113, S115, S117, S127, S128/128a, S112, S129, S30 von Korinth: *Corinth* IV, i, S. 24–29, Abb. 23–26, 28, 31; die Simen der Dächer 80, 81, 84 von Delphi: Le Roy 1967, S. 154–162, Taf. 59–70; oder aus der Argolis: Hübner 1975, S. 129–132, Taf. 69, 70; oder aus Olympia: *Olympia* II, S. 197–198, Taf. 121:5.

[30] *Corinth* I, iv, S. 83–88, Taf. 19, 20.

[31] *Olympia* II, S. 203, Abb. 28.

Heiden, J. 1987. *Korinthische Dachziegel. Zur Entwicklung der korinthischen Dächer*, Frankfurt am Main/Bern/New York/Paris

Hübner, G. 1973. "Dachterrakotten aus dem Kerameikos von Athen," *AM* 88, S. 67–143

———. 1975. "Dachterrakotten im Magazin des Museums von Nauplia," in *Tiryns* VIII, Mainz, S. 117–136

Koch, H. 1955. *Studien zum Theseustempel in Athen*, Berlin

Le Roy, Ch. 1967. *Les terres cuites architecturales* (*Fouilles de Delphes* II), Paris

*OlForsch* V = A. Mallwitz und W. Schiering, *Die Werkstatt des Pheidias in Olympia* (*Olympische Forschungen* V), Berlin 1964

*Olympia* II = W. Dörpfeld und R. Bormann, *Die Baudenkmäler* (*Olympia, Ergebnisse der von dem deutschen Reich veranstalteten Ausgrabungen* II), Berlin 1892

Orlandos, A. K. 1953–1954. «Ἡ γραπτὴ ἀρχιτεκτονικὴ διακόσμησις τοῦ ἐν Σουνίῳ ναοῦ τοῦ Ποσειδῶνος», ΑρχΕφ 1953–1954, Γ, S. 1–18

Schede, M. 1909. *Antikes Traufleistenornament*, Strassburg

Schuchhardt, W.-H. 1963. "Archaische Bauten auf der Acropolis von Athen," *AA* [*JdI* 78], S. 797–824

Thompson, H. A. 1940. *The Tholos of Athens and Its Predecessors* (*Hesperia* Supplement 4), Princeton

———. 1950. "Excavations in the Athenian Agora: 1949," *Hesperia* 19, S. 313–337

Van Buren, E. D. 1926. *Greek Fictile Revetments in the Archaic Period*, London

Walter, H. 1993. *Ägina. Die archäologische Geschichte einer griechischen Insel*, München

Welter, G. 1925. "Aegina," *AA* [*JdI* 40], S. 317–321

———. 1938a. *Aegina*, Berlin

———. 1938b. "Aeginetica I–XII," *AA* [*JdI* 53], S. 1–33

———. 1938c. "Aeginetica XIII–XXIV," *AA* [*JdI* 53], S. 480–538

Wolters, P. 1925a. "Ausgrabungen am Aphroditentempel in Ägina 1924," *Gnomon* 1, S. 46–49

———. 1925b. "Forschungen auf Ägina," *AA* [*JdI* 40], S. 1–12

KLAUS HOFFELNER

Berchtesgadnerstr. 50
A-5020 Salzburg
Austria

# ΑΡΧΙΤΕΚΤΟΝΙΚΕΣ ΤΕΡΡΑΚΟΤΕΣ ΑΠΟ ΤΗΝ ΑΡΧΑΙΑ ΣΙΚΥΩΝΑ

(PLATES 30–36)

ΑΠΟ ΤΗ ΔΕΥΤΕΡΗ ΜΕΓΑΛΗ ΚΑΙ ΓΝΩΣΤΟΤΑΤΗ από τις πηγές πολιτεία της Κορινθίας, τη Σικυώνα, προέρχεται το υλικό που παρουσιάζεται πολύ συνοπτικά στο δεύτερο συνέδριο για αρχιτεκτονικές τερρακότες της Αμερικανικής Σχολής Κλασσικών Σπουδών Αθηνών.[1] Ο χώρος της αρχαίας Σικυώνας με την ελληνιστική και ρωμαϊκή αγορά, το ωραιότατο θέατρο, το Στάδιο και τις πολυτελείς ρωμαϊκές επαύλεις καθώς και οι υποθεμελιώσεις των δύο επάλληλων ναών αρχαϊκού και ελληνιστικού έχει εντοπισθεί στο υψίπεδο όπου είναι χτισμένο το χωριό Βασιλικό. Η αρχαϊκή και κλασσική πόλη έχει με σιγουριά τοποθετηθεί στην πεδιάδα που ορίζεται από τα χωριά Βέλλο, Τραγάνα, Μούλκι και Βασιλικό.[2] Η τόσο σημαντική αυτή αρχαϊκή και κλασσική πόλη της ΒΔ Πελοποννήσου μέχρι σήμερα έχει αδικηθεί τόσο ανασκαφικά όσο και εκθεσιακά. Η αιτία για τη μομφή που διατυπώνω έγκειται (α) στο ότι ποτέ δεν δόθηκε από την Ελληνική Αρχαιολογική υπηρεσία η προσοχή που θα έπρεπε να έχει επικεντρωθεί σε ένα τόσο αρχαίο και πολύτιμο χώρο και (β) στο ότι η Κορινθία μόνη δεν έγινε αυτάρχης Εφορεία αλλά εξακολουθεί να παραμένει συνδεδεμένη με μιά Αρχαιολογική Εφορεία τέρας σε διαστάσεις, που καλύπτει διοικητικά και επιστημονικά την Επιδαυρία, την Αργολίδα και την Κορινθία.

Πολλά ερωτήματα για τη μεγάλη θέση της τέχνης της Σικυώνας παραμένουν αναπάντητα ενώ ο παραλληλισμός για τήν ακτινοβολία που μαζί με την Αρχαία Κόρινθο εξέπεμψε στις τρείς μεγάλες περιόδους Αρχαϊκή-Κλασσική-Ελληνιστική είναι ελλιπής.

Είναι απώλεια για την επιστήμη και για τον ίδιο τον τόπο και τη σύγχρονη Ελλάδα το ότι οι συχνές αλλαγές καλλιέργειας της πεδιάδας και το «λεπτόγεω» του υψιπέδου έχουν ήδη από την αρχή του αιώνα καταστρέψει αρχαία σπίτια, ναούς, τεμένη, εν μέρει το θέατρο και ίσως και το στάδιο που ακόμη δεν έχει ούτε δειγματοληπτικά ανασκαφεί.

---

[1] Θα ήθελα να ευχαριστήσω τον Διευθυντή της Αμερικανικής Σχολής Κλασσικών Σπουδών William Coulson καθώς και την υπεύθυνη της βιβλιοθήκης της Σχολής Nancy Winter, για την πρόσκληση να λάβω μέρος στο τόσο ενδιαφέρον και σοβαρώτατα οργανωμένο δεύτερο αυτό συνέδριο με θέμα τις αρχιτεκτονικές τερρακότες.

Θα ήθελα επίσης να τονίσω την επιτυχία και την άριστη διεξαγωγή που επετεύχθη χάρη στην έντονη προσωπική προσπάθεια της Nancy Winter. Εύχομαι να συνεχιστεί με την ίδια επιτυχία η διεξαγωγή αυτών των μικρών συνεδρίων πάνω σε συγκεκριμένα θέματα, γιατί είναι γνωστό πόσο πολύτιμα είναι τα αποτελέσματα και η συμβολή τους στην επιστήμη.

[2] Γενική βιβλιογραφία έως τα 1970 βρίσκομε στην μονογραφία του Φαράκλα 1971. Πλούσια βιβλιογραφία έχομε και στην *ΕΑΑ* στο λήμμα Σικυών, τ. VII σελ. 276–279. Οι παραπέρα δημοσιεύσεις είναι η δημοσίευση του ψηφιδωτού του Γοργονείου: Votsis 1976, καθώς και η εκτενής δημοσίευση των ψηφιδωτών της Σικυώνας από τον Salzmann 1982. Σχετικά με την ανασκαφή του νεκροταφείου βλ. μικρή είδηση στο Κρυστάλλη-Βότση 1984, σελ. 65, πίν. 58 και για την ανασκαφή στο θέατρο και στους ναούς—Βότση 1984, σελ. 61–62, εικ. 93–95, και Βότση 1987β, σελ. 91, εικ. 104–105 και Βότση 1987α, σελ. 66–68, πίν. 53–57.

Η πρώτη Μουσειακή συλλογή καταρτίστηκε από ευρήματα περισυλλογής και μικρών ανασκαφικών ερευνών από αρχαιολόγους σκαπανείς της ελληνικής αρχαιολογικής επιστήμης όπως ο Α. Φιλαδελφεύς.[3]

Πολύ αργότερα ο Α. Ορλάνδος στέγασε την εμπλουτισμένη και με ευρήματα της πολύχρονης προσωπικής του ανασκαφής νέα συλλογή, σε τρεις χώρους ρωμαϊκού βαλανείου του 2ου μ.Χ. αιώνα ανυψώνοντας τους τοίχους[4] με σύγχρονα τούβλα κόκκινα και καλύπτοντάς το με κεραμοσκεπή στέγη.

Η επανέκθεση του μικρού Μουσείου που γνώρισα, είχε γίνει από τον τότε αγαπημένο συνεργάτη του Α. Ορλάνδου και σημερινό καθηγητή Γ. Δεσπίνη και από το ζεύγος Μαρία και Ανδρέα Γαβρίλη που στράφηκαν όμως προς τη Μέση Εκπαίδευση. Το συμπαθέστατο αυτό μουσείο, χωρίς εργαστήρια, χωρίς αποθηκευτικούς χώρους, χωρίς στοιχειώδεις ανέσεις επιστημονικής εργασίας θεωρείται εδώ και τουλάχιστον είκοσι χρόνια ανεπαρκέστατο.

Για τη μακρά προσωπική μου σχέση με την Σικυώνα, θα ήθελα να μου επιτραπεί να κάνω μιά μικρή αναδρομή. Ήδη από το 1965–1966 με τον πρώτο μου διορισμό σαν επιμελήτρια αρχαιοτήτων Αργολιδοκορινθίας είχα την ευκαιρία να αρχίσω να ασχολούμαι με την ανασκαφή του νεκροταφείου στην πεδιάδα.[5] Σε exposé στην École Pratique des Hautes Études στον τομέα του R. Martin του οποίου υπήρξα μαθήτρια εξέθεσα τις απόψεις μου για τα πιόσχημα ταφικά μνημεία του IV π.Χ. αιώνα με βάση το μνημείο της ανασκαφής του 1966.[6] Μετά την μεταπολίτευση το 1974 επανήλθα στη θέση μου και στον τόπο μου εγκαταλείποντας το C.N.R.S. (Γαλλικό Ίδρυμα Ερευνών) και το αγαπημένο Μουσείο του Λούβρου όπου εργάστηκα δίπλα στον μοναδικό Αρχαιολόγο και Άνθρωπο P. Devambez.[7]

Πρώτα σαν επιμελήτρια (1975–1977) και αργότερα σαν Έφορος Αργολιδοκορινθίας συνέχισα συστηματικά την ανασκαφή της εκτεταμένης νεκρόπολης από το 1976 έως το 1979 (τέλος 6ου έως και τον 1ον μ.Χ. αιώνα).[8] Η ολοκληρωμένη δημοσίευση του υλικού παρόλη τη μεγάλη προεργασία που έχει γίνει καθυστερεί επειδή το μικρό Μουσείο με τις διάφορες κτιριακές περιπέτειες και επισκευές που το κρατούν κλειστό επί επτά χρόνια δεν προσφέρεται για να γίνει η ταύτιση του υλικού των τάφων και των πυρών. Η παρουσίαση του υλικού αυτού, όταν οι δυσκολίες υπερνικηθούν, νομίζω ότι θα φωτίσει την κοινή Κορινθιακή Σικυώνια παράδοση για τις κατηγορίες των αγγείων

---

[3] Βλ. Φιλαδελφεύς 1926α, σελ. 46–50 και τον κατάλογο των εκθεμάτων του ίδιου στο Φιλαδελφεύς 1926β, σελ. 17–23. Αρχαιολογική Συλλογή Σικυώνος (εν τω σημερινώ χωρίω Βασιλικώ) όπου εκθέτει συγκινητικά πως κατήρτισε την πρώτη μικρή συλλογή στην οικία Π. Μανίκα.

[4] Ορλάνδος 1936, σελ. 18.

[5] Βλ. Κρυστάλλη 1967, σελ. 164–166, πίν. 124 ανασκαφή ταφικού μνημείου στο σημείο που πέρναγε η εθνική οδός Κορίνθου-Πατρών και πρώτη αποκάλυψη του ψηφιδωτού ανδρώνα στον αγρό Ι. Κόλλια.

[6] Martin 1972.

[7] Θεωρώ υποχρέωση να αναφέρω ότι η θερμή υποδοχή και συμπαράσταση που είχα στο Παρίσι από τους αγαπητούς συναδέλφους Lily Ghali-Cahil, Jean Pouilloux, Yvon Garlan, Roland Martin, και πάνω από όλα από τον ίδιο τον αξέχαστο Pierre Devambez, ήταν ό,τι καλύτερο μπορούσε να δώσει η συναδελφική και ανθρώπινη αλληλεγγύη.

[8] Κρυστάλλη-Βότση 1976, σελ. 65, πίν. 58.

και των ειδωλίων. Το έτος 1975 καθαρίστηκε, σχεδιάστηκε και δημοσιεύτηκε το ψηφιδωτό του αγρού Ι. Κόλλια.[9]

Όσο ο δάσκαλος Α. Ορλάνδος ζούσε, για λόγους δεοντολογίας, περιοριζόμουνα στο να περιβάλλω με στοργή και φροντίδα τον αρχαιολογικό χώρο της Σικυώνας.[10]

Παράλληλα του εξέθεσα προφορικά το ενδιαφέρον που είχα για τη Σικυώνα και έτσι μιά μέρα είχα τη χαρά να τον ακούσω να μου λέει ότι θα ήταν ευχαρίστησή του να με δεί να συνεχίζω το έργο του. Μετά το θάνατο του ακάματου αυτού επιστήμονα, έγινε δεκτή από την Αρχαιολογική Εταιρεία η αίτησή μου και μου χορηγήθηκε η άδεια ανασκαφής του Αρχαιολογικού χώρου Σικυώνας με ελάχιστα όμως δυστυχώς χρήματα.

Οι αρχιτεκτονικές τερρακότες που παρουσιάζονται εδώ είναι στρωτήρες ηγεμόνες, σίμες με γραπτή και ανάγλυφη διακόσμηση και τμήματα ηγεμόνων καλυπτήρων.

Στο υλικό αυτό συγκαταλέγονται τα αντικείμενα που έχουν περισυλλεγεί σποραδικά από διάφορους αγρούς από την ανασκαφή του Α. Φιλαδελφέως και από την πολυετή ανασκαφή του Α. Ορλάνδου που συνεχίστηκε μετά το τέλος του Β' Παγκοσμίου πολέμου. Αναφέρονται επίσης και τα νεώτερα ευρήματα από το 1984–1988 που βρέθηκαν στους χώρους που ανέσκαψα γύρω από τους δύο επάλληλους ναούς, αρχαϊκό και ελληνιστικό, με μικρές πιστώσεις της Αρχαιολογικής Εταιρείας.[11]

## ΑΡΧΑΪΚΟΙ ΑΚΡΟΚΕΡΑΜΟΙ ΗΓΕΜΟΝΩΝ ΚΑΛΥΠΤΗΡΩΝ ΚΑΙ ΣΙΜΕΣ

Γύρω στο 500 π.Χ. τοποθετούνται τα δύο ημίση ακροκεράμων καλυπτήρων (Pls. 30:a και b). Από το ένα διασώζεται μόνο τό ανθέμιο ενώ στο δεύτερο το κατώτερο τμήμα με τεμάχιο του σώματος του καλυπτήρα. Ένα άλλο τρίτο σώζεται ακέραιο (Pl. 30:c).

[9] Votsis 1976. Σήμερα αποκολλημένο για συντήρηση βρίσκεται στην ελληνική αποθήκη του παλαιού συνεταιρισμού στην Αρχαία Κόρινθο. Όλα τα μέχρι τώρα ανευρεθέντα κλασσικά ψηφιδωτά δάπεδα όπως και το ψηφιδωτό του αγρού Ι. Κόλλια, κατά μαρτυρία του αείμνηστου Α. Ορλάνδου, προέρχονται από την κλασσική πόλη της πεδιάδας. Όλα βρίσκονται ενσωματωμένα στη μονογραφία του Salzmann 1982.

[10] Αγωνίστηκα και πέτυχα τον ηλεκτροφωτισμό του Μουσείου και του χώρου ενώ προκάλεσα με τα διαβήματά μου την εκπόνηση μελέτης για τη συντήρηση των παρόδων του θεάτρου που κινδύνευαν και κινδυνεύουν ακόμη. Αισθάνομαι αμηχανία που το εκφράζω αλλά είναι γεγονός, ότι ενώ ο ικανότατος αρχιτέκτων του Υ.Π.Π.Ο. Α. Νακάσης έχει εκπονήσει προ πολλών ετών τη μελέτη της συντήρησης των παρόδων, η συντήρηση δεν έχει ακόμα επιτευχθεί.

[11] Τα νέα ευρήματα καθαρίστηκαν και συγκολλήθηκαν από τον πολύπειρο τεχνίτη Α. Μαυραγάνη στον οποίο εκφράζω θερμές ευχαριστίες από τη θέση αυτή.

Οι φωτογραφίες έγιναν από τις κυρίες Ι. Ιωαννίδου και Λ. Μπαρτζιώτη, τις τόσο γνωστές για την ευαίσθητη δουλειά τους και τα slides από τον Ι. Πατρικιάνο. Η φωτογραφία Plate 36:f είναι δική μου λήψη.

Τη θέση του στη δημοσίευση αυτή έχει και ο άντρας μου Ν. Βότσης που με βοήθησε οικονομικά για να παρουσιαστεί άψογα φωτογραφικά το υλικό αυτό. Την ηθική του συμπαράσταση την έχω πάντοτε.

Ανήκουν στον τύπο ανθέμιο και άνθος λωτού ελίκων.[12] Η ομοιότητα που εμφανίζουν με αντίστοιχα της Κορίνθου είναι εμφανέστατη.[13] Μεγάλη ομοιότητα έχομε και με ανάλογα δείγματα ακροκεράμων από τον πώρινο ναό της Μαρμαριάς των Δελφών.[14] Ο τρίτος ηγεμών με μαύρο και πορτοκαλλί χρώμα (Pl. 30:c) εμφανίζει καταπληκτική χρωματική και σχεδιαστική ομοιότητα με ανάλογους του θησαυρού των Μεγαρέων στην Ολυμπία[15] Η ομοιότητα αυτή ίσως δίνει μιά νέα διάσταση στο πρόβλημα της διακόσμησης του θησαυρού των Μεγαρέων από Κορινθίους τεχνίτες ενώ ο λόγος ανέγερσής του ηταν νίκη των Μεγαρέων επί των Κορινθίων.[16] Ο J. Heiden παρόλη την αντίφαση που πιστοποιεί, θεωρεί σίγουρη την Κορινθιακή προέλευση του πήλινου διάκοσμου του θησαυρού.[17]

Η νέα εκδοχή που μπορεί να διατυπωθεί, δεδομένου ότι και η Σικυώνα αναφέρεται σαν πολύ παλαιά κτιριακή παρουσία στο σύνολο των θησαυρών[18] της Ολυμπίας είναι η σκέψη ότι ο διάκοσμος του θησαυρού των Μεγαρέων έγινε ισως από Σικυώνιους τεχνίτες. Έτσι κερδίζουμε από την Σικυώνια γη τρεις άριστης κατασκευής ηγεμόνες καλυπτήρες για τους οποίους ισχύουν απόλυτα οι εσωτερικοί γεωμετρικοί νόμοι που διέπουν τα αρχαϊκά αρχιτεκτονικά πήλινα διακοσμητικά των στεγών μέρη.[19]

Ο 5ος π.Χ. αι. εκπροσωπείται και από τμήμα «μεγαρικής» σίμης με το χαρακτηριστικά κυρτωμένο προφίλ (Pl. 31:a). Φέρει τή χαρακτηριστική εναλλακτική διακόσμηση επτάφυλλων ανθεμίων και κλειστών μπουμπουκιών λουλουδιών λωτού που διακοσμούν και τις δύο ζώνες. Το επίχρισμα των λουλουδιών είναι κίτρινο ενώ ο πηλός είναι κιτρινοπράσινος με μεγάλα μαύρα χαλίκα. Και εδώ η κατάφωρη ομοιότητα με τμήμα της αετωματικής σίμης του θησαυρού των Μεγαρέων γίνεται αμέσως αντιληπτή.[20] Παράλληλα έχομε και στην στέγη 45 των Δελφών[21] και στο S. 28 από την Κόρινθο.[22]

## ΣΙΜΕΣ 4ου π.Χ. ΑΙΩΝΑ ΓΡΑΠΤΕΣ

Οι γραπτές σίμες του 4ου π.Χ. αιώνα είναι τέσσαρες. Η σίμη α (Pl. 31:b) με καμπύλη διατομή εμφανίζει αρμονική διάταξη ενδεκάφυλλων ανθεμίων με ροπή των πετάλων προς

---

[12] Για τον τύπο αυτό των ηγεμόνων καλυπτήρων με την οργανωμένη παράθεση απόψεων και την συνολική έως πρόσφατα βιβλιογραφία πολλά προσφέρει η διατριβή της Βλαχοπούλου-Οικονόμου 1986, σελ. 19.

[13] *Corinth* IV, i και Roebuck 1990, σελ. 59–63, πίν. 7, 8. Για αρχαϊκά ανθέμια βλ. και Winter 1990, σελ. 13–32.

[14] Le Roy 1967, toit 45, σελ. 103, πίν. I έγχρωμη απεικόνιση και pl. 39. Ο Christian Le Roy χαρακτηριστικά αναφέρει "argile jaune couverte crème."

[15] Heiden 1987, σελ. 83 και πίν. 10:2 και Winter 1990, σελ. 13–32, ωραιότατη σχεδιαστική αναπαράσταση της στέγης του Θησαυρού των Μεγαρέων, fig. 7, όπου και εδώ διακρίνεται το ωραίο χέρι και η ευαισθησία του αγαπητού φίλου και εκλεκτού ζωγράφου Κ. Ηλιάκη.

[16] Παυσανίας, Ηλιακά 6,19,4.

[17] Heiden 1987, σελ. 84.

[18] Παυσανίας, Ηλιακά 6,19,1.

[19] Ρωμαίος 1951, σελ. 108–120. Κολοκοτσάς 1990, σελ. 141–148, εικ. 5.

[20] Heiden 1987, πίν. 10:1, σελ. 84.

[21] Le Roy 1967, σελ. 122, πίν. 43.

[22] *Corinth* IV, i και ανάλογα FA 3, FA 19, FA 430, 452 (Roebuck 1990, σελ. 46–47).

τα έξω που εναλλάσσονται με σχηματοποιημένα στεγνά άνθη λωτού με ανοιγμένα έντονα τα σέπαλα. Η βλαστόσπειρα που συνδέει τα δύο φυτικά μοτίβα είναι ακόμη αρκετά χυμώδης. Στην ανώτερη έξεργη ταινία δεν διακρίνεται διακόσμηση. Η κατώτερη ζώνη που εισέχει ελαφρά κοσμείται με την γνωστή σύνθεση του μαιάνδρου και του αβακωτού κοσμήματος. Όμοια διακόσμηση έχομε από την Ν. Στοά της Κορίνθου.[23] Το ίδιο περίπου θέμα έχομε και στη στέγη 81 των Δελφών.[24] Επισημαίνεται επίσης η σχέση με την γραπτή σίμη τύπου ΣΙa από το ιερό του Άμμωνα Δία στην Άφυτη της Χαλκιδικής.[25]

Χαρακτηριστικό και σ'αυτή την περίπτωση είναι, όπως και με το μάτι φαίνεται, αλλά και όπως παραδέχεται ο Καλτσάς, ότι η πήλινη διακόσμηση του ναού πρέπει να είναι κορινθιακής προέλευσης εισηγμένη ή κατασκευασμένη επί τόπου από Κορίνθους τεχνίτες.[26] Τώρα πιά θα μπορούσαμε ίσως να προσθέσουμε πλάϊ στους Κορίνθιους και τους Σικυώνιους τεχνίτες.

Η μοναδική εμπειρία που έχω από την πολύχρονη πείρα και παρατήρηση του υλικού της Κορίνθου και της Σικυώνας με ωθεί στο συμπέρασμα ότι είναι αδύνατος ο διαχωρισμός Κορινθιακών και Σικυώνιων εργαστηρίων.

Σοβαρώτατο στοιχείο για τον ισχυρισμό αυτό είναι, εκτός από το διακοσμητικό αρχιτεκτονικό υλικό που παραθέτουμε εδώ, το πολύ μεγάλο σε αριθμό υλικό που έχει έρθει στο φώς με συστηματικές ανασκαφές από ένα μικρό σχετικά τμήμα της παρατακτικά διατεταγμένης νεκρόπολης της Αρχαίας Σικυώνας που ανέσκαψα επί σειρά ετών.

Γεωμετρικά αγγεία, ειδώλια και αγγεία τέλους 6ου, αρχών 5ου π.Χ. αι., εγχώριες λευκές λήκυθοι, εγχώρια ερυθρόμορφα αγγεία 4ου π.Χ. αι., αξιολογώτατης εκτέλεσης καθώς και μεγάλη ποικιλία ελληνιστικών αγγείων και ειδωλίων που καλύπτουν τη χρονική περίοδο μέχρι και τον 1ο π.Χ. αιώνα καθιστούν σαφή την ταυτότητα των εργαστηρίων των δύο αυτών σημαντικών πόλεων της Β.Δ. Πελοποννήσου.[27]

Σαν σίμη β (Pl. 31:c) αναφέρεται τμήμα με την ίδια διακόσμηση με τη διαφορά ότι σ'αυτήν τα ανθέμια και τα λωτόμορφα άνθη ζωγραφίζονται αμελέστερα και δίνουν την εντύπωση ότι η εσωτερική γεωμετρική σχέση που έδενε τα φυτικά μοτίβα μεταξύ τους έχει διαλυθεί.[28] Στην επάνω ταινία υπάρχει αστράγαλος.

Στη συνέχεια αναφερόμαστε στη σίμη γ (Pl. 31:d) που στην άνω ταινία υπάρχει φέρει κυμάτιο με λογχόσχημα ενδιάμεσα φύλλα ενώ στην κεντρική ζώνη λυγερόκορμα ανθέμια του φλογωτού ρυθμού[29] εναλλασσόμενα με ημίκλειστα άνθη λωτού με πριονωτά σέπαλα. Η κατώτερη εισέχουσα ταινία φέρει τον τύπο σύνθετου μαίανδρου και τετράγωνο με αβακωτό κόσμημα.

---

[23] Corinth I, iv, σελ. 85-86, πίν. 20:3 (two pieces of raking sima) και 20:4 (two types of eaves tiles from south half of Stoa roof [S.90]).
[24] Le Roy 1967, σελ. 156, πίν. 59.
[25] Καλτσάς 1988, σελ. 44 και σχέδιο IV πίν. 5:δ, ε, 6:α.
[26] Καλτσάς 1988, σελ. 68-75 και κύρια σελ. 75.
[27] Θέλω να ελπίζω ότι η τόσο πολύτιμη μελέτη και παρουσίαση του υλικού αυτού δεν θα καθυστερήσει για πολύ.
[28] Φιλαδελφεύς 1926α (αποκάλυψις θεμελίων ναού 1920-1926), σελ. 46-50, εικ. 4.
[29] Le Roy 1967, toit 84, σελ. 173, πίν. 69, 70.

Το επόμενο τμήμα σίμης δ (Pl. 31:e) καθώς και νέο μικρό τμήμα (Pl. 31:f) φαίνεται ότι ανήκει στον ίδιο τύπο σίμης και κοσμείται με γραπτό κυμάτιο. Εδώ στην κύρια ζώνη έχουμε καλογραμμένα φουντωτά ανθέμια που εναλλάσσονται με την ίδια μορφή του ημίκλειστου άνθους λωτού που εκφύεται από τα πριονωτά σέπαλα όπως και στην προηγούμενη σίμη. Η κατώτερη ζώνη φέρει το θέμα σύνθετος μαίανδρος-αβακωτό κόσμημα. Στις δύο σίμες γ και δ πρέπει να επισημανθεί η χρήση στη διακόσμηση λευκοκίτρινου επιχρίσματος. Η κάτω επιφάνεια, όπως φαίνεται στο τεμάχιο από τις πρόσφατες ανασκαφές (Pl. 31:f), θα έφερε διακοσμητική ζώνη αστραγαλοειδούς κοσμήματος.

Χαρακτηριστική είναι η ομοιότητα που παρουσιάζουν οι σίμες γ και δ με τον διάκοσμο της στέγης 84 των Δελφών που ο Le Roy χρονολογεί στο τέλος του 4ου/αρχές του 3ου π.Χ. αιώνων.[30]

## ΣΙΜΕΣ ΜΕ ΑΝΑΓΛΥΦΟ ΔΙΑΚΟΣΜΟ 4ου π.Χ. ΑΙΩΝΑ

Στον 4ο π.Χ. αιώνα εμφανίζεται η σίμη με επίπεδο μέτωπο διακοσμημένο με ανάγλυφες σπείρες και φυτικά θέματα.[31]

Πρώτα θα αναφερθώ στο τμήμα σίμης μακράς πλευράς με ακέραιη λεοντοκεφαλή υδρορρόη (Pls. 32:a και b) που βρέθηκε σε παλαιές ανασκαφές. Δίπλα στη λεοντοκεφαλή από πολύνευρο καυλό άκανθας εκφύονται δύο ελικοειδή φυτικά κοσμήματα. Επάνω διογκωμένη ζώνη με κυμάτιο που αχνοφαίνεται. Η κατώτερη ζώνη λείπει. Η λεοντοκεφαλή αποτελεί έξοχο δείγμα ρεαλιστικής απόδοσης. Πάνω και δίπλα από τα βαθειά χωμένα αλλά έντονα μάτια, εμφανίζονται διογκώσεις από τη σύσπαση των μυών του αγριεμένου θηρίου. Έντονες αυλακώσεις πάνω από την άνω σιαγόνα αποδίδουν και αυτές ρεαλιστικά την ένταση του αγριμιού. Οι τρίχες του μουστακιού αποδίδονται και αυτές έντονα. Στο σημείο αυτό σώζονται ίχνη ιώδους και μελανόφαιου επιχρίσματος ενώ πάνω από τα μάτια έχομε κιτρινωπό επίχρισμα. Ο πηλός είναι ερυθρωπός. Τα πλαινά δόντια της άνω και κάτω σιαγόνας σώζονται ανά δύο. Η χαίτη δηλώνεται με δύο σειρές βοστρύχων που φέρουν ισχυρές αυλακώσεις. Η πρώτη σειρά έχει μία απόλυτη συμμετρία στη διάταξη και μιά χαρακτηριστική λεπτομέρεια, στοιχείο που χαρακτηρίζει το λιοντάρι αυτό. Η συγκεκριμμένη αυτή λεπτομέρεια είναι ότι στο ύψος της άκρης του ματιού και αντίστοιχα πάνω από το μέτωπο, δύο θύσσανοι τριχών συγκλίνουν και εμφανίζουν ένα επίμηκες βάθεμα.

Η δεύτερη σειρά της χαίτης δηλώνεται με θυσσάνους τριών ή τεσσάρων αυλακώσεων που κινούνται δεξιά και αριστερά του κεντρικού άξονα της λεοντοκεφαλής. Τα αυτιά είναι σχετικά μικρά και όχι ιδιαίτερα αιχμηρά.

Οι λεοντοκεφαλές της Ν. Στοάς της Κορίνθου,[32] που εργαστηριακά και χρονολογικά βρίσκονται πολύ κοντά, έχουν στα ίδια σημεία τα βαθουλώματα που

[30] Le Roy 1967, toit 84, σελ. 173, πίν. 69, 70. Έχομε τη διαφορά ότι στους Δελφούς τα σέπαλα δεν είναι πριονωτά.
[31] Καλτσάς 1988, ΣΙΙΙ α σελ. 52, υπ. 33 όπου παραθέτει και πλούσια βιβλιογραφία.
[32] *Corinth* I, iv, σελ. 84, πίν. 20:1. Εδώ πρέπει να αναφερθεί ότι η χρονολόγηση της Ν. Στοάς μετά από νέα στοιχεία που προέκυψαν μετατεθέται στο 320 π.Χ. Williams 1980, σελ. 107–108, και Καλτσάς 1988, σελ. 71.

δημιουργούνται από τη σύγκλιση δύο θυσσάνων της χαίτης. Τό ίδιο χαρακτηριστικό παρουσιάζει και το απότμημα λεοντοκεφαλής από κρηναίο οικοδόμημα του Κεραμεικού που η G. Hübner θεωρεί επείσακτο από την Κόρινθο.[33] Στις πολύ κοντινές σίμες του Εθνικού Αρχαιολογικού Μουσείου αρ. 19565, αγνώστου προελεύσεως, που δεν αφήνουν όμως αμφιβολία για την Κορινθιακή ή Σικυώνια προέλευσή τους,[34] το χαρακτηριστικό αυτό δεν εμφανίζεται, γεγονός που σημαίνει ότι προέρχονται από άλλη μήτρα. Μεγάλη είναι η ομοιότητα που παρουσιάζει και με τη σίμη Σ III α από το Μακεδονικό ιερό του ΄Αμμωνα-Δία στην ΄Αφυτη της Χαλκιδικής.[35]

Από άλλη σίμη έχομε μόνο τη λεοντοκεφαλή υδρορρόη από πηλό κιτρινωπό όχι καλά ψημένο που θρυμματίζεται εύκολα (Pl. 32:c). Η χαίτη αναδεικνύεται με δύο σειρές βοστρύχους και με τη χαρακτηριστική αυλάκωση στη θέση του κεντρικού άξονα που τέμνει και το μέτωπο. Τα μάτια είναι χαρακτηριστικά δουλεμένα με ισχυρά έκτυπο το περίγραμμα. Στον λέοντα αυτόν σώζονται εξαιρετικά καλά τα μπροστινά δόντια της άνω σιαγόνας.

Σπάραγμα ωραιότατης λεοντοκεφαλής υδρορρόης ήρθε στο φώς στο αγρόκτημα Καμπάρδη στην πεδιάδα του Βασιλικού σε ανασκαφική έρευνα που έγινε το καλοκαίρι του 1977 (Pl. 32:d). Μεταφέρθηκε στην ελληνική αποθήκη του Μουσείου της Αρχαίας Κορίνθου όπου όμως δεν κατέστη δυνατή η ανεύρεσή του προφανώς επειδή έχει συσσωρευθεί πληθώρα ανασκαφικού υλικού.[36]

Στον αγρό Καμπάρδη είχαμε την ευχάριστη έκπληξη της ανεύρεσης σε κάποια γωνιά σε καθαρά ελληνιστικό στρώμα—φερμένο όπως φαίνεται με νεροκατεβασιές από μακρύτερα—ενός μικρού χάλκινου αρχαϊκού βοδιού μήκους 0,20 εκ.[37]

Αξίζει να σημειωθεί ότι με τη ζωγραφική αλλά και τή γλυπτική απόδοση των λιονταριών οι Κορίνθιοι είχαν μεγάλη εξοικείωση. Αυτό φαίνεται καθαρά στα μεγαλόπρεπα λιοντάρια του ώριμου Κορινθιακού ρυθμού αλλά και στα αρχαϊκά όπως π.χ. το λιοντάρι του βωμού του ζωγράφου των βωμών.[38]

΄Αλλη επιβεβαίωση για την άριστη κατασκευή αλλά και την ιδιοτυπία των γλυπτών Κορινθιακών Λιονταριών έχομε στο πόρινο της Βοστώνης από την Περαχώρα[39] καθώς και στα δύο μαρμάρινα λιοντάρια από τό Λουτράκι στήν Ny Carlsberg Glyptothek τής Κοπεγχάγης.[40]

Τη σειρά αυτή πλουτίζει το μισό πόρινο τμήμα αρχαϊκού λιονταριού με κατεστραμμένο δυστυχώς το πρόσωπο που βρέθηκε από την γράγουσα σε ταραγμένα ελληνιστικά στρώματα στην πεδιάδα της Αρχαίας Σικυώνας σχετικά κοντά στον αγρό Καμπάρδη, όπου βρέθηκε και το χάλκινο αρχαϊκό βόδι. Θά ήταν πραγματικά πολύ ωραίο άν η αδελφότητα των τεχνιτών του θησαυρού των Σικυωνίων στους Δελφούς μάς

---

[33] Hübner 1973, σελ. 97–99, πίν. 63:1.
[34] Καλτσάς 1988, πίν. 12:β, γ και 13:α-δ.
[35] Καλτσάς 1988, σελ. 52–54 (πίν. 1:α-3, 2:α-δ) σχέδιο I.
[36] Η έγχρωμη διαφάνεια που είδαμε στο συνέδριο είχε γίνει πριν από χρόνια για να χρησιμοποιηθεί για διάλεξη με θέμα την Αρχαία Σικυώνα.
[37] Το μικρό αλλά σημαντικό χάλκινο αρχαϊκό βόδι καθώς και το πόρινο μισό αρχαϊκού λιονταριού για το οποίο γίνεται λόγος αμέσως παρακάτω, θα δημοσιευθούν σύντομα από τη γράφουσα.
[38] Βλ. Amyx 1988, σελ. 272–273, πίν. 124, όπου παρατίθεται και η σχετική βιβλιογραφία.
[39] Caskey 1925, σελ. 15–18, no. 10, και Gabelman 1965, σελ. 66, πίν. 5.
[40] Payne 1931, σελ. 243, πίν. 50:3, 4 και Gabelman 1965, σελ. 45 και 115, 58 πίν. 8.

έχει αφήσει ένα μικρό αντικατοπτρισμό της ιδιαιτερότητας της Σικυώνιας γλυπτικής στην ίδια την πατρίδα τους.

Από τις πρόσφατες ανασκαφές στη βόρεια πλευρά των ναών έχομε τμήμα άριστα τεχνουργημένης σίμης (Pl. 33:a) που διασώζει σε έξεργο ανάγλυφο τις γνωστές φυτικές ελικοειδείς απολήξεις που εκφύονται από πολύνευρο βλαστό και δύο θαλερά φύλλα άκανθας. Δίπλα στο πλούσιο αυτό φυτικό διάκοσμο σώζεται το ένα τρίτο λεοντοκεφαλής όπου η χαίτη δηλώνεται με τρείς σειρές φλογωτούς θυσσάνους. Το αυτί του ζώου είναι μικρό και αιχμηρό.

Και η σίμη αυτή τοποθετείται θεματικά πολύ κοντά στη ΣΙΙΙ α από την ΄Αφυτη,[41] σε εκείνη του Λεωνίδαιου της Ολυμπίας,[42] στις σίμες 19565 του Εθνικού Αρχαιολογικού Μουσείου, και φυσικά και σε εκείνη της Ν. Στοάς της Κορίνθου.[43]

Μικρό αλλά χαρακτηριστικό νέο εύρημα είναι και τεμάχιο σίμης (Pl. 33:b) που διασώζει πολύ καλά τα χρώματα. Στην επάνω ταινία ωά και λογχοειδή φύλλα ενώ στη μεσαία με ιδιαίτερο βάθος ζώνη διασώζεται φυτική ελικοειδής βλαστόσπειρα με έντονες φωτοσκιάσεις. Στο ένα άκρο διαφαίνεται η στρογγυλάδα που θα καλυπτόταν από την λεοντοκεφαλή. Στην ασυνήθιστα πλατειά τρίτη ζώνη σώζεται ο σύνθετος μαίανδρος και ενδιάμεσα το τετράγωνο με το αβακωτό κόσμημα.[44] Στην από κάτω ορατή επιφάνεια υπάρχει αστράγαλος γραπτός με δύο μικρές και μιά μεγάλη χάνδρα. Τα χρώματα που κυριαρχούν είναι το μαύρο και το ιώδες της Κορινθίας.

Τελευταίο αναφέρεται μικρό τμήμα σίμης με σύνθεση φύλλων άκανθας κλωνάρι και ελικοειδείς απολήξεις, που όμως δείχνει πλαδαρή εκτέλεση (Pl. 33:c). Το μεταλλικό μαύρο βάθος και η στεγνή σχετικά εκτέλεση την τοποθετεί στο τέλος 4ου/αρχές 3ου π.Χ. αιώνα. Πρόκειται για εύρημα από παλαιά ανασκαφή.

## ΑΚΡΟΚΕΡΑΜΟΙ

Στις ακροκεράμους κατατάσσονται κορυφαίες αμφίγραφοι (Pls. 34:a και b) σχετικές με της Ν. Στοάς της Κορίνθου,[45] που ίσως προέρχονται από επισκευή, καθώς και από τους Δελφούς[46]

Ακολουθούν δύο κομψότατα δείγματα ακροκεράμων ηγεμόνων (Pls. 34:c και d) που έχουν μεγάλη ομοιότητα με της Κορίνθου[47] από την Ν. Στοά και με της Επιδαύρου που έφερε στο φώς ο Β. Λαμπρινουδάκης από το ιερό του Μαλεάτα.[48] ΄Ομοια έχομε και από την ΄Αφυτη την οποία ο Καλτσάς θεωρεί εισηγμένη από την Κόρινθο[49] καθώς και άλλα δείγματα από την ΄Ηπειρο.[50]

---

[41] Καλτσάς 1988, σελ. 52 και σχέδιο Ι.
[42] Heiden 1987, 6 πίν. 17:1, Olympia, Leonidaion, Rankensima.
[43] Βλ. *Corinth* I, iv, σελ. 85–86, πίν. 20:3.
[44] Βότση 1987β, σελ. 91, εικ. 104.
[45] Βλ. *Corinth* I, iv, σελ. 85–86, πίν. 19:1 και 21:3 (two ridge palmettes from repair).
[46] Le Roy 1967, πίν. 74:1 F.8.
[47] *Corinth* I, iv, πίν. III.
[48] Λαμπρινουδάκης 1975, σελ. 167, πίν. 143, υποσημ. 2.
[49] Καλτσάς 1988, αρ. κατ. 31 και σελ. 64, σχ. VI αναπαράσταση του ηγεμόνα καλυπτήρα τύπου Κ.Ι. από το ιερό του ΄Αμμωνα Δία.
[50] Βλαχοπούλου-Οικονόμου 1986, σελ. 20–21, πίν. 2:α. Ανδρέου 1983, πίν. 6, 7.

Τον τύπο αυτό η Α. Βλαχοπούλου-Οικονόμου τον θεωρεί σταθμό του τέλους του ανάγλυφου ανθεμίου με λωτόσχημο κόσμημα στό κάτω μέρος και πιστεύω ότι έχει απόλυτο δίκαιο.

Στα δύο αυτά δείγματα από την Σικυώνα του τύπου αυτού με το ενδεκάφυλλο ανθέμιο και το ανεστραμμένο κλειστό άνθος λωτού η καρδιά στο μέν ένα είναι λογχόσχημη ενώ στο δεύτερο ωοειδής.

Παρουσιάζεται επίσης κορυφαία ακροκέραμος εξαιρετικής τέχνης με διπλό έξεργο επάλληλο ανθέμιο που εκφύεται από φύλλο άκανθας (Pl. 35:a). Το θέμα επαναλαμβάνεται αντιθετικά.

Σχεδόν όμοια μορφή έχομε από το Λεωνίδαιο της Ολυμπίας,[51] ενώ η ομοιότητα με κορυφώσεις επιτυμβίων στηλών του 4ου π.Χ. αι. είναι εμφανέστατη.[52] Ομοιότητα επίσης αναγνωρίζεται στα κορυφαία μικρά ανθέμια του χρυσού γυναικείου διαδήματος από τή Βεργίνα.[53] Σε ολόκληρο το διάδημα άλλωστε τα θέματα που κυριαρχούν, φυτόμορφες ελικοειδείς απολήξεις, φύλλα άκανθας και λουλούδια, αποτελούν επανάληψη των θεμάτων που στολίζουν τις αρχιτεκτονικές τερρακότες, τα δάπεδα, τις επιτύμβιες στήλες και τα αγγεία του 2ου μισού του 4ου π.Χ. αιώνα.

Στην ακροκέραμο της Σικυώνας μεγάλη σημασία έχει και η εργασία της προπαρασκευής της βασικής επιφάνειας για νά κολλήσουν επάνω της τα φύλλα του ανθεμίου που έβγαιναν από μήτρα.

Άλλη ακροκέραμος (Pl. 35:b) με απλουστευμένο ενδεκάφυλλο ανθέμιο που καλύπτει ολόκληρη την επιφάνεια μπορεί, κρίνοντας από την μεταλικότητα του μαύρου βάθους, να συγγενεύει με το τμήμα της σίμης της Plate 33:c. Σε άλλη σειρά ηγεμόνων ακροκεράμων[54] θα ανήκει η ακροκέραμος της Plate 35:c που προφανώς θα αποτελεί παραφθορά της κλασσικής κατά κάποιο τρόπο ακροκεράμου της σειράς Κ III του Καλτσά με έλικες, άκανθα με συγκλίνοντα φύλλα και μικρό ανθεμωτό πυρήνα που απαντάται πολύ συχνά στη Μακεδονία.

Η ακροκέραμος της Σικυώνας εικονίζει το θέμα: βάση τρία ή τέσσερα φύλλα άκανθας από όπου εκφύονται ελικοειδείς και κρινοειδείς μίσχοι, ενώ στο μέσο περίπου του ύψους της επιφάνειας αναπτύσσεται έντονα έκτυπο οκτάφυλλο ανθέμιο ενώ από το κεντρικό φύλλο της ακάνθινης βάσης αναδύεται λεπτός μίσχος που καταλήγει σε μαργαριτοειδές άνθος. Ανάλογο έχομε από τους Δελφούς[55] ενώ στη μαρμάρινη διακόσμηση των ναών της Μ. Ασίας βρίσκομε πολλές ανάλογες συνθέσεις.[56] Δείγμα παρεμφερών φυτικών διακοσμητικών θεμάτων σε εγχώριο πωρόλιθο μάς δίνει τμήμα σίμης[57] που απόκειται στην αυλή του μικρού Μουσείου της Σικυώνας (Pl. 35:d).

Άλλο είδος αρχιτεκτονικού διακόσμου που πρέπει να αναφερθεί είναι οι στρωτήρες ηγεμόνες με γραπτή διακόσμηση στην κάτω επιφάνεια.

---

[51] Heiden 1987, Taf. 17:1.
[52] Βλ. πολλά παραδείγματα στο έργο του Möbius 1929 σε στήλες 4ου π.Χ. αιώνα.
[53] Ανδρόνικος 1984, σελ. 196–197.
[54] Καλτσάς 1988, σελ. 65, σχ. XIX, πίν. 15:α, υποσημ. 168. Βλ. και δημοσίευση Μακαρόνας και Γιούρη 1989, πίν. 11 (φωτ. και σχέδιο Χρ. Λεφάκη), και Παντερμαλής 1987, σελ. 579–605, πίν. 117, 118.
[55] Le Roy 1967, πίν. 83:1, Α.152.
[56] Βλ. Charboneaux, Martin, και Villard 1970, σελ. 31, im. 26. Didymes, temple d'Apollon, chapiteau de pilastre à decor floral (détail).
[57] Lauter 1986, πίν. 38:b.

Από τις νέες ανασκαφές έχομε τμήμα (Pl. 36:a) που εύκολα μπορεί νά συγκριθεί με τη στέγη 81 των Δελφών[58] καθώς και άλλα δύο αποτμήματα με εναλλασσόμενα ανθέμια και κλειστό στο ένα ανοιχτό στο άλλο λουλούδια λωτού (Pls. 36:b και c). Τέλος αναφέρονται άλλα δύο τμήματα στρωτήρων ηγεμόνων με λυγερόκορμα άνθη (φλογωτός ρυθμός) και ανοιχτά άνθη λωτού που αναδύονται από πριονωτά σέπαλα (Pls. 36:d και e).[59] Στο ένα (Pl. 36:d) όλα τά φύλλα έχουν γραμμικά περιγράμματα.[60]

Αξίζει να αναφερθεί ότι ως πρόφατα δεν είχαμε στοιχεία για την ύπαρξη κεραμεικών εγχωρίων εργαστηρίων εκτός βέβαια από τη μαρτυρία της γραπτής παράδοσης.

Τώρα όμως και ιδιαίτερα μετά το έτος 1978 σε δοκιμαστική ανασκαφή στον αγρό Χατζηδάκη επάνω στο οροπέδιο βρέθηκε πλήθος ύστερων ακροκέραμων, μεγάλα κομμάτια κακοψημένου πηλού, πολλά τμήματα από λεοντοκεφαλές υδρορρόες (Pl. 36:f) καθώς και μήτρα ομοιώματος ψαριού.

Το υλικό αυτό χρειάζεται καθαρισμό και συντήρηση πρίν από την ολοκληρωμένη δημοσίευση, η σημασία όμως εντοπισμού εργαστηρίου στη Σικυώνα είναι μεγάλη.

Από το υλικό που παρουσιάζεται στο συνέδριο αυτό με τρόπο συνοπτικό πιστεύω ότι αρχίζει σιγά σιγά να αναδύεται η αυτοτέλεια της Σικυώνας δίπλα στη μεγάλη παρουσία της Κορίνθου.

Από τη Σικυώνα και την Κόρινθο φαίνεται πιά ολοκάθαρα ότι θα ξεκινούσαν τα συνάφια των τεχνιτών για ολόκληρη τήν Πελοπόννησο αλλά και την Βόρεια Ελλάδα, Θεσσαλία, Μακεδονία.

Τα έξοχα ψηφιδωτά των ανδρώνων των οικιών της Σικυώνας[61] με τα λεπταίσθητα ανθέμια και εκείνη την ατελείωτη ευφορία των άνθινων πλοχμών στο ψηφιδωτό του ύστερου 4ου π.Χ. αι., που υπάρχει τοποθετημένο σέ μιά από τις αίθουσες του τοπικού Μουσείου, που ολοφάνερα αναπαράγονται στα ψηφιδωτά δάπεδα οικιών και στις γραπτές διακοσμήσεις τάφων της Μακεδονίας, θεωρώ, ήδη από πολλά χρόνια, ότι αποτελούν αναντίρρητη μαρτυρία για την επίδραση που άσκησαν στην διακοσμητική γλώσσα της Μακεδονίας αλλά και της Ηπείρου.

Οι μονογραφίες, του Ν. Καλτσά για τις κεραμώσεις της Μακεδονίας,[62] η μελέτη των οικιών της Πέλλας[63] καθώς και η μονογραφία της Α. Βλαχοπούλου-Οικονόμου για την Ήπειρο[64] θαρρώ ότι οδεύουν πρός την άποψη αυτή. Πιστεύω ότι στο τόσο χρήσιμο αυτό συνέδριο για τις αρχιτεκτονικές τερρακότες θα καταδειχθούν από όλους τους συναδέλφους που μελετούν το ίδιο θέμα τα κοινά υπόγεια ρεύματα που διέτρεχαν την γλυκύτατη Ιωνία, την αυστηρή Πελοπόννησο, τήν κρυστάλλινη Αττική και μεταφέρονταν με μονοπάτια ορεινά και θαλασσινά στην Φωκίδα, Ακαρνανία, Ήπειρο καθώς και στη Θεσσαλία, Μακεδονία. Αυτή ακριβώς την πραγματικότητα

---

[58] Le Roy 1967, toit 81, πίν. 62 et 64 (τέλους 4ου π.Χ. αιώνα).

[59] Βλ. σχετική ομοιότητα με τμήμα σίμης από περισυλλογή από την Άφυτη, Καλτσάς 1988, αρ. κατ. 19, σχέδιο V ΣΙβ από το ιερό του Άμμωνα Δία και σχέδια ΧΙΙ, αριθ. κατ. 48 ΣΙVα από τη Βεργίνα.

[60] Σχετικά έχομε από τους Δελφούς στο Le Roy 1967, Α. 75, serie 64, πίν. 52.

[61] Votsis 1976, σελ. 575–578 σχέδιο Γοργονείου Κ. Ηλιάκη και γενικώτερη εργασία η μελέτη του Salzmann 1982.

[62] Καλτσάς 1988.

[63] Μακαρόνας και Γιούρη 1989.

[64] Βλαχοπούλου-Οικονόμου 1986.

του ζωντανού ιστού του ελλαδικού χώρου που μυρμήγκιαζε από τις εσώτερες διεργασίες του να δίνει και να παίρνει επιρροές που εμείς οι αρχαιολόγοι γνωρίζομε πολύ καλά, ίσως θα έπρεπε να τη δούν και να τη δεχτούν και επιστήμονες που κάτω από άλλου είδους αναγκαιότητες την ξεχνούν.

Βιβλιογραφία

Amyx, D. A. 1988. *Corinthian Vase Painting of the Archaic Period*, Berkeley
Ανδρέου, Η. 1983. «Το μικρό θέατρο της Αμβρακίας», Ηπειρωτικά Χρονικά 25, σελ. 9–23
Ανδρόνικος, Μ. 1984. *Βεργίνα. Οι βασιλικοί τάφοι*, Αθήνα
Caskey, J. 1925. *Catalogue of Greek and Roman Sculptures*, Cambridge
Charbonneaux, J., R. Martin, και F. Villard. 1970. *Grèce hellenistique*, Paris
*Corinth* I, iv = O. Broneer, *The South Stoa and Its Roman Successors* (*Corinth* I, iv), Princeton 1954
*Corinth* IV, i = I. Thallon-Hill και L. S. King, *Decorated Architectural Terracottas* (*Corinth* IV, i), Princeton 1929
Φαράκλας, Ν. 1971. «Αρχαία Σικυωνία. Αρχαίες ελληνικές πόλεις», Αθήνα
Φιλαδελφεύς, Α. 1926α. «Ανασκαφαί Σικυώνος», Δελτ 10, 1926 [1929], σελ. 46–50
———. 1926β. «Αρχαιολογική Συλλογή Σικυώνος», Δελτ 10, 1926 [1929] Παράρτημα, σελ. 17–23
Gabelman, H. 1965. *Studien zum frühgriechischen Löwenbild*, Berlin
Heiden, J. 1987. *Korinthische Dachziegel. Zur Entwicklung der korinthischen Dächer*, Frankfurt/Bern/New York/Paris
*Hesperia* 59 = *Proceedings of the First International Conference on Archaic Greek Architectural Terracottas, Athens, December 2–4, 1988* (*Hesperia* 59, 1990), N. A. Winter, επιμ.
Hübner, G. 1973. "Dachterrakotten aus dem Kerameikos von Athen. Ein Beiträge zur Bauornamentik des 5 und 4 Jhs. v. Chr.," *AM* 88, σελ. 67–143
Καλτσάς, Ν. 1988. *Πήλινες διακοσμημένες κεραμώσεις από τη Μακεδονία*, Αθήνα
Κολοκοτσάς, Κ. 1990. «Αρμονικαί χαράξεις στα αρχαϊκά αρχιτεκτονικά πήλινα του Άργους και της Επιδαύρου», εν *Hesperia* 59, σελ. 141–148
Κρυστάλλη, Π. 1967. «Σικυών», Δελτ 22, 1967, Β΄1 [1968], σελ. 164–166
Κρυστάλλη-Βότση, Π. 1976. «Ανασκαφή Σικυώνος», Δελτ 31, 1976, Β΄ [1984], σελ. 65
Λαμπρινουδάκης, Β. 1975. «Ιερόν Μαλεάτου Απόλλωνος εις Επίδαυρον», Πρακτικά 1975 [1977], σελ. 162–175
Lauter, H. 1986. *Die Architektur des Hellenismus*, Darmstadt
Le Roy, Ch. 1967. *Les terres cuites architecturales* (*Fouilles de Delphes* II), Paris
Μακαρόνας, Χ., και Ε. Γιούρη. 1989. *Οι οικίες αρπαγής της Ελένης και Διονύσου της Πέλλας*, Αθήνα
Martin, R. 1972. «Rapports sur les conférences de l'année scolaire 1971–1972», *Annuaire de l'École Pratiques des Hautes Études*, Paris, σελ. 233–237
Möbius, H. 1929. *Die Ornamente des griechischen Grabstelen*, Berlin
Ορλάνδος, Α. 1936. «Ανασκαφή Σικυώνος», Πρακτικά 1936 [1937], σελ. 86–94
Παντερμαλής, Δ. 1987. «Η κεράμωση των ανακτόρων στη Βεργίνα», Άμητος. Τιμητικός τόμος για τον καθηγητή Μανόλη Ανδρόνικο II, Θεσσαλονίκη, σελ. 579–605
Payne, H. 1931. *Necrocorinthia*, Oxford
Roebuck, M. C. 1990. "Archaic Architectural Terracottas from Corinth," εν *Hesperia* 59, σελ. 47–63
Ρωμαίος, Κ. 1951. *Κέραμοι της Καλυδώνος*, Αθήνα
Salzmann, D. 1982. *Untersuchungen zu den antiken Kieselmosaiken, von den Anfängen bis zum Beginn der Tesseratechnik* (*Archäologische Forschungen* 10), Berlin
Βλαχοπούλου-Οικονόμου, Α. 1986. *Ηγεμόνες και κορυφαίες κέραμοι με διακόσμηση από την Ήπειρο. Τύπος «άνθους λωτού-ελίκων».* (διδ. διατριβή), Ιωάννινα
Βότση, Π. 1984. Έργον 1984 [1985], σελ. 61–62
———. 1987α. «Ανασκαφή Σικυώνος», Πρακτικά 1987 [1991], σελ. 66–68
———. 1987β. Έργον 1987 [1988], σελ. 91–92
Votsis, K. 1976. "Nouvelle mosaïque de Sicyon," *BCH* 100, σελ. 575–588

Williams, C. K., II. 1980. "Corinth Excavations, 1979," *Hesperia* 49, σελ. 107–134
Winter, N. A. 1990. "Defining Regional Styles in Archaic Greek Architectural Terracottas," εν *Hesperia* 59, σελ. 13–32

CALLIOPI KRYSTALLI-VOTSI

Louki Akrita 38
Athens, Philothei 152 37
Greece

# DIE DACHTERRAKOTTEN VON AIGEIRA

(PLATES 37–40)

DIE FRÜHESTEN architekonischen Terrakotten lassen sich in Aigeira bis ins 7. Jh. v. Chr. zurückverfolgen. Der Langhausbau der Iphigeneia-Artemis auf der Akropolis (noch ohne Ringhalle) hatte Cellaausmaße von 6,00 × 20,00 m.[1] Trotz seiner Altertümlichkeit dürfte er bereits ein Terrakottadach besessen haben, da dem Gebäude mit ziemlicher Sicherheit Stroterfragmente zugewiesen werden dürfen,[2] die wie der Tempel in die Früharchaik zu datieren sind. Die Ziegel weisen einen rötlich gebrannten Ton auf (Munsell 7,5YR 7/6), was für eine lokale Produktion spricht.

Das älteste Terrakottadach von Aigeira würde gut zu den Befunden aus Korinth und Isthmia passen, wo jeweils schon im frühen 7. Jh. v. Chr. Tondächer nachzuweisen sind.[3]

In frühklassischer Zeit bekam der Bau ein neues Dach, welches seinen Vorgänger sicherlich weit an Schmuck und Farbenpracht übertraf. Die meisten Stücke wurden davon in einer 3,50 m tiefen Zisterne südlich des Baues gefunden.[4] Sämtliche Dachziegel folgen dem korinthischen Typus mit flachen Stroteren und eckigen Kalypteren. Darüberhinaus fanden sich bemalte Antefixe mit plastischem Palmettendekor, unplastisch bemalte Firstpalmetten sowie Randziegel von der Traufseite des Daches mit gemalten Randornamenten. Nach der Tonbeschaffenheit lassen sich zwei Gruppen voneinander unterscheiden: das Material der einen hat die typische korinthische Konsistenz in grünlich-gelber Färbung mit grobkörniger grauer bis schwarzer Magerung (Farbe: Munsell 10YR 8/6 bis 10YR 7/3, yellow bis pale brown) und ist mäßig hart gebrannt. Ein Vergleich mit Ziegeln aus Korinth zeigt, daß es sich um die gleiche Tonart handelt. Die zweite Gruppe weist einen rötlichen, nicht sehr hart gebrannten Ton mit weniger Magerung auf (Munsell 5YR 6 bis 5YR 7/4, light reddish brown bis pink), was auf eine einheimische Produktion schließen läßt. Jene Stücke der ersten Gruppe sind charakteristisch für das frühklassische Dach. Die zweite Gruppe umfaßt solche Stücke, die entweder späteren Gebäuden angehören oder im Zuge von Reparaturarbeiten angefertigt wurden.

Die Flachziegel weisen eine Breite von 63 cm auf.[5] Sie tragen an den seitlichen Stoßkanten leichte Aufbiegungen, sodaß der darüberliegende Kalypter gegen Verrutschen gesichert war. Zusätzlich, um eine optimale Fixierung insbesondere der untersten Ziegellage am Dachrand zu erreichen, wurden in den gebrannten Stroter Nacharbeitungen

---

[1] Zum Tempel B auf der Akropolis, siehe Alzinger 1985, S. 430–431, 446–451 sowie Abb. 23. Siehe auch Alzinger 1988, S. 20–23, Taf. 6.
[2] Alzinger 1985, S. 431, Abb. 27.
[3] Roebuck 1955, S. 156, Taf. 62:e–g; Robinson 1976, S. 231–235, Abb. 9; *Isthmia* I, S. 40–53.
[4] Zu den Architekturfunden aus der Zisterne, siehe Alzinger 1985, S. 431–451.
[5] Die Ziegellänge ist uns durch kein einziges Fragment erhalten.

vorgenommen. Vertiefungen in den seitlichen Aufbiegungen sollten jenen Halterungszapfen aufnehmen, der an der Unterseite sowohl der Antefixe als auch der gewöhnlichen Kalyptere vorhanden ist[6] (Pl. 37:a).

Die Randziegel der Traufseite mußten leicht über das darunter befindliche Steingeison vorspringen, um das Abtropfen des Regenwassers zu gewährleisten. Das läßt sich auch an der Unterseite der Hegemones ablesen: ihre äußerste Zone—nur der vorkragende, von unten sichtbare Teil—ist als glattgestrichener Saum ausgebildet und mit einem roten Unterstreif von 2,2 bis 3,3 cm Breite farblich abgesetzt. An den Traufseiten sind die Strotere mit gemalten Mäandern verziert, dazwischen liegen freistehende Rechtecke.[7]

Was den Zuschnitt der Traufziegel betrifft, so ist der untere Frontwinkel mit 76° anzunehmen vorausgesetzt, daß die Stirn senkrecht gestanden hat. Unter diesen Umständen ließe sich eine Dachschräge von 14° rekonstruieren.[8]

Die Enden der Kalyptere an den Traufseiten des Daches fanden mit plastisch geformten Antefixen ihren Abschluß. Insgesamt wurden bei den Grabungen elf Stirnziegel gefunden, deren erhabene Teile des Ornaments durch helle Ockerfarbe vom dunklen Hintergrund abgesetzt sind (hell-auf-dunkel-Technik)[9] (Pl. 37:b). Völlig abweichend in der Farbgebung, aber dem gleichen Model wie die "weißfigurigen" Antefixe entstammend, zeigt sich ein Stirnziegel (A1)[10] (Pl. 37:d), der in der archaischen Weise bemalt ist. Die Farben von Lotos und Palmette alternieren zwischen ockergelb und schwarz, der Hintergrund hat die Farbe des Tons. Das Dach gehört somit in die Zeit des Übergangs von der schwarz-, zur weißfigurigen Technik.

Das Motiv der Antefixe, die über einer Lotosblüte stehende Palmette, ist direkt von den spätarchaischen Antefixen abgeleitet.[11] Dennoch scheinen diese Ziegel Aigeiras der frühklassischen Periode anzugehören, da Heiden die frühesten rotfigurigen Simen erst in das fortgeschrittene erste Viertel des 5. Jh. v. Chr. datiert.[12] Die Übergangsphase, in der die korinthischen Werkstätten die rotfigurige Technik auf Dachterrakotten übertrugen, dokumentieren auch zwei Antefixe aus Kalaureia, die sich stilistisch sehr nahe stehen.[13] Eines ist in schwarzfiguriger Technik, das andere in der neuen Technik bemalt. Obzwar man lange an der Entstehungszeit der Stirnziegel im letzten Viertel des 6. Jh. v. Chr. festhielt,

---

[6] Zum Antefix A2 mit dem Zapfen zur Fixierung, siehe Alzinger 1985, S. 432, Abb. 29.

[7] Alzinger 1985, S. 441, Abb. 37.

[8] Zur Schrägstellung der Traufziegel im 6. und 5. Jh. v. Chr., siehe Buschor 1933, S. 3.

[9] Alzinger 1985, S. 435, Abb. 31.

[10] Alzinger 1985, S. 436, Abb. 32:a, b.

[11] Vorbildlich erscheinen hierfür die Antefixe des Megarerschatzhauses. Vgl. dazu *Olympia* II, S. 195, Taf. 119:5.

[12] Heiden 1987, S. 113–116. Bei den Simen aus Korinth (S27, S27a, S28, S52) und den delphischen Simen (S. 179/180 und S. 31/32) ist das Profil der abgesetzten Wellensima erstmals mit einer rotfigurigen Lotos-Palmetten Kette verziert. Zu Korinth, siehe *Corinth* IV, i, S. 22–24, Abb. 19:a, 20–22. Zu Delphi, siehe Le Roy 1967, S. 121–127, Taf. 43, 102.

[13] Van Buren 1926, S. 42, 151, Taf. VI, Abb. 16; Wide und Kjellberg 1895, S. 272–273, Abb. 4, 5; Welter 1941, S. 44, Taf. 31:b, c.

bringt sie Heiden zeitlich mit den übrigen in rotfiguriger Malerei ausgeführten Dächern in Verbindung und datiert sie somit ebenfalls in die Jahre um 480/475 v. Chr.[14] In dieser Zeit mag auch die Gestaltung des zweiten Tondaches vom Iphigeneia-Artemistempel in Aigeira erfolgt sein.[15]

Schon bald nach der Fertigstellung dürften Teile des Daches ausgebessert worden sein. Vermutlich beschädigte Stücke wurden durch einheimische Produkte ersetzt. Zwei aufgefundene Antefixe A12 und A13 bilden Beispiele hierfür.[16] Sie sind in der Tonart mit dem Material der aus einheimischen Manufakturen stammenden Keramik zu vergleichen. Auch ist die Technik im Vergleich zu den übrigen 11 Antefixen verschieden: sie besaßen keinen Halterungszapfen und waren insgesamt etwas schmäler (19 cm gegenüber durchschnittlich 20,5 cm). Im Vergleich zur ersten Serie zeigt sich auch beim Bruchstück A13, daß das Mittelblatt oben nicht spitz, sondern rund gestaltet ist.

Die Strotere des frühklassischen Daches waren an den Rändern der beiden Giebelseiten zu einer einfachen Sima aufgebogen, von der noch vier unterschiedlich große Teile erhalten sind[17] (Pl. 37:c). Die an die Sima angearbeiteten Strotere sind nicht mehr vorhanden. Alle Stücke bestehen aus grünlich-gelbem Ton und sind nach dem Schema der Sima des Schatzhauses von Megara in Olympia bemalt,[18] das um 510 v. Chr. datiert wird. Dieser schon im zweiten Viertel des 6. Jh. v. Chr. von den korinthischen Werkstätten erfundene Dachtypus, welcher den Wechsel vom Blattstabdekor zum Lotos-Palmetten Motiv vollzog,[19] hat sich bis zum Megarerschatzhaus gefestigt, und führt von dort unverändert in die Klassik.

Das Bindeglied zwischen Giebelseite und den Traufseiten bildeten in Aigeira ähnlich dem Megarerschatzhaus sicherlich Akroterkästen mit vorgeblendeten Löwenkopfwasserspeiern,[20] von denen zwar keine Überreste gefunden wurden, die aber dennoch vorausgesetzt werden dürfen.

Was schließlich den Dachfirst betrifft, so waren an den Kreuzungspunkten von Kalypter und Firstziegel jeweils Kombinationen von Deckziegeln angebracht, die alle hochgestellte Fächerpalmetten mit den Sichtseiten zu den beiden Traufseiten trugen[21] (Pl. 37:e). Die Palmettenblätter sind nur im Umriß modelliert, die Innenzeichnung ist gemalt, im Gegensatz zu den Antefixen nicht plastisch geformt. Die Technik zeigt bei allen Stücken die gleiche

---

[14] Heiden 1987, S. 124.

[15] Alzinger (1985, S. 440) hielt in seiner Publikation dieses Dach noch für älter und schlug aufgrund der Ornamentik und ihrer Bemalung einen zeitlichen Ansatz um 500 v. Chr. vor.

[16] Alzinger 1985, S. 437–438 mit Abb. 33:a, b und 34.

[17] Alzinger 1985, S. 438–439 mit Abb. 35:a, b.

[18] *Olympia* II, S. 195, Taf. 119:4.

[19] Als ältestes Dach, deren Torussima mit einer fortlaufenden Anthemienkette verziert ist, mag jenes des älteren Apollontempels von Korinth gelten, für dessen Dach man ein Entstehungsdatum um oder kurz nach 560 v. Chr. annehmen darf. Zur Datierung des Tempels, siehe Heiden 1987, S. 73; zu den Dachterrakotten, siehe Heiden 1987, S. 70–80 mit Lit. und Abb. Taf. 9.

[20] Vgl. dazu *Olympia* II, S. 195, Taf. 119:5 (Rekonstruktion); Mallwitz 1972, S. 175, Abb. 136.

[21] Alzinger 1985, S. 434, Abb. 30:a, b.

hell-auf-dunkel Malerei. Insgesamt wurden in der Zisterne acht gut erhaltene Stücke gefunden. Bei sechs Exemplaren sind die angearbeiteten Kalypterteile vollständig erhalten, bei keinem jedoch der Firstdeckziegel, der zumindest bei allen in Ansätzen vorhanden ist. Er ist nur an einer Seite angearbeitet und hatte vermutlich die Länge, die der Breite eines Stroters entsprach.[22]

Von späteren Ausbesserungen stammen vermutlich zwei Kalyptere (K1 und K2) aus korinthischem Ton, die beide an der Stirnseite den 2 cm hohen Abdruck eines Ringes aufweisen. Die Darstellung zeigt Amymone am Wasserkrug sitzend.[23] Die Stilistik des Bildes veranlaßt Alzinger dazu, den Ring und damit die erste Dachreparatur in das Jahrzehnt zwischen 460 und 450 v. Chr. zu datieren.[24] Aus einheimischem Ton (rosa-beige) mit gut geglätteter Oberfläche dürfte demgegenüber ein weiterer Kalypter sein, der an derselben Stelle zwei Ringabdrücke aufweist, mit der Darstellung eines Hundes, der einen Hasen beißt. Wie bei den Terrakotten A12 und A13, handelt es sich hier mit einiger Wahrscheinlichkeit um spätere Ausbesserungen einer einheimischen Manufaktur.

Aus dem gleichen Ton wie A12 und A13 ist der Firstziegel F17 gemacht.[25] Die etwas klobige Zeichnung, die Art der Darstellung erinnert an Firstpalmetten, wie sie uns von der Südstoa in Korinth bekannt sind.[26] Danach wäre der Firstziegel F17 in das dritte Viertel des 4. Jh. v. Chr. zu datieren und ist vielleicht der letzten Dachreparatur zuzuweisen.

Neben den Palmettenantefixen A1–A11 und den Nachformungen A12 und A13 wurden in der Zisterne noch vier weitere Antefixe gefunden, die zwar aus korinthischem Ton, jedoch aus vollkommen verschiedenen Modeln geformt sind (Pl. 38:a).[27] Bei diesen Stücken sitzt die krönende Palmette einem reich ornamentierten Sockel auf. Ihrem Aufbau nach sind diese Stirnziegel neben klassische Beispiele zu stellen wie die Antefixe der Pheidias Werkstatt in Olympia aus der zweiten Hälfte des 5. Jh. v. Chr.,[28] auf denen das früheste Auftreten des Dekorationssystems attischer Akrotere zu verzeichnen ist; sie dokumentieren die Übernahme des Akanthus in die korinthische Dachterrakottenornamentik.[29] Das klassische Antefix hat im Gegensatz zu den früheren Beispielen keinen Halterungszapfen.

Die Funde in der Zisterne reichen bis in die hellenistische Zeit, woraus zu folgern ist, daß damals das Dach des Tempels B abgetragen wurde. In der zweiten Hälfte des 3. Jh. war der Bau sicher nicht mehr in Verwendung, denn in seinem Westteil wurde eine Kalkwanne eingebaut. Darin lag eine Münze des Ptolemaios III (246–221).

Etwa 21 m nordwestlich der Skene des Theaters befindet sich ein kleiner Tempel, der Naiskos D, der als der von Pausanias angeführte Zeustempel identifiziert werden

---

[22] Zur Kombination von Dachziegel und Firstpalmette, vgl. Le Roy 1967, S. 174–175, Nr. 8 und 9, Taf. 70–72.
[23] Alzinger 1985, S. 442, Abb. 38.
[24] Alzinger 1985, S. 441.
[25] Alzinger 1985, S. 443, Abb. 39.
[26] *Corinth* I, iv, S. 86 und 96, Taf. 21.
[27] Alzinger 1985, S. 445, Abb. 40.
[28] *OlForsch* V, S. 116–117, Taf. 17 und 44:2.
[29] Zum attischen Einfluss, der sich an den meisten korinthischen Dächern der Hochklassik bemerkbar macht, siehe Heiden 1987, S. 112–113.

konnte.[30] Die erste Bauphase erfolgte in der ersten Hälfte des 3. Jh. v. Chr.,[31] als das hellenistische Zeusheiligtum mit einem Theater ausgestattet wurde. Diese Bautätigkeit war jene Konsequenz, die auf die Gründung des 2. achäischen Bundes (281/280 v. Chr.) und den etwas späteren Anschluß Aigeiras folgte,[32] da man aus politischen Gründen mit Repräsentationsbauten aufwarten wollte.

Von den verzierten Teilen des Naiskosdaches wurden Fragmente der Rankensima, welche die Traufränder schmückte gefunden,[33] ein Antefix sowie zahlreiche Fragmente von Löwenkopfwasserspeiern. Trotz der geringen Überreste läßt sich bei genauerer Betrachtung der Stücke, was den Aufbau der Sima, die Gestaltung der Ranken, Akanthusblätter und Löwenköpfe betrifft, eine gewisse Verwandtschaft zum Dach der Südstoa in Korinth erkennen,[34] die nach den neuesten Untersuchungen in den letzten Jahren des 4. Jh. v. Chr. entstanden sein muß.[35] Wie in Korinth wird auch in Aigeira jeder Simenblock einen geschlossenen Ornamentkreis gebildet haben. Das Rankensimenfragment E 5A (Pl. 38:b) vom Naiskos D ist deshalb so zu ergänzen, daß kannelierte Stengel hinter den Löwenköpfen aus einem Akanthusblatt entspringen. Aus einem geteilten Hüllenblatt, das durch einen Fruchtknoten gegen den Stengel abgesetzt ist, wachsen unmittelbar zwei flache Voluten. Die Südstoa zeigt noch die frühere Gliederung des Deckblattes, das in der gleichen Richtung wie die Stengelkannelierung verläuft und ihr mitunter sogar genau entspricht. Ab dem 3. Jh. v. Chr. wird ein Richtungsgegensatz der Deckblattfaltung angestrebt.[36] Dieses Schema ist auch auf den Simen Aigeiras vertreten.

Die stilistische Verwandtschaft zur Südstoa von Korinth zeigt sich vorwiegend in der Rankernornamentik. Allerdings weist die Traufsima des Naiskos D schon eine nachlässigere, auf derbe Reliefwirkung berechnete Bildung auf, was für das Dekor ab dem 3. Jh. v. Chr. bezeichnend ist. Ihre Beziehung zum zweigliedrigen hellenistischen Schema[37] spricht für eine Entstehung noch vor dem Ende 3. Jh. v. Chr.

Im Anschluß an die Südstoa soll auf drei weitere Simenfragmente aus Korinth hingewiesen werden, die ebenfalls dem Fragment E 5A vom Naiskos D sehr ähnlich sind. FS 433, das im Asklepieion gefunden wurde, kommt der Sima der Südstoa sehr nahe und ist aufgrund der Stratigraphie dem 4. oder 3. Jh. v. Chr. zuzuordnen.[38] FS 418 und FS 419 ohne Angabe

---

[30] Zu den Ausführungen des Pausanias, der im 2. Jh. n. Chr. Aigeira besuchte, siehe Pausanias 7,26,4–5, 10.
[31] Zum Naiskos D, siehe Gogos 1986, S. 32–38 mit Abb. 65, der Rekonstruktion des gesamten Theaterbereiches.
[32] Über den achäischen Bund des 3. Jh. v. Chr., siehe Urban 1979.
[33] Das Dach des Südost-Baues in Olympia ist nach dem 200 Jahre älteren Dach der Löwensima in Kalydon das älteste, das wieder eine Sima an der Traufseite zeigt. Mit der Wiedereinführung der Horizontalsima und den ersten Ansätzen, ein gemaltes Ornament in die Dreidimensionalität zu tragen, bildet das Dach des Südost-Baues, das in die Jahre nach 370 v. Chr. zu datieren ist, den Vorläufer der reliefierten Rankensima. Vgl. dazu Heiden 1987, S. 127–131 mit Lit. und Abb. Taf. 16.
[34] Siehe dazu *Corinth* I, iv, S. 83–88, 96, Taf. 19–22.
[35] Siehe dazu Heiden 1987, S. 141–142.
[36] Siehe dazu Schede 1909, S. 63.
[37] Schede 1909, S. 80–83.
[38] Herrn Professor Charles K. Williams, II, danke ich sehr herzlich, der mir eine Durchsicht der zum größten Teil unpublizierten Dachterrakotten von Korinth ermöglichte.

des Fundortes sind m.E. wegen ihrer bereits teigigen, schlaffen Formen später, eventuell ins ausgehende 3. Jh. v. Chr. zu datieren.[39]

Im Hellenismus verlieren die korinthischen Werkstätten völlig ihre Bedeutung für den außerkorinthischen Markt. Neue Impulse gibt es nicht, und die Handwerker zitieren nur noch ältere Dachränder. So haben sich die Bauleute von Aigeira nicht nur an den Ornamentformen Korinths orientiert, sondern nahmen auch Einflüsse aus Argos auf. Dies läßt sich an den Antefixen ablesen, die den Simen des Naiskos D aufsaßen.[40] E 24/88 (Pl. 38:c) ähnelt sehr dem Ziegel der Serie C 26659 aus Argos,[41] der sich keinem bestimmten Gebäude zuweisen läßt, und von Mde. Billot in das erste Drittel des 4. Jh. v. Chr. datiert wird.[42] Die argivische Werkstatt hat für den Stirnziegel das klassische Akroterornament stark abgewandelt.[43] An die Stelle des äußeren Volutenpaares treten lange Blütenstengel und die Voluten besitzen akanthisierte Deckblätter. An die klassischen Ziegel der Serie C 26659 schließt das Antefix C 2687 an, dessen reiche Gliederung und der zur Seite fallende Blütenstengel eine noch frühhellenistische Entstehung annehmen lassen.[44]

Die Tatsache, daß die gleichen Stirnziegel, wie sie dem frühen Naiskos zuzuordnen sind, auch im Theaterbereich gefunden wurden, legt nahe, das Bühnengebäude etwa gleichzeitig mit dem Naiskos D anzusetzen.[45] Was nun die Gestaltung der Tonsima der hellenistischen Skene betrifft, so läßt ein Vergleich mit der Sima des Naiskos D deutliche Parallelen erkennen. Eine Gegenüberstellung der Simenfragmente E 5A (Pl. 38:b) und ATK/87 Theater ATK 21/72 (Pl. 38:d) und ATK 19/72 (Pl. 38:e) zeigt, daß nicht nur bei den Antefixen, sondern auch bei der Simengestaltung dieselbe Art des Ornaments verwendet wurde. Die beiden zuletzt genannten Stücke sind zwar in der Ausführung der Deckblätter verschieden, dürften sich aber aufgrund ihrer sonstigen Ähnlichkeit zur selben Zeit am gleichen Gebäude befunden haben.[46] Die Löwenköpfe schließlich, Kopf E 6a/88 (Pl. 39:a) vom Naiskos D und ATK 3/72 vom Bühnengebäude gleichen einander so sehr, daß für beide das gleiche Model verwendet worden sein mag.

---

[39] Die Knospe im Zwickel der auseinanderstrebenden Voluten lässt sich erstmals auf der oberen Sima der Tholos zu Delphi feststellen, die um 380 v. Chr. errichtet wurde: Roux 1952, S. 442–454 mit Abb. Ab da wird sie zu einem häufigen Dekorationsmotiv, das auch gerne in Blütenform auftritt. Vgl. dazu die Sima der Tholos von Epidauros: Roux 1961, S. 140–145, 160–168, Taf. 43.

[40] Vgl. dazu Michaud 1973, S. 319, 321, Abb. 139.

[41] Vgl. das Antefix C 19226 aus dem Heiligtum des Apollon Pytheos: Vollgraff 1956, S. 18, Taf. V sowie den Stirnziegel vom "Dromos X": Deshayes 1966, S. 229, Taf. XLI:3, welche sich an die Serie C 26659 anschliessen.

[42] Herzlichen Dank schulde ich Mde. Billot für ihre freundlichen Auskünfte und das mir zur Vergügung gestellte Photomaterial.

[43] Einer Reduktion des Akroterschemas begegnen wir ab dem Ende des 5. Jh. v. Chr. des öfteren in Olympia, Delphi und Epidauros. Zu Olympia, siehe *OlForsch* V; zu Delphi, vgl. Le Roy 1967, Serie 69 (A. 109 und A. 95), S. 141, 146, 148, Taf. 53; zu Epidauros vgl. Harl 1971, S. 69, 109 (Serie E 18) mit Abb.

[44] Harl 1971, S. 91, 98 mit Abb.

[45] Vgl. dazu die neueste Untersuchung des Theaters von Gogos 1991, bes. S. 174–184, wo eine chronologische Abfolge der Bauphasen erstellt ist. Siehe auch Gogos 1986, S. 6–31.

[46] Aufgrund der sehr vagen Angabe des Fundortes zu Beginn der Grabung 1972 könnte das Fragment ATK 21/72 auch vom Naiskos D stammen.

Naiskos D erfuhr bereits kurz nach der Mitte des 2. Jh. v. Chr. einen Umbau, der mit der Aufstellung der Statue des Eukleides zusammenhing. In diese Periode, in der auch eine Neueindeckung des Daches erfolgte, gehört das Fragment ATK 1988 (Pl. 39:b). Dem Stück fehlt jede Feinheit der Linienführung. Die derben Formen haben jede Plastizität verloren, das Ornament ist in die Fläche gebannt. Wir befinden uns in einer Zeit, in der eine flächenhafte und linearbetonte Ornamentik im Vordringen begriffen ist. Das Schema auf der Sima des Naiskos D zeigt eine Abzweigung von der zweiten Volute nach oben, was an vergleichbare Stücke in Delphi erinnert, die allerdings der zweiten Hälfte des 3. Jh. v. Chr. angehören.[47] Dieser Dacherneuerung ist noch das Löwenkopffragment ATK 1986 zuzuweisen (Pl. 39:c), das die für das ausgehende 2. Jh. v. Chr. bezeichnende Richtung der Naturentfremdung und Tendenz zur Maskenhaftigkeit bereits andeutet.[48]

Zu einer letzten Umbauphase gehört das gut erhaltene Fragment eines Löwenkopfwasserspeiers ATK 1987 (Pl. 39:d). Für eine chronologische Einordnung von Interesse ist die Mähne, welche über der Kopfmitte gescheitelt ist. Vergleiche mit Löwenköpfen ähnlicher Haargestaltung weisen darauf hin, daß das Dach des Naiskos D im ausgehenden 1. Jh. v. Chr. erneuert worden sein muß.[49]

Mit dem Theaterbereich ist das Simenfragment 1/78 (Pl. 39:e) in Verbindung zu bringen, das eine Leiste mit einem Reliefmäander aufweist.[50] Aufgrund der Fundsituation mag zu ihm das Stirnziegelfragment ATK 1/72 (Pl. 39:f) gehören, welches die in der augusteischen Zeit so gängige Palmettengestaltung mit knopfartigen Einrollungen zeigt.[51] Somit hätte das hellenistische Bühnengebäude in der frühen Kaiserzeit eine Dachreparatur erfahren.[52] Obzwar der untere Teil vom Antefix weggebrochen ist läßt sich erkennen, daß das Ornament das Akroterschema eigenwillig reduziert wiedergibt. Typisch dafür sind die nach außen eingerollten Ranken, die ohne Verästelung aus dem Akanthuskelch aufwachsen.[53]

Der Naiskos F östlich des Theaters wurde als letzter der Naiskoi wahrscheinlich gegen Ende des 1. Jh. v. Chr. errichtet,[54] als im Heiligtum ausgedehnte Sanierungsarbeiten durchgeführt wurden. Von diesem Tempeldach haben sich nur geringfügige Ziegelreste erhalten. Das Antefixfragment ATK 18/72 (Pl. 40:a) und Na F 16/84, deren Palmettenblätter in Verdickungen enden dürften völlig gleich gestaltet gewesen sein wie das Antefix

---

[47] Vgl. dazu die Stücke S. 81, S. 123, S. 124 der Serie 89 bei Le Roy 1967, S. 179–182, Taf. 74.
[48] Vgl. dazu *OlForsch* IV, S. 70–74.
[49] Vgl. dazu den Löwenkopf von der Sima der Nordhalle in Korinth: *OlForsch* IV, S. 83–84, 86, Taf. 79, oder den Kopf einer schmucklosen Sima aus Olympia: *OlForsch* IV, S. 82–83, 86, Taf. 78.
[50] Der Reliefmäander als Dekoration auf Simen oder Verkleidungsplatten erfreute sich schon im 6. Jh. v. Chr. an der Westküste Kleinasiens grosser Verbreitung. Der Typus des Traufziegels mit Reliefmäanderverzierung an der Stirn tritt erst in hellenistische Zeit auf und wird vom griechischen Mutterland im frühen 2. Jh. v. Chr. übernommen. Vgl. dazu Metzger 1971, S. 78, Taf. 19, 185; Billot 1976, S. 105–106, Taf. 26:b, Abb. 3:c.
[51] Vgl. dazu Alzinger 1974, S. 109–118 mit Abb.
[52] Die Beobachtung stimmt mit den Ergebnissen der Bauuntersuchung von Gogos überein. Siehe dazu Anm. 45.
[53] Vgl. dazu Amn. 42. Stirnziegel mit ähnlichen Motiven finden sich in Olympia (spätes 5. Jh. v. Chr.): Harl 1971, S. 88, 135, mit Abb.; Mamousia (hell.): Petsas 1971, S. 186, Taf. 168; Patras (kaiserz.): Oikonomidou 1971, S. 163, Taf. 151; Sikyon (kaiserz.): Harl 1971, S. 88–89, 143–144 mit Abb. der Serien 6, 7, 8.
[54] Zum Naiskos F, siehe Gogos 1986, S. 45–49.

ATK 1/72 (Pl. 39:f) vom Theater; nur die äußeren Konturen weichen voneinander ab. Die große Ähnlichkeit der Antefixe vom Theater und vom Naiskos F läßt annehmen, daß beide Dächer gleichzeitig eingedeckt wurden, und daß Naiskos F eventuell die gleiche Reliefsima wie das Bühnengebäude hatte.

Auch vom Naiskos E gibt es nur eine bescheidene Anzahl von gefundenen Dachziegeln. Der Baubeginn dieses Tempels erfolgte noch im 3. Jh. v. Chr., etwas später als Naiskos D, also die Skene bereits aufrecht stand.[55] Dieser Bauperiode sind die beiden Simenranken ATK 169/79 und E 6/83 zuzuordnen, die im Gegensatz zu den fast gleichgestalteten des Bühnengebäudes und des Naiskos D eine engere Windung zeigen. Von den zugehörigen Antefixen hat sich nur ein bescheidenes Fragment mit einer gesprengten Palmette erhalten, ATK 11/72 (Pl. 40:b).[56] Ein Parallelstück hierfür gibt es in Delphi,[57] das Le Roy in die zweite Hälfte des 3. Jh. v. Chr. datiert. Dieser zeitliche Ansatz würde auch zu unserem Stück vom Naiskos E passen.

Das Traufziegelfragment ATK 88 mit dem breiten Astragal an der Unterseite, das zwischen den Naiskoi D und E gefunden wurde, möchte ich am Tempel E unterbringen, auch wenn die Südseite zum Theater hin mit einer Rankensima versehen war. Ähnlich der Südstoa von Korinth[58] könnte die hintere Dachfläche, die durch den knapp daneben befindlichen Naiskos D kaum gesehen wurde, mit einer Traufsima verkleidet gewesen sein.

Von den hellenistischen Giebelsimen wurde ein Fragment vom Naiskos E gefunden, ATK 1985/E (Pl. 40:d). Auffallend bei dieser flüchtig ausgeführten Blütentänie ist der durch ein Karo angegebene Palmettenkern; die Verbindungsranken zu den Lotosblüten daneben setzen nicht wie üblich unter der Palmette, sondern daneben an. Ein ähnlich gestalteter Ornamentstreifen begegnet uns nur im benachbarten Sikyon, wo diese Schmuckzone an der Unterseite eines Traufziegels zu finden ist.[59] Diese Beobachtung wirft die Frage auf, inwieweit eine Beeinflussung Aigeiras durch Sikyon auf künstlerischer Ebene erfolgte, das ebenfalls Mitglied des achäischen Bundes war, und wo gleichzeitig mit Aigeira im 3. Jh. v. Chr. eine rege Bautätigkeit nachzuweisen ist. Leider war mir bis jetzt der Zugang zu den Dachterrakotten von Sikyon nicht möglich.

Die zu Beginn der Kaiserzeit stattfindenden Erneuerungen im Theaterbereich dehnten sich auch auf den Naiskos E aus. Das Fragment eines Löwenkopfwasserspeiers ATK 3/77 (Pl. 40:c) weist bereits typische Merkmale der römischen Epoche auf: die Haarbüschel, Augenbrauen und Wimpern sind durch Furchen angedeutet, die man mit einem Stichel in den noch weichen Ton ritzte. Köpfe mit ähnlicher Bearbeitung finden sich frühestens im vorgerückten 1. Jh. v. Chr.[60] Stilistische Überlegungen zu Wasserspeiern in Korinth[61]

---

[55] Zum Naiskos E, siehe Gogos 1986, S. 39–45.

[56] Möbius (1968, S. 119, Anm. zu S. 88) hält Pheidias als Erfinder der geflammten Palmette. Von den Akroteren des Parthenon ausgehend wird diese Palmetteform in die Bauornamentik übernommen und findet sich als Stirnziegel im 4. Jh. v. Chr. am Dach der Tholos von Epidauros: Roux 1961, S. 140–145, 160–168, Taf. 43.

[57] Le Roy 1967, S. 180, Taf. 74 mit der Serie 89: S. 181, 182.

[58] Siehe dazu Anm. 34.

[59] Mylonas 1987, S. 91, Abb. 105.

[60] Vgl. dazu die Löwenkopfwasserspeier von einer Rankensima in Olympia: OlForsch IV, S. 82–83, 85–86, Taf. 94 sowie den Wasserspeier 7080 aus Ton in München: OlForsch IV, S. 87, Taf. 78.

[61] Vergleichend lassen sich die unpublizierten Stücke FS 295 und FS 933 heranziehen.

veranlassen letztlich dazu, den Löwenkopf vom Naiskos E in die augusteische Zeit zu datieren.

Als unter Max. Thrax (236–238 n. Chr.) das Bühnengebäude erneuert wurde,[62] versuchten die Handwerker die neuen Motive gleich in die Dachornamentik einzubringen. Nur wenige Fragmente, die sich zu einem Antefix zusammenfügen lassen, sind uns von der Skene erhalten, die zwar nie fertiggestellt wurde, deren Dachterrakotten man aber offensichtlich im voraus angefertigt hatte. Das Stirnziegelfragment Ξ 1/81 (Pl. 40:e) hat Parallelen in Olympia und auf Euböa, wo die Antefixe der späten Kaiserzeit ebenfalls zarte, dünne Palmettenblätter zeigen, offensichtlich ein Charakteristikum dieser Epoche.[63] Der untere Teil des Antefixes ATK 2/72 (Pl. 40:f) zeigt eine Leiste mit einem Eierstab, der sich etwa ab der Mitte des 1. Jh. v. Chr. von Italien ausgehend im ganzen römischen Imperium verbreitete, und mit der Staatsform auch auf die Peloponnes nach Korinth und nach Aigeira übergriff.[64]

## BIBLIOGRAPHIE

Alzinger, W. 1974. *Die augusteische Architektur in Ephesos*, Wien

———. 1985. "Aigeira-Hyperesia und die Siedlung Phelloë in Achaia (I). I. Die Bauten der nachmykenischen Zeit," *Klio* 67, S. 426–451

———. 1988. "Hyperesia-Aigeira. Der Wandel eines Heiligtums von spätmykenischer bis in klassische Zeit," Πρακτικά 1988 [1991], S. 20–23

Billot, M.-F. 1976. "Terres cuites architecturales du Musée Épigraphique," Δελτ 31, 1976, A' [1980], S. 87–135

Buschor, E. 1933. *Die Tondächer der Akropolis*, II, *Stirnziegel*, Berlin/Leipzig

*Corinth* I, iv = O. Broneer, *The South Stoa and Its Roman Successors* (*Corinth* I, iv), Princeton 1954

*Corinth* IV, i = I. Thallon-Hill und L. S. King, *Decorated Architectural Terracottas* (*Corinth* IV, i), Cambridge, Mass. 1929

Deshayes, J. 1966. *Argos. Les fouilles de la Deiras* (*Études péloponnésiennes* IV), Paris

Gogos, S. 1986. "Aigeira-Hyperesia und die Siedlung Phelloë in Achaia (II). I. Theater, II. Naiskoi beim Theater," *Klio* 68, S. 6–50

———. 1991. *Das Theater von Aigeira. Ein Beitrag zum antiken Theaterbau*, Wien

Harl, O. 1971. "Studien zu den Stirnziegeln der Peloponnes" (Diss. Graz-Universität 1971)

Heiden, J. 1987. *Korinthische Dachziegel. Zur Entwicklung der korinthischen Dächer*, Frankfurt am Main/Bern/New York/Paris

*Isthmia* I = O. Broneer, *The Temple of Poseidon* (*Isthmia* I), Princeton 1971

Le Roy, Ch. 1967. *Les terres cuites architecturales* (*Fouilles de Delphes* II), Paris

Mallwitz, A. 1972. *Olympia und seine Bauten*, Munich

Metzger, I. 1971. "Piräus-Zisterne," Δελτ 26, 1971, A' [1973], S. 41–94

Michaud, J. P. 1973. "Chronique des fouilles en 1972. Aigeira," *BCH* 97, S. 319–321

Möbius, H. 1968. *Die Ornamente der griechischen Grabstelen*, München

Mylonas, G. E. 1987. Ἔργον 1987 [1988], S. 91

Oikonomidou, M. 1971. «Πάτραι», Δελτ 26, 1971, B'1 [1974], S. 149–175

*OlForsch* IV = F. Willemsen, *Die Löwenkopfwasserspeier vom Dach des Zeustempels* (*Olympische Forschungen* IV), Berlin 1959

[62] Siehe dazu Anm. 45.

[63] Euböa: Sampson 1976, S. 139, Taf. 105:β. Olympia: Harl 1971, S. 94, 136, 137 mit Abb. (Antefixe 252 und 253).

[64] Vgl. dazu das früheste Antefix dieser Gattung in Padua: Strazzulla 1987, S. 295, Nr. 367, Taf. IV. In die mittlere bis späte Kaiserzeit ist das sehr ähnliche Fragment A 382 aus Korinth zuweisen. Es ist von schlechter Qualität mit stark degenerierten Ornamenten. Siehe dazu Harl 1971, S. 93, 124 mit Abb.

*OlForsch* V = A. Mallwitz und W. Schiering, *Die Werkstatt des Pheidias in Olympia* (*Olympische Forschungen* V), Berlin 1964

*Olympia* II = W. Dörpfeld und R. Bormann, *Die Baudenkmäler* (*Olympia, Ergebnisse der von dem deutschen Reich veranstalteten Ausgrabungen* II), Berlin 1892

Petsas, F. 1971. «Καλλιθέα», Δελτ 26, 1971, B′1 [1974], S. 185–186

Robinson, H. S. 1976. "Excavations at Corinth: Temple Hill, 1968–1972," *Hesperia* 45, S. 203–239

Roebuck, M. 1955. "Excavations at Corinth: 1954," *Hesperia* 24, S. 147–157

Roux, G. 1952. "Le toit de la Tholos de Marmaria et la couverture des monuments circulaires grecs," *BCH* 76, S. 442–483

———. 1961. *L'architecture de l'Argolide aux IV$^e$ et III$^e$ siècles avant J.-C.*, Paris

Sampson, A. 1976. «Χαλκίδα», Δελτ 31, 1976, B′1 [1984], S. 136–160

Schede, M. 1909. *Antikes Traufleistenornament*, Strassburg

Strazzulla, M. J. 1987. *Le terrecotte architettoniche della Venetia Romana*, Rom

Urban, R. 1979. *Wachstum und Krise des achäischen Bundes. Quellenstudium zur Entwicklung des Bundes von 280 bis 222 v. Chr.*, Wiesbaden

Van Buren, E. D. 1926. *Greek Fictile Revetments in the Archaic Period*, London

Vollgraff, W. 1956. *Le sanctuarie d'Apollon Pythéen à Argos* (*Études péloponnésiennes* I), Paris

Welter, G. 1941. *Troizen und Kalaureia*, Berlin

Wide, S., und L. Kjellberg. 1895. "Ausgrabungen auf Kalaureia," *AM* 20, S. 267–326

DORIS GNEISZ

Brucknergasse 23
A-7400 Oberwart
Austria

# KLASSISCHE DÄCHER AUS OLYMPIA

(Plates 41–47)

VIELE DER DÄCHER, die in archaischer Zeit die Gebäude Olympias deckten, waren im 5 Jh. v. Chr. bereits beschädigt oder ganz zerstört. Für einige Dächer wurden zur Reparatur Ersatzstücke angefertigt, andere mußten durch neue Dächer ersetzt werden.

Durch ein Erdbeben, welches in die 1. Hälfte des 5. Jh. v. Chr. datiert werden muß, ist der nahezu fertige, noch im Bau befindliche Zeustempel stark beschädigt worden.[1] Vermutlich haben aber auch kleinere Bauten in der Altis gelitten, denn nach dem Erdbeben ist eine derart rege Bautätigkeit zu verzeichnen, daß man von einer Neugestaltung des Heiligtums sprechen möchte: Der Zeustempel wurde fertiggestellt. Die beiden Apsisbauten des Bouleuterions wurden durch eine gemeinsame Vorhalle verbunden (s.u.). Im Westen und Nordwesten entstanden die griechischen Badeeinrichtungen und das Prytaneion. Das Stadion wurde deutlich vergrößert und erhielt dadurch seine endgültige Form (Phase IIIA). Große Schutt- und Abschlagschichten im Südosten des Heiligtums deuten darauf hin, daß dort die Bauhütten ihren Arbeitsplatz hatten. All diese Arbeiten müssen in die Mitte des 5. Jh. v. Chr. datiert werden. Es liegt nahe die vorausgegangenen Zerstörungen mit dem starken Erdbeben von 464 v. Chr., welches uns für Sparta überliefert ist, in Verbindung zu bringen.[2]

Ein besonders interessantes Dach wurde in Schuttschichten und den, in ihrer Funktion bis heute nicht erklärbaren, Steinzeilen im Südosten gefunden (s.o. Anm. 1). Die mysteriösen Steinzeilen, in die viele Ziegel des Daches verbaut waren, lassen sich in die Jahre um 460 v. Chr. datieren. Das Dach kann nicht lange sein Gebäude gedeckt haben, denn die Ornamentik von Giebelsima und Antefixen zeigt, daß es um 470 v. Chr. entstanden sein muß.[3] Auch das Gebäude dieses Daches wird beim Erdbeben von 464 v. Chr. gelitten haben. Auffälligstes Merkmal aller Ziegel dieses Daches ist, daß sie nicht rechtwinklig geschnitten sind.

Zu den verzierten Elementen des Daches gehören die Giebelsima (Pl. 41:a), die Traufziegel (Pl. 41:b), Antefixe (Pl. 41:c) und Firstziegel mit Firstpalmetten. Die Antefixe sitzen schräg an den Kalypteren. Die Traufziegel haben die Form von Parallelogrammen. Von den Antefixen und den Traufziegeln gibt es sowohl nach links als auch nach rechts gerichtete Exemplare.

Die Dachfläche war mit rautenförmigen (Pl. 42:a) und nahe dem First mit dreieckigen Ziegeln gedeckt. Diese Ziegel überlappten einander an ihren unteren Enden, so daß keine

---

[1] Bereits bemalte Antenkapitellfragmente und andere zerstörte Bauglieder des Zeustempels wurden in den sogenannten Steinzeilen im Südosten des Heiligtums gefunden. Der Keramikbefund aus den nicht leicht zu verstehenden Steinzeilen weist auf deren Datierung in die Jahre um 460 v. Chr. hin (demnächst ausführlich in: *OlBer* XI). Mallwitz 1981, S. 110–111.

[2] Neumann und Partsch 1885, S. 330–331; *RE* IIIA, S. 1387 (Ehrenberg); *RE* Suppl. IV, S. 351 (Capelle).

[3] Das Dach ist in der Ornamentik der Antefixe und seiner Struktur gut vergleichbar mit dem Dach der Tholos auf der Athener Agora. Die Tholos ist um 470 v. Chr. entstanden: Thompson 1940, S. 65–73; Miller 1988, S. 134–139, Taf. 45:1, 48:1, 2. Die Anthemienkette der Giebelsima ähnelt der Sima der Lesche der Knidier in Delphi: Le Roy 1967, S. 128–132, Taf. 1:46.

Deckziegel notwendig waren. Die Ziegel dieses Daches lassen sich zu einem keilartigen Dach, das ein Gebäude mit dreieckigem Grundriß deckte, zusammenfügen.

Nun stellt sich die Frage, welches Gebäude in Olympia mit diesem Dach gedeckt war, denn ein in seiner Grundfläche dreieckiges Gebäude ist uns vorderhand unbekannt. Einen ersten Hinweis auf die Lage des Gebäudes geben uns die Fundortangaben. Die Ziegelfragmente des Daches sind fast ausschließlich im Südosten des Heiligtums gefunden worden. Auf der Suche nach einem dreieckigen Gebäude in Olympia hilft uns Pausanias (5,15,5–6; 6,20,10) mit seiner sehr genauen Beschreibung des Hippodroms weiter.

Hierbei geht es vor allem um die komplizierte Startvorrichtung für die Pferdegespanne.[4] Zusammengefasst besteht die Startanlage aus der Agnaptoshalle und einer dreieckigen Konstruktion, die an die östliche Langseite der Halle anschließt. Pausanias betritt die Startvorrichtung und trennt bei der Beschreibung ausdrücklich zwischen dem Teil, der unter freiem Himmel liegt und der Spitze, dem Embolos (Keil), in den er von dem nicht gedeckten Teil aus hineingeht.

Als Architekten der Starteinrichtung nennt Pausanias uns den Athener Kleoitas. Er ist uns aus mehreren attischen Inschriften bekannt und lebte und wirkte in der Zeit unseres Daches.[5] Pausanias hat dieses Dach nicht gesehen, da es zu seiner Zeit zumindest zum Teil schon lange unter der Erde war. Der Embolos der Starteinrichtung ist aber nach dem Erdbeben wieder mit schrägen Ziegel, von denen sich einige Exemplare erhalten haben, ausgebessert worden. Das Embolosdach der Starteinrichtung dürfen wir als ersten konkreten Hinweis auf das im Mittelalter vom Alpheios weggerissene Hippodrom werten.

Ein weiteres, sehr ungewöhnliches Dach gehört zur Vorhalle des Bouleuterions von Olympia. Da fast alle Ziegel des Daches im oder vor dem Bouleuterion gefunden wurden, ist die Zuweisung so eindeutig wie in Olympia selten. Meist wurden die Ziegel eines Daches über das gesamte Heiligtum verstreut aufgefunden. Die Traufe des Daches besteht aus reliefierten Traufziegeln (Pl. 42:b), auf denen je zwei frei gearbeitete Voluten (Pl. 42:c) sitzen. Über der Fuge zweier Blöcke steht eine doppelte Palmette. Der Wasserabfluß in der Mitte ist sehr abwechslungsreich gestaltet.

Vermutlich wechselten sich in gleichmäßigem Rhythmus Löwenköpfe (Pl. 43:a), Gorgonen (Pl. 43:b) und Sonnenblumen miteinander ab. Im Gegensatz zu den Löwen waren die Sonnenblumen und die Gorgonen keine Wasserspeier, sie verdeckten nur den Ausfluß. Das Wasser lief hinter ihnen aus der Traufziegelöffnung heraus. Die stilistische Einordnung der Gorgo und der Löwen, aber auch die Fundumstände einiger Fragmente, die wohl schon beim Versetzen des Daches in die Erde gekommen sind, legen eine Datierung des Daches in das Jahrzehnt 460–450 v. Chr. nahe.[6]

Die Vorhalle ist dadurch datierbar geworden. Sie ist etwa 100 Jahre älter als bisher angenommen. Da in ihrem Fundament ein Geisonfragment des Zeustempels gefunden wurde, folgerte A. Mallwitz, daß die Vorhalle nach dem Erdbeben von 373 v. Chr., bei dem der Zeustempel beschädigt wurde, entstanden ist.[7] Das Geisonfragment kann aber ebenso

---

[4] Zuletzt: Wiegartz 1984; Ebert 1989.
[5] Hitzig und Blümner 1896, S. 268; Hitzig und Blümner 1901, S. 436.
[6] *Olympia* II, S. 195–196, Taf. 120; Floren 1977, S. 133–139; Moustaka 1984, S. 180.
[7] Mallwitz 1972, S. 239.

von dem schon erwähnten Erdbeben von 464 v. Chr. stammen. Die Vorhalle wird also bald danach errichtet worden sein.

Das Dach der um 430 v. Chr. entstandenen Pheidiaswerkstatt weist eine merkwürdige Eigenart auf. Alle Ziegelarten, von denen mehrere Stücke erhalten sind, lassen sich in zwei Serien, die sich nur in kleinen Details unterscheiden, trennen. Das betrifft die Antefixe, die Traufziegel und die Giebelsima. Die beiden Serien der Giebelsima (Pl. 43:c) unterscheiden sich durch das Profil, die Größe und geringfügig auch in der Bemalung. Die Traufziegel weisen eine voneinander abweichende Bemalung der Unterseite auf. Entweder ziert sie nur ein heller Astragal auf rotem Grund, oder sie tragen zusätzlich noch ein helles Band. Deutlich lassen sich die Antefixe trennen. Das üppige Rankengeschlinge der einen wächst aus einem fünfblättrigen (Pl. 44:a), der anderen aus einem dreiblättrigen (Pl. 44:b) Akanthuskelch.

Wie läßt es sich erklären, daß zu einem Dach von mehreren Ziegelarten zwei Serien existieren? Um eine wesentlich spätere Ausbesserung kann es sich nicht handeln, denn trotz aller Unterschiede sind sich die beiden Serien so ähnlich, daß sie uns gleichzeitig erscheinen und aus derselben Werkstatt stammen müssen. Die beiden Serien in zwei Dächer für zwei Gebäude zu trennen, verbietet sich, da alle Ziegel in der Regel den gleichen Fundort haben: in der Pheidiaswerkstatt oder in ihrer unmittelbaren Umgebung. Teilweise wurden die Fragmente in einer Schuttschicht bei der Pheidiaswerkstatt, der sogenannten Formenschicht, gefunden. Die Formenschicht mit dem Abfall der pheidiasischen Kultbildarbeiten wird in das Ende des 5. Jh. v. Chr. datiert.[8] Die Stücke deuten also auf eine frühe Beschädigung des Daches hin.

Vermutlich war die Geschichte des Daches folgendermaßen: Das Dach wurde um 430 v. Chr. gebrannt und versetzt. Kurz darauf wurde die Pheidiaswerkstatt beschädigt und dieselbe Tonwerkstatt hat den Auftrag zur Reparatur bekommen. So wären die Unterschiede, aber auch die annähernde Gleichzeitig der beiden Serien zu erklären.

Da in der Formenschicht auch Fragmente von mehreren anderen Dächern gefunden wurden, die auf die Beschädigung auch anderer Gebäude schließen lassen, ist zu vermuten, daß auch am Ende des 5. Jh. v. Chr. ein Erdbeben Olympia erschütterte. Dieses Erdbeben ist uns aber in den literarischen Quellen nicht überliefert.[9]

In dem Zeitraum zwischen dem Ende des 5. und dem beginnenden 3. Jh. v. Chr. sind in Olympia mehr als zehn kleine korinthische Dächern entstanden, die meist leider keinen Gebäuden zugewiesen werden können. Sie könnten zum Teil Ersatzdächer für solche Schatzhäuser gewesen sein, die ihre archaischen Eindeckungen bereits verloren hatten. Bisher nicht gefunden wurde ein Dach für das Metroon, obwohl gerade um 400 v. Chr., die Entstehungszeit des Metroons, mehrere korinthische Dächer hergestellt wurden. Sie scheinen aber für diesen Tempel zu klein zu sein.

Ein sehr interessantes Dach trug der SO-Bau. Er läßt sich nicht nur durch den Keramikbefund aus seinen Fundamentgräben datieren. Auch der SO-Bau ist nach einem Erdbeben entstanden. Er ist zum großen Teil aus umgearbeiteten Blöcken des Zeustempels, der beim Erdbeben von 373 v. Chr. stark beschädigt wurde, errichtet. Dieses berühmte Erdbeben

---

[8] Zuletzt: *OlForsch* XVIII, S. 1–4.
[9] Das Beben von 402 v. Chr. im nahegelegenen Elis (*RE* Suppl. IV, S. 350 [Capelle]) scheint für die Zerstörungen in Olympia zu spät zu sein.

in Achaia, beim dem Helike vom Meer verschlungen wurde und Bura in einer Erdspalte versank, ist in der antiken Literatur mehrfach erwähnt.[10] Da A. Mallwitz nachweisen konnte, daß der SO-Bau im Jahre 364 v. Chr. während einer Auseinandersetzung zwischen Arkadern und Eleern im Heiligtum bereits fertig war, muß er also in den Jahren um 370 v. Chr. entstanden sein.[11]

Der Dachrand des SO-Baus war an den Giebel- und den Traufseiten von der gleichen Sima eingefasst. An der Traufe waren die Simablöcke in ihrer Mitte durchbrochen und mit Wasserspeiern ausgestattet. Die Ornamentik der Giebelsima (Pl. 44:c) ist von der Traufsima nur durch ein kleines Detail zu unterscheiden. Das Mittelblatt des Lotosblütenkelches ist nicht gezackt umrandet. An der Traufe wechselten sich Blöcke mit Löwen- und mit Tüllenwasserspeiern (Pl. 45:a, b) ab. Die außergewöhnlichen Tüllen (Pl. 46:a) wachsen aus einem plastischen Akanthusbüschel und sind von einer Ranke eingefasst. Daher sind sie eher dem pflanzlichen als dem tierischen Bereich zuzuordnen.

Das Dach ist deswegen von Interesse, weil das gemalte Ornament erstmals in die dritte Dimension hervortritt. Man möchte diesen Dachrand entwicklungsgeschichtlich gerne für älter halten als die plastischen Rankensimen. Das scheint sich aber zu verbieten, denn die ersten Marmor-Rankensimen von Delphi und Epidauros müssen wohl doch etwas früher datiert werden.[12]

In der Mitte des 4. Jh. v. Chr. begann man, das olympische Heiligtum mit großen Gebäuden zu rahmen. Es entstanden das Leonidaion und die Südhalle. Die Echohalle im Osten wurde auch zu dieser Zeit geplant und begonnen, konnte aber erst in der frühen Kaiserzeit vollendet werden. Der Dachrand solcher hallenartiger Bauten wurde meist von Rankensimen begrenzt.[13] Allein aus der 2. Hälfte des 4. Jh. v. Chr. haben sich in Olympia Rankensimen von fünf verschiedenen Gebäuden erhalten.

Der bekannteste ist der mit fast 1000 Fragmenten vertretene Dachrandsschmuck des Leonidaions (Pl. 46:b). Die Rankensima ist im Laufe der Jahrhunderte öfters ausgebessert worden. Auch die Rankensima der Tafel 123:4 der Olympia-Publikation zählt zu einer solchen Ausbesserung, denn sie wiederholt in allen Motiven und Maßen exakt die älteren Stücke des Leonidaions. Diese Reparatur wird im 3. Jh. v. Chr. stattgefunden haben. Für die Südhalle, der R. Bormann diese Sima zuwies,[14] ist sie aber zu spät zu datieren. Eher gehört zur Südhalle eine Traufsima (Pl. 47:a), deren Rankenmotiv durch kleine zwischen den Voluten herabhängende Blüten bereichert ist.

Die wegen ihrer Tonfarbe sogenannte "Rote Rankensima" (Pl. 47:b) läßt sich mit Baugliedern einer ionischen Halle verbinden, da die Dübellöcher im Geison und in den Ziegeln sich in Form und Abstand gleichen. Wo allerdings diese Stoa gestanden hat, ist nicht bekannt. Keines ihrer Architekturfragmente wurde *in situ* gefunden.

---

[10] Neumann und Partsch 1885, S. 324–325; *RE* VII, S. 2855–2856 (Bölte); *RE* Suppl. IV, S. 350 (Capelle).
[11] Mallwitz 1981, S. 109–110.
[12] Heiden 1987, S. 130–131, 181–188.
[13] Heiden 1987, S. 198.
[14] *Olympia* II, S. 199.

## BIBLIOGRAPHIE

Ebert, J. 1989. "Neues zum Hippodrom und zu den hippischen Konkurrenzen in Olympia," *Nikephoros* 2, S. 89–107

Floren, J. 1977. *Studien zur Typologie des Gorgoneion*, Münster

Heiden, J. 1987. *Korinthische Dachziegel. Zur Entwicklung der korinthischen Dächer*, Frankfurt am Main/Bern/New York/Paris

Hitzig, H., und H. Blümner. 1896. *Des Pausanias Beschreibung von Griechenland* I, i, Leipzig

———. 1901. *Des Pausanias Beschreibung von Griechenland* II, i, Leipzig

Le Roy, Ch. 1967. *Les terres cuites architecturales* (*Fouilles de Delphes* II), Paris

Mallwitz, A. 1972. *Olympia und seine Bauten*, München

———. 1981. "Neue Forschungen in Olympia (Theater und Hestiaheiligtum in der Altis)," *Gymnasium* 88, S. 97–122

Miller, Stephen G. 1988. "Circular Roofing Systems and the Athenian Tholos," in Πρακτικά του XII Διεθνούς Συνεδρίου Κλασικής Αρχαιολογίας, Αθήνα, 4–10 Σεπτεμβρίου 1983, IV, Athens, S. 134–139

Moustaka, A. 1984. "Frühklassische Löwenplastik aus Olympia," *AM* 99, S. 177–183

Neumann, C., und J. Partsch. 1885. *Physikalische Geographie von Griechenland*, Breslau

*OlBer* XI = *Bericht über die Ausgrabungen in Olympia*, Berlin (in Vorbereitung)

*OlForsch* XVIII = W. Schiering, *Die Werkstatt des Pheidias in Olympia*, Zweiter Teil (*Olympische Forschungen* XVIII), Berlin 1991

*Olympia* II = W. Dörpfeld und R. Bormann, *Die Baudenkmäler* (*Olympia, Ergebnisse der von dem deutschen Reich veranstalteten Ausgrabungen* II), Berlin 1892

Thompson, H. A. 1940. *The Tholos and Its Predecessors* (*Hesperia* Supplement 4), Princeton

Wiegartz, H. 1984. "Zur Startanlage im Hippodrom von Olympia," *Boreas* 7, S. 41–71

JOACHIM HEIDEN

Deutsches Archäologisches Institut
Via Sardegna 79
I-00187 Roma
Italien

# HELLENISTIC ARCHITECTURAL TERRACOTTAS FROM MESSENE

(PLATES 48–56)

EXCAVATIONS at Messene[1] concentrated mainly in the central low area of the city and on the south slopes of Mount Ithome and brought to light buildings of religious and political character, not private residences; these buildings are (1) a small temple, of an unknown god or hero,[2] on the south slope of Ithome below the sanctuary of Zeus Ithomatas (Fig. 1, no. 10), (2) the sanctuary of Artemis Limnatis[3] (Fig. 1, no. 7), (3) part of the Theater[4] (Fig. 1, no. 1), (4) part of the North Stoa of the agora and a Fountain House nearby[5] (Fig. 1, no. 8), (5) the architectural complex of the Asklepieion[6] (Fig. 1, no. 2), (6) the Temple of Artemis Ortheia,[7] (7) the baths and latrines south of the Asklepieion,[8] and (8) the Stadium and the Heroon[9] at the southern end of the city on the fortification walls (Fig. 1, nos. 4 and 5). Excavations also yielded substantial quantities of architectural terracottas, the catalogue of which is being prepared by my collaborator Sappho Athanassopoulou. In this preliminary report I deal with classification and relative chronology of Laconian-type antefixes and Corinthian-type antefixes and simas as well as with their attribution to the roofs of excavated buildings.

## THE STAMPS

The stamps that occur exclusively on Laconian-type pan and cover tiles bear additional witness to the public and sacred character of the buildings. The most common stamp, represented by thirty-five examples, bears the adjective ΔΑΜΟΣΙΟΣ (= public tiling)[10] with

---

[1] Blouet 1831, I, pp. 27–33. Le Bas 1844, pp. 422–423. Sophoulis 1895, p. 27. Oikonomos 1909, 1925–1926. Orlandos 1963a, 1965, and the reports written by Orlandos for Πρακτικά, 1957–1975.

Unless otherwise indicated, all inventory numbers are those of the Museum at Messene.

The photographs for Plate 54:a and b come from Anastasios Orlandos' archives, kept by the Archaeological Society at Athens. All the rest are due to the photographer Vassilios Stamatopoulos. The topographical plan, Figure 1, was done by the topographer George Makris, while the plan, Figure 4, was done by the architect Dr. Athanasios Nakassis. The sima, Figure 19:a and b, was drawn by the painter Eustathios Androutsakis; all the rest were drawn in pencil by the author and inked by the drafter Evangelos Olympios.

[2] Themelis 1989, pp. 35–36, fig. 35.
[3] Themelis 1988, p. 72, fig. 15.
[4] Themelis 1987, pp. 73–79; Themelis 1988, pp. 45–52.
[5] Themelis 1990, pp. 26–27.
[6] Themelis 1987, pp. 79–90.
[7] Themelis 1990, p. 35, fig. 45.
[8] Themelis 1988, pp. 59–65.
[9] Themelis 1987, pp. 90–96; Themelis 1988, pp. 65–72; Themelis 1989, p. 37.
[10] Cf. the ΔΑΜΟΙΟ stamps at Nemea (see the article by Stephen G. Miller in this volume, pp. 85–98 above) and a ΔΗΜΟ[ΣΙΟΣ] stamp at Pella: Kaltsas 1988, p. 101, note 314, which refers to examples from Illyria,

relief letters 18 mm. high in an oblong frame 2.8 × 12 cm. (Fig. 2:a; Pl. 48:a, b). A second circular stamp, 6 cm. in diameter, of which only three examples exist, carries the ligature Δ (= ΔΑ<ΜΟΣΙΟΣ>)[11] and the initials ΕΥ underneath, most probably an archon's name (Fig. 2:b, Pl. 48:c). The third rectangular stamp, 5.4 × 13 cm., displays the words ΕΠΙ ΙΕΡΕΟΣ with relief letters 1.6 cm. high on the first line and a name in the genitive on the second (Fig. 2:c, d). Only the name ΦΙΛΙΠΠΟΣ, during whose priesthood these tiles were made and stamped, is better preserved on one of the six extant specimens; no doubt he was the priest of Zeus Ithomatas, who also functioned as eponymous of the year according to the testimony of certain inscriptions dealing with state and cult officials as Ἀγωνοθέται, Ἱεροθύται, Γραμματεῖς, Χαλειδοφόροι, Ἀγορανόμοι, and Ὑπαγορανόμοι.[12] The only Φίλιππος we know from Messene is the father of the famous sculptor Δαμοφῶν, mentioned in seven honorary decrees inscribed on a stone column found in the Asklepieion.[13] Philippos must have been active in the second half of the 3rd century B.C. and could have held the office of eponymous priest of the supreme god of the city during this period. The letter forms on the stamp do not contradict such a date.

A stone standard found in 1960 at the southwest corner of the agora, north of the Asklepieion and similar to those from the Athenian Agora and Assos,[14] shows the official size (L. 96 cm.) and shape of terracotta pan and cover tiles of Laconian type (Pl. 48:d).

## LACONIAN ANTEFIXES

The Laconian antefixes of Messene, less abundant than the Corinthian ones, can be classified in four main types according to form and especially according to the arrangement of decorative motifs. To Type 1 (Fig. 3, Pl. 48:e) belong some fragments found mainly in the area of the first Ortheia sanctuary (Fig. 4), which was constructed in the late 4th and abandoned in the early 2nd century B.C., according to recent contextual, architectural, and epigraphic evidence.[15] The main subject of the antefix decoration is the bust of a young goddess, possibly Artemis, flanked by two pairs of horizontal and vertical S-shaped scrolls and crowned with a palmette of seven plain leaves;[16] the pattern is framed by a thin astragal and plain relief bands. The simplicity and delicacy of the design, the spacious composition,

---

Piraeus, Athens, Tanagra, Sparta. The rarity of ΔΑΜΟΣΙΟΣ stamps in Macedonia, where the ΒΑΣΙΛΙΚΟΣ ones are the norm, has probably to do with the different political system there.

[11] A similar ligature Δ occurs on rectangular tile stamps from Illyria: Andrea 1976, p. 348, pl. XIV:14–16.

[12] *IG* V[1], 1467, 1468, 1469. Orlandos 1969, pp. 103–104, pl. 124:a; Themelis 1988, pp. 64–65.

[13] Orlandos 1972, pp. 137–138; Themelis 1989, p. 35, fig. 34; Themelis 1990, p. 32.

[14] Orlandos 1955, pp. 112–113, figs. 63, 64; Camp 1986, p. 128, fig. 106.

[15] Themelis 1991, pp. 28–30. The fill to the north of the Ortheia temple where fragments of Laconian antefix Type 1 were found contained pottery fragments of the 3rd/2nd century B.C., terracotta figurines, and two coin hoards dated to the middle of the 2nd century B.C. and related to the abandonment of the Ortheia temple and the construction of the Asklepieion complex in the first half of the 2nd century B.C.

[16] Cf. the terracotta Artemis heads on semicircular votive tablets from Ithaka in the National Museum: Kalligas 1979, pp. 59–61, pl. I, ΙΣΤ, especially ΙΖ΄ with incised S-shaped spirals around the head of Artemis Kyparissia (of South Italian inspiration?) and on a Laconian antefix of the 2nd century B.C. (Karapanos Collection 1148): Winter 1903, p. 166, fig. 4. Kalligas 1980, p. 26, fig. 18. For the presence of protomes and heads on architectural terracottas, see p. 153 below.

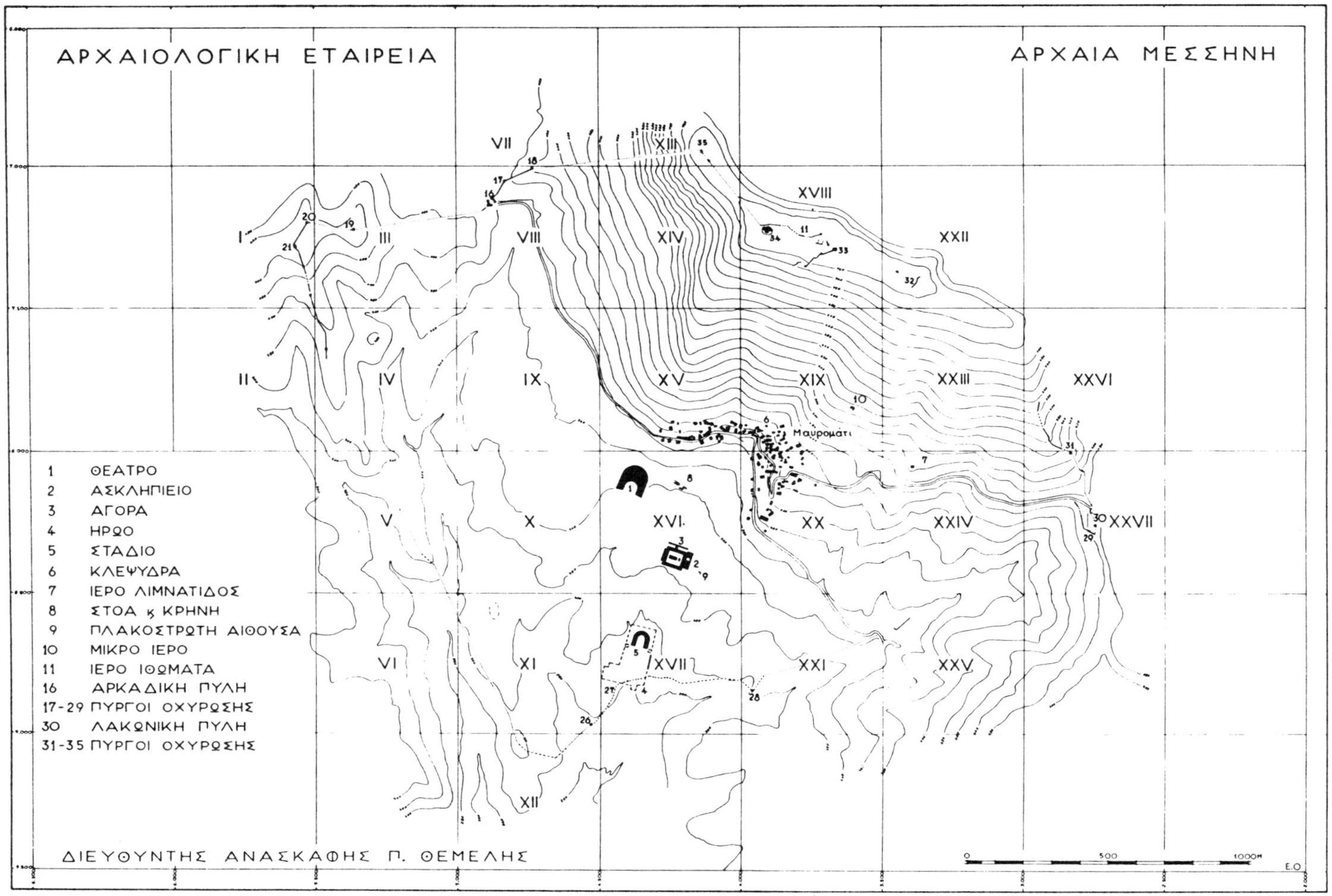

Fig. 1. Topographical plan of Messene, indicating the location of the excavated buildings: 1. Theater, 2. Asklepieion, 3. Agora, 4. Heroon, 5. Stadium, 6. Klepsydra, 7. Sanctuary of Limnatis, 8. North Stoa and Fountain House, 9. Paved Hall, 10. Small Temple, 11. Sanctuary of Zeus Ithomatas, 16. Arcadian Gate, 17–29. Towers, 30. Laconian Gate, 31–35. Towers

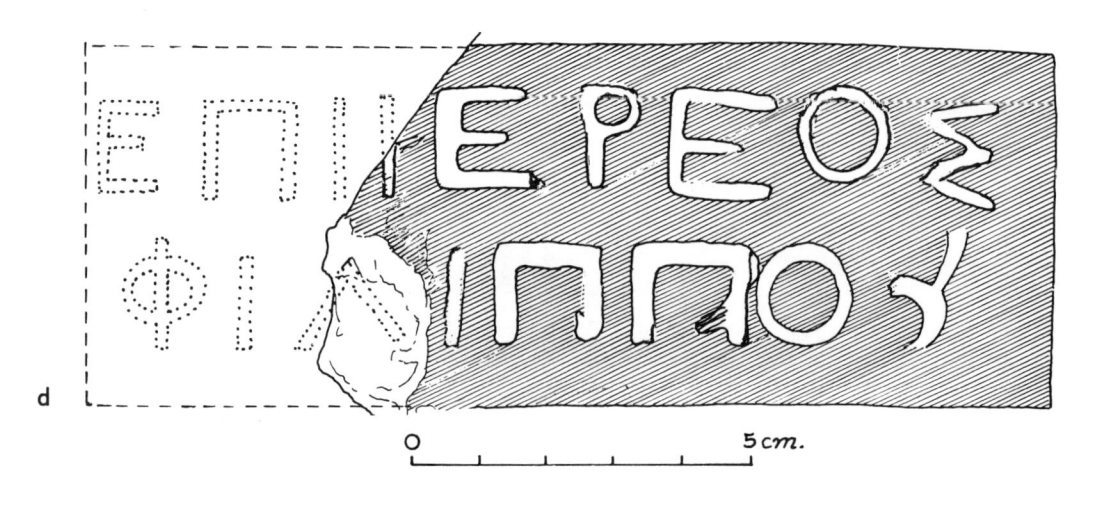

FIG. 2. Stamps occurring on Laconian pan and cover tiles from Messene

FIG. 3. Laconian antefix Type 1 with bust of Artemis

the slender almost triangular form of the antefix (with the vertical sides slightly convex) as well as the style of the goddess's head, the modeling of her face turned slightly to her left, and her hairdress bound with a stephane allow a date in the 3rd century B.C. and the attribution of this type of antefix to the roof of the small temple of Artemis Ortheia. Some of the ΕΠΙ ΙΕΡΕΟΣ stamps may come from the tiles of this temple.

Laconian antefixes of Type 2 (Fig. 5; Pl. 49:a) have been found on the north raised wing of the Asklepieion complex,[17] where most of the ΔΑΜΟΣΙΟΣ stamped tiles were also uncovered; in the West Parodos of the Theater, probably coming from the roof of the *skene*;[18] and at the east side of the Stadium, close to the stone thrones of the proedria (Pl. 49:b), deriving from the roof of a wooden shelter that protected the officials of the contests from sun and rain. Post holes at regular intervals have been brought to light on the pavement in front of and behind the stone seats.

The originality and high quality of this Messenian mold product are obvious; from a shaggy and voluminous tripartite acanthus emerges a dominating six-petaled flower and two

[17] This north wing, composed of two symmetrically disposed and divided large rooms on both sides of the north propylon, the original function of which was related to Asklepios' cult, was used as the Sebasteion or Caesareum in the Augustan period when the cult of this emperor and Roma found here an appropriate place to settle: *IG* V[1], 1444B, 1462. Groag 1939, p. 115; Orlandos 1959, pp. 170–171; Orlandos 1969, p. 103. *SEG* XXIII, 1968, p. 207; Migeotte 1985, pp. 597–607; Hänlein-Schäfer 1985, pp. 162–163, A 23; Themelis 1988, pp. 52–58.

[18] Themelis 1988, pp. 48–52, pl. 38:b.

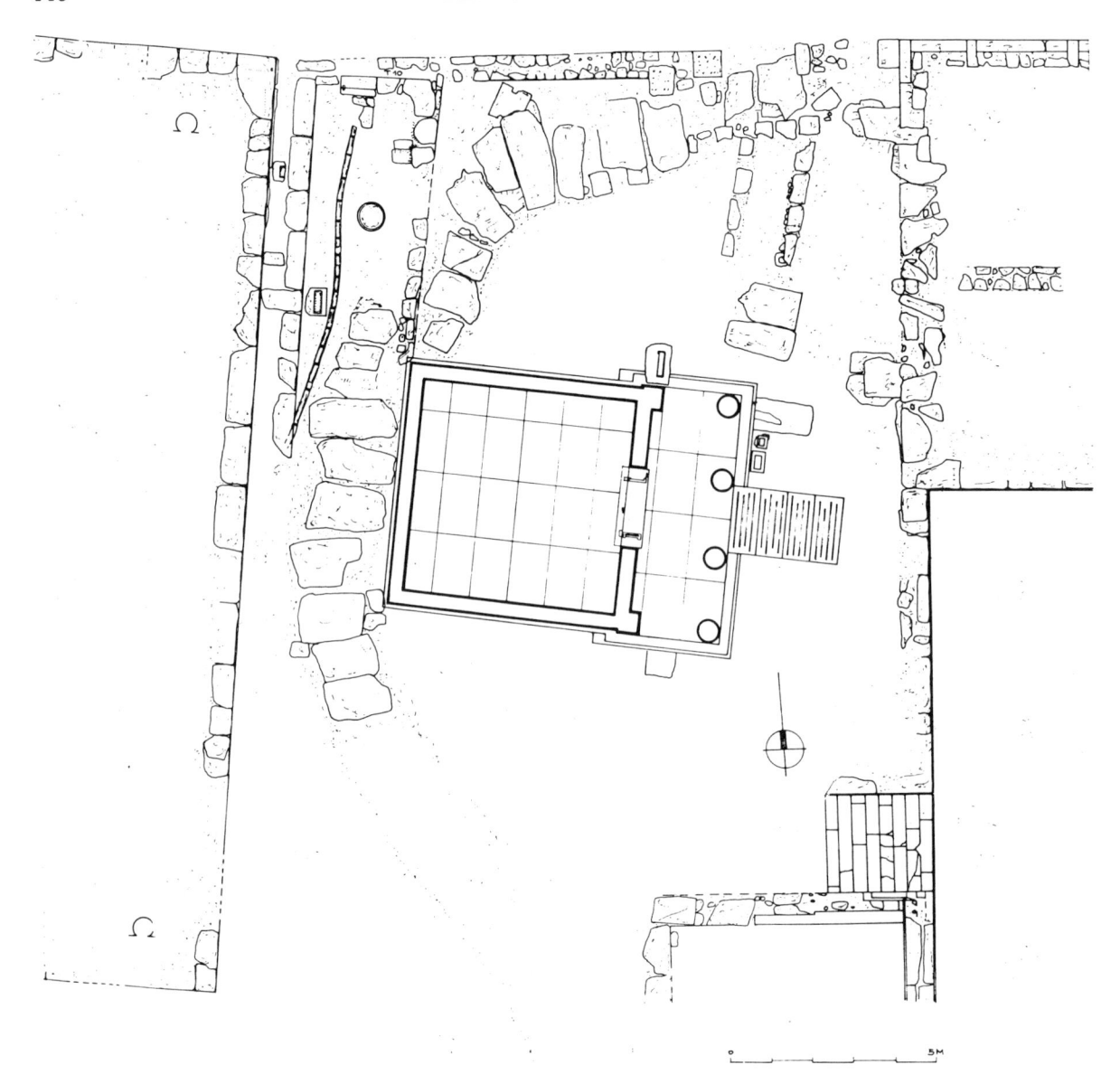

FIG. 4. Ground plan of the Ortheia sanctuary

antithetic spirals; the flower is flanked by two pairs of slender unequal spirals in mirror image. The central vegetal pattern is framed by a thin astragal and a broad projecting egg-and-dart molding. The boldness in treatment, the three-dimensionality, the torsion of spirals, and in general the baroque stylistic traits of the modeling assign this type of Laconian antefix to the early 2nd century B.C. This dating fits well the date of the Asklepieion complex, which must have been constructed in the first quarter of the 2nd century B.C., presumably before the final annexation of Messene by the Achaean League 183/2 B.C. This was a flourishing period for the city, with great building activity during which most of the above-mentioned buildings were erected, with the exception of the Ortheia temple, the North Stoa of the agora, the first phase of the Baths, and the Limnatis sanctuary; this is also the period of the

Fig. 5. Laconian antefixes Type 2

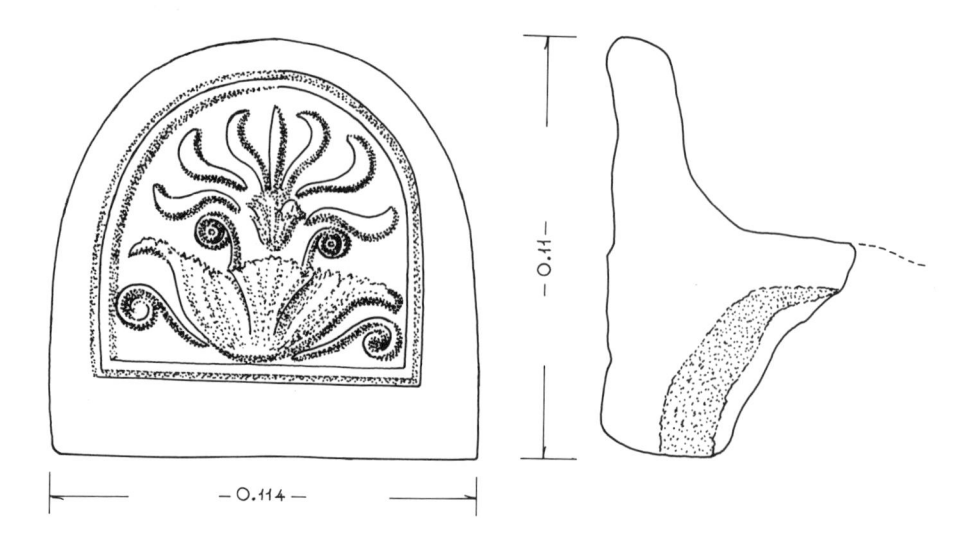

Fig. 6. Laconian antefix Type 3

greatest fame and sculptural production of Damophon, who made all the marble cult statues in the Asklepieion (Pausanias 4.31.10).[19] Fragments of Type 2 Laconian antefixes, as well as fragments of Laconian pan and cover tiles bearing the ΔΑΜΟΣΙΟΣ stamp, were found in fill to the east of the Sebasteion, rather securely dated on the basis of coins, pottery, and stamped amphora handles to the second half of the 2nd century B.C.,[20] a *terminus ante quem* for the dating of this type of antefix.

A fragment of Laconian antefix (inv. no. 1716) (Pl. 49:c) of rather poor workmanship constitutes a variant of Type 2. The linear and dry style of its design in low relief indicates a later date; it may be attributed to the repair of the horizontal cornice (παραετίς) of the Caesareum by the "Quaestor pro Praetore" Marcus Caesius Gallus in the 1st century after Christ.[21]

Type 3 Laconian antefix is represented by a chance find with no provenance and of small size, 11 cm. high (Fig. 6; Pl. 49:d). Its high relief decoration is composed of a thick tripartite acanthus from which two horizontal and two vertical spirals emerge; a broad seven-leaf palmette springs up from a central, higher placed, acanthus leaf. It is related to Type 2 as far as the high relief and the main elements of the design are concerned.

To the Type 4 Laconian antefix is ascribed a unique piece (Pl. 49:e) found by chance in the fields south of the city walls in an area of cemeteries. Its form is almost square (18.2 × 18 cm.) ending in a triangle with concave sides; it is decorated with the head of a Medusa (Rondanini

[19] The cult statues, as their bases indicate, are closely connected with the architecture and contemporary with it. The *floruit* of Damophon is assigned to 180–160 B.C.: Bol and Eckstein 1975, pp. 83–93; Lévy and Marcadé 1972, p. 986; *RE* Supplement XV, 1978, *s.v.* Messene, col. 288. (E. Meyer); Despinis 1966, pp. 378–385; Habicht 1985, p. 57. The decrees honoring Damophon (son of Philippos) mentioned above (p. 142) offer additional evidence concerning the areas and the *floruit* of his activity: Themelis 1990, pp. 31–32; Themelis 1993, pp. 34–39.

[20] Themelis 1988, pp. 54 (trial trench Z) and 74, pls. 41–44.

[21] *IG* V[1] 1462. Cf. Bardani 1986, pp. 79–81.

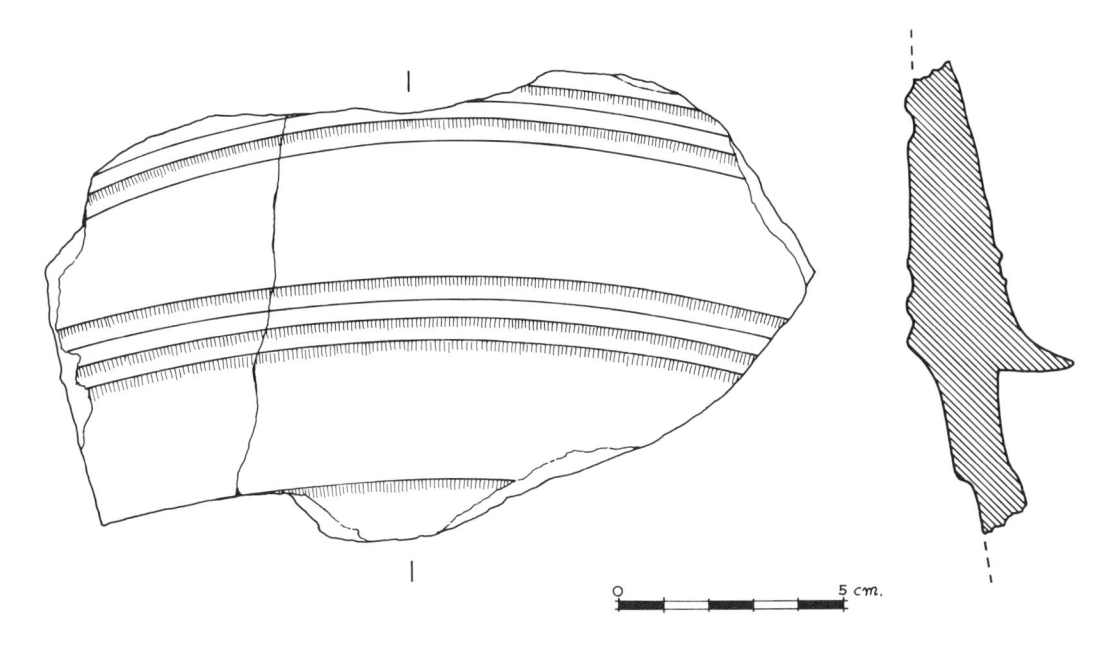

Fig. 7. Fragments of Laconian disc acroterion of the 6th century B.C. (inv. no. 1701)

type)[22] in high relief; the fleshy and rounded face of the female daemon is surrounded by snakes mingled with her hair, while two short wings sprout from her forehead. Despite weathering, the plastic virtues of the work are undeniable and comparable to classicizing sculptural works of the 2nd century B.C. and in particular to the Tritonesses on the throne of the Damophontian Lykosoura divinities.[23] The form of this Laconian antefix as well as the structure and motif of its decoration with a frontal Medusa head occupying the entire front plaque without vegetal decoration is unusual for the Greek mainland, where figural representations (heads, busts, whole figures, or animals) normally occupy the center and lower part of the pattern, being rather subordinated to the dominant vegetal design composed of spirals and palmettes. South Italy and Sicily seem to be the source of inspiration for this type of antefix; it will suffice to refer to the extensive series of Medusa-head antefixes in baroque style from Morgantina.[24] Some examples from Asia Minor and the Black Sea seem to derive from Italian prototypes as well.[25] The Medusa medallion on a bowl from Phaistos[26] dated to the period of Antiochos III (223–187 B.C.), of similar structure but more "pathetic" than ours, and the applied Medusa head in the middle of a vegetal relief frieze on polychrome

[22] Buschor 1958, pp. 26–27.
[23] Tritons and Tritonesses of Lykosoura: Karouzou 1967, p. 170, nos. 2171–2175, pl. 58.
[24] Uhlenbrock 1988, pp. 139–140; Kenfield 1994; cf. Brandes-Druba 1994.
[25] Cf. Stella G. Miller 1994; Zimmermann 1994; a peculiar type of Hellenistic antefix from Samos (frontal face of Gorgon-Medusa above horizontal spirals) suggesting a probable Italian source of inspiration: Kyrieleis 1978, p. 257, fig. 9. Cf. Buschor 1961–1962, p. 280, pl. 342 and the Gorgon head of a sima from Mieza (Macedonia): Kaltsas 1988, pp. 85–86, pl. 25 στ., no. 85. See also Andrén 1940, pp. 53, 56–57, pls. 20, 64–66.
[26] Callaghan 1983; p. 37; La Rosa 1990, p. 161, fig. 82:b.

painted ware from Centuripe[27] seem to form a chronological frame in which the Messenian Medusa head finds its place. The sepulchral symbolism of the Medusa head does seem to fit the use of our antefix on the roof of a grave monument of the naïskos type not unattested at Messene.

I close my brief account on the Laconian antefixes by presenting a few fragments of Archaic 6th-century pedimental disc acroteria from the area of the Asklepieion (Fig. 7; Pl. 49:f); they are covered with dark brown or black paint and are decorated with alternating bands and grooves. They belong to a type known from Olympia, Arcadia (Phigalia), and elsewhere,[28] and they witness the existence of Archaic structures at Messene earlier than the foundation of the new city in 369 B.C. Architectural remains of the Geometric and the Archaic periods were actually revealed in the courtyard of the Asklepieion by the northeast corner of the great temple[29] as well as under the cella of the Ortheia temple.

## CORINTHIAN ANTEFIXES AND SIMAS

The Corinthian antefixes can be tentatively divided into ten main types on the basis of their design and ornamental structure; seven of them have been associated with corresponding simas. These main types are distinguishable on the evidence of their common stylistic traits as four groups. Their relative chronological sequence is based partly on contextual evidence and partly on their attribution to the roofs of securely dated buildings.

Group A or "Classical Style," of the 4th century B.C. comprising one type of antefix (Fig. 8; Pl. 50:a).

Group B or "Plain Style," dating to the 3rd century B.C. and consisting of five types (Types 2–6) of antefixes and four simas (Figs. 9–17; Pls. 50:b–52).

Group C or "Rich Style," which dates to the first half of the 2nd century B.C. and comprises two types (Types 7 and 8) of antefixes and four simas (Figs. 19–23; Pls. 53, 55:a, b, 56:a, b).

Group D or "Late Style," comprising two types (Types 9 and 10) of antefixes (Figs. 24, 25; Pl. 56:c, d).

New finds will certainly enrich the material and will complete or modify the typology and the grouping.

### A. Classical Style

To Group A belongs the antefix Type 1 (Fig. 8; Pl. 50:a) represented by a few fragmentary examples uncovered to the northwest of the Asklepieion near the retaining wall of a sanctuary adjacent to the Ortheia temenos; this sanctuary, not mentioned by Pausanias, is not related to Athena Kyparissia, as we first suggested,[30] but to a hero cult, according to more recent

---

[27] The date of these vases is disputed, but a late 2nd-century date seems probable: Pollitt 1986, pp. 194–195, fig. 208, bib. no. 9.

[28] Themelis 1965, p. 207, pl. 213; Yalouris 1968, pp. 57–65 and note 1 with bibliography.

[29] Themelis 1987, pp. 87–88, fig. 12, pl. 68:b. E. Meyer's rather dogmatic statement that "irgendwelche älteren Siedlungsfunde liegen von der Stelle nicht vor" in *RE*, Supplement XV, 1978, *s.v.* Messene, p. 137 is not correct.

[30] Themelis 1988, p. 63; *SEG* XXIII, 1968, pp. 209–210.

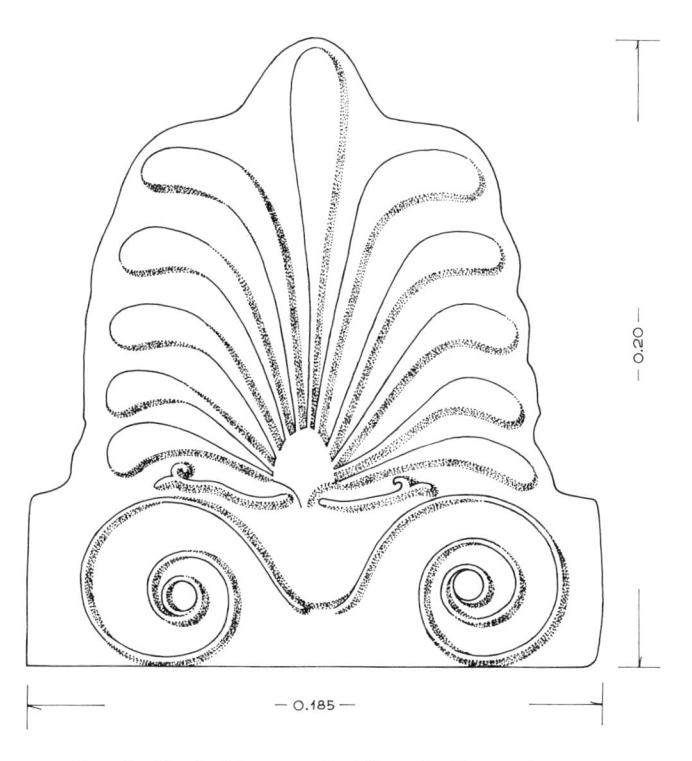

Fig. 8. Corinthian antefix Type 1, Group A

Fig. 9. Corinthian antefix Type 2, Group B

Fig. 10. Corinthian antefix Type 3, Group B

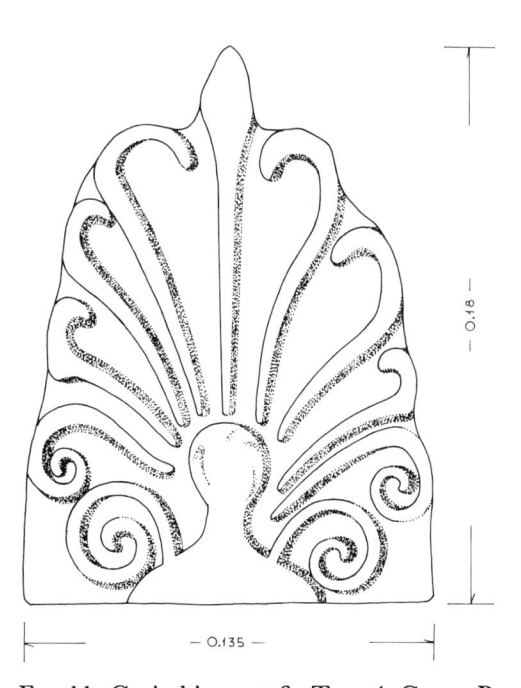

Fig. 11. Corinthian antefix Type 4, Group B

finds. The antefix is decorated with a pair of broad-eyed volutes joined by a channel to an acanthus; a quite accurately modeled and fine palmette of eleven leaves emerges from a tongue-shaped heart. Two modest stems spread horizontally to both sides of the heart below the palmette; the volute zone is low and wider than the anthemion one. The light ocher-painted relief contrasts with the dark-painted background. This type of antefix is attested mainly in the Argolid, where it is dated early in the 4th century B.C.[31] Our example cannot be earlier than 369 B.C., and a date in the second half of the 4th century seems rather secure; it is the earliest architectural terracotta found at Messene thus far, after the foundation of the new city.

B. PLAIN STYLE

To Group B or the plain-style group are attributed five types (2–6) of Corinthian antefixes and four corresponding simas (Figs. 9–17; Pls. 50:b–52). Common main features of the group are the low relief, the fine and clear design, the spacious composition, the dominant role of palmette and spiral, and the absence or more or less modest presence of the acanthus. The same features have been observed on the Laconian antefix Type 1 from the Ortheia temple, which we dated to the 3rd century B.C. Three of the simas display floral waterspouts, many fragments of which have been also found, while the fourth one has the usual form of a lion's head spout (Fig. 17).

The antefixes of Group B, products of local workshops, display stylistic and thematic affinities to a series of architectural terracottas produced by Corinthian workshops in the late 4th or early 3rd century B.C. and reproduced in variations dating to the 3rd century B.C. and later by local artisans in Perachora, Delphi, Epidauros, Lousoi, Dodona, Kassope, Pella, Olympia, Kerkyra,[32] and Illyria (Epidamnos, Antigonea, and Buthrot).[33] Stone simas of buildings dated in the 3rd century B.C. as, for example, the Arsinoeion of Samothrace[34] and the Aphrodite temple by Messa on Lesbos,[35] are stylistically comparable to the simas of Group B.

The antefix Type 2 of Group B (Fig. 9; Pl. 50:b) which occurs in two sizes (16 and 19 cm. high) is represented by abundant examples found at the Stadium, probably coming from the roofs of the stoas around it, in the Fountain House at the north side of the agora, and in the baths south of the Asklepieion. The leaves of the palmette are double, the S-shaped scrolls are paired in a lyre pattern and twice twisted as on the corresponding sima (Fig. 14:a; Pl. 50:c), where the spirals emerge from a horizontal fluted sheath, the cauliculus, crowned with an acanthus leaf. The profile of the sima is typical for the whole series, with a projecting egg-and-dart molding along the top edge and a smooth band or fascia below, usually plain on the front

[31] Waldstein 1902, p. 130, pl. 23; Deshayes 1966, p. 230, pl. 51.
[32] Billot 1976, p. 123, note 93 with bibliographic references. Kaltsas 1988, pp. 69–71, notes 200–205, colorplate VII, pls. 8, 9, 15, 20, 21; Vlachopoulou-Oikonomou 1986, pp. 114–187 and 279, pls. 10–15; Andreou 1983, pp. 20–21, pls. 6, 7, 8:a.
[33] Budina 1994.
[34] Bauer 1973, pl. 30:2; Ehrhardt 1985, p. 275, fig. 48.
[35] Hoepfner 1990, p. 7, fig. 10.

and with a painted astragal on the underside. The terracotta antefixes of the small temple of Pamisos at Aghios Floros in Messenia are similar to the ones from Messene (Fig. 18).[36]

The slightly larger antefix Type 3 of the same group (Fig. 10; Pl. 51:a) is similar to the previous one as far as composition and motifs are concerned. Different are the depressed lyre pattern, the appearance of acanthus half-leaves along the ground line and on both sides of the upper spirals on the antefix, as well as the single twist of the spirals on the sima and the emergence of acanthus and cauliculi from the angle between the fascia and waterspout (Fig. 15; Pl. 51:b, c).

Type 4 antefix and sima of Group B (Figs. 11, 16: Pls. 51:d, 52:a) consists only of one antefix and two fragments of simas, one of which was found at the sanctuary of Artemis Limnatis on the south slope of Ithome (Fig. 1, no. 7),[37] dated mainly on the basis of its architectural style to the late 3rd century B.C. The sima is similar to the previous one except for the smaller dimensions, but the antefix demands special attention: the combination of a female bust portraying a divinity, presumably Limnatis, with an abstract vegetal motif composed of a seven-leafed palmette that emerges from her head like a high crown and by pairs of spirals on both sides of her shoulders are closely related to the Laconian antefix Type 1 from the Artemis Ortheia temple as far as style and motifs are concerned. The bust of the goddess on both types occupies the central lower area replacing the heart of the palmette and the lyre pattern. This structural feature, with the palmette still dominating as the main ornamental element in contrast to the South Italian parallels, where the frontal face of the figure is the dominant decorative element occupying most of the plaque of the antefix,[38] suggests a rather mainland Greek and especially Peloponnesian source of inspiration.[39] Corinthian workshops of the late 4th or early 3rd century B.C. seem to have introduced figural subjects into the vegetal repertory of architectural terracottas attested since the Early Archaic period; the innovation spread quickly and was adopted by local workshops not only in the Corinthia and the Argolid but also in Arkadia, Messenia, Elis (and Olympia), Akarnania, Phokis, Epiros, Illyria, Kerkyra, and elsewhere.[40] The repertory is relatively rich, comprising divine or daemonic heads, busts, whole figure, and masks, as well as animals that are not confined to the antefixes but occasionally appear on the simas as well among vegetal motifs and continue to be reproduced down to the Roman Imperial period.

Even though most of the Hellenistic architectural terracottas (including the figural ones) from the above-mentioned regions still remain unpublished, the material known so far, although scanty, allows the following tentative conclusion: except for subjects with a general apotropaic and chthonic Dionysian character, such as Gorgon-Medusas, silens, satyrs, and

---

[36] Valmin 1938; Papachatzis 1979, p. 112, fig. 38.

[37] Le Bas 1844, pp. 422–423. *IG* V¹, 1442, 1458; Themelis 1988, p. 72, fig. 15.

[38] See notes 24 and 25 above.

[39] Cf. Billot 1976, pp. 131–132, notes 135–138; Hübner 1976, pp. 175–183; Pliny, *NatHist* 35.152 says that Butades of Sikyon "primus personas tegularum extremis imbricibus inposuit."

[40] Billot 1976, p. 423, note 93, p. 131, note 135, p. 133, note 146. Hübner 1976, pp. 175–183; Vlachopoulou-Oikonomou 1986, pp. 165–183, 192–210, pls. 17–19. Corinthian influence in Illyria through the Corinthian-Corcyraean colonies of Epidamnos and Apollonia dates from the late 7th and 6th century B.C. From the early 4th century B.C., however, South Italian elements were introduced in the region after the extended colonization under the leadership of the tyrant of Syracuse Dionysios the Elder who founded Issa (island of Vis) in 397–390 B.C. and Pharos (island of Hvar) in 385/384 B.C.: Stipcevic 1977, pp. 38–39.

FIG. 12. Corinthian antefix Type 5, Group B

FIG. 13. Corinthian antefix Type 6, Group B

maenads, most of the figures represented on Hellenistic architectural terracottas allude to local cults and divinities. It will suffice to refer here to the antefixes from Dodona and Kassope with the symbols of Zeus, the thunderbolt and the eagle, or with Ganymede's abduction by the eagle-Zeus, combined with palmettes and spirals, dated in the late 3rd or early 2nd century B.C.,[41] which are very characteristic and instructive examples.

Type 5 (Group B) architectural terracottas (Figs. 12, 17; Pl. 52:b, c), made with clay resembling Corinthian clay, are of fine workmanship; the group is represented by two complete antefixes found at the Limnatis sanctuary and abundant fragments of simas, many of them found north of the Ortheia temple and probably coming from the roof of the Ionic stoa along the west side of the precinct (Fig. 4). The contour of the antefix does not follow the curves of the palmette leaves, the cauliculi on the sima are not fluted, the end spirals are

---

[41] Evangelides and Dakaris 1959, pp. 166–168, pl. 11:c; Dakaris 1963, p. 37, pl. 19; Dakaris 1952, pp. 348–351, figs. 26–29; Dakaris 1954, p. 207, figs. 8, 9; Dakaris 1989, pp. 35, 37, 55–56, fig. 158:16a, b. Vlachopoulou-Oikonomou 1986, pp. 165–183, 192–210, pls. 17–19: Hübner 1976, pp. 180–183, pls. 63:3–5, 64:5–7. Cf. the antefixes with an Athena head in the center of the palmette at Pella: Makaronas and Youri 1989, p. 112, figs. 123, 125. Cf. also the Artemis bust between spirals on a terracotta pilaster capital from Myrina: Mollard-Besques 1963, p. 150, pl. 187:b, c; and the protomes on the crowning of two grave stelae in Kavala, Athens and Samikon (Elis): Jucker 1961, p. 164.

smaller, and a flower emerges from the junction of the spiral pairs.[42] Type 5, one of the latest of the Group, in my opinion, foreshadows the succeeding Group C.

Type 6 of Group B, comprising only antefixes, is a variant of Types 2 and 3 (Fig. 13; Pl. 52:d). The palmette leaves are not double, the lyre pattern is more distinct and adorned with delicate extensions; the bisected fork of the pendant central stem does not occur on the previous antefixes and the dental contour that continues down to the ground line does not exactly correspond to the curves of the design. Despite its formal affinities to Types 2 and 3, it is a rather later derivative of poor workmanship probably used in the repair of buildings epigraphically attested for the 1st century after Christ.[43] A defect in one of the molds used is responsible for the peculiar form of the lower left palmette leaf.

C. RICH STYLE

The two types (7 and 8) of antefixes and the four simas attributed to Group C are outstanding representatives of this style of the first half of the 2nd century B.C., a period during which Messenian arts and crafts, including architectural terracottas, reached their zenith (Figs. 19–23; Pls. 53, 55:a, b, 56:a, b).

Type 7 of this group is the best preserved, consisting of one antefix (Fig. 19:c) and many complete simas not only lateral but also raking (Fig. 19:a, b; Pl. 53:a–d), found mainly in the area of the agora north of the Asklepieion. The lateral sima of this type, although adorned with the typical motifs (for example, waterspouts in the form of a lion's head separated by double acanthus scrolls) is distinguished by the dense arrangement of motifs and the especially high relief; the stem of the spirals is partly twisted, while flowers emerge not only from the spiral contacts but also from the acanthus that crowns the cauliculus.[44] The lion's heads are freely modeled (not cast in a mold as is the case with the whole sima decoration) and applied separately to the spout opening before firing.[45] The deep depressions on both sides of the lion's forehead served for safer attachment. The turbulent manes cover most of the basic acanthus foliage and part of the start of the spirals. The free modeling presumably made by different hands produced different results apparent on the two better-preserved examples (Pl. 53:a), which would undoubtedly have led to falsely differentiated stylistic evaluation of the two animals' heads had they happened to be found detached from the sima.

The special features of the style are even better illustrated by the antefix (Fig. 19:c; Pl. 53:a) and especially the raking sima of the same Group C (Fig. 19:a, b; Pl. 53:b–d). No description could be considered satisfactory for such sculptural works in clay: two winged female figures very much like vegetal Nikai naked above the thighs are flying from both sides toward a floral centerpiece that forms the point of attraction or object of veneration; the lower part of each body is shaped into an elaborate and upward-curved acanthus leaf from which emerges a thorny spiral with double curl; similarly shaped are also their acanthus

---

[42] Forerunners of this type of sima and flower see in Kaltsas 1988, p. 75. Cf. also Dyggve, Poulsen, and Rhomaios 1934, fig. 47.

[43] See notes 17 and 21 above.

[44] See note 41 above. Cf. Billot 1976, nos. 14–21, pl. 25. Dyggve, Poulsen, and Rhomaios 1934, fig. 47; Kourouniotes 1911, p. 68, fig. 69; Hoepfner 1990, pp. 8–9, fig. 16 (= Artemision in Magnesia), p. 10, fig. 38 (= Smintheon in Troas).

[45] Cf. the lion's heads of similar modeling in Billot 1976, pl. 25. Gneisz 1994.

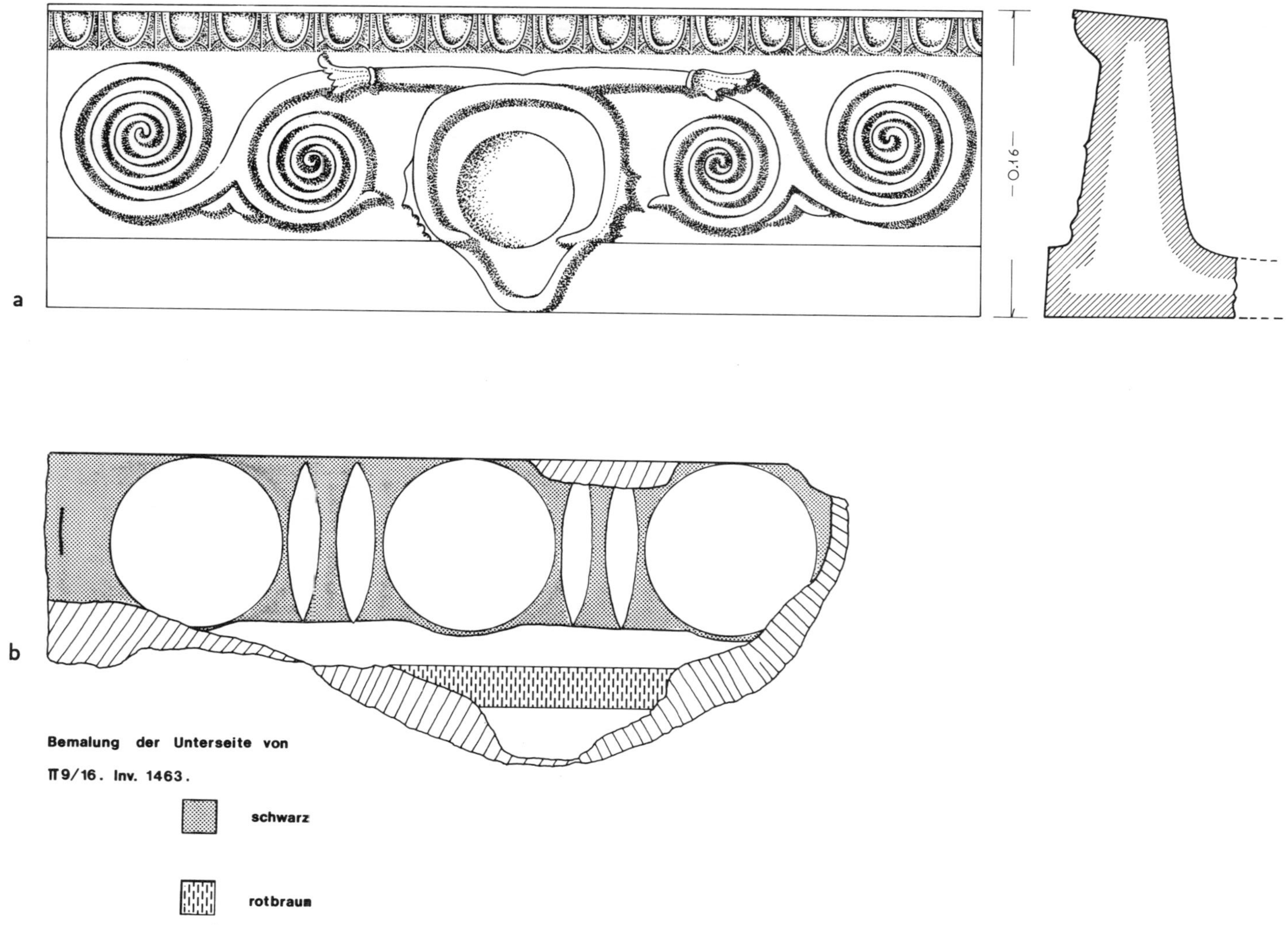

Bemalung der Unterseite von
π 9/16 . Inv. 1463.

schwarz

rotbraun

FIG. 14. Sima of Group B related to antefix Type 2. (a) Front view, reconstructed, (b) painted decoration of underside

wings. Both vegetal women touch or take hold with their outstretched hands (the right one with her right hand) the strongly curved and twisted sheaths of the cauliculi, which rise symmetrically on both sides of the central floral pattern and end in flowers. *Horror vacui* seems to have guided the artist's hand to fill all gaps between the vegetal Nikai and the central pattern with all sorts of large flowers that hang from long flexible stems springing up from the acanthi in all directions. The central floral pattern is repeated in larger scale and slightly variegated on the antefix (Pl. 53:a) of the lateral sima: two twisted S-shaped stems ending in spirals, acanthus, and flower buds between them spring up boldly from a tripartite asymmetric acanthus; a large cornucopia-like flower with a thorny calyx emerging from the central acanthus leaf occupies the space between the S-shaped stems.

The problem of origin and source or sources of inspiration of our vegetal theme combined with "plant figures" demands a more detailed analysis. Vegetal ornamentation in Greece experienced an essential structural transformation from the late 5th century B.C. onwards. Vigorous naturalistic and sometimes complex vegetal representations, including acanthus leaves, the lily, and other flowers, appear on the side or gradually take the place of the conservative and paratactic groups of ornaments in architecture and minor arts. The invention of the "Corinthian" capital (attributed to Kallimachos) probably had a share in its adaption of the new ornamental taste, while coroplasts and metalsmiths contributed to its diffusion. New vegetal themes with distinctive regional traits became especially popular in South Italy already in the early 4th century B.C., indicated by numerous examples mainly on the neck of red-figured Apulian vases. Thin volutes and spirals in perspective illusion and all sorts of large flowers in groups or in tiers ("Dreiblütengruppen", "Stockwerkblüten") and in various phases of growth as well as thin stems emerging from a central acanthus calyx often crowned with a human, usually female, head are some of the characteristics of South Italian subjects. South Italian ornamental taste seems to have had a certain influence (through imports, traveling artists, or pattern books) on Macedonian, Thracian, and especially central Italian architecture and minor arts (tomb painting, mosaics, textiles, jewelery, etc.) of the late 4th and early 3rd century B.C.[46] The influence was especially strong on Etrusco-Italic terracotta friezes with vegetal ornaments among which human heads also occasionally appear.[47]

The long strong tradition of vegetal themes on the Greek mainland did not allow the intrusion of South Italian or Italic vegetal systems in its ornamental repertory[48] and continued to inspire the peripheral workshops. Even in Macedonia where Italic influence is generally detectable, imitations or even imports of late 4th/early 3rd-century B.C. architectural terracottas from Athenian and Peloponnesian (especially Corinthian) workshops

---

[46] Klumbach 1937, pp. 29–30; Andrén, 1940, pp. 53–55; Toynbee and Ward Perkins 1950, pp. 1–4; Kraus 1953, pp. 31–32; Jucker 1961, p. 164; Lullies 1962, pp. 12–13; Zervoudaki 1968, pp. 1–88; Trumpf-Lyritzaki 1969, introduction; Börker 1973, pp. 287–288; Bauer 1973, pp. 9–13; Robertson 1975, pp. 440, 486–487, who suggests an origin of the vegetal motifs from the painting of the Sicyonian painter Pausias who, according to Pliny, *NatHist* 35.123, "ad numerossimam florum varietatem perduxit artem illam." Themelis 1979, pp. 136–137; Hamdorf 1979, pp. 31–41; Pfrommer 1982, pp. 119–130; Lauter 1986, p. 250; Lauter-Bufé 1987, p. 65; Sauron 1988, pp. 3–4, 10–19; Schauenburg 1989, pp. 36–37; Känel 1991, pp. 172–174.

[47] Känel 1991, pp. 173–174, note 28, 175.

[48] Pfrommer 1982, p. 167.

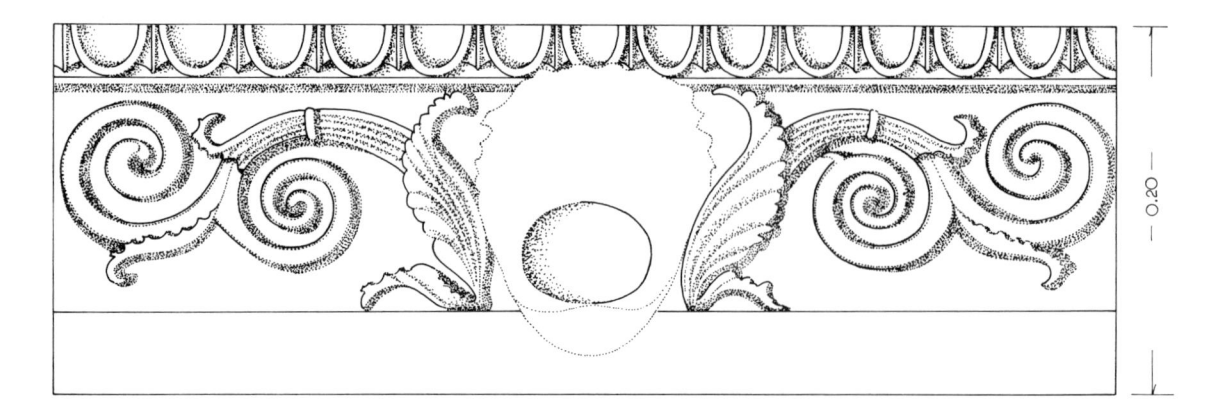

FIG. 15. Sima of Group B related to antefix Type 3

FIG. 16. Sima of Group B related to antefix Type 4

FIG. 17. Sima of Group B related to antefix Type 5

are well attested.[49] The diffusion of vegetal motifs during the Hellenistic period and the development of many regional styles makes detection of the possible sources of inspiration complicated and often fruitless. The lack of artistic tradition in Messene before 369 B.C. and its geographical situation would justify an Italic influence, as is probably the case with the Laconian antefix Type 2 described above. Certain features of the architectural terracottas in Group B, Type 7, as, for instance, the large size and form of flowers or flower buds hanging from long, thin, flexible stems on the raking sima, could be compared with Italic examples, but not exclusively because most of the motifs seem to derive from a Hellenistic vegetal "koine".[50] Consequently, a formal analysis of each motif separated from its ornamental context would be meaningless and probably misleading. The general design and effect, the composition of motifs on the antefix, and especially the raking sima displaying the two flying vegetal Nikai that flank the central floral system are unparalleled among architectural terracottas, earlier or contemporary, as far as I know. Thus it is reasonable to accept that we are dealing with the product of a local Hellenistic (2nd century B.C.) workshop closely related to workshops in western Greece comprising Elis, Arkadia, Achaia, and Illyria.

Semihuman, semivegetal figures ("plant divinities") winged or not, male or female, appear on various works of art from the second half of the 4th century B.C. on.[51] Most of them, however, are represented in rigid "archaistic" frontal postures not having any apparent morphological, iconographic, or stylistic affinity to these flying vegetal Nikai. I mention the gold diadem of the 3rd century B.C. with vegetal decoration from Kyme

---

[49] Kaltsas 1988, pp. 69–71. Eclecticism seems to characterize not only Macedonian architecture (Grobel-Miller 1971, pp. 228–229) but also mosaic floral patterns and architectural terracottas.

[50] Similar long, thin and flexible stems on a sofa capital in Rhodes: Konstantinopoulos 1969, p. 483, pl. 481:c and on western Greek tombstones: Fraser and Rönne 1957, pp. 52, 55–59; Fraser and Rönne 1971, pp. 53–54; Papapostolou 1975, pp. 291–292, fig. 1; cf. Dyggve, Poulsen, and Rhomaios 1934, p. 350, fig. 55.

[51] (1) Mosaic of the Vergina Palace: Petsas 1965, pp. 41–42, fig. 7; Andronikos, Makronas, Moutsopoulos, and Bakalakis 1961, pp. 21–22, pls. XVI, XVII; Salzmann 1982, p. 114, no. 130.

(2) The so-called Dionysos-Psilax winged figure on a marble throne found near the pronaos of the Parthenon (Akropolis Museum 1366) and a similar one in the Berlin Museum: Möbius 1926, pp. 117–124, pls. 18–20; Richter 1954, no. 4, pp. 271–276, pls. 47–50; Picard 1935, pp. 317–337; Picard 1963, pp. 961–962, 969, figs. 385, 386.

(3) A marble acroterion from South Russia in Leningrad: Möbius 1926, pl. 19; Picard 1963, fig. 386.

(4) A krater from Canicattini in the Syracuse Museum: Libertini 1950, pp. 97–98, figs. 2, 5; Schauenburg 1957, pp. 198–221.

(5) Stone helmet model from Mid-Rahineh (Egypt) in Amsterdam (Allard Pierson Museum 7866): Ponger 1942, p. 86, no. 177, fig. 4, pl. 39; Möbius 1964, p. 32; Neumann 1965, p. 149, note 28, pl. 59:1.

(6) Gold diadem from Irakleion, Crete (Coll. Metaxas no. 442): Alexiou 1963, p. 310, pl. 359; Neumann 1965, pp. 144–151, pls. 56:1, 57:3.

(7) Wall painting of Tomb No. 69 at Myra in Lycia: Fedak 1990, pp. 98–99, fig. 123:a, b.

(8) Sundial in Rhodes: Konstantinopoulos 1969, p. 466, pl. 471.

(9) Capital from Salamis, Cyprus: Smith 1900, pp. 263–266, no. 1510, pl. 27.

(10) Capital fragment in Cumae: Gabrici 1913, pp. 723–724, fig. 257.

(11) Pilaster capital in Kos: Neumann 1965, p. 149, note 27, pl. 58:1–3.

(12) Eros or Nike on two relief pillars and on moldmade bowls of the early 2nd century B.C. from Pergamon: de Luca 1990, pp. 595–597, pl. 93:2.

(13) Winged vegetal figure (Hekate, Enodoia?) on a pillar capital from Didyma: Voigtländer 1990, pp. 415–416, pl. 63:2.

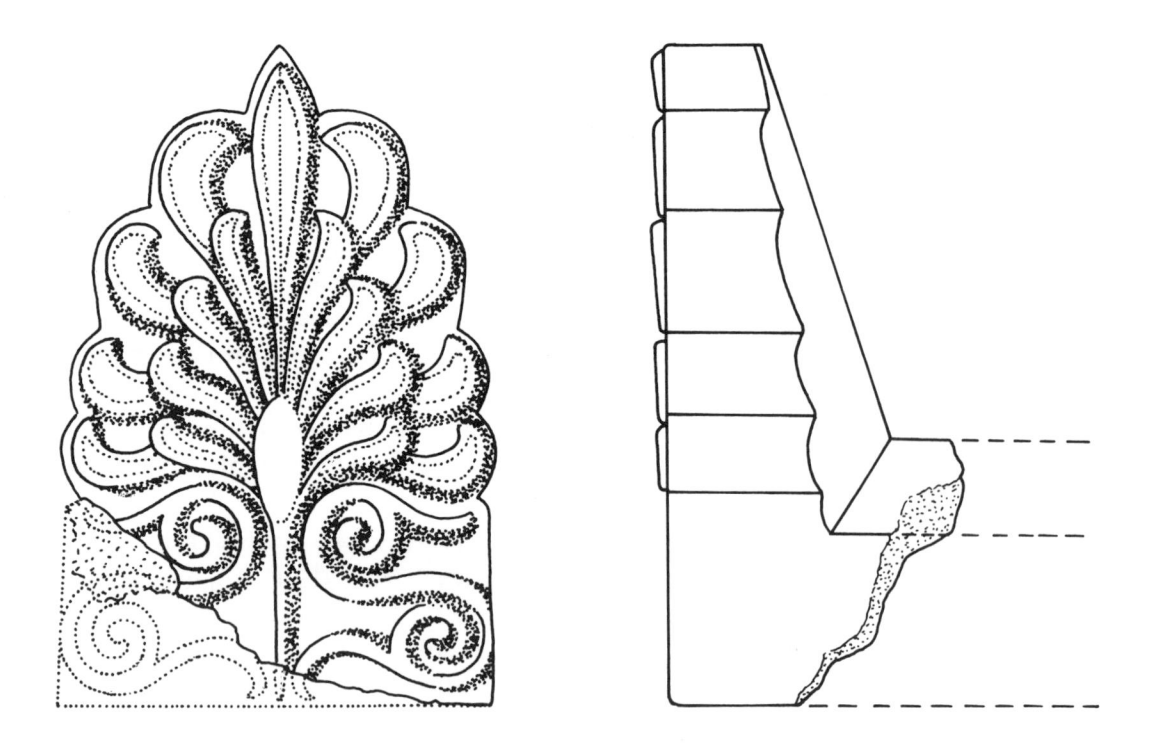

FIG. 18. Terracotta antefix from the temple of Pamisos at Aghios Floros in Messenia

(Aeolis)[52] representing two winged female figures seated on spirals on both sides of a central palmette and holding flower stems just because it combines vegetal motifs with two symmetrically placed winged figures, showing, however, no immediate connection to the Messenian terracotta frieze. The closest parallel is to be found on a grave stele of the 2nd century B.C. from Thebes (inv. no. 552), which displays a scroll running both ways from center, where an amphora (funerary urn?) is held or crowned by two flanking Erotes growing out of the scroll.[53] Fraser and Rönne compare it with the running acanthus scroll decorated with figures of Erotes on the Hephaisteion mosaic from Pergamon, arguing for a probable reflection of Pergamene art on the motif from Thebes.[54]

The vegetal Nikai as hybrid creatures participating in a fantasy scene could well be compared with Tritons and Tritonesses of the marine thiasos popular in Classical and Hellenistic art and usually connected with architecture.[55] Of special meaning are the double-tailed Tritonesses that support the throne of Demeter and Despoina at Lykosoura as well as the friezes with marine themes used with a decorative and symbolic content on

[52] Marshall 1911, p. 172, fig. 53, no. 1614; Neumann 1965, p. 147, pl. 56:b, d. Cf. the female figure seated on the spirals of a central acanthus pattern on the finial of a grave stele from Leukas: Kalligas 1969, p. 259, pl. 262:c.
[53] Fraser and Rönne 1957, p. 16, no. 24, pp. 52–53, pl. 7.
[54] Fraser and Rönne 1957, pp. 53 and 189, note 12.
[55] Lattimore 1976, pp. 31–32, 56–57, pls. IV–XIV, XXIV–XXIX; Karouzou 1974, pp. 26–28, fig. 1, pls. 8–12.

Fig. 19. Raking sima ([a] frontal view, [b] section) connected with antefix Type 7 (c)

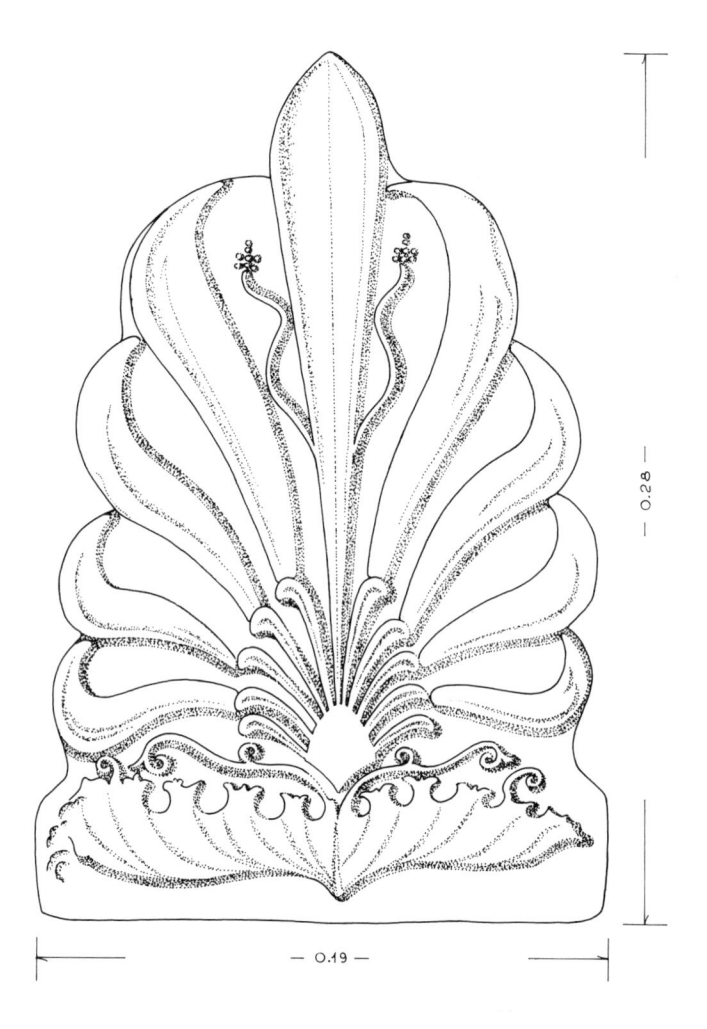

FIG. 20. Corinthian antefix Type 8, Group C

the sacred garment of Despoina;[56] both are attributed to the Messenian sculptor Damophon and dated to the early 2nd century B.C. Two types of figural Corinthian capitals of the same date found in the Asklepieion of Messene should also be mentioned here: they display the upper part of the naked body of winged Nikai and Erotes springing up from acanthus calyxes and holding spiral stems (Pl. 54:a, b).[57] The semihuman, semivegetal winged boys feeding lion griffins on relief plaques from Trajan's Forum[58] are splendid examples of the survival of analogous motifs in the Roman Imperial period.

[56] Cavvadias 1893, p. 11, pl. 4; Dickins and Kourouniotes 1906–1907, pl. 12; Dickins 1911, p. 311, fig. 2; Karouzou 1954, p. 170, nos. 2171–2175, pl. 58; Karouzou 1974, p. 33; Lattimore 1976, p. 56.
[57] Orlandos 1976, pp. 26, 38, figs. 13 and 37; Lauter 1986, p. 268, pl. 36:a, b.
[58] Goethert 1936, pp. 76–78; Bertoldi 1962, pp. 18–20; Borbein 1968, pp. 97–98, 102, note 506; Zanker 1970, p. 513, figs. 22, 23.

Fig. 21. Sima related to antefix Type 8, Group C

Fig. 22. Sima of Group C

Fig. 23. Sima of Group C

Parallels for the vegetal decoration of these simas are to be found on the sofa capitals of the Hellenistic grave stelai from western Greece[59] attested thus far in Elis, Achaia, Arcadia, and Kefallonia, in an area characterized by a certain cultural unity to which Messenia also belongs. The vegetal frieze on a sofa capital from Dyme in Achaia (Patras Museum, inv. no. 2731) dated in the 2nd century B.C.[60] provides the closest parallel to our raking sima despite the absence of the vegetal figures: two double cauliculi crowned with acanthus leaves spring antithetically from a central tripartite acanthus while thin flexible scrolled-up stems ending in large flowers emerge from the cauliculi.

The scene on the raking sima (Fig. 19:a) cannot be merely decorative; it should have a symbolic meaning as well; I would dare to call it "The Glorification of the Floral Symbol" and relate it to a divinity of the vegetal world. The temple of Aphrodite seen by Pausanias (4.31.6) in the agora (?) of Messene near the sanctuary of Poseidon would be an appropriate building to bear these architectural terracottas on its roof. A terracotta figurine of a winged Nike and two terracotta heads of Aphrodite with a flower stephane and flowers around the hair[61] are the only evidence we have concerning the iconography of this goddess at Messene (Pl. 54:c). The smaller head wears a thorny crown that shows formal similarities to the thorny ring of the central flower on the antefix and the raking sima.[62] The figural vases of Attic and Olynthian workshops found in Athens, Megara, the Corinthia, Chalkidike, Boiotia, Cimmerian Bosporus, Euboia, Phokis, Lokris, and Akarnania show an overwhelming preference for scenes of the circle of Aphrodite;[63] the goddess, Erotes, and winged female figures or busts are represented among acanthus spirals, leaves, and flowers or emerging from acanthus calyxes or seashells, thus testifying to the connection of Aphrodite, Eros, and winged women with acanthus motifs and flowers. The Apulian and Lucanian vases of the second half of the 4th century B.C. are also conclusive in this respect.[64]

Type 8 (Group C) of architectural terracottas is rather conservative and classicistic compared to the previous one. A special feature of the sima decoration is the very long two-storied cauliculus as well as the bell flowers (Fig. 21; Pl. 55:a), while on the antefix are the fleshy, sinewed palmette leaves, the second small palmette around the heart, the broad horizontal acanthus leaves along the bottom line, the modest spirals emerging from the acanthus, and the S-shaped thin stems ending in dotted flowers on both sides of the central palmette leaf (Fig. 20; Pl. 55:b). Similar Ω-shaped openings across the upper

---

[59] Papapostolou 1975, p. 292, fig. 1. Cf. the acanthus-spiral frieze with a winged Eros on a marble throne in the Castle of Kos: Neumann 1965, p. 151, pl. 59:2. Cf. McPhee 1979, pp. 159–162 (on a group of squat lekythoi in Agrinion and Ioannina decorated with figures surrounded by vegetal motifs also found on the Adriatic coast, attributed to local workshops of northwestern Greece bearing additional witness to the "cultural unity" of the region).

[60] Papapostolou 1975, p. 292, fig. 1.

[61] Messene Museum, inv. nos. 952, 955, 956, unpublished chance finds.

[62] For an earlier parallel to the thorny spirals on the raking sima, see the gold capital pin from the Peloponnese in the Museum of Fine Arts, Boston (inv. no. 96.718): Depper-Lippitz 1985, pp. 153–154, fig. 106.

[63] Trumpf-Lyritzaki 1969, pp. 126–131. In South Italy there are imitations of these vases: Trumpf-Lyritzaki 1969, p. 112: Plato, *Symposium* 196: οὗ δ' ἂν εὐανθής τε καὶ εὐώδης τόπος ᾖ, ἐνταῦθα δὲ καὶ ἵζει καὶ μένει.

[64] Trendall 1967, p. 159; Robertson 1975, p. 440; Sichtermann 1966, 54K-79, pl. 138. Cf. also the Nikai and Erotes on the gold wreath from Crumentum in Munich (inv. no. 2334): Hamdorf 1979, pp. 31–33, figs. 3, 6.

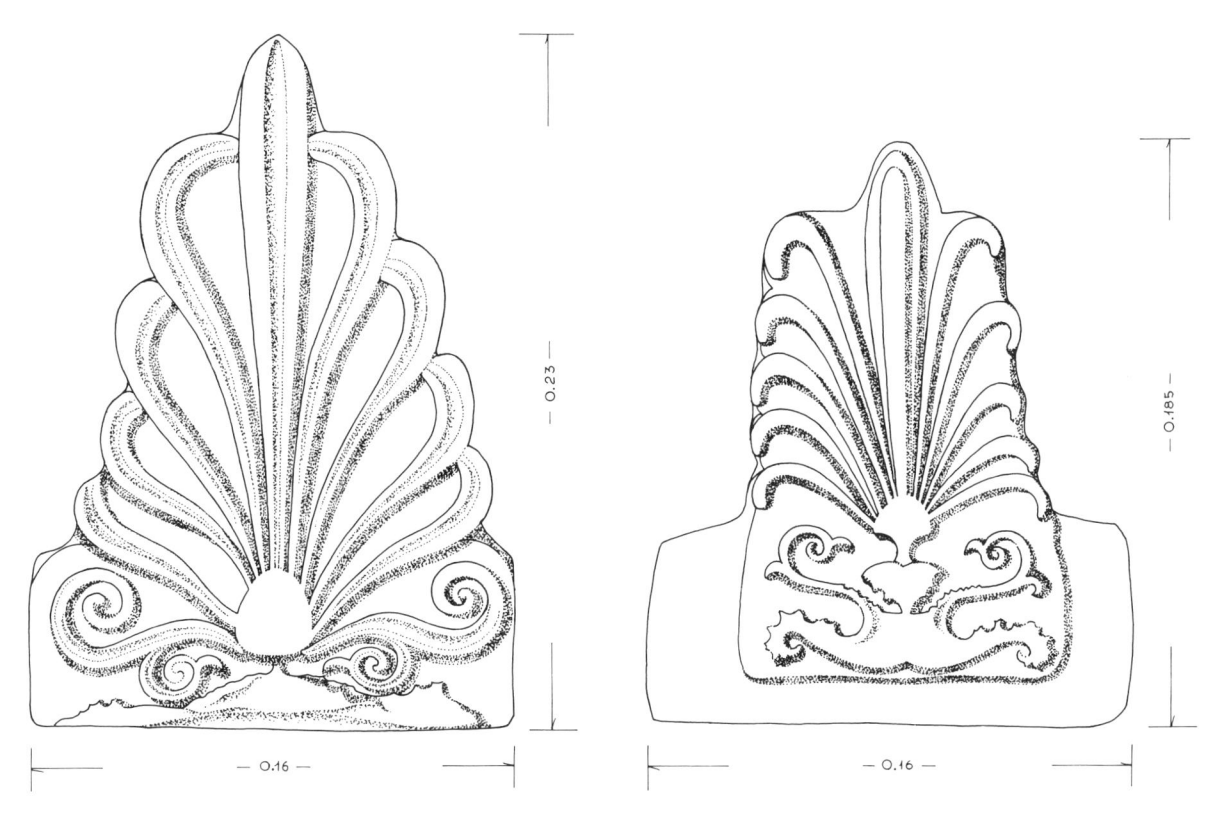

FIG. 24. Corinthian antefix Type 9, Group D

FIG. 25. Corinthian antefix Type 10, Group D

edge of the acanthus occur on the antefixes of the Stoa of Attalos (159–138 B.C.) as well as on the Corinthian capitals of the Olympieion in Athens from the period of Antiochos IV Epiphanes (176–165 B.C.).[65] The stone antefixes and simas from the stoas and the temple of the Asklepieion, dated to the 2nd century B.C.[66] are similar to these Messenian terracotta antefixes and simas (Pl. 55:c). Two more simas with no corresponding antefixes (Figs. 22, 23; Pl. 56:a, b) of the same Group C present slight differentiations as far as form and arrangement of flowers are concerned.

D. LATE STYLE (TYPES 9 AND 10)

Two antefixes without corresponding simas of rather poor workmanship (Figs. 24, 25; Pl. 56:c, d), Type 9 a chance find from the Stadium area, Type 10 of unknown provenance, are at this time the only representatives of Group D. Their motifs are related to earlier pieces. They may derive from buildings, especially stoas, which had been repaired during the 1st century after Christ.[67]

[65] Möbius 1926, p. 121, pl. 19:a, b. Cf. also the acanthi on the finial of the stele from Samikon dated to the 2nd century B.C.: Yalouris 1965, p. 210, pl. 234:b; Fraser and Rönne 1971, pp. 75–76, fig. 38; Papapostolou 1975, p. 294, no. 5.
[66] Orlandos 1969, p. 100, fig. 12, pl. 132:a, b.
[67] See notes 17 and 21 above.

## BIBLIOGRAPHY

Alexiou, S. 1963. «Ἀρχαιότητες καὶ μνημεῖα Κρήτης», Δελτ 18, 1963, Β′2 [1965], pp. 309–316

Andrea, Z. 1976. "Germimet Arkeologjike 1974/5," *Iliria* 4, 1971, pp. 347–349

Andrén, A. 1940. *Architectural Terracottas from Etrusco-Italic Temples* (*Acti Instituti Romani Regni Sueciae* VI), Lund/Leipzig

Andreou, E. 1983. «Τὸ μικρὸ θέατρο τῆς Ἀμβρακίας», Ἠπειρωτικὰ Χρονικὰ 25, pp. 9–23

Andronikos, M., C. Makaronas, N. Moutsopoulos, and G. Bakalakes. 1961. Τὸ ἀνάκτορο τῆς Βεργίνας, Athens

Bardani, V. 1986. «Εἰς *IG* V$^1$, 1462», *HOROS* 6, pp. 79–81

Bauer, H. 1973. *Korinthische Kapitelle des 4. und 3. Jhs. v. Chr.* (*Mitteilungen des Deutschen Archäologischen Instituts, Athenische Abteilung. Beiheft* 3), Berlin

Bertoldi, M. 1962. *Ricerche sulla decorazione architettonica nel Foro Traiano*, Rome

Billot, M.-F. 1976. "Terres cuites architecturales du Musée Épigraphique," Δελτ 31, 1976, Α′ [1980], pp. 87–135

Blouet, A. 1831. *Expédition scientifique de Morée* I, Paris

Börker, C. 1973. "Neuattisches und Pergaminisches an den Ara Pacis-Ranken," *JdI* 88, pp. 287–317

Bol, P., and F. Eckstein. 1975. "Das Polybios Stele in Kleitor," *AntP* 15, pp. 83–93

Borbein, A. H. 1968. *Campanareliefs. Typologische und stilkritische Untersuchungen* (*Mitteilungen des Deutschen Archäologischen Instituts, Römische Abteilung. Ergänzungsheft* 14), Mainz am Rhein

Brandes-Druba, B. 1994. "Einige tarentiner Architecturterrakotten," in *Hesperia* Supplement 27, pp. 309–325

Budina, D. 1994. "Architectural Terracottas from the Towns of Kaonia: Antigonea and Buthrot," in *Hesperia* Supplement 27, pp. 217–219

Buschor, E. 1958. *Medusa Rondanini*, Stuttgart

———. 1961–1962. "Die Grabung im Heraion vom Samos. Frühjahr 1961," Δελτ 17, 1961–1962, Β′1 [1963], pp. 279–280

Callaghan, P. J. 1983. "Stylistic Progression in Hellenistic Crete," *BICS* 30, pp. 31–39

Camp, J. M. 1986. *The Athenian Agora*, London

Cavvadias, P. 1893. *Fouilles de Lycosoura*, Athens

Dakaris, S. 1952. «Ἀνασκαφὴ Κασσώπης», Πρακτικὰ 1952 [1955], pp. 326–362

———. 1954. «Ἀνασκαφὴ Κασσώπης», Πρακτικὰ 1954 [1957], pp. 201–205

———. 1963. "Das Taubenorakel von Dodona und das Totenorakel bei Ephyra," *AntK-BH* 1, pp. 35–55

———. 1989. Κασσώπη, Νεώτεραι ἀνασκαφαὶ 1977–1983, Ioannina

De Luca, G. 1990. "Hellenistiche Kunst in Pergamon im Spiegel der megarischen Becher," in *Akten des XIII internationalen Kongresses für klassische Archäologie, Berlin 1988*, Mainz am Rhein, pp. 595–597

Depper-Lippitz, D. 1985. *Griechisches Goldschmuck*, Mainz am Rhein

Deshayes, J. 1966. *Argos. Les fouilles de la Deiras* (*Études péloponnésiennes* IV), Paris

Despinis, G. 1966. "Ein neues Werk des Damophon," *AA* [*JdI* 81], pp. 378–385

Dickins, G. 1911. "The Sandale in the Palazzo dei Conservatori," *JHS* 31, pp. 308–314

Dickins, G., and K. Kourouniotes. 1906–1907. "Damophon of Messene II," *BSA* 13, pp. 357–404

Dyggve, E., F. Poulsen, and K. Rhomaios. 1934. *Das Heroon von Kalydon*, Copenhagen

Ehrhardt, H. 1985. *Samothrake*, Stuttgart

Evangelides, D., and S. Dakaris. 1959. «Τὸ ἱερὸ τῆς Δωδώνης», ἈρχἘφ, pp. 1–176

Fedak, J. 1990. *Monumental Tombs of the Hellenistic Age: A Study of Selected Tombs from Pre-Classical to the Early Imperial Era*, Toronto

Fraser, P., and T. Rönne. 1957. *Boeotian and West Greek Tombstones*, Lund

———. 1971. "Some More Boeotian and West Greek Tombstones," *OpAth* 10, pp. 53–89

Gabrici, E. 1913. "Cuma," *MonAnt* 22, pp. 1–871

Gneisz, D. 1994. "Die Dachterrakotten von Aigeira," in *Hesperia* Supplement 27, pp. 125–134

Goethert, F.-W. 1936. "Trajanische Friese," *JdI* 51, pp. 72–81

Groag, E. 1939. *Die römischen Reichsbeamten von Achaia bis auf Diokletian*, Vienna

Grobel-Miller, S. 1971. "Hellenistic Macedonian Architecture: Its Style and Painted Ornamentation" (diss. Bryn Mawr College 1971)
Habicht, C. 1985. *Pausanias und seine "Beschreibung Griechenlands"*, Munich
Hänlein-Schäfer, H. 1985. *Veneratio Augusti. Eine Studie zu den Tempeln des ersten römischen Kaisers*, Rome
Hamdorf, F.-W. 1979. "Ein Goldkranz des 4. Jhs. v. Chr.," *MüJb* 30, pp. 31–41
*Hesperia* Supplement 27 = *Proceedings of the International Conference on Greek Architectural Terracottas of the Classical and Hellenistic Periods, Athens, December 12–15, 1991* (*Hesperia* Supplement 27), N. A. Winter, ed., Princeton 1994
Hoepfner, W. 1990. "Bauten und Bedeutung des Hermogenes," in *Hermogenes und die hochhellenistische Architektur, International Kolloquium in Berlin 1988*, W. Hoepfner and E.-L. Schwandner, eds., Mainz am Rhein, pp. 1–34
Hübner, G. 1976. "Antefixa Deorum Athenarum," *AM* 91, pp. 175–183
*IG* V[1] = *Inscriptiones Laconiae et Messeniae*, W. Kolbe, ed., Berlin 1913
Jucker, H. 1961. *Das Bildnis in Blätterkelch: Geschichte und Bedeutung einer römischen Porträtform* (*Bibliotheca Helvetica Romana* 3), Lausanne/Freiburg
Känel, R. 1991. "Zwei etruskisch-italische Terrakottaplatten mit vegetabilem Dekor in Genf," *AntK* 34, pp. 170–177
Kalligas, P. 1969. «Ἀρχαιότητες καὶ μνημεῖα Ἰωνίων Νήσων», Δελτ 24, 1969, Β'2 [1970], pp. 258–279
———. 1979. «Ἀρχαιολογικὰ εὑρήματα ἀπὸ τὴν Ἰθάκη», Κεφαλληνιακὰ Χρονικὰ 3, 1978–1979, pp. 45–69
———. 1980. «Τὸ ἱερὸ τοῦ Ἀπόλλωνος Ὑπερτελεάτα στὴ Λακωνία», in Πρακτικὰ τοῦ Α' Λακωνικοῦ Συνεδρίου, Σπάρτη-Γύθειο 7–11 Ὀκτ., 1977, Athens, pp. 10–30
Kaltsas, N. 1988. Πήλινες διακοσμημένες κεραμώσεις ἀπὸ τὴ Μακεδονία, Athens
Karouzou, S. 1954. Συλλογὴ γλυπτῶν, Athens
———. 1967. Συλλογὴ γλυπτῶν, Athens
———. 1974. «Ἡ μικρὴ ζωφόρος τῶν Θερμοπυλῶν καὶ ἡ ἔννοια τοῦ θαλάσσιου θιάσου», ἈρχΕφ, pp. 26–44
Kenfield, J. F. 1994. "High Classical and High Baroque in the Architectural Terracottas of Morgantina," in *Hesperia* Supplement 27, pp. 275–281
Klumbach, H. 1937. *Tarentiner Grabkunst* (*Tübinger Forschungen zur Archäologie und Kunstgeschichte* 13), Reutlingen
Konstantinopoulos, G. 1969. «Ἀρχαιότητες καὶ μνημεῖα Δωδεκανήσου», Δελτ 24, 1969, Β'2 [1970], pp. 457–485
Kourouniotes, K. 1911. Κατάλογος τοῦ Μουσείου Λυκοσούρας, Athens
Kraus, T. 1953. *Die Ranken der Ara Pacis: Ein Beitrag zum Entwicklungsgeschichte der augustäischen Ornamentik*, Berlin
Kyrieleis, H. 1978. "Ausgrabungen im Heraion von Samos 1978," *AA* [*JdI* 93], pp. 250–259
La Rosa, V. 1990. "Ceramiche ellenistiche da Festos: per il problema della distruzione finale della città," in Β' Ἐπιστημονικὴ Συνάντηση γιὰ τὴν Ἑλληνιστικὴ Κεραμεικὴ, Athens, pp. 160–166
Lattimore, S. 1976. *The Marine Thiasos in Greek Sculpture* (*Monumenta Archaeologica* 3; Monograph 9, Archaeological Institute of America), Los Angeles
Lauter, H. 1986. *Die Architektur des Hellenismus*, Darmstadt
Lauter-Bufé, H. 1987. *Die Geschichte des sikeliotisch-korinthischen Kapitells. Der sogennante italisch-republikanische Typus*, Mainz am Rhein
Le Bas, P. 1844. "Fouilles à Méssène," *RA* 1, pp. 422–426
Lévy, E., and J. Marcadé. 1972. "Au Musée de Lycosoura," *BCH* 96, pp. 968–1004
Libertini, G. 1950. "Grande cratere da Canicattini del Museo di Siracusa," *BdA* 35, pp. 97–107
Lullies, R. 1962. *Vergoldete Terrakotta-appliken aus Tarent*, Heidelberg
Makaronas, C., and E. Youri. 1989. Οἱ οἰκίες ἁρπαγῆς τῆς Ἑλένης καὶ Διονύσου τῆς Πέλλας, Athens
Marshall, F. H. 1911. *Catalogue of Jewellery in the British Museum*, London
McPhee, I. 1979. "The Agrinion Group," *BSA* 74, pp. 159–162
Migeotte, L. 1985. "Reparation des monuments publics à Messéne," *BCH* 190, pp. 597–607
Miller, Stella G. 1994. "Architectural Terracottas from Ilion," in *Hesperia* Supplement 27, pp. 269–273
Möbius, H. 1926. "Eine dreiseitige Basis in Athen," *AM* 51, pp. 117–124
———. 1964. *Alexandria und Rom*, Munich

Mollard-Besques, S. 1963. *Catalogue raisonné des figurines et reliefs en terre cuite grecques et romaines. Myrina*, Paris
Neumann, G. 1965. "Ein frühhellenistisches Golddiadem aus Kreta," *AM* 80, pp. 143–151
Oikonomos, G. 1909. «'Ανασκαφή έν Μεσσήνη», Πρακτικά 1909 [1910], pp. 201–205
———. 1925–1926. «'Ανασκαφή έν Μεσσήνη», Πρακτικά 1925–1926 [1929], pp. 55–66
Orlandos, A. 1955. Τα υλικά δομής των αρχαίων Ελλήνων κατά τους συγγραφείς, τας επιγραφάς και τα μνημεία, Α', Athens
———. 1957. «Ανασκαφή έν Μεσσήνη», Πρακτικά 1957 [1962], pp. 121–125
———. 1958. «Ανασκαφή Μεσσήνης», Πρακτικά 1958 [1965], pp. 12–183
———. 1959. «Ανασκαφή Μεσσήνης», Πρακτικά 1959 [1965], pp. 162–173
———. 1960. «Ανασκαφή Μεσσήνης», Πρακτικά 1960 [1966], pp. 210–227
———. 1962. «Ανασκαφή Μεσσήνης», Πρακτικά 1962 [1966], pp. 99–112ι
———. 1963a. «Ανασκαφή Μεσσήνης», Δελτ 18, 1963, Β' [1965], pp. 95–97
———. 1963b. «Ανασκαφή Μεσσήνης», Πρακτικά 1963 [1966], pp. 122–129
———. 1964. «Ανασκαφή Μεσσήνης», Πρακτικά 1964 [1966], pp. 96–101
———. 1965. «Δύο επιγραφαί έκ Μεσσήνης», ΑρχΕφ, pp. 110–121
———. 1969. «Ανασκαφή Μεσσήνης», Πρακτικά 1969 [1971], pp. 98–120
———. 1971. «Ανασκαφή Μεσσήνης», Πρακτικά 1971 [1973], pp. 157–171
———. 1972. «Ανασκαφή Μεσσήνης», Πρακτικά 1972 [1974], pp. 127–138
———. 1973. «Ανασκαφή Μεσσήνης», Πρακτικά 1973 [1975], pp. 108–111
———. 1974. «Ανασκαφή Μεσσήνης», Πρακτικά 1974 [1976], pp. 102–109
———. 1975. «Ανασκαφή Μεσσήνης», Πρακτικά 1975 [1977], pp. 176–177
———. 1976. Νεώτεραι έρευναι εν Μεσσήνη, 1957–1973, in *Neue Forschungen in griechischen Heiligtümern*, Tübingen, pp. 9–38
Papachatzis, N. 1979. Παυσανίου Ελλάδος περιήγησις. Μεσσηνιακά, Athens
Papapostolou, J. 1975. «Στήλες με ιωνικό επίκρανο στο Μουσείο της Πάτρας», *AAA* 8, pp. 291–304
Petsas, P. 1965. "Mosaics from Pella," in *La mosaïque gréco-romaine, Actes du Colloque International*, Paris, pp. 41–56
Pfrommer, M. 1982. "Grossgriechischer und mittelitalischer Einfluss in der Rankenornamentik frühhellenistischer Zeit," *JdI* 97, pp. 119–190
Picard, C. 1935. "Dionysos Psilax," in *Mélanges offerts à Octave Navarre*, Toulouse, pp. 317–337
———. 1963. *Manuel d'archéologie grecque. La sculpture* IV, ii, Paris
Pollitt, J. J. 1986. *Art in the Hellenistic Age*, Cambridge
Ponger, C. 1942. *Katalog der griechischen und römischen Skulpturen der stein. Gegenstände u. der Stuckplastik im Allard Pierson Museum*, Copenhagen
*RE* Supplement XV, 1978, s.v. Messene, col. 136–288 (E. Meyer)
Richter, G. M. A. 1954. "The Marble Throne on the Akropolis and Its Replicas," *AJA* 58, pp. 271–276
Robertson, M. 1975. *A History of Greek Art*, Cambridge
Salzmann, D. 1982. *Untersuchungen zu den antiken Kieselmosaiken von den Anfängen bis zum Beginn der Tessaratechnik* (*Archäologische Forschungen* 10), Berlin
Sauron, G. 1988. "Le méssage esthetique des rinceaux de l'Ara Pacis Auguste," *RA*, pp. 3–40
Schauenburg, K. 1957. "Zur Symbolik unteritalischer Rankenmotive," *RM* 64, pp. 198–221
———. 1989. "Zur Grabsymbolik apulischer Vasen," *JdI* 104, pp. 19–60
*SEG* = *Supplementum Epigraphicum Graecum*
Sichtermann, H. 1966. *Griechiesche Vasen in Unteritalien*, Tübingen
Smith, A. H. 1900. *British Museum Catalogue of Sculpture* II, London
Sophoulis, T. 1895. «Ανασκαφή εν Μεσσήνη», Πρακτικά 1895 [1896], p. 27
Stipcevic, A. 1977. *The Illyrians: History and Culture*, trans. by St. Čuliç Burton, Park Ridge, NJ
Themelis, P. 1965. «Αρχαιότητες και μνημεία Μεσσηνίας», Δελτ 20, 1965, Β'2 [1967], pp. 207–208
———. 1979. «Σκύλλα Ερετρική», ΑρχΕφ, pp. 118–153
———. 1987. «Ανασκαφή Μεσσήνης», Πρακτικά 1987 [1991], pp. 71–104
———. 1988. «Ανασκαφή Μεσσήνης», Πρακτικά 1988 [1991], pp. 41–79
———. 1989. «Μεσσήνη», Έργον 1989 [1990], pp. 30–37

———. 1990. «Μεσσήνη», Ἔργον 1990 [1991], pp. 26–35
———. 1991. «Μεσσήνη», Ἔργον 1991 [1992], pp. 28–35
———. 1993. "Damophon von Messene. Sein Werk im Lichte der neuen Ausgrabungen," *AntK* 36, pp. 24–40
Toynbee, J. M. C., and J. B. Ward Perkins. 1950. "Peopled Scrolls: A Hellenistic Motif in Imperial Art," *BSR* 18, pp. 1–43
Trendall, A. D. 1967. *The Red-figured Vases of Lucania, Campania and Sicily*, Oxford
Trumpf-Lyritzaki, M. 1969. *Griechische Figurenvasen des reichen Stils und der späten Klassik*, Bonn
Uhlenbrock, J. P. 1988. *The Terracotta Protomae from Gela*, Rome
Valmin, M. N. 1938. *The Swedish Messenia Expedition* (*Skrifter Utgivna av Kungl. Humanistiska Vetenskapssamfundet* 26), Lund
Vlachopoulou-Oikonomou, A. 1986. Ηγεμόνες και κορυφαίοι κέραμοι με διακόσμηση από την Ήπειρο, Ioannina (unpublished dissertation)
Voigtländer, W. 1990. "Vorklassische Baugedanken in spät- und nachklassicher Architektur Kleinasiens," *Akten des XIII internationalen Kongresses für klassische Archäologie, Berlin 1988*, Mainz am Rhein, pp. 414–416
Waldstein, C. 1902. *The Argive Heraeum* I, Boston
Winter, F. 1903. *Die Typen der figürlichen Terrakotten* II, Berlin
Yalouris, N. 1965. «Ἀρχαιότητες καὶ μνημεῖα Ἠλείας», Δελτ 20, 1965, Β'2 [1967], pp. 209–213
———. 1968. «Τὸ ἀκρωτήριον τοῦ Ἡραίου Ὀλυμπίας», in Χαριστήριον *A. Orlandos* IV, Athens, pp. 57–65
Zanker, P. 1970. "Trajansforum in Rom," *AA* [*JdI* 85], pp. 499–544
Zervoudaki, I. 1968. "Attische Polychrome Reliefkeramik des späten 5. und 4. Jhs. v. Chr.," *AM* 83, pp. 1–88
Zimmermann, K. 1994. "Traufziegel mit Reliefmäander aus dem Schwarzmeergebeit," in *Hesperia* Supplement 27, pp. 221–251

PETROS THEMELIS

UNIVERSITY OF CRETE
Department of History and Archaeology
74100 Rethymnon
Greece

# DIE KLASSISCHEN TEMPELDÄCHER VON KALAPODI (PHOKIS)

(PLATES 57–59)

DIE GRABUNGEN beim Dorf Kalapodi, in der im Altertum als Phokis bezeichneten Landschaft gelegen,[1] haben unter der Leitung von R. C. S. Felsch ein Heiligtum aufgedeckt,[2] das vermutlich mit dem bei Pausanias 10,53,36 genannten der Artemis von Hyampolis gleichzusetzen ist[3] und das, wie jedenfalls die Interpretation von Einzelfunden nahelegt,[4] in gleicher Weise auch dem Kult des Apoll diente. Es erfuhr in klassischer Zeit eine grundsätzliche architektonische Neugestaltung.[5] Wieweit dabei das gesamte archaische Temenos, dessen Tempel durch die Perser in Brand gesetzt und zerstört worden waren,[6] in seiner ursprünglichen Ausdehnung und Bauausstattung verändert, erneuert oder auch restauriert fortbestand, konnten die nur partiell durchgeführten Grabungen nicht im Einzelnen klären. Es gelang jedoch dem Ausgräber, die sich im Tempelbereich abzeichnenden Bauphasen eindeutig zu fassen und deren Chronologie durch stratigraphische Beobachtungen oder/und Münzfunde genauer voneinander abzugrenzen.[7]

Die Zuweisung von Dachterrakotten in die einzelnen Perioden beruht einerseits also auf den durch Felsch gewonnen Grabungsergebnissen, basiert aber andererseits auf Gruppierungen des Ziegelmaterials durch die Autorin, denen u.a. auch formal stilistische und typologische Kriterien zugrunde gelegt sind. Die Auswertung des erhaltenen Bestandes an Ziegeln, die sowohl dem sog. lakonischen wie korinthischen Deckungssystem angehören,[8] ergibt dabei, daß drei besonders umfangreiche Komplexe von Ziegelsorten korinthischen Dachzuschnittes mit drei unterschiedlich zu datierenden Dächern zu verbinden sind.

Die Fundorte selbst bestätigen die Scheidung des Materials nach Dachformen und ermöglichen außerdem die konkrete Identifikation von Bau und Dach. Im vorliegenden Zusammenhang heißt dies, daß im Heiligtum von Kalapodi vorallem die Tempel, als Behausung des Kultbildes und der heiligen Herdstätte, mit einem sog. korinthischen Dach geschmückt waren. In jedem Fall war die aufwendige Gestaltungsart, die dem Giebeldach in der literarischen Überlieferung zukommt und als Erfindung mit Korinth verknüpft

---

[1] Leekley und Efstratiou 1980, S. 123; Lauffer 1989, S. 271–273, *s.v.* Hyampolis.

Die Bildvorlagen zu Plates 57:a, b und 58 stammen von mir, alle übringen werden dem Deutschen Archäologischen Institut verdankt, nach Aufnahmen von A. Tzimas: 57:c (DAI 86/509), 59:a (DAI 86/511), b (DAI 86/520), und c (DAI 86/529). Die Zeichnungen, Figures 1, 2:a, b, und 4, stammen von mir, die Tuscheumzeichnung nahm Silke Mayerhofer vor. Die Rekonstucktionszeichnung, Figure 3, fertigte Florian Wiesler an.

[2] Felsch und Schuler 1980, S. 1–2, Anm. 1–5.
[3] Felsch und Siewert 1987, S. 686–687.
[4] Felsch 1988, S. 63; Felsch und Schuler 1980, S. 92.
[5] Kienast 1988, S. 100–103.
[6] Felsch und Schuler 1980, S. 84; Felsch 1991, S. 85–91.
[7] Felsch und Schuler 1980, S. 99 mit Anm. 203–207.
[8] Hübner 1980, S. 112–115.

wird,[9] in Kalapodi tatsächlich offenbar ausschließlich auf die Tempel selbst beschränkt. Der Grabungsbefund erwies freilich, daß dem nicht von Anfang an so gewesen war, wie die Schilfdächer der früharchaischen Tempel zeigten.[10] Erst im Zug einer Modernisierung hatten nämlich die beiden archaischen Tempel eine Terrakotta-Eindeckung erhalten, die allerdings eine ursprünglich, gemeinsame Konzeption verrät.[11] Für die ebenfalls verhältnismäßig große Anzahl an Ziegeln des sog. lakonischen Typus seit archaischer Zeit, für die aufgrund der Grabungssituation keine Architekturfundamente zu Verfügung stehen, wäre daher—sozusagen im Ausschlußverfahren—an Dächer von Baulichkeiten zu denken, die für alle, innerhalb eines heiligen Bezirkes notwendigen Belange (Schatzhaus, Priester- und Banketträume, Hallen) vorauszusetzen sind.

Wie das Heiligtum unmittelbar nach dem Abzug der Perser aussah, wissen wir nicht. Der archäologische Befund läßt offenbar sofort einsetzende Aufräumarbeiten und Trümmerbeseitigung vermuten. Ein heiliges Mal (?) im S-Tempel wurde zum Kultschacht umfunktioniert.[12] Die sakral bedeutsame Eschara in der ehemaligen Cella des archaischen N-Tempels erhielt dagegen eine Umbauung aus Spolien.[13] Dieser Einbau in die Ruinen des archaischen N-Tempels wurde peu à peu durch die Fundamentierung des ersten klassichen N-Tempels überlagert, dabei unterteilt und verkürzt ihn der Bau der klassischen Adyton-Quermauer,[14] doch betrug seine ursprüngliche Ausdehnung 5.17 × 8.88 m.[15] Dazu gehörte im westlichen unmittelbar vorgelagerten Areal ein offener, rituell genutzter Hof. Das Ganze diente von Anfang an als provisorische Kapelle, die die Kontinuität des Kultes in einer Zeit gewährleistete, in der der eigentliche Tempel noch fehlte.

Neben den oben bereits genannten Tempeldächern von korinthischem Zuschnitt fällt nun eine kleine Anzahl rotfiguriger Traufziegelfragmente im Bestand der Kalapodi-Ziegel auf. Ihre Fundorte liegen im ursprünglichen Innenbereich beider Tempel. Sie sind mit einem Lorbeerzweig, der nach links bzw. nach rechts gerichtet ist, dekoriert (Pl. 57:a, b). Keines der Fragmente läßt sich vervollständigen, man wird aber—in Analogie zu der durch die archaischen Traufziegel vorgegebenen Maßeinheit[16]—eine Frontbreite von *ca.* 0.58 m erwarten wollen. Dies bedeutete, daß die Schmuckbordüre aus acht alternierenden Motivpaaren (Fruchtstengel und Blättern) bestanden hätte. Die stilistische und typologische Einordnung einer solchen Ornamentik weist nach Athen.[17] Wenn aber dasgleiche Schmuckschema auf einer weißgrundigen Schale die Lippe ziert und dort pointiert ein Bild Apollons und einer

---

[9] Williams 1988, S. 227; Heiden 1987, S. 17; zur Terminologie s. Winter 1990, S. 13 mit Anm. 1.
[10] Felsch 1987, S. 14–15.
[11] Hübner 1990.
[12] Felsch 1987, S. 17, 25; vgl. S. 11 und die Abb. 2–3; 12; 26–27.
[13] Felsch und Schuler 1980, S. 98.
[14] Felsch und Schuler 1980, S. 88; Felsch 1988, S. 63.
[15] Felsch 1991, S. 88 Anm. 30.
[16] Hübner 1990, S. 170.
[17] Sie beginnt mit den rf. Simen-Beispielen, die keine Früchte aufweisen, Buschor 1929, S. 20–46, Taf. 1–4, 7–10; Vlassopoulou 1990, S. xxiii, no. 41–43; vgl. auch die Simen 56 und 65, Taf. B. Hinzu kommen Traufziegel mit diesem Ornament, Buschor 1933, S. 17–18; Vlassopoulou 1990, S. xxviii, no. 58. Vorläufig singulär ist das Beispiel mit auf das Blatt gesetzter Frucht aus dem Kerameikos, Hübner 1973, S. 73–77, Abb. 2, Taf. 57:2.

Muse vom Helikon umkränzt,[18] so wird man eine solche Koinzidenz auch als ikonographisches Indiz werten dürfen.[19]

In dem hier interessierenden Zusammenhang regen die gerade aufgezählten Gründe dazu an, diesen Traufziegeltypus mit dem provisorischen Kultbau zu verbinden. Getragen wird die Annahme nicht zuletzt durch den Umstand, daß die stilistische Datierung des Ornamentes, wie der Vergleich mit der erwähnten Schale zeigt, eine Zeitstufe impliziert, die mit dem Münzfund aus dem Fußboden des durch die Adytonmauer verkleinerten Kultraumes korrespondiert.[20] Tatsächlich ergäbe das oben postulierte Breitenmaß von 0.58 m pro Ziegel fünfzehnfach vervielfacht die Gesamtlänge des provisorischen Kultraumes, wobei ein Spielraum von je 0.012 m zwischen den Stoßfugen der jeweiligen Ziegellängsseiten hinzugerechnet werden muß. Die Schlüssigkeit der Beweisführung wird jedoch dadurch abgeschwächt, daß entsprechende Antefixformulierungen, die, jedenfalls attischer Typentradition folgend,[21] für diese Art von Traufziegeln zu fordern wären, nicht vorhanden sind, ja daß Antefixe überhaupt zu fehlen scheinen. Andrerseits sollten sie aber zu erwarten sein sogar dann, wenn lediglich ein hypaithrales Umfassungsgeviert mit einer tönernen Ziegelleiste abgeschlossen gewesen war.[22] Dieser Aporie ist nur durch die Vermutung zu begegnen, daß entweder die noch intakten archaischen Antefixe als krönendes Schlußglied verwendet oder daß die schon fertiggestellten Antefixe des ersten klassischen Tempels[23] bereits vorläufig hier versetzt waren. Wenn hier beide Lösungen erwogen werden, so geschieht dies deshalb, um die Aufmerksamkeit allgemein auf die Frage zu lenken, ob in dem vorgegebenen Rahmen, wie dies ein solcher Kultort darstellt, sichtbare Wiederverwendung resp. Kombination von dekorierten Dachterrakotten a priori möglich ist. Eine derartige Maßgabe setzt selbstverständlich eine inhärente metrologische Abhängigkeit von in situ aufeinanderfolgenden Bauten voraus.[24] Für die archaische Zeit hatte zumindest in Kalapodi gegolten, daß einem einzigen Kultgeschehen zwei Tempelgebäude zugewandt waren, deren Dächer in sich wechselweise, je nach Größe des Baus, verschiebbare resp. austauschbare Elemente besessen hatten.[25] Eine cum grano salis vergleichbare Hypothese für die direkte Nachfolgearchitektur in Betracht zu ziehen, mag daher vor diesem Forum legitim sein.

Der Unsicherheitsfaktor der Überlegungen wird freilich durch den fragmentarischen Zustand der Lorbeerzweig-Ziegel, deren Tiefenausdehnung in jedem Fall verloren ist, unterstrichen. Völlig spekulativ bleibt so die Frage nach einem (theoretisch möglichen) Giebel. Jedenfalls existieren keine Simenfragmente, deren Äußeres in Konsistenz und

---

[18] Boston, Museum of Fine Arts 00.356: Carpenter 1989, S. 283.
[19] Vgl. Philippart 1936, S. 77–81.
[20] Felsch und Schuler 1980, S. 88.
[21] Vgl. Hübner 1973, S. 73, Abb. 2.
[22] Vgl. z. B. auch die Ziegelbekrönung des Grabbezirks der Potamier, Wrede 1933, S. 36–37, Abb. 100; Knigge 1988, S. 134–135.
[23] Hübner 1990, Taf. 15:a.
[24] Derartige Abhängigkeiten sind nicht als absolute Massgleichheit aller Bauglieder zu verstehen, setzen aber die Möglichkeit dazu voraus, man vgl. etwa auch die Interdependenzen zwischen Vorparthenon und Parthenon, s. demnächst Korres (in Vorbereitung).
[25] Vgl. z.B. die Antefixe der archaischen Tempel, Hübner 1990, S. 170–171.

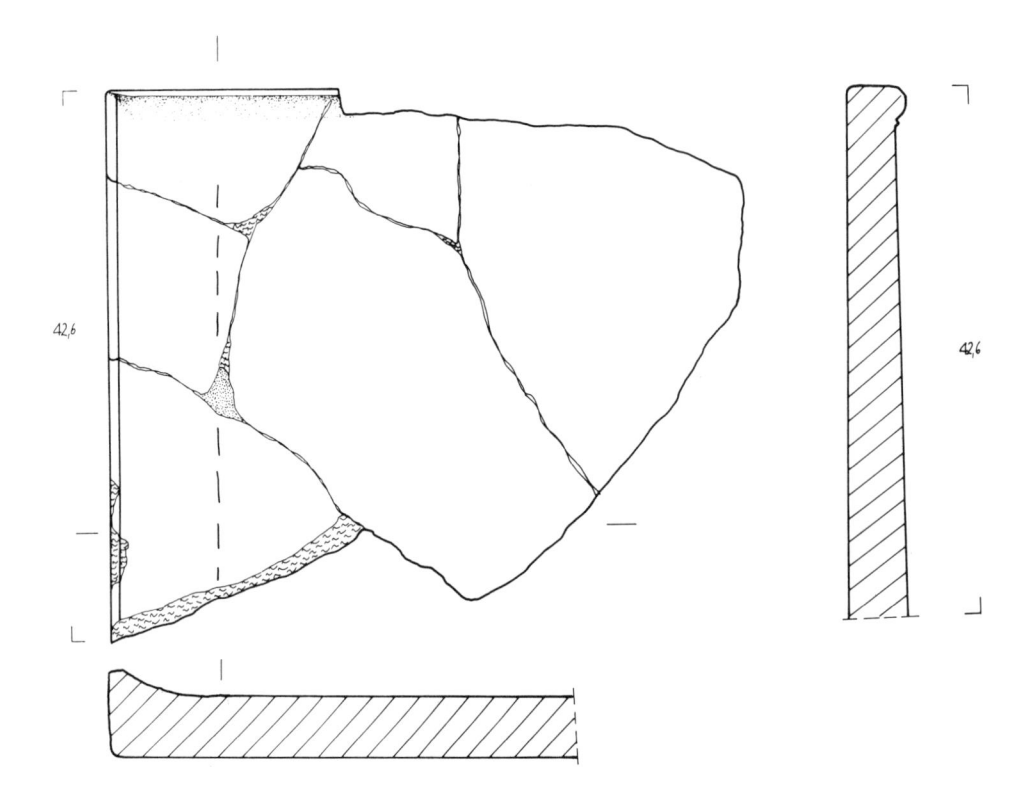

FIG. 1. Stroter des ersten klassischen Tempels (Z 673). Aufsicht. Maßstab 1:6

Bruchflächenfärbung den Lorbeerzweig-Ziegeln ähnelte, zumal diese im Bestand der Kalapodi-Ziegel überhaupt als Unikat zu gelten haben.

Der erste klassische Tempel erhob sich über der Ruine des archaischen N-Tempels und dem abgetragenen Kult-Provisorium. Das Ende seiner Bauzeit ist durch eine Münze datiert.[26] Die letzte Etappe der Bauarbeiten sah die Errichtung der Cella-Innensäulen vor, d.h. daß zu diesem Zeitpunkt das Dach selbst noch nicht verlegt war. Der archaische S-Tempel dagegen wurde nicht wieder aufgebaut.

Ein sozusagen spezifisches Aussehen kennzeichnet nun die Struktur der Tonmasse, aus denen die Schmuckglieder und ein Teil der übrigen Normalziegel (Fig. 1) dieses ersten klassischen Tempeldaches hergestellt sind. Im Ziegelbestand von Kalapodi kommt die rötlichbraune, großporige Körnung so rein nicht mehr vor, findet sich jedoch in übereinstimmender Weise an dem etwa hundert Jahre älteren Dach, das im antiken Opous eine Halle geziert hatte,[27] so daß für beide Dächer also eine lokrisch-phokidische Ziegelei nicht auszuschließen ist.

Der Dachschmuck des ersten klassischen Tempels folgt einem Dekorationsmuster, das in identischer Manier im großen panhellenischen Heiligtum dieser Landschaft, in Delphi,

[26] Felsch 1991, S. 89 mit Anm. 37.
[27] Dakoronia 1990, S. 175–179.

am Dach der Knidier-Lesche offenbar, verwendet worden war.[28] Er besteht aus einer rotfigurigen Giebelsima, die eine aufrechte, alternierende Lotos-Palmetten-Folge über liegender Wellenranke zeigt. Oben rahmt ein Astragal die Anthemienkette, unten bildet eine Schachbrett-Hakenmäander-Bordüre die Standleiste. Mit einer entweder an der rechten oder an der linken äußeren Kante angebrachten, nach hinten versetzten Nut waren die einzelnen Simenglieder miteinander, je nach Position am Giebel, verzahnt. Daß die Giebelspitze ein Akroter trug, ist wahrscheinlich, doch fehlt dafür jegliche Spur. Den First krönten beidseitig rotfigurig bemalte Palmetten-Reiter (Pl. 57:c). An den vier Ecken des Daches dienten Löwenkopf-Wasserspeier dazu, das Regenwasser abzuleiten. Ob sie gleichzeitig zu Akroter-Kästen gehört hatten, läßt sich nicht mehr entscheiden. Über die Längsseiten des Tempels ist, als Traufbandleiste, die Schachbrett-Mäander-Tänie hinweggeführt. Die Oberkante der Simen und Traufziegel wurde nach dem Brand und vielleicht während des Versetzens um *ca.* 0.05 m tief derart abgearbeitet, daß die schützende und wasserundurchlässige, gelb engobierte Oberfläche hier ganz und gar beseitigt wurde. Ein Grund für eine solche Maßnahme ist nicht einzusehen. Auf der Unterseite besitzen sie einen roteingefärbten Streifen, der den Überstand markiert. *Ca.* 0.18 m von ihm entfernt befinden sich in den Traufziegeln vor dem Brand gefertigte Aussparungen, in die Tonwürfel passen (Pl. 58:a, b). Die daran noch sichtbar erhaltenen mörtelartigen Überreste verraten, wie man um ihre Haftung im Hegemon bemüht war. Die Sicherung der übrigen Strotere (Fig. 1) auf ihrer Unterlage geschah z. T. durch Eisennägel,[29] in derselben Weise waren die Kalyptere auf den Stroteren befestigt (Pl. 58:c).

Kein Element der klassischen Dachglieder konnte, trotz zahlreicher Fragmente, bis jetzt vollständig zusammengesetzt werden. Ob dieselbe Kalkulation, mit der sich für das Dach in Delphi wenigstens die Ziegeltiefe = Simenbreite hatte annähernd bestimmen lassen,[30] auf die Fragmente des ersten und zweiten klassischen Daches zu übertragen sein wird, ist erst zu untersuchen. Komplett erhaltene oder rekonstruierbare Größen bietet vorläufig die Antefixhöhe, die entweder beim ersten klassischen Tempel mit 0.286 m (Fig. 2) oder mit *ca.* 0.38 m (Fig. 3:b) beim zweiten klassischen Tempel feststeht. Es scheint, als sei Nagelung beim zweiten klassischen Tempel prinzipiell aufgegeben.

Wenig mehr als ein Jahrzehnt war der erste klassische Tempel in Betrieb, als er, durch ein Erdbeben vermutlich, einstürzte.[31] Sofort wurde mit dem Wiederaufbau über einem, allerdings veränderten Grundriß, begonnen.[32] Es sind die Dimensionen der Normalstrotere und -kalyptere beider klassischer Dächer zu errechnen, auch liefern Engobierung und Tonstruktur eindeutige Zuordnungskriterien. Neben den beiden charakteristischen

---

[28] Le Roy 1967, Dach 56 (S. 128–132), S. 128–129, Taf. 46; Heiden 1987, S. 175, Abb. 6:4, Taf. 12:1. Dachglieder dieses Typus aus Kalapodi sind abgebildet in: Felsch und Kienast 1975, S. 9, Abb. 12; Hübner 1990, Taf. 15:a.
[29] Müller-Wiener 1988, S. 104, Abb. 55. Die in Kalapodi zahlreich zutage gekommenen Eisennägel gehören wahrscheinlich zum hölzernen Dachstuhl. Ihre Bearbeitung durch H.-O. Schmitt, Heidelberg, ist abgeschlossen. Gerade in der zweiten Hälfte des 5. Jhs. v. Chr. tritt Nagelung bei Terrakottaziegeln verhältnismässig häufig auf, vgl. z.B. auch die attischen Dächer, Hübner 1973, S. 89.
[30] Le Roy 1967, S. 131–132.
[31] Kienast 1980, S. 102; Felsch 1988, S. 63.
[32] Kienast 1988, S. 102.

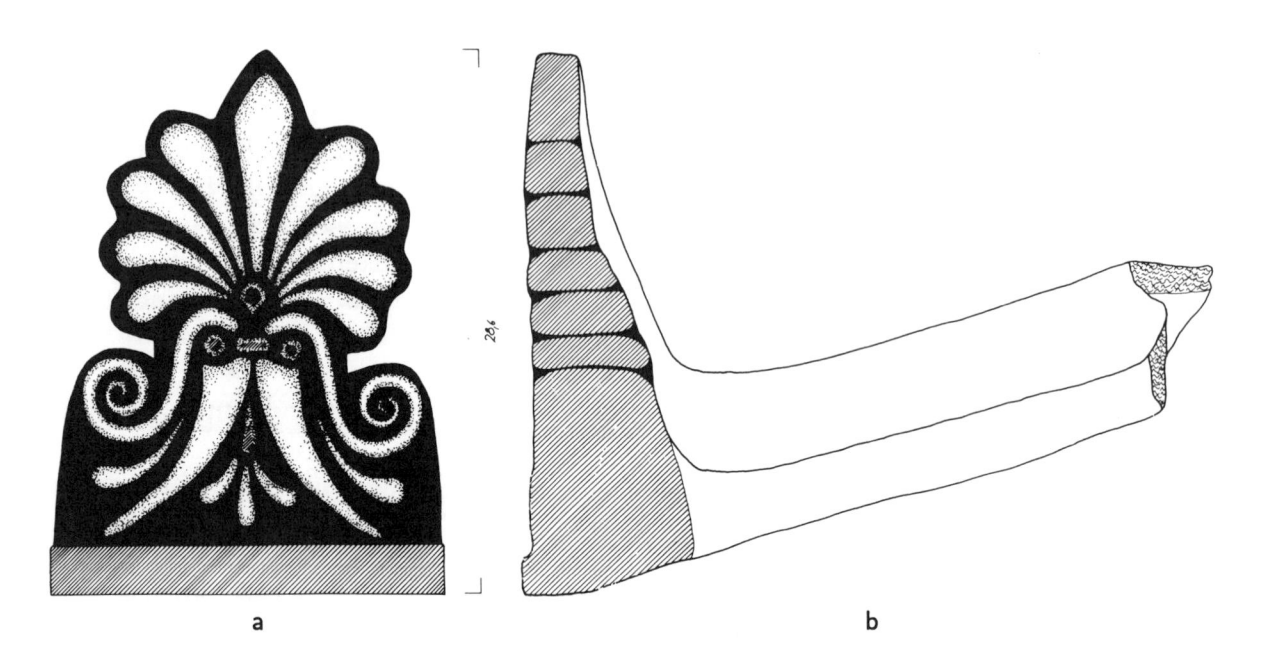

Fig. 2. (a) Antefix (Z 217), ergänzt, Ansicht, und (b) Kalypter mit Antefix (Z 211) des ersten klassischen Tempels, Seitenansicht. Maßstab 1:4

Ziegelgruppen existiert jedoch eine Variante, deren Aussehen und Konsistenz offenbar eine Mischung aus dem rötlich-braunen der ersten und dem cremefarbenen-gelben Tongemenge der zweiten klassischen Dacheindeckung darstellt. Symptomatisch ist in diesen Fällen ein rosafarbener, fast poliert zu nennender Überzug. Man ist geneigt, sie dem zweiten klassischen Dach zuzuweisen, da ein Teil der Traufrandglieder, die trotz gewisser formaler Variationen im Dekorschema diesem Tempeldaches angehören, in der beschriebenen Manier gehalten ist. Entweder handelt es sich um ziemlich gleichzeitig in Auftrag gegebene Ersatzstücke oder aber es stammen die einzelnen Dachhälften des zweiten klassischen Daches von Anfang an aus zwei unterschiedlich operierenden resp. brennenden Werkstätten.

Die ornamentale Dachrandgestaltung des zweiten klassischen Tempels lag offensichtlich in der architektonischen Neukonzeption des Gebäudes begründet. Das sehr helltonige Ziegelmaterial erscheint von den gleichen Schotterpartikelchen durchsetzt, die schon für die Magerung der archaischen Ziegel ein auffälliges Merkmal dargestellt hatten. Die technische Zurichtung der Giebelsima (Fig. 3:a) steht in der Tradition der Megara-Schatzhaus-Sima,[33] die ornamentale Ausgestaltung folgt offenbar attischem Dekorationsmuster. Für den Traufrand wurde eine Löwenkopf-Antefix-Sequenz gewählt, die so aufeinander abgestimmt war, daß den Löwenkopf jeweils beidseitig eine liegende S-Volute rahmte. Die Lage der Antefixe ist über den Traufziegel-Fugen, die durch Volutenkanten und -bruchstellen festliegen, bestimmt (vgl. Fig. 3:b). Sie krönen die gegenständig gerichteten Voluten,

[33] Herrmann 1974, S. 79, Taf. 38–39; Winter 1990, S. 21 mit Abb. 7.

Fig. 3. (a) Giebelsima und (b) Horizontalsima des zweiten klassischen Tempels, Rekonstruction. Maßstab 1:14.4

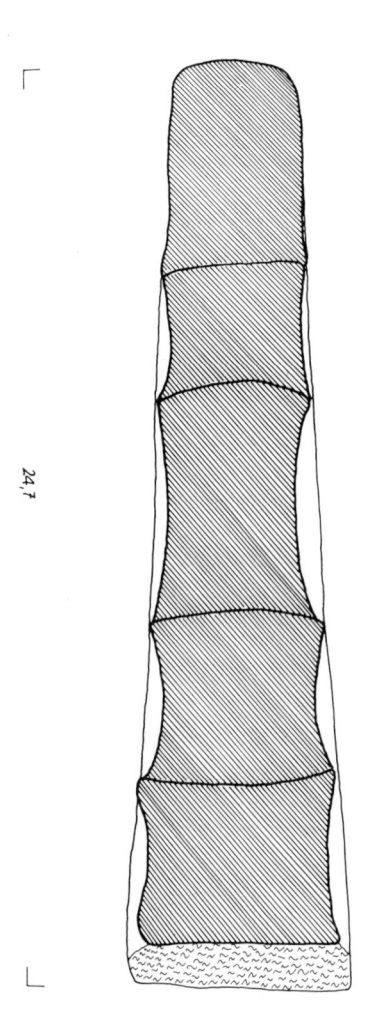

FIG. 4. Firstantefix (Z 597) des zweiten klassischen Tempels. Seitenansicht. Maßstab 1:2

die auf einem Schachbrett-Mäander-Band aufstehen, in das der Löwenkopf eingebunden ist (Pl. 59:a, b). Wie schon beim ersten klassischen Dach schließt das Schachbrett-Mäander-Band an die durch die Giebelsima (Fig. 3:a) vorgegebene Schmuckzone an, die so in beiden Fällen als Standleiste dient und optisch die verschiedenartigen Dekorelemente eint; denn gerade der Gegensatz zwischen der gemalten Blütenkette des Giebels (Fig. 3:a) und der plastischen Reliefierung der Traufe (Fig. 3:b) bedurfte besonders einer solchen Verknüpfung. Der insgesamt dünnwandige und feingliedrige Dekor splitterte leicht und läßt sich nur anhand seiner Bruchstücke rekonstruieren. Von besonderem Interesse ist dabei die Rekonstitution des Palmettenantefixes über dem Volutenstrang (Fig. 3:b). Es handelt sich hier um eine Schöpfung, die in den Umkreis attisch-ionisierender Ornamenterfindungen gehört und der die Anlage des Parthenonantefixes vorausgeht.[34] Sich aufrollende Bewegungsabläufe, allerdings eingebunden in einen anderen Fluß, kannte bereits die Archaik.[35]

Obwohl das wirkungsvolle Nebeneinander der konvexen und konkaven Elemente und die a-jour-gearbeitete Palmette an die sog. frühe Rankensima in Olympia oder jene des Telesterions in Eleusis erinnern könnten,[36] fehlen für diese Art von Umlaufbändern an Traufseiten jegliche Parallelen. Die farbliche Fassung, leuchtendes Gelb in dunklem Grund mit orangeroten Herz-Akzentuierungen in Palmette und Volute, betonte die filigrane Leichtigkeit der Bekrönung. Zugehörige Akrotere ließen sich in Fragmenten ausfindig machen. Doppelseitig bemalte Firstantefixe existieren (Fig. 4; Pl. 57:c), sie wiederholen den Ornamenttypus des ersten klassischen Firstantefixes. Sie saßen auf Kalypteren auf, die durch ein rot aufgemaltes Gittermuster dekoriert waren (Pl. 59:c).

Die Datierung dieses zweiten klassischen Daches beruht auf stilistischen Kriterien. Alle oben genannten klassischen Dachdekor-Varianten sind mit Sicherheit älter. Das Traufrand-Dekorsystem des zweiten klassischen Daches des Kalapodi-Tempels repräsentiert eine jener Vorstufen, die die Entwicklung der Rankensima peloponnesischer Prägung[37] ermöglichte. Die dicht aufeinanderfolgende Motivalternation an der Längsseite des Tempeldaches stellt nämlich selbst bereits eine rankenähnlich geschlossene Bordüre dar. In Anbetracht einer konservativ anmutenden Tradition, die Dachschmuck im 5. Jahrhundert v. Chr. kennzeichnet, wird man das zweite klassische Dach von Kalapodi in die beiden letzten Jahrzehnte dieses Jahrhunderts setzen.

## BIBLIOGRAPHIE

Buschor, E. 1929. *Die Tondächer der Akropolis*, I, *Simen*, Berlin/Leipzig
———. 1933. *Die Tondächer der Akropolis*, II, *Stirnziegel*, Berlin/Leipzig
Carpenter, Th. H. 1989. *Beazley Addenda: Additional References to* ABV, AVR² *and Paralipomena*, Oxford
Dakoronia, F. 1990. «Ἀρχαϊκές κεραμίδες ἀπό την Ἀνατολική Λοκρίδα», in *Hesperia* 59, S. 175–180

---

[34] Vgl. die Antefixe von Samos, Ohnesorg 1990, S. 188–189, Taf. 20:d ("Rhoikos" Antefix); S. 189 mit Anm. 12, Taf. 21:a (Südhalle), die archaischen Antefixe der Akropolis, vgl. Vlassopoulou 1990, S. xvi, no. 19, xx, no. 32, Taf. A. Zum Parthenonantefix zuletzt, Korres und Bouras 1983, S. 41.

[35] Die Voluten der Akropolisantefixe, s. Anm. 34, rollen sich bis zu einem gewissen Grad vergleichbar nach oben auf, bilden allerdings mit einem gegenläufigen Pendant eine geschlossene Schlaufe. Daß, in Analogie zu den Samosbeispielen und den Parthenonantefixen, die Voluten des Kalapodi-Antefixes sich aus der horizontalen Standleiste heraus nach oben entwickelt hätten, dann also um 90° gedreht vorgestellt werden müßten, verbieten die Breite und Laufrichtung der erhaltenen Volutenfragmente.

[36] Zur sog. Frühen Rankensima, s. Heiden, Kongress-Beitrag dieses Bandes; zur Telesterionsima, s. Schede 1909, S. 36–41, Taf. III, S. 21, Taf. IV, S. 22.

[37] Schede 1909, S. 41–75; dagegen Heiden 1987, S. 181–182. Die von Heiden vorgetragene Ableitung, S. 188–193 (d.h. die durch die vegetabilische Gestaltung klassischer Akrotere vorgeprägte, aber vertikal geführte Ausbildung wäre nur horizontal umgesetzt, dieser Schritt sei mit Isthmia vollzogen) erklärt und begründet nicht, warum die neu erfundene Dachrandgliederung mit anders aufgeteilten Ornamentkompartimenten und veränderten proportionalen Bedingungen operiert. Den Umstand, daß das Dekor-Verständnis eines derart geschlossen umlaufenden Ornamentbandes in funktionaler und struktureller Hinsicht sogar einen gewissen Archaismus repräsentiert, läßt Heiden außer Acht.

Felsch, R. C. S. 1987. "Bericht über die Grabungen im Heiligtum der Artemis Elaphebolos und des Apollon von Hyampolis 1978–1982," *AA* [*JdI* 102], S. 1–99

———. 1988. "Das Heiligtum bei Kalapodi in vor- und früklassischer Zeit," in Πρακτικά του XII Διεθνούς Συνεδρίου Κλασικής Αρχαιολογίας, Αθήνα, 4–10 Σεπτεμβρίου 1983, IV, Athen, S. 61–64

———. 1991. "Tempel und Altäre im Heiligtum der Artemis Elaphebolos von Hyampolis bei Kalapodi," in *L'éspace sacrificiel dans les civilisations mediterraneennes de l'antiquité*, Lyon, S. 85–91

Felsch, R. C. S., und H. J. Kienast. 1975. "Ein Heiligtum in Phokis," *AAA* 8, S. 1–24

Felsch, R. C. S., und H. Schuler. 1980. "Apollon und Artemis oder Artemis und Apollon? Bericht von den Grabungen im neu entdeckten Heiligtum bei Kalapodi 1973–1977," *AA* [*JdI* 95], S. 38–112

Felsch, R. C. S., und P. Siewert. 1987. "Inschriften aus dem Heiligtum von Hyampolis bei Kalapodi," *AA* [*JdI* 102], S. 681–687

Heiden, J. 1987. *Korinthische Dachziegel. Zur Entwicklung der korinthischen Dächer*, Frankfurt am Main/Bern/New York/Paris

Herrmann, K. 1974. "Die Giebelrekonstruktion des Schatzhauses von Megara," *AM* 89, S. 75–83

*Hesperia* 59 = *Proceedings of the First International Conference on Archaic Greek Architectural Terracottas, Athens, December 2–4, 1988* (*Hesperia* 59, 1990), N. A. Winter, ed.

Hübner, G. 1973. "Dachterrakotten aus dem Kerameikos von Athen," *AM* 88, S. 67–143

———. 1980. "Die Dachterrakotten," *AA* [*JdI* 95], S. 112–115

———. 1990. "Die Dachterrakotten der archaischen Tempel von Kalapodi (Phokis)," in *Hesperia* 59, S. 167–174

Kienast, H. J. 1980. "Die klassischen Tempel," *AA* [*JdI* 95], S. 99–108

———. 1988. "Die klassischen Tempel im Heiligtum bei Kalapodi," in Πρακτικά του XII Διεθνούς Συνεδρίου Κλασικής Αρχαιολογίας, Αθήνα, 4–10 Σεπτεμβρίου 1983, IV, Athen, S. 100–103

Knigge, U. 1988. *Der Kerameikos von Athen*, Athen

Korres, M. (in Vorbereitung). Συμβολή στην οικοδομική μελέτη των αρχαίων κιονών (Arbeitstitel)

Korres, M., und Ch. Bouras. 1983. Μελέτη αποκαταστάσεως του Παρθενώνος, Athen, S. 37–40

Lauffer, S. 1989. *Griechenland, Lexikon der historischen Stätten von den Anfängen bis zur Gegenwart*, S. Lauffer, ed., München

Le Roy, Ch. 1967. *Les terres cuites architecturales* (*Fouilles de Delphes* II), Paris

Leekley, D., und N. Efstratiou. 1980. *Archaeological Excavations in Central and Northern Greece*, Park Ridge, NJ

Müller-Wiener, W. 1988. *Griechisches Bauwesen in der Antike*, München

Ohnesorg, A. 1990. "Archaic Roof Tiles from the Heraion on Samos," in *Hesperia* 59, S. 181–192

Philippart, H. 1936. *Les coupes attiques à fond blanc*, Bruxelles

Schede, M. 1909. *Antikes Traufleistenornament*, Strassburg

Vlassopoulou, C. 1990. "Decorated Architectural Terracottas from the Athenian Acropolis," in *Hesperia* 59, S. vii–xxxi

Williams, C. K., II. 1988. "Corinthian Trade in Roof Tiles," in Πρακτικά του XII Διεθνούς Συνεδρίου Κλασικής Αρχαιολογίας, Αθήνα, 4–10 Σεπτεμβρίου, 1983, IV, Athen, S. 227–230

Winter, N. A. 1990. "Defining Regional Styles in Archaic Greek Architectural Terracottas," in *Hesperia* 59, S. 13–32

Wrede, W. 1933. *Attische Mauern*, Athen

GERHILD HÜBNER

INSTITUT FÜR BAUGESCHICHTE DER UNIVERSITÄT
Englerstr. 7
D-76128 Karlsruhe
Bundesrepublik Deutschland

# ΤΑ ΣΦΡΑΓΙΣΜΑΤΑ ΚΕΡΑΜΙΔΩΝ ΑΠΟ ΤΟ ΙΕΡΟ ΤΗΣ ΔΩΔΩΝΗΣ

(Plates 60–76)

ΣΤΗΝ ΕΡΓΑΣΙΑ αυτή[1] δημοσιεύονται 108 σφραγίσματα σε κεραμίδες στέγης που έχουν βρεθεί ως σήμερα κατά τις ανασκαφές του Ιερού της Δωδώνης[2] (Fig. 1).

Γενικά οι σφραγισμένες κεραμίδες είναι ελάχιστες[3] σε σύγκριση με τα σύνολα των κεραμίδων που συνήθως βρίσκονται σε μεγάλη αφθονία, ιδίως όταν πρόκειται για ανασκαφές κτηρίων. Όπως είναι γνωστό, σφραγίσματα έχουν χρησιμοποιηθεί ήδη από την Αρχαϊκή περίοδο,[4] κυρίως για να δηλώσουν τη θέση της κεραμίδας επάνω στη στέγη. Αργότερα χρησιμοποιήθηκαν και για άλλους σκοπούς και απέκτησαν ευρύτερο περιεχόμενο, όπως π.χ. ιερά σύμβολα ή σύντομες επιγραφές με αφιερώσεις και επικλήσεις στους θεούς, αναφορές του Ιερού ή του κτηρίου στο οποίο ανήκει

---

[1] Ευχαριστώ θερμά τον καθηγητή κ. Σ. Δάκαρη για την παραχώρηση της άδειας μελέτης και δημοσίευσης του σχετικού υλικού, καθώς και για τις πολύτιμες υποδείξεις του. Ευχαριστώ επίσης την καθηγήτρια κ. Β. Κοντορλίνη για την ανάγνωση του χειρογράφου και τις χρήσιμες διορθώσεις, καθώς και τους προϊσταμένους της ΙΒ΄ Εφορείας Αρχαιοτήτων κ. Ι. Ψυχογιού-Ανδρέου και κ. Η. Ανδρέου για τις διευκολύνσεις που μου παρείχαν κατά τη διάρκεια της έρευνας στο Μουσείο Ιωαννίνων. Οι φωτογραφίες των σφραγισμάτων οφείλονται στο φωτογράφο του Μουσείου Ιωαννίνων κ. Β. Πτηνόπουλο.

Στο κείμενο, εκτός από τις βιβλιογραφικές συντομογραφίες, χρησιμοποιούνται και τα παρακάτω σύμβολα:

Αρ.Μ.: Αριθμός ευρετηρίου του Μουσείου Ιωαννίνων.
Ε1: Ιερά Οικία στο Ιερό της Δωδώνης.
Ε2: Βουλευτήριο στο Ιερό της Δωδώνης.
Λ: Ναός Αφροδίτης στο Ιερό της Δωδώνης.
Μ: Οικία Ιερέων (;) στο Ιερό της Δωδώνης.
Ο, Ο1: Πρυτανείο στο Ιερό της Δωδώνης. Το Ο1 είναι προσθήκη στο αρχαιότερο οικοδόμημα Ο.

Στο κείμενο όλες οι χρονολογήσεις αναφέρονται στους προχριστιανικούς χρόνους, εκτός από αυτές που δηλώνονται. Οι διαστάσεις, που δίνονται, αναφέρονται στο σφράγισμα και όχι στο ενσφράγιστο απότμημα της κεραμίδας. Ο χαρακτηρισμός του χρώματος του πηλού γίνεται με βάση το *Munsell Soil Color Charts*, Baltimore, Maryland 1975.

Οι ενδείξεις των πινάκων αναφέρονται κατ'αρχήν στην ομάδα σφραγισμάτων (Α, Β, Γ), κατόπιν στην κατηγορία τους (Ι, ΙΙ, ΙΙΙ κλπ) και τέλος στον αύξοντα αριθμό των καταλόγων (1, 2, 3 κλπ).

[2] Για τις ανασκαφές στη Δωδώνη βλ. Δάκαρης 1960, σελ. 5, σημ. 2· Δάκαρης 1986β, σελ. 11–12, 155–157. Για τις πιο πρόσφατες έρευνες στο Ιερό βλ. Δάκαρης 1981α, σελ. 67–71· Δάκαρης 1982, σελ. 85–88· Δάκαρης 1983, σελ. 78–80· Δάκαρης 1985β, σελ. 39–44· Δάκαρης 1986γ, σελ. 100· Δάκαρης 1985α, σελ. 31–35· Δάκαρης 1986β, σελ. 64–66. Πρβ. επίσης Γραβάνη 1988–1989, σελ. 92, σημ. 13.

[3] Γενικά για τη σφράγιση των κεραμίδων βλ. Ορλάνδος 1955, σελ. 113–116· Martin 1965, σελ. 84–87· Guarducci 1969, σελ. 486–502. Πρβ. Βλαχοπούλου-Οικονόμου 1986, σελ. 261, σημ. 19. Για τις σφραγίδες που συνήθως ήταν ξύλινες, «ξύλινος τύπος» κατά τους αρχαίους, βλ. Ορλάνδος 1955, σελ. 113, σημ. 4, 5· Hübner 1973, σελ. 86–87. Πρβ. δύο πήλινες κυλινδρικές σφραγίδες των ύστερων γεωμετρικών χρόνων και της Ανατολίζουσας εποχής από τη Δωδώνη. Δάκαρης 1968, σελ. 57, πίν. 42:α.

[4] Γενικά για σφραγίσματα της Αρχαϊκής περιόδου βλ. Felsch 1979, σελ. 1–40, όπου και παλαιότερη βιβλιογραφία· Felsch 1990, σελ. 301–323.

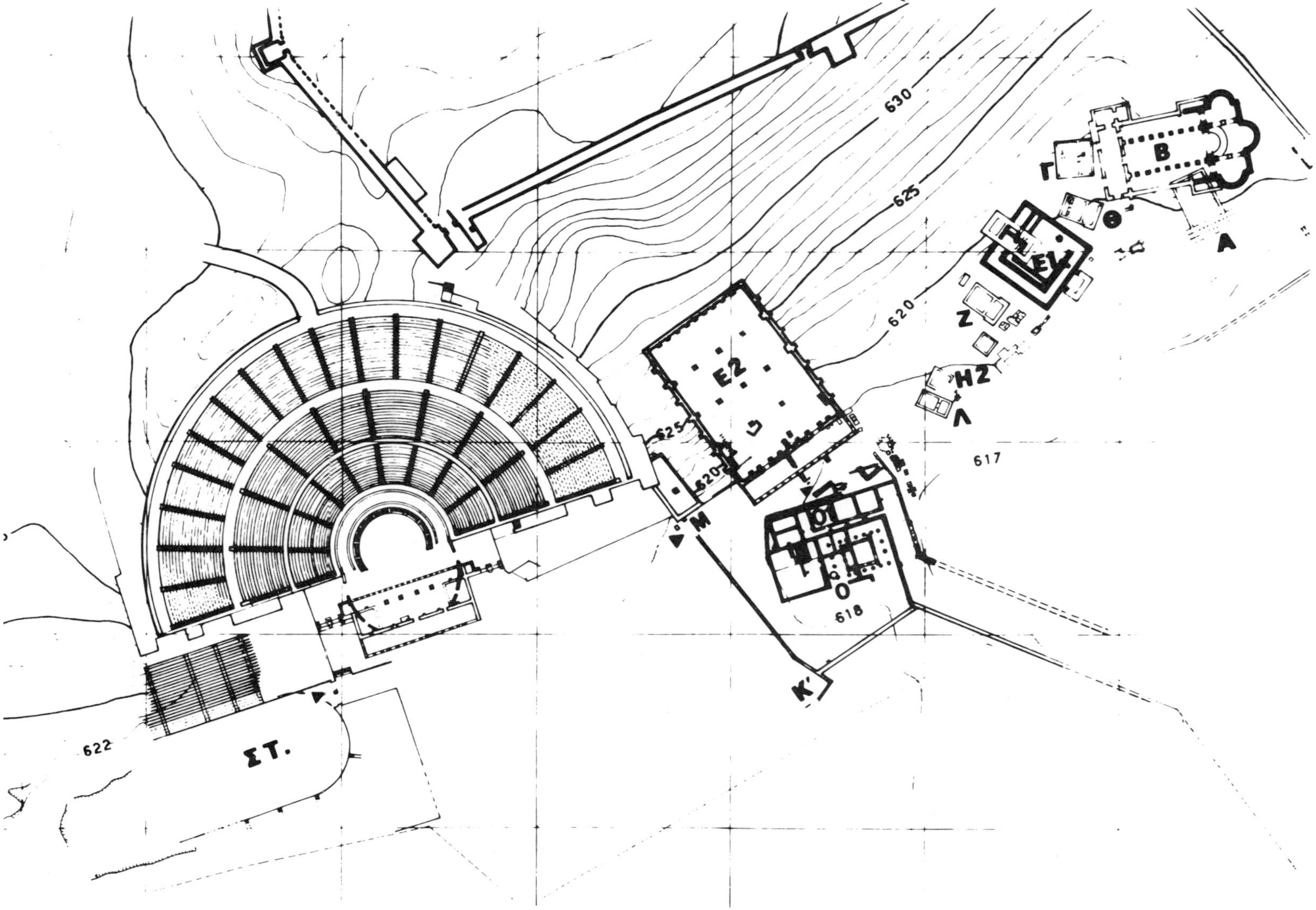

Fig. 1. Τοπογραφικό σχεδιάγραμμα του Ιερού της Δωδώνης

η κεράμωση, του κτήτορα του δημοσίου, του βασιλιά ή του επώνυμου άρχοντα, του τεχνίτη που τις κατασκεύασε κλπ.[5] Οι επιγραφές συνήθως ήταν σύντομες και περιείχαν μία ή δύο λέξεις. Κατά την Αρχαϊκή περίοδο σφραγιζόταν η κάτω, μη ορατή επιφάνεια της κεραμίδας,[6] σε αντίθεση με τις κεραμίδες της Ελληνιστικής περιόδου που ήταν σφραγισμένες στην επάνω ορατή επιφάνεια.[7] Τα σφραγίσματα αυτά δεν έχουν καμιά σχέση με τα τεκτονικά σήματα στις κεραμίδες, που ήταν συχνά κυρίως κατά την Αρχαϊκή περίοδο,[8] πιθανόν επειδή κατά τον 4ο αι. και μετά έχουν ελαττωθεί τα προβλήματα για την τοποθέτηση των κεραμίδων σε συγκεκριμένη θέση στη στέγη.[9]

Σφραγίσματα σε κεραμίδες κατά την Ελληνιστική περίοδο συναντώνται συχνά, ενώ κατά τη Ρωμαϊκή περίοδο είναι υπεράφθονα.[10] Έχει γίνει ήδη αποδεκτό ότι η σφράγιση των κεραμίδων κατά την Ελληνιστική περίοδο είχε σκοπό τη διευκόλυνση του ελέγχου από τον αρμόδιο άρχοντα ή την προστασία των έτοιμων κεραμίδων από την κλοπή.[11] Αντίθετα τα πρωιμότερα σφραγίσματα φαίνεται ότι εξυπηρετούσαν περισσότερο τις εσωτερικές ανάγκες των ίδιων των εργαστηρίων. Ας σημειωθεί ότι είναι δυνατόν στην ίδια κεραμίδα να υπάρχουν δύο σφραγίσματα, όπως η επιγραφή επί Κερκίωνος, όνομα επώνυμου άρχοντα σε στρωτήρα κέραμο από την Κασσώπη (Pl. 76:b).[12] Επομένως το σύνολο των σφραγισμάτων από τη Δωδώνη δεν αποδεικνύει κατ' ανάγκην και αντίστοιχο αριθμό κεραμίδων.

Τα 108 σφραγίσματα κεραμίδων από τη Δωδώνη, που δημοσιεύονται παρακάτω, αποτελούν ένα σημαντικό σύνολο σε σχέση με τα μέχρι σήμερα γνωστά σφραγίσματα από την Ήπειρο.[13] Με βάση το περιεχόμενό τους τα σφραγίσματα αυτά

---

[5] Πρβ. Καλτσάς 1988, σελ. 101.
[6] Βλ. Felsch 1990, σελ. 301.
[7] Hübner 1973, σελ. 86· Hübner 1976, σελ. 180, σημ. 29.
[8] Πέππα-Δελμούζου 1967-1968, σελ. 369-385.
[9] Καλτσάς 1988, σελ. 101.
[10] Hübner 1973, σελ. 86. Για σφραγίσματα Ρωμαϊκής περιόδου βλ. ενδεικτικά *Lateres Signati Ostienses*, σελ. 39 κεξ., με τη σχετική βιβλιογραφία στις σελ. 33-34.
[11] Felsch 1990, σελ. 301, σημ. 3.
[12] Δάκαρης 1989, σελ. 56, πίν. 12:β, γ. Βλ. επίσης διπλή σφράγιση σε στρωτήρα κέραμο από τη Βοιωτία. Πέππα-Δελμούζου 1970, σελ. 15, πίν. 10:γ. Σπανιότερα συναντώνται και περισσότερα σφραγίσματα στην ίδια κεραμίδα, όπως το τετραπλό σφράγισμα σε κεραμίδα από το ανάκτορο της Βεργίνας (Παντερμαλής 1987, σελ. 591 α). Για διπλή σφράγιση αρχαϊκών κεραμίδων βλ. Felsch 1990, σελ. 303, 309.
[13] Από τις σημαντικότερες ανασκαφές στο χώρο της Ηπείρου είναι γνωστά τα παρακάτω σφραγίσματα σε κεραμίδες:
Αμβρακίας: ΔΗΜΟΣΙΑ, ΔΑΜΟΣΙΑ, [ΔΑ]ΜΟ[ΣΙΟΝ] και ο βαίτυλος του Απόλλωνος Αγυιέος: Franke 1961, σελ. 312 (8), 315-316, πίν. 61:5· Τζουβάρα-Σούλη 1984, σελ. 432, σημ. 1· Τζουβάρα-Σούλη 1987-1988, σελ. 101, σημ 29. ΠΟΛΙΟΣ και ο βαίτυλος του Απόλλωνος Αγυιέος: Franke 1961, σελ. 312 (7), 315-316, πίν. 61:8· Βοκοτοπούλου 1967, σελ. 342· Τζουβάρα-Σούλη 1984, σελ. 432, σημ. 2, 4, πίν. 6:β. ΑΜΒΡ και ο βαίτυλος του Απόλλωνος Αγυιέος σε δάφνινο στεφάνι: Βοκοτοπούλου 1967, σελ. 342, πίν. 247:α· Τζουβάρα-Σούλη 1984, σελ. 432, σημ. 3, πίν. 6:α. ΛΥ: Χρυσοστόμου 1980, σελ. 309. ]ΡΑΚΛ[: Χρυσοστόμου 1980, σελ. 310. ...]ΙΟΣ: Χρυσοστόμου 1982, σελ. 262. ΖΩΠΥΡΟΣ: Χρυσοστόμου 1982, σελ. 263.
Κασσώπης: ΕΠΙ ΚΕΡΚΙΩΝΟΣ: Δάκαρης 1980γ, σελ. 31-32, πίν. 39:β, γ.
Καστρίτσας: ΔΗ[ΜΟΣΙΑ]: Δάκαρης 1952, σελ. 384· Franke 1961, σελ. 312 (6).

κατατάσσονται σε τρεις ομάδες: Α. Μονογράμματα. Β. Σφραγίσματα που έχουν σχέση με το Ιερό στο οποίο ανήκει η κεράμωση. Γ. Σφραγίσματα στα οποία αναγράφονται ονόματα άρχοντα ή τεχνίτη ή κεραμοποιού. Σχετικά σύμβολα ή διακοσμητικά στοιχεία συνοδεύουν πολλές φορές τις επιγραφές, όπως η παράσταση ενός αετού που πατά σε οριζόντιο κεραυνό, ένα δελφίνι, ένα ανθέμιο κλπ.

Στην Α' ομάδα ανήκει:
I. Το μονόγραμμα ΆΡ̄ (τέσσερα θραύσματα, βλ. παρακάτω σελ. 186–189, Pls. 60:b, 61, 62:a).

Στη Β' ομάδα εντάσσονται οι επιγραφές:
I. ΙΑΡΑ δεξιά και αριστερά από αετό που πατά σε κεραυνό με ωκύπτερο· όλη η παράσταση περιβάλλεται από στεφάνι βαλανιδιάς (δεκατρία θραύσματα, βλ. παρακάτω σελ. 189–194, Pls. 62:b, 63).
II. ΙΕΡΑ (δύο θραύσματα, βλ. παρακάτω σελ. 194–195, Pl. 64).
III. ΔΙΟΣ ΝΑΟΥ (τριάντα εννιά θραύσματα, βλ. παρακάτω σελ. 195–200, Pls. 65–69).

Στην Γ' ομάδα περιλαμβάνονται οι επιγραφές:
I. ΑΓΕΣΤΡΑΤΟΣ (τρία θραύσματα, βλ. παρακάτω σελ. 200–202, Pl. 70).
II. ΤΑ ΛΥΣΑΝΙΑ γύρω από ανθέμιο (επτά θραύσματα, βλ. παρακάτω σελ. 202–203, Pls. 71, 72:a).
III. ΑΠΟΛΛΟΔΩΡΟΥ ΛΥΣΑΝΙΑ γύρω από ανθέμιο (τέσσερα θραύσματα, βλ. παρακάτω σελ. 203–207, Pl. 72:b).
IV. ΝΙΚΟΜΑΧΟΥ γύρω από δελφίνι (πέντε θραύσματα, βλ. παρακάτω σελ. 207–210, Pl. 73).

---

Νεκρομαντείου: COS, P.CUR, P.CURT, ΟΥΙΟΣ: Δάκαρης 1963β, σελ. 61· Δάκαρης 1976, σελ. 83· Βλαχοπούλου-Οικονόμου 1979, σελ. 293.
Νικοπόλεως: ΛΥΤ.: Πέτσας 1950–1951, σελ. 39, αρ. 12, εικ. 16.
Ορράου: ΚΑΣ (= Κασσωπαίων): Δάκαρης 1986α, σελ. 143, πίν. 41:α, σημ. 78. ΜΟ και ο βαίτυλος επάνω σε αμφίκοιλο βάθρο: Δάκαρης 1986α, σελ. 143, σημ. 79–80.
Τιτάνης (Γκούμανης): [Δ]ΙΩΝΑΣ: Πέτσας 1952, σελ. 13, εικ. 24· Τζουβάρα-Σούλη 1979, σελ. 78. Εκτός από τις παραπάνω ήδη δημοσιευμένες σφραγισμένες κεραμίδες, στις αποθήκες του Μουσείου Ιωαννίνων και της Αρχαιολογικής Συλλογής Άρτας φυλάσσεται ένας αριθμός σφραγισμάτων που επιφυλασσόμεθα να παρουσιάσουμε στο μέλλον.
Το αντίστοιχο υλικό που προέρχεται από την Αλβανία είναι δυσπρόσιτο λόγω των γνωστών ιδιαιτεροτήτων της αλβανικής βιβλιογραφίας. (Για παλαιότερη βιβλιογραφία σχετική με τον καθορισμό των ορίων της αρχαίας Ηπείρου και για τις δυσχέρειες της αλβανικής βιβλιογραφίας βλ. Γραβάνη 1988–1989, σελ. 89–90, σημ. 2–3.) Ωστόσο ενδεικτικά βλ. Ugolini 1942, σελ. 231, 232, εικ. 241–244· Franke 1961, σελ. 312–315· Dautaj 1972, σελ. 149–157, εικ. 1, πίν. I, IV· Dautaj 1974, σελ. 445, πίν. II· Dautaj 1976, σελ. 390, πίν. I, II, IV(1)· Mano 1974, σελ. 205–211, εικ. 35· Andrea 1976, σελ. 348, πίν. XIV, σελ. 350, πίν. XVIII, 1· Papajani 1976, σελ. 421, εικ. 13· Tartari 1977–1978, σελ. 217, πίν. I:β1–3· Bereti 1977–1978, σελ. 286, πίν. III. Ιδιαίτερα βλ. 55 σφραγίσματα από την περιοχή ανάμεσα στους ποταμούς Αώο και Γενούσο: Ceka 1982, σελ. 103–130, πίν. I–VI. Βλ. επίσης Dautaj 1986, σελ. 101–109, πίν. II· Hidri 1986, σελ. 110, πίν. XIV· Tartari 1988, σελ. 96–98, πίν. IV· Dremsizova 1963, σελ. 386, πίν. 172, 173. Πρβ. επίσης Καλτσάς 1988, σελ. 103, σημ. 335.

V. ΕΠΙ ΦΟΡΜΙΣΣΚΟΥ[14] (τριάντα ένα θραύσματα, βλ. παρακάτω σελ. 210-213, Pls. 74-76:a).

Η προσπάθεια χρονολόγησης των σφραγισμάτων από τη Δωδώνη αντιμετωπίζει σοβαρά προβλήματα, καθώς δεν είναι δυνατό να στηριχθεί στη μελέτη της μορφής των γραμμάτων των επιγραφών[15] για τους παρακάτω λόγους: Οι επιγραφές αυτές δεν έχουν επίσημο χαρακτήρα, ώστε η μορφή των γραμμάτων να μπορεί να συσχετισθεί και να εξετασθεί παράλληλα με τα κείμενα των δημόσιων επιγραφών, επειδή συνήθως αποτελούν δημιουργήματα των ίδιων των τεχνιτών ή και των εργατών και όχι λιθοξόων ή ειδικευμένων στη γραφή.[16] Εξάλλου, όπως είναι φυσικό, το σφράγισμα σε πηλό διαφέρει από τη γραφή σε μάρμαρο. Περισσότερο ίσως χρήσιμη θα ήταν η συγκριτική αντιπαράθεση με τη γραφή των παπύρων, παρόλο που στην κατασκευή της σφραγίδας έχουμε μία πιο αργή διαδικασία και κατά συνέπεια μεγαλύτερες δυνατότητες για πιο προσεκτική εργασία. Επομένως η σφράγιση των κεραμίδων βρίσκεται ανάμεσα στις δύο ακραίες περιπτώσεις των επιγραφών σε μάρμαρο και των κειμένων σε πάπυρο.[17]

---

[14] Ο ανασκαφέας αναφέρει ότι «ευρέθησαν... και κεραμίδες με εκτύπους επιγραφάς, ἐπί Φορμίσσχου, Διός Νάου... ιδου», (Δάκαρης 1971, σελ. 126) και αλλού «Διός Νάου, ἐπί Φορμίσσχου, -ιδου» (Δάκαρης 1969β, σελ. 26· Δάκαρης 1969α, σελ. 19). Σφραγίσματα όμως με τα γράμματα -ιδου δεν έχουν βρεθεί, παρά την επισταμένη έρευνα, στις αποθήκες του Μουσείου Ιωαννίνων.

Εκτός όμως από τα παραπάνω σφραγίσματα, ανάμεσα στο ποικίλο υλικό από τη Δωδώνη βρέθηκε και ένα έντυπο σφράγισμα σε σχήμα τριγώνου, με εγγεγραμμένο κύκλο που διακοσμείται εσωτερικά με εξαφυλλο ρόδακα. Στις γωνίες του τριγώνου φέρονται «επί τα λαιά» τα γράμματα της επιγραφής ΔΗ|[ΜΟ|ΣΙ]Α. Τα γράμματα και η διακόσμηση είναι έκτυπα (Pl. 60:a). Το απότμημα της κεραμίδας δεν έφερε καμιά ανασκαφική ένδειξη και αριθμό Μουσείου. Κανονικά λοιπόν το παραπάνω σφράγισμα έπρεπε να ενταχθεί στη Β' ομάδα, αν κατά τη διάρκεια της έρευνας δε διαπιστώναμε ότι ίσως πρόκειται για το σφράγισμα που αναφέρει ο Δάκαρης (Δάκαρης 1952, σελ. 384) ότι έχει βρεθεί στην Καστρίτσα Ιωαννίνων και επαναλαμβάνει σύντομα ο Franke (Franke 1961, σελ. 312 [6]), χωρίς όμως φωτογραφία. Η επιγραφή ΔΗΜΟΣΙΑ συναντάται πολύ συχνά σε σφραγίσματα κεραμίδων και σημαίνει ότι η κεράμωση ανήκει στην ιδιοκτησία του δημοσίου. Βλ. σχετικά Ορλάνδος 1955, σελ. 114· Hübner 1976, σελ. 180, σημ. 29. Στη Μακεδονία απαντά συντομογραφημένη (ΔΗΜΟ) σε κεραμίδα από την Πέλλα (Καλτσάς 1988, σελ. 101, σημ. 314, 315), ενώ σώζεται επίσης σε σφραγίσματα από την Αλβανία και ειδικότερα από την περιοχή ανάμεσα στον Αώο και στο Γενούσο (Ceka 1982, σελ. 104, 105, 114, 116-118, όπου και παλαιότερη βιβλιογραφία. Πρβ. Andrea 1976, σελ. 348, πίν. XIV:2, 4). Βλ. επίσης τη λέξη Δαμόσιος σε πήλινη σφραγίδα του 3ου αι. (Albanien, σελ. 278, αρ. 150). Στην Ήπειρο είναι γνωστή από σφραγίσματα της Αμβρακίας με το σύμβολο της πόλης, δηλ. οβελίσκο (βαίτυλο) και από τις δύο πλευρές του τη λέξη [Δ]ΑΜΟ[Σ]ΙΑ (Franke 1961, σελ. 312 [8], 315, 316, πιν. 61:5· Τζουβάρα-Σούλη 1984, σελ. 432· Τζουβάρα-Σούλη 1987-1988, σελ. 101, σημ. 29). Επίσης στην Αμβρακία βρέθηκε τμήμα πήλινου υδροσωλήνα με έγκοιλα τα γράμματα ΔΑΜΟΣΙΟΝ (Βοκοτοπούλου 1976, σελ. 194), ενώ στην Κασσώπη βρέθηκαν 2 χάλκινα σταθμά (σπίτι 14) που φέρουν το ανάγλυφο μονόγραμμα ΔΑ[ΜΟΣΙΑ] (Δάκαρης 1989, σελ. 57, πίν. 17:a).

[15] Τα ίδια προβλήματα συναντά κανείς στην προσπάθεια να χρησιμοποιήσει ό,τι ισχύει για τις επίσημες επιγραφές ως χρονολογικό κριτήριο για τα τεκτονικά σημεία και τις επιγραφές που χαράσσονται από τους τεχνίτες. Πέππα-Δελμούζου 1967-1968, σελ. 383.

[16] Για σχετική βιβλιογραφία και για σημαντικές διαφορές στη μορφή των γραμμάτων όχι μόνο ανάμεσα σε επίσημες και λαϊκές επιγραφές, αλλά και ανάμεσα στα γράμματα επιγραφών της ίδιας περιόδου που προέρχονται από διαφορετικές περιοχές ή ακόμη και ανάμεσα στα γράμματα της ίδιας επιγραφής βλ. Βλαχοπούλου-Οικονόμου 1986, σελ. 257, 264, σημ. 28-30, σελ. 265, σημ. 31-36.

[17] Καλτσάς 1988, σελ. 104, όπου και σχετική βιβλιογραφία.

Για τους παραπάνω λόγους η μορφή των γραμμάτων υποδεικνύει μόνο το ευρύτερο χρονολογικό πλαίσιο στο οποίο μπορούν να ενταχθούν τα σφραγίσματα[18] και για την τεκμηρίωση σταθερότερων χρονολογήσεων απαιτείται η αναζήτηση άλλων στοιχείων που πιθανόν προσφέρει το κείμενο της επιγραφής.

Ωστόσο η καθυστερημένη εισαγωγή από τον βασιλιά Θαρύπα (432/22–390/85) του ελληνικού αλφαβήτου στην Ήπειρο,[19] όπου το αρχαιότερο προς το παρόν δείγμα γραφής είναι δύο τιμητικά ψηφίσματα του Κοινού των Μολοσσών που χρονολογούνται στα 370–368,[20] αποτελεί ένα σημαντικό *terminus post quem*. Στα χρηστήρια μολύβδινα ελάσματα της Δωδώνης[21] συναντώνται βέβαια διάφοροι τύποι αλφαβήτων του 6ου και του 5ου αι., που όμως χαράσσονταν από τους ίδιους τους προσκυνητές οι οποίοι προέρχονταν από διάφορα μέρη της Ελλάδας.[22] Η συνέχιση των ανασκαφών στη Δωδώνη με τις νέες στρωματογραφικές μεθόδους και η ανασκαφή στο κτήριο Μ με την «αιτωλική επίχωση»[23] ίσως προσφέρουν πρόσθετα στοιχεία που θα επιτρέψουν να τεκμηριωθούν ορισμένες από τις χρονολογήσεις που προτείνονται παρακάτω.

## Α' ΟΜΑΔΑ

I. Μονόγραμμα ⏶

Το μονόγραμμα ⏶ (Pls. 60:b, 61, 62:a) εμπεριέχεται σε τετράγωνο έντυπο σφράγισμα και περιλαμβάνει τα γράμματα Α, Ρ, Τ, Ν, Κ, επίσης έντυπα. Η εσωτερική κεραία του Α είναι τεθλασμένη, ενώ στην οριζόντια κεραία, που το επιστέφει, σώζονται ακρεμόνες που κατευθύνονται προς τα επάνω. Παρόλο που η μορφή και το μέγεθος των γραμμάτων είναι ίδια, ωστόσο οι διαστάσεις των έντυπων τετραγώνων ποικίλουν, πράγμα που πιθανόν σημαίνει ότι τα σφραγίσματα προέρχονται από διαφορετικές σφραγίδες. Έχουν βρεθεί τα παρακάτω σφραγίσματα:

1. Αρ.Μ.: 3506 β (Pl. 60:b).[24]
   Ύψ. 0,063 μ. Πλ. 0,06 μ.
   Πηλός ερυθρός (2.5YR 5/6).
   Θέση: Ε2· ανασκαφή 1968.
   Ολόκληρο το μονόγραμμα ⏶.

2. Αρ.Μ.: 273 (Pl. 61:a).[25]
   Ύψ. 0,052 μ. Πλ. 0,052 μ.
   Πηλός υπέρυθρος κιτρινωπός (5YR 6/8).
   Ανασκαφή 1935.
   Ολόκληρο το μονόγραμμα ⏶.

---

[18] Woodhead 1967, σελ. 65.
[19] Δάκαρης 1964α, σελ. 52–55· Δάκαρης 1972β, σελ. 79.
[20] Γραβάνη 1988–1989, σελ. 125, σημ. 217, όπου και σχετική βιβλιογραφία.
[21] Βοκοτοπούλου 1973, σελ. 60–65 και Δάκαρης 1986β, σελ. 92–94, πίν. 42.
[22] Γραβάνη 1988–1989, σελ. 125, σημ. 218.
[23] Για την «αιτωλική επίχωση» βλ. παρακάτω σελ. 193, σημ. 86.
[24] Δάκαρης 1968, σελ. 52, πίν. 38:β.
[25] Ευαγγελίδης 1935, σελ. 260, αρ. 43, εικ. 25:β (12)· Franke 1961, σελ. 312 (4), 315, πίν. 61:4.

3. Αρ.Μ.: 3491 (Pl. 62:a).
   ΄Υψ. 0,037 μ. Πλ. 0,078 μ.
   Πηλός υπέρυθρος κιτρινωπός (5YR 6/8).
   Θέση: Θέατρο· ανασκαφή 1959.
   Απότμημα του μονογράμματος ΆΡ.

4. Αρ.Μ.: 3506 α (Pl. 61:b).
   ΄Υψ. 0,058 μ. Πλ. 0,047 μ.
   Πηλός υπέρυθρος (2.5YR 6/8).
   Θέση: Ε2· ανασκαφή 1968.
   Αριστερό τμήμα του μονογράμματος ΆΡ.

Η συντετμημένη απόδοση ονομάτων και η χρήση μονογραμμάτων, που είναι απλά σήματα με το αρχικό της λέξης ή με τη μορφή συμπλέγματος γραμμάτων, είναι πολύ συχνή σε σφραγίσματα κεραμίδων,[26] λαβών[27] και πωμάτων[28] αμφορέων, νομισμάτων,[29] αγγείων[30] κλπ.

Κατά τον Δάκαρη[31] στο μονόγραμμα ΆΡ εμπεριέχονται τα γράμματα Α, Π, Ρ, Τ, Ν, Κ και είναι πιθανή η ανάγνωση Κ[ΟΙ]Ν[Ο]Ν ΑΠ[ΕΙ]Ρ[Ο]ΤΑΝ.[32] Η άποψη του Franke[33] ότι πρόκειται για τη συντομογραφία του ονόματος ενός επώνυμου άρχοντα,[34] αλλά και η πιθανότητα[35] να πρόκειται για το όνομα του τεχνίτη[36] μας οδηγούν να αναζητήσουμε την ερμηνεία του μονογράμματος σε μία σειρά Ηπειρωτικών ονομάτων που εμπεριέχουν τα παραπάνω γράμματα, όπως π.χ. τα ονόματα Ἀκραλέστων, Ἀνδροκάδας, Ἀνδρόκκας, Ἀνδροκλείδης, Ἀνδροκλείων, Ἄνδροκος, Ἀνδρόνικος, Ἀντίρκας, Ἀριστοκράτης κλπ.[37] Ας σημειωθεί η σύνδεση από τον Franke σχετικά όμοιου μονογράμματος ΆΡ με το όνομα Ἀνδρόνικος.[38]

[26] Για μονογράμματα σε σφραγίσματα κεραμίδων από τη Μακεδονία βλ. Καλτσάς 1988, σελ. 97-105 και από την Αλβανία βλ. Andrea 1976, σελ. 348, πίν. 14:14-16· Ugolini 1942, σελ. 232 (4), εικ. 244. Σε σχέση με το σύνολο των σφραγισμάτων σε κεραμίδες τα μονογράμματα συναντώνται σπανιότερα. Hübner 1973, σελ. 86. Για συμπλέγματα γραμμάτων από την Αττική και την Ελευσίνα βλ. Πέππα-Δελμούζου 1967-1968, σελ. 384, σημ. 28-30.

[27] Για μονογράμματα σε λαβές αμφορέων από το Νεκρομαντείο του Αχέροντα βλ. Βλαχοπούλου-Οικονόμου 1979, σελ. 293.

[28] Για μονογράμματα σε πώματα αμφορέων από το Νεκρομαντείο βλ. Δάκαρης 1964β, σελ. 57. Πρβ. Γραβάνη 1988-1989, σελ. 123, σημ. 206.

[29] Για μονογράμματα στα νομίσματα από την Ἤπειρο βλ. Franke 1961, σποραδικά.

[30] Για μονογράμματα σε λυχνάρια και αμφορείς από το Νεκρομαντείο βλ. Γραβάνη 1988-1989, σελ. 123, σημ. 204, 205.

[31] Δάκαρης 1968, σελ. 52.

[32] Πρβ. σφράγισμα με το σύμπλεγμα των τριών πρώτων γραμμάτων της λέξης Δυμ(αίων). Μαστροκώστας 1963, σελ. 96, πίν. 67:β.

[33] Franke 1961, σελ. 146, 312, 315.

[34] Πρβ. μονόγραμμα από την Αίγινα: Ἀ(ττάλου) Β(ασιλέως). Welter 1954, στ. 45, 46.

[35] Πρβ. την περίπτωση του μονογράμματος ΑΒ σε κεραμίδες από την Πέργαμο και τις διαφορετικές ερμηνείες που έχουν προταθεί. Wensler 1989, σελ. 38, σημ. 24-28.

[36] Για μονογράμματα κεραμοπλαστών από την Αλβανία βλ. Dautaj 1972, σελ. 154, πίν. IV· από την Πέλλα, καθώς και για μονογράμματα και συμπλέγματα σε νομίσματα, τα οποία αποδίδονται στο νομισματοκόπο βλ. Καλτσάς 1988, σελ. 103, σημ. 327· Papajani 1976, σελ. 421.
Για μονογράμματα σε λαβές αμφορέων που αναφέρονται σε ιδιοκτήτες εργαστηρίων ή σε υπεύθυνους άρχοντες της πόλης βλ. ενδεικτικά Nikolaidou-Patera 1986, σελ. 485-490. Για μονογράμματα, μερικά από τα οποία είναι παρόμοια, σε νομίσματα του Κοινού των Ηπειρωτών (234/3-168/7) βλ. Franke 1961, σελ. 172-217. Για μονογράμματα των τεχνιτών σε πήλινα ειδώλια από την Μύρινα βλ. Kassab 1988, σελ. 61 κεξ.

[37] Hammond 1967, Index I, σελ. 796-817.

[38] Franke 1961, σελ. 146.

Η έλλειψη στρωματογραφικών ενδείξεων και συνεπώς η αδυναμία να συσχετισθούν τα σφραγίσματα των κεραμίδων από τη Δωδώνη με άλλα ευρήματα αποδυναμώνει την προσπάθεια χρονολόγησής τους. Ωστόσο, οι ακρεμόνες που επιστέφουν το άλφα αποτελούν ένδειξη για τη χρονολογική τοποθέτηση των σφραγισμάτων στον 3ο ή στον 2ο αι. Οι ακρεμόνες θεωρούνται εύρημα της Ελληνιστικής περιόδου, κατά την οποία είναι ιδιαίτερα δημοφιλείς, ενώ κατά τη Ρωμαϊκή περίοδο, ως επί το πλείστον, εγκαταλείπονται.[39] Εξάλλου η γωνιώδης μορφή της εσωτερικής κεραίας του άλφα υποδηλώνει ότι μπορούμε να υποστηρίξουμε τη χρονολόγηση στον 3ο ή στον 2ο αι.,[40] καθώς παρόμοια μορφή του άλφα δεν μπορεί να γίνει αποδεκτή για επιγραφή αρχαιότερη του 3ου αι.[41]

Παρόμοια μορφή του άλφα διακρίνουμε επίσης σε σφραγίσματα κεραμίδων που προέρχονται από τις περιοχές της Διμάλλας και της Απολλωνίας και χρονολογούνται στον 3ο–2ο αι.[42] Η γωνιώδης εσωτερική κεραία του άλφα συναντάται στην Ήπειρο στα νομίσματα του Κοινού των Ηπειρωτών, αμέσως μετά το 234/3 και σε δύο λίθινα βάθρα τιμητικών ανδριάντων του τέλους του 3ου αι., τα οποία βρίσκονται στη ΝΑ γωνία του Βουλευτηρίου της Δωδώνης με ψηφίσματα του Κοινού και την υπογραφή του ανδριαντοποιού Αθηνογένους.[43] Επομένως είναι δυνατή η χρονολόγηση των σφραγισμάτων στα χρόνια του Κοινού των Ηπειρωτών (234/3–168/7),[44] την οποία ενισχύει και η ομοιότητα του μονογράμματος με άλλα αντίστοιχα στα νομίσματα του Ηπειρωτικού Κοινού.[45]

Κατά την περίοδο αυτή αναπτύχθηκε μεγάλη οικοδομική δραστηριότητα στο Ιερό. Η Ιερά Οικία, που είχε κατεδαφισθεί από τους Αιτωλούς (219),[46] αποκτά μνημειακή μορφή. Οι ναοί της Διώνης, της Θέμιδος, του Ηρακλέους, της Αφροδίτης και το Βουλευτήριο ανοικοδομούνται. Το θέατρο επισκευάζεται και συμπληρώνεται με ένα λίθινο προσκήνιο, δύο ιωνικά πρόπυλα και δύο μικρά παρασκήνια. Ένα μεγάλο λίθινο στάδιο κατασκευάζεται μπροστά από τα δυτικά πυργοειδή αναλήμματα του θεάτρου,[47] ενώ το οικοδόμημα Ο επισκευάζεται και επεκτείνεται.[48]

[39] Woodhead 1967, σελ. 64.
[40] Καλτσάς 1988, σελ. 105.
[41] Woodhead 1967, σελ. 65. Το άλφα με γωνιώδη εσωτερική κεραία σε επιγραφές βάσεων αγαλμάτων του τέλους του 4ου αι. από την Ολυμπία θεωρείται εξαίρεση. Fraser και Rönne 1957, σελ. 87, 88, σημ. 38–41.
[42] Ceka 1982, πίν. I–V.
[43] Δάκαρης 1967–1968, σελ. 388, σημ. 7, 8.
[44] Για το Κοινό των Ηπειρωτών και για τη μεγάλη οικοδομική δραστηριότητα που αναπτύχθηκε στη Δωδώνη βλ. Ευαγγελίδης και Δάκαρης 1959, σελ. 98–112· Δάκαρης 1960, σελ. 9–12, 28–32· Δάκαρης 1986β, σελ. 22, 46–49, 61, 64, 65, 72, 73.
[45] Franke 1961, σελ. 146.
[46] Κατά τον Πολύβιο (4.67.3) οι Αιτωλοί με το στρατηγό Δωρίμαχο κατέλαβαν αιφνίδια το Ιερό και προέβησαν σε λεηλασίες και καταστροφές: «τάς τε στοὰς ἐνέπρησε καὶ πολλὰ τῶν ἀναθημάτων διέφθειρε, κατέσκαψε δὲ καὶ τὴν ἱερὰν οἰκίαν». Το επόμενο έτος ο Φίλιππος ο Ε' εισέβαλε με μακεδονικό και Ηπειρωτικό στρατό στην Αιτωλία και κατέλαβε το Θέρμο (Πολύβ. 5.9.1–4). Με τα λάφυρα του Θέρμου ο Φίλιππος και το Κοινό των Ηπειρωτών ανοικοδόμησαν τα κατεστραμμένα Ιερά. Ευαγγελίδης και Δάκαρης 1959, σελ. 134, 135, 148· Δάκαρης 1960, σελ. 9, 10.
[47] Δάκαρης 1986β, σελ. 22.
[48] Δάκαρης 1981α, σελ. 70· Δάκαρης 1982, σελ. 87.

Η απόδοση των σφραγισμένων κεραμίδων με το μονόγραμμα Ἀε σε συγκεκριμένη στέγη κτηρίου της Δωδώνης δεν είναι δυνατό να τεκμηριωθεί, καθώς ο αριθμός τους είναι περιορισμένος και οι ανασκαφικές ενδείξεις ελλιπείς. Ωστόσο, το γεγονός ότι τα δύο από τα τέσσερα σφραγίσματα (αρ. 1, 4) προέρχονται από το Βουλευτήριο του Ιερού θα μπορούσε να χρησιμοποιηθεί ως ένδειξη απόδοσης των κεραμίδων αυτών στη στέγη του Βουλευτηρίου.[49]

## Β' ΟΜΑΔΑ

I. ΙΑΡΑ, στεφάνι βαλανιδιάς και αετός που πατά σε κεραυνό με ωκύπερο.

Στο κέντρο των στρογγυλών έντυπων σφραγισμάτων της Β'Ι κατηγορίας (Pls. 62:b, 63) παριστάνεται ένας αετός προς τα δεξιά που πατά στον κεντρικό δεσμό ενός οριζόντιου κεραυνού. Ο κεραυνός αποτελείται από δύο αντικόρυφα συμμετρικά λωτόμορφα μέρη με σαφή δήλωση των σεπάλων. Κάτω από τον κεντρικό δεσμό εικονίζεται ένα ωκύπτερο.[50] Όλη η παράσταση περιβάλλεται από στεφάνι βαλανιδιάς με δεσμό στο κάτω μέρος. Αριστερά και δεξιά από τον αετό φέρονται τα γράμματα ΙΑ και αριστερά και δεξιά από το ωκύπτερο τα γράμματα ΡΑ. Φέρεται επομένως η επιγραφή ΙΑΡΑ, δωρικός τύπος της λέξης ιερά.[51] Έχουν βρεθεί τα παρακάτω σφραγίσματα:

1.  Διάμ. 0,078 μ. (Pl. 62:b).[52]
    Πηλός ρόδινος (7.5YR 7/4).
    Ανασκαφή 1965.
    Ολόκληρο σφράγισμα.
    Ι|Α|Ρ|Α

2.  Διάμ. τόξου 0,069 μ. (Pl. 63:a, επάνω αριστερά).
    Πηλός υπέρυθρος κιτρινωπός (5YR 6/6).
    Ανασκαφή 1965.
    Τμήμα του στεφανιού βαλανιδιάς και ο αετός.
    Ι|Α|[Ρ|Α]

3.  Αρ.Μ.: 5727 (Pl. 63:a, κάτω αριστερά).
    Διάμ. τόξου 0,065 μ.
    Πηλός ρόδινος (7.5YR 7/4).
    Θέση: Ε2· ανασκαφή 1971.
    Τμήμα του στεφανιού βαλανιδιάς, ο αετός και το δεξιό τμήμα του κεραυνού με το δεσμό.
    [Ι]|Α|[Ρ|Α]

4.  Αρ.Μ.: 5724 (Pl. 63:a, επάνω δεξιά).
    Διάμ. τόξου 0,054 μ.
    Πηλός ρόδινος (7.5YR 7/4).
    Θέση: Ε2· ανασκαφή 1971.
    Τμήμα του στεφανιού βαλανιδιάς και ο αετός.
    [Ι]|Α|[Ρ|Α]

5.  Διάμ. τόξου 0,069 μ.
    Πηλός ελαφρά καστανός (7.5YR 6/4).
    Ανασκαφή 1965.
    Τμήμα του στεφανιού βαλανιδιάς, ο αετός και τμήμα του κεραυνού προς τα αριστερά.
    Ι|[Α|Ρ|Α]

---

[49] Για τις οικοδομικές φάσεις του Βουλευτηρίου και τις αντίστοιχες στέγες του βλ. Βλαχοπούλου-Οικονόμου 1986, σελ. 222, σημ. 41, σελ. 239, 244, 247, 248· Βλαχοπούλου-Οικονόμου 1988–1989, σελ. 84.

[50] Για τα ωκύπτερα βλ. Δάκαρης 1980β, σελ. 27–34.

[51] Βλ. Frisk 1960, στο λήμμα. Πρβ. Boisacq 1950, στο λήμμα, όπου και σχετική βιβλιογραφία για τη χρήση του άλφα και του έψιλον.

[52] Δάκαρης 1980β, σελ. 30, πίν. 4:2.

6. Αρ.Μ.: 3502 (Pl. 63:b, επάνω δεξιά).
   Διάμ. τόξου 0,065 μ.
   Πηλός υπέρυθρος κιτρινωπός (5YR 7/6).
   Ανασκαφή 1965.
   Τμήμα του στεφανιού βαλανιδιάς και του αετού.
   |[Ι]|Α|[Ρ|Α]

7. Αρ.Μ.: 5729 (Pl. 63:b, κάτω αριστερά).
   Διάμ. τόξου 0,065 μ.
   Πηλός υπέρυθρος κιτρινωπός (5YR 6/8).
   Θέση: Ε2· ανασκαφή 1971.
   Τμήμα του στεφανιού βαλανιδιάς, του αετού, του κεραυνού με το δεσμό και του ωκυπτέρου.
   Ι|[Α]|Ρ|[Α]

8. Διάμ. τόξου 0,045 μ. (Pl. 63:b, επάνω αριστερά).
   Πηλός υπέρυθρος κιτρινωπός (5YR 7/6).
   Ανασκαφή 1965.
   Τμήμα του στεφανιού βαλανιδιάς, του κεραυνού και το ωκύπτερο.
   [Ι|Α|Ρ]|Α

9. Διάμ. τόξου 0,055 μ. (Pl. 63:b, κάτω δεξιά).
   Πηλός υπέρυθρος κιτρινωπός (5YR 7/6).
   Ανασκαφή 1965.
   Τμήμα του στεφανιού βαλανιδιάς, το δεξιό τμήμα του κεραυνού με το δεσμό, τμήμα του ωκυπτέρου.
   [Ι]|Α|[Ρ]|Α

10. Διάμ. τόξου 0,071 μ.
    Πηλός ρόδινος (7.5YR 7/4).
    Θέση: Ο1· ανασκαφή 1981.
    Τμήμα του στεφανιού βαλανιδιάς, το αριστερό τμήμα του κεραυνού με το δεσμό και το ωκύπτερο.
    [Ι|Α]|Ρ|Α

11. Αρ.Μ.: 3548 (Pl. 63:a, κάτω δεξιά).
    Διάμ. τόξου 0,043 μ.
    Πηλός υπέρυθρος κιτρινωπός (5YR 7/6).
    Τμήμα του στεφανιού βαλανιδιάς και το δεξιό τμήμα του κεραυνού.
    [Ι|Α|Ρ]|Α

12. Διάμ. τόξου 0,072 μ.
    Πηλός υπέρυθρος κιτρινωπός (5YR 7/6).
    Ανασκαφή 1965.
    Τμήμα του στεφανιού βαλανιδιάς και η άκρη του αριστερού τμήματος του κεραυνού.
    [Ι|Α|Ρ|Α]

13. Αρ.Μ.: 3504.
    Διάμ. τόξου 0,063 μ.
    Πηλός υπέρυθρος κιτρινωπός (5YR 7/6).
    Ανασκαφή 1965.
    Αριστερό τμήμα του κεραυνού.
    [Ι|Α]|Ρ|[Α]

Η επιγραφή ἱερά συναντάται πολύ συχνά σε σφραγίσματα κεραμίδων[53] και καθορίζει ότι η κεράμωση ανήκει στην ιδιοκτησία του Ιερού. Υπονοείται η λέξη «κεραμίς», δηλ. «ἱερά κεραμίς», γι'αυτό και μερικές φορές συναντάται με τον τύπο ἱεροί, δηλ. «ἱεροί κέραμοι».[54] Η λέξη ἱερά απαντά και στην επόμενη κατηγορία σφραγισμάτων (Β΄II),[55] καθώς και σε μία μολύβδινη ψήφο ή εισιτήριο του τέλους του 3ου ή των αρχών του 2ου αι. από τη Δωδώνη.[56]

Για τον αετό, τον «τελειότατον πετεηνῶν»,[57] και τον κεραυνό, το «Ζηνός ἄγρυπνον βέλος, καταιβάτης ἐκπνέων φλόγα»,[58] είναι γνωστό ότι συνδέονται άμεσα με τη λατρεία του Διός.[59] Επομένως σε συνάρτηση με τη λέξη ἱαρά υπονοείται: «Ἱερά κεραμίς

---

[53] Ορλάνδος 1955, σελ. 114, σημ. 4, όπου και σχετική βιβλιογραφία. Συμπληρωματικά βλ. Daux 1959, σελ. 628· Lehmann 1960, σελ. 37, 38, 109–118· Πέππα-Δελμούζου 1967–1968, σελ. 384, σημ. 28, 31, όπου βλ. και για το σύμπλεγμα των γραμμάτων ΗΡ, που ίσως δηλώνει το επίθετο hιεροί ή hιερά.
[54] Ορλάνδος 1955, σελ. 114.
[55] Βλ. παρακάτω σελ. 194–195.
[56] Δάκαρης 1986β, σελ. 107.
[57] Ὅμηρ. Θ 247.
[58] Αἰσχ. Προμ. 358.
[59] Ο αετός, ως ιερό πτηνό του Διός, είναι πολύ γνωστός από έναν μεγάλο αριθμό έργων της πλαστικής, της μικροτεχνίας και της νομισματοκοπίας, όπου συνήθως παριστάνεται ο Ζευς να εξακοντίζει με το

του Δωδωναίου Διός».[60] Στην Ήπειρο[61] η παράσταση αετού που πατά σε κεραυνό είναι πολύ διαδεδομένο σύμβολο,[62] ιδίως ως έμβλημα νομισμάτων.[63] Στις κοπές της Ηπειρωτικής Συμμαχίας (342/40–234/3)[64] και του Κοινού των Ηπειρωτών (234/3–168/7)[65] αποτελεί το μόνιμο επίσημα.[66]

Το θέμα του αετού που πατά σε κεραυνό δεν υποδηλώνει μόνο το σύμβολο της δύναμης του Ναΐου Διός αλλά, όπως προκύπτει από την αρχαία παράδοση, ήταν και το έμβλημα της γενναιότητας των Μολοσσών και κατ' επέκταση της Ηπειρωτικής Συμμαχίας και του Κοινού των Ηπειρωτών.

Γενικά η ταξινόμηση σε σαφείς ξεχωριστούς τύπους απόδοσης του αετού δεν είναι δυνατή. Ο αετός αποδίδεται σε κατατομή προς τα δεξιά, με κλειστές φτερούγες, όπως στα νομίσματα του Κοινού των Ηπειρωτών.[67] Αντίθετα, για την παράσταση του κεραυνού στην αρχαία ελληνική τέχνη[68] έχουν διαπιστωθεί τρεις ευδιάκριτες παραλλαγές του λωτόμορφου σχήματος που στη διάρκεια των ελληνιστικών χρόνων χρησιμοποιούνται σχεδόν με την ίδια συχνότητα.[69] Ο τύπος του κεραυνού, που εικονίζεται στα σφραγίσματα την Β'I κατηγορίας, ανήκει κυρίως στην πρώτη παραλλαγή που χαρακτηρίζεται από την αντικόρυφη συμμετρική τοποθέτηση δύο ανθέων λωτού.

---

δεξί χέρι του τον κεραυνό, προβάλλοντας προς την κατεύθυνση αυτή το αριστερό χέρι, όπου συχνά κάθεται στο ανάστροφο της παλάμης ο αετός. Βλ. Oder, *RE* I, στ. 371–375.

[60] Για τα σύμβολα των ονομάτων βλ. Brommer 1988, σελ. 69, 70, όπου και σχετική βιβλιογραφία.

[61] Εκτός Ηπείρου αετός και επιγραφή ΟΙΩΝΟΣ εικονίζεται σε σφράγισμα κεραμίδας της Αρχαϊκής περιόδου από το Καλαπόδι Βοιωτίας (Felsch 1990, σελ. 303, εικ. 1:α, σελ. 316, Β2, πίν. 51) και αετός που αρπάζει ένα φίδι και επιγραφή P.ANILI.PF σε σφράγισμα ρωμαϊκής κεραμίδας από την Ιταλία (Del Chiaro 1989, σελ. 59).

[62] Για παραστάσεις αετού και κεραυνού στην Ήπειρο βλ. Βλαχοπούλου-Οικονόμου 1986, σελ. 192–201, 203, σημ. 13, σελ. 204, σημ. 14, σελ. 254–258.

[63] Η παράσταση αετού σε κεραυνό είναι γνωστή στην Ήπειρο κυρίως από τις ηλειακές αποικίες, επειδή αποτελούσε το συχνότερο έμβλημα στα νομίσματα των Ηλείων (Schrader 1937, σελ. 213, 214· Franke 1961, σελ. 94). Από τα τέλη του 5ου αι., επί Θαρύπα, και από το α' μισό του 4ου αι., επί Αλκέτα, οι Μολοσσοί υιοθετούν τον αετό και τον κεραυνό μαζί με την προτομή του Διός ως εθνικά τους σύμβολα. Τα δύο τελευταία χρησιμοποιούν συχνά ως εμβλήματα στον οπισθότυπο των νομισμάτων τους (Franke 1961, σελ. 89, πίν. 8:R3–R12, 9:R13, R14, 11). Στο β' μισό του 4ου αι. ο μολοσσός βασιλιάς Αλέξανδρος Α' (342–331/30), κατά τη διάρκεια της εκστρατείας του στην Κάτω Ιταλία, έκοψε μία σειρά χρυσών, ασημένιων και χάλκινων νομισμάτων με παράσταση αετού και κεραυνού, που αντιγράφουν τα σύμβολα των μολοσσικών νομισμάτων (Franke 1961, σελ. 89, 90, πίν. 55:12). Το παράδειγμά του ακολούθησε η Ηπειρωτική Συμμαχία (Franke 1961, πίν. 55:12, 14–16), ο Πύρρος (297–272) και το Κοινό των Ηπειρωτών (Franke 1961, πίν. 20–31). Για τις παραστάσεις του αετού σε κεραυνό, που χρησιμοποιείται ως έμβλημα σε όλα σχεδόν τα νομίσματα των Πτολεμαίων της Αιγύπτου βλ. Βλαχοπούλου-Οικονόμου 1986, σελ. 198, 206, σημ. 23, σελ. 207, σημ. 24, 25 και για τις παραστάσεις σε μακεδονικά νομίσματα (Φιλίππου Ε' και Περσέως) βλ. Βλαχοπούλου-Οικονόμου 1986, σελ. 199, 207, σημ. 28, σελ. 208, σημ. 36.

[64] Για τη χρονολόγηση της σύστασης της Συμμαχίας βλ. Δάκαρης 1986α, σελ. 118 και σημ. 32, 33.

[65] Για το Κοινό των Ηπειρωτών, βλ. παραπάνω σελ. 188, σημ. 44.

[66] Δάκαρης 1980α, σελ. 26.

[67] Franke 1961, πίν. 20–31.

[68] Για τον κεραυνό στην αρχαία ανατολική και ελληνική τέχνη βλ. Jacobsthal 1906, σελ. 39 κεξ.

[69] Για την τυπολογία του κεραυνού και για τις παραλλαγές του σχήματός του κατά την Ελληνιστική περίοδο βλ. Βλαχοπούλου-Οικονόμου 1986, σελ. 205, σημ. 17, όπου και σχετική βιβλιογραφία.

Με μικρές διαφορές⁷⁰ ο ίδιος τύπος κεραυνού απαντά στον οπισθότυπο πολλών νομισμάτων του Κοινού των Ηπειρωτών[71] και στα ανθεμωτά μέτωπα ηγεμόνων και κορυφαίων κεράμων της ίδιας περιόδου από την Κασσώπη.[72] Σε σχέση με τις παραστάσεις σε αρχαιότερα παραδείγματα, όπως στα νομίσματα που έκοψε ο Αλέξανδρος Α' (334-330) στην Κάτω Ιταλία,[73] ο αετός στα νομίσματα του Κοινού και ιδιαίτερα στα σφραγίσματα των κεραμίδων εικονίζεται χωρίς οργανικότητα, δύναμη και ζωή.[74] Τόσο ο αετός, όσο και ο κεραυνός και το στεφάνι της βαλανιδιάς έχουν ατονίσει και τυποποιηθεί εξαιτίας της μηχανικής επανάληψης.

Το θέμα του κεραυνού με τα ωκύπτερα είναι μία βραχυγραφία του αετού σε κεραυνό, το οποίο, αν και είναι σε χρήση στα ηλειακά νομίσματα,[75] δεν έχει ωστόσο υιοθετηθεί στα νομίσματα των Ηπειρωτών.[76]

Το στεφάνι βαλανιδιάς, που περιβάλλει την παράσταση, συνδέεται επίσης άμεσα με τη λατρεία του Δωδωναίου Διός. Η «ὑψίκομος δρῦς» θεωρείται το ιερό δέντρο του Ναΐου Διός[77] όχι μόνο από τον Όμηρο,[78] αλλά και από πολλούς αρχαίους συγγραφείς, όπως τον Ησίοδο, τον Πλάτωνα, τον Σοφοκλή, τον Στράβωνα και τον Παυσανία.[79] Κλαδιά βαλανιδιάς εικονίζονται σε πάρα πολλές αρχαίες Ηπειρωτικές παραστάσεις, όπως στις κοπές των νομισμάτων,[80] σε χάλκινα ευρήματα από τη Δωδώνη,[81] στο πορτρέτο του βασιλιά Πύρρου,[82] σε επιτύμβιες στήλες[83] κ.α. Εξάλλου η ύπαρξη της ιερής βαλανιδιάς στην Ιερά Οικία έχει βεβαιωθεί ανασκαφικά από μία μεγάλη κοιλότητα στο έδαφος και ταυτόχρονα αποδεικνύεται από τη μελέτη της αρχιτεκτονικής σύνθεσης της Ιεράς Οικίας.[84]

---

[70] Η ελικοειδής κίνηση των εσωτερικών στελεχών που φυτρώνουν από την κεντρική γλωχίνα δε συναντάται στα σφραγίσματα των κεραμίδων.

[71] Franke 1961, σποραδικά και ιδιαίτερα σελ. 147, 148, πίν. 32-34.

[72] Σε αντίθεση, ο αετός στα μέτωπα αυτά παριστάνεται σε κίνηση, σα να είναι έτοιμος να πετάξει, με σώμα κατά τρία τέταρτα και πολύ ψηλά και ραδινά σκέλη. Βλαχοπούλου-Οικονόμου 1986, σελ. 192-201.

[73] Franke 1961, σελ. 321, πίν. 55:5, 12.

[74] Πρβ. τον μεγαλοπρεπή και γεμάτο δύναμη χάλκινο αετό από τη Δωδώνη, έργο χαλκοπλαστικής με ξεχωριστή ποιότητα, της ώριμης αρχαϊκής τέχνης (Βοκοτοπούλου 1973, σελ. 55) ή του αυστηρού ρυθμού (Δάκαρης 1986β, σελ. 107).

[75] Schrader 1937, σελ. 213, 214, εικ. 9, 11.

[76] Δάκαρης 1980β, σελ. 30.

[77] Για τη βαλανιδιά (φηγό) που αποτέλεσε τον πυρήνα της λατρείας του Διός στη Δωδώνη, είτε με τη μορφή δενδρολατρίας, είτε ως ενσάρκωση της προελληνικής θεάς Γης βλ. Ευαγγελίδης και Δάκαρης 1959, σελ. 12, σημ. 2, σελ. 13, σημ. 1, σελ. 127, 130· Δάκαρης 1967-1968, σελ. 386-405· Δάκαρης 1986β, σελ. 25-31.

[78] Όμηρ. ξ 327-330, τ 296-299.

[79] Franke 1961, σελ. 317, σημ. 4.

[80] Franke 1961, σποραδικά.

[81] Carapanos 1878, πίν. 49:12· Ευαγγελίδης 1935, σελ. 238, αρ. 63, εικ. 12.

[82] Lévêque 1957, πίν. IV.

[83] Από τον 3ο αι. και μετά, τα κλαδιά βαλανιδιάς είναι ένα αγαπητό κόσμημα στις επιτύμβιες στήλες της Δυτικής Ελλάδας και της Αλβανίας, σε αντίθεση με άλλες περιοχές όπου είναι σχεδόν άγνωστα. Για τη σύνδεσή τους με το Ιερό της Δωδώνης βλ. Fraser και Rönne 1957, σελ. 184, πρβ. Δάκαρης 1967-1968, σελ. 389.

[84] Δάκαρης 1986β, σελ. 43, 49.

Κατά τον Δάκαρη[85] οι κεραμίδες χρονολογούνται πριν από το 219 από τη μορφή των γραμμάτων και επειδή έχουν βρεθεί στην «αιτωλική επίχωση»,[86] η οποία σχηματίσθηκε μεταξύ του Βουλευτηρίου (Ε2) και του θεάτρου, με την απόθεση χωμάτων μετά την αιτωλική καταστροφή (219).[87] Χαρακτηριστικό στοιχείο των γραμμάτων είναι η μορφή του άλφα με καμπύλη την εσωτερική κεραία, η οποία θεωρείται[88] μεταγενέστερη από τη μορφή του άλφα με οριζόντια την εσωτερική κεραία και προγενέστερη από τη μορφή του άλφα με τεθλασμένη την εσωτερική κεραία.[89] Κατά τους Fraser και Rönne[90] είναι σε χρήση κατά τον 3ο αι.

Η πλειονότητα των σφραγισμάτων προέρχεται από τη στέγη του Βουλευτηρίου (Ε2).[91] Εφόσον λοιπόν θεωρούμε ως δεδομένο ότι προέρχονται από τη στέγη, η οποία προϋπήρχε της αιτωλικής καταστροφής του 219,[92] προκύπτει το εύλογο ερώτημα αν πρέπει να θεωρήσουμε ότι ανήκουν στη στέγη που συνδέεται με την ίδρυση του Ε2 στις αρχές του 3ου αι.[93] Με βάση τα μέχρι σήμερα ανασκαφικά δεδομένα δεν έχει διαπιστωθεί κάποια επισκευή της στέγης του Ε2 κατά τη διάρκεια του 3ου αι. και πριν από την ανοικοδόμησή του κατά τον επόμενο χρόνο μετά την αιτωλική καταστροφή (218).[94] Ωστόσο είναι πιθανές επισκευές της στέγης[95] εξαιτίας του μεγάλου όγκου της[96] και των καιρικών συνθηκών που επικρατούν στην «δυσχείμερον» κατά τον Όμηρο[97] Δωδώνη.

[85] Δάκαρης 1980β, σελ. 30.
[86] Για την «αιτωλική επίχωση» του κτηρίου Μ, το οποίο ισοπεδώθηκε με τα απορρίμματα και τα αρχιτεκτονικά συντρίμματα του Ιερού βλ. Δάκαρης 1963α, σελ. 149· Βοκοτοπούλου 1975, σελ. 216· Δάκαρης 1986β, σελ. 63, 64.
[87] Για την αιτωλική καταστροφή βλ. παραπάνω σελ. 188, σημ. 46.
[88] Fraser και Rönne 1957, σελ. 83–90.
[89] Ωστόσο, βλ. Fraser και Rönne 1957, σελ. 83, σημ. 5, όπου παραδείγματα για την ταυτόχρονη χρήση όλων των μορφών του άλφα στην ίδια λέξη. Βλ. επίσης, για διαφορετική χρονολόγηση του άλφα με καμπύλη την εσωτερική κεραία σε επιγραφές από την Ολυμπία, Fraser και Rönne 1957, σελ. 87, 88.
[90] Fraser και Rönne 1957, σελ. 85.
[91] Οι ανασκαφικές ενδείξεις των θραυσμάτων αρ. 1, 2, 5, 6, 8, 9, 12, 13 αναφέρουν «ανασκαφή του 1965», η οποία έγινε στη ΝΑ γωνία του Ε2 και στο χώρο ανάμεσα στο Ε2 και στο ναΐσκο Λ (Δάκαρης 1965, σελ. 53).
[92] Βλ. παραπάνω σελ. 188, σημ. 46.
[93] Η σύγχρονη κατασκευή του Ε2 και της στοάς είναι μεταγενέστερη από τον αρχικό εξωτερικό περίβολο, που έχουν αποκόψει κατά την κατασκευή τους, και σύγχρονη με την κατασκευή των πυργοειδών αναλημμάτων του θεάτρου και την επένδυση του κτηρίου Μ. Επειδή το Μ χρονολογείται στον 4ο αι. και τα αναλήμματα του κοίλου πιθανότατα στους χρόνους του Πύρρου (297–272), η κατασκευή του Ε2 χρονολογείται στις αρχές του 3ου αι. Επίσης, η χρησιμοποίηση του αμμολίθου για τους κίονες, που είναι γνωστή από τις αρχές του 3ου αι. και η ομοιότητα του Ε2 και της στοάς, ως προς την τοιχοδομία με τη σκηνή του θεάτρου και ως προς τη μορφή με τη στοά της σκηνής, ενισχύουν τη χρονολόγηση του Ε2 και της στοάς στις αρχές του 3ου αι. Δάκαρης 1966, σελ. 80, 81.
[94] Βλ. παραπάνω σελ. 188, σημ. 46.
[95] Πρβ. επιδιόρθωση της στέγης της Ιεράς Οικίας κατά το δ' τέταρτο του 4ου αι., όταν δημιουργείται ο ισοδομικός περίβολος σε αντικατάσταση του κυκλικού περιβόλου με τους τρίποδες. Βλαχοπούλου-Οικονόμου 1986, σελ. 100, 101, 110, σημ. 51.
[96] Για τη στήριξη της τεράστιας στέγης, η οποία είχε πλάτος 30,20 μ., εκτός από τις αντηρίδες κατά μήκος όλων των τοίχων του Ε2, στο εσωτερικό του υπήρχαν δύο σειρές από 3 ιωνικούς κίονες, οι οποίοι κατά την ανοικοδόμηση μετά την αιτωλική καταστροφή (218) αυξήθηκαν με την προσθήκη άλλων δύο. Δάκαρης 1986β, σελ. 58–61.
[97] Όμηρ. Π 233–235.

Οι μελλοντικές ανασκαφές του Ε2[98] ίσως θα επιτρέψουν μία τεκμηριωμένη απόδοση των σφραγισμάτων σε στέγη του Ε2, η οποία συνδέεται είτε με την ίδρυσή του ή με κάποια οικοδομική φάση κατά τη διάρκεια του 3ου αι.

## ΙΙ. ΙΕΡΑ

Η επιγραφή ΙΕΡΑ (Pl. 64) εμπεριέχεται σε ορθογώνιο έντυπο σφράγισμα που ορίζεται από λεπτή ταινία και εξωτερικά αστραγαλωτή διακόσμηση, η οποία αποτελείται από εναλλασσόμενη διπλή κάθετη ταινία και κομβίο. Η διακόσμηση και τα γράμματα είναι έκτυπα. Έχουν βρεθεί τα παρακάτω σφραγίσματα:

1. Αρ.Μ.: 5730 (Pl. 64:a).[99]
   Ύψ. 0,027 μ. Μήκ. 0,065 μ.
   Πηλός υπέρυθρος κιτρινωπός (7.5YR 7/6).
   Θέση: Ε2· ανασκαφή 1969.
   ΙΕΡΑ

2. Αρ.Μ.: 3503 (Pl. 64:b).
   Ύψ. 0,027 μ. Μήκ. 0,07 μ.
   Πηλός υπέρυθρος κιτρινωπός (7.5YR 7/6).
   Ανασκαφή 1965.
   ΙΕΡΑ

Κατά την άποψη του Δάκαρη[100] το σφράγισμα με τη λέξη ἱερά ανήκει στα τέλη του 4ου ή τις αρχές του 3ου αι. Ωστόσο, ανεξάρτητα από τις ήδη διατυπωμένες επιφυλάξεις για τη δυνατότητα χρονολόγησης των σφραγισμάτων με βάση τη μορφή των γραμμάτων,[101] τα γράμματα του συγκεκριμένου σφραγίσματος δεν προσφέρουν καμιά ασφαλή χρονολογική ένδειξη. Το άλφα π.χ. με οριζόντια την εσωτερική κεραία ναι μεν προϋπάρχει του άλφα με τεθλασμένη την εσωτερική κεραία, αλλά εξακολουθεί να είναι σε ταυτόχρονη χρήση όχι μόνο σε επιγραφές του 3ου αι.,[102] αλλά και κατά τη διάρκεια του 2ου και του 1ου αι.[103]

Εξάλλου η έλλειψη στρωματογραφικών ενδείξεων, σε συνάρτηση με τις παραπάνω δυσκολίες, αποτρέπει την ασφαλή χρονολόγηση των σφραγισμάτων. Μόνον ένα *terminus ante quem* μπορεί να δοθεί και αυτό είναι η ρωμαϊκή καταστροφή του 168/7,[104] καθώς ο ανασκαφέας αναφέρει[105] ότι το σφράγισμα με τη λέξη ἱερά βρέθηκε στο «συνεχές στρώμα της ρωμαϊκής καταστροφής, με άφθονα συντρίμματα κεράμων στέγης» που διαπιστώθηκε σε όλη την έκταση του νότιου τμήματος του Ε2. Ο μικρός αριθμός

---

[98] Η ανασκαφή του Ε2 δεν έχει ολοκληρωθεί. Δάκαρης 1986β, σελ. 62.
[99] Δάκαρης 1969α, σελ. 19, 20.
[100] Δάκαρης 1969α, σελ. 19, 20· Δάκαρης 1969β, σελ. 26.
[101] Βλ. παραπάνω σελ. 185, 186.
[102] Fraser και Rönne 1957, σελ. 88.
[103] Βλαχοπούλου-Οικονόμου 1986, σελ. 257, 264, σημ. 29.
[104] Είναι γνωστό ότι το 168 οι Ρωμαίοι υπό τον Αιμίλιο Παύλο εισέβαλαν στην Ήπειρο και μετά από απόφαση της ρωμαϊκής συγκλήτου κατέστρεψαν 70 Ηπειρωτικές πόλεις και φρούρια και πούλησαν ως δούλους 150.000 ανθρώπους. Πολύβ. 30.15· Στράβ. 7.7.3· Livy 45.34· Πλούτ., Αιμ. Παύλ. 29· Pliny, *NatHist* 4.39. Ο αντίκτυπος της τρομαχτικής καταστροφής που υπέστη το Ιερό της Δωδώνης ήταν ακόμη αισθητός κατά την εποχή του Στράβωνος (7.7.9) που περιγράφει ως εξής την κατάσταση του Ιερού: «ἐκλέλοιπε δέ πως καὶ τὸ μαντεῖον τὸ ἐν Δωδώνῃ καθάπερ τἆλλα». Πρβ. Δάκαρης 1960, σελ. 33, 34· Δάκαρης 1964α, σελ. 155, 156· Δάκαρης 1987, σελ. 11–21.
[105] Δάκαρης 1969β, σελ. 26.

ΤΑ ΣΦΡΑΓΙΣΜΑΤΑ ΚΕΡΑΜΙΔΩΝ ΑΠΟ ΤΟ ΙΕΡΟ ΤΗΣ ΔΩΔΩΝΗΣ 195

των ευρημάτων και οι πενιχρές ανασκαφικές ενδείξεις[106] υποδεικνύουν μόνο την πιθανότητα οι ενσφράγιστες αυτές κεραμίδες να προέρχονται από κάποια στέγη του Βουλευτηρίου.[107] Μόνο το κοινό περιεχόμενο με τα σφραγίσματα της Β΄Ι κατηγορίας[108] (η επιγραφή ἱαρά-ἱερά), θα μπορούσε να αποτελέσει μία ένδειξη ώστε να θεωρήσουμε την Β΄ΙΙ κατηγορία σύγχρονη με τη Β΄Ι και επομένως να τη συσχετίσουμε είτε με την ίδρυση του Βουλευτηρίου κατά την περίοδο της βασιλείας του Πύρρου (297–272) είτε με κάποια επιδιόρθωση της στέγης κατά τη διάρκεια του 3ου αι.[109]

### III. ΔΙΟΣ ΝΑΟΥ

Στα ορθογώνια έντυπα σφραγίσματα της Β΄ΙΙΙ κατηγορίας (Pls. 65–69) εμπεριέχεται η επιγραφή ΔΙΟΣ ΝΑΟΥ. Έχουν βρεθεί τα παρακάτω σφραγίσματα:

1. Αρ.Μ.: 5750 (Pl. 65:a, αριστερά).
   Ύψ. 0,02 μ. Μήκ. 0,09 μ.
   Πηλός ελαφρά καστανός (7.5YR 6/4).
   Θέση: Ε2· ανασκαφή 1969.
   ΔΙΟCΝΑΟΥ

2. Αρ.Μ.: 3518 (Pl. 65:b, αριστερά).
   Ύψ. 0,02 μ. Μήκ. 0,09 μ.
   Πηλός υπέρυθρος κιτρινωπός (5YR 6/6).
   Θέση: Ε2· ανασκαφή 1966.
   ΔΙΟC[ΝΑΟΥ]

3. Αρ.Μ.: 5749 (Pl. 65:a, δεξιά).
   Ύψ. 0,02 μ. Μήκ. 0,05 μ.
   Πηλός υπέρυθρος κιτρινωπός (5YR 6/6).
   Θέση: Ε2· ανασκαφή 1969.
   ΔΙΟC[ΝΑΟΥ]

4. Αρ.Μ.: 5722 (Pl. 65:b, δεξιά).
   Ύψ. 0,02 μ. Μήκ. 0,05 μ.
   Πηλός ελαφρά καστανός (7.5YR 6/4).
   Θέση: Ε2· ανασκαφή 1970.
   ΔΙΟC[ΝΑΟΥ]

5. Ύψ. 0,02 μ. Μήκ. 0,04 μ.
   Πηλός υπέρυθρος κιτρινωπός (5YR 6/4).
   Ανασκαφή 1967.
   Δ[ΙΟCΝΑΟΥ]

6. Αρ.Μ.: 5721.
   Ύψ. 0,02 μ. Μήκ. 0,07 μ.
   Πηλός υπέρυθρος κιτρινωπός (5YR 6/8).
   Θέση: Ε2· ανασκαφή 1970.
   [ΔΙΟ]CΝΑΟΥ

7. Αρ.Μ.: 5733.
   Ύψ. 0,02 μ. Μήκ. 0,05 μ.
   Πηλός ανοικτός καστανός (7.5YR 6/4).
   Θέση: Ε2· ανασκαφή 1969.
   [ΔΙΟCΝ]ΑΟΥ

8. Αρ.Μ.: 3696.
   Ύψ. 0,02 μ. Μήκ. 0,05 μ.
   Πηλός υπέρυθρος κιτρινωπός (5YR 7/6).
   Θέση: Στοά του Ε2· ανασκαφή 1968.
   [ΔΙΟCΝΑ]ΟΥ

9. Ύψ. 0,03 μ. Μήκ. 0,09 μ.
   Πηλός υπέρυθρος (10YR 6/8).
   Θέση: Ο· ανασκαφή 1983.
   [ΔΙ]ΟCΝΑ[ΟΥ]

10. Ύψ. 0,02 μ. Μήκ. 0,16 μ. (Pl. 66:a).
    Πηλός υπέρυθρος κιτρινωπός (5YR 6/4).
    ΔΙΟCΝΑΟΥ

11. Αρ.Μ.: 3485 (Pl. 66:b).
    Ύψ. 0,02 μ. Μήκ. 0,06 μ.
    Πηλός υπέρυθρος κιτρινωπός (7.5YR 7/6).
    Θέση: Θέατρο· ανασκαφή 1959.
    ΔΙΟ[CΝΑΟΥ]

---

[106] Το σφράγισμα αρ. 1 προέρχεται από την ανασκαφή του νότιου τμήματος του Ε2 (Δάκαρης 1969β, σελ. 26) και το σφράγισμα αρ. 2 προέρχεται από την ανασκαφή του 1965, που έγινε στο χώρο ανάμεσα στη ΝΑ γωνία του Ε2 και του ναΐσκου Λ προς Α (Δάκαρης 1965, σελ. 53).
[107] Για τις οικοδομικές φάσεις του Ε2 και τις αντίστοιχες στέγες του βλ. παραπάνω σελ. 189, σημ. 49.
[108] Βλ. παραπάνω σελ. 189–194.
[109] Βλ. παραπάνω σελ. 193.

12. Ὕψ. 0,02 μ. Μήκ. 0,06 μ.
    Πηλός υπέρυθρος κιτρινωπός (5YR 7/6).
    Θέση: Ανατολικά του Ε2· ανασκαφή 1965.
    ΔΙΟΣ[ΝΑΟΥ]

13. Αρ.Μ.: 5745 (Pl. 67:a).
    Ὕψ. 0,01 μ. Μήκ. 0,04 μ.
    Πηλός υπέρυθρος κιτρινωπός (5YR 7/6).
    Ανασκαφή 1971.
    [ΔΙΟΣ]ΝΑΟ[Υ]

14. Ὕψ. 0,02 μ. Μήκ. 0,04 μ.
    Πηλός υπέρυθρος κιτρινωπός (5YR 7/6).
    [ΔΙΟΣΝΑ]ΟΥ

15. Ὕψ. 0,02 μ. Μήκ. 0,05 μ.
    Πηλός υπέρυθρος κιτρινωπός (5YR 7/8).
    Ανασκαφή 1959.
    [ΔΙΟΣ]ΝΑΟ[Υ]

16. Ὕψ. 0,083 μ. Μήκ. 0,21 μ.
    Πηλός υπέρυθρος κιτρινωπός (5YR 6/8).
    Θέση: Ο· ανασκαφή 1990.
    [ΔΙ]ΟΣΝΑΟΥ

17. Ὕψ. 0,011 μ. Μήκ. 0,11 μ.
    Πηλός υπέρυθρος κιτρινωπός (5YR 6/8).
    Θέση: Ο· ανασκαφή 1990.
    [ΔΙΟΣΝ]ΑΟΥ

18. Αρ.Μ.: 4086 (Pl. 67:b, αριστερά).
    Ὕψ. 0,02 μ. Μήκ. 0,04 μ.
    Πηλός υπέρυθρος κιτρινωπός (5YR 6/4).
    Θέση: Θέατρο· ανασκαφή 1959.
    Δ[ΙΟΣΝΑΟΥ]

19. Αρ.Μ.: 5726 (Pl. 67:b, δεξιά).
    Ὕψ. 0,02 μ. Μήκ. 0,11 μ.
    Πηλός υπέρυθρος κιτρινωπός (5YR 6/8).
    Ανασκαφή 1971.
    [ΔΙΟΣ]ΝΑΟ[Υ]

20. Αρ.Μ.: 3484 (Pl. 68:b, επάνω αριστερά).[110]
    Ὕψ. 0,05 μ. Μήκ. 0,09 μ.
    Πηλός υπέρυθρος (2.5YR 6/8).
    Θέση: Θέατρο· ανασκαφή 1959.
    ΔΙΟΣ[ΝΑΟΥ]

21. Αρ.Μ.: 3486 (Pl. 69:a, αριστερά).
    Ὕψ. 0,05 μ. Μήκ. 0,06 μ.
    Πηλός υπέρυθρος κιτρινωπός (5YR 6/8).
    Θέση: Θέατρο· ανασκαφή 1959.
    ΔΙΟΣ[ΝΑΟΥ]

22. Αρ.Μ.: 5725.
    Ὕψ. 0,04 μ. Μήκ. 0,07 μ.
    Πηλός υπέρυθρος κιτρινωπός (7.5YR 6/6).
    Θέση: Ε2· ανασκαφή 1971.
    ΔΙΟΣ[ΝΑΟΥ]

23. Αρ.Μ.: 4095.[111]
    Ὕψ. 0,05 μ. Μήκ. 0,07 μ.
    Πηλός υπέρυθρος κιτρινωπός (5YR 6/8).
    Θέση: Ε2· ανασκαφή 1966.
    ΔΙΟ[ΣΝΑΟΥ]

24. Ὕψ. 0,05 μ. Μήκ. 0,07 μ. (Pl. 68:a, αριστερά).
    Πηλός υπέρυθρος κιτρινωπός (5YR 7/8).
    Θέση: Στοά του Ε2· ανασκαφή 1972.
    ΔΙΟ[ΣΝΑΟΥ]

25. Αρ.Μ.: 3487 (Pl. 69:b, δεξιά).[112]
    Ὕψ. 0,03 μ. Μήκ. 0,08 μ.
    Πηλός υπέρυθρος κιτρινωπός (5YR 6/8).
    Θέση: Θέατρο· ανασκαφή 1959.
    ΔΙΟΣ[ΝΑΟΥ]

26. Αρ.Μ.: 5736.
    Ὕψ. 0,04 μ. Μήκ. 0,05 μ.
    Πηλός υπέρυθρος κιτρινωπός (5YR 6/6).
    Θέση: Ε2· ανασκαφή 1968.
    ΔΙΟ[ΣΝΑΟΥ]

27. Ὕψ. 0,05 μ. Μήκ. 0,05 μ. (Pl. 68:a, μέσον).
    Πηλός υπέρυθρος (2.5YR 6/6).
    Θέση: Ο1, δωμάτιο δ· ανασκαφή 1982.
    ΔΙΟΣ[ΝΑΟΥ]

28. Ὕψ. 0,04 μ. Μήκ. 0,05 μ.
    Πηλός υπέρυθρος κιτρινωπός (5YR 7/6).
    Θέση: Ε2· ανασκαφή 1971.
    Δ[ΙΟΣΝΑΟΥ]

29. Ὕψ. 0,05 μ. Μήκ. 0,06 μ.
    Πηλός υπέρυθρος κιτρινωπός (5YR 7/6).
    Θέση: Θέατρο· ανασκαφή 1959.
    ΔΙΟΣ[ΝΑΟΥ]

30. Αρ.Μ.: 5744 (Pl. 68:b, επάνω δεξιά).
    Ὕψ. 0,047 μ. Μήκ. 0,087 μ.
    Πηλός υπέρυθρος κιτρινωπός (5YR 6/8).

---

[110] Δάκαρης 1960, σελ. 32, πίν. 12:γ· Franke 1961, σελ. 312 (5), 315, πίν. 61:1α.
[111] Δάκαρης 1966, σελ. 82, πίν. 82:α.
[112] Δάκαρης 1960, σελ. 32, πίν. 12:γ.

Θέση: Θέατρο· ανασκαφή 1959.
[ΔΙ]ΟΣ[ΝΑΟΥ]

31. Αρ.Μ.: 5735.
῾Υψ. 0,03 μ. Μήκ. 0,06 μ.
Πηλός υπέρυθρος κιτρινωπός (5YR 6/8).
Θέση: Ε2· ανασκαφή 1968.
[Δ]ΙΟΣ[ΝΑΟΥ]

32. Αρ.Μ.: 5741 (Pl. 69:a, δεξιά).
῾Υψ. 0,049 μ. Μήκ. 0,077 μ.
Πηλός υπέρυθρος κιτρινωπός (5YR 6/6).
Θέση: Θέατρο· ανασκαφή 1959.
[Δ]ΙΟΣΝ[ΑΟΥ]

33. Αρ.Μ.: 5738.
῾Υψ. 0,02 μ. Μήκ. 0,06 μ.
Πηλός υπέρυθρος (2.5YR 6/8).
[ΔΙΟ]ΣΝΑ[ΟΥ]

34. ῾Υψ. 0,049 μ. Μήκ. 0,07 μ. (Pl. 68:a, δεξιά).
Πηλός υπέρυθρος κιτρινωπός (5YR 6/6).
Θέση: Ο1· δωμάτιο δ· ανασκαφή 1982.
[ΔΙΟ]ΣΝΑ[ΟΥ]

35. Αρ.Μ.: 5742 (Pl. 69:b, αριστερά).
῾Υψ. 0,048 μ. Μήκ. 0,078 μ.
Πηλός υπέρυθρος (2.5YR 6/8).
Θέση: Θέατρο· ανασκαφή 1959.
[ΔΙΟ]ΣΝΑΟ[Υ]

36. Αρ.Μ.: 3670 (Pl. 68:b, κάτω δεξιά).
῾Υψ. 0,034 μ. Μήκ. 0,07 μ.
Πηλός υπέρυθρος κιτρινωπός (5YR 6/8).
[ΔΙΟΣ]ΝΑ[ΟΥ]

37. Αρ.Μ.: 3917 (Pl. 68:b, κάτω αριστερά).[113]
῾Υψ. 0,048 μ. Μήκ. 0,13 μ.
Πηλός υπέρυθρος καστανός (2.5YR 5/4).
Θέση: Θέατρο· ανασκαφή 1959.
[ΔΙΟΣ]ΝΑΟΥ

38. ῾Υψ. 0,049 μ. Μήκ. 0,068 μ.
Πηλός ερυθρός (2.5YR 5/6).
Θέση: Ο1· ανασκαφή 1981.
[ΔΙΟΣΝ]ΑΟΥ

39. ῾Υψ. 0,048 μ. Μήκ. 0,07 μ.
Πηλός υπέρυθρος (2.5YR 6/8).
Θέση: Ο1, δωμάτιο α· ανασκαφή 1981.
[ΔΙΟΣΝ]ΑΟΥ

Τα σφραγίσματα της Β΄ΙΙΙ κατηγορίας, σύμφωνα με το μέγεθος και τη μορφή των γραμμάτων, είναι δυνατόν να ταξινομηθούν σε τέσσερις υποκατηγορίες που υποδεικνύουν τη χρήση τουλάχιστον τεσσάρων διαφορετικών σφραγίδων. Στην α΄ υποκατηγορία περιλαμβάνονται τα θραύσματα αρ. 1-9 (Pl. 65). Το σφράγισμα είναι έντυπο ορθογώνιο με έκτυπα γράμματα,[114] ύψους ±0,014 μ. Στη β΄ υποκατηγορία περιλαμβάνονται τα θραύσματα αρ. 10-17 (Pls. 66, 67:a). Το σφράγισμα είναι έντυπο ορθογώνιο με έκτυπα γράμματα, ύψους ±0,014 μ., τα οποία ορίζονται κατά μήκος από δύο έκτυπες οριζόντιες παράλληλες ταινίες, που εφάπτονται σχεδόν στην κορυφή και στο πέρας των γραμμάτων.[115] Διακοσμητικός οφθαλμός[116] προηγείται των λέξεων

---

[113] Δάκαρης 1960, σελ. 32, πίν. 12:β· Franke 1961, σελ. 312 (5), 315, πίν. 61:1β.

[114] Το δέλτα αποδίδεται με αμβλεία την κορυφαία γωνία, το σίγμα είναι μηνοειδές, το νι αποδίδεται αντίστροφα (για αντίστροφη επιγραφή σε ανθεμωτό μέτωπο από την Κασσώπη πρβ. Βλαχοπούλου-Οικονόμου 1986, σελ. 256 και παρακάτω σελ. 208), το άλφα έχει τεθλασμένη την εσωτερική κεραία, το όμικρον είναι στρογγυλό και ισομέγεθες με τα υπόλοιπα γράμματα και το ύψιλον έχει ανοιχτές κεραίες.

[115] Το δέλτα αποδίδεται με ακρεμόνα στην προέκταση προς τα επάνω της δεξιάς πλάγιας κεραίας και αμβλεία την κορυφαία γωνία, το γιώτα με ακρεμόνες, το σίγμα με παράλληλα τα δύο σκέλη και ακρεμόνες στην ένωση των δύο πλάγιων εσωτερικών κεραιών, το νι με ακρεμόνες και το άλφα με γωνιώδη την εσωτερική κεραία και ακρεμόνα προς τα κάτω στην αριστερή κεραία της εσωτερικής γωνίας. Το όμικρον είναι στρογγυλό και ισομέγεθες. Μόνο στο σφράγισμα αρ. 10 (Pl. 66:a) διακρίνεται αδιάγνωστο τριγωνικό σχήμα (πιθανόν δέλτα) στο κενό ανάμεσα στην πλάγια δεξιά κεραία του δέλτα και το γιώτα, με το κάτω σκέλος παράλληλο προς τη δεξιά κεραία του δέλτα. Με επιφύλαξη επίσης εκφράζεται η πιθανότητα να πρόκειται για τη συντομογραφία της λέξης δ(αμοσία), η οποία συναντάται συχνά στα σφραγίσματα των κεραμίδων (βλ. παραπάνω σελ. 185, σημ. 14 και παρακάτω σελ. 206).

[116] Πρβ. δύο διακοσμητικά τρίγωνα ανάμεσα στα γράμματα της επιγραφής Γυμνασίου, σε σφράγισμα κεραμίδας από την Αλβανία: Ceka 1982, σελ. 109, πίν. ΙΙΙ:31.

Διός και Νάου. Στο όλο σφράγισμα είναι αισθητή μία αυξημένη διακοσμητική τάση. Στην γ' υποκατηγορία (Pl. 67:b) εντάσσονται μόνο δύο αποτμήματα (αρ. 18, 19), από τα οποία στο πρώτο διασώζεται μόνο το γράμμα δέλτα. Το σφράγισμα είναι έντυπο ορθογώνιο με έκτυπα γράμματα,[117] ύψους ±0,0118 μ. Στην δ' υποκατηγορία περιλαμβάνονται τα θραύσματα αρ. 20–39 (Pls. 68, 69). Τα γράμματα[118] είναι έντυπα, ύψους ±0,024 μ., και ορίζονται κατά μήκος από δύο παράλληλες, επίσης έντυπες ταινίες.

Η επίκληση του Διός της Δωδώνης ως Νάιος ή Νᾶος ή Νάος είναι πάρα πολύ γνωστή. Η παλαιότερη μνεία στη γραπτή παράδοση ανάγεται στον 4ο αι., αλλά επιγραφικά αποδεικνύεται αρχαιότερη.[119] Τα επίθετα, κατά την άποψη του Ευαγγελίδη και του Δάκαρη,[120] πρέπει να συσχετισθούν με τις λέξεις ναίω-ναός (= ιερά οικία) που δηλώνουν την κατοικία του θεού, η οποία έχει διαπιστωθεί φιλολογικά και ανασκαφικά,[121] αντίστοιχα προς τη λέξη Φηγωναῖος (= αυτός που κατοικεί στη φηγό[122]). Η γραφή Νάος[123] έχει αποδειχθεί επιγραφικά επικρατέστερη. Στα σφραγίσματα με την επιγραφή Διός Νάου πιθανόν υπονοείται η λέξη ἱερά (δηλ. «Ἱερά κεραμίς Διός Νάου»).[124] Πολύ κοινή είναι η χρήση μόνο του επιθέτου ἱερά[125] ή μόνο της γενικής κτητικής του θεού ή της θεάς ή των θεών.[126]

---

[117] Το δέλτα αποδίδεται με οξεία την κορυφαία γωνία, το νι με παράλληλα τα δύο σκέλη, το άλφα είναι φθαρμένο, ωστόσο φαίνεται πιθανότερο να έχει οριζόντια την εσωτερική κεραία, το όμικρον είναι στρογγυλό και ισομέγεθες.

[118] Το δέλτα έχει οξεία την κορυφαία γωνία, το γιώτα φέρει ακρεμόνες, το όμικρον είναι ισομέγεθες αλλά ωοειδές, το σίγμα έχει παράλληλα τα δύο σκέλη με ακρεμόνες και ιδιαίτερα μακρές τις εσωτερικές πλάγιες κεραίες οι οποίες σχηματίζουν οξεία γωνία στην επαφή τους. Το νι με κάθετες τις παράλληλες κεραίες φέρει ακρεμόνες, το άλφα έχει οριζόντια την εσωτερική κεραία και φέρει ακρεμόνες στις απολήξεις των εξωτερικών πλάγιων σκελών και το ύψιλον φέρει στην απόληξη της κατακόρυφης κεραίας ακρεμόνα προς τα δεξιά.

[119] Ευαγγελίδης και Δάκαρης 1959, σελ. 142, σημ. 1. Για το πλήθος των αναθηματικών και χρηστήριων επιγραφών από το Ιερό με το επίθετο Νάιος ή Νάιος βλ. SGDI, αρ. 1347, 1351, 1368, 1371, 1373–1375, 1557, 1560, 1562–1565, 1567, 1568, 1572, 1574, 1575, 1578, 1579, 1581–1583, 1585, 1586, 1588, 1590–1592, 1596, 1597· πρβ. Τζουβάρα-Σούλη 1979, σελ. 70, 72, σημ. 483, όπου και σχετική βιβλιογραφία.

[120] Ευαγγελίδης και Δάκαρης 1959, σελ. 142, 143, όπου βλ. αναλυτικά για την ετυμολογία και την ερμηνεία των λέξεων, με αντίστοιχη βιβλιογραφία. Πρβ. Cabanes 1988, σελ. 51–53.

[121] Δάκαρης 1986β, σελ. 40–43.

[122] Πρβ. το χωρίο του Ησιόδου (Fr. 240 M-W) «ναῖον δ' ἐν πυθμένι φηγοῦ».

[123] Από το Νάος προήλθε το Νάιος, όπως από το Ζεύς Κεραυνός το Ζεύς Κεραύνιος. Ευαγγελίδης και Δάκαρης 1959, σελ. 143, σημ. 1.

[124] Πρβ. επιγραφές σε σφραγίσματα από το Ιερό της Σαμοθράκης: Ἱερά Θεῶν (Lehmann 1960, σελ. 110, 111, 114, 118), από το Επιγραφικό Μουσείο Αθηνών: Ἱερά Νυμφῶν (Πέππα-Δελμούζου 1970, σελ. 14, πίν. 8:β) και από την Αγορά των Αθηνών: Ἱερά Ἡφαίστου (Shear 1939, σελ. 214, 215, εικ. 12.).

[125] Βλ. παραπάνω σελ. 189–195.

[126] Πρβ. Δ]ιώνας από την Τιτάνη (Γκούμανη) (Τζουβάρα-Σούλη 1979, σελ. 78, σημ. 530, 531), Δεσποίνας, Ἀπόλλωνος ἐν Ἀμυκλαίοι (Ορλάνδος 1955, σελ. 114, σημ. 6, 12· Hübner 1976, σελ. 180), Ἀπόλλωνος (Ρωμαίος 1933, σελ. 14), Σεμνῶν Θεῶν (Ζαχαριάδου, Κυριακού και Μπαζιωτοπούλου 1985, σελ. 50, εικ. 12).

Τα σφραγίσματα όλων των υποκατηγοριών έχουν χαρακτηριστικές μορφές γραμμάτων, οι οποίες υποδεικνύουν μία χρονολόγηση από τον 3ο αι. και μετά. Στην α' υποκατηγορία η μορφή του άλφα με γωνιώδη την εσωτερική κεραία[127] και η χρήση του μηνοειδούς σίγμα[128] και του ύψιλον με ανοιχτές κεραίες.[129] Στη β' υποκατηγορία η αφθονία των ακρεμόνων[130] και το άλφα με γωνιώδη την εσωτερική κεραία. Στην δ' υποκατηγορία η αφθονία των ακρεμόνων· το άλφα έχει οριζόντια την εσωτερική κεραία, αλλά μόνο το στοιχείο αυτό δεν μπορεί να αποτελέσει τεκμήριο για διαφορετική χρονολόγηση.[131]

Και στις τέσσερις υποκατηγορίες η μορφή του νι με κάθετες ισομεγέθεις κεραίες και στη β' και δ' υποκατηγορία η μορφή του σίγμα με οριζόντιες κεραίες[132] επιτρέπουν τη χρονολογική ένταξη των σφραγισμάτων στα χρόνια του Κοινού των Ηπειρωτών (234/3–168/7),[133] την οποία έχει ήδη υποδείξει ο ανασκαφέας.[134] Η χρονολόγηση αυτή ενισχύεται από το γεγονός ότι μερικά από τα σφραγίσματα, που προέρχονται από το νότιο τμήμα του Ε2, έχουν βρεθεί στο συνεχές στρώμα της ρωμαϊκής καταστροφής,[135] στοιχείο το οποίο καθορίζει τη χρονολογία 168/7 ως ένα *terminus ante quem*.[136] Η προέκταση της δεξιάς πλάγιας κεραίας του δέλτα προς τα επάνω στα σφραγίσματα της β' υποκατηγορίας θα μπορούσε να αποτελέσει ένδειξη για μία νεότερη χρονολόγηση στον 1ο αι., χωρίς όμως να αποτελεί ασφαλές τεκμήριο για να αποκλεισθεί η χρονολόγηση στο 2ο αι.[137] Περισσότερη όμως επιμονή για τεκμηρίωση της χρονολογικής ένταξης με βάση τη μορφή των γραμμάτων είναι παρακινδυνευμένη.

---

Για το όνομα του Διός με αντίστοιχες επικλήσεις όπως Διός 'Ολυμπίου από την Ολυμπία και μερικά γράμματα από την επιγραφή Ζεύς 'Ελλάνιος από την Αίγινα βλ. Franke 1961, σελ. 315, σημ. 14, 15. Για το όνομα Διός σε σφράγισμα κεράμου από την Αλβανία βλ. Ceka 1982, σελ. 105, αρ. 12, σελ. 120, πίν. Ι:12.

[127] Για τη χρήση του Α με γωνιώδη την εσωτερική κεραία βλ. παραπάνω σελ. 188, σημ. 40–43.

[128] Για το μηνοειδές σίγμα βλ. Klaffenbach 1957, σελ. 43. Πρβ. Πέτσας 1961, σελ. 40. Σφραγίσματα μακεδονικών κεραμίδων με μηνοειδές σίγμα χρονολογούνται στα έτη της βασιλείας του Φιλίππου Ε' (Μπακαλάκης 1934, σελ. 104–113, εικ. 5–8), ενώ επιγραφή από τη Δωδώνη, στην οποία συναντάται μηνοειδές σίγμα ανάμεσα σε άλλα τετρασκελή, χρονολογείται από τον Ευαγγελίδη στα 370 (Ευαγγελίδης 1956, σελ. 4). Στις αργυρές δραχμές όμως του Κοινού των Ηπειρωτών της περιόδου 215–195 χρησιμοποιείται το μηνοειδές σίγμα. Franke 1961, σελ. 142–145.

[129] Καλτσάς 1988, σελ. 105.

[130] Για τη χρήση των ακρεμόνων ως χρονολογικό κριτήριο βλ. παραπάνω σελ. 188, σημ. 39.

[131] Για την ταυτόχρονη χρήση του άλφα με οριζόντια την εσωτερική κεραία και του άλφα με γωνιώδη βλ. παραπάνω σελ. 194, σημ. 102, 103.

[132] Δάκαρης 1967–1968, σελ. 388. Για το σίγμα με οριζόντιες κεραίες πρβ. Woodhead 1967, σελ. 64. Βλ. επίσης για το σίγμα και το νι Βλαχοπούλου-Οικονόμου 1986, σελ. 257.

[133] Για το Κοινό των Ηπειρωτών βλ. παραπάνω σελ. 188, σημ. 44.

[134] Δάκαρης 1960, σελ. 32· Δάκαρης 1966, σελ. 82· Δάκαρης 1969β, σελ. 26· Δάκαρης 1969α, σελ. 19· Δάκαρης 1971, σελ. 126.

[135] Δάκαρης 1969β, σελ. 26.

[136] Βλ. παραπάνω σελ. 194, σημ. 104.

[137] Fraser και Rönne 1957, σελ. 89.

Με βάση τις ανασκαφικές ενδείξεις[138] τα σφραγίσματα πρέπει να προέρχονται από τις στέγες του Βουλευτηρίου και της σκηνής του θεάτρου.[139] Πιθανόν ανήκουν στην οικοδομική φάση που ακολούθησε την αιτωλική καταστροφή του 219 με τις επιδιορθώσεις και ανοικοδομήσεις των κτηρίων.[140]

Κατά τον Ορλάνδο[141] η αναγραφή του ονόματος του θεού ή της θεάς κατά γενική πτώση σε κεραμίδες, που προέρχονται από Ιερά, πιστοποιεί και την ύπαρξη στο αντίστοιχο Ιερό εργαστηρίων κατασκευής κεράμων. Για τη λειτουργία σχετικών εργαστηρίων[142] στη Δωδώνη τίθεται το ερώτημα με βάση ορισμένες ενδείξεις, όπως η ανεύρεση κεραμεικού κλιβάνου των υστεροελλαδικών χρόνων[143] και η διαπίστωση της λειτουργίας χαλκουργείων[144] και νομισματοκοπείου[145] στο Ιερό.

## Γ' ΟΜΑΔΑ

### Ι. ΑΓΕΣΤΡΑΤΟΣ

Στη Γ'Ι κατηγορία (Pl. 70) εμπεριέχεται η επιγραφή ΑΓΕΣΤΡΑΤΟΣ σε ορθογώνιο έντυπο σφράγισμα που ορίζεται από διπλές παράλληλες λεπτές ταινίες,[146] οι οποίες

---

[138] Από τα εννιά θραύσματα (αρ. 1–9) της α' υποκατηγορίας τα εφτά (αρ. 1–4, 6–8) προέρχονται από το Ε2, ένα (αρ. 5) από ανασκαφή του 1967, η οποία επίσης έγινε στη στοά του Ε2 και στην περιοχή ανατολικά μέχρι το ναΐσκο Λ (Δάκαρης 1967, σελ. 33) και ένα (αρ. 9) από το Ο που βρίσκεται νότια του Ε2. Επομένως τα σφραγίσματα της α' υποκατηγορίας προέρχονται χωρίς αμφιβολία από το Ε2. Η ίδια ανεπιφύλακτη απόδοση δεν ισχύει για τα σφραγίσματα των υπόλοιπων υποκατηγοριών. Από τα έξι θραύσματα (αρ. 10–15) της β' υποκατηγορίας δύο (αρ. 10, 14) είναι χωρίς στοιχεία, ένα (αρ. 11) προέρχεται από το θέατρο, ένα (αρ. 12) από το Ε2, ένα (αρ. 13) από ανασκαφή του 1971, κατά την οποία διερευνήθηκε το δυτικό τμήμα του Ε2 (Δάκαρης 1971, σελ. 124) και ένα (αρ. 15) είναι αμφισβητούμενο, επειδή προέρχεται από την ανασκαφή του 1959, κατά την οποία διερευνήθηκε τόσο το θέατρο όσο και ο χώρος νότια των αναθηματικών βάθρων, ανάμεσα στην Ιερά Οικία και το ναό της Θέμιδος (Ευαγγελίδης 1959, σελ. 114). Από τα δύο θραύσματα (αρ. 16, 17) της β' υποκατηγορίας το ένα (αρ. 16) προέρχεται από το θέατρο και το άλλο (αρ. 17) από την ανασκαφή του 1971, κατά την οποία διερευνήθηκε το δυτικό τμήμα του Ε2 (βλ. παραπάνω). Από τα είκοσι θραύσματα (αρ. 18–37) της γ' υποκατηγορίας οκτώ (αρ. 18, 19, 23, 27, 28, 30, 33, 35) προέρχονται από το θέατρο, έξι (αρ. 20–22, 24, 26, 29) από το Ε2, τέσσερα (αρ. 25, 32, 36, 37) από το Ο1 και δύο (αρ. 31, 34) είναι χωρίς στοιχεία.

[139] Δάκαρης 1966, σελ. 82· Δάκαρης 1969β, σελ. 26· Δάκαρης 1960, σελ. 32.

[140] Βλ. παραπάνω σελ. 188, σημ. 46, σελ. 189, σημ. 49. Για τις στέγες του Ε2 και της σκηνής του θεάτρου μετά την αιτωλική καταστροφή βλ. Βλαχοπούλου-Οικονόμου 1988–1989, σελ. 84, 87.

[141] Ορλάνδος 1955, σελ. 115. Αντίθετα η Καρύδη θεωρεί ότι συνήθως στα Ιερά δεν έχουμε ιδιαίτερα εργαστήρια. Walter-Karydi 1981, σελ. 45.

[142] Γενικότερα για τοπικά εργαστήρια κεραμεικής στην Ήπειρο και ιδιαίτερα στην Αμβρακία, όπου έχουν βρεθεί πήλινες μήτρες για την κατασκευή ακροκεράμων (Βλαχοπούλου-Οικονόμου 1986, σελ. 30–33, 184–186) και ειδωλίων (Δάκαρης 1964γ, σελ. 311, 312· Daux 1967, σελ. 681), καθώς και στην Κασσώπη, όπου έχουν αποκαλυφθεί εγκαταστάσεις σιδηρουργείου και χαλκουργείων (Δάκαρης 1989, σελ. 35, 51, 57) βλ. Γραβάνη 1988–1989, σελ. 119, 120.

[143] Δάκαρης 1967, σελ. 40–42, εικ. 5· Δάκαρης 1986β, σελ. 60.

[144] Δάκαρης 1986β, σελ. 101· Κουλεϊμάνη-Βοκοτοπούλου 1975, σελ. 165.

[145] Franke 1961, σελ. 123, 124, 150· Hammond 1967, σελ. 638· Δάκαρης 1986β, σελ. 23· Δάκαρης 1987, σελ. 14–16. Πρβ. Γραβάνη 1988–1989, σελ. 121, όπου, εκτός των άλλων, βλ. και σχετικά με την αλληλοεξάρτηση των επαγγελμάτων που υποδεικνύει τη λειτουργία κεραμουργείων σε συγκροτήματα εργαστηρίων (χαλκουργείων, νομισματοκοπείων κλπ.).

[146] Για ορθογώνιο πλαίσιο που ορίζεται από διπλή ταινία βλ. σφράγισμα από την Αλβανία: Dautaj 1972, σελ. 154, πίν. IV.

συνδέονται εσωτερικά με μικρές παράλληλες λεπτές ταινίες. Η διακόσμηση και τα γράμματα είναι έκτυπα. Έχουν βρεθεί τα παρακάτω σφραγίσματα:

1. Ύψ. 0,025 μ. Μήκ. 0,10 μ. (Pl. 70:a).[147]
   Πηλός ερυθρός (2.5YR 5/8).
   Θέση: Ο1· ανασκαφή 1981.
   Ολόκληρο σφράγισμα.
   ΑΓΕΣΤΡΑΤΟΣ

2. Αρ.Μ.: 271.[148]
   Ύψ. 0,026 μ. Μήκ. 0,069 μ.
   Πηλός ελαφρά υπορόδινος καστανός (5YR 6/4).
   Ανασκαφή 1935.
   [ΑΓΕ]ΣΤΡΑΤΟΣ

3. Αρ.Μ.: 3557 (Pl. 70:b).[149]
   Ύψ. 0,026 μ. Μήκ. 0,032 μ.
   Πηλός υπέρυθρος κιτρινωπός (5YR 7/6).
   Ανασκαφή 1958–1959.
   [ΑΓΕΣΤΡΑΤ]ΟΣ

Το όνομα Ἀγέστρατος συναντάται στην αρχαία ελληνική ονοματολογία,[150] σε αντίθεση με την Ηπειρωτική προσωπογραφία, όπου δεν είναι γνωστό.

Το όνομα Ἀγέστρατος μπορεί να είναι όνομα άρχοντα[151] ή τεχνίτη ή κεραμοποιού. Επειδή όμως εκφέρεται στην ονομαστική πτώση θεωρείται πιθανότερο ότι υπονοείται το ἐπόει, το οποίο όμως δεν προσγράφεται.[152] Η παρουσία στα σφραγίσματα κυρίου ονόματος, γνωστή και από άλλες περιοχές, θα πρέπει να συνδεθεί ή με το εργαστήριο στο οποίο κατασκευάσθηκαν οι κεραμίδες ή με κάποιο πρόσωπο που έπαιξε βασικό ρόλο στην ανοικοδόμηση του κτηρίου. Για τη δεύτερη περίπτωση ωστόσο έχουμε σε άλλα παραδείγματα συνήθως τον τύπο του ονόματος μαζί με τη λέξη ἐργώνης ἠ ἀρχιτέκτων.[153] Από την Ήπειρο μέχρι σήμερα έχουν διασωθεί ελάχιστα ονόματα τεχνιτών. Από την Κασσώπη προέρχεται το μοναδικό δείγμα Ηπειρωτικής ακροκεράμου που φέρει στο ανθεμωτό μέτωπο το όνομα του τεχνίτη Κάσσανδρος, καθώς και ένα μικρό θραύσμα πήλινης μήτρας με επιγραφή Σωκρ[άτης].[154] Επίσης σε αγγεία[155] από την Κασσώπη διασώζονται δύο ονόματα τεχνιτών: σε ένα άωτο σκυφίδιο

---

[147] Δάκαρης 1981β, σελ. 31, εικ. 50.
[148] Ο Ευαγγελίδης (Ευαγγελίδης 1935, σελ. 260, αρ. 42, εικ. 25:β, 1) συμπληρώνει: ΣΩ]ΣΤΡΑΤΟΣ, ενώ ο Franke (Franke 1961, σελ. 312[3], 314, πίν. 61:3) συμπληρώνει το όνομα ως ΗΓΕ-, ΚΛΕ-, ΜΕΝΕ-, ή ΑΡΕ]ΣΤΡΑΤΟΣ. Η συμπλήρωση ΑΓΕ]ΣΤΡΑΤΟΣ βεβαιώνεται από το σφράγισμα αρ. 1, Plate 70:a, στο οποίο σώζεται ολόκληρη η επιγραφή.
[149] Franke 1961, σελ. 312 (3β), 314.
[150] Pape και Benseler 1911, στο λήμμα. Πρβ. σε ευρήματα από τη Ρόδο και την Τήλο: Fraser και Matthews 1987, στο λήμμα· ιδιαίτερα βλ. Grace 1963, σελ. 328, σημ. 20· Grace 1985, σελ. 8, 9.
[151] Ο Franke θεωρεί το όνομα Ἀγέστρατος ως όνομα επώνυμου άρχοντα (Franke 1961, σελ. 314). Για τους επώνυμους άρχοντες του Κοινού των Ηπειρωτών βλ. Δάκαρης 1965, σελ. 54.
[152] Ορλάνδος 1955, σελ. 115. Πρβ. *Agora* XIV, σελ. 36, 37, πίν. 30:c.
[153] Καλτσάς 1988, σελ. 103, σημ. 332, 333, 335, όπου και σχετική βιβλιογραφία για σφραγίσματα από την Αλβανία, με ονόματα σε ονομαστική και γενική πτώση. Για την έννοια της λέξης τέκτων, η οποία θεωρείται ότι σήμαινε τόσο τον ξυλουργό, όσο και τον τεχνίτη (ή καλλιτέχνη) και για την έννοια του όρου ἀρχιτέκτων (δηλ. του επικεφαλής των εργατών κλπ.) βλ. Πέππα-Δελμούζου 1967–1968, σελ. 380, σημ. 19, όπου και σχετική βιβλιογραφία.
[154] Βλαχοπούλου-Οικονόμου 1986, σελ. 254–258, πίν. 20:α, β, σχέδ. 24 και σελ. 263, σημ. 23.
[155] Για την παρουσία ή την απουσία των υπογραφών στα αγγεία βλ. Γραβάνη 1988–1989, σελ. 124, σημ. 216, σελ. 125, σημ. 219, όπου και σχετική βιβλιογραφία. Ειδικότερα για τις λιγοστές επιγραφές που διασώζονται επάνω σε αγγεία από την Ήπειρο (εκτός βέβαια από τις ενσφράγιστες λαβές των

το όνομα Λυκώτας[156] και σε μερικά ερυθροβαφή πινάκια το όνομα Σωτηρίχου,[157] ενώ στο περιχείλωμα μιας μήτρας ειδωλίου του 4ου αι. από την Αμβρακία είναι χαραγμένο το όνομα του κοροπλάθου σε γενική: Σατύρου.[158]

Τα σφραγίσματα της Γ'Ι κατηγορίας έχουν χρονολογηθεί από τον ανασκαφέα στους χρόνους πριν από τη ρωμαϊκή καταστροφή (168/7).[159] Η χρονολόγηση αυτή δεν ανατρέπεται από τη μελέτη της μορφής των γραμμάτων, καθώς το άλφα έχει γωνιώδη την εσωτερική κεραία και το σίγμα παράλληλα τα δύο σκέλη.[160]

## II. ΤΑ ΛΥΣΑΝΙΑ, ανθέμιο

Τα ορθογώνια έντυπα σφραγίσματα της Γ'ΙΙ κατηγορίας (Pls. 71, 72:a) κοσμούνται από ένα κατακόρυφο σχηματοποιημένο επτάφυλλο ανθέμιο[161] που φυτρώνει από τον κεντρικό στρογγυλό δεσμό δύο οριζοντίων ζευγαριών σπειρών, οι οποίες κινούνται αντιθετικά. Ανάμεσα από τις σπείρες και παράλληλα προς τα στελέχη τους φέρεται οριζόντιο επίμηκες στέλεχος, ενώ ο στρογγυλός δεσμός εφάπτεται με την κορυφή οξυκόρυφου τριγωνικού σχήματος. Δεξιά και αριστερά από την κορυφή του ανθεμίου φέρονται τα γράμματα ΤΑ, κατά μήκος της αριστερής του πλευράς τα γράμματα ΛΥ, κατά μήκος της δεξιάς του πλευράς τα γράμματα ΣΑ και στην κάτω πλευρά των σφραγισμάτων τα γράμματα ΝΙΑ με το νι αντίστροφο.[162] Σώζεται επομένως η επιγραφή ΤΑΛΥΣΑΝΙΑ, με γράμματα «επί τα λαιά». Τα γράμματα και η διακόσμηση είναι έκτυπα. Έχουν βρεθεί τα παρακάτω σφραγίσματα:

1.  Αρ.Μ.: 3573 (Pl. 71:a, αριστερά).
    Ύψ. 0,075 μ. Πλ. 0,047 μ.
    Πηλός υπέρυθρος κιτρινωπός (5YR 7/8).
    [ΤΑ]|ΛΥ|[ΣΑ]|ΝΙΑ

2.  Ύψ. 0,075 μ. Πλ. 0,047 μ. (Pl. 72:a, αριστερά).
    Πηλός υπέρυθρος (2.5YR 6/8).
    ΤΑ|ΛΥ|[Σ]Α|[ΝΙΑ]

3.  Αρ.Μ.: 3489 (Pl. 72:a, δεξιά).
    Ύψ. 0,068 μ. Πλ. 0,049 μ.
    Πηλός υπέρυθρος κιτρινωπός (7.5YR 7/6).
    Θέση: Θέατρο· ανασκαφή 1959.
    [ΤΑ|Λ]Υ|ΣΑ|[ΝΙΑ]

4.  Αρ.Μ.: 5739 (Pl. 72:a, μέσον).
    Ύψ. 0,04 μ. Πλ. 0,04 μ.
    Πηλός ρόδινος (7.5YR 7/4).
    [ΤΑ|ΛΥ|ΣΑ|ΝΙΑ]

5.  Αρ.Μ.: 3672 (Pl. 71:b).
    Ύψ. 0,082 μ. Πλ. 0,046 μ.
    Πηλός υπέρυθρος κιτρινωπός (7.5YR 6/6).
    Θέση: Ε2· ανασκαφή 1968.
    ΤΑ|[ΛΥ]|ΣΑ|ΝΙΑ

---

αμφορέων που είναι επείσακτοι: Βλαχοπούλου-Οικονόμου 1979, σελ. 279–298) βλ. Γραβάνη 1988–1989, σελ. 123, 124.

[156] Gravani 1986, σελ. 126, πίν. 126:6.
[157] Gravani 1986, σελ. 129, πίν. 133:3.
[158] Τζουβάρα-Σούλη 1987–1988, σελ. 118, σημ. 167, εικ. 16.
[159] Δάκαρης 1981β, σελ. 30, 31, εικ. 50.
[160] Βλ. παρακάτω σελ. 207, σημ. 208, 209.
[161] Η παράσταση ανθεμίου είναι γνωστή σε σφραγίσματα κεραμίδων ήδη από τον 5o αι. Felsch 1990, σελ. 305, πίν. 52. Πρβ. σφράγισμα από το Ιερό της Αρτέμιδος στους Λουσούς. Reichel και Wilhelm 1901, σελ. 64, εικ. 142. Βλ. επίσης το ανθέμιο σε σφράγισμα αμφορέα από τη Θάσο. Garlan 1986, σελ. 239:d.
[162] Για αντίστροφα γράμματα και επιγραφές βλ. παραπάνω σελ. 197, σημ. 114 και παρακάτω σελ. 208.

6. Αρ.Μ.: 3488 (Pl. 71:a, δεξιά).
Ύψ. 0,064 μ. Πλ. 0,044 μ.
Πηλός υπέρυθρος κιτρινωπός (5YR 6/8).
Θέση: Θέατρο· ανασκαφή 1959.
Τ[Α|ΛΥ]|ΣΑ|[ΝΙΑ]

7. Αρ.Μ.: 3490
Ύψ. 0,076 μ. Πλ. 0,048 μ.
Πηλός υπέρυθρος κιτρινωπός (7.5YR 6/6).
Θέση: Θέατρο· ανασκαφή 1959.
[ΤΑ|ΛΥ|ΣΑ|ΝΙΑ]

Τα σφραγίσματα της κατηγορίας Γ΄ΙΙ θα συνεξετασθούν με τα σφραγίσματα της επόμενης κατηγορίας Γ΄ΙΙΙ, επειδή έχουν κοινά στοιχεία, από τα οποία το σημαντικότερο είναι το ίδιο κύριο όνομα <u>Λυσανίας</u> και η χρήση παρόμοιου διακοσμητικού θέματος, ενός ανθεμίου.

## III. ΑΠΟΛΛΟΔΩΡΟΥ ΛΥΣΑΝΙΑ, ανθέμιο

Στα ορθογώνια έντυπα σφραγίσματα την Γ΄ΙΙΙ κατηγορίας (Pl. 72:b) κατά μήκος της δεξιάς μακράς πλευράς φέρεται η επιγραφή ΑΠΟΛΛΟΔΩΡΟΥ, παρεμβάλλεται ένα σχηματοποιημένο εννιάφυλλο ανθέμιο και κατά μήκος της αριστερής μακράς πλευράς φέρεται η επιγραφή ΛΥΣΑΝΙΑ. Το ανθέμιο φυτρώνει ανάμεσα από δύο αντιθετικά κινούμενες σιγμοειδείς έλικες[163] που κοσμούν το κεντρικό τμήμα στο κάτω μέρος του σφραγίσματος. Φυλλάριο,[164] με μορφή μηνίσκου,[165] ακουμπά στα κορυφαία άκρα των ελίκων, ενώ λεπτότερο φυλλάριο φυτρώνει από το μέσον περίπου των επάνω σπειρών.[166] Τα γράμματα και η διακόσμηση είναι έκτυπα. Έχουν βρεθεί τα παρακάτω σφραγίσματα:

1. Αρ.Μ.: 3530 (Pl. 72:b, μέσον).[167]
Ύψ. 0,064 μ. Πλ. 0,052 μ.
Πηλός υπέρυθρος κιτρινωπός (7.5YR 6/6).
Ανασκαφή 1953.
[ΑΠΟΛΛΟΔΩΡΟΥ|ΛΥ]ΣΑΝΙΑ

2. Αρ.Μ.: 3492 (Pl. 72:b, δεξιά).
Ύψ. 0,05 μ. Πλ. 0,052 μ.
Πηλός υπέρυθρος κιτρινωπός (7.5YR 6/6).
Θέση: Θέατρο· ανασκαφή 1959.
[ΑΠΟ]ΛΛΟ[ΔΩΡΟΥ|ΛΥΣΑΝΙΑ]

3. Αρ.Μ.: 3576 (Pl. 72:b, αριστερά).
Ύψ. 0,07 μ. Πλ. 0,053 μ.
Πηλός υπέρυθρος κιτρινωπός (7.5YR 6/6).
ΑΠΟΛΛΟΔ[ΩΡΟΥ|ΛΥΣΑΝΙΑ]

4. Μήκ. 0,16 μ.[168]
ΑΠΟΛΛΟΔΩΡΟΥ|ΛΥΣΑΝΙΑ

---

[163] Για τη γένεση και εξέλιξη των ελίκων στη βάση των ανθεμωτών μετώπων κεράμων βλ. Βλαχοπούλου-Οικονόμου 1986, σελ. 15–21.
[164] Για φυλλάρια ως διακοσμητικά στοιχεία ελίκων βλ. Βλαχοπούλου-Οικονόμου 1986, σποραδικά.
[165] Πρβ. Βλαχοπούλου-Οικονόμου 1986, σελ. 168, 175, σημ. 18.
[166] Ας σημειωθεί ότι στο σχέδιο του σφραγίσματος αρ. 4 από τον Καραπάνο (Carapanos 1878, σελ. 111, αρ. 6, πίν. 61:11) το ανθέμιο αποδίδεται ως επτάφυλλο, ενώ είναι εννιάφυλλο και δε δηλώνονται οι λεπτομέρειες στις έλικες, οι οποίες όμως διακρίνονται σαφώς στο θραύσμα αρ. 1.
[167] Franke 1961, σελ. 312 (1β), πίν. 61:2.
[168] Carapanos 1878, σελ. 111 (6), πίν. 61:11· Franke 1961, σελ. 312 (1α). Παρά την επισταμένη έρευνα το θραύσμα δεν έχει βρεθεί στις αποθήκες του Μουσείου Ιωαννίνων.

Το όνομα Λυσανίας είναι πολύ γνωστό και σε άλλα μέρη της Ελλάδας,[169] αλλά και στην περιοχή της Ηπείρου, όπου είναι διαδεδομένο[170] και μαρτυρείται επιγραφικά. Εκτός των άλλων διασώζεται σε επιγραφή του τέλους του 4ου αι.,[171] και σε τρεις επιγραφές από τη Δωδώνη (*SGDI*, αρ. 1339, 1350 και 1360). Από αυτές οι δύο πρώτες (*SGDI*, αρ. 1339 και 1350) χρονολογούνται από τον Hammond[172] λίγο πριν το 170. Ο Λυσανίας, ο οποίος αναφέρεται στις επιγραφές αυτές (*SGDI*, αρ. 1339 και 1350) μπορεί να είναι το ίδιο πρόσωπο. Ας σημειωθεί εξάλλου ότι το όνομα Λυσανίας συναντάται σε δραχμή του Κοινού των Ηπειρωτών,[173] καθώς και σε μολύβδινο έλασμα από τη Δωδώνη με κατάλογο πολιτών οι οποίοι είχαν προσφέρει χρηματικά ποσά για την ανοικοδόμηση του Ιερού μετά την αιτωλική καταστροφή (219).[174] Θα είχε ιδιαίτερο ενδιαφέρον αν ήταν δυνατό να ταυτίσουμε τον Λυσανία των σφραγισμάτων με τον Λυσανία των επιγραφών *SGDI*, αρ. 1339, 1350, της δραχμής του Ηπειρωτικού Κοινού[175] και του μολύβδινου ελάσματος[176] ή να διαπιστώσουμε κάποια συγγενική σχέση μεταξύ τους.[177]

Το όνομα Ἀπολλόδωρος, που συνυπάρχει με το όνομα Λυσανίας στα σφραγίσματα της Γ΄ΙΙΙ κατηγορίας, συναντάται ιδιαίτερα συχνά στην αρχαία ελληνική ονοματολογία,[178] σε αντίθεση με την Ηπειρωτική προσωπογραφία, όπου είναι σπάνιο.[179] Η σχέση των δύο ονομάτων μεταξύ τους δεν πρέπει να είναι η σχέση πατέρα και γιου, καθώς δεν έχουμε δείγματα αναγραφής πατρωνυμικού σε σφραγίσματα κεραμίδων.[180] Κατά τον Ορλάνδο[181] τα ονόματα αυτά είναι τα ονόματα των ἐργώνων ή των εργοστασιαρχών

---

[169] Pape και Benseler 1911, στο λήμμα. Πρβ. Fraser και Matthews 1987, στο λήμμα· Πέτσας 1961, σελ. 27, σημ. 3.

[170] Hammond 1967, Index I, σελ. 808· Cabanes 1976, σελ. 621. Πρβ. Γραβάνη 1988–1989, σελ. 123, σημ. 205.

[171] Ευαγγελίδης 1935, σελ. 245· Hammond 1967, σελ. 564, 565.

[172] Hammond 1967, σελ. 649, 650. Πρβ. Franke 1961, σελ. 145 και Cabanes 1976, σελ. 364, 456.

[173] Franke 1961, σελ. 314. Για το Κοινό των Ηπειρωτών βλ. παραπάνω σελ. 188, σημ. 44.

[174] Αντωνίου 1991, σελ. 131.

[175] Στην Κέρκυρα, στην Απολλωνία και στο Δυρράχιο συναντάται το όνομα του ίδιου επωνύμου σε σφραγίσματα κεραμίδων και σε νομίσματα. Franke 1961, σελ. 314.

[176] Αντωνίου 1991, σελ. 131.

[177] Πρβ. τη σχέση παππού και εγγονού μεταξύ του Αντινόου, ο οποίος αναφέρεται σε επιγραφή του τέλους του 4ου αι. (*SGDI*, αρ. 1338) και του Αντινόου, ο οποίος αναφέρεται σε επιγραφή (*SGDI*, αρ. 1339) που χρονολογείται γύρω στο 170 (Hammond 1967, σελ. 648). Γνωστό εξάλλου είναι ότι ο Χάροψ, γιος του Μαχατά (Πολύβ. 20.3), ο οποίος βοήθησε τον Φλαμινίνο στις επιχειρήσεις κατά του Περσέα (Δάκαρης 1986β, σελ. 22) είχε έναν εγγονό με το ίδιο όνομα. Δάκαρης 1968, σελ. 48–51.

[178] Pape και Benseler 1911, στο λήμμα. Πρβ. Fraser και Matthews 1987, στο λήμμα· Fraser και Rönne 1957, σελ. 16, αρ. 25. Πρβ. την επιγραφή Ἐπὶ Ἀπολλοδώρου σε δύο σφραγίσματα κεραμίδων ελληνιστικών χρόνων από την Κέρκυρα. Δοντάς 1966, σελ. 87, πίν. 83:α.

[179] Βλ. σε επιγραφή από την Άρτα. Hammond 1967, Index I, σελ. 798.

[180] Franke 1961, σελ. 314.

[181] «Σπανιώτερον μνημονεύουσιν αι επί πλίνθου ή κεράμου επιγραφαί και το όνομα του ἀρχιτέκτονος, συχνά δε το του ἐργώνου, ενός ή και δύο ... ή τέλος το του εργοστασιάρχου της κατασκευής των». Ορλάνδος 1955, σελ. 115, 116, σημ. 1.

των κεραμίδων.[182] Αντίθετα ο Franke[183] θεωρεί ότι πρόκειται για τα ονόματα δύο αρχόντων, συνήθεια γνωστή και από τα Ηπειρωτικά νομίσματα, όπου αναγράφονται τα ονόματα ή οι συντομογραφίες των ονομάτων δύο ή τριών αρχόντων ταυτόχρονα. Το ίδιο φαινόμενο συναντάται σχετικά συχνά και σε σφραγίσματα κεραμίδων από την Αλβανία.[184] Η άποψη του Franke ενισχύεται από το περιεχόμενο των μέχρι σήμερα άγνωστων σφραγισμάτων της Β'ΙΙ κατηγορίας. Τα γράμματα ΤΑ που σώζονται στην κορυφή του ανθεμίου φαίνεται πιθανότερο ότι δεν είναι τα αρχικά κύριου ονόματος,[185] αλλά τα αρχικά της λέξης τα(μίας).[186] Είναι γνωστό ότι στα σφραγίσματα κεραμίδων συνηθίζεται η αναγραφή του επώνυμου άρχοντα, που θυμίζει τις μεσοποταμιακές πήλινες επενδύσεις των ανακτόρων, στις οποίες γράφονταν τα ονόματα των μοναρχών. Τις πιο πολλές φορές συνοδεύονται με την πρόθεση ἐπί[187] ή χωρίς πρόθεση με απλή αναγραφή του κύριου ονόματος σε γενική πτώση.[188] Η αναγραφή του τίτλου συναντάται σχετικά σπάνια,[189] όπως σε σφράγισμα από την Κέρκυρα: Ἀστυνομοῦντος Συνωπίωνος[190] ή σε σφράγισμα από την Ολυμπία: [ἐπι]μ[ελητοῦ] Ἀχεμάχου.[191]

Σύμφωνα λοιπόν με τα παραπάνω ο Λυσανίας δεν είναι ο τεχνίτης ή ο εργοστασιάρχης των κεράμων, αλλά ένα δημόσιο πρόσωπο που στα σφραγίσματα της Γ'ΙΙ κατηγορίας χαρακτηρίζεται από την ιδιότητά του (ταμίας), ενώ στα σφραγίσματα της Γ'ΙΙΙ κατηγορίας συνοδεύεται με το όνομα ενός άλλου προσώπου, του Ἀπολλοδώρου, που μπορεί επίσης να είναι δημόσιο πρόσωπο. Επειδή όμως σε σφραγίσματα κεραμίδων είναι δυνατόν το όνομα του επώνυμου άρχοντα να συνοδεύεται με το όνομα του κεραμουργού,[192] δεν μπορούμε να αποκλείσουμε την πιθανότητα ο Ἀπολλόδωρος να μην είναι άρχοντας, αλλά ο κατασκευαστής των κεραμίδων.

Ενδιαφέρον είναι το διακοσμητικό θέμα των αντιθετικά κινούμενων οριζόντιων σπειρών κάτω από το ανθέμιο της Γ'ΙΙ κατηγορίας, που δε συναντάται στις διακοσμήσεις της βάσης στα ανθεμωτά μέτωπα ηγεμόνων και κορυφαίων καλυπτήρων

---

[182] Για δύο κύρια ονόματα σε γενική πτώση στην ίδια επιγραφή βλ. σε σφράγισμα από τη Σπάρτη: ἐργώνων Νικίωνος (κ)α(ὶ) Ξενάρχου (IG V¹ 889, 890) και σε σφραγίσματα από τη Δημητριάδα: Μυσανίου και Μενωνίδου (Αρβανιτόπουλος 1928, σελ. 120, εικ. 145, σελ. 121, εικ. 146).

[183] Franke 1961, σελ. 314.

[184] Ceka 1982, σελ. 109, αρ. 27, σελ. 110, αρ. 38, 39, 41, σελ. 111, αρ. 49, 52, σελ. 117.

[185] Hammond 1967, Index I.

[186] Πρβ. σφράγισμα με την επιγραφή ΕΠΙΤΑΜΙΑ από το Λάφριο της Καλυδώνας. Dyggve και Poulsen 1948, σελ. 198, σημ. 5. Στα σφραγίσματα κεραμίδων των Διμαλλιτών από την Αλβανία ο άρχοντας, που αποδίδεται με τη μορφή μονογράμματος, μπορεί να είναι Γραμματέας ή Ταμίας. Albanien, σελ. 277, αρ. 142. Για τον τίτλο του ταμία βλ. RE στο λήμμα. Για τη λέξη ταμίας σε επιγραφές βλ. Guarducci 1969, σελ. 729, και σε νομίσματα βλ. Icard 1968, σελ. 483, στο λήμμα.

[187] Ορλάνδος 1955, σελ. 115, σημ. 7.

[188] Βλ. παρακάτω σελ. 208, σημ. 223.

[189] Αντίθετα η λέξη ἐργώνας σε γενική πτώση συνοδεύει το κύριο όνομα σε πληθώρα παραδειγμάτων. Ορλάνδος 1955, σελ. 115, σημ. 10.

[190] Ορλάνδος 1955, σελ. 115, σημ. 7.

[191] Franke 1961, σελ. 314, σημ. 9.

[192] Μέμνονος [ἐ]πί Αἰνίππου. Guarducci 1969, σελ. 496.

από την Ήπειρο, όπου οι έλικες έχουν ως επί το πλείστον κατακόρυφη τοποθέτηση.[193] Θα μπορούσε κανείς να υποθέσει ότι πρόκειται για τη γραμμική απόδοση ενός εκφυλισμένου οριζόντιου κεραυνού,[194] όπου τα αντικόρυφα συμμετρικά τοποθετημένα άνθη λωτού αποδίδονται εντελώς σχεδιαστικά,[195] με πέταλα που έχουν τη μορφή σπειρών.[196] Σε συνάρτηση με την πιθανότητα αυτή το τριγωνικό σχήμα κάτω από τον κεντρικό δεσμό του «κεραυνού» είναι δυνατόν να θεωρηθεί ως ένα εκφυλισμένο ωκύπτερο.[197] Με τις ίδιες όμως επιφυλάξεις εκφράζεται και η άποψη ότι πρόκειται για τη συντομογραφία της λέξης Δ(αμοσία), η οποία συναντάται πολύ συχνά στα σφραγίσματα των κεραμίδων.[198]

Με βάση τη μορφή των γραμμάτων τα σφραγίσματα εντάσσονται σε ένα ευρύτερο χρονολογικό πλαίσιο από τον 3ο αι. και μετά. Στα σφραγίσματα της Γ΄ΙΙ κατηγορίας (Τα Λυσανία) το άλφα αποδίδεται με οριζόντια την εσωτερική κεραία[199] και το νι με παράλληλα και ισομεγέθη τα δύο σκέλη.[200] Στα σφραγίσματα της Γ΄ΙΙΙ κατηγορίας (Ἀπολλοδώρου Λυσανία) το άλφα αποδίδεται με οριζόντια την εσωτερική κεραία, το πι με ισομεγέθη τα δύο σκέλη,[201] το όμικρον μικρότερο από τα άλλα γράμματα,[202] το δέλτα με αμβλεία την κορυφαία γωνία[203] και το νι με παράλληλα και ισομεγέθη τα δύο σκέλη. Σύμφωνα με τη σχεδιαστική αναπαράσταση του σφραγίσματος αρ. 4 από τον Καραπάνο,[204] το ωμέγα παριστάνεται με οριζόντια τα κάτω σκέλη.[205] Διακρίνεται επίσης η χρήση ακρεμόνων,[206] τουλάχιστον στα αρχικά γράμματα άλφα και πι του ονόματος Ἀπολλοδώρου.

Η σημαντικότερη διαφορά στα γράμματα των σφραγισμάτων των δύο κατηγοριών εντοπίζεται στην απόδοση του σίγμα που στα σφραγίσματα της Γ΄ΙΙ κατηγορίας (Τα Λυσανία) παριστάνεται με ανοιχτά σκέλη, ενώ στα σφραγίσματα της Γ΄ΙΙΙ κατηγορίας (Ἀπολλοδώρου-Λυσανία) με οριζόντια και παράλληλα σκέλη. Η απόδοση του

---

[193] Βλαχοπούλου-Οικονόμου 1986, σποραδικά. Πρβ. Βλαχοπούλου-Οικονόμου 1988–1989, σελ. 67–87.
[194] Για την παράσταση του κεραυνού βλ. παραπάνω σελ. 191, 192.
[195] Πρβ. γραμμική απόδοση κεραυνού στη λαβή ξίφους από χάλκινο ανδριάντα στρατηγού, που απολήγει σε κεφάλι θηλυκού πάνθηρα από το Βουλευτήριο της Δωδώνης. Βοκοτοπούλου 1973, πίν. 27.
[196] Για κεραυνό με σπειροειδή μορφή πετάλων βλ. τις παραστάσεις σε μελανόμορφη κύλικα που βρίσκεται στο Βερολίνο (Cook 1965, σελ. 776, εικ. 740) και σε νομίσματα από την Ολυμπία (Cook 1965, πίν. XXXVI).
[197] Για τα ωκύπτερα βλ. παραπάνω σελ. 189, σημ. 50, σελ. 192, σημ. 75, 76.
[198] Βλ. παραπάνω σελ. 185, σημ. 14. Για δέλτα (Δ) σε σφράγισμα κεραμίδας βλ. Hidri 1986, σελ. 110, πίν. XIV:4.
[199] Για ταυτόχρονη χρήση του άλφα με οριζόντια και με γωνιώδη την εσωτερική κεραία βλ. παραπάνω σελ. 194, σημ. 102, 103.
[200] Fraser και Rönne 1957, σελ. 89.
[201] Fraser και Rönne 1957, σελ. 89· Franke 1961, σελ. 121, 321.
[202] Η μικρότερη απόδοση του όμικρον σε σχέση με τα υπόλοιπα γράμματα απαντά σε όλη τη διάρκεια της Ελληνιστικής και της πρώιμης Ρωμαϊκής περιόδου. Βλαχοπούλου-Οικονόμου 1986, σελ. 257, σημ. 35.
[203] Βλ. παραπάνω σελ. 197, σημ. 115.
[204] Carapanos 1878, σελ. 111 (αρ. 6), πίν. 61:11.
[205] Για τη μορφή του ωμέγα κατά την Ελληνιστική περίοδο βλ. Fraser και Rönne 1957, σελ. 86, 87.
[206] Για τη χρήση των ακρεμόνων ως χρονολογικό κριτήριο βλ. παραπάνω σελ. 188, σημ. 39.

σίγμα με ισχυρή απόκλιση στις κεραίες του είναι χαρακτηριστική για τον 3ο αι.,[207] ενώ κατά τον 2ο αι., αν και δεν εγκαταλείπεται εντελώς,[208] ωστόσο βαθμηδόν απομακρύνεται και αντικαθίσταται από την απόδοση του σίγμα με παράλληλες κεραίες.[209] Η παραπάνω παρατήρηση θα μπορούσε να αποτελέσει μία ένδειξη ότι πρόκειται για σφραγίσματα τα οποία πρέπει να τοποθετηθούν στο μεταίχμιο ανάμεσα στον 3ο και το 2ο αι., με όλες όμως τις επιφυλάξεις που συνοδεύουν τη χρονολόγηση των επιγραφών των σφραγισμάτων με βάση τη μορφή των γραμμάτων.[210] Η χρονολογική αυτή τοποθέτηση ενισχύεται από την πιθανότητα της ταύτισης του Λυσανία των σφραγισμάτων με τον Λυσανία που μαρτυρείται επιγραφικά και χρονολογείται πριν από το 170.[211]

Ωστόσο η μορφή των ανθεμίων στα σφραγίσματα και των δύο κατηγοριών και ιδιαίτερα της Γ'ΙΙ κατηγορίας (Τα Λυσανία), όπου αποδίδεται εντελώς γραμμικά, συναντάται συνήθως από τα μέσα του 2ου αι. και μετά. Τα ανθέμια χαρακτηρίζονται από την ομοιότητα με φτερό ή κλαδί,[212] με φύλλα λεπτόμισχα και επιμήκη, τα οποία καταλήγουν στα άκρα τους σε ισχυρή συστροφή. Τα φύλλα δε βλαστάνουν από έναν κεντρικό πυρήνα, αλλά από τον επιμήκη μίσχο του κορυφαίου λογχόσχημου φύλλου.

Στα σφραγίσματα της Γ'ΙΙΙ κατηγορίας (Ἀπολλοδώρου Λυσανία) τα δύο χαμηλότερα φύλλα του ανθεμίου προς τα δεξιά και αριστερά είναι φλογοειδή,[213] με τόσο ισχυρές συστροφές που ομοιάζουν με σιγμοειδείς έλικες. Ενώ τα στελέχη των τριών προς τα επάνω φύλλων είναι υψηλά και κινούνται παράλληλα προς το κεντρικό φύλλο, το χαμηλότερο φύλλο προς τα δεξιά και αριστερά έχει σχεδόν οριζόντια τοποθέτηση.

Με βάση τη συγκριτική αντιπαράθεση με τη μορφή των ανθεμίων και των ελίκων, που κοσμούν τα μέτωπα ηγεμόνων και κορυφαίων καλυπτήρων από την Ήπειρο, διαπιστώνεται ομοιότητα μόνο με τη διακόσμηση είκοσι έξι αποτμημάτων μετώπων ηγεμόνων καλυπτήρων,[214] τα οποία προέρχονται από τη στέγη της διώροφης σκηνής του θεάτρου στη Δωδώνη, που χρονολογείται μετά τα μέσα του 2ου αι.[215]

IV. ΝΙΚΟΜΑΧΟΥ, δελφίνι

Στο μέσο των ορθογώνιων έντυπων σφραγισμάτων της Γ'ΙV κατηγορίας (Pl. 73) παριστάνεται ένα σχηματοποιημένο δελφίνι προς τα δεξιά, με κυρτή ράχη και ψαλιδωτή

[207] Fraser και Rönne 1957, σελ. 88.
[208] Σε νομίσματα του Πτολεμαίου V (τέλη 3ου–αρχές 2ου αι.) συναντάται το σίγμα άλλοτε με ανοιχτές κεραίες και άλλοτε με παράλληλες κεραίες. Kyrieleis 1973, σελ. 219, εικ. 3, σελ. 294, εικ. 5, 6, σελ. 225, εικ. 7, σελ. 226, εικ. 9, σελ. 227, εικ. 10, 11, σελ. 231, εικ. 17–19.
[209] Woodhead 1967, σελ. 64.
[210] Βλ. παραπάνω σελ. 185, 186.
[211] Βλ. παραπάνω σελ. 204, σημ. 172–174.
[212] Για την παρομοίωση ανθεμίου ως «κλάδου φυτού» βλ. Ευαγγελίδης και Δάκαρης 1959, σελ. 172. Πρβ. Βλαχοπούλου-Οικονόμου 1986, σελ. 255, 259, σημ. 4, σελ. 272.
[213] Για «φλογοειδή» ανθέμια, τα οποία κατά τον Le Roy 1967, σελ. 165, στις ακροκεράμους εμφανίζονται από τον 3ο αι. και μετά, βλ. Βλαχοπούλου-Οικονόμου 1986, σελ. 166, 167, 173, σημ. 3–9.
[214] Βλαχοπούλου-Οικονόμου 1986, σελ. 266–274, πίν. 27:β-δ, 28:α–γ, 29:α, σχέδ. 29.
[215] Συμπίπτει με μερικές πρόχειρες επισκευές του προσκηνίου και της σκηνής του θεάτρου, οι οποίες έχουν αποδειχθεί από τα λείψανα τοίχου ρωμαϊκών χρόνων από αργούς λίθους. Δάκαρης 1960, σελ. 34, πίν. 7, σχέδ. 8.

ουρά, ενώ ανά δύο πτερύγια διακρίνονται στην επάνω και στην κάτω πλευρά του σώματός του. Κατά μήκος της επάνω μακράς πλευράς των σφραγισμάτων φέρονται τα γράμματα ΝΙΚΟ και κατά μήκος της κάτω μακράς πλευράς τα γράμματα ΜΑΧΟΥ, αντίστροφα και «επί τα λαιά». Έχουν βρεθεί τα παρακάτω σφραγίσματα:

1. Ύψ. 0,052 μ. Μήκ. 0,073 μ. (Pl. 73:a).
Πηλός υπέρυθρος κιτρινωπός (5YR 7/8).
Θέση: Ο1, διάδρομος ε· ανασκαφή 1982.
ΝΙΚΟ|ΜΑΧΟΥ

2. Ύψ. 0,051 μ. Μήκ. 0,055 μ.
Πηλός υπέρυθρος κιτρινωπός (5YR 6/8).
Θέση: Ο1, δωμάτιο δ1· ανασκαφή 1982.
[ΝΙΚΟ|ΜΑΧΟ]Υ

3. Ύψ. 0,052 μ. Μήκ. 0,078 μ. (Pl. 73:b).[216]
Πηλός υπέρυθρος κιτρινωπός (5YR 6/8).

Θέση: Ο1, δωμάτιο ε· ανασκαφή 1982.
ΝΙΚΟ|ΜΑΧΟΥ

4. Ύψ. 0,047 μ. Μήκ. 0,065 μ.
Πηλός υπέρυθρος κιτρινωπός (5YR 6/8).
Θέση: Ο1, δωμάτιο ε· ανασκαφή 1982.
Ν[ΙΚΟ]|Μ[ΑΧΟΥ]

5. Ύψ. 0,048 μ. Μήκ. 0,069 μ.
Πηλός υπέρυθρος κιτρινωπός (5YR 6/8).
Θέση: Ο1, δωμάτιο ε· ανασκαφή 1982.
ΝΙΚΟ|ΜΑΧΟΥ

Το δελφίνι είναι ένα θέμα ιδιαίτερα αγαπητό στην αρχαία ελληνική τέχνη.[217] Ενώ καταρχήν χρησιμοποιήθηκε ως σύμβολο της θάλασσας, γρήγορα έχασε αυτό το χαρακτήρα και κατά την Ελληνιστική περίοδο καθιερώθηκε ως αυτοδύναμο διακοσμητικό θέμα. Σε σφραγίσματα κεραμίδων συναντάται ήδη από τον 6ο αι. στην Αίγινα[218] και το Καλαπόδι.[219]

Το όνομα Νικόμαχος συναντάται συχνά στην αρχαία ελληνική ονοματολογία[220] και δεν είναι άγνωστο στην Ηπειρωτική προσωπογραφία.[221] Τα στοιχεία που έχουμε στη διάθεσή μας δεν επιτρέπουν να διευκρινίσουμε με βεβαιότητα την ιδιότητα του Νικομάχου. Κατά τον Ορλάνδο[222] το όνομα του αρχιτέκτονα ή του εργώνου εκφέρεται σε γενική ή σε ονομαστική πτώση (οπότε υπονοείται το ἐπόει), ενώ του επώνυμου άρχοντα συνοδεύεται από την πρόθεση ἐπί. Στα σφραγίσματα όμως της Γ΄ΙΙ κατηγορίας[223] αποδείχθηκε ότι έχουμε όνομα δημόσιου άνδρα που εκφέρεται σε γενική πτώση. Ενδιαφέρουσα θα ήταν η πιθανότητα σύνδεσης του Νικομάχου των σφραγισμάτων με το Νικόμαχο που μαρτυρείται σε απελευθερωτικό ψήφισμα του τέλους του 3ου και των αρχών του 2ου αι. από τη Δωδώνη[224] και σε μολύβδινο έλασμα από τη Δωδώνη

[216] Δάκαρης 1982, σελ. 87, πίν. 62:α.
[217] Βλ. Stubbing 1929, σποραδικά· Rumpf 1969, σελ. 90 κεξ., 97 κεξ., όπου και άφθονη βιβλιογραφία για τις παραστάσεις δελφινιού στην αρχαία ελληνική τέχνη.
[218] Welter 1938, στ. 486, εικ. 9.
[219] Felsch 1979, σελ. 26, 32, 33, εικ. 5:2, 3· 10:1-3, πίν. 2:7, 8· 5:6.
[220] Pape και Benseler 1911, στο λήμμα. Πρβ. Fraser και Matthews 1987, στο λήμμα.
[221] Hammond 1967, Index I, σελ. 810. Πρβ. το όνομα σε σφράγισμα από την Αλβανία. Ceka 1982, σελ. 112, αρ. 58.
[222] Ορλάνδος 1955, σελ. 115. Πρβ. παραπάνω σελ. 204, σημ. 181.
[223] Βλ. παραπάνω σελ. 205. Πρβ. σφραγίσματα κεραμίδων από τη ρωμαϊκή οικία των ιερέων («σκανά») στο Ιερό του Απόλλωνος Μαλεάτα της Επιδαύρου με το όνομα του συγκλητικού Αντωνίνου (2ος αι. μ.Χ.) σε γενική πτώση. Λαμπρινουδάκης 1990, σελ. 14, εικ. 16.
[224] SGDI, αρ. 1349. Πρβ. Δάκαρης 1969β, σελ. 35· Cabanes 1976, σελ. 472, 554, 589, αρ. 75.

που χρονολογείται μετά το 219.[225] Ωστόσο η άφθονη μίκα που εμπεριέχει ο πηλός όλων των αποτμημάτων των κεραμίδων της Γ'IV κατηγορίας, σε συνάρτηση με την παράσταση του δελφινιού, που ίσως διατηρεί τη συμβολική σύνδεση με τη θάλασσα και τις θαλάσσιες δραστηριότητες,[226] θα μπορούσε να μας οδηγήσει στην υπόθεση ότι πρόκειται για κεραμίδες οι οποίες προέρχονται από παράλιο κεραμουργείο και επομένως το όνομα Νικόμαχος μπορεί να ανήκει στον εργώνη ή στον εργοστασιάρχη της κατασκευής τους.[227]

Κατά τον ανασκαφέα[228] τα γράμματα των σφραγισμάτων της Γ'IV κατηγορίας ανήκουν στον 4ο ή στις αρχές του 3ου αι. Ωστόσο, το νι με ισομήκη και παράλληλα τα δύο σκέλη, το άλφα με οριζόντια την εσωτερική κεραία, το όμικρον μικρότερο από τα άλλα γράμματα και το μι με ελαφρά ανοιχτές κεραίες συναντώνται εξίσου συχνά και αργότερα.[229]

Τα σφραγίσματα προέρχονται από την πτέρυγα Ο1 που αποτελεί προσθήκη στη βόρεια πλευρά του Πρυτανείου (Ο) της Δωδώνης.[230] Με βάση τα ανασκαφικά δεδομένα η κατασκευή του οικοδομήματος Ο είναι σύγχρονη με του Βουλευτηρίου (Ε2)[231] στις αρχές του 3ου ή στα τέλη του 4ου αι. Στα τέλη του 3ου αι., κατά την περίοδο του Κοινού (234/3–168/7), χρονολογείται η νέα πτέρυγα Ο1[232] που χρησίμευε για την εστίαση και τη διανυκτέρευση των αρχόντων του Κοινού. Τα σφραγίσματα προέρχονται από τη στέγη αυτής της πτέρυγας[233] και μία χρονολόγησή τους στον ύστερο 3ο αι. θα συνέπιπτε με το χρόνο κατασκευής του κτηρίου. Η περίοδος αυτή έχει σχέση με τη μεγάλη άνθηση του Ιερού και την ανάπτυξη του Κοινού των Ηπειρωτών, το οποίο είχε την έδρα του στο Βουλευτήριο της Δωδώνης. Την επέκταση επέβαλαν

---

[225] Βλ. παραπάνω σελ. 204, σημ. 174.
[226] Όπως στα σφραγίσματα αμφορέων της Θάσου και της Ρόδου, όπου συναντάται ιδιαίτερα συχνά. Fraser 1977, σελ. 40, 41, σημ. 234.
[227] Πρβ. τα άφθονα σφραγίσματα κεραμίδων από τις ανασκαφές στην Πέλλα, που φέρουν ένα κύριο όνομα σε πτώση γενική, το οποίο θεωρείται ως όνομα των ιδιοκτητών ή των επικεφαλής των κεραμουργείων (Παπακωνσταντίνου-Διαμαντούρου 1971, σελ. 71 [αρ. 7], 72 [αρ. 18, 19], 74 [αρ. 38, 40], 76 [αρ. 55, 58], 77 [αρ. 64, 69], 78 [αρ. 82, 84]. Πρβ. Καλτσάς 1988, σελ. 97–105) και το όνομα του κατασκευαστή κεραμίδων από τη Ρόδο: Διονυσίου (Kantzia και Zimmer 1989, σελ. 513). Για ονόματα τεχνιτών σε μέτωπα ηγεμόνων καλυπτήρων από την Ακρόπολη, την Αγορά των Αθηνών και τον Κεραμεικό βλ. Watzinger 1901, σελ. 311, εικ. 4· Buschor 1933, σελ. 58–61, εικ. 82, 83· Agora V, σελ. 43, 71, 107, πίν. 49· Hübner 1976, σελ. 178–180, πίν. 63:6, 7.
[228] Δάκαρης 1982, σελ. 87.
[229] Βλαχοπούλου-Οικονόμου 1986, σελ. 257. Βλ. επίσης παραπάνω σελ. 206.
[230] Για το Ο-Ο1 βλ. Δάκαρης 1972α, σελ. 94–98· Δάκαρης 1973, σελ. 87–98· Δάκαρης 1974, σελ. 73–78· Δάκαρης 1981α, σελ. 67–71· Δάκαρης 1982, σελ. 85–88· Δάκαρης 1983, σελ. 78–80· Δάκαρης 1985β, σελ. 39–44· Δάκαρης 1986γ, σελ. 100· Δάκαρης 1986β, σελ. 64–66.
[231] Βλ. παραπάνω σελ. 193, σημ. 93.
[232] Ας σημειωθεί ότι στη διάρκεια των ανασκαφών στο εσωτερικό του Ο (καλοκαίρι 1989) δεν έχει βρεθεί άλλο σφράγισμα της Γ'IV κατηγορίας, πράγμα που αποδεικνύει ότι τα σφραγίσματα αυτά δεν έχουν καμιά σχέση με τη στέγη του κυρίως Πρυτανείου, αλλά ανήκουν αναμφισβήτητα στη στέγη της νέας πτέρυγας Ο1.
[233] Βλ. Βλαχοπούλου-Οικονόμου 1988–1989, σελ. 77, 78.

οι αυξημένες ανάγκες του Ιερού, που στους χρόνους αυτούς παρουσιάζει μεγάλη οικοδομική και πολιτική δραστηριότητα.[234]

Τα σφραγίσματα έχουν βρεθεί στο στρώμα της ρωμαϊκής καταστροφής[235] του 167, που αποτελεί ένα *terminus ante quem* για τη χρονολόγησή τους. Εξάλλου μετά τη ρωμαϊκή καταστροφή η βόρεια πτέρυγα (Ο1) φαίνεται από τα μέχρι σήμερα ανασκαφικά δεδομένα ότι δεν ανοικοδομήθηκε.[236]

## V. ΕΠΙ ΦΟΡΜΙΣΣΚΟΥ

Κατά μήκος των ορθογώνιων έντυπων σφραγισμάτων της Γ΄V κατηγορίας (Pls. 74–76:a) φέρεται έκτυπη η επιγραφή ΕΠΙΦΟΡΜΙΣΣΚΟΥ. Έχουν βρεθεί τα παρακάτω σφραγίσματα:

1. Αρ.Μ.: 5734.
   ΄Υψ. 0,02 μ. Μήκ. 0,08 μ.
   Πηλός ρόδινος (5YR 7/4).
   Θέση: Στοά του Ε2· ανασκαφή 1968.
   ΕΠΙΦΟΡΜ[ΙΣΣΚΟΥ]

2. Μήκ. 0,06 μ.[237]
   ΕΠΙΦ[ΟΡΜΙΣΣΚΟΥ]

3. ΄Υψ. 0,02 μ. Μήκ. 0,06 μ.
   Πηλός ωχρός καστανός (10YR 7/4).
   Θέση: Στοά του Ε2· ανασκαφή 1967.
   ΕΠΙΦΟ[ΡΜΙΣΣΚΟΥ]

4. Αρ.Μ.: 3505 (Pl. 75:b, κάτω).
   ΄Υψ. 0,02 μ. Μήκ. 0,07 μ.
   Πηλός υπέρυθρος κιτρινωπός (7.5YR 7/6).
   Θέση: Δυτικά του Ε2· ανασκαφή 1965.
   ΕΠΙΦΟΡ[ΜΙΣΣΚΟΥ]

5. Αρ.Μ.: 3585 (Pl. 75:a, αριστερά).
   ΄Υψ. 0,02 μ. Μήκ. 0,10 μ.
   Πηλός ρόδινος (7.5YR 7/4).
   Θέση: Ε2· ανασκαφή 1966.
   ΕΠΙΦΟΡΜΙ[ΣΣΚΟΥ]

6. Αρ.Μ.: 3517.
   ΄Υψ. 0,02 μ. Μήκ. 0,05 μ.
   Πηλός υπέρυθρος (2.5YR 6/6).
   Θέση: Ε2· ανασκαφή 1966.
   ΕΠΙΦ[ΟΡΜΙΣΣΚΟΥ]

7. ΄Υψ. 0,02 μ. Μήκ. 0,04 μ.
   Πηλός υπέρυθρος κιτρινωπός (5YR 7/6).
   Θέση: Ε2· ανασκαφή 1967.
   ΕΠ[ΙΦΟΡΜΙΣΣΚΟΥ]

8. Αρ.Μ.: 4091 (Pl. 74:b, επάνω).[238]
   ΄Υψ. 0,02 μ. Μήκ. 0,14 μ.
   Πηλός ρόδινος (7.5YR 7/4).
   Θέση: Στοά του Ε2· ανασκαφή 1966.
   Ε]ΠΙΦΟΡΜΙΣΣΚΟΥ

9. Αρ.Μ.: 4101.
   ΄Υψ. 0,02 μ. Μήκ. 0,09 μ.
   Πηλός υπέρυθρος κιτρινωπός (5YR 7/6).
   Θέση: Στοά του Ε2· ανασκαφή 1966.
   ΕΠΙΦΟΡ[ΜΙΣΣΚΟΥ]

10. Αρ.Μ.: 4089 (Pl. 74:b, κάτω).[239]
    ΄Υψ. 0,02 μ. Μήκ. 0,14 μ.
    Πηλός ρόδινος (7.5YR 7/4).
    Θέση: Ε2· ανασκαφή 1966.
    [Ε]ΠΙΦΟΡΜΙΣ[Σ]ΚΟ[Υ]

11. Αρ.Μ.: 4090 (Pl. 76:a, επάνω αριστερά).[240]
    ΄Υψ. 0,02 μ. Μήκ. 0,05 μ.
    Πηλός ρόδινος (7.5YR 7/4).
    Θέση: Ε2· ανασκαφή 1966.
    [Ε]ΠΙΦΟ[ΡΜΙΣΣΚΟΥ]

---

[234] Δάκαρης 1982, σελ. 87. Πρβ. παραπάνω σελ. 188.
[235] Δάκαρης 1982, σελ. 85. Για τη ρωμαϊκή καταστροφή βλ. παραπάνω σελ. 194, σημ. 104.
[236] Δάκαρης 1986β, σελ. 65.
[237] Carapanos 1878, σελ. 112 (7), πίν. 61:10· Franke 1961, σελ. 312 (2), 314. Παρά την επισταμένη έρευνα το θραύσμα αυτό δεν έχει βρεθεί στις αποθήκες του Μουσείου Ιωαννίνων.
[238] Δάκαρης 1966, σελ. 82, πίν. 82:β (επάνω δεξιά).
[239] Δάκαρης 1966, σελ. 82, πίν. 82:β (κάτω).
[240] Δάκαρης 1966, σελ. 82, πίν. 82:β (επάνω αριστερά).

## ΤΑ ΣΦΡΑΓΙΣΜΑΤΑ ΚΕΡΑΜΙΔΩΝ ΑΠΟ ΤΟ ΙΕΡΟ ΤΗΣ ΔΩΔΩΝΗΣ

12. Αρ.Μ.: 4100 (Pl. 74:a, επάνω).
 Ύψ. 0,02 μ. Μήκ. 0,11 μ.
 Πηλός υπέρυθρος κιτρινωπός (5YR 7/8).
 Θέση: Στοά του Ε2· ανασκαφή 1966.
 [Ε]ΠΙΦΟΡΜΙC[CΚΟΥ]

13. Αρ.Μ.: 5728 (Pl. 74:a, κάτω αριστερά).
 Ύψ. 0,02 μ. Μήκ. 0,05 μ.
 Πηλός υπέρυθρος κιτρινωπός (5YR 7/8).
 Θέση: Ε2· ανασκαφή 1971.
 [ΕΠ]ΙΦΟΡΜ[ΙCCΚΟΥ]

14. Αρ.Μ.: 3698 (Pl. 75:b, επάνω δεξιά).
 Ύψ. 0,02 μ. Μήκ. 0,09 μ.
 Πηλός ρόδινος (7.5YR 7/4).
 [ΕΠ]ΙΦΟΡΜΙ[CCΚΟΥ]

15. Ύψ. 0,02 μ. Μήκ. 0,15 μ. (Pl. 75:a, δεξιά).
 Πηλός υπέρυθρος κιτρινωπός (7.5YR 7/6).
 Θέση: Ε2· ανασκαφή 1967.
 [ΕΠ]ΙΦΟΡΜΙCCΚ[ΟΥ]

16. Αρ.Μ.: 4104 (Pl. 74:a, κάτω μέσον).
 Ύψ. 0,02 μ. Μήκ. 0,05 μ.
 Πηλός ρόδινος (7.5YR 7/4).
 Θέση: Ε2· ανασκαφή 1966.
 [ΕΠΙΦ]ΟΡΜΙC[CΚΟΥ]

17. Αρ.Μ.: 5828.
 Ύψ. 0,02 μ. Μήκ. 0,02 μ.
 Πηλός ρόδινος (7.5YR 7/4).
 Θέση: Ε2· ανασκαφή 1966.
 [ΕΠΙΦ]ΟΡ[ΜΙCCΚΟΥ]

18. Αρ.Μ.: 5731 (Pl. 75:b, επάνω αριστερά).
 Ύψ. 0,02 μ. Μήκ. 0,09 μ.
 Πηλός ρόδινος (7.5YR 7/4).
 Θέση: Ε2· ανασκαφή 1969.
 [ΕΠΙΦΟ]ΡΜΙC[C]Κ[ΟΥ]

19. Ύψ. 0,02 μ. Μήκ. 0,12 μ.
 Πηλός υπέρυθρος κιτρινωπός (7.5YR 7/6).
 Θέση: Ε2· ανασκαφή 1967.
 [ΕΠΙΦΟ]ΡΜΙCCΚ[ΟΥ]

20. Ύψ. 0,02 μ. Μήκ. 0,08 μ.
 Πηλός υπέρυθρος κιτρινωπός (7.5YR 7/6).
 Θέση: Ο1· ανασκαφή 1981.
 [ΕΠΙΦΟΡ]ΜΙC[C]ΚΟΥ

21. Ύψ. 0,02 μ. Μήκ. 0,09 μ.
 Πηλός ρόδινος (7.5YR 7/4).
 Θέση: Ε2· ανασκαφή 1967.
 [ΕΠΙΦΟΡ]ΜΙCCΚΟΥ

22. Αρ.Μ.: 5746 (Pl. 74:a, κάτω δεξιά).
 Ύψ. 0,02 μ. Μήκ. 0,04 μ.
 Πηλός ρόδινος (7.5YR 7/4).
 Θέση: Ε2· ανασκαφή 1969.
 [ΕΠΙΦΟ]ΡΜΙCC[ΚΟΥ]

23. Ύψ. 0,02 μ. Μήκ. 0,07 μ.
 Πηλός υπέρυθρος κιτρινωπός (5YR 7/8).
 Θέση: Ε2· ανασκαφή 1967.
 [ΕΠΙΦΟΡΜ]ΙCCΚΟΥ

24. Αρ.Μ.: 3695 (Pl. 76:a, κάτω αριστερά).
 Ύψ. 0,01 μ. Μήκ. 0,05 μ.
 Πηλός ρόδινος (7.5YR 7/4).
 Θέση: Στοά του Ε2· ανασκαφή 1968.
 [ΕΠΙΦΟΡ]ΜΙC[ΚΟΥ]

25. Αρ.Μ.: 4103.
 Ύψ. 0,02 μ. Μήκ. 0,08 μ.
 Πηλός ρόδινος (5YR 7/4).
 Θέση: Νότια του Ε2· ανασκαφή 1966.
 [ΕΠΙΦΟΡΜΙ]CCΚΟΥ

26. Αρ.Μ.: 5732.
 Ύψ. 0,02 μ. Μήκ. 0,08 μ.
 Πηλός υπέρυθρος κιτρινωπός (5YR 6/8).
 Θέση: Ε2· ανασκαφή 1969.
 [ΕΠΙΦΟΡΜΙ]C[C]ΚΟΥ

27. Ύψ. 0,02 μ. Μήκ. 0,06 μ.
 Πηλός ρόδινος (7.5YR 7/4).
 Θέση: Ε2· ανασκαφή 1967.
 [ΕΠΙΦΟΡΜΙC]CΚΟΥ

28. Αρ.Μ.: 5737 (Pl. 76:a, επάνω δεξιά).
 Ύψ. 0,02 μ. Μήκ. 0,05 μ.
 Πηλός υπέρυθρος (2.5YR 6/8).
 Θέση: Ε2· ανασκαφή 1968.
 [ΕΠΙΦΟΡΜΙCC]ΚΟΥ

29. Ύψ. 0,02 μ. Μήκ. 0,03 μ.
 Πηλός υπέρυθρος κιτρινωπός (5YR 7/8).
 Θέση: Ε2· ανασκαφή 1967.
 [ΕΠΙΦΟΡΜΙCCΚ]ΟΥ

30. Ύψ. 0,02 μ. Μήκ. 0,08 μ.
 Πηλός υπέρυθρος κιτρινωπός (5YR 6/8).
 Ανασκαφή 1967.
 [ΕΠΙΦΟΡΜΙCCΚ]ΟΥ

31. Αρ.Μ.: 5747 (Pl. 76:a, κάτω δεξιά).
 Ύψ. 0,02 μ. Μήκ. 0,04 μ.
 Πηλός ρόδινος (7.5YR 7/4).
 Θέση: Ε2· ανασκαφή 1969.
 [ΕΠΙΦΟΡΜΙCC]ΚΟΥ

Η χρήση της πρόθεσης ἐπί υποδεικνύει ότι το όνομα Φορμίσσκος είναι χωρίς αμφιβολία το όνομα ενός επώνυμου άρχοντα,[241] και όχι το όνομα του κεραμουργού. Η αναζήτηση του ονόματος Φορμίσκος ή Φορμίσσκος στα σχετικά ονοματολογικά λεξικά της υπόλοιπης Ελλάδας, εκτός Ηπείρου, έχει αποβεί άγονη. Συγγενικό όνομα, από το οποίο πρέπει να προέρχεται το Φορμίσκος είναι το Φορμίων,[242] το οποίο συναντάται συχνά. Πρέπει λοιπόν να θεωρηθεί ως τοπικό όνομα της Δυτικής Ελλάδας, όπου μαρτυρείται σε μία επιγραφή από το Ροδοτόπι (Πασσαρών) του α' μισού του 2ου αι.[243] και σε δύο μολύβδινα ελάσματα από τη Δωδώνη.[244] Ας σημειωθεί ότι τα αρχικά ΦΟΡ, από τα οποία υπονοείται πιθανόν το όνομα Φορμίων ή το όνομα Φορμίσκος, σώζονται σε αργυρές δραχμές των χρόνων του Κοινού των Ηπειρωτών.[245] Κατά τον Δάκαρη[246] η μορφή των γραμμάτων στα νομίσματα και τα σφραγίσματα των κεραμίδων είναι ίδια.

Τα γράμματα των σφραγισμάτων είναι τυπικά της Ελληνιστικής περιόδου. Το έψιλον αποδίδεται με τη χαρακτηριστική για τους τρεις τελευταίους προχριστιανικούς αιώνες μηνοειδή μορφή.[247] Το πι αποδίδεται με ισοϋψείς τις κατακόρυφες κεραίες, το όμικρον ισομέγεθες με τα άλλα γράμματα, το μι με παράλληλα τα δύο σκέλη[248] και το σίγμα μηνοειδές.[249] Ο διπλασιασμός συμφώνων και ιδιαίτερα του σίγμα μπροστά από το ταυ ή το κάπα, όπως στην περίπτωση της επιγραφής ἐπί Φορμίσσκου των σφραγισμάτων, συναντάται συχνά στην Ήπειρο.[250]

Ο Δάκαρης[251] χρονολογεί τις κεραμίδες με την επιγραφή Ἐπί Φορμίσσκου στους χρόνους της Δημοκρατίας (234/3-168/7) και πιθανόν μετά την αιτωλική καταστροφή,[252] άποψη η οποία ενισχύεται από την πιθανότητα ταύτισης του Φορμίσσκου των σφραγισμάτων με τον Φορμίσκο της δραχμής του Ηπειρωτικού Κοινού και των

---

[241] Πρβ. Ἐπί Κερκίωνος από την Κασσώπη. Δάκαρης 1980γ, σελ. 31, 32, πίν. 39:β, γ. Για την πρόθεση ἐπί + το όνομα επώνυμου άρχοντα βλ. Ορλάνδος 1955, σελ. 115, σημ. 7· Franke 1961, σελ. 314 και σε άφθονα σφραγίσματα από την Αλβανία: Andrea 1976, σελ. 350, πίν. XVIII:1· Tartari 1977-1978, σελ. 217, πίν. I:β1-3· Ceka 1982, σελ. 110, αρ. 38, πίν. III:39· Hidri 1986, σελ. 110, πίν. XIV:2 και ιδιαίτερα Tartari 1988, σελ. 96-98, πίν. IV.

[242] Όπως από το Παρμένων προέρχεται το Παρμενίσκος. Fraser και Rönne 1957, σελ. 167. Για το Φορμίων βλ. Fraser και Rönne 1957, σελ. 142 (3)· Pape και Benseler 1911, στο λήμμα· Fraser και Matthews 1987, στο λήμμα. Για την Ήπειρο βλ. Hammond 1967, Index I, σελ. 816.

[243] Ευαγγελίδης 1914, σελ. 239. Πρβ. Cabanes 1976, σελ. 552, αρ. 29 και Hammond 1967, σελ. 651, σημ. 2 και Index I, σελ. 816.

[244] SGDI, αρ. 1359. Πρβ. Carapanos 1878, σελ. 57, πίν. 30:1. Για το δεύτερο έλασμα με κατάλογο πολιτών οι οποίοι είχαν προσφέρει χρηματικά ποσά για την ανοικοδόμηση του Ιερού μετά την αιτωλική καταστροφή (219) βλ. παραπάνω σελ. 204, σημ. 174. Στο έλασμα αυτό το όνομα Φορμίσκος αναφέρεται δύο φορές και πιθανόν πρόκειται για παππού και εγγονό.

[245] Franke 1961, σελ. 156, 174, πίν. 24:V 85 (ομάδα II, σειρά 20).

[246] Δάκαρης 1966, σελ. 82, πίν. 82:β.

[247] Στον 4ο αι. συναντάται σποραδικά. Klaffenbach 1957, σελ. 43.

[248] Για τη μορφή του πι, του όμικρον και του μι κατά την Ελληνιστική περίοδο βλ. παραπάνω σελ. 206, σημ. 201, 202, σελ. 209, σημ. 229.

[249] Για το μηνοειδές σίγμα βλ. παραπάνω σελ. 199, σημ. 128. Πρβ. Franke 1961, σελ. 142.

[250] Ευαγγελίδης 1914, σελ. 234, όπου και σχετικά παραδείγματα. Πρβ. Hammond 1967, σελ. 735.

[251] Δάκαρης 1966, σελ. 82.

[252] Για την ανοικοδόμηση του Ιερού μετά την αιτωλική καταστροφή βλ. παραπάνω σελ. 188, σημ. 46.

μολύβδινων ελασμάτων από τη Δωδώνη. Ας σημειωθεί ότι πρόκειται για τη μοναδική κατηγορία σφραγισμάτων από τη Δωδώνη, η οποία με βεβαιότητα προέρχεται από τη στέγη του Βουλευτηρίου (Ε2).[253]

## ΒΙΒΛΙΟΓΡΑΦΙΑ

*Agora* V = H. S. Robinson, *Pottery of the Roman Period: Chronology* (*Athenian Agora* V), Princeton 1959
*Agora* XIV = H. A. Thompson και R. E. Wycherley, *The Agora of Athens* (*Athenian Agora* XIV), Princeton 1972
*Albanien* = *Albanien. Schätze aus dem Land der Skipetaren*, Mainz 1988
Andrea, Z. 1976. "Gërmimet arkeologjike të viteve 1974–75," *Iliria* 6, σελ. 331–366
Αντωνίου, Α. 1991. Δωδώνη. Συμβολή Ηπειρωτών στην ανοικοδόμηση κτισμάτων του Ιερού της Δωδώνης (μετά το 219 π.Χ.), Αθήναι
Αρβανιτόπουλος, Α. 1928. Αι γραπταί στήλαι Δημητριάδος Παγασών, Αθήναι
Bereti, V. 1977–1978. "Gërmime në Triport," *Iliria* 7–8, σελ. 285–288
Boisacq, E. 1950. *Dictionnaire étymologique de la langue grecque*, Heidelberg
Brommer, F. 1988. "Redende Zeichen," *AA* [*JdI* 103], σελ. 69–70
Buschor, E. 1933. *Die Tondächer der Akropolis*, II, *Stirnziegel*, Berlin/Leipzig
Cabanes, P. 1976. *L' Épire de la mort de Pyrrhos à la conquête romaine (272–167 av. J.C.)*, Paris
———. 1988. "Les concours des NAIA de Dodone," *Nikephoros* 1, σελ. 49–84
Carapanos, C. 1878. *Dodone et ses ruines*, Paris
Ceka, N. 1982. "Vula antike mbi tjegulla në trevën ndërmjet Aosit dhe Genusit," *Iliria* 12:1, σελ. 103–130
Χρυσοστόμου, Π. 1980. «ΙΒ΄ Εφορεία Προϊστορικών και Κλασικών Αρχαιοτήτων», Δελτ 35, 1980, Β΄1 [1988], σελ. 307–311
———. 1982. «ΙΒ΄ Εφορεία Προϊστορικών και Κλασικών Αρχαιοτήτων», Δελτ 37, 1982, Β΄2 [1989], σελ. 260–263
Cook, A. 1965. *Zeus. A Study in Ancient Religion* II, New York
Δάκαρης, Σ. 1952. «Ανασκαφή εις Καστρίτσαν Ιωαννίνων», Πρακτικά 1952 [1955], σελ. 362–386
———. 1960. «Το Ιερόν της Δωδώνης», Δελτ 16, 1960 [1962], σελ. 4–40
———. 1963α. «Αρχαιότητες και μνημεία Ηπείρου», Δελτ 18, 1963, Β΄2 [1965], σελ. 149–157
———. 1963β. «ΗΠΕΙΡΟΣ. Νεκυομαντείον Ἐφύρας», Ἔργον 1963 [1964], σελ. 57–64
———. 1964α. Οι γενεαλογικοί μύθοι των Μολοσσών, εν Αθήναις
———. 1964β. «ΗΠΕΙΡΟΣ. Νεκυομαντείον Ἐφύρας», Ἔργον 1964 [1965], σελ. 51–64
———. 1964γ. «Αρχαιότητες και μνημεία Ηπείρου», Δελτ 19, 1964, Β΄3 [1967], σελ. 305–314
———. 1965. «Ανασκαφή του Ιερού της Δωδώνης», Πρακτικά 1965 [1967], σελ. 53–65
———. 1966. «Ανασκαφή του Ιερού της Δωδώνης», Πρακτικά 1966 [1968], σελ. 71–84
———. 1967. «Ανασκαφή του Ιερού της Δωδώνης», Πρακτικά 1967 [1969], σελ. 33–54
———. 1967–1968. «Επιτύμβιος στήλη (ή περί δρυολατρείας)», Χαριστήριον εις Αν. Κ. Ορλάνδον, τόμ. Δ΄, Αθήναι, σελ. 386–405
———. 1968. «Ανασκαφή του Ιερού της Δωδώνης», Πρακτικά 1968 [1970], σελ. 42–59
———. 1969α. «Δωδώνη», Ἔργον 1969 [1970], σελ. 19–28
———. 1969β. «Ανασκαφή του Ιερού της Δωδώνης», Πρακτικά 1969 [1971], σελ. 26–35
———. 1971. «Ανασκαφή του Ιερού της Δωδώνης», Πρακτικά 1971 [1973], σελ. 124–129
———. 1972α. «Ανασκαφή του Ιερού της Δωδώνης», Πρακτικά 1972 [1974], σελ. 94–98
———. 1972β. «Θεσπρωτία», Αρχαίες ελληνικές πόλεις 15, Αθήναι
———. 1973. «Ανασκαφή του Ιερού της Δωδώνης», Πρακτικά 1973 [1975], σελ. 87–98
———. 1974. «Ανασκαφή του Ιερού της Δωδώνης», Πρακτικά 1974 [1976], σελ. 73–78
———. 1976. «Αχέρων–Εφύρα», Ἔργον 1976 [1977], σελ. 80–88
———. 1980α. «Οι αρχές της νομισματοκοπίας στην αρχαία Ήπειρο», Ηπειρωτικά Χρονικά 22, σελ. 21–26

---

[253] Για τις οικοδομικές φάσεις του Ε2 και τις αντίστοιχες στέγες του βλ. παραπάνω σελ. 189, σημ. 49.

———. 1980β. «Ωκύπτερα», Ηπειρωτικά Χρονικά 22, σελ. 27–34

———. 1980γ. «Ανασκαφή στην Κασσώπη Ηπείρου», Πρακτικά 1980 [1982], σελ. 21–32

———. 1981α. «Ανασκαφή στο Ιερό της Δωδώνης», Πρακτικά 1981 [1983], σελ. 67–71

———. 1981β. «Δωδώνη», Έργον 1981 [1982], σελ. 30–31

———. 1982. «Ανασκαφή Δωδώνης», Πρακτικά 1982 [1984], σελ. 85–88

———. 1983. «Ανασκαφή στο Ιερό της Δωδώνης», Πρακτικά 1983 [1986], σελ. 78–80

———. 1985α. «Δωδώνη», Έργον 1985 [1986], σελ. 31–35

———. 1985β. «Ανασκαφή Δωδώνης», Πρακτικά 1985 [1990], σελ. 39–44

———. 1986α. «Το Όρραον. Το σπίτι στην αρχαία Ήπειρο», ΑρχΕφ, σελ. 108–146

———. 1986β. Δωδώνη. Αρχαιολογικός Οδηγός, Ιωάννινα

———. 1986γ. «Ανασκαφή Δωδώνης», Πρακτικά 1986 [1990], σελ. 100

———. 1987. «Η ρωμαϊκή πολιτική στην Ήπειρο», στα Πρακτικά του Α΄ Διεθνούς Συμποσίου για τη Νικόπολη, Ευ. Χρυσός, επιμ., Πρέβεζα, σελ. 1–21

———. 1989. Κασσώπη. Νεότερες ανασκαφές 1977–1983, Ιωάννινα

Dautaj, B. 1972. "La cité illyrienne de Dimale," *Iliria* 2:2, σελ. 149–157

———. 1974. "Rezultatet e gërmimeve arkeologjike të vitit 1973 në Dimal," *Iliria* 3, σελ. 443–446

———. 1976. "Dimale à la lumière des données archéologiques," *Iliria* 4:1, σελ. 385–398

———. 1986. "Organizimi politik e shoqëror i bashkësisë dimalite në shek. III–II p.e. sonë," *Iliria* 16:1, σελ. 101–109

Daux, G. 1959. "Chronique des fouilles en 1958," *BCH* 83, σελ. 568–793

———. 1967. "Chronique des fouilles et découvertes archéologiques en Grèce en 1966," *BCH* 91, σελ. 623–889

Del Chiaro, M. A. 1989. "Villa with a View," *Archaeology* 42, σελ. 58–61

Δοντάς, Γ. 1966. «Ανασκαφαί Κερκύρας», Πρακτικά 1966 [1968], σελ. 85–94

Dremsizova, C. 1963. «Tuiles à estampilles de la Nécropole d'Apollonia», *Apollonia, Les fouilles dans la Nécropole d'Apollonia en 1947–1949*, σελ. 321–324, 286, 387, Sofia

Dyggve, E., και F. Poulsen. 1948. *Das Laphrion. Der Tempelbezirk von Kalydon* (Arkaeologisk-Kunsthistoriske Skrifter I, ii), København

Ευαγγελίδης, Δ. 1914. «Επιγραφαί εξ Ηπείρου», ΑρχΕφ, σελ. 232–241

———. 1935. «Ηπειρωτικαί Έρευναι. Ι. Η ανασκαφή της Δωδώνης 1935», Ηπειρωτικά Χρονικά, σελ. 192–260

———. 1956. «Ψήφισμα του βασιλέως Νεοπτολέμου εκ Δωδώνης», ΑρχΕφ, σελ. 1–13

———. 1959. «Ανασκαφαί Δωδώνης», Πρακτικά 1959 [1965], σελ. 114

Ευαγγελίδης, Δ., και Σ. Δάκαρης. 1959. «Το Ιερόν της Δωδώνης. Α. Ιερά Οικία», ΑρχΕφ, σελ. 1–176

Felsch, R. 1979. "Boiotische Ziegelwerkstätten archaischer Zeit," *AM* 94, σελ. 1–40

———. 1990. "Further Stamped Roof Tiles from Central Greece, Attica and the Peloponnese," στα *Proceedings of the First International Conference on Archaic Greek Architectural Terracottas, Athens, December 2–4, 1988* (Hesperia 59, 1990), N. A. Winter, επιμ., σελ. 301–323

Franke, P. 1961. *Die antiken Münzen von Epirus*, Wiesbaden

Fraser, P. M. 1977. *Rhodian Funerary Monuments*, Oxford

Fraser, P. M., και E. Matthews. 1987. *A Lexicon of Greek Personal Names* I, Oxford

Fraser, P. M., και T. Rönne. 1957. *Boeotian and West Greek Tombstones* (Acta Instituti Atheniensis Regni Sueciae, 4°, vi), Lund

Frisk, Hj. 1960. *Griechisches etymologisches Wörterbuch*, Heidelberg

Garlan, V. 1986. "Quelques nouveaux ateliers amphoriques à Thasos," στα *Actes du colloque international organisé par le Centre National de la Recherche Scientifique, l'Université de Rennes II et l'École Française d'Athènes (Athènes, 10–12 Septembre 1984). Recherches sur les amphores grecques* (BCH Supplement 13), J.-Y. Empereur και Y. Garlan, επιμ., σελ. 201–276

Grace, V. 1963. "Notes on the Amphoras from the Koroni Peninsula," *Hesperia* 32, σελ. 319–334

———. 1985. "The Middle Stoa Dated by Amphora Stamps," *Hesperia* 54, σελ. 1–54

Gravani, K. 1986. "Die Keramik von Kassope. Ein vorläufiger Überblick," στο *Wohnen in der klassischen Polis*, I, *Haus und Stadt im klassischen Griechenland*, W. Hoepfner και E.-L. Schwandner, επιμ., München, σελ. 123–134

Γραβάνη, K. 1988–1989. «Κεραμεική των ελληνιστικών χρόνων από την Ήπειρο», Ηπειρωτικά Χρονικά 29, σελ. 89–132

Guarducci, M. 1969. *Epigrafia greca*, II, *Epigrafi di carattere pubblico*, Roma

Hammond, N. 1967. *Epirus. The Geography, the Ancient Remains, the History and the Topography of Epirus and Adjacent Areas*, Oxford

Hidri, H. 1986. "Nekropoli antik i Dyrrahut," *Iliria* 16:2, σελ. 99–113

Hübner, G. 1973. "Dachterrakotten aus dem Kerameikos von Athen," *AM* 88, σελ. 67–143

———. 1976. "Antefixa Deorum Athenarum," *AM* 91, σελ. 175–183

Icard, S. 1968. *Dictionary of Greek Coin Inscriptions*, Chicago

*IG* = *Inscriptiones Graecae*

Jacobsthal, P. 1906. *Der Blitz in der orientalischen und griechischen Kunst*, Berlin

Καλτσάς, N. 1988. Πήλινες διακοσμημένες κεραμώσεις από τη Μακεδονία, Αθήνα

Kantzia, Ch., και G. Zimmer. 1989. "Rhodische Kolosse," *AA* [*JdI* 104], σελ. 497–523

Kassab, D. 1988. *Statuettes en terre cuite de Myrina. Corpus des signatures, monogrammes, lettres et signes* (Bibliothèque de l'Institut Français d'Études Anatoliennes d'Istanbul XXIX), Paris

Klaffenbach, G. 1957. *Griechische Epigraphik*, Göttingen

Κουλεϊμάνη-Βοκοτοπούλου, Ι. 1975. Χαλκαί κορινθιουργείς πρόχοι, Αθήναι

Kyrieleis, H. 1973. "Die Porträtmünzen Ptolemaios' V und seiner Eltern," *JdI* 88, σελ. 213–246

Λαμπρινουδάκης, Β. 1990. «Επίδαυρος», Έργον 1990 [1991], σελ. 11–21

*Lateres Signati Ostienses* (Acta Instituti Finlandiae v. 7:1–2), Roma 1978

Le Roy, Ch. 1967. *Les terres cuites architecturales* (Fouilles de Delphes II), Paris

Lehmann, K. 1960. *The Inscriptions on Ceramics and Minor Objects* (Samothrace II, ii), New York

Lévêque, P. 1957. *Pyrrhos*, Paris

Mano, A. 1974. "Nekropoli i dystë i Apolonisë," *Iliria* 3, σελ. 153–238

Martin, R. 1965. *Manuel d'architecture grecque* I, Paris

Μαστροκώστας, Ευθ. 1963. «Ανασκαφή του Τείχους Δυμαίων», Πρακτικά 1963 [1966], σελ. 93–98

Μπακαλάκης, Γ. 1934. «Ανασκαφή εν Φλωρίνη της Άνω Μακεδονίας», Πρακτικά 1934 [1935], σελ. 91–114

Nikolaidou-Patera, M. 1986. "Un nouveau centre de production d'amphores timbrées en Macédoine," στα *Actes du colloque international organisé par le Centre National de la Recherche Scientifique, l'Université de Rennes II et l'École Française d'Athènes (Athènes, 10–12 Septembre 1984). Recherches sur les amphores grecques* (BCH Supplement 13), J.-Y. Empereur και Y. Garlan, επιμ., σελ. 485–490

Ορλάνδος, Α. 1955. Τα υλικά δομής των αρχαίων Ελλήνων κατά τους συγγραφείς, τας επιγραφάς και τα μνημεία, Α', Αθήναι

Παντερμαλής, Δ. 1987. «Η κεράμωση του ανακτόρου της Βεργίνας», Αμητός. Τιμητικός τόμος για τον καθηγητή Μανόλη Ανδρόνικο ΙΙ, Θεσσαλονίκη, σελ. 579–605

Papajani, L. 1976. "La cité illyrienne de Klos," *Iliria* 4:1, σελ. 411–422

Παπακωνσταντίνου-Διαμαντούρου, Δ. 1971. Πέλλα. Ιστορική επισκόπησις και μαρτυρίαι, εν Αθήναις

Pape, W., και G. Benseler. 1911. *Wörterbuch der griechischen Eigennamen*, Braunschweig

Πέππα-Δελμούζου, Ντ. 1967–1968. «Τεκτονικά σημεία και επιγραφαί επί μαρμαρίνων αρχιτεκτονικών μελών», Χαριστήριον εις Αν. Κ. Ορλάνδον, τομ. Δ', Αθήναι, σελ. 369–385

———. 1970. «Επιγραφική Συλλογή Αθηνών», Δελτ 25, 1970, Β'1 [1972], σελ. 14–15

Πέτσας, Φ. 1950–1951. «Ειδήσεις εκ της 10ης αρχαιολογικής περιφερείας (Ηπείρου)», ΑρχΕφ, σελ. 31–49

———. 1952. «Ειδήσεις εκ της 10ης αρχαιολογικής περιφερείας (Ηπείρου)», ΑρχΕφ, σελ. 1–15

———. 1961. «Ωναί εκ της Ημαθίας», ΑρχΕφ, σελ. 1–57

*RE* = *Real-Encyclopädie der classischen Altertumswissenschaft*, Stuttgart 1893 κεξ.

Reichel, W., και A. Wilhelm. 1901. "Das Heiligthum der Artemis zu Lusoi," *ÖJh* 4, σελ. 1–89

Ρωμαίος, Κ. 1933. «Εκ του αρχαιοτέρου ναού της Φιγαλείας», ΑρχΕφ, σελ. 1-25
Rumpf, A. 1969. *Die Meerwesen auf den antiken Sarkophagreliefs* (*Die antiken Sarkophagreliefs* V, i), Roma
Schrader, H. 1937. "Zur Chronologie der elischen Münzen," ΑρχΕφ, σελ. 208-216
*SGDI* = H. Collitz και A. Fick. 1899. *Sammlung der griechischen Dialekt-Inschriften* II, Göttingen
Shear, T. L. 1939. "The Campaign of 1938," *Hesperia* 8, σελ. 201-246
Stubbing, S. 1929. *The Dolphin in the Literature and Art of Greece and Rome*, Menasha
Tartari, F. 1977-1978. "Hedhurinë me qeramikë lokale nga Durrësi," *Iliria* 7-8, σελ. 217-222
———. 1988. "Godinë e lashtë banimi në sheshin e parkut 'Rinia', Durrës," *Iliria* 18:1, σελ. 91-108
Τζουβάρα-Σούλη, Χρ. 1979. Η λατρεία των γυναικείων θεοτήτων εις την αρχαίαν Ήπειρον (διδ. διατριβή), Ιωάννινα
———. 1984. «Λατρεία του Απόλλωνα Αγυιέα στην Ήπειρο», Δωδώνη 13, σελ. 427-442
———. 1987-1988. «Κορινθιακές επιδράσεις στη λατρεία της αρχαίας Ηπείρου», στα Πρακτικά Γ' Διεθνούς Συνεδρίου Πελοποννησιακών Σπουδών, Αθήναι, σελ. 97-120
Ugolini, L. 1942. "L'Acropoli di Butrinto," *Albania Antica* 3, σελ. 1-291
Βλαχοπούλου-Οικονόμου, Α. 1979. «Έντυπες σφραγίδες σε λαβές αμφορέων από το Νεκυομαντείο του Αχέροντα και τη Δωδώνη», Δωδώνη 8, σελ. 279-298
———. 1986. Ηγεμόνες και κορυφαίες κέραμοι με διακόσμηση από την Ήπειρο. Τύπος «άνθους λωτού-ελίκων» (διδ. διατριβή), Ιωάννινα
———. 1988-1989. «Διακοσμημένα μέτωπα ηγεμόνων κεράμων από τη Δωδώνη. Τύπος ελίκων», Ηπειρωτικά Χρονικά 29, σελ. 67-87
Βοκοτοπούλου, Ι. 1967. «Αρχαιότητες και μνημεία Ηπείρου», Δελτ 22, 1967, Β'2 [1969], σελ. 339-349
———. 1973. Οδηγός Μουσείου Ιωαννίνων, Αθήνα
———. 1975. «Αρχαιότητες και μνημεία Ηπείρου», Δελτ 30, 1975, Β'2 [1983], σελ. 209-217
———. 1976. «Εφορεία Κλασικών Αρχαιοτήτων Ηπείρου», Δελτ 31, 1976, Β' 2 [1984], σελ. 193-199
Walter-Karydi, E. 1981. "Bronzen aus Dodona—Eine epirotische Erzbildnerschule," *JbBerlMus* 23, σελ. 11-48
Watzinger, C. 1901. "Die Ausgrabungen am Westabhange der Akropolis," *AM* 26, σελ. 305-332
Welter, G. 1938. "Aeginetica XIII-XXIV," *JdI* 53, στ. 480-540
———. 1954. "Aeginetica XXV-XXXVI," *AA* [*JdI* 69], στ. 28-48
Wensler, A. 1989. "Zur Datierung des Temenos für den Herrscherkult in Pergamon," *AA* [*JdI* 104], σελ. 33-42
Woodhead, A. 1967. *The Study of Greek Inscriptions*, Cambridge
Ζαχαριάδου, Ο., Δ. Κυριακού, και Ε. Μπαζιωτοπούλου. 1985. «Σωστική ανασκαφή στον ανισόπεδο κόμβο Λένορμαν-Κωνσταντινουπόλεως», ΑΑΑ 18, σελ. 39-50

AMALIA VLACHOPOULOU-OÏKONOMOU
DEPARTMENT OF CLASSICAL ARCHAEOLOGY
University of Ioannina
Ioannina, Greece

# ARCHITECTURAL TERRACOTTAS FROM THE TOWNS OF KAONIA: ANTIGONEA AND BUTHROT

(PLATES 77, 78)

ACCORDING TO literary sources, Kaonia was situated along the coast in southern Albania, from the Akrokeraun mountains in the north to the Thyamis river in the south. Its interior stretched through the valley of the Drinos river to the Aoos river, which separates Illyria from Epeiros.[1] Historical and archaeological sources reveal an intensely populated area during antiquity with great economic and cultural prosperity reflected in its early and intensive urbanization.[2]

Buthrot, Antigonea, and Foenike rank among the most important urban centers. Systematic, long-term excavations in these towns have shed light on different aspects of the cities' rich cultural life. Archaeologists have uncovered monumental architecture as well as local and imported works of art that reflect high cultural, economic, and artistic activity.[3]

Among the decorative finds some architectural terracottas, treated for the first time in this paper, attract attention. Twenty fragments of antefixes are examined, giving (1) classification by characteristic features, (2) identification of techniques and prototypes, (3) description by center of origin and motifs, and (4) approximate dating, based on the type of decoration and comparison to related finds.

In Antigonea, although tiles were excavated in great numbers, antefixes are very rare; all in all only six pieces have been found, of which only two are fairly complete and well preserved, the others being fragmentary. All are made of red clay mixed with lime granules. Their composition and color are the same as those tiles found in other buildings, an indication not only of the existence of local workshops for producing tiles but also of local production of antefixes.

According to decorative motifs, the antefixes of Antigonea fall into two groups. The first variant of Group 1 includes antefixes with a palmette in relief on the front (Pl. 77:a). The palmette has as its heart a bud from which ten petals radiate, five on each side. The petals are arched at their tips and end in a spiral. Below the palmette are two symmetrical spirals, almost horizontal, accompanied by other leaves.

The second variant, which is rather fragmentary, has the same motif: the palmette, with its heart in the form of a rhombus from which petals branch out on both sides (Pl. 77:b). There are also lateral floral motifs in the form of a spiral. Both of these architectural terracottas of Group 1 were found on the main street of the agora of the town, which is well dated to the beginning of the 3rd century B.C.[4]

---

[1] Budina 1969.
[2] Prendi and Budina 1970, pp. 67–87.
[3] Ugolini 1932; Ugolini 1942; Budina 1972.
[4] Budina and Stamati 1989, pp. 135–140.

The second group of antefixes is composed of four fragments, which are decorated with floral motifs combined with spirals (Pl. 77:c–f). These antefixes of Group 2 bear some resemblance to those found in Buthrot. They have been found in strata belonging to the 3rd century B.C.

Dating of the antefixes from Antigonea does not constitute a problem, for they come from a well-dated stratum belonging to the 3rd to 2nd century B.C. Even the name of Antigonea itself is helpful here, for it suggests a foundation by Pyrrhus between the years 297 and 280 B.C.[5] Because of the town's violent end near the middle of the 2nd century B.C., as a result of the war with Rome, the archaeological data do not go beyond this time. The town was destroyed and there was no later occupation. The antefixes thus belong to the period before the destruction of the city. Their style and decoration can be compared to the antefixes found in Foenike, Buthrot, Apollonia, and other Illyrian towns of the Hellenistic period.

The architectural terracottas of Buthrot, in particular those discovered in recent years in different parts of the town, include fifteen fragments of antefixes that are important for their decoration. These objects were found in mixed strata, and archaeological data is not available for their dating. All antefixes are made of pure clay, yellow-ocher or red or pink in color. There are several variants, based on decoration. Their common feature is the type of decoration, a palmette and spirals, similar to the antefixes of Antigonea. By the stylistic treatment of these decorative elements, we can identify other variants with human or animal heads combined with spirals or floral motifs.

The first variant has as its decoration a palmette in relief opening in both directions, radiating from a heart in the form of a rhombus or circle (Pl. 78:d). Below the palmette there are two or more antithetical spirals. In contrast to the most common style, one of the antefixes has a palmette in deeper relief (Pl. 78:f). On the front surface is a slip of red color, characteristic of the Hellenistic period.

In the second variant the antefixes have as decoration a rosette combined with spirals. The better-preserved fragment (Pl. 78:a) presents a rosette with lines following the contours of the petals. In the center is a circular bud from which nine petals radiate. Below is a pair of volutes ending in spirals. There are traces of red on the front surface, and the clay is pure ocher. Another antefix of this variant (Pl. 78:e) has the same decoration, but the color of its clay is different, being dark gray, probably because it was overfired or, more likely, was a remainder in the local workshop.

The third variant (Pl. 78:b, c) of the Buthrot group is composed of antefixes that have as the main decoration a palmette emerging from a bud. At the center of the palmette on one of these examples is the head of a bearded man (Pl. 78:c), probably Zeus. Both of these examples are made of pure clay that is red to light pink in color. Judging from the composition and color of the clay, the antefixes appear to be the same as other tiles found in abundance in the excavations. In this group we must include five other fragments of antefixes (Pl. 78:g–i), all made of pure clay, yellow-ocher in color. The main design is the spiral combined with floral motifs. On two other fragments we can see, besides the S-shaped spiral, a woman's head (Pl. 78:i), very damaged but similar in style to an example found

[5] Budina 1984, p. 159.

here long ago by Italian excavators, dated to the Hellenistic period.[6] On another fragment (Pl. 78:g), the contours of an animal head are visible, probably the head of the ox Buthrots, mentioned frequently in ancient sources.[7]

Dating the Buthrot antefixes, in contrast to the Antigonea examples, presents some difficulties because of the lack of stratagraphic data. Nevertheless, dating may be done on the basis of stylistic comparisons with antefixes of the Hellenistic period from neighboring towns, such as Antigonea and Foenike,[8] and other towns outside of Kaonia, such as Apollonia,[9] Dimal,[10] Kerkyra, the towns of Magna Graecia, and Macedonia,[11] their similarity consisting of both the motifs and to a certain extent the technical particularities. The motif of the palmette is found early on painted pitchers of Dyrrachium and Apollonia but also occurs on finds from the Roman period in these towns. All these comparisons help to date the antefixes of Buthrot to the Hellenistic period.

As far as the origin of their form is concerned, it must be said that such antefixes are typologically and stylistically derived from the major center of such production in Corinth.[12] Nevertheless, the local features of the clay, which is the same as that of the plain tiles in the above-mentioned centers, indicate that these antefixes were produced locally. The decorative concept, following Corinthian models, shows cultural links that existed between these important Epirote centers and Corinth during the Hellenistic period. This phenomenon has been observed in Buthrot as early as the Archaic period, to judge from Archaic pottery found on the acropolis there.[13]

## BIBLIOGRAPHY

Budina, D. 1969. "Disa rezultate të gjurmimeve në vendbanimet e lashta ilire të Kaonisë," in *Konferenca e dytë e studimeve Albanologjike* II, Tirana

———. 1972. "Antigonée," *Iliria* 2, pp. 269–348

———. 1984. "Le lieu et le rôle d'Antigonea dans la vallée du Drino," in *l'Illyrie méridionale et l'Épire dans l'antiquité*, P. Cabanes, ed., Clermont/Ferrand, pp. 159–166

———. 1989. *Vorrömisches Butrint*, Buthrot/Tirana

Budina, D., and F. Stamati. 1989. "Disa objekte bronxi nga Antigonea," *Monumentet* 2, pp. 135–140

Kaltsas, N. E. 1988. Πήλινες διακοσμημένες κεραμώσεις από τη Μακεδόνια, Athens

Prendi, F., and D. Budina. 1970. "La civilisation illyrienne de la vallée du Drino," *Studio Albanica* 2, pp. 67–87

Ugolini, L. M. 1932. "L'Acropoli di Fenice," *Albanica antica* 2

———. 1942. "L'Acropoli di Butrino," *Albanica antica* 3

Zeqo, M. 1986. "D'anciens temoignages de l'art à Durrës, *Iliria* 1986:1, p. 185

DHIMOSTEN BUDINA

QENDRA E KËRKIMOVE ARKEOLOGJIKE
Tirana
Albania

[6] Ugolini 1942, p. 192.
[7] Virgil 1.55; Aristotle, *Hist. Anim.* 8; Athenaios 9.18, etc.
[8] Ugolini 1932.
[9] Muzeum Nacional inv. no. 76.
[10] Archeological Museum inv. no. 573.
[11] Kaltsas 1988, p. 79.
[12] Kaltsas 1988, p. 79; Zeqo 1986:1, p. 185.
[13] Budina 1989, p. 21, with earlier bibliography.

# TRAUFZIEGEL MIT RELIEFMÄANDER AUS DEM SCHWARZMEERGEBIET

(PLATE 79)

VON MEHREREN FUNDPLÄTZEN der nördlichen und westlichen Schwarzmeerküste ist eine Reihe griechischer Dachterrakotten bekanntgeworden, die sich im Bereich des Pontos Euxeinos offenbar besonderer Beliebtheit erfreut haben: Traufziegel mit Reliefmäander.[1] Diese flachen, auf Grund ihrer Zurichtung direkt am vorspringenden Dachrand angebrachten, deshalb allgemein als Hegemones bezeichneten Dachziegel verfügen über eine leistenartig ausgebildete und herabhängende, durch ihre Dekoration auf Ansicht berechnete Front. Der Schmuck dieser auch als Taenia anzusprechenden Frontleiste ist in Relief ausgeführt. Es handelt sich dabei um ein Ornamentsystem, bei dem zwei sich überlagernde Mäanderbänder so auseinandergezogen sind, daß in regelmäßigen Abständen Platz für annähernd quadratische Felder entsteht, die ihrerseits unterschiedlich gefüllt sein können. Dieses charakteristische Dekorationsschema von Traufziegeln kommt, gemessen am Publikationsstand, vornehmlich im Schwarzmeergebiet,[2] vereinzelt aber auch an anderen Fundorten der griechischen Welt vor. Dabei wird dieser Dachterrakottentyp bevorzugt hellenistisch datiert.

Am ältesten griechischen Siedlungsplatz im Schwarzmeergebiet, dem von Milet gegründeten westpontischen Histria,[3] sind bisher 31 Beispiele dieses Typs aufgetaucht, allerdings meist außerhalb gut beobachteter Grabungszusammenhänge. Trotzdem kann festgehalten werden, daß diejenigen Stücke, für die Fundnachrichten vorliegen, alle aus solchen Bereichen Histrias stammen, in denen griechische Schichten berührt wurden: aus dem innerhalb der eigentlichen "Festung Histria" vom 6.–1. Jh. v. Chr. existierenden Tempelbezirk T (Zona sacra); von der nur auf einem kurzen Abschnitt Z₂ ausgegrabenen Befestigungsmauer klassischer Zeit; aus dem Sektor X auf dem in archaischer Zeit entstandenen Plateau, wo sich bis in hellenistische Zeit zivile Siedlungsbereiche gehalten haben. Da die überwiegende Mehrzahl dieser Traufziegel mit Reliefmäander bisher unpubliziert blieb,[4] darf von ihrer hier beabsichtigten Vorstellung Aufschluß zu einigen Fragen erwartet werden, die sich ganz allgemein mit diesem durch gleichartige Zurichtung

---

[1] Der Beitrag stellt die überarbeitete Fassung eines Kapitels meiner ungedruckten Habilitationsschrift dar: Zimmermann 1983, Kapitel VI/5. Teilergebnisse waren bereits im Oktober 1978 auf dem Eirene-Kongress in Nesebâr, Bulgarien vorgetragen worden: "Hellenistische Architekturterrakotten von der westlichen Schwarzmeerküste." Alle Fotos und Vorlagen für die Zeichnungen stammen vom Autor; die Reinzeichnungen fertigten H.-J. Roloff und A. Rehbein, beide Rostock.

[2] Vgl. Åkerström 1966; Zeest 1966; Ognenova-Marinova 1980.

[3] Zu Histria vgl. zuletzt zusammenfassend: Alexandrescu und Schuller 1990 (mit Gesamtbibliographie).

[4] Je 1 Stück abgebildet bei Pârvan 1916, S. 703–704, Nr. 61:b, mit Abb.; Canarache 1957, S. 171, Nr. 457, mit Abb.; 5 weitere Stücke in *Histria* V, Taf. 11:88–92; 2 weitere bei Zimmermann in Alexandrescu und Schuller 1990, S. 169, Abb. 8, S. 177, Abb. 23.

und Verzierung charakterisierten Dachterrakottentyp verbinden. Dem steht allerdings erschwerend gegenüber, daß nicht einer dieser Hegemones komplett erhalten ist.

Alle aufgeführten Fragmente (**1–31**) vertreten durch die gleiche allgemeine Zurichtung—es handelt sich um Flachziegel mit herabhängender Front und Stegen über den Seiten, die ein wenig auf die Front umbiegen—und den von eingestreuten Feldern aufgelockerten Reliefmäander denselben Typ. Trotzdem scheitert die wünschenswerte weitere typologische Gruppierung dieses Materials daran, daß sich die Stücke in vielen Punkten unterscheiden, sei es in Ton, Überzug und Farbgebung, sei es in der unterschiedlichen Fronthöhe und anderen Abmessungen, sei es in Ornamentdetails. Gehören sie auch alle zu demselben Typ, läßt sich dennoch bei keinem einzigen Fragment eine derartige Übereinstimmung mit einem anderen feststellen, daß eine Gruppenbildung voll gerechtfertigt wäre.[5] Deshalb folgt die Anordnung der Fragmente im Katalog ihrem Funddatum bzw. anderweitigen Bekanntwerden.

Der in der Regel matt ziegelrote, bisweilen nach Gelb (**7, 17, 27**), Ocker (**15, 16**) und/oder Braun (**2, 5, 14, 17, 21**) neigende, meist verschmutzte Ton ist in Abhängigkeit von der Menge, Größe und Verteilung der Zuschläge unterschiedlich dicht bzw. porös. Neben Glimmer kommen weißliche, schwärzliche und rötliche Magerungsteilchen—letztere auch in gröberer Form und vereinzelt als Ziegelsplitter an der Oberfläche bloßliegend (**10, 14**)—in unterschiedlichen Mischungsverhältnissen vor. Auch finden sich gelegentlich im Ton Schnecken oder Muscheln (**4**[?]) bzw. Abdrücke von letzteren (**17**). Ist das Ausgangsmaterial sandig, so wirkt noch das fertige Produkt weich und leidet unter erhöhtem Abrieb, andere Stücke sind dagegen sehr hart gebrannt (**5, 27**). Zwei Fragmente (**6, 18**) fallen durch ihre Tonbeschaffenheit aus dem beschriebenen Rahmen: Sie haben zwar alle die üblichen Zuschläge, dabei aber eine rötlich-violette Grundfarbe mit vielen, fast zitronengelben Einsprenkelungen—darin ähnelt der Ton demjenigen der Amphoren aus Sinope;[6] es wird sich also bei ihnen um Import von dort handeln. Sie verfügen auch über einen ganz charakteristischen, ursprünglich kräftig gelben, ins Grünliche tendierenden Überzug, der alle Oberflächen erfaßt, aber unterschiedlich erhalten blieb.[7] Auch an anderen Stücken finden sich einheitliche Überzüge, teils in der Art einer gelblichen Engobe (**4**[?], **7, 14, 16, 23**[?]), teils als braun- bis violettroter Farbauftrag (**8, 15**[?], **19, 27**). Gerade von letzterem sind nur geringe Spuren erhalten (**10, 12, 21, 31**), so daß sich schwer entscheiden läßt, ob einst immer das ganze Stück damit überzogen war. Es kommt hinzu, daß eine Reihe von Stücken stark versintert ist (**3, 5**[?], **20, 24, 26**), wodurch ein Überzug möglicherweise verdeckt wird. Trotzdem möchte man annehmen, daß dieser Dachterrakottentyp ursprünglich generell farbige Überzüge besessen hat.

Auch bei der insgesamt einheitlichen Zurichtung, die sich aus zwei größeren Fragmenten (**15, 25**) noch am besten erschließen läßt, begegnet man laufend kleineren Abweichungen.

---

[5] So spricht z.B. die unterschiedliche Fronthöhe dagegen, alle Stücke mit Buchstaben zusammenzufassen, zumal sich diese auch in ihrer Anbringung unterscheiden; möglicherweise bilden **1** und **19** eine Gruppe, da die Höhe von 6,0 cm und der Sitz des Buchstabens auf einer leicht angehobenen Platte übereinstimmen—doch läßt sich eine solche Vermutung nicht anderweitig erhärten, solange das von Pârvan veröffentlichte Stück verschollen bleibt.

[6] Vgl. Coja in *Histria* V, S. 53 zu Nr. 91/2.

[7] Dieser Überzug wird auch bei **14** verwendet, doch unterscheidet sich der Ton von den Stücken vermuteter Provenienz aus Sinope.

Die Oberseite des sich rückwärts verjüngenden Flachziegels ungleicher Plattenstärke (im Ansatz 2,4 cm bei **12** bis 3,3 cm bei **3**) ist in der Regel ganz eben und geglättet (Ausnahmen: **4, 10, 13, 20**), kann aber auch ein wenig gewölbt sein (**27**). Sie biegt, wenn nicht beschädigt, in knapper Rundung zur geraden, in einem Falle gewölbten (**7**) Front um, die entweder genau im rechten Winkel ansetzt (**5, 6, 14, 16, 17, 20**) oder diesen knapp, dabei niemals mehr als *ca.* 5° unter- bzw. überschreitet (spitzwinklig = **4, 10, 12**; stumpfwinklig = **3, 13, 15, 18, 19, 21, 25, 26, 27, 30, 31**). Im Ganzen gesehen sind diese Unregelmäßigkeiten so gering, daß davon ausgegangen werden kann, es sei immer ein rechter Winkel beabsichtigt gewesen. Die Höhe der herabhängenden Front schwankt—auch wenn man von den aufgesetzten Stegen an den Eckstücken absieht, also nur den den Reliefmäander tragenden Teil zugrundelegt— dagegen stärker und reicht von 5,4 cm (**4**) bis 9,0 cm (**7**). Auch ihre Unterkante, deren Breite von 1,0 auf 3,0 cm steigen kann, nimmt—wenn sie nicht parallel zur Oberseite liegt (**15, 23, 25**)—entweder abgerundete Form an (**6, 7, 13, 17, 21**) oder ist in der Mehrzahl der Fälle unterschiedlich schräg nach hinten angehoben, bildet also eine Wassernase. Die Rückseite der Front ist nur ausnahmsweise einer schrägen Fläche verpflichtet (**14**), leitet aber sonst in einer unterschiedlich starken, gelegentlich abgestuften Wölbung zum rückwärtigen Flachziegel über. Alle diese Teile der Unterseite sind nur allgemein angelegt, also geebnet und leicht geglättet.

Die Eckstücke—es sind sowohl linke (**6, 13, 15, 20, 26, 31**) als auch rechte (**2, 3, 7**) vorhanden—weisen eine Besonderheit auf, die die Verwendung des Typs eindeutig festlegt. Über ihren Seiten erheben sich nämlich bis 3,2 cm (**20**) hohe und bis 3,7 cm (**31**) breite Stege, die meist etwas schmaler, aber in derselben Höhe auf die Front umbiegen, diese aber nicht in ähnlicher Weise begleiten, sondern nach maximal 8,5 cm (**31**)[8] abbrechen. Da es kein Eckstück gibt, das in diesem Bereich der Front nicht über einen solchen Steg oder zumindest geringe Überbleibsel bzw. Brüche eines solchen[9] verfügt, hat es mit ihnen eine bestimmte Bewandtnis. Diese wird von histrianischen Traufziegelfragmenten ohne Frontschmuck bzw. aus einer Ergänzung[10] ähnlicher, in Olbia gefundener Fragmente mit Reliefornamenten ersichtlich: Werden diese Hegemones aneinandergerückt, bilden die jeweils sich berührenden Frontstege zweier solcher Dachziegel das Widerlager für einen ihre Stoßfuge überdeckenden Kalypter, dessen untere, geschlossene Stirn zu diesem Zweck unten eine wenig ausklinkt, während sein oberer Teil auf den Frontstegen des Traufziegels aufliegt. Die Fragmente des hier vorgestellten histrianischen Dachterrakottentyps sind wegen derselben Konstruktion also mit Sicherheit Überreste von Traufziegeln und nicht—wie gelegentlich bezeichnet— Simen;[11] ihr horizontales Auflager, die herabhängende, schmale Front mit eingliedrigem Ornamentstreifen und einer zur Wassernase ausgebildeten Unterkante bieten die für diese Zweckbestimmung außerdem notwendige Zurichtung.

[8] **6** = 5,6 cm; **7** = 5,9 cm; **15** = 6,8 cm; **20** = 6,1 cm; **26** = 7,1 cm.
[9] **2** bietet in seiner Zerstörung nur noch einen Stumpf über dem rechten Eckbereich, das Mittelstück **12** dort noch eine kleine Aufwölbung über der Oberseite. **3** ist an der rechten Ecke oben auf eine Breite von mindestens 6 cm bis in den Mäander hinein ausgebrochen; nach den Maßen in Anm. 8 kann hier also ein Frontsteg vorhanden gewesen sein.
[10] Vgl. Zeest 1966, Taf. 31:1–4.
[11] Während Pippidi 1962, S. 154, Anm. 32, sogar von Sima spricht, bezeichnet sie Coja in *Histria* V, S. 53 zu Nr. 88, als "tuile de frise."

Zu dieser gehört offenbar auch, daß die gelegentlich (**6, 26**) rechtwinklig zur Front abbiegenden Seitenflächen sonst nach hinten leicht zurückgenommen, d.h. einwärts gestellt werden (**3, 7, 15, 20**), um so ein besseres Anpassen der Traufziegel untereinander zu erreichen. In einem bestimmten Abstand zur Front wird bei einem Fragment (**7**) die Seitenfläche sogar noch zusätzlich zurückgesetzt. Ein anderes Beispiel (**15**) zeigt noch zwei weitere Vorrichtungen, die offenbar der Gefahr des Verrutschens vorbeugen sollen: Einmal springt in Höhe des unteren Mäandersteges ein zapfenartiger Wulst über die linke Seitenfläche hinaus und müßte theoretisch am Nachbarstück auf eine entsprechende Einkerbung gestoßen sein; zum anderen tritt—in ziemlicher Entfernung von der Front— vor die schräg nach hinten zurückweichende Seitenfläche ein zwar schmaler, hier aber die gesamte Ziegelhöhe einnehmener Steg hervor, dessen Stirn genau im rechten Winkel zur Front liegt und folglich das Pendant am ebenso konstruierten Nachbarstück flächig berühren soll. Ein ähnliches, mit Anathyrose vergleichbares punktuelles Aneinanderstoßen ist auch andernorts bei Dachziegeln beobachtet worden.[12]

Natürlich werden auch diese am Dachrand liegenden Traufziegel angenagelt gewesen sein, doch reicht die maximal erhaltene Tiefe (**25** = 15,9 cm) offenbar bei keinem Fragment bis in diesen Bereich. Nach Aussage des breitesten Fragments (**15** = 32,2 cm) mit nur einer erhaltenen Ecke muß die Frontbreite dieses Traufziegels mindestens 40 cm gemessen haben. In Olbia, wo auch keine kompletten Traufziegel dieses Typs aufgetaucht sind, hat man eine Breite von *ca.* 55 cm erschlossen.[13]

Die Fronten aller Fragmente ziert als einheitlicher Schmuck ein Reliefmäander, der— wie schon beschrieben—aus zwei einzelnen, sich kreuzenden Mäanderbändern mit dadurch regelmäßig wiederkehrendem Swastika-Ornament und zwischen diesen eingestreuten rechteckigen Feldern besteht. Die Reliefstege sind durchschnittlich 0,5–0,7 cm breit und im allgemeinen 0,3–0,4 cm hoch, zeigten ursprünglich einen rechteckigen Querschnitt—einmal kommt Trapezform vor (**25**)—mit scharfen Kanten und sind heute meist abgeschliffen gerundet. Gewöhnlich liegt die Grundfläche der gesamten Front auf einem einheitlichen Niveau. Nur an einem Eckstück (**20**) ist die Vorderseite des oben auf die Front umbiegenden Steges auf die Höhe der Mäanderstege gehoben, so daß das Ornament an dieser Stelle weniger aufgesetzt als ausgeschnitten wirkt. Die Ansichtsseiten jener die Frontecken überragenden Stege sind entweder mit einem Eierstab in schwachem Relief dekoriert (**6, 7, 15, 26**), der seinerseits nach oben sowie an der zur Mitte hin gewandten Seite gerahmt ist,[14] oder mit einem spiralartig aufgerollten Pflanzenornament geschmückt (**31**), wie es auch an Beispielen aus Olbia vorkommt. Alle diese Reliefornamente müssen aus der Form gewonnen sein, was auch daraus ersichtlich wird, daß bisweilen Mäanderstege und Oberkante der Front nicht parallel liegen (**20, 21**) oder Stege beim Abnehmen der Front verrutscht (z.B. **15**) bzw. anderweitig deformiert sind (z.B. **8**). Zwischen den Mäanderstegen kann— offenbar auf Grund schlechter Ausformung—sogar Ton stehenbleiben (**2, 3**).[15] Wegen des

---

[12] Vgl. Buschor 1929, S. 30; Hübner 1975, S. 124 zu Taf. 66:5, 6.

[13] Vgl. Brašinskij, in Zeest 1966, S. 40 mit Anm. 27.

[14] Am besten an **7** zu erkennen; bei **6** bzw. **15** scheint wenigstens noch der Ansatz der seitlichen Rahmung erhalten zu sein, während **26** in allen Randbereichen zu stark zerstört ist.

[15] Da es sich bei beiden Eckstücken um ein kleines Feld an gleicher Stelle handelt, könnte man versucht sein, an eine Herstellung aus derselben Form zu denken; dem steht gegenüber, daß dieser Bereich bei **2** bis auf die Höhe der Mäanderstege gefüllt ist, bei **3** jedoch nicht.

schlechten Erhaltungszustandes lassen sich keine Spuren nachträglichen Korrigierens dieser Unregelmäßigkeiten mehr feststellen. Die Verwendung des Modellierholzes kann an den histrianischen Fragmenten überhaupt nur einmal (**31**), dazu noch an der schrägen Unterseite der Wassernase, beobachtet werden.

Die in das fortlaufende Mäanderband eingestreuten Rechteckfelder sind dem Quadrat angenähert. Sie bestehen gewöhnlich aus einem rahmenden Steg mit unterschiedlicher Füllung, seltener aus einer dann nur wenig angehobenen, nicht die Höhe der Reliefstege erreichenden quadratischen Platte (**1, 19, 31**). Die gerahmten Rechteckfelder können leer bleiben (**12, 15**[?], **16, 25**[?]), fünf quadratische oder abgerundete, wie beim Würfel angeordnete Punkte (**2**[?], **3, 10, 14, 15, 25**[?]), oder aber sternartige Rosetten aufnehmen, die unterschiedlich viele, nämlich vier (**3, 8**), fünf (**15, 20**[?], **26**) oder acht (**10, 13, 20**[?]) strahlenförmige Blattspitzen haben. Schließlich können in diesen gerahmten Rechteckfeldern (**4, 6, 25**) oder auf den leicht angehobenen quadratischen Platten (**1, 19, 31**) aus Reliefstegen gebildete griechische Buchstaben einzeln oder in Paaren Aufnahme finden: A (**1, 31**), Δ (**31**), E (**4, 25**), H (**19**), Υ (**6**), K[A?] (**28**), OΥ (**11**). Trotz des Fragmentcharakters aller Stücke ist ersichtlich, daß Rosetten- und Punktfüllung nebeneinander auftreten (**3, 10, 15**), möglicherweise auch mit leeren Feldern (**15, 29**) kombiniert sein können, während sie für eine Verbindung der Buchstaben untereinander oder mit den genannten Füllungen nichts hergeben (vgl. **25**).[16] Bei den Eckstücken muß nicht nur der fortlaufende Mäander, sondern können auch Rechteckfelder geschnitten sein (**15, 26**); diese werden sich—wie der Eierstab und dessen Rahmung am oberen Frontsteg—auf dem benachbarten Traufziegel fortgesetzt haben. Wie dieses Problem beim Fragment **6** gelöst war, bleibt fraglich, da einerseits bis zur seitlichen Begrenzung des Traufziegels gerade noch Platz wäre, um das den Buchstaben rahmende Rechteck zu schließen, andererseits das Υ innerhalb des Feldes soweit rechts sitzt, daß die Existenz eines oder mehrerer weiterer Buchstaben links von ihm notwendig zu werden scheint.

Es gibt von anderen nord- und westpontischen Fundorten genügend Dachterrakotten mit diesem Ornamentsystem, teils in unmittelbaren Parallelen, teils in anderen Kombinationen. Von ihnen sind vielleicht auch Hinweise zu erwarten, die den Sinn der eingestreuten Buchstaben erhellen. Dieses charakteristische Dekorationsschema mit seinen Variationen kommt nämlich entweder—wie in Histria—als Frontschmuck von Traufziegeln oder aber als solcher von Simen vor, bei denen es dann nur den unteren, etwa der Stärke des rückwärtigen Flachziegels entsprechenden Streifen einnimmt.

In Olbia[17] wurden neben Traufziegeln, deren Fronten mit Eier- und Perlstäben geschmückt sind,[18] vor allem solche mit dem in Histria bekannten Reliefmäander gefunden, deren eingestreute Rechtecke ganz ähnliche Füllungen aufweisen: verschiedene Rosettenformen,[19] Einzelbuchstaben im rahmenden Rechteck[20] bzw. auf leicht angehobener

---

[16] Der knappe Überrest könnte einer der 5 "Würfel"-Punkte, aber ebensogut der Ansatz einiger weniger griechischer Buchstaben (Z, T) sein.
[17] Brašinskij, in Zeest 1966, S. 39–40 mit Anm. 30: 4.–2. Jh. v.
[18] Zeest 1966, Taf. 30:8, 31:3; Åkerström 1966, S. 2, Taf. 1:2. Ähnliche Stücke aus dem Bosporanischen Reich: Zeest 1966, Taf. 36:3, 39:1, 2.
[19] Åkerström 1966, S. 2, Taf. 1:7.
[20] Zeest 1966, Taf. 30:10. Buchstaben: M, O.

Platte.²¹ Die auf die Front umbiegenden Stege darüber sind entweder glatt oder tragen das auch in Histria vorhandene pflanzliche Ornament. Die olbianischen Stücke zeigen, daß die Reliefbuchstaben immer nur mit ihresgleichen, niemals mit anderen Füllungen kombiniert werden und daß die auf Platten gesetzten Lettern bisweilen spiegelbildlich erscheinen können. In Histria scheint dies bisher nicht der Fall zu sein: Denn die Lettern unsymmetrischer Form wie E (**4, 25**) und K (**28**) zeigen die übliche rechtsläufige Leserichtung; und stehen die anderen vorkommenden, ganz symmetrisch gebildeten Buchstaben A, Δ, H, O, Υ allein, ist dies nicht mit Sicherheit zu entscheiden.

Das in Mesambria (Nesebâr) gefundene diesbezügliche Material²² ist erheblich reicher und umfaßt sowohl Traufziegel (unter denen wie in Olbia auch wieder solche mit ionischem Kymation und Astragal an der Frontfläche vorkommen²³) als auch Simen, die beide den Reliefmäander mit eingestreuten Feldern als Schmuck benutzen. In den Rechtecken tauchen entweder vierteilige Rosetten (Traufziegel, Simen),²⁴ ein einzelner knopfartiger Punkt in der Mitte des Feldes (Simen)²⁵ oder aber Buchstaben (Traufziegel, Simen)²⁶ auf. Diese sitzen hier zwar niemals auf angehobenen Platten, werden dafür aber—wie in Histria—sowohl einzeln (Simen nur so) als auch in zwei Lettern nebeneinander angeordnet. Hinsichtlich der Kombinationsfähigkeit der einzelnen Füllungen bieten die Stücke aus Mesambria ebenso wenig Neues wie ein in der Nähe von Burgas am See Mandren gefundenes Einzelstück,²⁷ das auch einen Buchstaben aufweisen soll.

Während der Sinn dieser sicher nicht zufälligen Buchstaben bzw. Buchstabenfolgen bis vor kurzem noch unklar war, höchstens apotropäischer Charakter zugestanden wurde,²⁸ hat L. Ognenova-Marinova unlängst eine Deutung dieser rätselhaften Inschriften vorgeschlagen.²⁹ Danach können durch Positionsbestimmung der Fragmente und durch solche mit mehreren Buchstaben (für die sie als umfangreichstes Beispiel ein unpubliziertes Stück aus Odessos (Varna)³⁰ mit vier Buchstabenfeldern (A]N-ΘE-ΣT-HP-[..) heranzieht) auch anderweitig, nämlich auf Flachziegeln, Amphoren, Münzen und Steininschriften ganz oder teilweise belegte Personennamen wie Moschos, Euphamidas, Anthesterios und als thrakischer Name Rebas/Rebada gewonnen werden. Der Charakter aller dieser Denkmälergruppen legt nahe, daß es sich bei den Genannten weniger um Handwerksmeister bzw. Werkstattbesitzer, sondern um städtische Beamte (Magistrate, vielleicht

---

[21] Zeest 1966, Taf. 30:11, 31:1, 4; Åkerström 1966, S. 2, Taf. 1:8. Buchstaben: P-H-B-A-Δ-A, links- und rechtsläufig.

[22] Ognenova 1975, Abb. S. 55, 61, 65, 87. Ognenova-Marinova 1980.

[23] Ognenova-Marinova 1980, S. 113–115, Nr. 9–12, Abb. 7–10.

[24] Ognenova-Marinova 1980, S. 115–116, Nr. 13–17, Abb. 11 = Traufziegel; S. 145, Nr. 74, Abb. 65 = Sima.

[25] Filow 1915, Sp. 235, Abb. 13; Ognenova-Marinova 1980, S. 130–138 *passim* Nr. 48, 48:a, 50–52, 58–60, 62–63, Abb. 37, 38, 40–42, 48–50, 52, 53.

[26] Ognenova-Marinova 1980, S. 116–120, Nr. 18–34, Abb. 12–24 = Traufziegel mit Einzelbuchstaben: Υ, N, O, Silben: PO, HP (Ligatur), TI, MI, ΔA, AN, ΣT, bzw. Silben-Kombination: MI-ΔA, AN-ΘE-ΣT, S. 143–145, Nr. 72, 75, Abb. 62–63, 66 = Simen mit Einzelbuchstaben: B bzw. deren Kombination: P-H-B.

[27] Karajotov 1975, S. 26, 27 obere Abb.; angeblich mit Buchstaben A.

[28] Vgl. Brašinskij, in Zeest 1966, S. 40 mit Anm. 28.

[29] Ognenova-Marinova 1980, S. 147–155.

[30] Ognenova-Marinova 1980, S. 154, Abb. 75.

auch Wohltäter—im Falle des Euphamidas wohl zugleich ein nachgewiesener Architekt) handeln wird, zu deren Pflichten u.a. auch die Bauaufsicht gehörte. Die Traufziegel und Simen mit Buchstabenfeldern sind deshalb in gewisser Weise mit den auf Flachziegeln vorkommenden Astynomoi-Stempeln zu vergleichen. Ob dies in gleichem Maße auch für diejenigen Hegemones mit Reliefmäander zutrifft, in deren Feldern nur Einzelbuchstaben erscheinen (also auch für die meisten der histrianischen Beispiele gilt), konnte angesichts ihrer hier geringen Zahl bisher nicht entschieden werden. Doch ein im Sommer 1991 in Histria aufgefundenes Fragment mit den Buchstabenfeldern A-Δ nahe dem linken Seitenrand (**31**) stellt sich nun so unmittelbar neben die olbianischen Beispiele mit dem rechts- oder linksläufig vorkommenden Namen thrakischer Herkunft P-H-B-A-Δ-A, scheint wegen der vollkommenen Ähnlichkeit sogar aus derselben Form hergestellt worden zu sein, daß auch für die histrianischen Stücke der Schluß naheliegt, in diesen Buchstabenfolgen bestimmte Namen zu sehen.

Dennoch ließe sich noch eine andere Deutungsmöglichkeit anführen: In Pergamon kommen an Flachziegelstirnen komplett eingestempelte und als Bestimmungsinschriften[31] erkannte Buchstabenfolgen vor, durch die die Anfertigung für bestimmte Bauwerke dokumentiert wird.

Traufziegel (und Simen) mit Reliefmäander sind jedoch nicht nur im Schwarzmeergebiet verbreitet, sondern haben sich auch in Kleinasien nachweisen lassen: Å. Åkerström erwähnt bzw. bildet eine Reihe von Stücken aus Assos,[32] Pergamon,[33] Chios,[34] und unbekanntem Fundort[35] ab; hinzu kommen Beispiele aus Priene,[36] angeblich Kappadokien,[37] doch ist damit bei weitem noch nicht alles erfaßt.[38] In den Reliefmäander einbezogene Buchstaben finden sich bei allen diesen Stücken bisher nicht, dafür aber die anderen, bereits in Histria beobachteten Varianten der Felderfüllung: knopfartiger Punkt in der Mitte (Assos), 5 "Würfel"-Punkte (Priene), vierteilige Rosette auf angehobener Platte (Kappadokien), achtteilige Rosette (Pergamon), leeres Feld (Assos, unbekannter Fundort), angehobene, aber leere Platte (unbekannter Fundort).

Die Traufziegel mit Reliefmäander werden im allgemeinen in hellenistische Zeit datiert,[39] stammen ja oft auch von Fundorten, die in dieser Epoche blühten oder (wie Priene nach der Mitte des 4. Jh. v.) neu gegründet wurden. Für stilistische Vergleiche eignen sich die rein geometrischen Formen des außerdem meist stark abgeriebenen, wenn nicht

---

[31] Vgl. *AvP* VIII, ii, S. 399–401; *AvP* IX, S. 133; *AvP* X, S. 40–46.

[32] Åkerström 1966, S. 13, 14, 15, Taf. 7:1, 3 (3 steht sicher auf dem Kopf); weitere Stücke im Museum of Fine Arts, Boston.

[33] *AvP* IX, S. 133, Taf. 42:b; Åkerström 1966, S. 22 mit Anm. 78.—Kenntnis und Fotos von 2 unpublizierten Stücken in Berlin, Staatl. Museen P 716 bzw. P 718 verdanke ich V. Kästner/Berlin.

[34] Åkerström 1966, S. 35.

[35] Åkerström 1966, S. 45, Taf. 17:4, 5; 6 Stücke im Museum von Smyrna/Izmir.

[36] Wiegand und Schrader 1904, S. 227, Abb. 220.

[37] Paris, Louvre CA 6229: Hinweis und Foto verdanke ich der Freundlichkeit von M.-F. Billot/Paris.

[38] Vgl. hier die Beiträge von Gneisz (1994), Kästner (1994), und Stella Miller (1994), aber auch derartige Stücke vom griechischen Festland, etwa in Athen, Epigraphisches Museum: Billot 1976, S. 99, Abb. 3:c, S. 105–106, Nr. 23, Taf. 26:b; aus dem Piräus: Metzger 1971, S. 78, Nr. 185, Taf. 19; aus Delos: *Delos* V, S. 108, Abb. 142.

[39] Vgl. Åkerström 1966, S. 19 mit Anm. 58; und andernorts (hier in Anm. 18, 33, 35).

beschädigten Dekors kaum. Die an den Vorderflächen der zur Front umbiegenden Stege angebrachten ionischen Kymatien (**6, 7, 15, 26**) mit ihren stark zugespitzten Eikörpern, fast linear verkümmerten Rahmenstäben sowie durchlaufenden, bisweilen tropfenförmigen Blattspitzen stehen in ihrer das Ganze auflösenden Tendenz ziemlich am Ende einer langen Entwicklung und können den späten Zeitansatz in gewisser Weise unterstützen. L. Ognenova-Marinova schlägt vor,[40] mittels der an den Dachterrakotten von Mesambria (Nesebâr) vorkommenden Gesichtsmasken (Athena, Medusa, Satyr, Nymphe, Herakles) unterschiedlicher Typik und vom 5.–2. Jh. v. reichender Entwicklungsstufen auch die Simen mit Reliefmäander zeitlich zu gruppieren, ohne es dann im Detail durchzuführen. Für die sich selbst typologisch nicht mehr erkennbar verändernden Reliefmäander der Traufziegel gibt der Vergleich mit denen der Simen aber nichts her.

Bedauerlicherweise gibt es bisher fast keine in ihrem Fundzusammenhang publizierten Dachterrakotten mit Reliefmäander, die eine präzisere zeitliche Eingrenzung dieses Typs oder doch einiger seiner Vertreter gestatten würden. So ist ein ganz unscheinbares, als Stukkatur-Fragment[41] beschriebenes Stück mit Reliefmäander von der Taman-Halbinsel bekanntgemacht worden, das stratigraphisch in einen vom 2. Viertel des 3. bis zur Mitte des 2. Jh. v. reichenden Zeitraum gehört. Und leider ist auch in Histria nur für einige wenige der Traufziegelfragmente mit Reliefmäander die Fundlage genauer erfaßt und dadurch in einigen Fällen eine annähernde Datierung möglich: **15** = 1. Hälfte des 3. Jh. v.,[42] **22** = 3./2. Jh. v.,[43] **19**[44] und **21**[45] = allgemein hellenistisch. Daraus scheint ersichtlich, daß, wie in Olbia, dieser Typ von Dachterrakotten auch in Histria etwa vom ausgehenden 4. bis mindestens ans Ende des 2. Jh. v. gebräuchlich gewesen ist, und deshalb mit den übrigen hier gefunden hellenistischen Stroteren und Kalypteren in Verbindung gebracht werden kann.

Die auffällige Verbreitung der Traufziegel (und Simen) mit Reliefmäander im kleinasiatischen und Schwarzmeerraum wirft die Frage nach den Orten ihrer Herstellung, damit nach dem Zusammenhang von lokaler Produktion und Export auf. Auf Grund der an ihnen auftauchenden, auch anderweitig belegten Personennamen ist es L. Ognenova-Marinova

---

[40] Ognenova-Marinova 1980, S. 152–153; vgl. Ognenova 1960, S. 225, Abb. 3, 229 mit Anm. 2; Filow 1915, Sp. 235. Die in Nesebâr gemachten Funde scheinen generell etwas zu hoch angesetz zu sein; das trifft z.B. für die Mauern zu, die sich (wie Alexandrescu 1982 mitteilt) gut mit der hellenistischen Mauer von Histria vergleichen lassen und deshalb herabdatiert werden müssen.

[41] Sokol'skij 1976, S. 46, Abb. 32:2.

[42] Nach Auskunft von M. Coja bedeutet −1.50 m. das unterste, also das früheste hellenistische Niveau (1. Hälfte 3. Jh. v.); aus dem gleichen Niveau stammen—wenn auch an anderer Stelle des Sektors $Z_2$ ausgegraben—von ihr an den Anfang des 3. Jh. v. datierte kannelierte und glatte Schwarzfirnis-Kantharoi wie z.B. *Histria* V, S. 45, Nr. 12, 13, S. 37, Abb. 2, Taf. 2:12, 13; die von ihr vorgeschlagene Datierung des Traufziegels in das 4. Jh. v. ist also zu berichten.

[43] Wie die Fundkomplexe Histria 1972 T ([obiecte] 54–57, 59) zusammen mit dem Keramik-Komplex Histria 1972 T (29) gefunden, der gemischte Keramik mit Schwarzfirnis und Kanneluren sowie West-Slope-Ware vornehmlich des 3./2. Jh. v., aber auch ein Stück des ausgehenden 4. Jh. v. enthält.

[44] Fundinventar nicht vorhanden; befand sich in einem Kasten mit Funden Histria 1966 T, der Pseudo-Kos-Amphoren und Keramik des 1. Jh. v. enthält, wobei nicht sicherzustellen ist, ob der Kasteninhalt einen Fundzusammenhang wiedergibt.

[45] Nach Auskunft von M. Coja bedeutet "Wohnung mit Pflaster" an diesem Fundplatz ein Niveau mit Bautrümmern, das über der Schicht des 4. Jh. v. liegt, also hellenistisch zu datieren wäre.

möglich,[46] Dachterrakotten, die den Namen des Moschos (ca. 3. Viertel des 4. Jh. v.) tragen,[47] mit Olbia, diejenigen mit dem des Euphamidas dagegen mit Mesambria (Nesebâr) zu verbinden; auch für die in Odessos (Varna) und Mesambria (Nesebâr) gefundenen, wohl in der gleichen Matrize geformten Stücke mit dem Namen des Anthesterios ergibt sich auf diese Weise westpontische Provenienz, die man auch für den in Olbia, Histria und Mesambria (Nesebâr) gleichermaßen vorkommenden thrakischen Namen Rebas annahmen möchte. Neben jeweils lokaler Produktion von Dachterrakotten in Olbia, Histria und Mesambria (Nesebâr) bestehen also zwischen diesen Städten auch Exportbeziehungen, die natürlich nicht auf diese beiden Orte beschränkt bleiben. Denn für Olbia[48] werden auf der Basis kleinerer Unterschiede in der Zurichtung, Ornamentik und Tonzusammensetzung nicht nur verschiedene lokale, vielleicht nacheinander arbeitende Werkstätten, sondern auch Import aus Sinope und Herakleia wahrscheinlich gemacht. Dafür bieten die zwei Traufziegelfragmente aus Histria (**6, 18**), die sich durch ihre Tonbeschaffenheit als Importstücke aus Sinope zu erkennen geben, eine willkommene Bestätigung. Weitere Aussagen zum wichtigen Problem der Austauschbeziehungen zwischen den Griechenstädten des Schwarzmeergebietes in hellenistischer Zeit lassen sich aus dem hier vorgestellten histrianischen Material vorerst nicht gewinnen, zugleich wird aber deutlich, welchen Beitrag zu dessen Lösung Tonanalysen leisten können.

Die in Histria bei den Traufziegeln mit Reliefmäander durch kleine Abweichungen in Zurichtung und Ornament angetroffene Vielfalt macht deutlich, daß es sich bei ihnen um Überreste einer größeren Zahl von Dachrändern handeln muß. In keinem Fall gibt es jedoch Nachrichten darüber, ob in der Nähe ihrer Fundorte auch Gebäudereste angetroffen wurden, deren Aufbau sie dann mit gewisser Sicherheit zugeordnet werden könnten. Vermutlich haben die Bauwerke, zu denen sie einst gehörten, nicht oder nur im Sockel aus Stein, im übrigen aus vergänglichem Material bestanden. Denn auch über das sonstige Aussehen der Dächer ist nichts weiter zu ermitteln, als daß die zur Front umbiegenden Seitenstege eine bestimmte Form von Traufkalypteren erforderlich machen. Von solchen an der Stirnseite geschlossenen und wohl ebenfalls mit Reliefdekor geschmückten, vor allem aber im unteren Auflageteil ausgeklinkten Traufkalypteren hellenistischer Zeit sind, im Gegensatz zu Olbia, aus Histria bisher keine Überreste bekanntgeworden. Hingegen lassen sich die Wurzeln des zumindest im Schwarzmeergebiet die tönernen Dachränder hellenistischer Bauten häufig zierenden, hier also besonders beliebten Reliefmäanders mit eingestreuten Feldern bis zum normalerweise gemalten Hakenmäander spätarchaischer Zeit zurückverfolgen.[49] In der späteren Zeit ist ihm eine große Verbreitung als Dekorationsglied mit Aufnahme sogar in den Monumentalbau beschieden.

---

[46] Ognenova-Marinova 1980, S. 153–154.

[47] Vgl. Brašinskij, in Zeest 1966, S. 39.—Ognenova-Marinova macht darauf aufmerksam (7.10.1978), daß in Nesebâr inzwischen sogar eine Dachterrakotte (Inv. 1789; Traufziegel oder Sima ?) mit dem komplett eingestempelten Namen des Moschos entdeckt worden sei, die wegen des späteren Fundes jedoch nicht mehr in *Nessèbre* II habe Aufnahme finden können.

[48] Vgl. Brašinskij, in Zeest 1966, S. 40, Anm. 29–30.

[49] Einen spätarchaischen Hakenmäander in Relief zeigt ein Antefix aus Mytilene/Lesbos: Koch 1915, S. 29, 30, Abb. 11; Åkerström 1966, S. 25, 26, Taf. 12:1: Ende 6. Jh. v. Zwei weitere ostgriechische Beispiele der 2. Hälfte des 6. Jh. v. in Hornbostel 1980, S. 26, Nr. 19, 20, mit Abb. S. 25, 27.

# KATALOG

Die Stücke sind chronologisch nach ihrem Funddatum oder anderweitigen Bekanntwerden aufgeführt. Die Figuren finden sich alle zusammen am Ende des Katalogs.

Abkürzungen: Br = Breite, H = Höhe, T = Tiefe; alle Maße in cm; T = Tempelzone, $Z_2$ = Bereich der klassischen Mauer, X = Grabungssektor X; (xx) = Fundkomplex innerhalb eines Grabungsareals und Fundjahres.

**1.** Histria, 1914/15      Figs. 1, 2
[Verbleib unbekannt]

Nach Pârvan aus der 'Festung', "găsit pe cetate, spre Mare," also vermutlich Sektor T.
Pârvan 1916, S. 703, 704 Nr. 61:b, mit Abb.; Pippidi 1962, S. 154 Anm. 32.
Br = 8,7 ; H = 6,0; T = 5,0 (Pârvan).

Mittelstück mit Rest der Oberseite, hinten gebrochen. Reliefmäander mit eingestreuter, leicht angehobener viereckiger Platte (*ca.* 3 × 3 cm): Buchstabe A.

**2.** Histria, (Alte Funde) 1927–1942      Fig. 3
(altes Inv. B 2602)

Aufschrift mit Bleistift: Histria; mit Tinte: B 2602.
Br = 12,5; H = 8,8; T = 6,2.

Ton matt rötlich bis graubraun; sehr kleine rötliche Magerungsteilchen, Glimmer.

Rechtes Eckstück mit Teil der geglätteten Seitenfläche, sonst allseitig gebrochen und sehr stark bestoßen. Reliefmäander mit eingestreutem Feld: möglicherweise Rest von 5 "Würfel"- Punkten.

**3.** Histria, 1954 Plateau      Fig. 4
(Inv. V 6181)

Aus Schnitt ZV$_3$.[50]
Br = 26,1; H = 7,9–8,2; T = 10,0.

Ton dicht, matt ziegelrot; wenige schwärzliche Magerungsteilchen, Glimmer; leichte Sinterspuren.

Aus 3 Fragmenten zusammengesetztes rechtes Eckstück, links und hinten gebrochen; überall sehr stark beschädigt; rechte Seitenfläche nach hinten leicht zurückgenommen. Reliefmäander mit 2 eingestreuten Feldern: vierteilige Rosette, 5 "Würfel"-Punkte.

**4.** Histria, 1954 Sektor X      Figs. 1, 5
Aufschrift: M [ ] 3 B –0,40.[51]
Br = 10,8; H = 5,4; T = 7,4.

Ton fein, orange bis matt ziegelrot; porös durch weißliche, rötliche und schwärzliche Magerungsteilchen, Glimmer; Reste von Muscheln oder Schnecken (?). Gelblich-grauer Überzug (?) an Front.

Mittelstück mit roh geebneter Oberseite, unten und hinten gebrochen. Reliefmäander mit eingestreutem Feld: Buchstabe E.

**5.** Histria, 1954 Sektor X      Fig. 6
(Inv. V 17 142)

Aufschrift: M [] 2c –0,40.[52]
Br = 8,3; H = 7,7; T = 1,9.

Ton rötlich-braun, sehr hart gebrannt; weißliche und rötliche Magerungsteilchen, Glimmer; Reste von Sinter (?).

Mittelstück mit schmalem Streifen der Oberseite, unmittelbar hinter Front gebrochen. Reliefmäander.

**6.** Histria, 1954 Sektor X      Figs. 1, 7
Aufschrift: [] 3 –0,45.[53]
Coja 1962a, S. 24 Abb. 3:5; Coja 1962b, S. 120 Abb. 3:5; Coja in *Histria* V, S. 53 Nr. 92, Taf. 11:92.
Br = 9,8; H = 11,4; T = 10,1.

Ton rötlich-violett mit vielen, fast zitronengelben Einsprenkelungen; außerdem unterschiedlich große schwärzliche, rötliche und wenige weißliche Magerungsteilchen, Glimmer. Überall ursprünglich kräftig

---

[50] Nach Auskunft von M. Coja zwischen 1949 und 1951 ohne stratigraphischen Zusammenhang im weiteren Umfeld der klassischen Mauer Z$_2$ gefunden und offenbar 1955 von ihr "rückwirkend" beschriftet.
[51] In der römischen Nekropole (M = mormînt = Grab), also in Sekundärlage angetroffen.
[52] Wie oben Anm. 51.
[53] Nach Auskunft von M. Coja in oberster hellenistischer Schicht, angeblich aber nicht in ungestörter Fundlage aufgetaucht.

gelber, ins Grünliche tendierender Überzug, am besten an Unterseite bewahrt; an Unterkante zusätzliche dunkelrote Farbspuren.

Linkes Eckstück, rechts und hinten gebrochen, überall stark bestoßen; über Ziegelplatte erhebt sich ein *ca.* 2,5 cm hoher und *ca.* 2,2 cm breiter Steg, der 5,6 cm auf die Front umbiegt; diese *ca.* 9 cm hoch. Reliefmäander mit eingestreutem, möglicherweise durch Seitenbegrenzung angeschnittenem Feld: Buchstabe Υ; Frontsteg darüber mit teilweise gerahmtem, seitlich geschnittenem Eierstab.

7. Histria, 1954 Sektor X                    Fig. 8
   Br = 9,0; H = 11,4; T = 9,2.

Ton fein, sandig, gelblich bis matt rötlich; sehr kleine weißliche, rötliche und schwärzliche Magerungsteilchen. Hellgelber Überzug in Spuren an Front und Oberseite.

Rechtes Eckstück, links und hinten gebrochen, stark abgerieben; weitgehend geglättete, nach hinten leicht zurückweichende Seitenfläche nach *ca.* 5 cm abgesetzt und etwas tiefer fortgeführt; über Ziegelplatte erhebt sich ein *ca.* 2,4 cm hoher, in der Breite differierender Steg, der 5,9 cm und etwas schmaler auf die Front umbiegt; diese 9,0 cm hoch. Reliefmäander; Frontsteg darüber mit teilweise gerahmtem Eierstab.

8. Histria, 1954 Sektor X                    Pl. 79:d
   [Verbleib unbekannt]
   Br = 10,0; H = 5,5; T = 7,4.

Ton rötlich. Überall dunkelroter Überzug, an Front nur noch in Vertiefungen erhalten.

Mittelstück, hinten gebrochen. Reliefmäander mit eingestreutem Feld: vierteilige Rosette.

9. Histria, 1954 Sektor X                    Pl. 79:e
   [Verbleib unbekannt]
   Br = 4,5; H = 3,7; T = 2,9.
   Ton rötlich.

Mittelstück, außer oben allseitig gebrochen. Reliefmäander.

10. Histria, 1956 T (43)[54]                  Fig. 9
    Br = 16,1; H = 7,7; T = 10,2.

Ton matt ziegelrot; vereinzelt mittelgroße dunkelrote, auch weißliche Magerungsteilchen, etwas Glimmer. Spuren von Braunrot an "Würfel"-Punkten inzwischen verloren.

Mittelstück, hinten gebrochen; Front stark bestoßen und abgerieben. Reliefmäander mit 2 eingestreuten Feldern: 5 "Würfel"-Punkte, Reste einer achtteiligen Rosette.

11. Histria, vor 1957                         Figs. 1, 10
    (Inv. V 2445)
    Aufschrift, schwarz: H V. 2445.
    Canarache 1957, S. 171 Nr. 457, mit Abb.
    Br = 6,1; H = 4,7; T = 3,2.

Ton weich, sandig, hellrot; viele kleine weißliche, gelbliche, rötliche und schwärzliche Magerungsteilchen.

Allseitig, auch hinten gebrochenes Fragment. Reliefmäander mit eingestreutem Feld: Buchstabengruppe ΟΥ.

12. Histria, 1959 Sektor $Z_2$                Fig. 11
    (Inv. V 20 531)
    Aus Schnitt S4.
    Br = 9,9; H = 5,7; T = 8,0.

Ton sandig, dicht, matt ziegelrot; rötliche Magerungsteilchen, Glimmer. Weinrote Farbtupfen an Oberseite neben Aufwölbung.

Mittelstück, unten und hinten gebrochen; auf glatter Oberseite rechts nahe der Front kleine Aufwölbung (0,2 cm) als Überrest eines aufragenden Steges; Front stark bestoßen. Reliefmäander mit Rest eines eingestreuten leeren Feldes.

13. Histria, 1959 Sektor $Z_2$                Fig. 12
    Aus Schnitt S4.
    Br = 14,4; H = 7,3; T = 10,2.

Ton sandig, dicht, hell ziegelrot; wenige weißliche Beimengungen, sehr viel Glimmer.

Linkes Eckstück mit stark beschädigter Seitenfläche, hinten gebrochen; Front sehr stark beeinträchtigt. Reliefmäander mit eingestreutem Feld: Rest einer achtteiligen Rosette.

14. Histria, 1960 T (18 [?])[55]              Fig. 13
    Br = 15,0; H = 7,0; T = 6,2.

---

[54] Fundinventar nicht vorhanden.
[55] Fundinventar nicht vorhanden.

Ton matt ziegelrot bis bräunlich; unterschiedlich große ziegelrote, wenige weißliche Magerungsteilchen, Glimmer. Gelbgrauer Überzug mit Stich ins Grünliche an Oberseite, Front und deren Unterkante; schwarze Flecke vor allem an Rückseitenbruch modern.

Mittelstück, hinten gebrochen; Front sehr stark bestoßen. Reliefmäander mit eingestreutem Feld: 5 "Würfel"-Punkte.

**15.** Histria, 1963 Sektor Z$_2$    Fig. 14; Pl. 79:a–c
(Inv. V 25 536)
Aus Schnitt S6a, Süd-Profil, −1,50 m.[56]
Coja, in *Histria* V, S. 53 Nr. 88, Taf. 11:88.
Br = 32,2; H = 10,0; T = 16,0.
Ton fein, sandig, ockerfarben bis rötlich; an Flächen aufgerauht, sonst porös durch bröckelige rötliche Magerungsteilchen, Glimmer. Möglicherweise tonfarbener Überzug (Coja).

Aus 2 Fragmenten zusammengesetztes linkes Eckstück, rechts und hinten gebrochen, überall bestoßen; geglättete linke Seitenfläche nach hinten leicht zurückgenommen; in 11,6 cm Tiefe springt ein senkrechter, 3,4 cm breiter Steg vor, dessen Stirn in der Ebene der linken Frontbegrenzung liegt (rechter Winkel); hier im unteren Frontbereich zapfenförmiger Vorsprung über die Seitenfläche hinaus; über Ziegelplatte erhebt sich ein *ca.* 3 cm breiter, heute an seiner Oberfläche völlig abgerundeter, noch *ca.* 2,4 cm hoher Steg, der weniger breit und mindestens 6,8 cm auf die Front umbiegt. Reliefmäander mit mehreren eingestreuten Feldern (von rechts): wegen Bruch Füllung unsicher, 5 "Würfel"-Punkte, fünfteilige Rosette, leeres (?) Feld an linker Seite geschnitten; Frontsteg darüber mit Eierstab.

**16.** Histria, 1963 (?) Sektor Z$_2$    Fig. 15
*Passim.*
Coja, in *Histria* V, S. 53 Nr. 89, Taf. 11:89.
Br = 11,0; H = 6,3; T = 6,0.
Ton ockerfarben bis hell ziegelrot; weißliche, vereinzelt rötliche und schwärzliche Magerungsteilchen, Glimmer. Gelblicher Überzug an Unterkante und Wölbung kräftiger, an Front nur in den tieferliegenden Partien bewahrt.

Mittelstück, hinten gebrochen, überall stark beschädigt bzw. abgerieben; Unterkante der Front durch Abrieb nicht komplett (originale Fronthöhe dehalb bei 6,4–6,5 cm). Reliefmäander mit eingestreutem leeren Feld.

**17.** Histria, 1963 (?) Sektor Z$_2$    Fig. 16
*Passim.*
Coja, in *Histria* V, S. 53 Nr. 90, Taf. 11:90 (um 90° zu drehen).
Br = 7,0; H = 7,8; T = 7,2.
Ton fein, gelblich-braun; Glimmer; ein deutlicher Muschelabdruck.

Mittelstück, hinten gebrochen, überall stark abgerieben, besonders an Unterkante (Fronthöhe deshalb vielleicht etwas höher). Reliefmäander.

**18.** Histria, 1963 (?) Sektor Z$_2$    Fig. 17
*Passim.*
Coja, in *Histria* V, S. 53 Nr. 91, Taf. 11:91 (steht auf dem Kopf); Zimmermann, in Alexandrescu und Schuller 1990, S. 177 Abb. 23.
Ton und Überzug einschließlich Verteilung **6** nächst verwandt.

Mittelstück mit glatter Oberseite, hinten gebrochen; Front bestoßen. Reliefmäander mit Rest vom Rahmen eines eingestreuten Feldes.

**19.** Histria, 1966 T (65)[57]    Figs. 1, 18
Br = 8,7; H = 6,0; T = 5,0.
Ton matt ziegelrot; unterschiedlich große rötliche Magerungsteilchen, Glimmer (?). Rötlicher bis violetter Überzug an Oberseite, Front und deren rückwärtiger Wölbung; an Front größtenteils abgeplatzt.

Mittelstück, hinten gebrochen; Front stark beschädigt. Reliefmäander mit eingestreuter, leicht angehobener quadratischer Platte (2,5 × 2,5 cm): Buchstabe H.

**20.** Histria, 1966 T[58]    Fig. 19
Br = 13,5; H = 10,4; T = 7,2.
Ton dicht, matt ziegelrot; wenige weißliche Beimengungen, kaum Glimmer; vollkommen weißgrau versintert.

---

[56] Wie oben Anm. 42.
[57] Wie oben Anm. 44.
[58] Fundinventar nicht vorhanden.

Aus 2 Fragmenten zusammengesetztes linkes Eckstück, rechts und hinten gebrochen, überall sehr stark bestoßen; linke Seitenfläche nach hinten leicht zurückgenommen; über Ziegelplatte erhebt sich ein max. 3,2 cm hoher Steg, der 6,1 cm auf die Front umbiegt; diese ca. 7,5 cm hoch. Reliefmäander mit eingestreutem Feld: Reste einer fünf- oder achtteiligen (?) Rosette.[59]

**21.** Histria, 1970 Sektor Z₂      Fig. 20
Aus Schnitt S12. Aufschrift: Loc. cu pav.[60]
Br = 6,0; H = 5,9; T = 4,0.
Ton fein, sandig, hellbraun bis matt ziegelrot; selten weißliche Beigaben, Glimmer; blaugrauer Einschluß in einem Bruch. Geringste rote Farbspuren an Oberseite und Front.
Aus 2 Fragmenten zusammengesetztes, überall stark bestoßenes Mittelstück, hinten gebrochen. Reliefmäander mit eingestreutem, offenbar leerem Feld.

**22.** Histria, 1972 T ([obiecte] 58)      Fig. 21
Aus S IV₂[]1, unmittelbar unter Brandschicht 2 (sog. Burebista-Brandschicht).[61]
4,6 × 4,3.
Ton matt ziegelrot; weißliche und schwärzliche Magerungsteilchen, etwas Glimmer.
Allseitig, auch hinten gebrochenes Fragment unklarer Position. Reliefmäander.

**23.** Histria, 1973 T (49)      Fig. 22
Aus Raum a über den Anten des Aphrodite-Tempels, Nivellierungsschicht über Brandschicht 2 (sog. Burebista-Brandschicht).
Br = 19,9; H = 7,3–7,5; T = 9,8.
Ton matt ziegelrot; dunkelgraue und ziegelrote Magerungsteilchen, wenig Glimmer. Vereinzelte Reste eines gelbgrauen Überzuges (?) mit Stich ins Olivfarbene.
Mittelstück, hinten gebrochen. Reliefmäander mit eingestreutem Feld: achtteilige Rosette.

**24.** Histria      Fig. 23
[1977 im Depot aufgetaucht]
Br = 10,7; H = 6,1; T = 4,1.

Ton fein, sandig, matt ziegelrot; porös durch viele weißliche, rötliche und schwärzliche Magerungsteilchen, Glimmer; teilweise versintert.
Mittelstück, außer oben allseitig gebrochen; kleine Partie der geglätteten Oberfläche und von Wölbung der Rückseite erhalten; Front stark bestoßen und Ornament weitgehend abgerieben. Reliefmäander, rechts Ansatz eines eingestreuten Feldes.

**25.** Histria      Figs. 1, 24
[1978 im Depot aufgetaucht]
Zimmermann, in Alexandrescu und Schuller 1990, S. 169 Abb. 8.
Br = 23,3; H = 6,0; T = 15,9.
Ton ziegelrot; weißliche, rötliche und schwärzliche Magerungsteilchen.
Mittelstück, hinten gebrochen. Reliefmäander mit 2 eingestreuten Feldern: Buchstabe E, am rechten Bruch Rest einer Füllung mit Punkten oder weiterem Buchstaben.[62]

**26.** Histria      Fig. 25
[1981 im Depot aufgetaucht]
Br = 14,4; H = 8,8; T = 14,8.
Ton matt ziegelrot; teils versintert, besonders an Front als weißgrauer Überzug.
Linkes Eckstück, sonst allseitig gebrochen; sehr stark bestoßen und abgerieben; im rechten Winkel zur Front ansetzende Seitenfläche geglättet, oben einwärts geneigt; über Ziegelplatte erhebt sich ein 2,5 cm hoher und 3,5 cm breiter, oben glatter Steg, der 7,1 cm auf die Front umbiegt und ursprünglich ca. 3 cm breit war. Reliefmäander mit 2 eingestreuten Feldern: links geschnitten, fünfteilige Rosette; Frontsteg darüber mit Resten eines Eierstabes.

**27.** Histria      Fig. 26
[1981 im Depot aufgetaucht]
Br = 11,8; H = 4,0; T = 12,7.
Ton gelbgrau bis rötlich, hart gebrannt; rötliche und schwärzliche Magerungsteilchen; Brüche und Unterseite stark versintert. Dunkler, braunroter, teils zu Schwarz neigender Überzug an Front und stark abschiefernd an Oberseite.

---

[59] Zum Teil außerordentlich schwach, scheinen sich fünf Rosettenblätter sicher und möglicherweise zwei weitere abzuzeichnen.
[60] Wie oben Anm. 45.
[61] Vgl. oben Anm. 43.
[62] Wie oben Anm. 16.

Mittelstück, außer oben allseitig gebrochen. Reliefmäander.

**28.** Histria    Figs. 1, 27
[1983 im Depot aufgetaucht]
Br = 13,1; H = 5,5; T = 6,4.

Ton sehr fein, orange bis ziegelrot; wenige weißliche und schwärzliche Magerungsteilchen, Glimmer.

Mittelstück, hinten gebrochen. Reliefmäander mit eingestreutem Feld: Buchstabengruppe K[A ?].

**29.** Histria, 1990 Plateau    Fig. 28
*Passim.*
Br = 9,8; H = 6,5; T = 10,7.

Ton ziegelrot; vereinzelt weißliche Beimengungen. Spuren eines gelblichen Überzuges (?) an Oberfläche und Teilen der Front.

Mittelstück, hinten gebrochen. Reliefmäander mit Rest eines eingestreuten leeren Feldes.

**30.** Histria, 1991 Plateau    Fig. 29
Aus dem Bereich Sektor X 1966–1968, *passim*.
Br = 23,4; H = 7,1; T = 9,4.

Ton dunkel ziegelrot; viele weißliche, gelegentlich schwärzliche Beimengungen, vereinzelt Glimmer.
Mittelstück, hinten gebrochen; Front erheblich abgerieben; Oberfläche der Ziegelplatte beidseitig geringfügig ansteigend. Reliefmäander mit 2 eingestreuten Feldern: achtteilige Rosette, 5 "Würfel"-Punkte.

**31.** Histria, 1991 Sektor T    Figs. 1, 30
Aus römisch-byzantinischen Schichten südöstlich des Aphrodite-Tempels, *passim*.
Br = 17,3; H = 9,5; T = 8,2.

Ton matt ziegelrot; vereinzelt dunkelrote und schwärzliche Magerungsteilchen. Reste eines weitgehend abgeriebenen weinroten Überzuges an gesamter Oberseite, Front und Unterseite der Wassernase.

Linkes Eckstück, rechts und hinten gebrochen; links allerdings nur ein kleiner Streifen der nach oben leicht einwärts geneigten Seitenfläche erhalten; über Ziegelplatte erheben sich Reste eines Steges, der max. 8,5 cm auf die Front umbiegt, hier *ca.* 3,7 cm hoch ist und Trapezform annimmt; Spuren des Modellierholzes an Wassernase. Reliefmäander mit 2 eingestreuten, leicht angehobenen quadratischen Platten (2,6 × 2,6 cm): Buchstaben A, Δ; Frontsteg darüber mit stilisiertem spiralartigen Pflanzenornament.

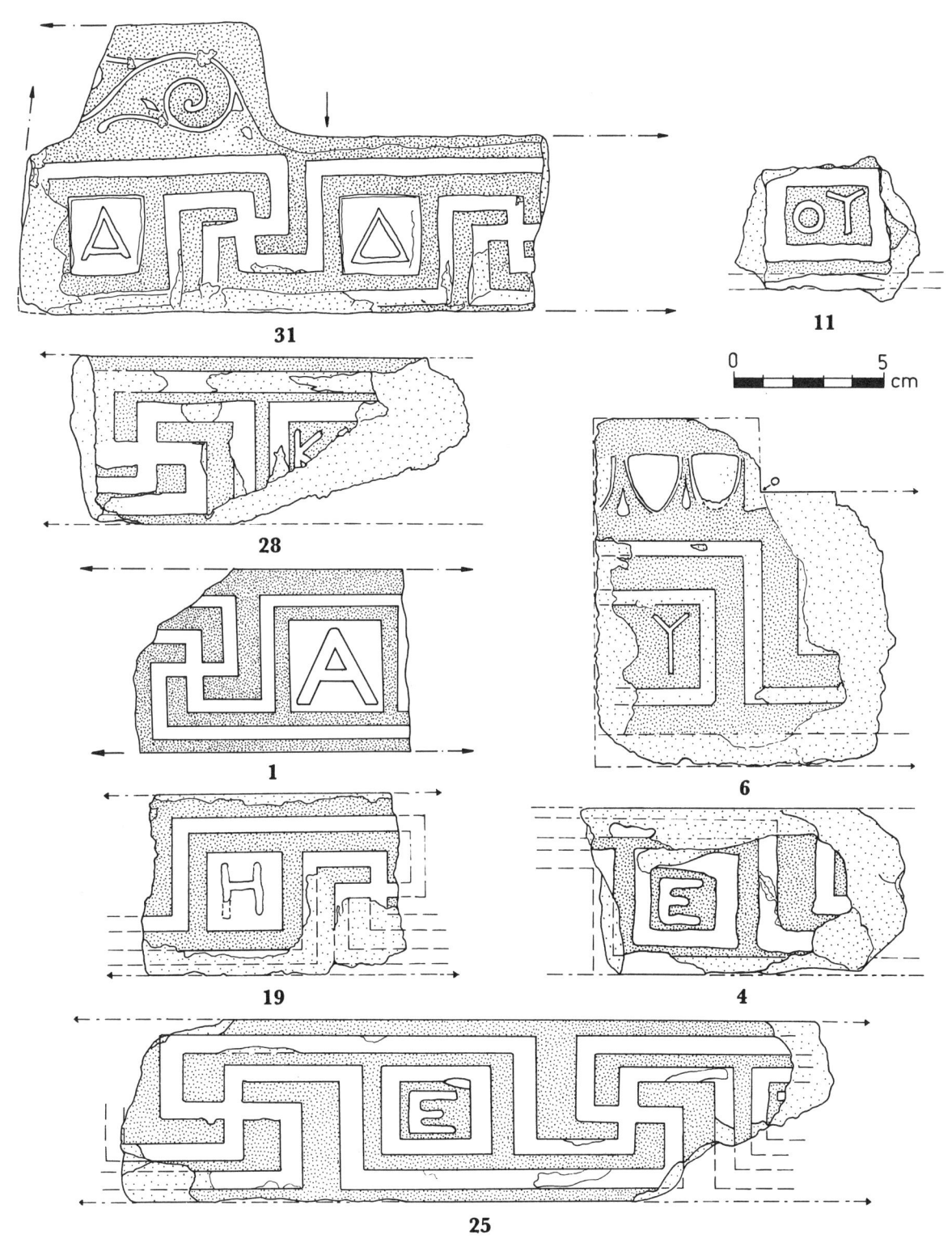

FIG. 1. Zusammenstellung von Traufziegeln mit Reliefmäander und eingestreuten Buchstaben: Fronten von **31, 11, 28, 1, 6, 19, 4, 25**

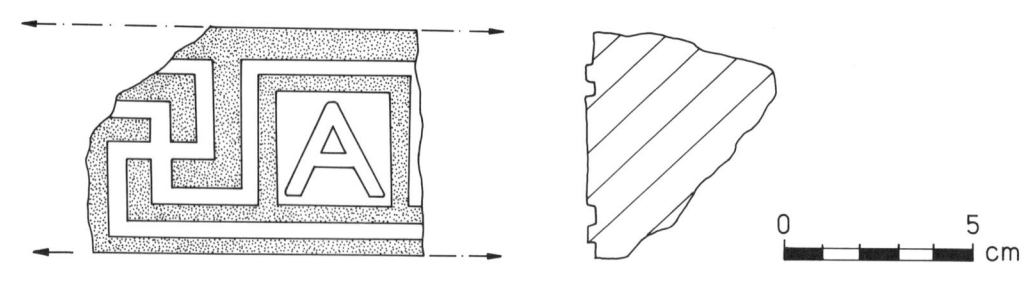

FIG. 2. **1**: Front, Schnitt

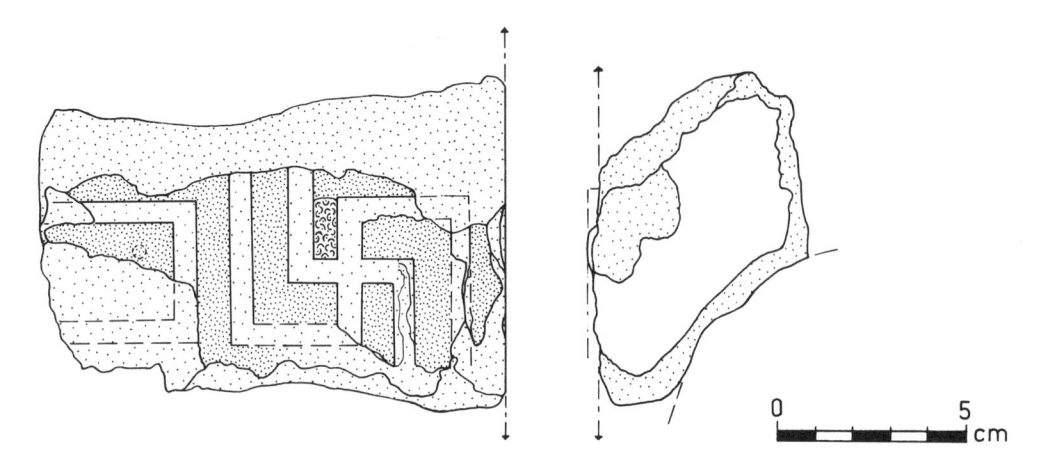

FIG. 3. **2**: Front, Seitenansicht rechts

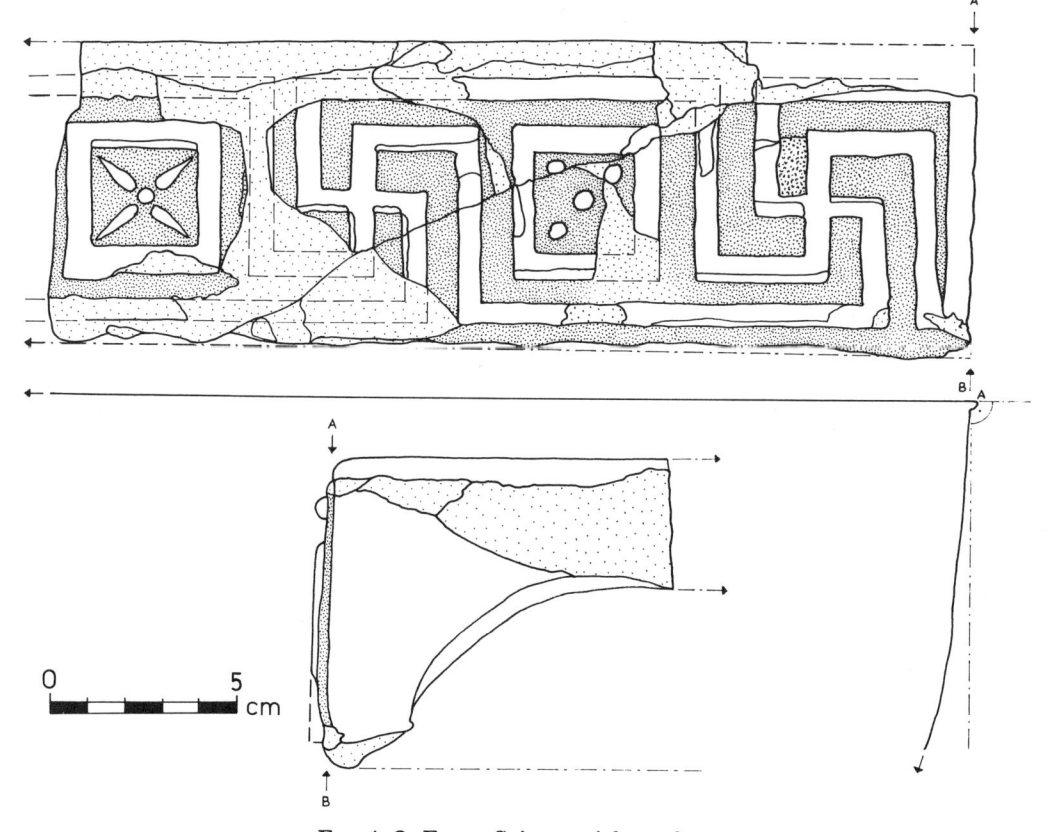

FIG. 4. **3**: Front, Seitenansicht rechts

# TRAUFZIEGEL MIT RELIEFMÄANDER AUS DEM SCHWARZMEERGEBIET 237

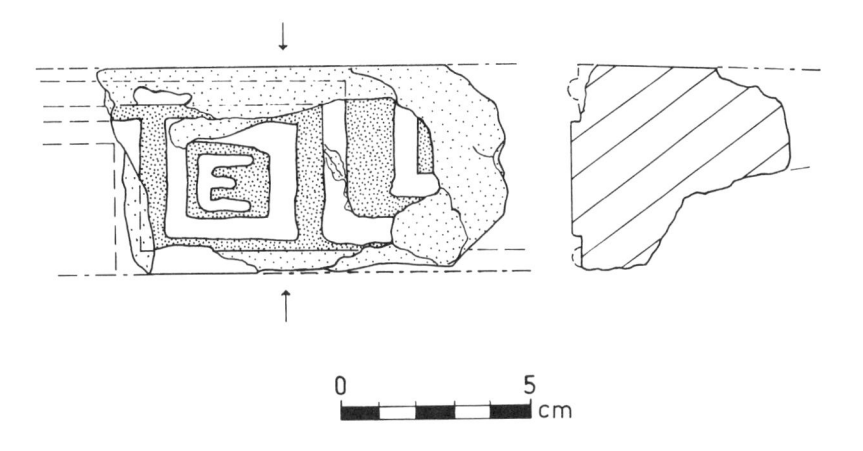

Fig. 5. **4**: Front, Schnitt

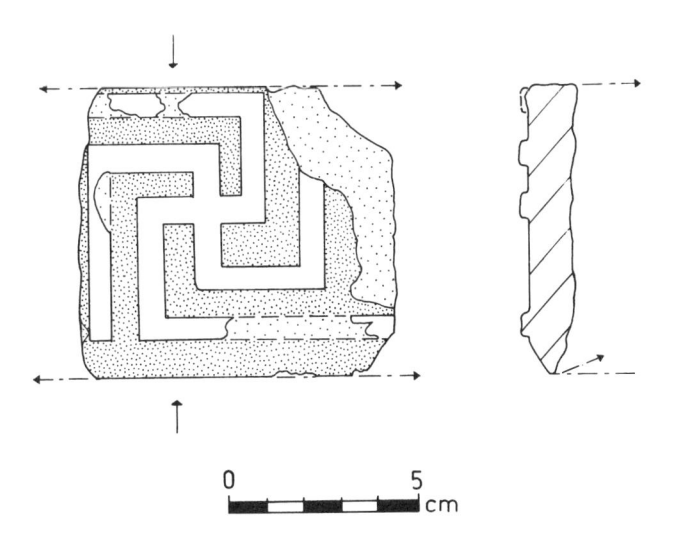

Fig. 6. **5**: Front, Schnitt

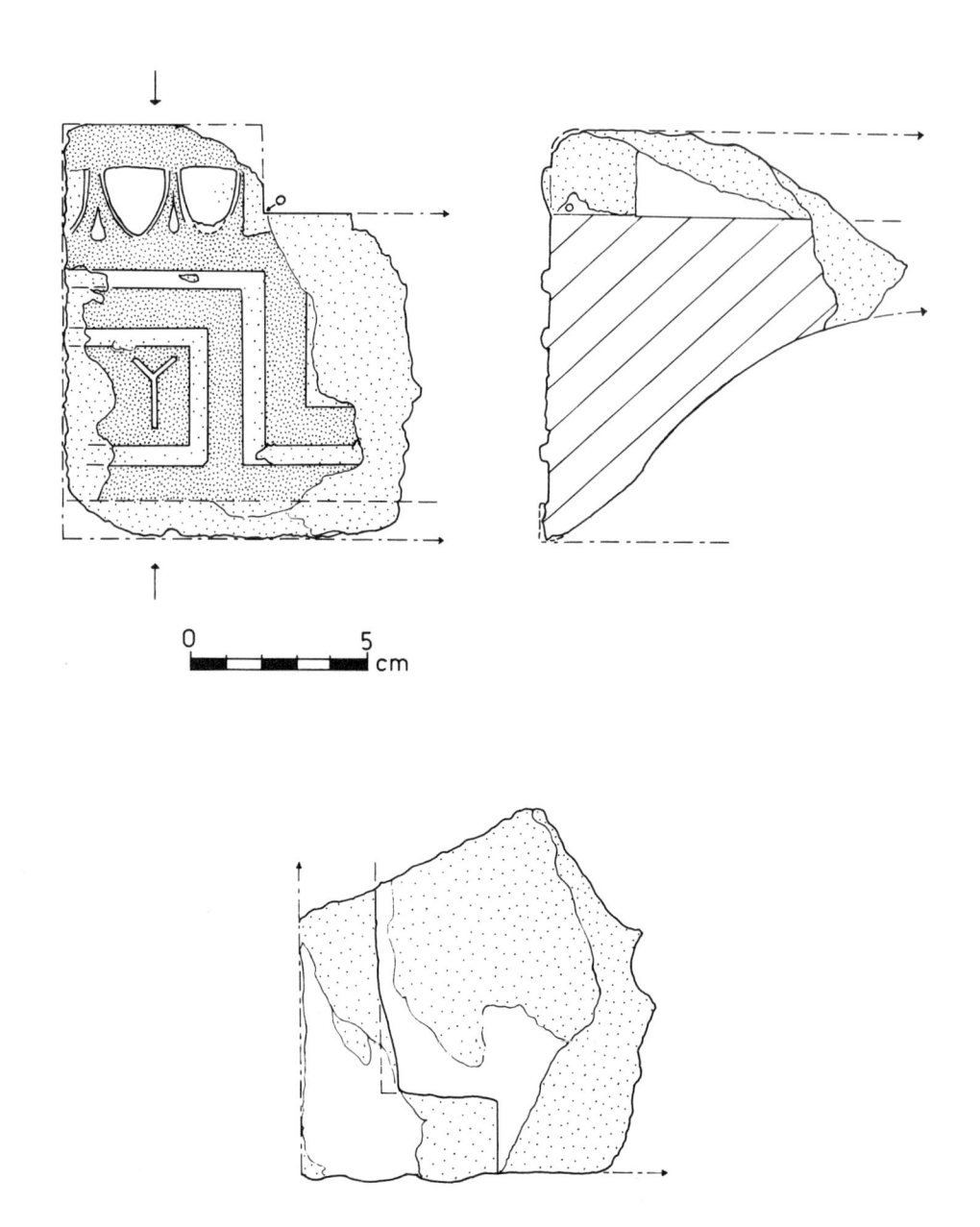

FIG. 7. **6**: Front, Schnitt, Aufsicht

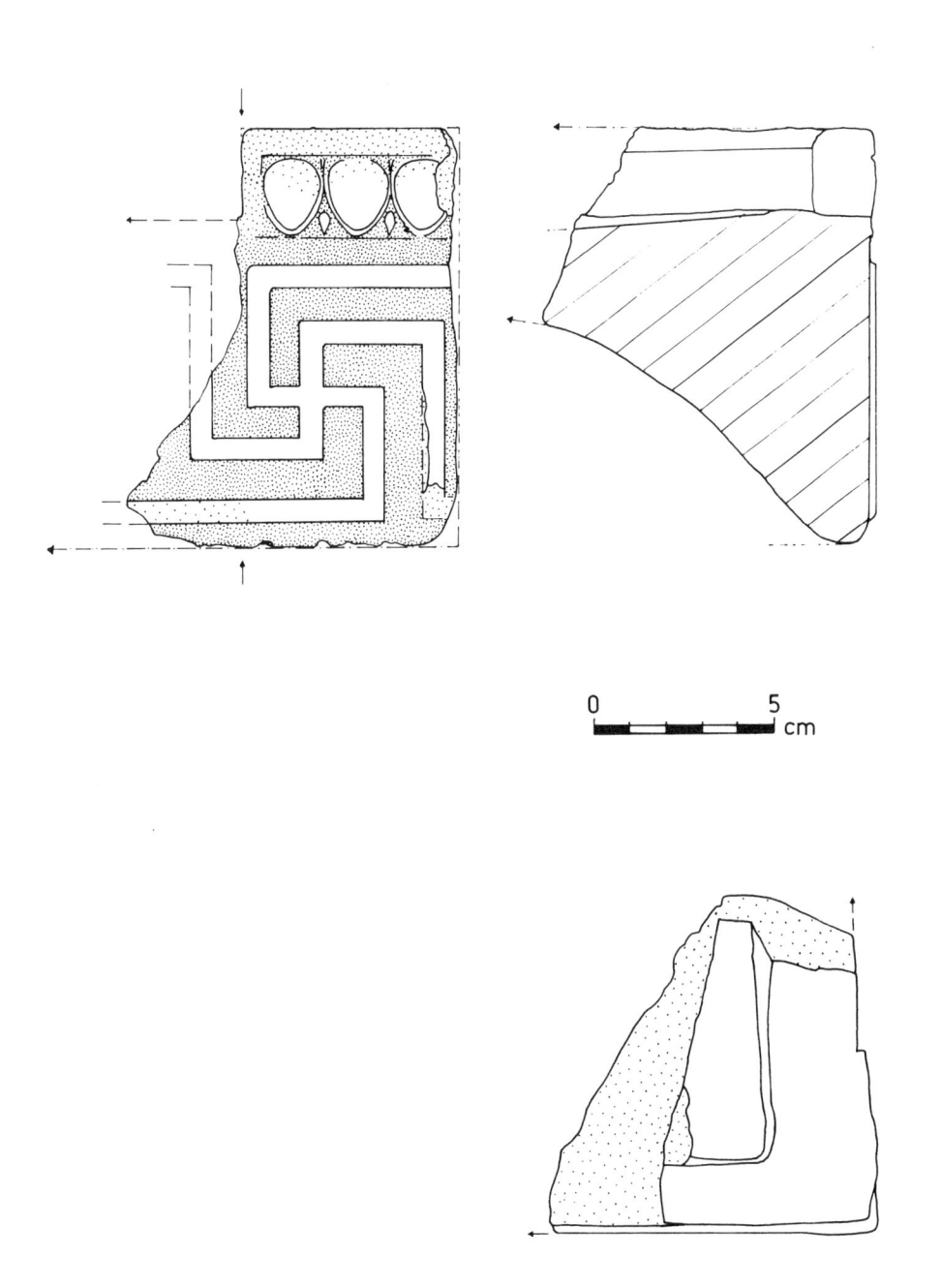

Fig. 8. **7**: Front, Schnitt, Aufsicht

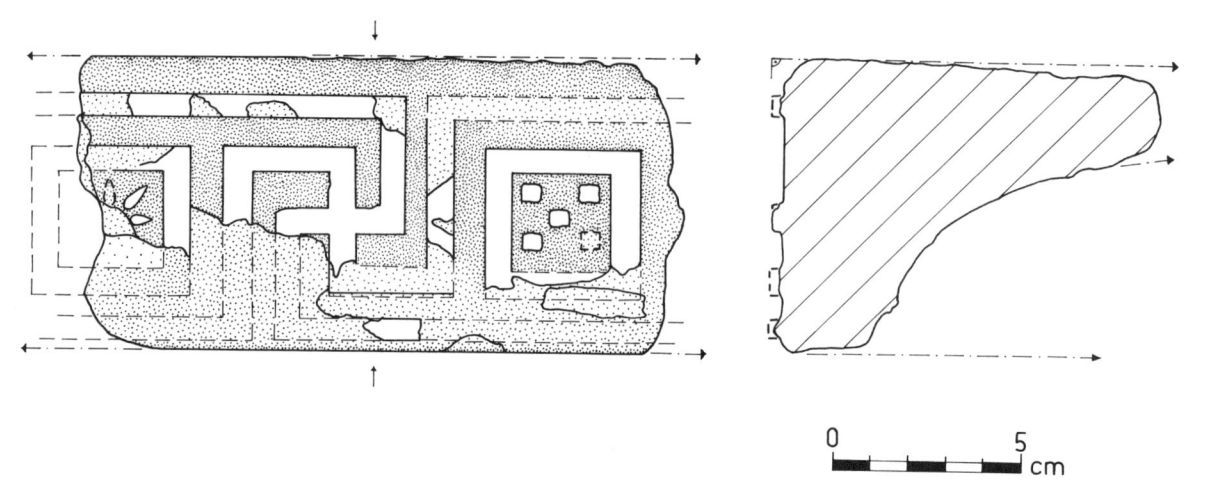

Fig. 9. **10**: Front, Schnitt

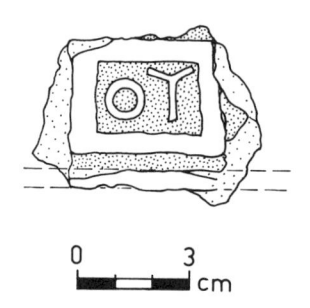

Fig. 10. **11**: Front

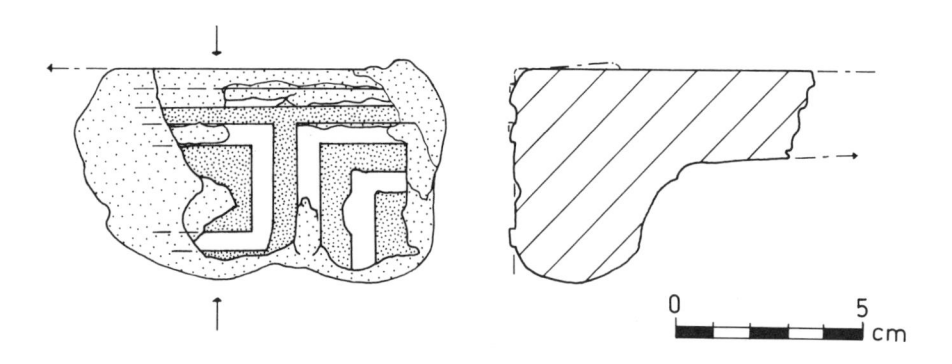

Fig. 11. **12**: Front, Schnitt

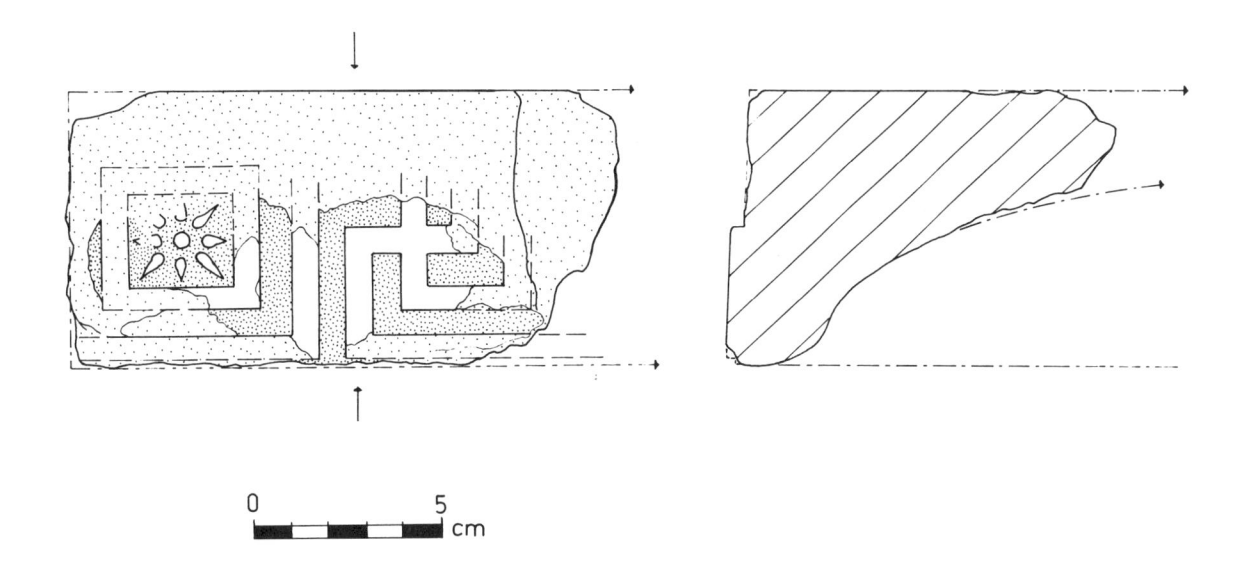

FIG. 12. **13**: Front, Schnitt

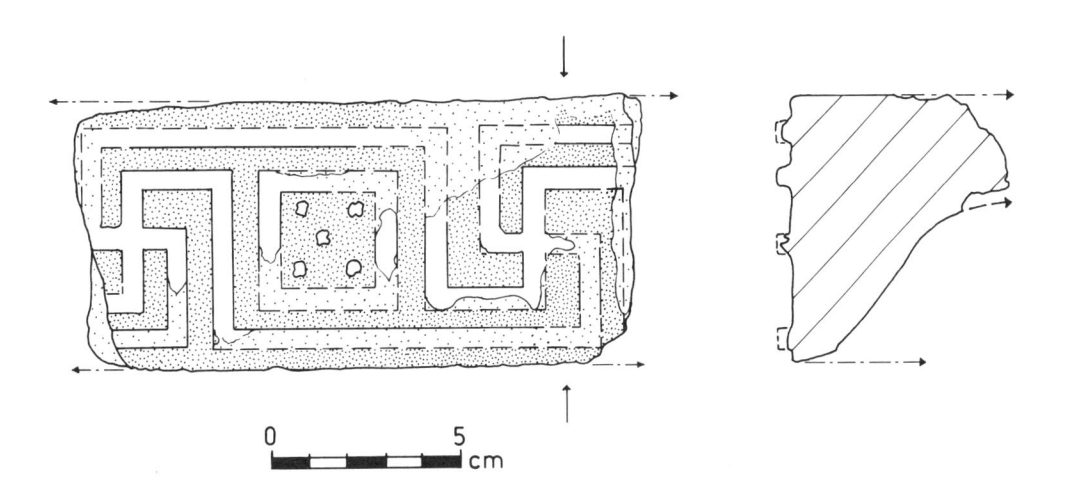

FIG. 13. **14**: Front, Schnitt

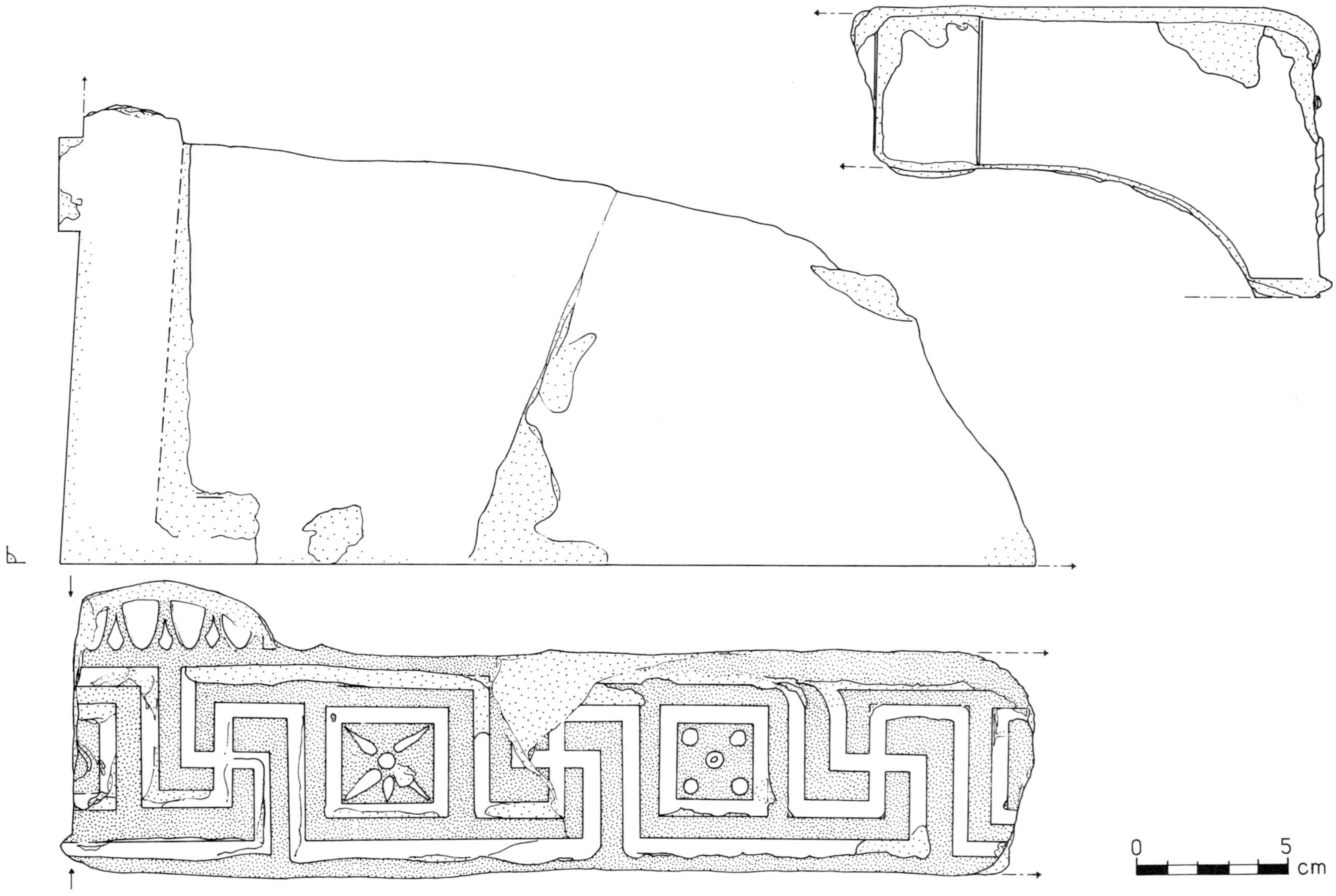

FIG. 14. **15**: Aufsicht, Seitenansicht links, Front

# TRAUFZIEGEL MIT RELIEFMÄANDER AUS DEM SCHWARZMEERGEBIET

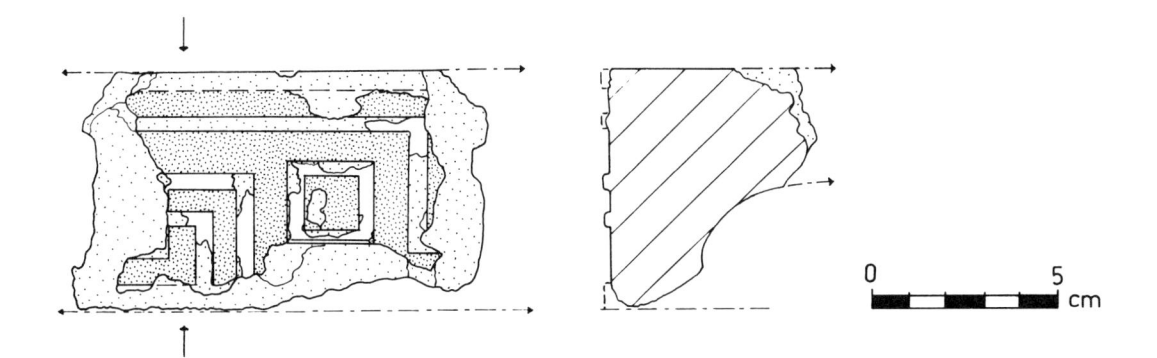

FIG. 15. **16**: Front, Schnitt

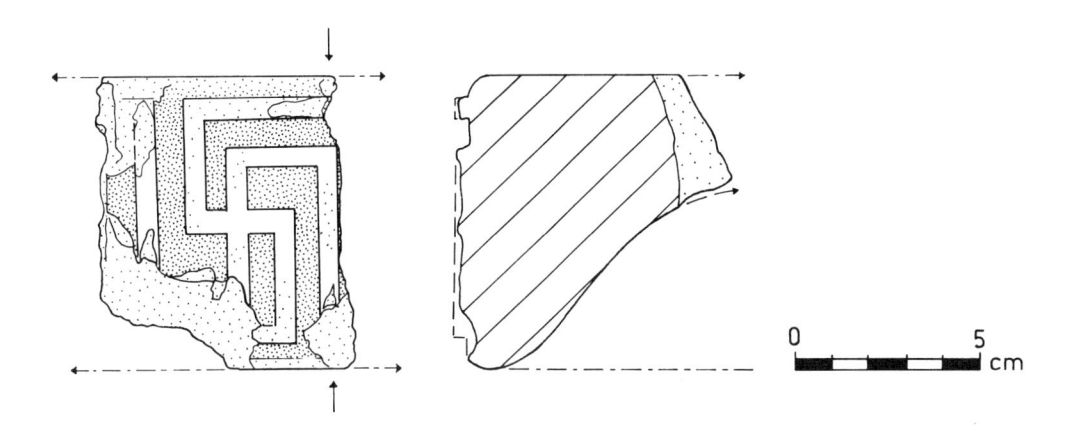

FIG. 16. **17**: Front, Schnitt

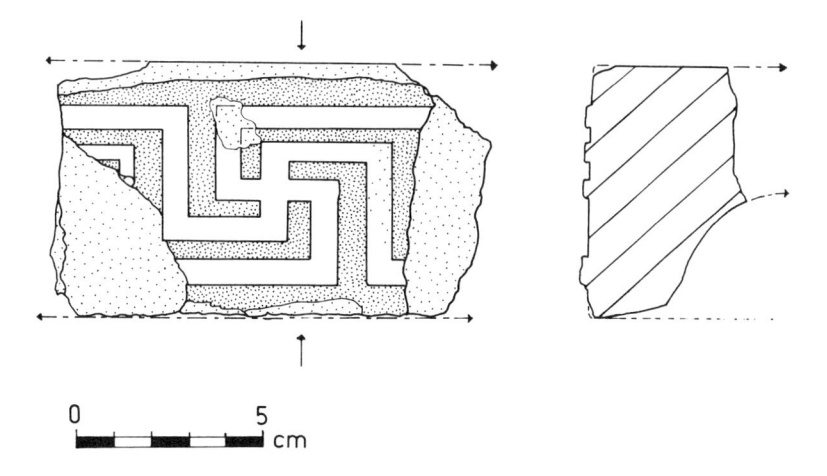

FIG. 17. **18**: Front, Schnitt

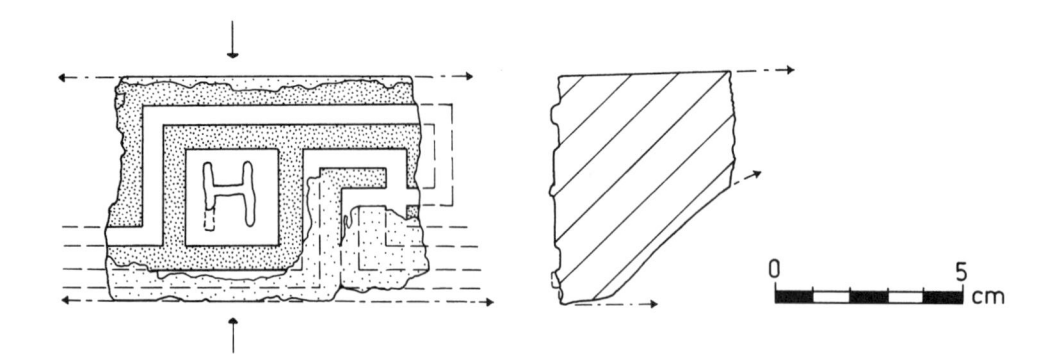

Fig. 18. **19**: Front, Schnitt

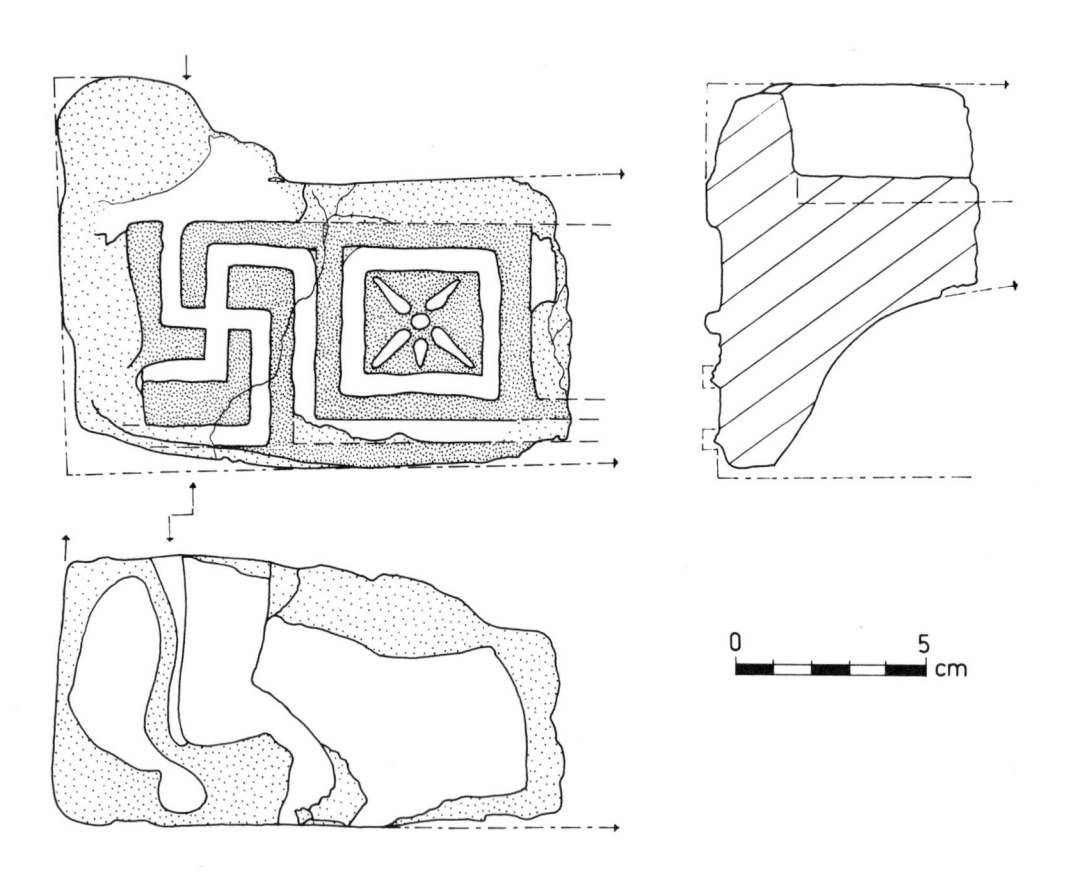

Fig. 19. **20**: Front, Schnitt, Aufsicht

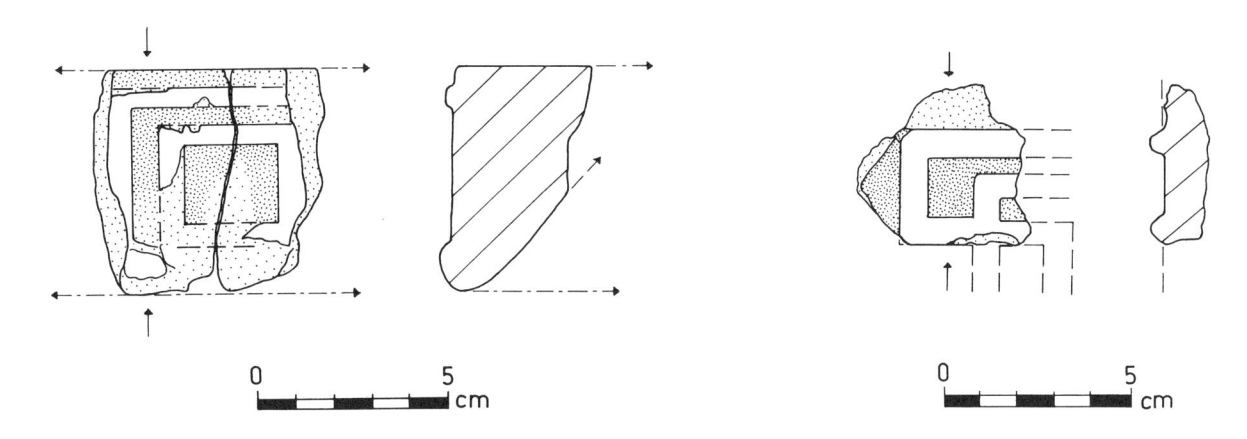

FIG. 20. **21**: Front, Schnitt

FIG. 21. **22**: Front, Schnitt

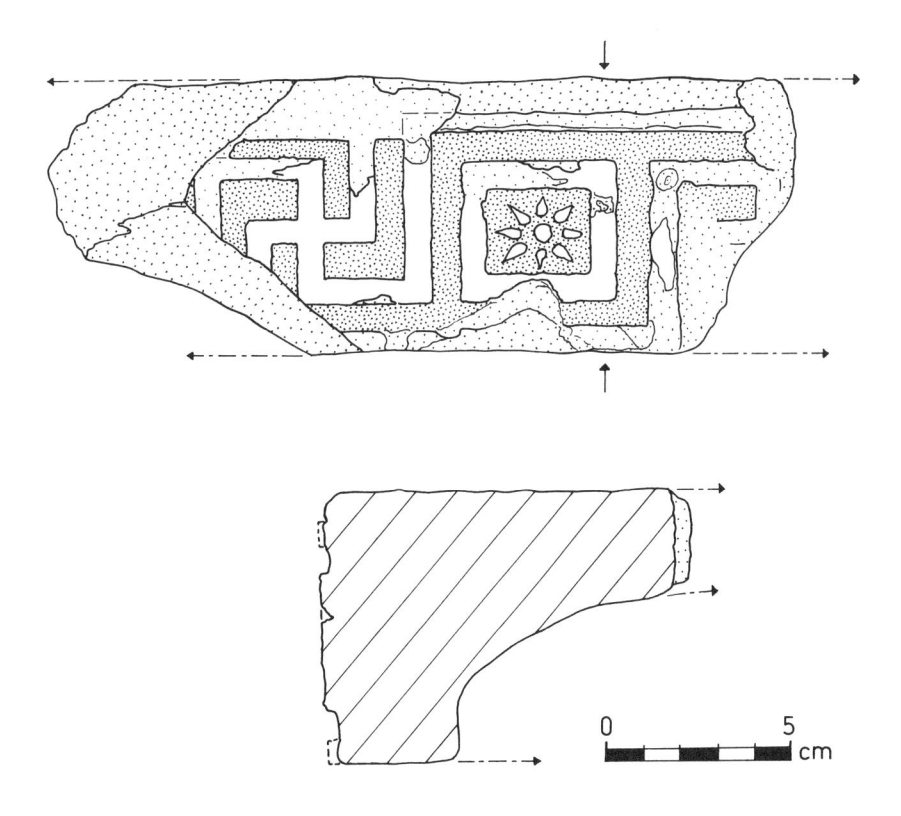

FIG. 22. **23**: Front, Schnitt

246   KONRAD ZIMMERMANN

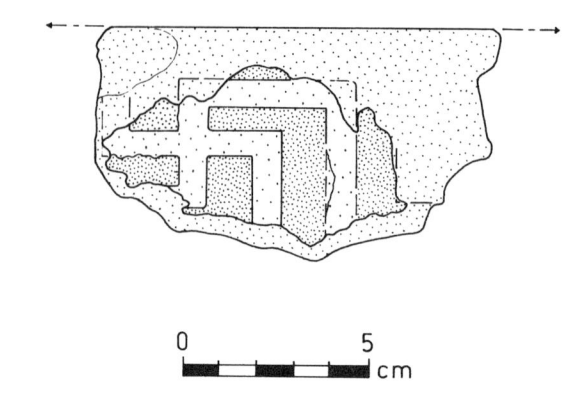

Fig. 23. **24**: Front

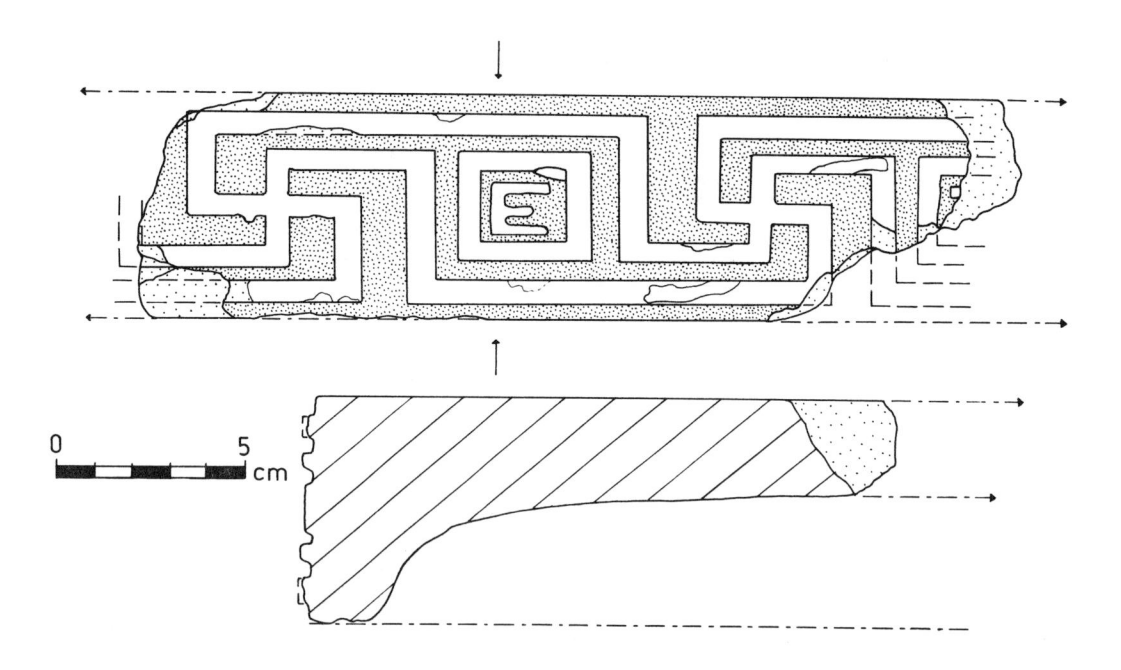

Fig. 24. **25**: Front, Schnitt

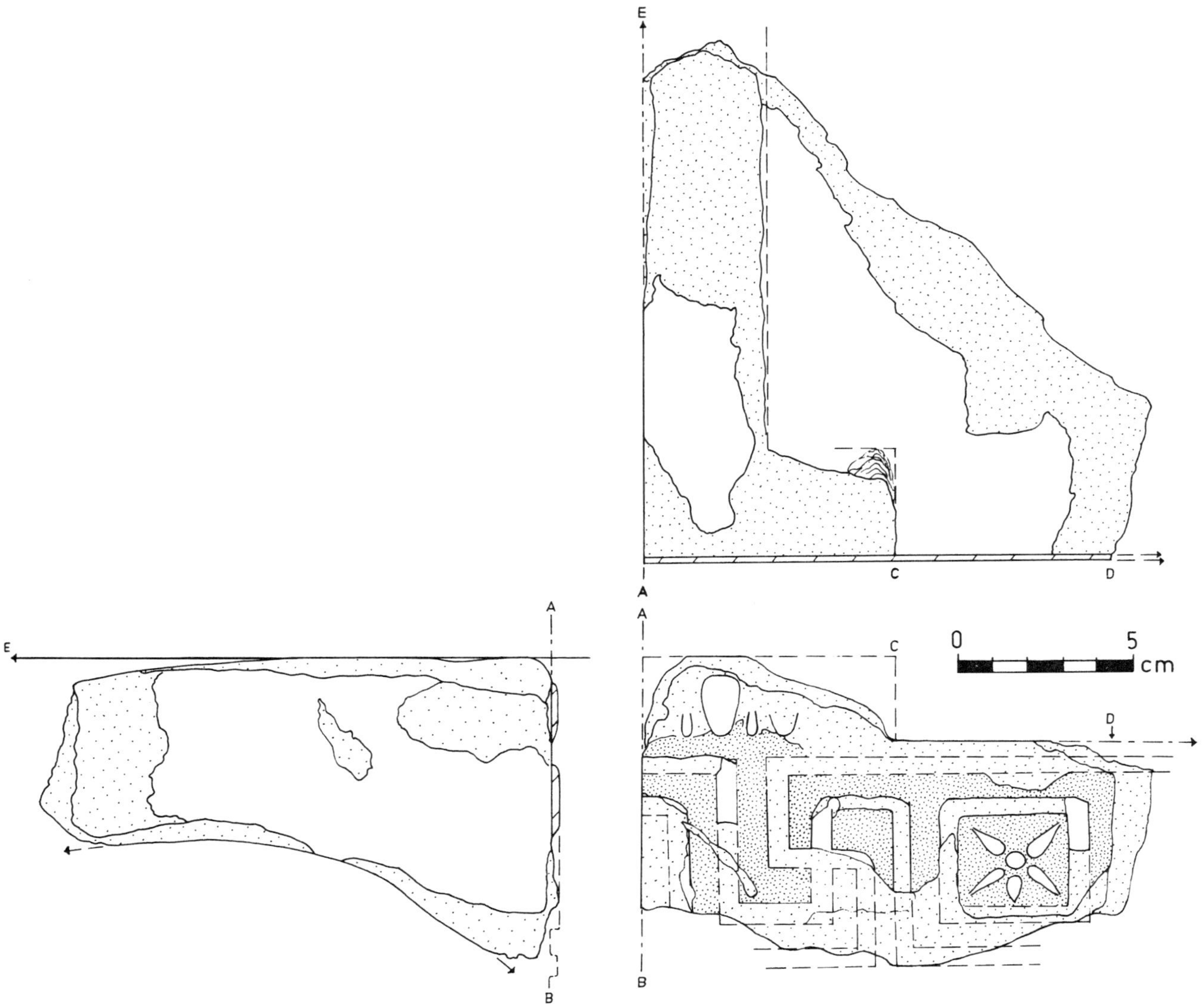

FIG. 25. **26**: Aufsicht, Seitenansicht links, Front

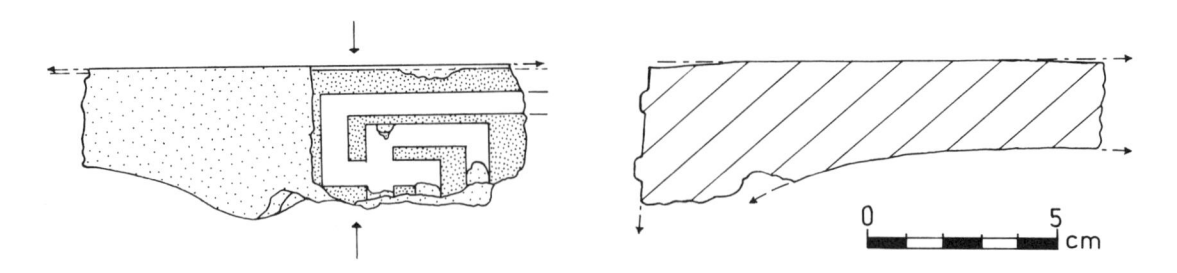

FIG. 26. **27**: Front, Schnitt

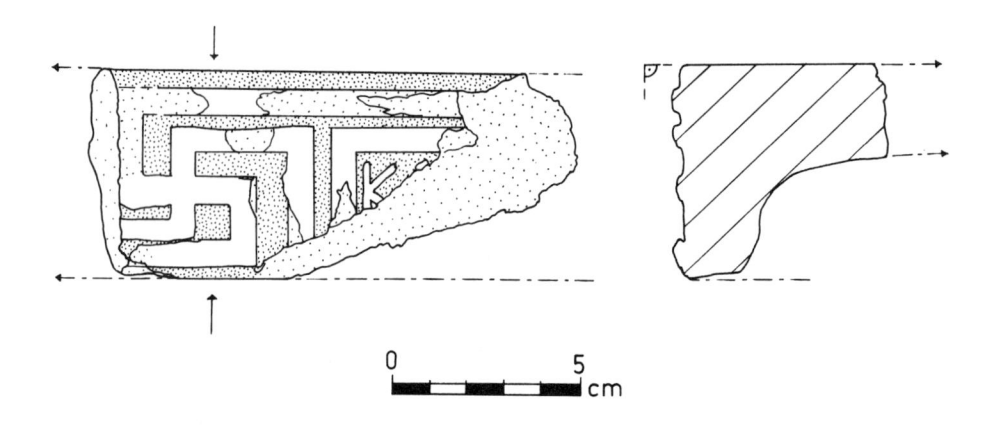

FIG. 27. **28**: Front, Schnitt

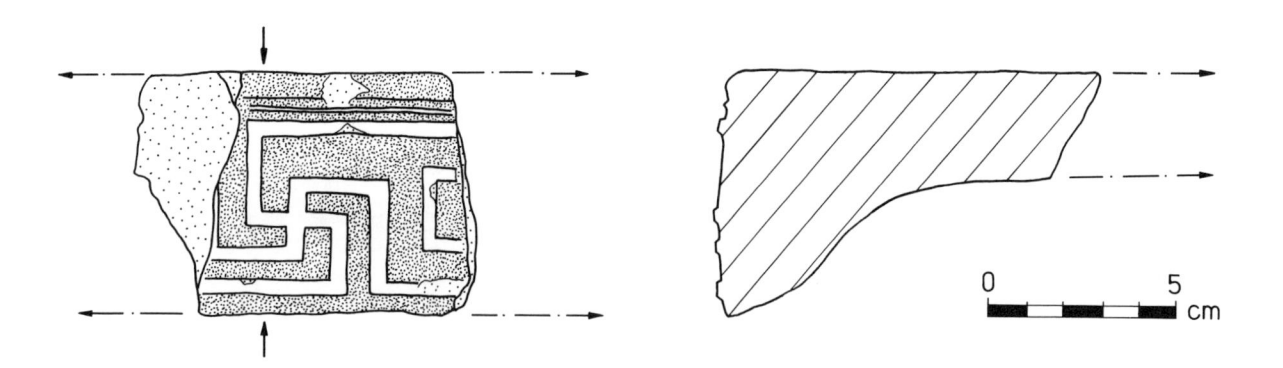

FIG. 28. **29**: Front, Schnitt

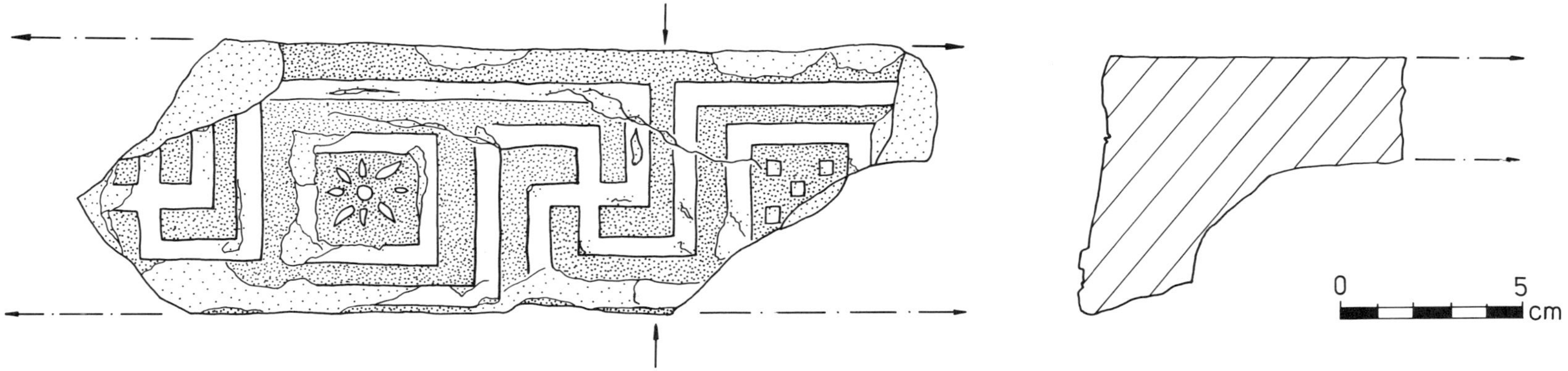

Fig. 29. **30**: Front, Schnitt

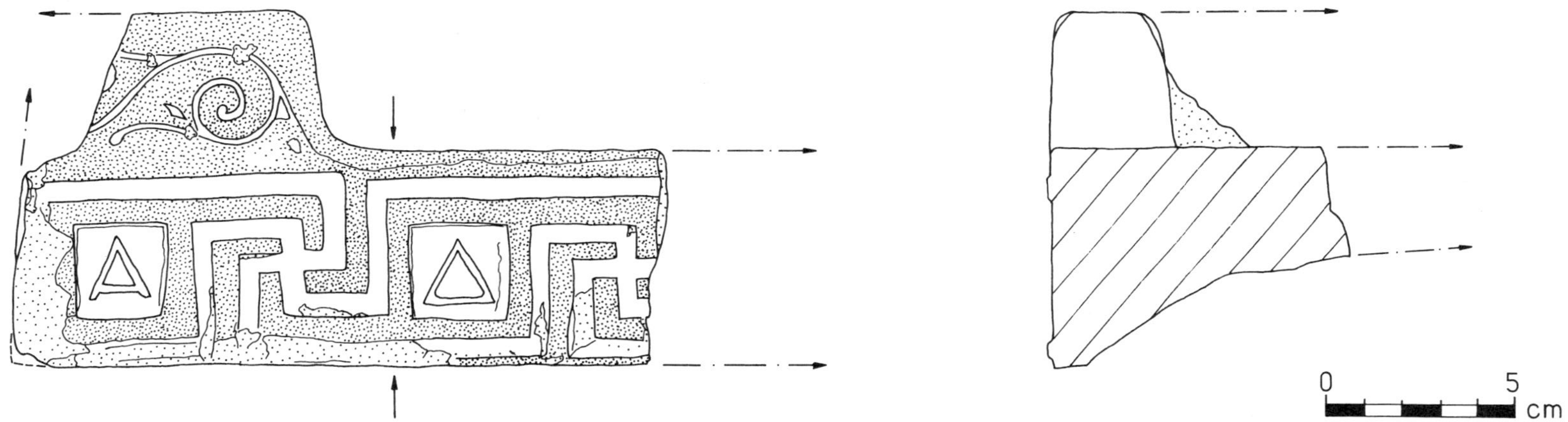

Fig. 30. **31**: Front, Schnitt

## BIBLIOGRAPHIE

Åkerström, Å. 1966. *Die architektonischen Terrakotten Kleinasiens* (Acta Instituti Athenienses Regni Sueciae XI), Lund

Alexandrescu, P. 1982. Rezension zu *Nessèbre* II in *Pontica* 15, S. 47–55

Alexandrescu, P., und W. Schuller. 1990. *Histria. Eine Griechenstadt an der rumänischen Schwarzmeerküste* (Xenia. Konstanzer Althistorische Vorträge und Forschungen 25) [darin S. 155–157: K. Zimmermann, "Zu den Dachterrakotten griechischer Zeit aus Histria"], P. Alexandrescu und W. Schuller, Hrsg., Konstanz

*AvP* VIII, ii = E. Fabricius und C. Schuchhardt, *Die Inschriften von Pergamon* (Altertümer von Pergamon VIII, ii), M. Fränkel, Hrsg., Berlin 1895

*AvP* IX = E. Boehringer und F. Krauss, *Das Temenos für den Herrscherkult, "Prinzessinnen Palais"* (Altertümer von Pergamon IX), Berlin 1937

*AvP* X = A. von Szalay und E. Boehringer, *Die hellenistischen Arsenale* (Altertümer von Pergamon X), Berlin 1937

Billot, M.-F. 1976. "Terres cuites architecturales du Musée Épigraphique," Δελτ 31, 1976, A' [1980], S. 87–135

Buschor, E. 1929. *Die Tondächer der Akropolis*, I, *Simen*, Berlin/Leipzig

Canarache, V. 1957. *Importul amforelor stampilate la Histria*, București

Coja, M. 1962a. "Activitatea meșteșugărească la Histria în sec. VI–I î.e.n.," *Studii și cercetări de istorie veche [și arheologie]* 13, S. 19–46

———. 1962b. "L'artisanat à Histria du VI<sup>e</sup> au I<sup>er</sup> siècle avant notre ère," *Dacia* n.s. 6, S. 115–138

*Delos* V = F. Courby, *Portique d'Antigone ou du nord-est* (Delos V), Paris 1912

Filow, B. 1915. "Bulgarien," *AA* [*JdI* 30], Sp. 218–236

Gneisz, D. 1994. "Die Dachterrakotten von Aigeira," in *Hesperia* Supplement 27, pp. 125–134

*Hesperia* Supplement 27 = *Proceedings of the International Conference on Greek Architectural Terracottas of the Classical and Hellenistic Periods, Athens, December 12–15, 1991* (Hesperia Supplement 27), N. A. Winter, Hrsg., Princeton 1994

*Histria* V = M. Coja und P. Dupont, *Ateliers céramiques* (Histria V), București/Paris 1979

Hornbostel, W. 1980. *Museum für Kunst und Gewerbe Hamburg: Aus Gräbern und Heiligtümern. Die Antikensammlung W. Kropatscheck*, Mainz

Hübner, G. 1975. "Dachterrakotten im Magazin des Museums von Nauplia," in *Tiryns* VIII, Mainz, S. 117–136

Kästner, V. 1994. "Kleinasien und Griechenland: Dachterrakotten nacharchaischer Zeit aus Pergamon," in *Hesperia* Supplement 27, pp. 253–268

Karajotov, I. 1975. "Trakijska krepost na severnija brjag na Mandrenskoto ezero," *Izkustvo* (Sofija) 25:3–4, S. 25–29

Koch, H. 1915. "Studien zu den campanischen Dachterrakotten," *RM* 30, S. 1–115

Metzger, I. 1971. "Piraeus-Zisterne," Δελτ 26, 1971, A' [1973], S. 41–94

Miller, Stella G. 1994. "Architectural Terracottas from Ilion," in *Hesperia* Supplement 27, pp. 269–273

Ognenova, L. 1960. "Les fouilles de Mesambria," *BCH* 84, S. 221–232

———. 1975. "Podvodna archeologija v Nesebăr," *Vekove* 1975:3, S. 43–48

Ognenova-Marinova, L. 1980. "Tuiles et terres cuites architecturales," in *Nessèbre* II, V. Velkov, Hrsg., Sofia, S. 110–155

Pârvan, V. 1916. *Histria IV* (Analele Academiei Române, Memoriile Secțiunii Istorice, ser. 2, 38), București

Pippidi, D. M. 1962. "Gli scavi nella zona sacra di Histria," *Dacia* n.s. 6, S. 139–156

Sokol'skij, N. I. 1976. *Tamanskij tolos i rezidencija Chrisaliska*, Moskva

Wiegand, Th., und H. Schrader. 1904. *Priene. Ergebnisse der Ausgrabungen und Untersuchungen in den Jahren 1895–1898*, Berlin

Zeest, I. B. 1966. *Keramičeskoe proizvodstvo i antičnye keramičeskie stroitel'nye materialy = Archeologija SSSR. Svod archeologičeskix istočnikov G 1-20* [darin S. 36–45: I. B. Brašinskij, "Ol'vija"], I. B. Zeest, Hrsg., Moskva

Zimmermann, K. 1983. *Dachterrakotten griechischer Zeit aus Histria. Untersuchungen zur Typologie, Datierung und Verbreitung keramischer Bauelemente im Schwarzmeergebiet*, Berlin (ungedruckt)

KONRAD ZIMMERMANN

UNIVERSITÄT ROSTOCK
Institut für Altertumswissenschaften
Fachgebiet Klassische Archäologie
Universitätsplatz
D-18051 Rostock
Bundesrepublik Deutschland

# KLEINASIEN UND GRIECHENLAND
# DACHTERRAKOTTEN NACHARCHAISCHER ZEIT AUS PERGAMON

(Plates 80–83)

SEIT DEM BEGINN der Grabungen im Jahre 1878 ist die wissenschaftlichen Literatur über die Architektur von Pergamon zwar beachtlich angewachsen. Die dekorative Baukeramik nimmt darin jedoch nur einen sehr bescheidenen Platz ein. Abgesehen von einem ausführlichen Kapitel über die Inschriften gestempelter Ziegel[1] wird sie nur beiläufig erwähnt. Dies mag einerseits damit zu begründen sein, daß verzierte Dachziegel in der Fundstatistik kaum in Erscheinung treten und dürfte andererseits daran liegen, daß die geringe handwerkliche Qualität der gefundenen Ziegel kaum zu einer eingehenderen wissenschaftlichen Bearbeitung anregte.[2] Außerdem lassen sich die aus Schuttablagerungen geborgenen oder in sekundärer Verwendung als Grababdeckung vorkommenden Ziegel auch kaum eindeutig bestimmten Bauwerken zuordnen. Auffallend bleibt jedoch die geringe Funddichte, die vielleicht damit zu erklären ist, daß die repräsentativen Bauten der Akropolis von Pergamon bereits früh mit steinernen Antefixen—aus Andesit (Athenatempel?) oder seit der Königszeit dann aus Marmor (Ionischer Tempel beim Gymnasion, Heratempel, Zeusaltar?)—versehen wurden. Die Dächer der übrigen Bauten müssen mit sehr einfachen hellenistischen Ziegelformen eingedeckt gewesen sein. In dem erwähnten Inschriftenband der Altertümer von Pergamon werden neben den aufgrund der Stempelform der Königszeit zugewiesenen Fragmenten auch zwei vollständige Ziegel genannt, die nach Berlin gelangt sind:[3]

**Dachziegel**
Die Ziegel bestehen aus hellrotem Ton und sind auf der Oberseite mit einem dunkelroten Überzug versehen. Der *Flachziegel* ist 57 cm breit und 65 cm lang. Die Ränder sind 5,8 cm hoch rechtwinklig aufgebogen, die Oberseite zeigt am hinteren Ende einen schmalen Arretierungssteg und an der Vorderkante eine unten überstehende Verdickung von etwa dreieckigem Querschnitt. Deren Vorderseite ist bei den *Traufziegeln* häufig mit eingedrückten Schriftzügen (βασιλικη, βασιλειων,

---

[1] *AvP* VIII, ii, S. 393–422.

Fotonachweis: Staatliche Museen zu Berlin, E.-M. Borgwaldt (Pls. 80:a, c, 81:a); Reproduktionen (Pls. 82:d, 83:a) und alle übrigen Aufnahmen vom Verfasser.

Die vorliegende Abhandlung verdankt zu einem guten Teil ihre Entstehung der Möglichkeit, originale Fundstücke der Pergamon-Grabung am Ort selbst und Vergleichsmaterial im Kerameikos studieren zu können. Für das dabei gezeigte großzügige Entgegenkommen und die gewährte Hilfe mit Rat und Tat danke ich besonders W. Radt, dem Ehepaar Raeck und G. de Luca sowie U. Knigge und A. Schöne.

[2] Eine Ausnahme bilden lediglich Fragmente eines archaischen Daches, die Conze in den *AvP* I, ii, S. 160, Beiblatt 9 veröffentlichte.

[3] *AvP* VIII, ii, S. 393–394.

ιερων, ιερεων, τειχων) versehen, die sich offenbar auf die Zugehörigkeit zu bestimmten Kategorien von Bauwerken beziehen.

Ein *Flachziegelfragment* (Inv. P 752; 1600×)[4] (Pl. 80:a) aus der im Jahre 1904 ausgeräumten Fundamentkammer des Zeusaltares besitzt sogar drei Stempelabdrücke (zweimal τειχ[ων und einmal βασ[ιλειων), die wahrscheinlich auf die Zugehörigkeit zur königlichen Stadtmauer hinweisen.

Der innen runde und außen pentagonale *Kalypter* ist 55,4 cm lang, zeigt am hinteren Ende eine leicht vertiefte Auflagefläche und schließt vorn mit einer glatten unverzierten Antefixplatte (14,3 cm breit und 9,3 cm hoch) ab.

Ein ähnliches gestempeltes *Fragment* in der Berliner Antikensammlung läßt daneben vielleicht noch Spuren einer einfachen linearen Verzierung erkennen.[5]

Neben diesem unverzierten und dank der Stempel einigermaßen zeitlich fixierbaren Material gibt es jedoch auch einige reliefierte Dachziegel, von denen Fragmente in der Berliner Antikensammlung und in den Depots der Pergamongrabung aufbewahrt werden. Dies sind zunächst Traufziegel mit einer im Querschnitt etwa dreieckigen nach unten überhängenden Nase. Auf der Oberseite sitzen die üblichen im Querschnitt rechteckigen Seitenstege, die knapp vor der Traufe enden und der Arretierung der Antefixkalyptere dienten. Die Antefixe stehen in diesem Fall auf der Traufziegelkante. Die Stirnseite der Ziegel schmückt ein reliefierter Swastika-Blütenstern-Mäander. In Berlin befinden sich vier Fragmente einer Variante dieses Typus (Inv. P 716–P 719). Ein Fragment (Inv. P 717) gehört zur rechten vorderen Ecke eines Traufziegels (Pl. 80:b)[6] und läßt auf der Oberseite noch Spuren des Steganwaltzes erkennen. Ton und Überzug entsprechen den vorgenannten unverzierten hellenistischen Dachziegeln:

### Traufziegelfragment
Antikensammlung, Inv. P 716 (1616×; Zettelinventar Nr. 390)
Swastikamäander mit alternierendem Blütensternquadrat (vom Stern nur geringe Spuren erhalten).
Höhe: 7,9 cm; Länge (erh.): 15,6 cm; Tiefe (erh.): 8,5 cm.

### Traufziegelfragment
Antikensammlung, Inv. P 717
Rechtes Eckstück; Dekoration wie P 716 aber mit einem gut erhaltenem Blütenstern (mit Punkt in der Mitte).
Höhe (erh.): 7,7 cm; Länge (erh.): 20,6 cm; Tiefe (erh.): 8,3 cm.

### Traufziegelfragment
Antikensammlung, Inv. P 718 (155×; Zettelinventar Nr. 390) (Pl. 80:c)
Dekoration wie P 716.
Höhe (erh.): 7,7 cm; Länge (erh.): 14,2 cm; Tiefe (erh.): 4,5 cm.

---

[4] *AvP* I, ii, S. 279; Schmidt 1990, S. 146, Taf. 90 (oben).
[5] *AvP* VIII, ii, S. 406 Nr. 681 (Inv. 41); nach S. 396–397 aus der Zeit Attalos I (?).
[6] Gleiche Randstücke wurden im Herrscherkult-Temenos (*AvP* IX, S. 133, Taf. 42:b) und bei der Olivenhainhalle im Asklepieion gefunden (Inv. OH 67 T 408/175).

**Traufziegelfragment**
Antikensammlung, Inv. P 719
Dekoration wie P 717.
Höhe (erh.): 6,7 cm; Länge (erh.): 14,5 cm; Tiefe (erh.): 9,1 cm.

Die Ziegeldicke beträgt allgemein 2,4–2,7 cm und die Stirnseite war wohl bei allen aufgeführten Bruchstücken ursprünglich 7,9 cm hoch. Somit gehörten diese Exemplare zu einem einzigen Ziegeltypus und wurden vielleicht auch zusammen auf dem Burgberg gefunden. Daneben konnten andere Fragmente desselben Typs im Herrscherkult-Temenos[7] und im Olivenhain beim Asklepieion geborgen werden.[8] Weitere pergamenische Fundstücke variieren das Ornament und haben ein kleineres Format—so ein Ziegel aus dem Herscherkultbezirk mit Kreuzstern-Quadrat und ein Mäander ohne Blütenstern aus dem Asklepieion.[9] Derartige Traufziegel mit reliefiertem Mäandermuster waren besonders im kleinasiatischen Ambiente (Ilion, Assos, Erythrai, Priene, Chios, Samos) und im Schwarzmeergebiet weit verbreitet.[10] Das Ornament erschien dabei in verschiedenen Varianten (Mäanderrapporte mit Quadratfeldern, Schachbrettmustern, Buchstabenfeldern und verschiedene Sternformen) oder wurde um weitere Zusätze bereichert (ionische Kymatien, Anthemien).[11] Datiert werden diese Ziegel allgemein in hellenistische Zeit. Sollten die Mäandertraufziegel aus Priene wirklich mit der ersten Phase des dortigen >Ekklesiasterions< zu verbinden sein, dann wäre wenigstens an diesem Ort eine engere zeitliche Fixierung eines Mäanderziegeldaches in die Zeit vom Ende des 3. bis zum Anfang des 2. Jh. v. Chr. möglich.[12] Das Mäanderornament mit Blütensternen war in gemalter Form auf Ziegeln aber bereits seit archaischer Zeit (Histria) bekannt und einfache reliefierte Mäandermuster traten in Verbindung mit Simen und Verkleidungsplatten ebenfalls schon im 6. Jh. v. Chr. in Kleinasien auf (Milet, Mylasa, Sardes).[13] Dies und der Mangel an gesicherten Fundzusammenhängen erschweren es bisher, die Anfänge der besonderen hellenistischen Ausprägung des Mäanderziegels zeitlich genauer einzugrenzen.

Zu den einfachsten reliefierten Stirnziegeln im hellenistischen Kleinasien und im Schwarzmeergebiet zählen die fünfeckigen Verschlußplatten der korinthischen Kalyptere mit aufgeprägten Palmettenmustern. In Pergamon wurde ein Antefix dieses Typs im Asklepieion gefunden:

---

[7] *AvP* IX, S. 133 Nr. 1–5, Taf. 42:b; Höhe (erh.): 7,6–6,7 cm.
[8] *AvP* XI, ii, S. 119, 125, Nr. 638 (Inv. OH 67 T 408/175); Höhe (erh.): 7,5 cm; Breite (erh.): 16 cm. Die beiden zusammengehörigen Ziegelfragmente wurden aus den Verschüttungsmassen der langen hellenistischen Halle im Olivenhain geborgen, die im 1. Drittel des 2. Jh. v. Chr. errichtete wurde und bis in das 4. Jh. in Benutzung blieb (ebd. S. 32–44, 84–85).
[9] *AvP* IX, S. 133, Nr. 7:b und *AvP* XI, ii, S. 125, Nr. 639.
[10] Zu Kleinasien vgl. Åkerström 1966, S. 2, 13–15, 35, 100, Taf. 1:7–8, 7:1 und 3, 17:4–5; zu den Mäanderziegeln im Schwarzmeergebiet siehe den Beitrag von K. Zimmermann (1994). Weitere Hinweise auf Reliefziegel, z.B. auch aus Abdera, Athen und Delos, nennt Billot 1976, S. 105–106 mit Taf. 26:b (Athen). Reliefmäander lassen sich außerdem auch in Süditalien nachweisen (vgl. z.B. eine Sima aus Sybaris: *Sibari* IV, S. 355, Nr. 153, Abb. 335).
[11] Z.B.: *Samos* XIV, S. 42–44 (A 540), Abb. 80.
[12] Åkerström 1966, S. 100.
[13] Åkerström 1966, S. 104, Abb. 33, Taf. 43:1, 44:1, 59:1.

## Pentagonalantefix

Bergama, Asklepieion-Depot (ohne Nr.) (Pl. 81:b)

Kalypterfragment mit Antefix aus versintertem roten Ton. Der Deckziegel ist innen halbrund und schließt mit einer fünfeckigen Antefixplatte ab. Das Antefix zeigt eine flachreliefierte Flammenpalmette über liegenden S-Voluten.

Höhe: 9 cm; Breite: 13,5 cm; Tiefe (erh.): 9,5 cm.

Auch zu diesem Stück können zahlreiche vergleichbare Beispiele angeführt werden. Variiert wurde das zentrale Palmettenmuster als auch das begleitende Rankenwerk, manchmal bereichert um Blüten und Halbpalmetten (Exemplare aus Ilion, Sardes, Priene, Didyma, Samos/Castro Tigani, Histria und Olbia).[14] Die Oberseiten waren bisweilen konkav gekrümmt oder konnten auch leicht über den Ziegel hinausragen (Samos, Histria). Aufgrund der Ornamentik werden diese Stirnziegel trotz der konservativen Grundform kaum vor dem 3.–2. Jh. v. Chr. entstanden sein.

Eine weitere bis in die Archaik zurückverfolgbare Typenreihe bilden die ostionischen Antefixe mit einer über Voluten aufwachsenden Palmette.[15] Als hellenistische Variante dieses Grundtypus kann ein in Berlin aufbewahrtes Antefix aus Pergamon angesehen werden:

## Palmettenantefix

Antikensammlung, Inv. P 712 (Burgberg, Fundort unbekannt)[16] (Pl. 81:a)

Spitzbogige Antefixplatte mit reliefierter neunblättriger Flammenpalmette. In der linken unteren Ecke eine kleine Volute, deren Ranke sich von unten anlaufend im Uhrzeigersinn einrollt. Oben ein abzweigendes Blatt (?). Unten nach rechts ansteigende Bruchkante, Ausbrüche im Palmettenfeld und rückseitiger Ansatz des in einem Mittelgrat auslaufenden dachförmigen Kalypters. Ton grau verfärbt mit gleichfarbigem Überzug (sekundärer Brandschaden?).

Höhe (erh.): 14,7 cm; Breite (erh.): 13,5 cm; Tiefe (erh.): 4,5 cm.

Die allgemeine Gestalt dieses Antefixes erinnert an hellenistische Firstpalmetten aus Assos.[17] Ähnliche spitzbogige Antefixe (mit Randleiste) und großen Voluten wurden auch in Ilion gefunden.[18] Leider fehlt der untere Abschluß des pergamenischen Antefixes, so daß eine exakte typologische Bestimmung schwierig ist. Am Ort selbst wären für diese gedrungene Form einige steinerne Stirnziegel anzuführen, darunter ein Andesitfragment, das Richard Bohn dem Athenatempel zuweisen möchte.[19] Die heute schmucklos glatte Fläche dieses Fragmentes wird ursprünglich sicher ein aufgemaltes Palmettenmuster getragen haben. Die anderen Stücke besitzen dagegen das übliche Palmettenrelief, bieten aber leider keine Anhaltspunkte mehr für eine Ergänzung des unteren Abschlusses:

---

[14] Åkerström 1966, S. Taf. 1:3, 36:4, 52:4, 59:3 und 5; *Samos* XIV, S. 43–44, Abb. 81; Zimmermann 1983, S. 288, Typ A IV/1–2, 290–292. (Datierung 2.–3. Jh. v. Chr.), Taf. 24.

[15] Frühe Beispiele aus dem samischen Heraion (Buschor 1933b, S. 22–46); vgl. auch Harl 1971, S. 63–71 (Voluten-Typus).

[16] Archiv der Antikensammlung Inv. 37 (Sculptur Baracke II), Nr. 117.

[17] Åkerström 1966, Taf. 8:4 und 6.

[18] DAI Athen, Foto Tro. 168.

[19] *AvP* II, S. 10 (mit Zeichnung).

### Stirnziegel aus Andesit

Antikensammlung, vorläufige Inv. Nr. 138/1 (Fig. 1:a)

Dachförmiger Andesitziegel (Höhe *ca.* 10 cm) mit aufragender paraboloider Antefixplatte. Die Unterseite ist konkav ausgehöhlt.

Höhe (erh.): 18,5 cm; Breite: 17,2 cm; Tiefe (erh.): 7,9 cm.

### Firstpalmette aus weißem Marmor

Im Theater gefunden. Bergama (?); Skizze in der Antikensammlung[20] (Fig. 1:b)

Beidseitig ausgearbeitete neunblättrige Palmetten mit rund geschlosenen nach außen schwingenden Blättern.

Höhe (erh.): 18 cm.

### Palmettenantefix aus Kalkstein

Antikensammlung, ohne Inv. Nr., Fundort unbekannt (Pl. 81:c)

Fragment eines Antefixes aus phokäischem Kalkstein mit reliefierter Flammenpalmette. Die Palmette zeigt auf der ovalen bestoßenen Platte wenigstens sieben Blätter, links eine Brandschwärzung.

Höhe (erh.): 9,3 cm; Breite (erh.): 10,9 cm; Tiefe (erh.): 7,9 cm.

### Palmettenantefix aus >Trachyt<

Westlich unterhalb des Athenaheiligtums gefunden; Skizze in der Antikensammlung (Fig. 1:d)[21]

Halbovaler Stirnziegel mit reliefierter Flammenpalmette aus >Trachyt<. Die Palmette entspringt einem kelchförmigem Herzstück und besaß wahrscheinlich neun Blätter. Kalypter dachförmig.

Höhe (erh.): 12,5 cm; Breite: 12,5 cm.

Auch die jüngeren Marmorantefixe des von Attalos II (159–138 v. Chr.) gestifteten Heratempels besitzen unter der frei gearbeiteten siebenblättrigen Flammenpalmette noch zwei sich nach außen einrollende Voluten (Fig. 1:e).[22] Bemerkenswert und mit Stirnziegeln aus Assos vergleichbar ist das kelchförmige Herzstück dieses Antefixes.[23] Weitere allerdings im Palmettenmotiv abweichende Marmorantefixe befinden sich im pergamenischen Grabungsdepot (Pl. 81:d). Der Blattfächer zeigt je vier in der Mitte gekerbte Blätter, die beiderseits eines ebenso gekerbten senkrecht aufsteigenden Mittelstengels nach außen schwingen, wobei die Blattenden jetzt abgebrochen sind. Darunter biegen vom Herzstück ausgehend zwei dünne Volutenranken nach außen und rollen sich nach oben ein. Die gerade abgeschnittene Unterseite war wohl zum Aufsetzen auf eine Sima gedacht. Sehr ähnliche Palmettenmotive zeigen auch hellenistische Tonantefixe aus Didyma, Histria und Korinth,[24] ohne daß aus dem Erhaltenen eine genauere Vorstellung vom oberen Abschluß des Motivs gewonnen werden könnte.

Neben der Palmette über einem Volutenpaar kennen wir aus Kleinasien als Dachschmuck die Palmette über stehenden S-Voluten (Volutenleier).[25] Das Motiv begegnet uns schon in

---

[20] Archiv der Antikensammlung Nr. 110; in Pergamon verbliebene kleine Architekturteile II, Zettel Nr. 210.
[21] Grabungsarchiv Pergamon Nr. 110; in Pergamon verbliebene kleine Architekturteile II, Zettel Nr. 137.
[22] *AvP* VI, S. 106, Taf. XXXIV:15; Breite: 23,5 cm.
[23] Åkerström 1966, Taf. 7:4, 5.
[24] *Didyma* I, S. 150, Taf. 223 (F 675 unten links); Zimmermann 1983, S. 283, Typ A III/4, Taf. 24; *Corinth* IV, i, S. 17, Abb. 12:1, 54, Nr. A 66–67.
[25] Harl 1971, S. 47–62 (Lyra-Typ).

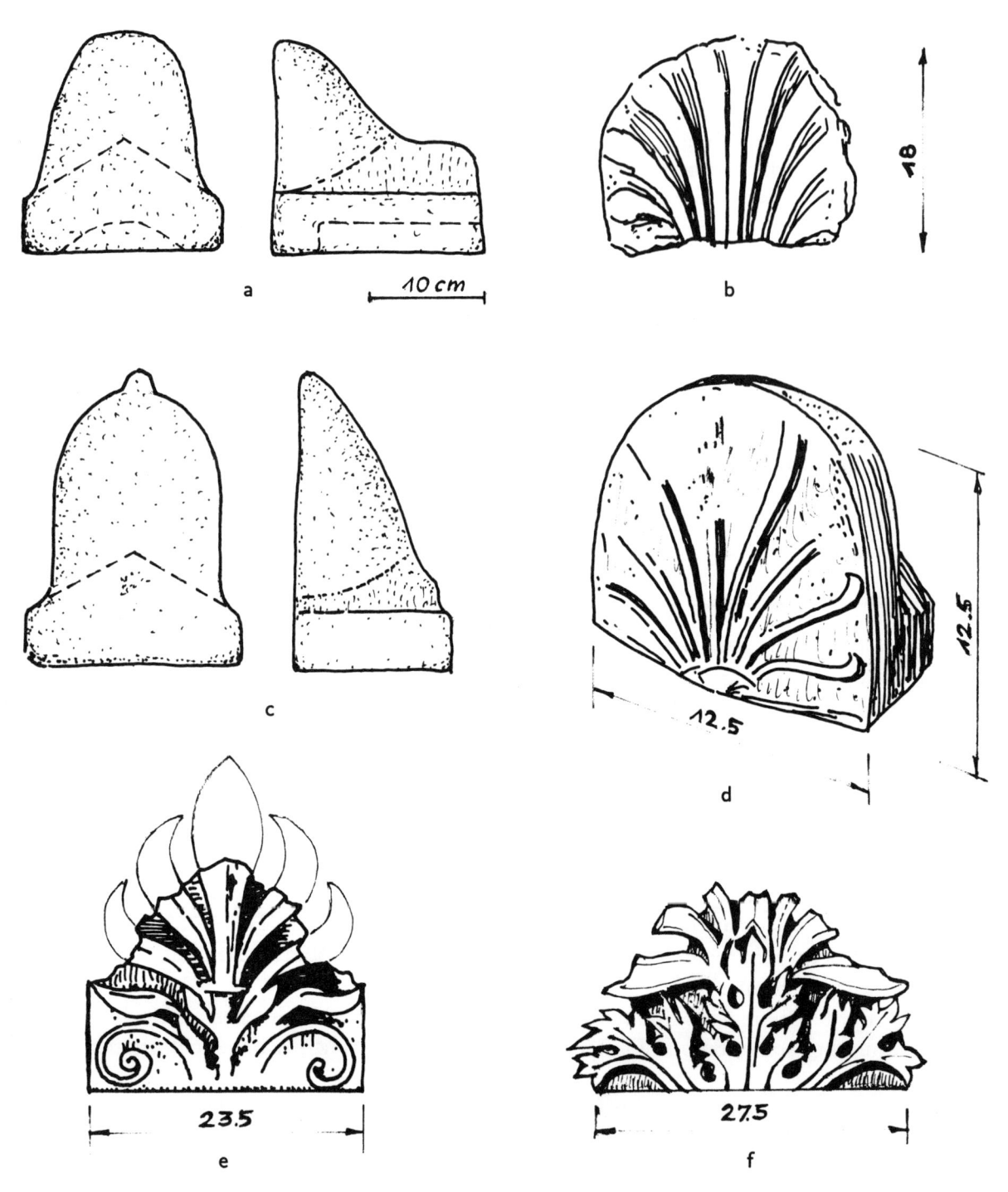

FIG. 1. a. Andesitantefix Inv. 138/1. b. Firstpalmette aus Marmor. c. Andesitantefix Inv. 138/2. d. Antefix aus >Trachyt<. e. Marmorantefix des Heratempels. f. Marmorantefix des ionischen Tempels beim Gymnasion.

archaischer Zeit als Akroter in Assos[26] oder als Reliefmuster auf kleinasiatischen Simaplatten[27] und daneben besonders in Kleinasien und Attika als Grabstelenbekrönung.[28] Auf Antefixen erscheint dieses Ornament im mutterländischen Ambiente seit etwa 500 v. Chr. meist mit nahzu waagerecht liegenden S-Voluten (Jüngerer Aphaiatempel Aigina, Stiermonument auf Delos, Olympia etc.).[29] Die östlichen Antefixen zeigen dagegen eine analog den Stelenbekrönungen und Firstpalmetten[30] gestaltete Variante des Motivs mit aufgerichteten S-Voluten, wie sie zum Beispiel in gemalter Form sicher auch die Marmorziegel des Niketempels auf der Athener Akropolis schmückte.[31] Ein Antefixfragment aus dem athenischen Kerameikos, das nach G. Hübner den Eindruck erweckt, als wäre es „geradezu von einem Ionier gemacht", ließe sich hier anschließen.[32] Weitere Stirnziegel mit dieser Ornamentvariante wurden in Olynth[33] und Abdera[34] gefunden. Dabei kann gerade bei den abderitischen Dachterrakotten allgemein schon in archaischer Zeit eine starke Abhängigkeit von kleinasiatischen und nesiotischen Werkstätten beobachtet werden,[35] was letztlich die Vermutung bekräftigt, daß der Ursprung des >Lyratyps< in ebendiesem Ambiente zu lokalisieren ist.[36]

Seiner äußeren Form nach läßt sich diesen Palmettenantefixen des >Lyratyps< vermutlich ein weiteres Andesitfragment aus Pergamon anschließen:

**Stirnziegel aus Andesit**
Antikensammlung, vorläufige Inv. Nr. 138/2 (Fig. 1:c)
Spitzbogiges Andesitantefix mit dachförmigem Kalypteransatz. Unterseite nicht ausgehöhlt.
Höhe: 23,5 cm; Breite: 18 cm; Tiefe (erh.): 13,8 cm.

Auch bei diesem Andesitfragment ist die vorauszusetzende Bemalung völlig verschwunden. Aber die schlank proportionierte Platte mit ihrem spitzbogigen Abschluß, aus dem noch die Spitze des Mittelblattes emporragt, läßt eine Dekoration in Form einer Flammenpalmette über einer Volutenleier vermuten. Vielleicht noch älter als dieser Steinziegel könnte das Bruchstück eines tönernen Antefixes in der Antikensammlung sein:

---

[26] Clark 1898, S. 136–137, Abb. 33, 270–272, Abb. 63.
[27] Z.B. auf einer Sima aus Sardes in New York (Metropolitan Museum): Åkerström 1966, Taf. 44:2.
[28] Hiller 1967, S. 20–26.
[29] Aigina: Harl 1971; Delos: Harl 1971, S. 53 und Daux 1965, S. 996, Abb. 5; Olympia: *Olympia* II, S. 199, Taf. 124 (1:a/b) sowie mit dreieckig ausgeschnittener Unterseite und Flammenpalmette aus der Palästra, *Olympia* II, S. 143–144, Taf. 91:7; weitere Beispiele aus Argos (Vollgraff 1956, S. 17–19, Taf. V oben links und unten rechts, Taf. VI oben rechts), Megalopolis (Firstpalmette des Thersileion: Gardner u.a. 1892, S. 33, Abb. 22) und Süditalien (Antefix aus Sybaris: *Sibari* III, S. 58, Nr. 175, Abb. 40).
[30] Vgl. z.B. die tönerne Firstpalmette des Aphaiatempels: Furtwängler 1906, S. 41, Abb. 13, Taf. 48:3, 3a.
[31] Züchner 1936, Sp. 320–323, Abb. 10, 11.
[32] Hübner 1973, S. 114–115, 136 (Katalog E), Nr. 2 (Inv. Z 147), Taf. 66:6.
[33] *Olynthus* XII, S. 91, Taf. 84:1–4.
[34] Kaltsas 1988, S. 20, Anm. 33, Taf. 27:g, d; Lazarides 1965, S. 456, Taf. 543:g; Skarlatidou 1982, S. 334, Taf. 222:g.
[35] Vgl. dazu auch Koukouli-Chrysanthanki 1970, S. 358.
[36] Veilleicht kann man Palmettenantefixe mit S-förmig nach aussen schwingenden Volutenenden (Südbau im samische Heraion: Åkerström 1966, S. 99, Abb. 30, 31; Ohnesorg 1990, S. 189, Taf. 21:a; Athenatempel in Assos: Åkerström 1966, S. 13–15, Taf. 5:1) als unmittelbare Vorläufer des >Lyratyps< ansehen, der dann in den letzten Jahrzehnten des 6. Jh. v. Chr. in Kleinasien entstanden sein dürfte.

### Fragment eines Palmettenantefixes
Antikensammlung, Inv. P 709; Hochburg, Nordostecke[37] (Pl. 81:e)

Oberes Bruchstück einer abgerundeten Antefixplatte mit flachreliefierter 13-blättriger Palmette über großen Voluten und rhomboiden Herzstück. Oben rechts und unten gebrochen. Hellroter, versinterter Ton.

Höhe (erh.): 10 cm; Breite (erh.): 13,5 cm (ergänzt *ca.* 15 cm); Tiefe (erh.): 4,7 cm.

Die breiten, flach gewölbten Blätter der Palmette dieses Stirnziegels haben spitze Enden und sind dicht gestaffelt. Von den darunter liegenden Voluten sind zwar nur die oberen Ränder erhalten, sie lassen aber noch ein konvexes Volutenband mit Randstegen erkennen. Außerdem beginnt der rückseitige Ziegelansatz erst in der Höhe der unteren Bruchkante, was auf eine größere Antefixhöhe schließen läßt, die genug Fläche für eine Volutenleier böte. Würde man das pergamenische Fragment mit einer Volutenleier ergänzen, so wäre es typologisch mit den Antefixen aus Abdera zu vergleichen, deren Palmetten aber teilweise noch archaisch strukturiert erscheinen.[38] Der Form der Palmette unseres Fragmentes ähnelt dagegen stilistisch eher den Blattfächern einer Rankensima aus Eleusis, die in das dritte Viertel des 5. Jh. v. Chr. datiert wird.[39]

Die übrigen pergamenischen Antefixe des >Lyratyps< übernehmen dann die Form der üblichen hellenistischen Flammenpalmette:

### Palmettenantefix aus weißem Marmor
Bergama, Asklepieion-Depot, Inv. A 58/27 (Pl. 82:a)

Kleines Antefix mit neunblättriger Flammenpalmette über einem Volutenpaar. Die Palmettenblätter sind gekerbt und wachsen aus einem kleinen Herzstück hervor. Die Voluten besitzen Augen, ihre Bänder biegen nach außen bis zum Abbruch der jetzt fehlenden Antefixunterkante. Die Oberfläche ist versintert.

Höhe (erh.): 14 cm; Breite (erh.): 8 cm; Tiefe (erh.): 8 cm.

### Fragment eines Palmettenantefixes
Antikensammlung, Inv. P 710 (Pl. 82:b)

Fragment einer Flammenpalmette aus hellrotem Ton mit dunkelroter Engobe. Beiderseits des kräftig modellierten Mittelblattes biegen je vier dünnere S-förmige Blätter nach außen. Sie wachsen aus einem kelchförmigen Herzstück hervor, dem auch Ranken entspringen, die sich nach unten zu Voluten (?) einrollen. Oben und unten gebrochen, seitlich bestoßen.

Höhe (erh.): 11,8 cm; Breite: 12,8 cm; Tiefe (erh.): 7,7 cm.

### Fragment eines Palmettenantefixes
Bergama, Asklepieion-Depot, Inv. T 59/92 (Streufund vom Festplatz des Asklepieions)

Mittelstück eines tönernen Palmettenantefixes. Zwischen Voluten wächst ein Stiel hervor, der in einen Kelch mit weit ausbiegenden Blättern einmündet. Dem Kelch entspringt eine Flammenpalmette.

Höhe (erh.): 9,5 cm.

---

[37] Archiv der Antikensammlung Inv. 37, Nr. 155.
[38] Skarlatidou 1982, S. 334, Taf. 222:g.
[39] Hübner 1973, S. 111–112, Abb. 11; vgl. auch die Palmette des Mittelakroters vom Satrapensarkophag aus Sidon bei Kleemann 1958, S. 72–73, 86, Taf. 18:a.

### Fragmente eines Palmettenantefixes

Bergama, Asklepieion-Depot, Inv. T 59/82 (F.Nr. 385), T 61/55 (F.Nr. 791), T 61/131 (F.Nr. 0; alle Fragmente aus dem Asklepieion)[40] (Pl. 82:c)

Die beiden letztgenannten Fragmente sind Bruchstücke von elfblättrigen Flammenpalmetten, das erstgenannte besteht aus dem Unterteil des Antefixes mit Volutenleiern und dem Ansatz des dachförmigen, innen gerundeten Kalypters (Höhe: 8 cm; Breite: 16,5 cm). Die Voluten besitzen konvexe Augen und obere nach außen weisende siebenblättrige Zwickelpalmetten. Das rhomboide Herzstück der Hauptpalmette ist nach unten stielartig verlängert als Ansatz einer neunblättrigen Palmette, die zwischen den Voluten herabhängt. Darunter sitzen auf der abschließenden Standleiste zwei gegenständige schneckenartige Ornamente.

Der Ton ist hellrot und trägt einen rotbraunen Überzug.

Höhe (ergänzt): *ca.* 21 cm; Breite (ergänzt): 16,5 cm; Tiefe (erh.): 10 cm.

### Fragment einer Firstpalmette (?)

Inventar der Pergamon-Grabung 1908 Nr. 113 (Foto DAI Athen, Nr. 1644.b) (Pl. 82:d)

Spitzbogige, unten leicht eingezogene Platte mit neunblättriger Flammmenpalmette, die über Voluten aus einem stilisierten Akanthuskelch hervorwächst. Die Voluten werden außen von schlanken knospenartigen Blüten flankiert. Unterseite abgebrochen, Spitze bestoßen.

Abmessungen des Fragmentes nach der Fotografie: etwa 14 × 12 cm.

Die Palmette des recht gut gearbeiteten Marmorantefixes läßt sich mit einem älteren Stirnziegel aus der Unterstadt von Assos[41] vergleichen und steht offenbar dem Anthemionornament eines Antenkapitells vom didymäischen Naiskos stilistisch sehr nahe. Ähnlich geformt sind hier wie dort die außen an die Palmettenvoluten angesetzten Blattgebilde mit kleinen Knospen.[42] Danach wäre eine Datierung noch in das dritte Jahrhundert und vielleicht die Verbindung mit einem Tempelbau im Asklepieion denkbar.

Auch die übrigen oben aufgeführten pergamenischen Ziegel entsprechen weitgehend den hellenistischen Funden aus der Unterstadt von Assos. So ähnelt das Antefix in Berlin (Inv. P 710) in der blütenkelchartigen Gestaltung des Palmetten-Herzstückes den Fragmenten Inv. P 4132–P 4135 in Boston.[43] Für die Exemplare aus dem Asklepieion-Depot können wir neben den Ziegeln aus Assos auch noch Stirnziegel aus Larisa am Hermos und Erythrai zum Vergleich heranziehen. Offenbar war dieser Typus in nur gering voneinander abweichenden Varianten in den Küstenstädten der Troas und der Aeolis sehr verbreitet. Nach der Anordnung der kleinen Palmette zwischen den Volutenleiern kann

---

[40] Frau Gioia de Luca verdanke ich die nachfolgenden näheren Angaben zur Fundsituation: Inv. T 59/82 stammt aus dem Gebiet der älteren hellenistischen Osthallen—vermutlich aus einer Schicht, die vor der Anlage der jüngeren Osthöfe entstand (aus demselben Gebiet, allerdings aus gestörter Schicht, ein Fragment eines entsprechenden Stirnziegels); T 61/55 vom Vorgelände des Asklepiostempels auf der Felsbarre (Gebiet des sogenannten Altarhauses) und Inv. T 61/131 wurde als Streufund innerhalb des Gevierts der kaiserzeitlichen Hallen des Festplatzes gefunden.

[41] Åkerström 1966, S. 15, 20, Taf. 6.

[42] Pfrommer 1989, S. 433–434, Taf. 42:3; vgl. weiterhin Antefixe aus Erythrai (*Erythrai* II, S. 122, Nr. 89, Taf. 48:2; Åkerström 1966, S. 36, Nr. 2, Abb. 10:1) und einen Stirnziegel aus Atalanti (aus dem Gebiet Kaphassi mit Bauten des 2.–1. Jh. v. Chr.), wo die Voluten aber bereits aus einem Akanthuskelch hervorwachsen (Pariente 1990, S. 770, Abb. 90.)

[43] Åkerström 1966, S. 15–16, Taf. 7:4, 5; die blütenförmige Palmetten-Herzstücke sind bei den Firstpalmetten (Åkerström 1966, S. 17, Taf. 8:4 und 6) noch deutlicher erkennbar.

man wenigstens zwei Hauptformen unterscheiden. Die vielleicht ältere Variante besitzt eine hängende Innenpalmette wie das Asklepieion-Antefix und kommt auch in Assos und Larisa vor.[44]

Die zweite möglicherweise etwas jüngere aber ebenfalls hellenistische Spielart zeigt dagegen eine aufrecht stehende Palmette auf der Antefixbasis zwischen den unteren Voluten. Dabei kann diese Innenpalmette (wie bei einem Antefix aus Erythrai)[45] auch auf nach innen abzweigenden kleinen Voluten sitzen. Als Rudiment läßt sich dieses Volutenmotiv außerdem auch an dem Asklepieion-Fragment T 59/82 beobachten, obwohl hier die Innenpalmette hängend angeordnet ist.

Die Antefixe mit stehender Leierpalmette wurden in Erythrai, Larisa am Hermos sowie zusammen mit reliefierten Mäandertraufziegeln und Firstpalmetten bei der Südhalle, dem >Bazaar<, der Agora von Assos gefunden. Dieses zweischiffige und mehrstöckige Bauwerk steht offenbar in der Tradition der spezifisch-pergamenischen Hallenbauten[46] und dürfte wie diese während der ersten Hälfte des 2. Jh. v. Chr. entstanden sein. Mit dem Dach der Südhalle von Assos ergäbe sich auch ein Anhaltspunkt für die Datierung der Fragmente aus dem pergamenischen Asklepieion. Letztere gehören sicher zu einem Antefixtyp, der aufgrund seiner konserativer wirkenden Struktur älter ist als der kleinteiliger gegeliederte Südhallenstirnziegel aus Assos, andererseits aber nach den Palmettenformen kaum vor dem Ende des 3. Jh. v. Chr. entstanden sein wird.

Auch das vermutlich zu einer Firstpalmette gehörende Bruchstück, das 1908 bei der Pergamongrabung gefunden wurde, läßt sich gut mit dem Firstziegeln der Südhalle von Assos vergleichen. Bemerkenswert ist hier jedoch der Akanthuskelch unter der Palmette, der dieses Fragment mit den nun folgenden pergamenischen Funden verbindet.

Während die bisher behandelten Ziegeltypen sich gut in das allgemeine konservative Bild der kleinasiatisch-ionischen Baukeramik einfügen, verkörpert der abschließend zu besprechende Typus einen Sonderfall, für den keine Vorstufen in dieser Region existieren. Mehrere Fragmente dieses Ziegeltyps traten als Grababdeckung im Arsenalbezirk und in den Schuttschichten der Trajaneumsubstruktionen auf:

**Antefixfragment**
Fotoinventar Pergamon 1927 Nr. 108: von einem byzantinischen Grab über Arsenal IV[47] (Pl. 83:a)
Unterteil eines Palmettenantefixes mit Akanthuskelch und Volutenranken.

---

[44] Assos: Åkerström 1966, S. 15, 20, Taf. 6; Larisa am Hermos: Åkerström 1966, S. 50, Taf. 17:1.
[45] Åkerström 1966, S. 36, Nr. 1, Abb. 10:2.
[46] Coulton 1976, S. 70–71. Die hier vorgeschlagene Datierung um die Mitte des 2. Jh. v. Chr. gibt nur den spätesten möglichen Zeitpunkt der Entstehung der Südhalle an, da deren Anlage einerseits baugeschichtlich in einem engen Zusammenhang mit den pergamenischen Hallenbauten in Athen und der Nordhalle des Athenaheiligtums in Pergamon zu sehen ist und sie andererseits ein wesentliches Element der in das 3.–2. Jh. v. Chr. datierten Marktanlage darstellt.
[47] *AvP* X, S. 29, Taf. 26:b.

**Antefixfragmente**

Antikensammlung, Inv. P 711 und P 720, P 715; >zwischen den beiden Caesarentempeln<[48] (Pl. 83:b)

Zwei zusammengehörige Fragmente vom Oberteil eines Antefixes mit gesprengter doppelter Flammenpalmette (>Rosettentypus<) und Bruchstück einer Antefixbasis wie oben.

**Antefixfragmente**

Bergama, Trajaneumgrabung 1983 (aus umgelagertem hellenistischen Bauschutt in den römischen Substruktionen etwa fünf Fragmente von Palmettenantefixen des gleichen Typs wie oben)[49]

Die aufgeführten Fragmente bestehen aus hellrotem Ton und besitzen eine graugelbe Engobe. Die erschließbaren Maße eines vollständigen Antefixes betragen: Höhe 24 cm und Breite 18 cm. Der dachförmige Deckziegel ist 12 cm hoch und 18 cm breit; der Ziegel endet mit einem Mittelgrat auf der Rückseite der Antefixplatte.

Die Gestalt des Stirnziegels läßt sich aus den Bruchstücken vollständig wiedergewinnen. Das Relief zeigt einen dreiblättrigen Akanthuskelch, aus dem ein herzförmiges Volutenpaar emporwächst, das seitlich von weiteren sich gabelnden und zu Voluten einrollenden Ranken gestützt wird. Aus den Zwickeln zwischen Haupt- und Seitenranken sprießen schräg nach oben gerichtete kleine siebenblättrige Palmetten. Zwischen den oberen Voluten hängt eine kleine Blüte. Über den Voluten erhebt sich die gesprengte doppelte Flammenpalmette. Sie besteht aus zweimal sechs großen äußeren und zweimal fünf kleineren inneren spitz zulaufenden gratigen Blättern. In der Palmettenspitze sitzt eine kleine achtblättrige Rosette.

Die Beschaffenheit des Tones, die Abmessungen und die ornamentale Struktur dieses Antefixes entsprechen offenbar den attischen Stirnziegeln des >Rosettentypus<, wie sie beispielsweise im Kerameikos bei der Pompeiongrabung gefunden wurden. G. Hübner hat diesen Typus in der Pompeionpublikation vorgestellt und bereits auf seine Abhängigkeit von den Antefixen des Erechtheions—die aber leider nur durch ihre inferioren römischen Ersatzstücke überliefert sind—hingewiesen.[50] Es handelt sich damit also um die hellenistische Fassung eines Antefixmotivs, das im griechischen Mutterland bis nach Makedonien und darüber hinaus eine außerordentliche Verbreitung gefunden hat.[51] Im kleinasiatisch-pergamenischen Ambiente ist mit dem Import dieses Typus wahrscheinlich auch die Übernahme des Akanthuskelches in der Stirnziegelornamentik verbunden.

---

[48] Archiv der Antikensammlung Inv. 37, Nr. 116 (P 715) und Nr. 118 (P 720); außerdem als weitere hier zugehörige Fragmente, deren Aufbewahrungsort nicht mehr zu ermitteln ist: Nr. 119 (Fragment der linken oberen Volute mit Palmettenresten, 7 cm breit) mit derselben Herkunftsangabe, die sich auf den Hang zwischen dem Trajaneum und dem Tempel auf der Theaterterrasse bezieht. Bei dem letztgenannten Tempel wurden zwei weitere Fragmente dieses Antefixtypus gefunden: Nr. 121 (linke Seitenpalmette, 7,5 cm breit) und Nr. 149 (Mittelstück mit linker oberer Volute, 19 cm hoch).

[49] Informationen und Fotos von diesen noch unpublizierten Neufunde verdanke ich W. Raeck.

[50] Hübner 1973, S. 71, 121, 127, 143, Taf. 70:6 und in *Kerameikos* X, S. 233, 236, Abb. 260:a (Z 42); zu den Erechtheionantefixen vgl. Züchner 1936, Sp. 323–327, Abb. 14–17.

[51] Billot 1976, S. 116–117, Nr. 52 und 52, Taf. 28:e, f; Kaltsas 1988, S. 35, Nr. 68 (aus Pella), Taf. 21:b, S. 84 (Typ K V).

Das bis zu den Parthenonakroteren zurückverfolgbare Schema der >gesprengten Palmette< läßt sich im 4. Jh. und 3. Jh. v. Chr. mehrfach nicht nur in der steinernen Bauornamentik sondern auch auf Stirnziegeln beobachten (z.B. in Delphi, Olympia und Kalaureia).[52] So wird man den >Rosettentypus< nach seiner Palmettengestaltung dieser Zeit—wie dies auch schon vorgeschlagen wurde—zuweisen und ihn in frühhellenistische Zeit datieren können.[53]

Die in Pergamon gefundenen Antefixe können damit und nach den gesicherten Fundplätzen nur mit einem Dach verbunden werden, das zu einem wichtigeren älteren Gebäude im oberen Akropolisterrrain gehörte. In Frage käme dann wahrscheinlich der Palastkomplex I in seinem Zustand vor dem Umbau im 2. Jh. v. Chr.

An die Fragmente des >Rosettentypus< lassen sich noch zwei weitere Ziegelbruchstücke anschließen, die das Motiv variieren und deren Fundort nicht mehr zu ermitteln ist. Aber ausgehend vom Tonmaterial und im Vergleich mit den übrigen Architekturterrakotten unserer Sammlung möchte ich doch annehmen, daß es sich auch um pergamenische Fundstücke handelt:

**Antefixfragmente**
Zwei Stücke ohne Inv. Nr. (Pergamon ?) (Pl. 83:c)
Unterteile eines Palmettenantefixes mit gegenständigen S-förmigen Voluntenranken über einem dreiblättrigen stark verschliffenen Akanthuskelch. Die oberen Voluten besitzen ein konvexes Auge, während die unteren spiralig aufgerollt sind und in äußere Blütengebilde auslaufen. Zwischen den oberen Voluten befindet sich ein Blütenkelch mit einer kleinen herabhängenden Palmette. Über dem Blütenkelch ist der Ansatz einer Innenpalmette erkennbar und rechts daneben strebt das unterste Blatt des jetzt nur noch im Ansatz erkennbaren äußeren Palmettenfächers nach oben und biegt in Höhe der Bruchkante nach außen. Im Zwickel zwischen dem Palmettenblatt und der Voluntenranke sitzt eine neunblättrige Seitenpalmette.

Die Fragmente bestehen aus hellrotem Ton und sind mit einer dunkelroten Engobe überzogen, wie sie allgemein für die hellenistischen Ziegel in Pergamon charakteristisch ist. Der innen gerundete, außen dachförmige Kalypter (8,5 cm hoch und 16 cm breit) läuft mit einem kräftigen Grat auf der Rückseite der Antefixplatte aus.

A. Höhe (erh.): 14,6 cm; Breite: 16,2 cm; Tiefe (erh.): 13 cm.
B. Höhe (erh.): 12,2 cm; Breite (erh.): 11,3 cm; Tiefe (erh.): 7 cm.

Das Relief dieser Stirnziegel läßt sich offenbar aus der Verknüpfung traditionell kleinasiatischer Gestaltungsweisen mit dem aus Attika übernommenen neuen Antefixtyp erklären. Die teigig und schwerfällig modellierten Ornamente verleihen dem Ziegel allerdings einen altertümlichen Charakter. Nach der gröberen Ausführung zu urteilen wird man wohl die beiden Fragmente als Ersatzstücke für beschädigte Antefixe des >Rosettentypus< eingesetzt haben.

---

[52] Delphi, marmorne Traufsima des Apollontempel VI (366–320 v. Chr.): *Samothrace* IV, ii, S. 88–89, Abb. 83; Olympia, nordöstlich des Zeustempels gefundene Antefixe (>Diadochenzeit<): *Olympia* II, S. 143, Taf. 91:6; Kalaureia, Bau G (l. Hälfte 3. Jh. v. Chr.): Wide und Kjellberg 1895, S. 284–285, Abb. 15.

[53] Ein bisher unpubliziertes Palmettenfragment, das wahrscheinlich zu einem Ziegel des >Rosettentypus< gehören dürfte, wurde im Bau Z 3 (Knigge 1988, S. 93–94) des Kerameikos gefunden. Danach wäre dieser Typ in Athen bereits in der zweiten Hälfte des 4. Jh. v. Chr. nachweisbar.

Das mit diesen Ziegeln eingeführte Motiv des Akanthuskelches wurde in der Folgezeit dann besonders bei Marmorantefixen verwendet. Zu erwähnen in diesem Zusammenhang sind mehrere Fragmente eines Kalyptertyps von der Terrasse des Zeusaltars (Pl. 83:d, Fig. 2) und ein Palmettenstirnziegel vom ionischen Gymnasiontempel (Fig. 1:f):

**Marmorkalypter mit Antefix**
Antikensammlung, vorl. Inv. Nr. 125.a[54]
Dachförmiger Marmorkalypter. Die Stirnseite schmückt ein aufbiegendes Akanthusblatt, aus dem seitlich mit Knospen besetzte seilförmig gedrehte Ranken und oben ein Blattbündel hervorwachsen. Die Blätter sind über dem Kalypter abgebrochen. Die Unterseite zeigt eine kreuzförmige Vorritzung und ist in einem Abstand von *ca.* 1 cm von der Kalypterstirn *ca.* 3,5 cm tief ausgehöhlt. Auf dem glatten Teil der Unterseite befindet sich seitlich ein kreisförmiges Loch für einen runden Dübel (Durchmesser *ca.* 13 mm).
Höhe (Kalypter): 10 cm; Breite: 16 cm.

**Marmorkalypter mit Antefix**
Antikensammlung, vorl. Inv. Nr. 125.b
Marmorziegel wie Inv. Nr. 125.a. Die seitlichen Ranken sind jedoch glatt und die Aushöhlung der Unterseite beginnt 19 cm hinter der Kalypterstirn. Rest des Bronze(?)dübels.

**Marmorkalypter mit Antefix**
Antikensammlung, vorl. Inv. Nr. 205
Marmorziegel wie Inv. Nr. 125.b mit anpassendem kleinen Fragment des bekrönenden Blattstandes. Die Aushöhlung beginnt *ca.* 21 cm hinter der Kalypterstirn.

**Palmettenantefix aus Marmor**
Akropolis von Pergamon, beim ionischen Gymnasiontempel[55]
Marmorantefix mit durchbrochen gearbeitetem dreiteiligen Akanthuskelch, aus dem eine siebenblättrige Flammenpalmette hervorwächst. Die Palmettenblätter sind über dem an der Unterseite ausgehöhlten dachförmigen Kalypter abgebrochen.
Höhe (Kalypter): 14 cm; Breite (Kalypter): 27,5 cm.

Bei den erstgenannten drei Marmorkalypteren glaubte J. Schrammen, daß sie nicht zum Zeusaltar gehören würden, da die Unterseiten nicht vollständig für die Falze der marmornen Dachkassetten ausgearbeitet sind. Wenn man jedoch berücksichtigt, daß einigen Kassettenplatten, deren Stirnflächen auf Anschluß gearbeitet sind, möglicherweise noch Werkstücke vorgeblendet waren,[56] ließe sich dieser Einwand widerlegen. Die Kalyptere, die nach ihren Abmessungen sehr gut zum Dach des Altars passen würden, wären dann auf den jetzt fehlenden Vorsatzsteinen mit ihrer glatten Unterseite verdübelt gewesen. Beim unfertigen Zustand des Altarbaues wird aber wohl nur ein Teil des Daches (wahrscheinlich an der Ostseite) mit diesen Kalypteren geschmückt gewesen sein.

Die Marmorziegel selbst können mit weiteren im Altargebiet gefundenen Fragmenten von Blütenständen (Pl. 83:e) ergänzt werden. Das am besten erhaltene Bruchstück eines solchen Blütenstengels ist 12,3 cm hoch und an drei Seiten (die Rückseite blieb roh und ist

---

[54] *AvP* VII, ii, S. 385, Nr. 43.
[55] *AvP* VI, S. 75–76, Beiblatt 3:9.
[56] *AvP* III, i, S. 43, Abb. d., 44.

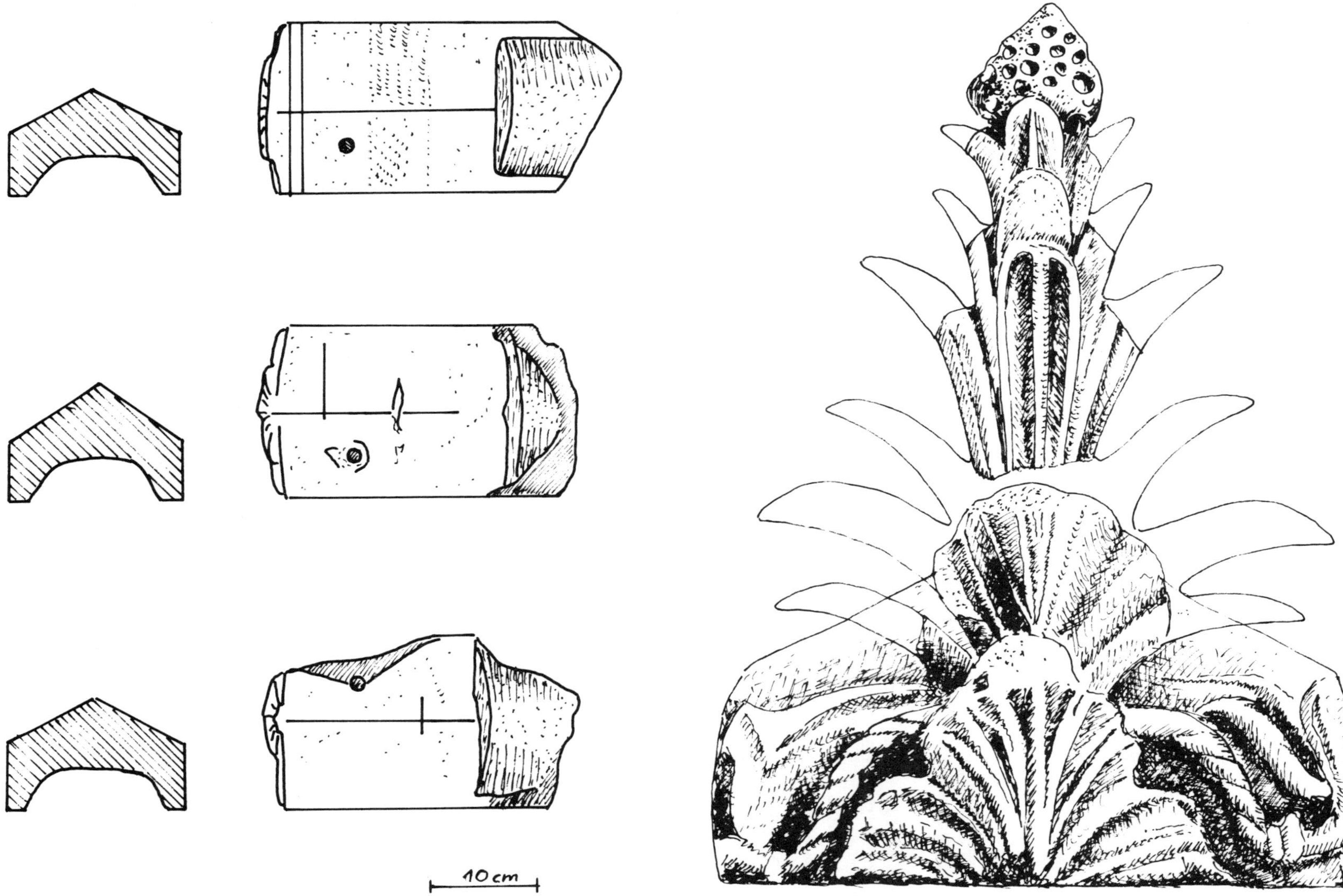

Fig. 2. Marmorantefixe von der Alterterrasse. Schnitte, Unterseiten und Rekonstructionsversuch

verwittert) von dreifach gestaffelten, ausbiegenden Schilfblättern umgeben. Die Oberfläche des kegelförmigen Blütenstandes ist durch Bohrungen aufgelöst.

Ein ähnlich filigranes Gebilde wie dieser Antefixtyp von der Altarterrasse stellte auch das Antefix des Gymnasiontempels dar. Es gehört zu jenen hellenistischen Antefixtypen, bei denen unter Auslassung der Voluten die Palmette direkt mit dem Akanthuskelch verbunden wurden.[57] Damit ist bei diesem Stirnziegltyp der Aufbau noch stärker reduziert als bei den Marmorantefixen der Attalosstoa in Athen,[58] wo ähnlich wie beim Altarantefix noch rudimentäre Rankenschößlinge unter der Palmette erhalten sind. Gerade im attischen Umkreis fällt jedoch die derbere Formensprache der Antefixe der Attalosstoa im Vergleich zu den feingliedrigeren Nachfolgetypen der Erechtheion-Stirnziegel besonders auf. Vielleicht können wir hier ebenso wie in der Hallenarchitektur Rückwirkungen jener intensiven Kontakte erkennen, die das Attalidenreich mit Athen unterhielt und aus denen es zu einem erheblichen Teil seine kulturelle Identität bezog.

## BIBLIOGRAPHIE

Åkerström, Å. 1966. *Die architektonischen Terrakotten Kleinasiens* (*Acta Instituti Athenienses Regni Sueciae* XI), Lund

*AvP* I, ii = A. Conze, *Stadt und Landschaft* (*Altertümer von Pergamon* I, ii), Berlin 1912

*AvP* II = R. Bohn, *Das Heiligtum der Athena Polias Nikephoros* (*Altertümer von Pergamon* II), Berlin 1885

*AvP* III, i = J. Schrammen, *Der grosze Altar der Obere Markt* (*Altertümer von Pergamon* III, i), Berlin 1906

*AvP* VI = P. Schazmann, *Das Gymnasion der Tempelbezirk der Hera Basileia* (*Altertümer von Pergamon* VI), Berlin 1923

*AvP* VII, ii = F. Winter, *Die Skulpturen mit Ausnahme der Altarreliefs* (*Altertümer von Pergamon* VII, ii), Berlin 1908

*AvP* VIII, ii = E. Fabricius und C. Schuchhardt, *Die Inschriften von Pergamon* (*Altertümer von Pergamon* VIII, ii), M. Fränkel, ed., Berlin 1895

*AvP* IX = E. Boehringer und F. Krauss, *Das Temenos für den Herrscherkult, "Prinzessinnen Palais"* (*Altertümer von Pergamon* IX), Berlin 1937

*AvP* X = A. von Szalay und E. Boehringer, *Die hellenistischen Arsenale* (*Altertümer von Pergamon* X), Berlin 1937

*AvP* XI, ii = O. Ziegenaus und G. De Luca, *Das Asklepieion, II, Der nördliche Temenosbezirk und angrenzende Anlagen in hellenistischer und frührömischer Zeit* (*Altertümer von Pergamon* XI, ii), Berlin 1975

Billot, M.-F. 1976. "Terres cuites architecturales du Musée Épigraphique," Δελτ 31, 1976, A′ [1980], S. 87–135

Buschor, E. 1933a. *Die Tondächer der Akropolis*, II, *Stirnziegel*, Berlin/Leipzig

———. 1933b. "Altsamische Grabstelen," *AM* 58, S. 22–46

Clark, J. Th. 1898. *Report on the Investigation at Assos 1882, 1883*, New York

*Corinth* IV, i = I. Thallon-Hill und L. S. King, *Decorated Architectural Terracottas* (*Corinth* IV, i), Cambridge, Mass. 1929

Coulton, J. J. 1976. *The Architectural Development of the Greek Stoa*, Oxford

Daux, G. 1965. "Chronique des fouilles 1964," *BCH* 89, S. 683–1007

*Didyma* I = H. Knackfuss, *Die Baubeschreibung* (*Didyma* I), Berlin 1941

*Erythrai* II = C. Bayburtluoğlu, *Terracottas in Erythrai* (*Erythrai* II), Ankara 1977

Furtwängler, A. 1906. *Aegina, das Heiligtum der Aphaia*, Munich

Gardner, E. A., W. Loring, G. C. Richards, und W. J. Woodhouse. 1892. *Excavations at Megalopolis* (*JHS* Supplement 1), London

Harl, O. 1971. "Studien zu den Stirnziegeln der Peloponnes" (Diss. Graz-Universität 1971)

Hiller, F. 1967. "Zur Berliner Ritzstele," *MarbWPr* [1968], S. 18–26

Hübner, G. 1973. "Dachterrakotten aus dem Kerameikos von Athen," *AM* 88, S. 67–143

---

[57] Z.B. bei den Marmorantefixe vom Naiskos des didymäischen Apollontempels: Pfrommer 1987, S. 177–179, Taf. 53:3; vgl. auch Mitsopoulou-Leon 1967, S. 124–131 (Nr. 3–11).

[58] Travlos 1971, S. 514, Abb. 646 und 647; vgl. auch das Fragment bei Buschor 1933a, S. 61, Abb. 84 rechts.

Kaltsas, N. 1988. Πήλινες διακοσμημένες κεραμώσεις από τη Μακεδονία, Athens
*Kerameikos* X = W. Hoepfner, *Das Pompeion und seine Nachfolgerbauten (Kerameikos* X), Berlin 1976
Kleemann, I. 1958. *Der Satrapen-Sarkophag aus Sidon (Istanbuler Forschungen* 20) Berlin
Knigge, U. 1988. *Der Kerameikos von Athen*, Athen
Koukouli-Chrysanthaki, H. 1970. "Sarcophages en terre cuite d'Abdere," *BCH* 94, S. 327–360
Lazarides, D. I. 1965. "'Άβδηρα," Δελτ 20, 1965, Β'3 [1967], S. 453–461
Mitsopoulou-Leon, V. 1967. "Beobachtungen zu einigen Ton-Antefixen aus Elis," in *Festschrift Fritz Eichler (ÖJh* Beiheft 1), Wien, S. 124–131
Ohnesorg, A. 1990. "Archaic Roof Tiles from the Heraion on Samos," in *Proceedings of the First International Conference on Archaic Greek Architectural Terracottas, Athens, December 2–4, 1988 (Hesperia* 59, 1990), N. A. Winter, Hrsg., S. 181–192
*Olympia* II = W. Dörpfeld and R. Bormann, *Die Baudenkmäler (Olympia, Ergebnisse der von dem deutschen Reich veranstalteten Ausgrabungen* II), Berlin 1892
*Olynthus* XII = D. M. Robinson, *Domestic and Public Architecture (Excavations at Olynthus* XII), Baltimore 1946
Pariente, A. 1990. "Chronique des fouilles en 1989," *BCH* 114, S. 703–939
Pfrommer, M. 1987. "Überlegungen zur Baugeschichte des Naiskos im Apollontempel zu Didyma," *IstMitt* 37, S. 145–185
———. 1989. "Zum Fries des Dionysostempels in Milet," *IstMitt* 39, S. 433–439
*Samos* XIV = R. Tölle, *Das Kastro Tigani (Samos* XIV), Bonn 1974
*Samothrace* IV, ii = K. Lehmann und J. Spittle, *The Altar Court (Samothrace* IV, ii), New York 1964
Schmidt, Th.-M. 1990. "Der späte Beginn und der vorzeitige Abbruch der Arbeiten am Pergamonaltar," in *Phyromachosprobleme (Mitteilungen des Deutschen Archäologischen Instituts, Römische Abteilung. Ergänzungsheft* 31), B. Andreae, Hrsg., Berlin, S. 141–162
*Sibari* III = *NSc* 1970 Supplement
*Sibari* IV = *NSc* 1974 Supplement
Skarlatidou, E. 1982. "'Άβδηρα," Δελτ 37, 1982, Β'2 [1989], S. 334
Travlos, J. 1971. *Bildlexikon zur Topographie des antiken Athen*, Tübingen
Vollgraff, W. 1956. *Le sanctuaire d'Apollon Pythéen à Argos (Études péloponnésiennes* I), Paris
Wide, S., und L. Kjellberg. 1895. "Ausgrabungen auf Kalaureia," *AM* 20, S. 267–326
Zimmermann, K. 1983. *Dachterrakotten griechischer Zeit aus Histria. Untersuchungen zur Typologie, Datierung und Verbreitung keramischer Bauelemente im Schwarzmeergebiet*, Habilitationsschrift, Humboldt-Universität, Berlin
Züchner, W. 1936. "Fragmente auf der Akropolis und im Asklepieion zu Athen," *AA* [*JdI* 51], Sp. 305–384

VOLKER KÄSTNER

STAATLICHE MUSEEN ZU BERLIN
Antikensammlung
Bodestr. 1-3
D-10178 Berlin
Bundesrepublik Deutschland

# ARCHITECTURAL TERRACOTTAS FROM ILION

(PLATE 84)

DOZENS OF architectural terracottas have been discovered and inventoried since renewed excavations started at Troy in 1988.[1] As of this writing these include stamped roof tiles, decorated eaves tiles, and an assortment of antefixes. They derive from three basic types of context: first, archaeological dump fills of earlier excavations; second, trenches opened to explore buildings on or near the citadel partially uncovered in previous investigations; and third, new areas spreading southward below the citadel in the Lower City.[2] The material retrieved thus far appears to date to Ilion's Hellenistic and Roman phases, not always at this point distinguishable one from the other. Preliminary assessment is based, with few exceptions, on stylistic considerations as most of the specimens are floating chronologically in ill-defined contexts.[3] The following pages are intended to serve as a typological introduction to the subject.

Architectural terracottas recovered from the site raise specific questions to be addressed as excavations proceed. One concerns evaluating a relevant piece of testimony attributed to Demetrios of Skepsis by Strabo (13.1.27). Demetrios, on a youthful visit to Ilion early in the 2nd century B.C., is said to have found the city so neglected that its roofs were not even tiled.[4] Hyperbole or fact? Another major question concerns the roofing of those

---

[1] It is a pleasure to thank Nancy Winter and the American School of Classical Studies for organizing and hosting the conference on Classical and Hellenistic architectural terracottas. By prior agreement a résumé of my communication is presented here with the proceedings of this conference in anticipation of a fuller study to follow in *Studia Troica*. The bibliography on earlier excavations is extensive and includes not only the several books on Troy by Schliemann and Dörpfeld but also the series entitled *Troy* published under Blegen's direction. Major publications with regard to the Classical and Roman phases include sections of Dörpfeld 1902 and Blegen *et al.* 1958. They most specifically include Goethert and Schleif 1962 on the temple and two monographs in the *Troy* series: Bellinger 1961 on the coins and Thompson 1963 on the terracotta figurines. In addition, Blegen's preliminary reports published through most of the 1930's in *AJA* contain otherwise inaccessible information. For further bibliography and reports on current work the reader is directed to forthcoming issues of *Studia Troica*. Architectural terracottas from Ilion have a double set of numbers. The first refers to the excavation's master list of Post-Bronze Age finds started in 1988, with AT standing for architectural terracotta. The second number is a field notation incorporating a sequential number within the grid square of its discovery.

[2] For the general site plan, see Korfmann 1991, p. 23, fig. 23, pl. 4:2; also Korfmann 1992, p. 7, fig. 3.

[3] For comments on the problems of mixed fills, see Miller 1991, pp. 39–41, 54–55. Among architectural terracottas exceptional as deriving from identifiable context are a tile stamped ΘΕΑΤΡΟΝ, probably from the skene of the Roman renovation of Theater A, and an eaves tile stamped ΔΗΜΟΣΙΑ, found by Blegen just west of the Bouleuterion and probably belonging to its Roman configuration (on these, see Rose 1992, pp. 48, fig. 4 and 49 with fig. 10, respectively).

[4] The passage has been commented upon repeatedly: see, notably, Leaf 1923, pp. xxvii–xxxiv, 144–146 and Bellinger 1961, p. 8.

Classical and Roman buildings uncovered in earlier excavations. The Temple of Athena is a prime example.[5] Little roofing material was mentioned in reports of earlier excavations, and indeed many once-discarded architectural terracottas are reappearing in excavation dumps currently under investigation. Interesting as pieces from such sources may sometimes be, they obviously provide little information about their original use. Consequently, the more important sources are the new trenches now being opened, particularly those in the Lower City. Here an abundance of Hellenistic material exists, although typically it is discovered thoroughly churned up by Roman activity directly above.

Among the architectural terracottas recovered so far are numerous eaves tiles with meanders in relief which, judging from their varied findspots, were widely used throughout the city. Small variations occur in the patterning and they appear in different fabrics. One example suffices to illustrate the type (Pl. 84:a).[6] This is a familiar sort of eaves tile, and in the immediate area of the Troad it is found, for instance, at nearby Assos.[7]

Antefixes at Ilion are represented by a considerable array of the palmette variety. A selection of three, all preserved only in their upper parts, will serve to suggest something of the range. The first, and surely the earliest of them, is relatively tall and compact (Pl. 84:b).[8] Its palmette is executed in high relief with graduated, drooping frond tips forming the outer edge. The second is an arched plaque with raised border surrounding a flatter palmette with upturned tips (Pl. 84:c).[9] And finally, the third has a broader, borderless surface as background for an almost spidery palmette whose tips here are markedly curved upward (Pl. 84:d).[10] A significant technical feature of many of Ilion's antefixes concerns a handlelike strut at the back that originally joined the cover tile below and served to buttress the relatively thin upper part of the palmette.[11] A reverse view of the last example shows the remaining stump of its strut (Pl. 84:e). This distinctive arrangement as employed on Hellenistic antefixes is otherwise best known in Campania.[12]

At present we continue to rely heavily on Åke Åkerström's book on the architectural terracottas of Asia Minor for relevant regional *comparanda*. From the Troad he collected

---

[5] On the problem of the temple roofing, see Goethert and Schleif 1962, p. 18. Note that the temple in general remains poorly understood (see Hoepfner 1969, pp. 165–181). For a recent reconsideration of the dating of the temple, based on the style of its metopes, see Schmidt-Dounas 1991, pp. 363–415.

[6] AT 19, K 17.79 (p.L. 0.181 m.) comes from the Lower City in mixed context containing remains of Hellenistic material from a terracotta figurine factory (see Miller 1991, pp. 40–41, Context III). Another fragment of the type was found in the same context. AT 4, D 9.33 (p.L. 0.16 m.) comes from excavation dump fill of Schliemann and Dörpfeld (on this, see Miller 1991, pp. 39–40, Context I).

[7] Åkerström 1966, p. 15, nos. 3 and 4, pl. 7:1 and 3 respectively. For examples from the Black Sea region, see the paper by Zimmermann (1994).

[8] AT 30, D 9.735 (p.H. 0.128 m.) from excavation dump fill on the citadel.

[9] AT 17, K 17.55 (p.H. 0.097 m.) from mixed fill in the Lower City.

[10] AT 10, D 9.134 (p.H. 0.13 m.) from excavation dump fill on the citadel.

[11] Lacking this strut is a mended and virtually complete specimen, AT 59, I 17.74, Çanakkale Museum inv. no. 5544 (illustrated by Korfmann 1991, p. 25, fig. 26:1).

[12] For discussion of these struts, see Koch 1912, p. 6 with fig. 10, Hellenistic antefixes from Capua.

various palmette antefixes from the Lower City at Assos, but these, like ours, remain unassigned to specific buildings and consequently resist precise dating.[13] Interestingly enough, although several of them are typologically related to those of Ilion, none appears to have the strut arrangement on the rear.

The most unusual antefix type from Ilion is quite different from those just noted. It features a bust of Athena in relief against a rimmed, arched background (Pl. 84:f). The goddess wears a crested helmet with horns projecting from either side, while a spearhead appears at her right.[14] In the field to either side of her face are three rounded protrusions. The back preserves the stump of the usual supporting strut. Two similar but much more fragmentary pieces of the type have been found.[15] All three come from trenches spread across a distance of more than a hundred meters in the Lower City. And all three were found in mixed fills of Hellenistic to Late Roman date.

Another such antefix is recorded as belonging to the collection of Frank Calvert. Hans Thiersch in his unpublished, illustrated manuscript of this collection documents that the antefix in question resembles ours but adds an owl to the spearhead at the left of Athena's head.[16] We have no idea where exactly it was found other than generally "at Ilion". But if nothing else, this variant indicates that more than one mold was involved in production of the antefix type. What kind of building or buildings these antefixes may have adorned and what the dating might be remain to be determined.

The tradition of human-headed architectural terracottas is firmly rooted in Italy, and indeed Nancy Winter has argued persuasively that it emanated from there.[17] She has also pointed out that whereas the notion was transplanted to Northwestern Greece in Archaic times, it was favored only relatively briefly in that area. In their Italian homeland, by contrast, human-headed architectural terracottas survived, at least in some areas, through the Hellenistic period.[18] The subject has never been systematically studied in the rest of the Greek world, although sporadic examples have been noted from time to time.[19] A general impression based on cursory observation of unpublished material suggests that by Late Hellenistic times antefixes with human heads, usually small and embedded in vegetal surroundings, were fairly widespread. But it can also be observed on the basis of isolated published examples, particularly in the Black Sea area,[20] that there is an earlier tradition of antefixes in certain regions of the eastern Greek world that has heads as the dominant

---

[13] Åkerström 1966, pp. 15–21, pls. 6, 7:4–8, and 8:3.

[14] AT 21, M 18.330 (p.H. 0.128 m.).

[15] AT 18, K 17.68.3 (p.H. 0.112 m.) and AT 29, H 17.38.3 (p.H. 0.132 m.).

[16] Thiersch 1902, p. 42, no. 167.

[17] Winter 1978, pp. 27–58.

[18] For numerous examples, see Koch 1912, *passim*. For Tarentine specimens, see Laviosa 1954, pp. 240–243, 245–247 and Higgins 1954, nos. 1361–1366 (mid-4th century).

[19] See Hübner 1976, pp. 175–183 with references.

[20] See, for instance, a relatively large Athena head from Mesembria (Bouzek 1990, p. 141, fig. 40:1). Among relatively smaller heads, see one from Sinope (Akurgal and Budde 1956, p. 28, pl. 11:a).

feature. The subject deserves further investigation to determine, among other things, just how the human-headed antefixes of the Alexander Sarcophagus are related to these[21] and where the Athena antefixes from Ilion fit into the broader picture.

Iconographically, an Athena wearing a horned helmet in the manner of the Ilion pieces is clearly out of the ordinary,[22] and it seems logical to conclude that some very specific image was intended by it. Actual helmets with cow (or bull) horns are known,[23] and at Macedonian Pella there is a series of 2nd-century figurines of Athena wearing this type of headgear.[24] The Pella figurines have been much discussed, and at least one theory connects them with the city's foundation myth involving a wandering cow.[25] Ilion too has just such a story: according to Apollodoros (*Bibl.* 3.12.3), the eponymous hero Ilos founded the city at a spot to which a certain dappled cow had led him. Whether the sacrifice of a cow at the cult statue of Athena Ilias seen on local coins somehow commemorates this event is debatable.[26] Sacrifice of bovines to Athena is obviously not unusual,[27] but finding allusion to it assimilated to the goddess's iconography (if, indeed, that is what we are seeing) most certainly is. However that may be, it is evident that many different images of Athena were current at Ilion.[28] It is also becoming increasingly apparent that waves of influence reached Ilion from various sources, from both East and West.

The rather curious fact that two of the major temples of the Troad, those at Assos and Ilion, are of the non-Asiatic Doric order has often been noted. And terracotta figures, of which Ilion is producing an increasing body of material, also go their own way; they are quite different, for instance, from those of Pergamon.[29] Clearly, ongoing excavations at Ilion will expand the repertoire of architectural terracottas and add to the growing corpus of its physical remains as a basis for cultural assessment. We can hope not only for a greater typological range but most particularly for contextual circumstances to provide chronological fixed points and enable assignment to roofs of specific buildings.

---

[21] Von Graeve (1970, p. 30, pls. 4:3 and 5:1) sees the antefixes of the Alexander Sarcophagus as unrelated to those of the Black Sea region.

[22] Contrast the Athena-headed antefixes, where the goddess is more traditionally helmeted, collected by Hübner 1976, pl. 63:1–3 and one from Mesembria (Bouzek 1990, p. 141, fig. 40:1).

[23] For a 4th-century B.C. horned helmet from Brjastovec in Bulgarian Thrace, see *Traci*, no. 114. For Celtic horned helmets, see Dintsis 1986, p. 156, and for Bactrian rulers wearing horned helmets on coins, Dintsis 1986, p. 79 with note 12.

[24] Conveniently illustrated in Yalouris *et al.* 1980, no. 150.

[25] See *Pella* I, pp. 39, 51–54. Cows are also particularly connected with Athena in Boiotia (see Schachter 1981, pp. 130–134).

[26] For discussion, see von Fritze 1902, pp. 514–516 and Bellinger 1961, pp. 31 and 54. The ritual sacrifice of the cow to Athena first appears on coins dated by Bellinger 1961, pl. 4, nos. T80, T81 to the 2nd century B.C. The fate of the cow is more graphically rendered on coins of Faustina the Younger (Bellinger 1961, pl. 8, nos. T166, T167).

[27] On the sacrificial cow at the Panathenaic festival of Ilion, see testimonia collected by Frisch 1975, e.g., nos. 5, 6, and 42.

[28] For a discussion of basic Athena types at Ilion, see Miller 1991, pp. 44–45 with notes 18–24.

[29] See comments in *Pergamon* III, p. 172.

## BIBLIOGRAPHY

Åkerström, Å. 1966. *Die architektonischen Terrakotten Kleinasiens* (*Acta Instituti Athenienses Regni Sueciae* XI), Lund

Akurgal, E., and L. Budde. 1956. *Vorläufiger Bericht über die Ausgrabungen in Sinope*, Ankara

Bellinger, A. R. 1961. *Troy. The Coins* (Supplementary Monograph 2), Princeton

Blegen, C., C. G. Boulter, J. L. Caskey, and M. Rawson. 1958. *Troy IV. Settlements VIIa, VIIb and VIII*, Princeton

Bouzek, J. 1990. *Studies of Greek Pottery in the Black Sea Area*, Prague

Dintsis, P. 1986. *Hellenistische Helme*, Rome

Dörpfeld, W. 1902. *Troja und Ilion. Ergebnisse der Ausgrabungen in den vorhistorischen und historischen Schichten von Ilion 1870–1894*, Athens

Frisch, P. 1975. *Die Inschriften von Ilion*, Bonn

Fritze, H. von. 1902. "Die Münzen von Ilion," in Dörpfeld 1902

Goethert, F. W., and H. Schleif. 1962. *Der Athenatempel von Ilion*, Berlin

Graeve, V. von. 1970. *Der Alexandersarkophag und seine Werkstatt* (*Istanbuler Forschungen* 28), Berlin

Higgins, R. A. 1954. *Catalogue of the Terracottas in the Department of Greek and Roman Antiquities British Museum*, repr. Oxford 1969

Hoepfner, W. 1969. "Zum Entwurf des Athena-Tempels in Ilion," *AM* 84, pp. 165–181

Hübner, G. 1976. "Antefixa Deorum Athenarum," *AM* 91, pp. 175–183

Koch, H. 1912. *Dachterrakotten aus Campanien*, Berlin

Korfmann, M. 1991. "Troia: Reinigungs- und Dokumentationsarbeiten 1987, Ausgrabungen 1988 und 1989," *Studia Troica* 1, pp. 1–34

———. 1992. "Troia-Ausgrabungen 1990 und 1991," *Studia Troica* 2, pp. 1–41

Laviosa, C. 1954. "Le antefisse fittili di Taranto," *ArchCl* 6, pp. 217–250

Leaf, W. 1923. *Strabo on the Troad*, Cambridge

Miller, Stella G. 1991. "Terracotta Figurines: New Finds at Ilion, 1988–1989," *Studia Troica* 1, pp. 39–68

*Pella* I = D. Papakonstantinou-Diamantourou, Ιστορική επισκοπήσεις και μαρτυρίαι (Πέλλα I), Athens 1971

*Pergamon* III = E. Töpperwein, *Terrakotten von Pergamon* (*Pergamenische Forschungen* III), Berlin 1976

Rose, C. B. 1992. "The 1991 Post-Bronze Age Excavations at Troia," *Studia Troica* 2, pp. 43–60

Schachter, A. 1981. *Cults of Boiotia*, I, *Acheloos to Hera* (*Bulletin of the Institute of Classical Studies of the University of London* Supplement 38.1), London

Schmidt-Dounas, B. 1991. "Zur Datierung der Metopen des Athena-Tempels von Ilion," *IstMitt* 41, pp. 363–415

Thiersch, H. 1902. *Katalog der Sammlung Calvert in den Dardanellen und in Thymbra* (Handwritten catalogue)

Thompson, D. B. 1963. *Troy: The Terracotta Figurines of the Hellenistic Period* (Supplementary Monograph 3), Princeton

*Traci* = *Arte e cultura nelle terre di Bulgaria dalle origini alla tarda romanità* (Exhibition catalogue, Venice 1989), Milan

Winter, N. A. 1978. "Archaic Architectural Terracottas Decorated with Human Heads," *RM* 86, pp. 27–58

Yalouris, N., M. Andronikos, K. Rhomiopoulou, A. Herrmann, and C. Vermeule. 1980. *The Search for Alexander* (Exhibition catalogue, Washington/Chicago/Boston/San Francisco 1980–1982), Boston

Zimmermann, K. 1994. "Traufziegel mit Reliefmäander aus dem Schwarzmeergebiet," in *Proceedings of the International Conference on Greek Architectural Terracottas of the Classical and Hellenistic Periods, Athens, December 12–15, 1991* (*Hesperia* Supplement 27), N. A. Winter, ed., Princeton, pp. 221–251

STELLA G. MILLER

BRYN MAWR COLLEGE
Department of Classical and Near Eastern Archaeology
Bryn Mawr, PA 19010

# HIGH CLASSICAL AND HIGH BAROQUE IN THE ARCHITECTURAL TERRACOTTAS OF MORGANTINA

(PLATE 85)

THE END of Morgantina's Archaic phase was abrupt.[1] Most areas of the city, both intramural and extramural, show signs of violent destruction by fire. The ceramic evidence associated with these destruction strata dates this event to late in the second quarter of the 5th century B.C., and since Diodoros (11.78.1) tells us that the Sikel nationalist Douketios took Morgantina in 459, it seems reasonable to connect the material and literary evidence.[2]

When Morgantina reappears physically, it has been refounded on the Serra Orlando ridge a short distance to the west of the Cittadella, the site of the intramural Archaic city.[3] The positive features that appear at the Serra Orlando site (the civic and religious monuments in and around the agora, the domestic structures and sanctuaries to the east, west, and north of the agora), all aligned according to an orthogonal plan, and even the city walls are products of an intensive rebuilding program perhaps begun during the Timoleontic revival of Hellenic Sicily in the second half of the 4th century. This program reached its climax in the second quarter of the 3rd, when Morgantina was a large and prosperous outpost of the kingdom of Hieron II of Syracuse.[4]

Between the Archaic and Hellenistic phases, then, the material record at Morgantina appears to have left two major and potentially related lacunae. The first is the issue of the unknown fate of the population of Archaic Morgantina, and the second is the apparent absence of monumental architecture dating to the Classical phases at either the Cittadella or the Serra Orlando sites.

At the Cittadella there is no evidence for reoccupation until the second half of the 4th century.[5] The extramural necropoleis, however, continued in use into the second half of the 5th century, though at a diminished level in frequency of use and in the richness of the grave offerings.[6] In addition, Archaic Morgantina's most prominently positioned and splendidly

---

[1] Thanks are due to the following individuals and institutions: Shari Taylor Kenfield, Curator of Research Photographs in the Department of Art and Archaeology at Princeton University, for invaluable research assistance; Professor Malcolm Bell III of the University of Virginia and Director of the Morgantina Excavations, for helpful discussions as always; Dr. Nancy A. Winter of the American School of Classical Studies at Athens, for arranging and hosting this conference; the Rutgers University Council on Research and Sponsored Programs and the Department of Art History at Rutgers University, for making possible my attendance at this conference; the American School of Classical Studies at Athens, for its generous hospitality.

[2] Bell 1988, pp. 313–316; Sjöqvist 1973, pp. 51–52.

[3] Perhaps the best complete plan of both the Cittadella and the Serra Orlando sites can be found in Bell 1981, pl. 1.

[4] Bell 1988, pp. 316 and 338.

[5] Sjöqvist 1973, pp. 51–52; Sjöqvist 1958, pp. 155–158; Stillwell 1959, pp. 171–173; Allen 1970, p. 378.

[6] Lyons, forthcoming, *Morgantina Studies* V. See now Lyons, in press, *Bolletino di Archeologia*. Thanks to Dr. Lyons for manuscript versions of both these forthcoming publications and for many helpful conversations over the years.

decorated temple atop Farmhouse Hill, the summit of the Cittadella, apparently continued to be maintained and used until the early years of the 4th century.[7]

At the Serra Orlando site some coins and sherds dating to the second half of the 5th century and found in wash contexts seemed to indicate continued habitation there during that period,[8] but the apparent lack of monumental architecture seemed to express a marginal existence for the Classical community.[9]

The evidence from both the Cittadella and the Serra Orlando sites thus suggests a greatly diminished human presence at the site in the second half of the 5th century and the first half of the 4th. Huddled around the open area that would become the Hellenistic agora, these inhabitants continued to make sporadic use of the necropoleis on the slopes of the Cittadella, maintained the still standing temple at the Cittadella's summit, and perhaps still used the Cittadella as a place of refuge in times of danger.[10] Literary evidence, however, indicates that there had to be something of value at Morgantina in the second half of the 5th century for it to have been awarded to Kamarina at the Congress of Gela in 424, though it could have been the *chora* of this *polis axiologos*, as Diodoros labels Morgantina, rather than its *asty* that made it a bargaining chip.[11] In addition, Diodoros tell us that Dionysios I took the city in 396,[12] and Morgantina's apparent pre-Timoleontic importance is documented by a rare and remarkable series of silver tetradrachms, which also seem to illustrate the Late Classical city's dependence on Syracuse.[13]

This shadowy picture of Morgantina's Classical phases took an abrupt turn in the summer of 1982 with the discovery of a single antefix (Pl. 85:a) in the fill behind the back wall of the Northeast Fountain House.[14] The style of this face immediately brings to mind the female heads from the metopes of the Temple of Zeus at Olympia and, closer to home, the female heads from the metopes of Temple E at Selinous.[15] These comparanda appear to date the antefix to the 460's or the early 450's, but the more pronounced mu-shape of the upper lip inclines me to place it at the lower end of this suggested chronology or slightly later.[16]

In fact, other antefix fragments, invariably battered lower faces that proved to belong to this set, had been discovered in previous seasons of excavation (Pl. 85:d). Even in these

---

[7] Allen 1970, p. 378. For the most in-depth discussion of this building, see Kenfield 1990, pp. 265–274.

[8] Sjöqvist 1960b, pp. 292–300; Bell 1981, p. 5, note 12; Bell 1988, pp. 314–316. Recent excavations on the east side of the Lower Agora have also revealed a potter's kiln dating to the second half of the 5th century; see Bell 1988, pp. 319–321.

[9] See, for example, comments by Finley 1968, p. 64.

[10] Allen 1970, p. 378, notes 34 and 35.

[11] Thucydides 4.65 for the Congress of Gela and Diodoros 11.78.1 for the description of the Morgantina taken by Douketios as a *polis axiologos*.

[12] Diodoros 14.78.7; Sjöqvist 1973, pp. 56–59.

[13] Bell 1981, p. 5, note 15; Buttrey *et al.* 1989, pp. 4–8, pl. 1, figs. 7–10.

[14] Bell 1988, pp. 333–334, note 66, fig. 28.

[15] Discussions with complete bibliographies to dates of publication can be found in Ridgway 1970, pp. 12–28; Holloway 1975, pp. 19–26, figs. 125–151.

[16] In the lively discussion following the presentation of this paper, opinions concerning the date of this antefix as manifested by its style varied widely, from the 470's to the first quarter of the 4th century.

fragments the classicism is readily apparent, but the dearth of monumental architecture dating to the Early and High Classical periods led to the assumption that these fragments belonged to a set of classicizing Hellenistic female-head antefixes.

The discovery of a nearly complete antefix revealed that stylistically the entire set should probably be dated soon after Douketios' taking of Archaic Morgantina. This conclusion seems to entail a number of other assumptions. If, for example, this earlier dating is correct, then Morgantina must have been refounded on the Serra Orlando ridge almost immediately after the destruction of the Archaic city, and, since Douketios is known to have founded and refounded other cities, it is tempting to add Morgantina to his list.[17]

With whom, then, did Douketios populate this refounded city? The findspot of this relatively complete antefix suggests an answer. Its proximity to the North Stoa I, apparently the only public building of Morgantina's High Classical phase of which there are any remains, indicates that it might have belonged to the roof of that building.[18]

The scrappy remains of the North Stoa I were discovered in the excavations of the east end of the overlying North Stoa II.[19] The strata associated with the North Stoa I contained coins of Syracuse and Kamarina as well as Attic black-glazed sherds dating to the second half of the 5th century. The coins and sherds, of course, supply a date for the use of the building, and the sherds further indicate that providing a formal setting for drinking parties was one of the principal functions of North Stoa I. The remains of the walls of the building show that they were about 0.75 m. thick and constructed of stone, mostly rubble, but with the occasional use of ashlar blocks, especially at the corners. The rooms of the building seem to have been nearly square in plan and ranged side by side along the northeastern side of the agora. These rooms do not seem to have communicated with each other, but each apparently gave onto the open space to the south and perhaps onto a street to the north.

Each of these features of the North Stoa I corresponds to the earlier remains of a building on the southeastern side of the Archaic agora, a building which I have addressed on several occasions in other contexts.[20] The eaves of this Archaic building were decorated sequentially with two sets of female-head antefixes. The early examples date to the early years of the third quarter of the 6th century, when a sizable group of Greeks arrived and settled at the previously indigenous site.[21] Later, probably in the 470's, the roof was damaged and

[17] Diodoros 11.88.6 for Menai and Palike; Diodoros 12.8.2 for Kale Akte. See Bell 1988, pp. 319–321; Finley 1968, pp. 63–64. Indeed, the House of the Silver Hoard, an architecturally undistinguished domicile in spite of the glamor of the eponymous find of Roman silver coins deposited in its cistern, is located immediately to the east of the Upper Agora and may date as early as the second half of the 5th century. If so, its alignment suggests that the orthogonal plan that determined the layout of the Hellenistic city may have been a feature of the Douketian refounding. Bell 1988, pp. 320 and 338, fig. 1; Tsakirgis 1983, pp. 42–46, 424. This dissertation has been updated and rewritten and is to appear as *Morgantina Studies* VII, forthcoming, Princeton University Press.

[18] Bell 1988, p. 334, note 66.

[19] Sjöqvist 1962, pp. 136–137; Sjöqvist 1964, pp. 138–140; Allen 1970, p. 364.

[20] Initial reports on this building appear in Sjöqvist 1958, pp. 155–158; Stillwell 1959, pp. 171–173; Sjöqvist 1960a, pp. 133–135; Kenfield 1993b.

[21] Kenfield 1993a; Mertens-Horn 1991, pp. 11–12, fig. 3.

repaired with more up-to-date female-head antefixes.[22] Clearly there was a desire to keep the decoration of the eaves of this Archaic civic building as au courant as possible. It seems reasonable to assume that this desire was also applied to its apparent Early and High Classical successor, the so-called North Stoa I.[23]

That a building appears in the early 450's at Classical Morgantina, which is more or less identical in placement, plan, construction technique, decoration, and function to what was arguably Archaic Morgantina's most important civic building, suggests that Douketios transferred the surviving population from the Archaic site to the Classical site.[24] Perhaps it is not accidental that the position of this new building, the North Stoa I, was the best on the agora for affording a view of the new civic center immediately to the south and a view of the old city in the distance to the east.

In the 5th century, with the advent of classicism and its correlative humanism, a conflation of forms occurred in the two types of antefixes most prevalent in the Western Greek world.[25] The canonical Archaic gorgoneion with its broad, flat face (betraying its origins in the graphic arts) and its grimacing mouth, fangs, and protruding tongue is abandoned for what is essentially a female head in much higher relief and more closely related to monumental freestanding sculpture. Indeed, the only indication that this new kind of gorgoneion antefix really represents Medusa is the continued appearance of flanking snakes, that feature of the Archaic gorgoneion which is the last to disappear. The necessity for the Medusa to inspire fear in the viewer, thus performing her apotropaic function, is now accomplished not through her monstrous appearance as in the past but through her wildly demented demeanor.

At first the timeless sobriety of High Classicism is maintained and the dementia is communicated through the disheveled hair into which the snaky locks of earlier gorgoneia have metamorphosed. Always in step with development in the more monumental plastic arts, the face gradually becomes more mobile, more fleeting in its expression. The lips part, the eyes are set more deeply into their orbital cavities, and the forehead develops a horizontal crease that causes it to project forward on two planes. The use of these techniques enables the sculptor to communicate dementia and thus inspire fear through apparent emotion rather than through symbol, though the hair remains invariably wild and unkempt.

It is interesting that none of these High and Late Classical Medusa head antefixes appear at Morgantina. In fact, the female-head antefixes under discussion are the only

---

[22] Kenfield 1993b, p. 26; Stillwell 1961, pp. 280–281, fig. 12, pl. 94; Winter 1978, pp. 36–38, pl. 14, figs. 3 and 4; Albanese Procelli 1990, pp. 7–16; Mertens-Horn 1991, p. 12. My proposed date for the antefixes in this series is considerably later than the dates proposed by Winter, Albanese Procelli, or Mertens-Horn.

[23] It is interesting to note that this civic building on the southeast side of the Archaic agora was, in spite of its destruction in 459, never further dismantled or built over when the area was reoccupied in the 4th century, perhaps suggesting a continued reverence for the ruins of the building down into at least the Late Classical period. See Stillwell 1959, p. 173.

[24] There has been much speculation on the specifics of Douketios' program. See, most recently, Rizzo 1970, pp. 158–169; Adamesteanu 1962. A potter's kiln firing Sikulo-Geometric pottery but associated with Attic black-glazed sherds dating to the second half of the 5th century has been discovered on the southeast side of the Classical/Hellenistic agora at the Serra Orlando site, thus apparently demonstrating the continued ethnic mix of the community at the Serra Orlando site. See Bell 1988, pp. 319–321.

[25] The best general examinations of this development remain Laviosa 1954, pp. 228, 235–243, pls. LXXII, LXXIII and Floren 1977, pp. 116–217.

architectural terracottas from Morgantina that can be definitely associated with the Early and High Classical phases of the site. Other revetments discovered in contexts similar to these Classical female heads are typologically Archaic, thus raising the issue of whether they belonged to buildings of the Early and High Classical phases decorated in an old-fashioned, conservative manner, or to extramural Archaic sanctuaries.[26] It is possible that the people of Classical Morgantina preferred Archaic decoration for their sanctuaries and, as we have already seen, up-to-date decoration for their civic buildings, but it can hardly be claimed, in light of the female-head antefixes, that only worn, outmoded molds were available at sites in the *mesogeia*.[27] Unfortunately, the intensive building activity of the Hellenistic phases has for the most part obliterated the buildings these revetments decorated.

Hellenistic Morgantina is practically as rich in the number and variety of its antefixes as its Archaic predecessor. By way of illustration, I present two examples, a dramatic mask antefix of high quality (Pl. 85:b) and a female-head antefix (Pl. 85:c) also of high quality, worthy progeny of her Archaic and Classical forebears. Unfortunately, the taking of Morgantina by the Romans in 212/11 and the subsequent occupation and cleanup by Rome's Spanish mercenaries have made it impossible to associate any of these antefixes with other revetments of the roofs to which they belonged or even, for that matter, with any specific buildings.[28]

In any event, the most prominent series among these antefixes is the previously discussed Medusa-head type, present at the site in five different sets. The antefixes of one of these sets are interesting (Pl. 85:e), not because they are particularly fine pieces of sculpture (they were, indeed, clearly produced in a worn mold) but because each antefix of the set displays a scarlike ridge running diagonally across the face from lower left to upper right.[29] Since the breadth of this ridge varies from antefix to antefix, the technical reason for its existence is clear: the coroplast was using a broken mold. When pushing the clay down into the mold, he was forced to hold the two pieces of the mold together. Some of the clay was, of course, bound to be forced down into the crack. The breadth and height of the resulting ridge depended on how closely together the two pieces were held. What is surprising is that the coroplast did not bother to trim off the ridge before firing. Perhaps he reasoned that the flaw would not be apparent to the viewer when the antefix was painted and mounted on the eaves of its roof. A more romantic interpretation would see his decision to retain the ridge as a means of increasing the horrifying power of the image.

The most spectacular set of these Medusa-head antefixes (Pl. 85:f) arguably provides the finest examples of Hellenistic sculpture from the site. Unlike their scar-faced sisters, their crisp features bespeak early production in a first-generation mold. Now the artist confronts

[26] For a definition of intramural, extramural, suburban, and extraurban sanctuaries, see Edlund 1987, pp. 41, 95–125, 142–143; Malkin 1981, pp. 290–325.

[27] A claim made by Albanese Procelli 1990, p. 9.

[28] The classic example of this phenomenon is the baroque Medusa antefixes presented below (Pl. 85:f). These were found dumped into the cistern of the House of the Antefixes, a shabby structure to the roof of which these beautiful revetments could hardly have belonged. The assumption, then, has been that these antefixes originally decorated the roof of a nearby and much more splendidly appointed domicile such as the House of the Official. See Tsakirgis 1983, pp. 152–155; Allen 1970, pp. 361–363.

[29] Besides the examples of this antefix discovered in the American excavations at Morgantina, a number were recovered by Paolo Orsi and are housed uncatalogued in the Museo Archeologico Regionale in Syracuse.

the viewer with the ultimate statement of Medusa's wild-eyed dementia, a look as terrifying as, perhaps even more terrifying than, that of her Archaic forebears. The High Baroque style of these antefixes is apparent. These antefixes probably date to the second quarter of the 3rd century and must, in any event, antedate the catastrophe of 212/11.[30]

Considering what is now known about the early gestation of the Hellenistic baroque in the Western Greek world,[31] it is unlikely that the stylistic impulses responsible for the appearance of these antefixes lie in the eastern Mediterranean or even on the Italian mainland.

In the 3rd century, Syracuse is the most likely source of inspiration for the baroque style manifested in these antefixes. Indeed, one of the most intriguing aspects of these antefixes is that they can perhaps be seen as providing a glimpse at the largely unknown art of Hieronian Syracuse.[32]

In any event, these antefixes show once again that in spite of Morgantina's remote position and the humble, moldmade nature of the objects, Morgantina remained very much in touch with the latest stylistic developments in the sculpture of the Hellenic world.

## BIBLIOGRAPHY

Adamesteanu, D. 1962. "L'ellenizzazione della Sicilia ed il momento di Ducezio," *Kokalos* 7, pp. 167–198

Albanese Procelli, R. M. 1990. "Antefisse a protome femminile dal centro indigeno del Mendolito di Adrano," *SicArch* 23, pp. 7–31

Allen, H. L. 1970. "Excavations at Morgantina (Serra Orlando), 1967–1969: Preliminary Report X," *AJA* 74, pp. 359–383

Bell, M., III. 1981. *The Terracottas (Morgantina Studies* I), Princeton

———. 1988. "Excavations at Morgantina, 1980–1985: Preliminary Report XII," *AJA* 92, pp. 313–342

Buttrey, T. V., K. T. Erim, T. D. Groves, and R. Ross Holloway. 1989. *The Coins (Morgantina Studies* II), Princeton

Edlund, I. E. M. 1987. *The Gods and the Place: Location and Function of Sanctuaries in the Countryside of Etruria and Magna Graecia (700–400 B.C.)*, Stockholm

Finley, M. I. 1968. *Ancient Sicily to the Arab Conquest*, London

Floren, J. 1977. *Studien zur Typologie des Gorgoneion*, Münster Westfalen

Holloway, R. Ross. 1975. *Influences and Styles in the Late Archaic and Early Classical Sculpture of Sicily and Magna Graecia*, Louvain

Kenfield, J. F. 1990. "An East Greek Master Coroplast at Late Archaic Morgantina," in *Proceedings of the First International Conference on Archaic Greek Architectural Terracottas, Athens, December 2–4, 1988* (*Hesperia* 59, 1990), N. A. Winter, ed., pp. 265–274

———. 1993a. "The Case for a Phokaian Presence at Morgantina as Evidenced by the Site's Archaic Architectural Terracottas," in *Les grands ateliers d'architecture dans le monde égéen du VI$^e$ siècle av. J.-C. Actes du colloque d'Istanbul, 23–25 mai 1991* (*Varia Anatolica* III), J. des Courtils and J.-C. Moretti, eds., Paris, pp. 261–269

---

[30] See Tsakirgis 1983.

[31] Ridgway 1990, pp. 150–154, 180–185 esp. 181, and 315–316, with complete bibliography to date of publication.

[32] See, for example, Wescoat 1989, p. 110, nos. 34 and 35, the only objects (coins) in the catalogue dated to the reign of Hieron II; Bell 1981, pp. 43–44. Langlotz 1965, p. 301, no. 155 presents a limestone head in a baroque style from Megara Hyblaia which he dates to the 2nd century. In light of these Medusa-head antefixes from Morgantina, it would perhaps be preferable to see this head as an example of the sculpture of Syracuse in the 3rd century.

———. 1993b. "A Modelled Terracotta Frieze from Archaic Morgantina: Its East Greek and Central Italian Affinities," in *Deliciae Fictiles: Proceedings of the First International Conference on Central Italic Architectural Terracottas, Rome, 10–12 December, 1990*, E. Rystedt, C. Wikander, Ö. Wikander, eds., Stockholm, pp. 21–28

Langlotz, E. 1965. *Ancient Greek Sculpture of South Italy and Sicily*, New York

Laviosa, C. 1954. "Le antefisse fittili di Taranto," *ArchCl* 6, pp. 217–250

Lyons, C. L. In press. "Modalità di acculturazione a Morgantina," *Bolletino di Archeologia*

———. Forthcoming. *The Archaic Necropolis (Morgantina Studies V)*, Princeton

Malkin, I. 1981. "Religion and the Founders of Greek Colonies" (Diss. University of Pennsylvania 1981)

Mertens-Horn, M. 1991. "Una nuova antefissa a testa femminile da Akrai ed alcune considerazioni sulle Ninfe di Sicilia," *Bolletino di Archeologia* 66, pp. 9–28

Ridgway, B. S. 1970. *The Severe Style in Greek Sculpture*, Princeton

———. 1990. *Hellenistic Sculpture*, I, *The Styles of ca. 331–200 B.C.*, Madison

Rizzo, F. P. 1970. *La repubblica di Siracusa nel momento di Ducezio*, Palermo

Sjöqvist, E. 1958. "Excavations at Serra Orlando (Morgantina): Preliminary Report II," *AJA* 62, pp. 155–164

———. 1960a. "Excavations at Morgantina (Serra Orlando) 1959: Preliminary Report IV," *AJA* 64, pp. 125–135

———. 1960b. "Perchè Morgantina?" *RendLinc* 15, pp. 291–300

———. 1962. "Excavations at Morgantina (Serra Orlando) 1961: Preliminary Report VI," *AJA* 66, pp. 135–143

———. 1964. "Excavations at Morgantina (Serra Orlando) 1963: Preliminary Report VIII," *AJA* 68, pp. 137–147

———. 1973. *Sicily and the Greeks*, Ann Arbor

Stillwell, R. 1959. "Excavations at Serra Orlando 1958: Preliminary Report III," *AJA* 63, pp. 167–173

———. 1961. "Excavations at Morgantina (Serra Orlando) 1960: Preliminary Report V," *AJA* 65, pp. 277–281

Tsakirgis, B. 1983. "The Domestic Architecture of Morgantina in the Hellenistic and Roman Periods" (Diss. Princeton University 1983)

Wescoat, B. D., ed. 1989. *Syracuse: The Fairest Greek City*, Rome

Winter, N. A. 1978. "Architectural Terracottas Decorated with Human Heads," *RM* 85, pp. 27–58

JOHN F. KENFIELD

DEPARTMENT OF ART HISTORY
Rutgers University
Voorhees Hall
Hamilton Street
New Brunswick, NJ 08903

# LE TERRECOTTE ARCHITETTONICHE DI ELEA-VELIA DALL'ETÀ ARCAICA ALL'ETÀ ELLENISTICA

(PLATES 86–88)

LE VICENDE STORICO-POLITICHE che portarono alla fondazione di Elea, sulle coste del Tirreno, da parte dei Focei di Asia Minore, sono narrate con ricchezza di particolari da Erodoto e Strabone.[1]

Il racconto erodoteo ci fornisce innanzitutto la data di fondazione della nuova polis ionica intorno al 540 a.C., immediatamente dopo la battaglia di Alalia contro Etruschi e Cartaginesi; di maggior interesse peraltro è il riferimento ad altre città coloniali dell'Italia meridionale quali Reggio e Poseidonia che ebbero un ruolo determinante, non semplicemente limitato alla scelta del sito, nella nascita del nuovo insediamento.[2] Da una lettura critica del passo erodoteo si ricava che la fondazione di Elea va inserita nella complessa realtà dell'area tirrenica nella seconda metà del VI sec. a.C., dove già esistevano delicati equilibri tra le poleis italiote precedentemente insediate e che essa costituisce piuttosto l'epilogo di un lungo processo che ha visto la frequentazione ionica in generale, e focea in particolare, interessare il bacino del Mediterraneo occidentale sin dai primi decenni del VI sec. a.C.[3]

Questa premessa è necessaria se si pensa che, generalmente, viene attribuito ad Elea un ruolo preponderante nella diffusione di prodotti, motivi e modelli di impronta ionica in area tirrenica e che alla presenza dei Focei ad Elea si fa risalire la trasmissione di "prototipi" dall'area greco-orientale.[4] In particolare è proprio intorno a problematiche specifiche delle terrecotte architettoniche che, nonostante una notevole penuria di materiali editi provenienti da Velia, il dibattito degli studiosi è andato via via arricchendosi di contributi stimolanti.[5]

In realtà la storia degli scavi di Elea è quanto mai scarna. Dalle prime descrizioni dell'Antonini nel '700[6] bisognerà attendere il 1889 quando lo Schleuning pubblicò la prima planimetria generale e studiò il circuito murario della città;[7] ma soltanto nel 1927 A. Maiuri iniziò una prima campagna di esplorazione archeologica rimasta peraltro isolata.[8] Negli anni '50 P. Sestieri diede l'avvio a campagne più sistematiche e continuative[9] che avrebbero

[1] Gigante 1966, pp. 295–315.
[2] Lepore 1966, p. 258.
[3] Morel 1982, pp. 479–500.
[4] Johannowsky 1983, p. 74.
[5] Colonna 1980–1981, pp. 160–161.
[6] Fiorelli 1882.
[7] Schleuning 1889, pp. 179–194.
[8] Maiuri 1926–1927, pp. 15–29.
[9] Sestieri 1949, n. 1961; Sestieri 1951, n. 2634; Sestieri 1952, n. 2114; Sestieri 1953, n. 2270; Sestieri 1954, n. 3047; Sestieri 1955, n. 2174.

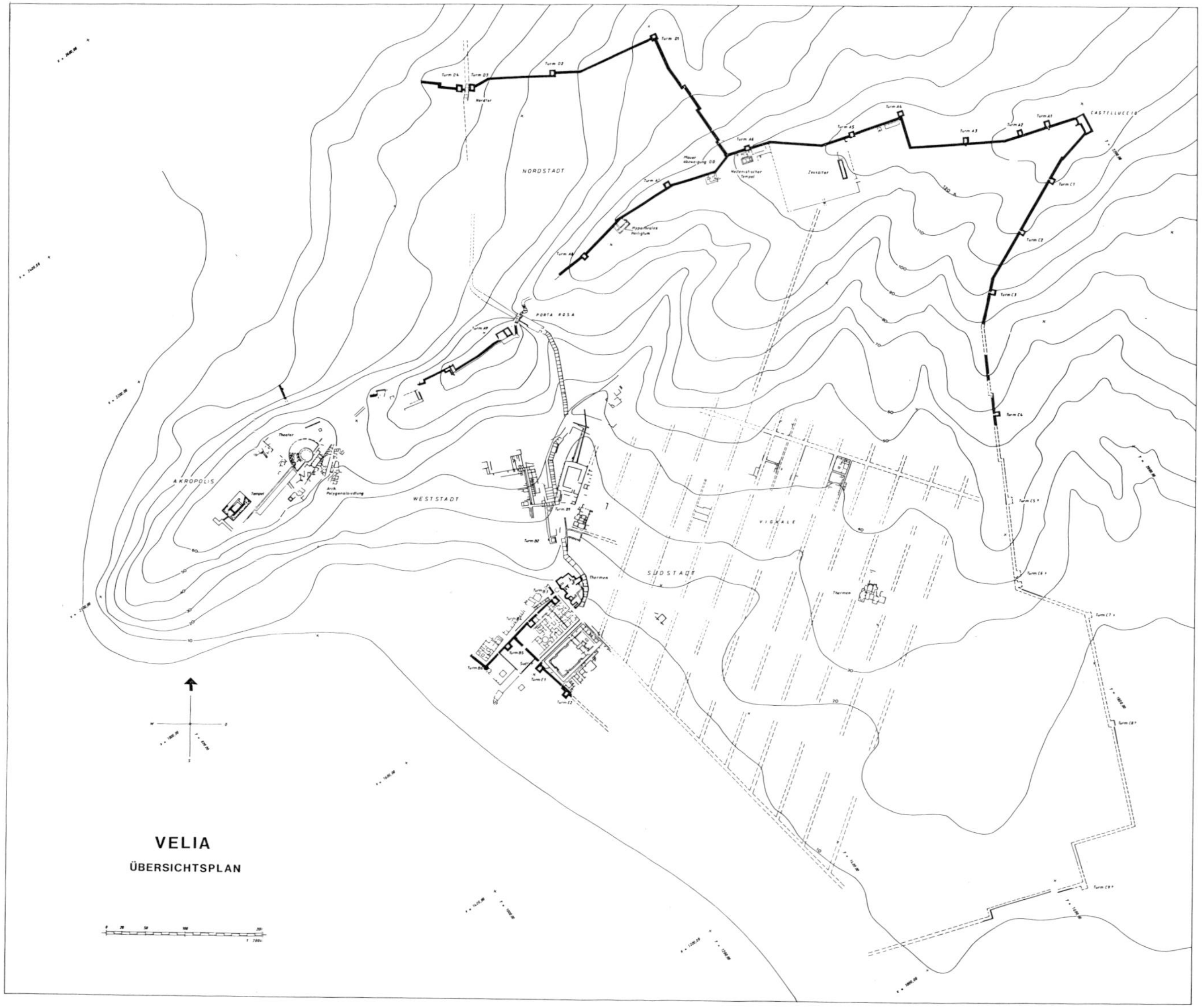

Fig. 1: Elea. Planimetria della città

trovato poi in M. Napoli, nel corso degli anni '60, un entusiasta e attivo ricercatore, teso ad esplorare il tessuto urbano della città, la sua estensione ed i suoi rapporti con l'interno.[10]

Degli scavi realizzati in quegli anni rimangono le analisi topografiche ed urbanistiche di M. Napoli[11] (Fig. 1) e, più recentemente, un quadro di sintesi di W. Johannowsky,[12] mentre del tutto inediti sono a tutt'oggi i materiali e i loro contesti di provenienza.

Accanto dunque ad un dibattito storico sempre più approfondito e ad un quadro urbanistico via via più chiaro, grazie anche alle sistematiche indagini che l'Istituto di Archeologia dell'Università di Vienna va conducendo,[13] va annotata questa carenza nello studio e nella sistemazione dei materiali velini.

Da ciò è scaturita pertanto la necessità di un ampio programma di studio avviato in questi anni dalla Soprintendenza Archeologica di Salerno-Avellino-Benevento, contemporaneamente alla ripresa sistematica dell'esplorazione della città antica.[14]

Uno dei primi lavori in via di realizzazione interessa le terrecotte architettoniche rinvenute nel corso degli scavi tra gli anni '30 e gli anni '70, sollecitato proprio dalla necessità di fornire materiali editi al dibattito relativo alla comparsa di particolari tipologie della decorazione architettonica fittile nell'area del basso e medio Tirreno nella seconda metà del VI sec. a.C.[15]

Il materiale è stato organizzato per classi tipologiche dal momento che purtroppo, soprattutto per i pezzi provenienti dagli scavi più vecchi, mancano quasi del tutto i dati di provenienza. Anche nei casi in cui è stato possibile individuare i contesti di provenienza o addirittura le quote di profondità del ritrovamento, i dati non sono mai sufficienti per attribuire le terrecotte architettoniche recuperate ad un determinato edificio nè per ricostruire dei "sistemi" decorativi completi. Si può solo ipotizzare la presenza di una serie di tetti con copertura di tegole e coppi, decorati, ai lati terminali, da elementi di protezione fittile, di cui rimangono frustuli più o meno ricomponibili.

## ETÀ ARCAICA

Le più antiche terrecotte architettoniche rinvenuta ad Elea, riferibili tutte ai primi decenni di vita della città, sono esclusivamente tegole di gronda dipinte ed antefisse. Mancano del tutto, allo stato attuale della ricerca, elementi attribuibili a sime o a lastre di rivestimento.

Gli edifici arcaici di Elea, prevalentemente case, presentavano uno zoccolo in muratura costruito con blocchetti di arenaria in opera poligonale a giunture curve, secondo una tradizione costruttiva chiaramente importata dalla Ionia di Asia; le parti alte erano in mattoni crudi ed i tetti dovevano prevalentemente essere in argilla battuta e legno, ancora

---

[10] Napoli 1966, pp. 191–226; Napoli 1970, pp. 226–235.
[11] Napoli 1969, pp. 151–163.
[12] Johannowsky 1982, pp. 225–246.
[13] Krinzinger 1987, p. 19.
[14] Tocco 1991.
[15] Winter 1978, pp. 27–57; Kästner 1982a; Knoop 1987; Bonghi Jovino 1989, pp. 666–682; Greco 1990a, pp. 59–63.

secondo una tradizione orientale, peraltro confermata dal fatto che la documentazione archeologica non attesta una particolare abbondanza di tegole e coppi di età arcaica.[16]

Accanto a questi edifici ve ne erano tuttavia altri che, pur conservando lo zoccolo in muratura poligonale e l'elevato in mattoni crudi, avevano un tetto pesante con tegole piane a bordo rialzato, coppi decorati nella parte terminale da antefisse semicircolari e tegole di sponda con la faccia iposcopica dipinta. Questi tetti riflettono una tradizione decorativa peculiare dell'area tirrenica la quale si innesta su una tecnica struttiva puramente ionica.[17]

Le antefisse arcaiche sono a lastra semicircolare con nimbo baccellato e presentano tre diversi motivi decorativi: palmetta dritta, palmetta pendula, testina femminile. Esse sono pertinenti ad almeno quattro tetti differenti, mentre le varianti individuate per l'antefissa a palmetta pendula possono appartenere sia a riparazioni dello stesso tetto, sia a più tetti diversi.

Le antefisse sono tutte a stampo, con ritocchi a stecca e con una ricca policromia. Anche ad un semplice esame autoptico sono distinguibili gli esemplari realizzati in argilla locale da quelli invece ricavati da un'argilla del tutto differente, di cui soltanto le analisi in corso potranno precisare l'area di provenienza.

*Antefissa a palmetta ritta entro nimbo baccellato* (Pl. 86:a). La lastra, semicircolare, è decorata con una palmetta a nove lobi convessi, rigidi e allungati, fuoriuscenti da un elemento semicircolare di base; un nastro piatto segna la cornice liscia, terminante con un bordo dentellato, sulla quale era dipinta la decorazione baccellata in colore bruno e crema.[18]

L'antefissa ripete esattamente un tipo attestato a Cuma, Ischia e Capua e si inserisce perfettamente nella seriazione di recente operata da Knoop, il quale individua in Ischia e Cuma i centri propositivi per questo tipo, collocando cronologicamente la palmetta dritta senza base (tipo 4) al secondo quarto del VI sec. a.C. e considerandola l'antecedente del motivo a palmetta pendula.[19]

La discussione sulla priorità o meno del tipo di antefissa con palmetta dritta, ripresa recentemente anche dalla Bonghi Jovino,[20] poggia purtroppo su seriazioni teoriche o su analisi stilistiche, mentre mancano dati archeologici stratigrafici sicuramente affidabili.

Il problema è strettamente connesso a quello della nascita del nimbo, considerato dalla maggioranza degli studiosi un apporto del mondo greco-orientale per il confronto con alcuni esemplari noti da tempo, provenienti da Neandria, Taso e Gordium, che presentano una cornice dentellata.[21]

Va tuttavia osservato che antefisse semicircolari sono ben attestate anche nella Grecia continentale: l'esempio più noto e calzante è quello di Sparta, dipinto con un motivo elicoidale circondato da una cornice liscia dipinta a denti di lupo.[22] Antefisse circolari senza nimbo sono presenti in Sicilia[23] e in Etruria[24] già nel primo quarto del VI sec. a.C.

---

[16] Martin 1970, pp. 93–107; Morel 1970, pp. 131–145; Neutsch 1970, pp. 146–152.
[17] Knoop 1987, pp. 186–187.
[18] N. inv. 43531. Alt. 13,5; largh. 21,2; argilla non locale.
[19] Knoop 1987, p. 139, con bibliografia precedente.
[20] Bonghi Jovino 1989, p. 672; Kästner 1982b, pp. 90–100.
[21] Åkerström 1966; Greco 1990b.
[22] Winter 1990, pp. 13–32, pl. 1:c.
[23] Cfr. *infra*, nota 26.
[24] Wikander 1981, pp. 124–125.

e durano per un lungo periodo, sino a sviluppare una grande varietà di tipologie in età ellenistica.[25] Considerare dunque la semplice antefissa semicircolare con palmetta il primo anello all'origine del tipo può essere fuorviante, così come non sempre è chiaro il rapporto tra motivo "a rilievo" e motivo "dipinto".

È opinione diffusa che il "dipinto" preceda il "plastico" e che pertanto anche la cornice semplicemente dipinta sia l'antecedente di quella con foglie plastiche. In realtà, anche solo sfogliando i classici repertori di terrecotte architettoniche a nostra disposizione, risulta evidente come, soprattutto nelle fasi iniziali della sperimentazione e della produzione di un tipo, il rapporto tra "rilievo" e "pittura" sia piuttosto articolato e mai costretto in una rigida successione di "prima" e "dopo". Basti pensare, per limitarsi all'area greco-occidentale, ai materiali cumani dove si alternano nello stesso lasso cronologico elementi a rilievo o dipinti; e ad Agrigento e Gela, dove antefisse dipinte con palmette coesistono con palmette a rilievo nel corso della metà del VI sec. a.C.[26]

Il tentativo dunque di porre in uno sviluppo seriale l'antefissa semicircolare con palmetta dritta dipinta, poi plastica, a cui si aggiunge la cornice prima dipinta e poi plastica e da cui ha infine origine il motivo della palmetta pendula con cornice plastica non sembra, allo stato attuale delle ricerche, suffragato da elementi probanti e può considerarsi solo un'ipotesi di lavoro.[27]

Ad Elea i due tipi coesistono e si collocano entrambi nella seconda metà del VI sec. a.C., così come anche a Pompei, nella decorazione del tempio di Apollo, l'antefissa a palmetta dritta, in ben quattro varianti e repliche, con nimbo, è datata alla fine del VI sec. ed è considerata contemporanea al tipo con palmetta pendula.[28] Le antefisse pompeiane sembrano appartenere tutte, per la presenza del listello di base e del nimbo plastico aggettante, ad una variante leggermente più recente rispetto all'esemplare eleate, che viceversa è privo di base, con cornice liscia a curvatura appena accennata.

L'antefissa di Elea, realizzata con ogni probabilità con argilla di area vesuviana, si data ai primi decenni di vita della città (540–520) e trova un confronto particolarmente stretto, sia per modulo che per elementi decorativi, con un esemplare proveniente da Capua, datato dalla Bonghi al secondo quarto del VI sec. a.C.[29] e da Johannowsky nel terzo quarto dello stesso secolo.[30] In mancanza di elementi oggettivi, non è possibile decidere se la cronologia del tipo debba essere appiattita sul dato eleate, oppure se esso sia da considerare il caso attardato di modello già formato nei decenni centrali del VI sec. a.C.

In questa sede interessa sottolineare due riflessioni scaturite dall'analisi dell'esemplare eleate: il tipo a palmetta dritta coesiste e si alterna con quello a palmetta pendula ancora nei decenni finali del VI secolo, mantenendo il "dipinto" quando il "plastico" è pienamente affermato; ad Elea l'esemplare è giunto insieme alla prima generazione di coloni ed è un prodotto di officina campana al quale vanno associate le più antiche tegole di sponda, anch'esse dipinte, con ogni probabilità provenienti dalla stessa officina. Non è da escludere

---

[25] Laviosa 1954, pp. 214–250.
[26] De Miro 1965, p. 74, fig. 3; Fiorentini 1977, p. 109 tav. XXV:5; Andrén 1940, pp. CLXII–CLXIII.
[27] Kästner 1982a, pp. 23–30.
[28] De Caro 1986, pp. 37–38.
[29] Bonghi Jovino 1989, p. 672.
[30] Johannowsky 1983, p. 74.

che qui esso abbia costituito un prototipo da cui sarà stata forse ricavata una serie locale, purtroppo non attestata dai frammenti a nostra disposizione.

*Antefissa a palmetta pendula entro nimbo baccellato* (Pl. 86:b). La lastra semicircolare poggia su una fascia piana dipinta; il motivo centrale è costituito da una palmetta capovolta a 7 lobi fuoriuscente da un nucleo centrale a bottone plastico; essa è retta da una coppia di volute disposte in senso orizzontale e legate tra loro da un elemento lanceolato che funge da riempitivo nel punto di congiunzione. Il nimbo è costituito da 17 lobi appena incurvati, terminanti a giorno, contornati da un sottile bordo a rilevo e poggianti su un cordolo plastico.[31] Sono attestate due varianti distinte per modulo e resa plastica e pittorica, mentre una variante più tarda (A II c) è caratterizzata dalla palmetta impressa al negativo sulla lastra.

Il tipo è notissimo, attestato da una ricca serie cumana[32] e presente, con le medesime caratteristiche all'interno della Campania, nel Lazio meridionale e in Sicilia.[33] Purtroppo i materiali cumani, ischitani[34] e capuani, privi di contesto di provenienza, non possono fornire elementi precisi per l'inquadramento cronologico del tipo, mentre puntualizzazioni migliori vengono dalle recenti analisi sulle terrecotte architettoniche di Satricum, Pompei e Himera.

A Satricum la sostanziale integrità del sistema di copertura consente a Knoop di attribuire l'antefissa a palmetta pendula entro nimbo al terzo venticinquennio del VI sec. a.C., mentre G. Colonna tende a fissare intorno al 520 la seconda fase decorativa del tempio.[35]

A Pompei alcuni esemplari provenienti dagli scavi di A. Maiuri nell'area del tempio di Apollo vennero datati dallo studioso agli inizi del VI a.C.[36] Una recente sistemazione di tutti i materiali del tempio ha permesso a S. De Caro di datare le terrecotte architettoniche negli ultimi decenni del VI sec., attribuendole al periodo di massimo splendore del santuario,[37] in associazione con ceramiche d'importazione che ne confermano la cronologia.

A Himera esemplari di antefisse a palmetta pendula provengono dagli scavi nell'abitato e nell'area dei templi C e D e vengono datate a partire dal terzo venticinquennio del VI sec.[38]

Alla diffusa opinione che segna dunque come limiti cronologici per questo particolare tipo di antefissa gli anni tra il 550 e il 520 a.C. si oppone la Bonghi Jovino, che lo considera un'elaborazione più antica che "non scavalca il limite cronologico della metà del VI sec. a.C."[39] L'ipotesi della Bonghi poggia sul presupposto che l'antefissa nimbata con testa dedalica costituisca il *terminus ante quem* per le sequenze delle antefisse a palmetta; dal

---

[31] Alt. 25,8; largh. 30; alt. base 4,7; largh. base 22,5; alt. lobo 5.
[32] Cfr. Scatozza 1971, pp. 45–111.
[33] Per la carta di distribuzione del tipo cfr. Cristofani 1987, p. 107; Knoop 1987, p. 96.
[34] Da Ischia provengono alcuni esemplari di antefissa a palmetta dritta e a palmetta capovolta entro nimbo spesse volte citati dagli studiosi, ma purtroppo inediti. Nel piccolo museo di S. Restituta sono esposti due esemplari, di cui uno a palmetta dritta ed uno a palmetta capovolta, provenienti dagli scavi di Lacco Ameno, ma privi del relativo contesto. I due esemplari, che rientrano perfettamente nella tipologia cumano-capuana, sembrano tuttavia leggermente più recenti e sono certamente di produzione locale. Su questi materiali è in corso uno studio da parte di L. Cicala che ha discusso una tesi di laurea sull'argomento, presso l'Università di Salerno.
[35] Colonna 1984, pp. 396–397.
[36] Maiuri 1949, pp. 120–121.
[37] De Caro 1986, p. 33.
[38] Bonacasa 1970, p. 222, fig. 12; Epifanio 1977, p. 164, tav. XLIX:1.
[39] Bonghi Jovino 1989, p. 674.

momento che la prima viene datata prima della fondazione di Elea, queste ultime non possono scendere al di là della metà del secolo.

Se proviamo però ad affrancare la tipologia dell'antefissa con nimbo, in questa prima fase di sperimentazione, dal rigido schema seriale che costringe ovviamente a determinare successivi passaggi di una derivazione, si nota come è solo la comparsa del nimbo l'elemento più nuovo e dirompente rispetto a tipologie già circolanti tanto nella Grecia continentale quanto in quella orientale e occidentale. Sostanzialmente i motivi decorativi (palmetta dritta, palmetta pendula e testa femminile) seguono un percorso quasi parallelo e in molti casi coesistono nello stesso lasso cronologico.[40] Sarà necessario dunque spostare il nostro interesse sul problema della comparsa del nimbo e sull'area dove tale innovazione è avvenuta.[41]

Ad Elea l'antefissa a palmetta pendula coesiste, come già si è detto, con quella a palmetta dritta e costituisce anch'essa un portato della officine cumane. È interessante notare come in successione ad esemplari importati compaiono quelli in argilla locale che documentano la ripetizione del modello (variante C). Una verifica cronologica di notevole interesse proviene dai recenti sondaggi stratigrafici realizzati dall'Istituto Archeologico di Vienna.[42] Nella zona bassa della città è stata individuata, negli strati più profondi a contatto con la sabbia sterile, una serie di strutture abitative caratterizzate dallo zoccolo in opera poligonale a giunture curve e dall'elevato in mattoni crudi, con un tetto pesante rinvenuto in crollo: oltre a tegole ed a coppi semicircolari, sono stati recuperati esemplari quasi integri di tegole di sponda con tracce di pittura ed alcuni frammenti di nimbo pertinenti al tipo II b dell'antefissa a palmetta pendula. L'associazione con frammenti ceramici sia d'importazione che prodotti localmente consente una datazione delle strutture agli anni tra il 540 ed il 520 a.C.

*Antefissa a testa femminile entro nimbo baccellato* (Fig. 2). La testa poggia su una fascia piana di cui rimane parzialmente l'attacco. Il busto femminile, frontale, con capelli a bande sulla fronte e treccioline sul collo, è incorniciato da un nimbo a 17 lobi leggermente incurvati e poggianti su un cordolo plastico. Una ricca policromia ne completa la decorazione.[43]

L'esemplare, noto da tempo, aveva circolato nei testi scientifici solo come frammento del busto e della testa.[44] Nella recente ricognizione nei magazzini di Velia abbiamo avuto la fortuna di recuperare tre frammenti del nimbo con attacco, che hanno consentito il restauro e la ricostruzione completa del tipo.[45]

L'antefissa non pone grossi problemi di inquadramento cronologico e tipologico, trovando confronti molto stretti con esemplari cumani e capuani,[46] mentre si discosta leggermente da quelli satricani. Il Kästner data l'esemplare velino intorno al 530 a.C., sulla base di convincenti confronti con l'acconciatura dei capelli delle korai dell'Acropoli,

---

[40] Cristofani 1987, p. 106.
[41] Greco 1990b.
[42] Ringrazio il prof. F. Krinzinger per avermi illustrato gli ultimi risultati, inediti, delle sue ricerche. Una nota preliminare in Tocco 1991.
[43] N. inv. 43130 + 86397 + 86395. Alt. att. 24,5; largh. ric. 34.
[44] Sestieri 1955, n. 2174; D'Agostino 1974, p. 197, tav. 74; Riis 1981, p. 18, tav. 1, 5E (erroneamente detta da Capua).
[45] I frammenti provenivano tutti dal riempimento del grande muro di terrazzamento realizzato al momento della costruzione del tempio sull'acropoli: cfr. Morel 1970, p. 144.
[46] Koch 1912, tavv. VIII, IX.

Fig. 2: Antefissa arcaica a testa femminile

e lo considera leggermente più recente della nota serie Capua-Satricum.[47] La cronologia all'ultimo quarto del VI sec. a.C. è accolta anche dalla Winter, che considera l'antefissa di Elea un prodotto di officina campana.[48] Il dibattito è arricchito dal fatto che altri studiosi agganciano la cronologia delle antefisse a testa femminile a questo esemplare di Elea e considerano la città come il centro propulsore di una tipologia che genericamente viene definita "greco-orientale".[49] Senza voler entrare nella problematica relativa alla comparsa dell'antefissa a testa femminile, già trattata in altra sede,[50] va ancora una volta sottolineato che il dato più significativo è la presenza del nimbo che, nell'esemplare di Elea, circonda una testa i cui caratteri formali sono improntati a quel diffuso ionismo che informa di sè quasi tutti i prodotti dell'artigianato artistico nel corso del VI sec. a.C. e che alla fine del secolo raggiungerà una più capillare diffusione.[51]

È inoltre probabile che l'esemplare eleate, eseguito in argilla non locale, sia anch'esso un prodotto d'importazione, giunto nella città focea insieme agli esemplari a palmetta pendula o dritta, attestando un interesse "campano" non certo irrilevante da parte dei primi coloni.

[47] Kästner 1982a, p. 47.
[48] Winter 1978, p. 40, tav. 18:4.
[49] Johannowsky 1983, p. 74; Scatozza 1971, p. 54; D'Agostino 1974, p. 198.
[50] Greco 1990a, p. 61; Greco 1990b.
[51] *Les céramiques, passim*; Croissant 1983; Gras 1985.

In conclusione, se è pur vero che i Focei hanno avuto un ruolo preminente nella diffusione dei prodotti e dei motivi ionici in area greco occidentale, ciò non è certo da ricollegarsi con la fondazione di Elea, ma è da ricercarsi piuttosto in momenti precedenti, quando essi detengono quasi il monopolio del commercio greco-orientale e si installano a Marsiglia o sulla costa iberica e sono tra i principali frequentatori dell'emporio di Gravisca.[52]

È viceversa in area campana, tra Pitecusa e Cuma,[53] che nel corso del VI sec. si vanno sperimentando nuove tipologie di rivestimento fittile dei tetti e si va realizzando un "sistema" unitario che verrà largamente esportato nelle zone di influenza e di interesse cumano. Di tutte le sperimentazioni che le officine cumane realizzano, la più innovativa e originale è certamente il nimbo, quale corona di foglie posta ad enfatizzare il motivo centrale della lastra;[54] e nelle prime fasi della sperimentazione la cornice, sia dipinta che plastica, si alterna in diversi modi sino a giungere alla sua definizione che unisce in un unico elemento i due motivi fondamentali della decorazione fittile architettonica del mondo greco, la palmetta e la testa femminile o gorgonica. Alla canonizzazione del tipo si giunge rapidamente, attraverso innovazioni progressive che vanno analizzate nel complesso unitario del sistema: gli stessi elementi costituitivi della palmetta (palmetta pendula volute riempitivo centrale romboidale, bottone plastico) si ritrovano identici nelle lastre di rivestimento,[55] così come i motivi dipinti sullo zoccolo delle antefisse sono gli stessi che decorano la faccia iposcopica delle tegole di sponda.

È dunque all'interno di una stessa officina, o tra artigiani di identica estrazione culturale, che motivi strutturali e formali del mondo greco vengono rielaborati, interpretati ed enfatizzati, fino a comporre un sistema nuovo che, diffondendosi largamente, segnerà se non altro una leadership tecnica e stilistica dell'area di produzione. Le officine pitecusane-cumane, per il ruolo preminente rivestito nella produzione artigianale del VI sec. a.C. in area tirrenica, possono pertanto, a buon diritto, essere considerate le protagoniste della creazione di questo sistema decorativo architettonico che troverà ampia ricezione tanto in area etrusco-laziale quanto nelle aree interne.[56] La presenza in Sicilia dei tipi cumani è già stata messa in relazione con un circuito distributivo indiscutibilmente calcidese, con i punti focali nell'area Pitecusa-Cuma, e con un quadro molto articolato dei rapporti Campania-Sicilia che porteranno ben presto ad un'egemonia siracusana nel golfo cumano.[57]

Altrettanto intensi e precoci dovettero essere i rapporti con Elea la cui fondazione coinvolge come si è detto Reggio e Poseidonia, inserendosi nel delicato equilibrio tra le città italiote ed etrusco-campane nell'area del mare Tirreno.[58]

---

[52] "I Focei".
[53] Ridgway 1984, pp. 134–135; Buchner 1985, pp. 82–83.
[54] Il nimbo, trasposizione plastica delle baccellature dipinte di tradizione orientalizzante, può essere assunto come modello dei processi "combinatori" tipici delle officine italiote. L'ipotesi che esso costituisse un'elaborazione della più nota palmetta è stata già esposta in Greco 1990b.
[55] Knoop 1987, p. 186.
[56] Colonna 1980–1981, p. 160; Frederiksen 1984, pp. 174–179; Johannowsky 1969, p. 280.
[57] Lepore 1967, pp. 151–170.
[58] Pugliese Carratelli 1966, pp. 155–163.

## L'ETÀ CLASSICA

La documentazione relativa alle terrecotte architettoniche di età classica registra viceversa un notevole vuoto. L'esemplare di maggiore interesse è costituito da un'*antefissa a testa femminile entro nimbo baccellato* (Pl. 86:c).

La testa è di impianto classico, con volto ovale, lineamenti regolari e capelli riportati in due bande divise da una scriminatura centrale, con due ciocche laterali che ricadono sulle spalle. Al collo una collana con pendente centrale. La testa è incorniciata da una doppia voluta e da un nimbo a baccellature piatte e rigide, separate tra loro da una costolatura rilevata.[59]

L'antefissa ripete piuttosto fedelmente i tratti canonici dei tipi arcaici a testa femminile, dallo zoccolo di base, al nimbo, mentre cambia il volto, che qui ha tratti classici, come l'ovale slargato e pieno, i capelli ondulati, la collana.

Fenomeni di sopravvivenza e di ripresa intenzionale delle tipologie arcaiche sono largamente attestati a Capua come a Fratte o nel Sannio ed hanno sempre un carattere di conservatorismo legato alle profonde valenze attribuite ai modelli più antichi.[60]

La nostra antefissa trova uno stetto confronto con un esemplare di Neapolis, tratto molto probabilmente da una matrice gemella e datato da M. Napoli alla fine del V sec. a.C., da W. Johannowsky alla prima metà del IV a.C.[61] L'antefissa napoletana è eseguita in un'argilla rossa, molto depurata, assai simile a quella di Elea. Sebbene soltanto un'analisi petrografica lo potrà definire con certezza, è assai suggestiva l'ipotesi che essa sia un prodotto di officina eleate, a conferma degli intensi rapporti intercorrenti tra le due città in questo periodo.[62] Da rivedere piuttosto è la cronologia del tipo che per resa stilistica richiama piuttosto prodotti della statuaria e della coroplastica della prima metà del IV sec. a.C.: valga l'esempio della piccola statua marmorea di Hera trovata nell'edificio quadrato all'Heraion alla Foce del Sele, che suggerisce peraltro un incipiente processo di "sannitizzazione" della cultura figurativa eleate.[63]

G. Greco

## ETÀ ELLENISTICA

Le terrecotte architettoniche eleati di età ellenistica comprendono numerosi tipi di antefisse, delle sime di gronda, oltre ad alcuni pezzi con funzione acroteriale. Non essendo possibile, in questa sede, procedere ad una presentazione sistematica dei singoli tipi, per i quali si demanda al catalogo di prossima pubblicazione, si è necessariamente operata una scelta

---

[59] Alt. ric. 25; largh. ric. 22. Del tipo si sono recuperati 8 frammenti pertinenti alla stessa matrice e due pertinenti ad altro modulo, derivato da una diversa generazione. L'argilla è quella rossa tipica di Velia.

[60] Cfr. *infra*, n. 69–71.

[61] Da uno scavo nei pressi di via Duomo: Napoli 1967, p. 600; Johannowsky 1960, p. 501, fig. 7; Johannowsky 1985, p. 213; Morel 1986, p. 311, tav. XVIII:2.

[62] Che vanno dall'adozione del piede foceo nella monetazione di Neapolis alla comunanza dei culti: cfr. Lepore 1967, pp. 158–170.

[63] Colonna 1960, pp. 264–266; D'Agostino 1988, pp. 531–589.

di quegli esemplari che risultano maggiormente indicativi delle tendenze generali della produzione in tale periodo.

Una prima considerazione riguarda il fatto che possiamo riscontrare una notevole vitalità nel campo della produzione delle terrecotte architettoniche ellenistiche eleati. Essa è documentata da una maggiore rilevanza numerica del materiale rispetto a quello piuttosto limitato di età arcaica, ed a quello decisamente scarso di età classica. I numerosi pezzi rinvenuti, più di un centinaio, sono inquadrabili in una progressione cronologica che abbraccia tutta l'età ellenistica e giunge sino al momento in cui, nell'89 a.C., Elea otterrà la cittadinanza romana, trasformando il suo nome in Velia, con un prolungamento sino alla piena età imperiale.

È assai probabile che motivi di ordine economico siano alla base del fenomeno nel suo aspetto più generale: numerosi indizi inducono a ritenere che, contrariamente a quanto si verifica nel caso della maggior parte dei centri della Magna Grecia, Elea avesse continuato a godere di una relativa floridezza economica, in parte dovuta ai suoi buoni rapporti con Roma, in parte all'espletamento di attività commerciali di ampio respiro.[64]

Il numero dei modelli, nonchè le numerose varianti e riduzioni dei singoli tipi, tutti eseguiti nell'inconfondibile argilla locale, costituiscono un interessante corollario a quanto già da tempo si conosceva circa l'attività delle officine laterizie della città. Sin dagli inizi del III secolo a.C. è attestata infatti ad Elea una particolarissima produzione di mattoni cotti,[65] di dimensioni e forma assai tipici, contraddistinti da uno spessore abbastanza alto e da una serie di scanalature interne, oltre che dalla presenza di bolli. Ricorrente è la sigla ΔΗ(ΜΟΣΙΑ), accoppiata a una seconda sigla, variabile, generalmente di due o tre lettere e di più difficile interpretazione: se la prima infatti indica sicuramente un interesse ufficiale dello stato nella produzione dei laterizi, la seconda è stata variamente riferita a magistrati eponimi, a proprietari o ai diversi responsabili della produzione. In attesa di ulteriori chiarimenti, derivanti da una maggiore attenzione stratigrafica all'utilizzo dei mattoni eleati, sottolineamo come andrebbe in ogni caso approfondita l'interessante osservazione di W. Johannowsky che riferisce alcune sigle a santuari (AΘH, AΠO).[66] Una migliore conoscenza dei contesti di provenienza sia dei laterizi bollati che delle terrecotte architettoniche potrebbe inoltre utilmente aiutarci a comprendere il ruolo e la funzione di queste ultime nell'ambito di una produzione che si presenta fortemente subordinata al controllo pubblico.

Antefisse

Per quanto riguarda le antefisse, la continuità dei modelli più antichi è documentata da una ricca varietà di tipi che, in forme diverse, ripetono il modello della palmetta ritta di tradizione arcaica.

---

[64] Sulle attività edilizie nella città nel III e nel II sec. a.C. cfr. Johannowsky 1982, pp. 236–238; sulla vitalità del porto nel II sec. a.C., Bencivegna Trillmich 1984, pp. 20–33; Leiwo 1985, pp. 494–499 circa la presenza di *negotiatores* eleati a Delo.

[65] Schleuning 1889, pp. 184–190; Mingazzini 1954, pp. 21–60; Gallo 1966, pp. 366–377; Johannowsky 1982, pp. 235–237.

[66] Johannowsky 1982, pp. 235–236. Tale osservazione si potrebbe facilmente estendere anche ad altre sigle, quali ΑΙΣ. oppure HPM.

Fig. 3: Antefissa ellenistica a palmetta ritta e nimbo baccellato

Di particolare interesse è il caso di un'*antefissa entro cornice baccellata* (Fig. 3): la palmetta a cinque lobi, di cui quello centrale corposo e lanceolato, è inserita in un cordolo rilevato che inferiormente si chiude in due volute a ricciolo. Da quest'ultimo si diparte una specie di nimbo, costituito da baccellature profonde incavate e molto irregolari. La terminazione inferiore era costituita da una fascia piatta leggermente arretrata rispetto al campo decorativo.[67] È molto probabile che in questo caso ci si trovi di fronte a una ripresa intenzionale del modello arcaico, pur in una versione assai tarda e degenerata, attraverso una reinterpretazione degli elementi essenziali di questo: le baccellature del nimbo sono incavate e rese quasi al negativo, il cordolo e le volute laterali diventano parte sostanziale del campo decorativo, venendosi a fondere in un unico elemento con la soprastante palmetta. La ripresa di un modello arcaico, come già nel caso delle antefisse a testa femminile, esaminato in questa sede da G. Greco,[68] è un dato ampiamente attestato in alcune aree dell'entroterra lucano di cultura indigena, quale occasionale fenomeno di recezione di tipologie e modelli propri

---

[67] Se ne conservano 7 frammenti, pertinenti a due diverse varianti. L'altezza ricostruita del tipo è di cm. 25. L'argilla è locale.
[68] *Supra*, n. 59–60.

FIG. 4: Antefissa ellenistica a palmetta ritta e bordo lenticolare

dell'ambiente italiota sin dagli inizi del V sec. a.C.[69] e si fa evidente nel corso del IV sec. a.C anche in centri campani, come Fratte e Poseidonia,[70] quale esito di un processo di parziale penetrazione di elementi lucani.[71] In questa chiave risulta di estremo interesse riscontrare lo stesso fenomeno in un centro come Elea, che tradizionalmente viene considerata, insieme a Neapolis, una sorta di roccaforte culturale della grecità contro le pressioni dei Lucani, i quali nel corso degli ultimi decenni del V secolo avevano già occupato la vicina Poseidonia.[72]

Un esempio opposto è riscontrabile anche nel caso di un'*antefissa a palmetta, con bordo a decorazione lenticolare* (Pl. 86:d; Fig. 4), che viceversa si presenta come una ripresa particolarmente elegante degli antichi motivi.

---

[69] *Popoli anellenici*, pp. 76, 129, tavv. 22, 56; Greco 1977, pp. 131–146; Mazzei 1981, pp. 17–39; Greco 1982, pp. 74–75, figg. 18, 19.

[70] Greco 1990a, p. 73, figg. 95, 96.

[71] Cfr. Zancani Montuoro 1965–1966, pp. 36–37; Lepore 1967, pp. 194–215; Cordano 1971; Pugliese Carratelli 1973, pp. 3–6; Pugliese Carratelli 1974, pp. 7–12; Pontrandolfo Greco 1979, pp. 36–37.

[72] Per una discussione del passo di Strabone (6.1.2) relativo alle lotte contro i Lucani e i Poseidoniati, Lepore 1966, p. 263.

Fig. 5: Antefissa semicircolare con palmetta

Fig. 6: Antefissa semicircolare con palmetta

L'antefissa, attestata in quattro varianti diverse,[73] è decorata da una palmetta a cinque lobi estroflessi, fuoriuscendo da una coppia di volute e da un nucleo centrale di forma allungata. Tra i lobi superiori erano inseriti due elementi vegetali simili a foglie spinose. Di particolare interesse, ai fini dell'inquadramento tipologico del pezzo, è il bordo ondulato, decorato con una serie di elementi concavi lenticolari, nei quali sembra di poter leggere l'ultima reminiscenza dell'antico nimbo baccellato. Più difficile la definizione cronologica del tipo: la base, soprattutto nella prima variante, quella più curata, presenta un kyma ionico sotto il quale corre una fila di perle e astragali. Entrambi i motivi sono frequentemente attestati in alcuni esemplari romano-urbani di impronta atticistica della prima età imperiale, ma tuttavia, in questi ultimi, non risultano mai adottati contestualmente nell'ambito di una stessa antefissa.[74] Sembra più probabile pensare invece che il tipo costituisca una redazione classicistica di età ellenistica avanzata che, così come nella reminiscenza del nimbo, riprende anche nei particolari secondari elementi già noti nelle terrecotte architettoniche magnogreche di età tardo-arcaica e classica.[75]

Un caso diverso è quello di alcune *antefisse a palmetta* (Figs. 5, 6), documentate da un gran numero di esemplari, attribuibili a non meno di 7 diverse varianti:[76] elemento costante

[73] Nr. inv. 43147 e 86457: alt. ric. 26; largh. max. 18; largh. base 14. Argilla locale.

[74] Cfr. Pensabene e Sanzi Di Mino 1983, tav. 82, n. 415; tav. 89, n. 486; tav. 103, n. 385; tav. 108, nn. 670, 672; tav. 125, nn. 808–809; tav. 134, nn. 880 (per il motivo con perle e astragali); tav. 84, n. 433; tav. 89, nn. 488, 495; tav. 102, n. 583; tav. 104, n. 634; tav. 118, nn. 737–739; tav. 119; tav. 122; tav. 123, nn. 792–795; tav. 139, n. 923; tav. 141, n. 928 (motivo del kyma ionico).

[75] Cfr. il medesimo motivo di perle e astragali insieme al kyma ionico in area metapontina, sia su alcune terrecotte architettoniche che nelle arule: Lo Porto 1966, p. 151, fig. 11 (sima), p. 154, fig. 14 (arula); Mertens 1974, tav. 53 (tetto B, tetto A); Mertens 1983, tav. XXV:c (tempio ionico).

[76] Sono stati raccolti più di 20 frammenti, pertinenti ad altrettanti esemplari e provenienti sia dall'acropoli che dalla parte bassa della città (scavi 1935, 1953, 1973). In tutti gli esemplari l'argilla è locale.

è la forma, semicircolare, e la presenza al centro di una grande palmetta a sette lobi che si incurvano elegantemente verso l'interno, fuoriuscendo da una coppia di volute di base disposte in senso orizzontale. Cambiano, nelle diverse varianti, i motivi decorativi accessori, costituiti da un kyma ionico, oppure da un motivo ad onda corrente alla base, o ancora da un kyma ionico che in alcuni esemplari corre lungo il profilo esterno. La forma armoniosa della palmetta, che si inserisce equilibratamente nel campo dell'antefissa, riflette un aggiornamento stilistico e l'adeguamento ai nuovi canoni decorativi di età ellenistica, che rendono suggestivo, per quanto molto probabilmente casuale, il confronto con alcuni esemplari non lontani cronologicamente di area greca.[77] Più diretto il rapporto con alcune antefisse tarantine del III sec. a.C., dove ritroviamo sia la forma semicircolare dell'antefissa, sia il motivo della palmetta singola, per quanto rappresentato in una forma più slanciata e verticale.[78]

Nel corso dell'età ellenistica numerosi e costanti rimangono comunque i legami con l'area settentrionale campana, in particolare con Capua.

Un'*antefissa a profilo pentagonale*, contornata da una cornice piatta leggermente rilevata, presenta un motivo decorativo centrale a fiore con calice spinoso e corolla compatta, probabilmente identificabile con un cardo, il quale fuoriesce da una coppia di volute disposte in senso orizzontale ed è fiancheggiato da due rami ricurvi e spinosi (Pl. 87:a). A Velia il tipo è attestato in due varianti, la prima delle quali dà origine ad almeno due riduzioni.[79] Alcune antefisse identiche, ricavate da una matrice molto fresca, sono state ritrovate a Capua. Qui il tipo si arricchisce, in una delle sue varianti, di alcuni motivi decorativi che sono il frutto dell'abbinamento reciproco di matrici diverse: il piano pentagonale dell'antefissa viene inserito, quale elemento di base, in una lastra più grande, decorata al centro con una testa femminile con kalathos o con berretto frigio, ai due lati da una coppia di eroti nudi, non rappresentati in posizione simmetrica, bensì entrambi sbilanciati verso destra,[80] evidentemente desunti da matrici altrimenti utilizzate per piccole statue votive. L'elemento figurato in questo casi fornisce i più concreti elementi per la cronologia del pezzo al III sec. a.C.[81]

Ad ambiente capuano riporta anche un altro tipo di antefissa con profilo a forma di echino nella parte inferiore e con la terminazione superiore cuspidata.[82] Il campo è decorato al centro da una testina con berretto frigio che ricade con due cocche ai lati del volto. La testina è inquadrata da due volute coricate di base, collegate mediante una barretta trasversale e che si diramano, ai lati, in due tralci vegetali ondulati terminanti in una rosetta

---

[77] Si vedano ad esempio alcune antefisse da Assos: Åkerström 1966, pp. 13–15, tav. 7:7, 8:1–3, di incerta datazione.

[78] Cfr. Laviosa 1954, pp. 249–250, tav. LXXVIII:2–4; Pensabene e Sanzi Di Mino 1983, p. 136, n. 247, tav. 65, dove si menzionano anche alcuni esemplari inediti dalle terme di via S. Aloe a Vibo Valentia.

[79] 9 frammenti, pertinenti ad almeno 7 pezzi diversi. Nella variante A l'altezza è di cm. 15, la larghezza 16. L'argilla è locale.

[80] Koch 1912, p. 29, fig. 38, tav. V:2, 4; Bedello Tata 1990, p. 104, tav. XV:1, 2.

[81] Per la testina cfr. Bedello Tata 1976, p. 68, tav. XVIII:1, tipo A XXIII A 1, riproducente, sia pure in dimensioni maggiori, un busto con caratteristiche analoghe. Le figurine di eroti trovano confronti generici nel materiale capuano edito. Si veda ad es. Mollard Besques 1986, p. 9, tav. 6:d, p. 10, tav. 7:e, p. 11, tav. 8:d.

[82] N. inv. 20089; alt. 14; largh. 19; argilla locale.

a quattro petali (Pl. 87:b). Tanto la forma, quanto la decorazione centrale trovano riscontro, più che non in altre terrecotte architettoniche, nella produzione di arule che, nel corso del IV e del III secolo a.C., appare caratteristica del centro campano.[83]

SIME

Di particolare interesse tra il materiale eleate di età ellenistica è inoltre la presenza di un cospicuo gruppo di sime fittili.

I frammenti superstiti sono pertinenti a non meno di 10 tipi diversi, distinti l'uno dall'altro sia per le dimensioni che per il profilo e gli elementi decorativi, che ne rendono probabile l'attribuzione ad un arco cronologico abbastanza ampio e ad una serie di edifici differenti tra loro. Ciononostante sembra possibile, almeno per la maggior parte di essi, enucleare alcune caratteristiche comuni che costituiscono l'unico elemento valido, nella quasi totale mancanza di dati di scavo, per un inquadramento di massima nell'ambito della produzione fittile del centro.

In almeno 7 dei 10 tipi che sono stati classificati l'altezza oscilla tra cm. 17 e cm. 20. Il profilo è generalmente bombato e la sima termina superiormente con una fascia piana frontale, risultando priva della tacca per l'inserimento del coronamento soprastante, che caratterizza invece pezzi analoghi in ambiente laziale ed etrusco. La decorazione è costituita di regola da palmette alternate a fiori di loto, collegati tra loro da motivi a spirale (Pl. 88:a). In un unico caso è sicuramente documentata la presenza di un doccione passante, probabilmente a protome leonina.[84] Altri tipi presentano un motivo di palmette alternate tra loro e differenziate nella disposizione dei lobi (Pl. 88:b), oppure inframmezzate a tralci naturalistici (Pl. 88:c).

In linea di massima sembra possibile affermare che le sime di Elea-Velia, sia per struttura che per motivi decorativi, appaiono collegate ad una tradizione fittile squisitamente magnogreca, che trova i suoi precedenti nella numerosa serie di sime, prevalentemente utilizzate nella decorazione templare, attestate in siti quali Crotone, Caulonia e Metaponto.[85]

Più in particolare potremmo registrare l'influenza della vicina cultura poseidoniate, nell'adozione del profilo a kyma recta verticale con una larga e prominente curva inferiore, qui attestato sino dalla fine del VI secolo a.C. nella sima litica del tempio di Athena[86] e destinato a mantenersi a secoli di distanza nella sima in terracotta del tempio italico del Foro.[87]

In definitiva, allo stadio attuale della nostra conoscenza, le sime di Elea, insieme con il tipo di antefissa semicircolare a palmetta che abbiamo sopra ricordato (Figs. 5, 6), sembrano rappresentare quanto di più strettamente legato alla cultura magno-greca il centro abbia prodotto nel campo della decorazione architettonica fittile. Esse risultano assai diverse dagli esemplari tardo-classici ed ellenistici di area campana di Fratte di Salerno,[88]

---

[83] Per le arule del Museo Campano si veda Bedello Tata, Casolo, e Baroni 1990, pp. 58–69, tavv. 10–15. Più in generale Van Buren 1918, pp. 15–53, in part. p. 40, n. 4, per un tipo simile alla nostra antefissa; Jastrow 1938, pp. 1–28; Jastrow 1946, pp. 67–80; Ricciotti 1979.

[84] N. inv. 20095, tipo C II, alt. 18,5.

[85] Per il materiale di Metaponto cfr. Mertens 1974, pp. 216–224, tavv. XLIX, LII, LIII; per Crotone, Mertens 1986, pp. 200–206, 213–221.

[86] Cfr. Shoe 1952, pp. 171–173, tav. XXX:3, 4.

[87] Shoe 1952, tav. XXX:5: cfr. Krauss 1939, pp. 14, 35, tavv. 7, 34:2, 35:1.

[88] Greco 1990a, p. 66, figg. 71, 72.

Pompei, Foro triangolare[89] e di Capua, caratterizzati dalla costante di un inserimento tra le palmette di testine femminili con berretto frigio o arricchite di volute e viticci.[90] Le forme capricciose delle palmette e l'eleganza naturalistica dei petali dei fiori di loto consentono un inquadramento generico della maggior parte di questi tipi nel corso della media età ellenistica (III-II sec. a.C.): maggiormente significativo in questo caso è il confronto con una sima a piccola gronda leonina, decorata con palmette e fiori di loto, sempre da Fratte,[91] la cui probabile cronologia (III sec. a.C.) trova confronto nei dati stratigrafici emersi da recenti scavi a Pompei.[92]

Un diverso inquadramento cronologico, così come un differente riferimento ambientale deve essere proposto per l'ultimo tipo di sima considerato (Pl. 88:c).

La sima, a profilo rettilineo, è limitata superiormente da un kyma ionico abbastanza regolare sopra una fila di dentelli quadrati. Il campo decorativo è occupato da un motivo di grandi palmette a 7 petali, quella centrale a petali introflessi, le due laterali a petali alternativamente introflessi ed estroflessi. Le palmette fuoriescono da un calice stilizzato e piatto e sono alternate ad eleganti tralci ondulati da cui pendono piccoli frutti di melograno. Il ritrovamento di un esemplare integro permette di escludere la presenza del doccione leonino.[93]

Le caratteristiche generali del tipo (profilo rettilineo, bordo dentellato, forma inorganica della palmetta) riportano ancora una volta all'ambiente campano e trovano confronto in alcuni esemplari di Capua[94] e, soprattutto, di Pompei, databili nel corso del I sec. a.C. e della prima età imperiale:[95] in particolare si veda la sima a doccione leonino, decorata con motivo di palmette e tralci di acanto che fuoriescono dai lobi, anch'essa con profilo rettilineo e bordo superiore a dentelli,[96] o ancora quella con doccione a forma di maschera e palmette di forma molto simile a quella del nostro esemplare, dai cui petali fuoriescono sottili tralci vegetali.[97]

ACROTERI

Solo pochi pezzi infine, nella ricca produzione eleate, risultano il prodotto di un maggiore impegno decorativo e sembrano da attribuire a edifici sacri o comunque di carattere pubblico.

Il primo frammento è pertinente ad un acroterio centrale di forma circolare, decorato con una testa maschile barbata: rimane solamente la parte inferiore del volto con piccole labbre dischiuse e una folta barba a morbidi riccioli ritorti che si dispongono simmetricamente ai lati

---

[89] Le terrecotte del tempio dorico del Foro triangolare di Pompei sono ancora inedite. Una descrizione, priva purtroppo di apparato fotografico in Richardson, Jr. 1974, pp. 281–290, con una datazione eccessivamente bassa, al II sec. a.C.

[90] Bedello Tata 1978, pp. 210–218, tavv. LXXXI, LXXXII.

[91] Greco 1990a, p. 69, fig. 84, con ampia discussione sull'evoluzione della sima.

[92] Bedello Tata 1984, p. 251, tav. 141:4 (anteriore al II sec. a.C.).

[93] Alt. 23,5, largh. 51. Numerosi frammenti provengono dallo scavo dell'abitato nel quartiere meridionale della città.

[94] Koch 1912, tav. XXIII, XXIV; De Franciscis 1952, p. 311, fig. 3.

[95] In mancanza di un'adeguata edizione del materiale il punto di riferimento rimane ancora la vecchia edizione di von Rohden 1880, pp. 6–15, figg. 3, 4, 6, 7, 9, 10; tavv. VII–IX.

[96] Von Rohden 1880, p. 32, tav. VII:1, dalla casa dei Niobidi (alt. 32).

[97] Von Rohden 1880, p. 14, fig. 9 (alt. 22).

di una scriminatura centrale. Inferiormente il pezzo presenta una terminazione arrotondata, a sezione obliqua, che doveva formare la fascia piatta di contorno dell'acroterio.[98]

L'utilizzazione di acroteri circolari a decorazione della testata del columen, ampiamente documentata in Sicilia e Magna Grecia, così come in ambiente campano sin dall'età arcaica,[99] si prolunga in età classica ed ellenistica: oltre allo splendido pezzo da Fratte di Salerno con Eracle in lotta col leone nemeo, probabilmente eseguito da un'officina italiota, che ne costituisce l'esemplare di maggior rilievo,[100] vanno ricordati alcuni tipi capuani, con testa femminile coperta da berretto frigio e a maschera, quest'ultimo di esecuzione estremamente corsiva.[101]

La cronologia del nostro esemplare, unicamente basata sui pochi elementi che si possono trarre dal trattamento stilistico della barba, a boccoli corposi e resi con un rilievo profondamente chiaroscurato, sembrerebbe circoscrivibile tra la fine del IV ed il II secolo a.C. Il diametro ricostruibile (circa cm. 40) ne consente l'attribuzione ipotetica ad un edificio di medie dimensioni.[102] Altrettante incertezze permangono per quanto riguarda l'identificazione del soggetto: a livello di pura ipotesi potremmo pensare ad una ripresa del tipo dell'Acheloo, ampiamente documentato in area campana in età arcaica,[103] nella versione umanizzata con fluente barba a boccoli che si afferma nell'iconografia della divinità sin dalla fine del V secolo.[104]

Un secondo frammento è pertinente ad un grosso muso di cinghiale, plasmato a mano,[105] di cui si conserva solo la parte anteriore, con il pelame a folte ciocche ondulate, eseguito con fitti colpi di stecca, le narici ottenute mediante due impressioni concave contornate da due linee semicircolari e l'attacco della dentatura nella bocca spalancata (Pl. 88:d). Sia per fattura che per dimensioni il pezzo appare identico all'esemplare più completo rinvenuto a Fratte di Salerno, databile alla fine del IV–inizi III secolo e considerato di probabile officina italiota, che ipoteticamente G. Greco attribuisce a un edificio sacro, forse il medesimo cui apparteneva il celebre acroterio circolare con Eracle in lotta con il leone nemeo.[106]

Un'idea più precisa della sua originaria struttura e funzione ci può essere fornita da un doccione angolare integro di Pompei,[107] presumibilmente rinvenuto nell'area del Foro, dove avrebbe decorato uno degli edifici pubblici di età sannitica. Per quanto di dimensioni leggermente minori,[108] esso rivela la medesima cura e la stessa freschezza di modellato dei

[98] N. inv. 7488; alt. att. 14, largh. att. 21; argilla locale.
[99] Kästner 1990, pp. 251–264; Greco 1990a, pp. 63–65.
[100] Greco 1990a, p. 69, fig. 78.
[101] Koch 1912, pp. 76–77, tav. XXII:3, figg. 85, 86.
[102] Nettamente inferiore all'esemplare con Eracle di Fratte (Greco 1990a, p. 68: diametro interno 62/64, esterno 78/81), si accosta viceversa per dimensioni al tipo arcaico con testa di Acheloo, rinvenuto nello stesso sito (Greco 1990a, pp. 63–65: diam. ricostruito 44 circa).
[103] A Capua: Koch 1912, pp. 74–76, tav. XXII:2; a Fratte: Greco 1990a, pp. 60–63.
[104] Cfr. Isler 1970, pp. 40–43, nn. 10–12; n. 91, tav. XII; n. 92, tav. XIII; n. 272, tav. XXI.
[105] N. inv. 9455; alt. att. 9, largh. att. 14,5; argilla locale.
[106] Greco 1990a, p. 68, fig. 79. La popolarità del motivo nella decorazione architettonica di Fratte è attestato dalla presenza di altri due frammenti di modello identico, ma realizzati in tufo (pp. 81–82, nn. 44–45, figg. 117, 118). Nel pezzo di Fratte l'altezza è di cm. 45, la lunghezza totale di cm. 52.
[107] Von Rohden 1880, p. 32, tav. IV.
[108] Alt. 40; lunghezza testa 35.

nostri esemplari. La testa in questo caso emerge da una lastra piatta quadrata di base che doveva essere affrancata allo spiovente del tetto, ad una delle estremità angolari.

In conclusione il quadro che emerge dalla rapida analisi che abbiamo effettuato delle terrecotte architettoniche di Elea in età ellenistica ci consente di enucleare alcune tendenze assai chiare: una di esse, senza dubbio la più colta e raffinata, si rifà a modelli di sicura matrice magno-greca, che filtrano elaborazioni ampiamente sperimentate nelle officine dell'Italia meridionale e che trovano in questo periodo in Taranto il loro maggiore centro di diffusione. La seconda tendenza riconferma invece la gravitazione tirreno-campana di Elea che aveva caratterizzato il momento arcaico della città: essa si mantiene assai viva e costante anche in età ellenistica, come documentano i numerosi confronti che si sono di volta in volta istituiti con Capua, Pompei e Fratte di Salerno.

Resta da comprendere, come compito principale della ricerca ancora in corso, l'effettivo ruolo sostenuto da Elea tanto nella recezione quanto nella diffusione di questi modelli: il volto culturale della città in questo periodo è assai composto, con aperture al più raffinato linguaggio figurativo di impronta greca che coesistono con manifestazioni formali più corsive, caratteristiche dei centri campani ormai pienamente sannitici. Ciò rende assai suggestiva e probabile l'ipotesi che la produzione delle terrecotte eleati non sia rimasta confinata ad un livello prevalentemente ricettivo, ma che, viceversa, essa abbia rivestito un importante ruolo di elaborazione autonoma e di successiva diffusione dei nuovi tipi.

M. J. STRAZZULLA

## BIBLIOGRAFIA

Åkerström, Å. 1966. *Die architektonische Terrakotten Kleinasiens* (*Acta Instituti Atheniensis Regni Sueciae* XI), Lund

Andrén, A. 1940. *Architectural Terracottas from Etrusco-Italic Temples* (*Acta Instituti Romani Regni Sueciae* VI), Lund/Leipzig

*Atti Taranto* = *Atti del Convegno di studi sulla Magna Grecia*, Taranto

Bedello Tata, M. 1976. *Capua preromana*, III, *Le terrecotte votive*, Roma

———. 1978. "Osservazioni in margine ad alcune terrecotte architettoniche capuane di età ellenistica," *ArchCl* 30, pp. 210–218

———. 1984. "Le terrecotte architettoniche," in *Ricerche a Pompei. Insula V, regio VI dalle origini al 79 d.C.*, Roma, pp. 249–257

———. 1990. "Botteghe artigiane a Capua," in *Artigiani e Botteghe nell'Italia preromana*, Roma, pp. 97–122

Bedello Tata, M., V. Casolo, e S. Baroni. 1990. *Capua preromana IV. Oscilla, thymiateria, arulae*, Firenze

Bencivegna Trillmich, C. 1984. "La ceramica iberica da Velia. Contributo allo studio della diffusione della ceramica iberica in Italia," *MM* 25, pp. 20–33

Bonacasa, N. 1970. *Himera I. Campagne di scavo 1963–1965*, Roma

Bonghi Jovino, M. 1989. "La produzione fittile in Etruria ed i suoi riflessi nell'Italia antica," in *II Congr. Int. Etrusco (Firenze 1985)*, Roma, pp. 666–682

Buchner, G. 1985. "L'emporion di Pithecusa," in *Napoli antica* (*Catalogo della Mostra*), Napoli, pp. 79–86

*Les céramiques* = *Les céramiques de la Grèce de l'Est et leur diffusion en Occident*, Napoli 1978

Colonna, G. 1960. *EAA* IV, 1960, pp. 251–274 (*s.v.* Italica Arte)

———. 1980–1981. "La Sicilia ed il Tirreno nel V e nel IV sec.," *Kokalos* 26–27, pp. 157–191

———. 1984. "I templi del Lazio sino al V sec. a.C.," *QArchEtr* 8, pp. 396–411

Cordano, F. 1971. *Fonti greche e latine per la storia dei Lucani e Brettii e di altre genti indigene della Magna Grecia*, Potenza

Cristofani, M. 1987. "I santuari: tradizioni decorative," in *Etruria e Lazio arcaico*, Roma, pp. 95–120

Croissant, F. 1983. *Les protomes féminines archaïques*, Paris

D'Agostino, B. 1974. "Il mondo periferico della Magna Grecia," in *Popoli e Civiltà dell'Italia antica* II, Roma, pp. 179–271

———. 1988. "Le genti della Campana antica," in *Italia omnium terrarum alumna*, Milano, pp. 531–589

De Caro, S. 1986. *Saggi nell'area del tempio di Apollo a Pompei* (*AION, St. Ant., Quad.* 3), Napoli

De Franciscis, A. 1952. "S. Maria Capua Vetere," *NSc*, p. 311

De Miro, E. 1965. "Terrecotte architettoniche agrigentine," *CronCatania* 4, pp. 39–78

Epifanio, E. 1977. "Nuovi rivestimenti fittili ad Himera," in *Il tempio greco in Sicilia. Architettura e culti* (*CronCatania* 16), pp. 165–173

Fiorelli, G. 1882. *Regio III (Lucania et Britti). XII. Velia (Comune di Ascea)*, *NSc*, pp. 388–390

Fiorentini, G. 1977. "Sacelli sull'acropoli de Gela," in *Il tempio greco in Sicilia. Architettura e culti* (*CronCatania* 16), pp. 105–114

"I Focei" = "I Focei dall'Anatolia all'oceano," *PP* 37, 1982, pp. 161–500

Frederiksen, M. 1984. *Campania*, Roma

Gallo, G. 1966. "I bolli sui mattoni di Velia," *PP* 21, pp. 366–377

Gigante, M. 1966. "Il logos erodoteo sulle origini di Elea," *PP* 21, pp. 295–315

Gras, M. 1985. *Trafics Tyrrhéniens archaïques*, Roma

Greco, G. 1977. "Antefisse gorgoniche da Lavello," *RendNap* 52, pp. 131–146

———. 1982. "Lo sviluppo di Serra di Vaglio nei secoli V e IV," *MEFRA* 94, pp. 74–75

———. 1990a. "Le terrecotte architettoniche," in *Fratte. Un insediamento etrusco-campano*, Modena, pp. 59–86

———. 1990b. "Le terrecotte architettoniche e votive di Fratte," in *La presenza etrusca nella Campania meridionale (Salerno 1990)* (in corso di stampa)

Greco Pontrandolfo, A. 1979. "Segni di transformazioni sociali a Poseidonia tra la fine del V e gli inizi del III sec. a.C.," *DialArch*, pp. 27–50

*Hesperia* 59 = *Proceedings of the First International Conference on Archaic Greek Architectural Terracottas, Athens, December 2–4, 1988* (*Hesperia* 59, 1990), N. A. Winter, ed.

Isler, H. P. 1970. *Acheloos. Eine Monographie*, Bern

Jastrow, E. 1938. "Abformung und Typenwandel in der antiken Tonplastik," *OpArch* 1, pp. 1–28

———. 1946. "Two Terracotta Reliefs in American Museums," *AJA* 50, pp. 67–80

Johannowsky, W. 1960. "Problemi archeologici napoletani con particolare riferimento alle zone interessate dal risanamento," in *La città di Napoli dalle origini al 1860*, G. Russo, ed., Napoli, p. 501

———. 1969. "Intervento," in *VII AttiTaranto*, p. 280

———. 1982. "Considerazioni sullo sviluppo urbano e sulla cultura materiale di Velia," *PP* 37, pp. 225–246

———. 1983. *Materiali di età arcaica dalla Campania*, Napoli

———. 1985. "Una terracotta architettonica da via Duomo," in *Napoli antica (Catalogo della Mostra)*, Napoli, p. 213

Kästner, V. 1982a. "Archaische Baukeramik der Westgriechen" (diss. Humboldt-Universität Berlin-Ost 1982)

———. 1982b. "Die frühe Architektur Pompejis und die Dachterrakotten Produktion des griechischen Kampanien," in *Pompeji 79–1979, Beiträge zum Vesuvausbruch und seiner Nachwirkung*, Stendal, pp. 90–100

———. 1990. "Scheibenförmige Akrotere in Griechenland und Italien," in *Hesperia* 59, pp. 251–264

Knoop, R. R. 1987. *Antefixa Satricana*, Assen

Koch, H. 1912. *Dachterrakotten aus Campanien*, Berlin

Krauss, F. 1939. *Der korinthisch-dorische Tempel am Forum von Paestum*, Berlin

Krinzinger, F. 1987. "Velia. Grabungsbericht 1987," *Römische Historiche Mitteilungen* 29, p. 19

Laviosa, C. 1954. "Le antefisse fittili di Taranto," *ArchCl* 6, pp. 214–250

Leiwo, M. 1985. "Why Velia Survived through the 2nd Century B.C. Remarks on the Economic Connections with Delos," *Athenaeum* 63, pp. 494–499

Lepore, E. 1966. "Elea e l'eredità di Sibari," *PP* 21, p. 255–278

———. 1967. "La vita politica e sociale," in *Storia di Napoli* I, Napoli, pp. 141–371

Lo Porto, G. F. 1966. "Metaponto. Scavi e ricerche archeologiche," *NSc*, pp. 136–231
Maiuri, A. 1926–1927. "Velia, prima ricognizione ed esplorazione," in *Campagna della Società Magna Grecia*, Roma, pp. 15–29
———. 1949. *Introduzione allo studio di Pompei*, Napoli
Martin, R. 1970. "Le problème de l'appareil polygonal à Vélia," *PP* 25, pp. 93–107
Mazzei, M. 1981. "Appunti preliminari sulle antefisse fittili 'etrusco-campane' nella Daunia pre-romana," *Taras* 1, pp. 17–39
Mertens, D. 1974. "L'architettura," in *Metaponto, XIII AttiTaranto*, pp. 187–235
———. 1983. "Per l'urbanistica e l'architettura della Magna Grecia," in *Megale Hellas, XXI AttiTaranto*, pp. 97–135
———. 1986. "I Santuari di Capo Colonna e Crimisa: aspetti dell'architettura crotoniate," in *Crotone, XXIII AttiTaranto*, pp. 189–230
Mingazzini, P. 1954. "Velia. Fornace di mattoni e antichità varie," *AttiMGrecia* 1, pp. 21–60
Mollard Besques, S. 1986. *Catalogue raisonné des figurines et reliefs en terrecuite grecs, étrusques et romains* IV, Paris
Morel, J. P. 1970. "Sondages sur l'acropole de Vélia," *PP* 25, pp. 131–145
———. 1982. "Les Phocéens d'Occident: nouvelles données, nouvelles approches," *PP* 37, pp. 479–500
———. 1986. "Remarques sur l'art et l'artisanat de Naples antique," *XXV AttiTaranto*, p. 311
Napoli, M. 1966. "La ricerca archeologica a Velia," *PP* 21, pp. 191–226
———. 1967. "Le arti figurative," in *Napoli antica* I, Napoli, p. 593–622
———. 1969. *Civiltà della Magna Grecia*, Roma
———. 1970. "Intorno alla pianta di Velia," *PP* 25, pp. 226–235
Neutsch, B. 1970. "Neue archäologische Untersuchungen am Südhang der Akropolis von Elea," *PP* 25, pp. 146–152
Pensabene, P., e M. R. Sanzi Di Mino. 1983. *Museo Nazionale Romano. Le terrecotte*, III, i, *Antefisse*, Roma
*Popoli anellenici* = *Popoli anellenici in Basilicata (Catalogo della Mostra)*, Napoli 1971
Pugliese Carratelli, G. 1966. "Greci d'Asia in Occidente tra il secolo VII e il VI," *PP* 21, pp. 155–163
———. 1973. "Problemi della storia di Paestum," in *La monetazione in bronzo di Poseidonia-Paestum, Atti III Convegno internazionale di Studi Numismatici (Napoli 1971)*, Roma, pp. 3–11
———. 1974. "Le genti della Lucania antica e le loro relazioni con i Greci d'Italia," in *Atti Convegno omonimo (Potenza Matera 1971)*, Roma, pp. 7–12
Ricciotti, D. 1979. *Le terrecotte votive dell'Antiquarium Comunale. I: le arule*, Roma
Richardson, L., Jr. 1974. "The Archaic Doric Temple of Pompeii," *PP* 29, pp. 281–290
Ridgway, D. 1984. *L'alba della Magna Grecia*, Milano
Riis, P. J. 1981. *Etruscan Types of Heads*, Copenhagen
Scatozza, L. 1971. "Le terrecotte architettoniche cumane di età arcaica," *Klearchos* 13, pp. 45–111
Schleuning, W. 1889. "Velia in Lucanien," *JdI* 4, p. 179–194
Sestieri, C. P. 1949. *FA* 4, n. 1961
———. 1951. *FA* 6, n. 2634
———. 1952. *FA* 7, n. 2114
———. 1953. *FA* 8, n. 2270
———. 1954. *FA* 10, n. 3047
———. 1955. *FA* 11, n. 2174
———. 1956. *FA* 11, n. 2174
Shoe, L. T. 1952. *Profiles of Western Greek Mouldings (Papers and Monographs of the American Academy in Rome* 14), Roma
Tocco, G. 1991. "Relazione," *XXXI AttiTaranto* (in corso di stampa)
Van Buren, E. D. 1918. "Terracotta Arulae," *MAAR* 2, pp. 15–53
Von Rohden, H. 1880. *Die Terrakotten von Pompeji*, Stuttgart
Wikander, Ch. 1981. *Acquarossa. Painted Architectural Terracottas from Acquarossa (Acta Instituti Romani Sueciae* XXXVIII, i), Stockholm

Winter, N. 1978. "Architectural Terracottas with Human Heads," *RM* 85, pp. 27–58
———. 1990. "Defining Regional Styles in Archaic Greek Architectural Terracottas," in *Hesperia* 59, pp. 13–32
Zancani Montuoro, P. 1965–1966. "L'edificio quadrato nello Heraion alla Foce del Sele," *AttiMGrecia* 6–7, pp. 27–193

Giovanna Greco

Università degli Studi d'Napoli Federico II
Dipartimento di Discipline Storiche
via Porta di Massa, 1
80133 Napoli
Italia

Maria José Strazzulla

Università degli Studi di Roma «La Sapienza»
Dipartimento di Scienze Storiche, Archeologiche e Antropologiche dell'Antichità
Piazzali Aldo Moro 5
I-00185 Roma
Italia

# EIN ARCHITEKTONISCHES TERRAKOTTAFRAGMENT HELLENISTISCHER ZEIT AUS REGGIO CALABRIA

(Plates 89, 90)

IM MUSEO NAZIONALE von Reggio Calabria ist ein im Stadtgebiet von Reggio Calabria, das sich über den Ruinen der griechischen Kolonie Rhegion erstreckt, gefundenes Terrakottafragment aufbewahrt (Pls. 89, 90),[1] welches bis jetzt fast keine Beachtung gefunden hat. Von R. Spadea wurde das Stück unter den architektonischen Terrakotten von Reggio Calabria erwähnt, ohne auf dessen Funktion einzugehen:[2] "Esse sono di età ellenistica, come un bel frammento in cotto con parte di una figura, seduta probabilmente su una roccia."

Das Bruchstück besteht aus zwei im Winkel von etwa 90° zueinander stehenden Tonplatten, deren originale rechte Seitenkante und hintere Kante erhalten sind, während der linke Teil und der obere Abschnitt abgebrochen sind. Im Gegensatz zum hinteren Rand ist der rechte Rand des Fragments nicht gerade geschnitten, sondern der Ton wurde an der Kante wenig sorgfältig mit der Hand verstrichen. In die rechte Seitenkante ist im Bereich der Kante zwischen den beiden Platten eine waagrechte Höhlung eingelassen. Bei einer horizontalen Lage der unteren Platte beträgt die Breite des Fragmentes 22,3 cm, die Höhe 16,7 cm und die Tiefe 23,8 cm. Die obere Platte ist 2,5 bis 3 cm dick, die untere ungefähr 4 cm. Die Außenseiten der Platten sind mit Reliefs verziert. Die nicht für die Ansicht bestimmte Innenseite ist auf sehr grobe Weise geglättet. Die Oberfläche der Außenseiten wird von einer Schicht fein geschlämmten Tons gebildet. Reste einer Bemalung sind nicht sichtbar.

Die Oberfläche der unteren Platte wird von unregelmäßig geformten Buckeln gebildet, welche durch Kehlungen geringer Tiefe getrennt sind. Die höchsten Teile der Buckel sind ungefähr in einer Ebene angeordnet. Die Anordnung von Buckeln von verschiedener Größe und Form entspricht der Darstellung von Felsen in der klassischen und hellenistischen Kunst.[3]

Auf der Vorderseite der oberen Platte ist in hohem Relief eine menschliche Figur wiedergegeben, welche an der Kante ein wenig auf die untere Platte übergreift. Die Relieftiefe beträgt 8–9 cm. Von der Figur sind der untere Teil des Bauches, der Ansatz des rechten Beines, das linke Bein mit Ausnahme des Fußes und ein Teil des linken Armes im Bereich des Ellbogens erhalten. Das rechte Bein war zur rechten Seite der Figur ausgestreckt. Der linke Oberschenkel ist ganz leicht zu seiner Linken gedreht. Der linke Unterschenkel

---

[1] Inv. Nr. 3266 c. Für die Möglichkeit zur Untersuchung dieses Stückes dankt der Verfasser Liliana Costamagna, Silvana Cilione und Beatrice Nucera von der Soprintendenza Archeologica della Calabria, für die Genehmigung zur Publikation der Soprintendentin Elena Lattanzi.

Der Verfasser dankt ferner allen, welche sich nach dem Vortrag in Athen an der Diskussion beteiligten, wobei besonders die Beiträge von Rudolf Känel und Volker Kästner zur architektonischen Funktion des Fragmentes und von Gerhild Hübner zur Ikonographie hervorzuheben sind.

Die Photographien wurden vom Verfasser aufgenommen und von Gerhard Feitzinger vergrößert.

[2] Spadea 1987, S. 94.

[3] Carroll-Spillecke 1985, S. 56–63.

ist angewinkelt und zur rechten Seite der Figur gerichtet. Die Figur ist also in sitzender Haltung mit zur Seite gestreckten Beinen und auf den linken Ellbogen gestütztem Körper dargestellt. Der Bauch ist nicht von Gewand bedeckt. Vom Ellbogen verläuft das um den Arm geschlungene Himation in einem Bogen zum Ansatz der Beine. Ein Zipfel des Himations hängt vom Ellbogen herab. Die Beine sind zur Gänze vom Gewand verhüllt.

Da die Reliefdarstellung die beiden im Winkel von etwa 90° zueinander stehenden Platten zur Gänze ausfüllt, waren beide Seiten für die Ansicht bestimmt. Aufgrund der Position der Figur steht fest, daß der obere Abschnitt des Bruchstückes senkrecht und der untere waagrecht angeordnet war, sodaß beide Ansichtsseiten nur bei einem tieferen Standpunkt des Betrachters sichtbar waren. Das weist ebenso wie die Tonqualität und die Dicke der Platten auf eine architektonische Funktion hin. Wahrscheinlich handelt es sich um das Fragment der Verkleidung eines aus Holz bestehenden Architekturelementes, dessen Unterseite nicht oder nicht zur Gänze auf einem anderen Bauglied auflag.

Obwohl aufgrund der fragmentarischen Erhaltung und des Fehlens von Vergleichsbeispielen ein sicheres Urteil nicht möglich ist, kann in Erwägung gezogen werden, daß das Terrakottabruchstück aus Reggio Calabria der Verkleidungsplatte eines *columen* oder *mutulus* angehört. Diese Form architektonischer Terrakotten ist nicht nur in Etrurien und Latium,[4] sondern, wie der Sarkophag des Athleten aus Tarent[5] zeigt, auch in der Magna Graecia nachgewiesen. Der horizontale Teil des Bruchstücks bedeckte also vielleicht die aus der Tympanonwand ragende Unterseite, der vertikale Abschnitt hingegen die Stirnseite eines in Längsrichtung des Gebäudes angeordneten Dachbalkens.

Wegen des Erhaltungszustandes ist die Rekonstruktion und Deutung der dargestellten Szene problematisch. Das Motiv der auf einem Felsen sitzenden Figur entspricht Darstellungen der Aphrodite[6] sowie anderer Gottheiten und Menschen männlichen und weiblichen Geschlechts[7] in der klassischen und hellenistischen Kunst. Ohne Kenntnis des Gebäudes, zu dessen Ausstattung das Terrakottafragment gehört, und ohne Kenntnis weiterer Bruchstücke ist eine Identifizierung der Figur nicht möglich.

Wenn auch nicht mit Sicherheit feststeht, welche architektonische Funktion das Bruchstück aus Reggio Calabria hat, so ist es mit größter Wahrscheinlichkeit das Zeugnis für eine bisher einzigartige Form von Architekturdekoration, welche nach der Bildung der Falten, die mit jener von tarentinischen Terrakottastatuetten vergleichbar ist, der frühhellenistischen Zeit angehört. Es zeigt ebenso wie die Drachenköpfe aus Reggio Calabria,[8] welchen ähnliche Beispiele in Sandstein aus Gela entsprechen,[9] daß auch in hellenistischer Zeit in der Magna Graecia neue Formen architektonischer Terrakotten geschaffen wurden. Es sind also auch die architektonischen Terrakotten ein Zeugnis dafür, daß in hellenistischer Zeit im Bereich der westgriechischen Architektur die schöpferische Kraft nicht erloschen ist, auch wenn sich in der Tempelarchitektur am Ende des 5. Jhs. v. Chr. ein Nachlassen der Kreativität

---

[4] Andrén 1940, S. LX–LXII.
[5] Mura Sommella 1987, S. 50–54, 63 Nr. 17.
[6] *LIMC* II, i 1984, S. 92–95, Nr. 857–898, *s.v.* Aphrodite (A. Delivorrias).
[7] Carroll-Spillecke 1985, S. 56–63.
[8] Spadea 1987, S. 94.
[9] Gela: Adamesteanu und Orlandini 1956, S. 346, Abb. 7, 8. Morgantina: Allen 1973, S. 78, Nr. 5, 6, Abb. 17–26.

feststellen läßt.[10] Vielmehr wurden in der hellenistischen Zeit, besonders im 3. Jh. v. Chr., eigenständige Architekturformen, z. B. Theaterbauten[11] und Grabnaiskoi,[12] sowie Architekturelemente, wie das sikeliotisch-korinthische Kapitell,[13] und Bauplastik, wie der als Mittelakroter dienende Adler aus Megara Hyblaea,[14] und die Atlanten und Karyatiden,[15] geschaffen, welche zum Teil eine starke Ausstrahlung auf die mittelrepublikanische Baukunst Mittelitaliens ausübten.[16]

## BIBLIOGRAPHIE

Adamesteanu, D., und H. Dilthey. 1992. *Macchia di Rossano, Il santuario della Melfitis. Rapporto preliminare*, Galatina

Adamesteanu, D., und P. Orlandini. 1956. "Gela (Sicilia). Ritrovamenti vari," *NSc*, S. 203–401

Allen, H. L. 1973. "Morgantina Sea Monsters, Lions and 'Baroque' Sicilian Workshops," *OpRom* 9, S. 73–84

Andrén, A. 1940. *Architectural Terracottas from Etrusco-Italic Temples* (Acta Instituti Romani Regni Sueciae VI), Lund/Leipzig

Bonacasa, N. 1985. "Le arti figurative. L'ellenismo e la tradizione ellenistica," in *Sikanie*, G. Pugliese Carratelli, Hrsg., Milano, S. 277–347

Carroll-Spillecke, M. 1985. *Landscape Depictions in Greek Relief Sculpture*, Frankfurt am Main

Carter, J. C. 1975. *The Sculpture of Taras* (Transactions of the American Philological Association, n.s. 65, no. 79), Philadelphia

D'Amicis, A., A. Dell'Aglio, E. Lippolis, und G. A. Maruggi. 1991. *Vecchi Scavi. Nuovi Restauri*, Taranto

Isler, H. P. 1981. "Contributi per una storia del teatro antico. Il teatro greco di Iatas e il teatro di Segesta," *NumAntCl* 10, S. 131–164

———. 1985. "Una cariatide dal teatro greco di Solunto," *SicArch* 18:59, S. 65–70

Klumbach, H. 1937. *Tarentiner Grabkunst*, Reutlingen

Lattanzi, E. 1987. *Il Museo Nazionale di Reggio Calabria*, Roma/Reggio Calabria

Lauter-Bufé, H. 1987. *Die Geschichte des sikeliotisch-korinthischen Kapitells*, Mainz

*LIMC* II, i = *Lexicon Iconographicum Mythologiae Classicae* II, i, Zürich/München 1984

Lippolis, E. 1987. "Organizzazione delle necropoli e struttura sociale nell' Apulia ellenistica. Due esempi: Taranto e Canosa," in *Römische Gräberstraßen*, H. von Hesberg und P. Zanker, Hrsg., München, S. 139–154

Martorano, F. 1991. "Catalogo dei modelli locresi," in *I ninfei di Locri Epizefiri. Architettura. Culti erotici. Sacralità delle acque*, F. Costabile, Hrsg., Catanzaro, S. 63–94

Martorano, F., und F. Costabile. 1991. "I modelli fittili dei ninfei," in *I ninfei di Locri Epizefiri*, F. Costabile, Hrsg., Catanzaro, S. 45–62

---

[10] Mertens 1984, S. 202–205; Mertens 1990, S. 383.

[11] Isler 1981.

[12] Carter 1975; Lippolis 1987.

[13] Lauter-Bufé 1987.

[14] *Mégara Hyblaea* IV, S. 26, Taf. 46:1, 3; 64, 65.

[15] Schaller 1973, S. 69–72, Nr. 180–183, 185–187, 189; Schmidt-Colinet 1977, S. 227–228, W 28–32; S. 242–244, M 2, 3, 5, 7–9.

Canosa: Pensabene 1990, S. 292–293, 315–316, Nr. 97–99, Taf. 131:1–5. Tarent: Klumbach 1937, S. 66–67, Nr. 158, Taf. 25. Ferner sind im Museo Archeologico Nazionale von Tarent das Bruchstück eines Atlanten (Inv. 6162) und einer Karyatide aufbewahrt. Vaste: D'Amicis et al. 1991, S. 149–158. Macchia di Rossano: Adamesteanu und Dilthey 1992, S. 77, Taf. 53. Montescaglioso: Lattanzi 1987, S. 194. Solunt: Pace 1922, Sp. 225–226, Abb. 17, 18; Isler 1985, S. 65–70. Monte Iato: Ribi und Isler Kerenyi 1976, S. 13–48, Taf. 1–19. Segesta: Rizzo 1923, S. 103, Abb. 45. Centuripe: Bonacasa 1985, S. 332, Abb. 355, 356, 389–392. Syrakus: Aten. V, 208b (Schiff Hierons II.); Rizzo 1923, S. 97–105, Abb. 42–44, Taf. 6 (Theater).

Karyatiden sind ferner auf Modellen von Nymphäen wiedergegeben: Lokri: Martorano 1991, S. 80, Nr. C1.1, Abb. 135–139. Tarent: Martorano und Costabile 1991, S. 51, 58, Abb. 71:a, b.

[16] Lauter-Bufé 1987, S. 90–91.

*Mégara Hyblaea* IV = G. Vallet und F. Villard, *Le temple du IV<sup>e</sup> siècle (Mégara Hyblaea* IV), Paris 1966

Mertens, D. 1984. *Der Tempel von Segesta und die dorische Tempelbaukunst des griechischen Westens in klassischer Zeit*, Mainz

———. 1990. "Some Principal Features of West Greek Colonial Architecture," in *Greek Colonists and Native Populations. Proceedings of the First Australian Congress of Classical Archaeology Held in Honour of Emeritus Professor A. D. Trendall*, J.-P. Descoedres, Hrsg., Canberra/Oxford, S. 373–386

Mura Sommella, A. 1987. "Gli atleti della Magna Grecia e la Tomba dell'Atleta di Taranto," in *'Athla' e atleti nella Grecia classica*, A. Mura Sommella, E. Talamo, und M. Cima, Hrsg., Milano

Pace, B. 1922. "Il tempio di Giove Olimpico in Agrigento," *MonAnt* 28, Sp. 173–252

Pensabene, P. 1990. "Il tempio ellenistico di S. Leucio a Canosa," in *Italici in Magna Grecia. Lingua, insediamenti e strutture*, M. Tagliente, Hrsg., Venosa, S. 269–337

Ribi, E. A., und C. Isler-Kerenyi. 1976. "Die Stützfiguren des griechischen Theaters von Iaitas," in *Studia Ietina* I, H. Bloesch und H. P. Isler, Hrsg., Erlenbach/Zürich, S. 13–48

Rizzo, G. E. 1923. *Il teatro greco di Siracusa*, Milano

Schaller, F. 1973. *Stützfiguren in der griechischen Kunst*, Wien

Schmidt-Colinet, A. 1977. *Antike Stützfiguren*, Frankfurt am Main

Spadea, R. 1987. "Le terrecotte architettoniche," in Lattanzi 1987, S. 92–94


PETER DANNER

UNIVERSITÄT SALZBURG
Institut für Klassische Archäologie
Residenzplatz 1
A-5020 Salzburg
Austria

# EINIGE TARENTINER ARCHITEKTURTERRAKOTTEN

(PLATES 91–93)

DIE TARENTINISCHE KULTURGESCHICHTE basiert in ihren Einzelfragen mehr auf Annahmen denn auf beweisbaren Grundlagen.[1] Ursache für diese definitorischen Unsicherheiten sind fehlende literarische Quellen sowie ausreichende exakte Grabungsbefunde[2] im antiken Tarentiner Stadtbereich, der heute modern überbaut und für systematische archäologische Arbeiten weitgehend unzugänglich ist.[3] Trotz dieser Unzulänglichkeiten läßt sich die materielle Hinterlassenschaft dieses unteritalischen Kulturzentrums der Magna Graecia[4] im klassischen und frühhellenistischen Zeitraum einigermaßen begründet sortieren und verläßlich bewerten. Fortschritte konnten auf den zahlreichen Kongressen in Tarent[5] und in der Vorlage des archäologischen Materials in Sonderschauen verzeichnet werden.[6] Antefixe (Stirnziegel)[7] aus diesem Gebiet haben als Hauptuntersuchungsgegenstand jedoch bisher für die Bewertung tarentinischer Phänomene eher eine periphere Rolle gespielt und zu Recht nicht im Mittelpunkt des Interesses gestanden, da die unzureichende Funddokumentation insbesondere für diese Gattung nach wie vor weitere Aufschlüsse erschwert.[8] Trotz der Bemerkung von R. M. Cook über die tarentinischen Terrakotten im allgemeinen, daß "though artistically the material is not appetizing and its importance is only parochial,"[9] erscheint die nähere Beschäftigung mit tarentinischen Antefixen aufgrund ihrer Quantität sowie plastischen und ikonographischen Qualität wünschenswert. Eingehendere Besprechungen dieses tarentinischen Materials erfolgten für die archaische Zeit u.a. schon bei Kästner und Winter, für die klassische bei Herdejürgen und Laviosa.[10]

Die hier vorgelegten Antefixe aus Kiel sind hinsichtlich Größe, Stil und Typus Vertreter der in vielen Sammlungen der Welt bekannten Art, die bisher jedoch nur vereinzelt publiziert wurden.[11] Die Kieler Antefixe wurden Mitte der 20er Jahre aus einer Hand geschlossen für die dortige Antikensammlung bezogen.[12] Es handelt sich bei diesen Stücken ausschließlich um Terrakotta-Antefixe,[13] die nach Ausweis der an den Plattenrückseiten der Antefixe in

[1] Wuilleumier 1939; vgl. auch die neuere Arbeit von Brauer 1986, sowie kürzlich Graepler 1990.
[2] Vgl. z.B.: Viola 1881; Lenormant 1881–1882, S. 25–53, 83–127; Bartoccini 1936; Orsi 1933, S. 71.
[3] Zu einer "Rekonstruktion" alter Grabungsdokumente s. Graepler 1984; Graepler 1988; Graepler 1990.
[4] Phillips 1968a, S. 23.
[5] S. die laufenden Kongreßberichte *AttiTaranto*, ab Jahrgang 1961.
[6] S. z.B.: Forti 1966; Belli 1970; De Juliis und Laiacono 1985; Andreassi u.a. 1986; Guzzo u.a. 1988; De Juliis 1985; *Kat. Tarent.*
[7] Zum Terminus s. Andrén 1940, S. LXXXIII, Anm. 4, sowie *EAA* I, 1958, S. 404, *s.v.* Antefissa (A. Andrén).
[8] Eine frühe kurze Bearbeitung bei Anderson 1883.
[9] Cook 1974, S. 159.
[10] Kästner 1982; Kästner 1989; Winter 1978; Herdejürgen 1971; Herdejürgen 1978; Herdejürgen 1982. Laviosa 1954.
[11] S. z.B.: Breitenstein 1941; Higgins 1954; Laviosa 1954; Herdejürgen 1971, Taf. 18; Kingsley 1976.
[12] S. dazu Brandes 1988, S. 2.
[13] Wegen des nachweislichen Mangels an guten Marmor- oder anderen geeigneten Werksteinmaterialien für den Architekturbereich in der antiken Magna Graecia ist die Verwendung von Terrakotta eine verbreitete

Fragmenten noch befindlichen Kalypteransätze Bestandteile der Architekturdekoration von Sanktuar- oder Sepulkralbauten des 5. und 4. Jh. v. Chr. in Tarent waren.

Zunächst einmal seien die Kieler Objekte kurz in Tabellenform vorgestellt. Die Tonfarbwertbestimmungen sind nach international akzeptierten Farbskalen[14] zur Vermeidung subjektiver und schwerlich nachvollziehbarer Beurteilungen[15] vorgenommen worden.[16] Alle hier aufgeführten Terrakotta-Antefixe stammen aus Matrizen.[17] Absolute Datierungsansätze sind grundsätzlich wegen der fehlenden äußeren Datierungsmöglichkeiten problematisch und hier nur als ungefähre Einordnungen zu verstehen.

| Inv.-Nr. | Höhe/Breite (cm) | Kalypter[a] | Tonfarbwert[b] | Datierung[c] | Plate |
|---|---|---|---|---|---|
| B 346 | 17/19 | halbrund | 10YR 8/4 | *ca.* 360 | 91:a |
| B 347 | 18/17 | halbrund | 10YR 8/4 | *ca.* 320 | 91:b |
| B 348 | 20/19 | halbrund | 10YR 8/6 | 370–350 | 91:c |
| B 349 | 19/17 | halbrund | 5YR 7/4 | *ca.* 340 | 92:a, b |
| B 350 | 15/20 | halbrund | 10YR 7/4 | 420–410 | 92:c |
| B 351 | 16/18 | halbrund | 10YR 8/4 | *ca.* 360 | 92:d |
| B 407 | 19/21 | pentagonal | 2,5YR 5/8 | *ca.* 320 | 93:a |
| B 408 | 19/20 | halbrund | 10YR 8/4 | 370–350 | 93:b |

[a] Form des Kalypteransatzes an der planen Rückseite der Antefixplatte. Diese setzen jeweils mehrere cm unterhalb der Oberkante des Antefixes an und wirken teilweise wie abgeschnitten. Das Kieler Antefix B 349 besitzt noch ein zurückspringendes Kalypterfragment von *ca.* 13 cm Länge.

[b] Lt. Munsellnotierungen; die Tonfarbwerte ergeben sich aus dem am Objekt dominanten Farbton, der möglichst an Bruchkanten der Terrakotta erschlossen werden sollte, um etwaige Überlagerungen durch Kalk, Farbreste oder Versinterungen auszuschließen; vgl. auch die mikro- und makroskopischen sowie petrographischen Untersuchungen bei Knoop 1987, im Tafelteil und in Appendix Teil B, S. 227, sowie ähnliche Maßnahmen bei Wiederkehr 1990, S. 119.

[c] Zur Datierungsproblematik s. weiter unten.

TABELLE DER KIELER ANTEFIXE

Der Fundort der Objekte war beim Ankauf nicht mitgeteilt worden, doch spricht schon sowohl die Auffindung von zahlreichen Antefixen gleichen oder ähnlichen Typus, Stils sowie entsprechender Abmessungen in den Nekropolen des antiken Tarents für die dortige

---

Erscheinung; s. hierzu z.B. Mertens-Horn 1988, S. 115, die von "alternativer" Technologie spricht; vgl. auch Mertens 1990, S. 374–375, sowie kürzlich Todisco 1990, S. 915.

[14] Vgl. *Munsell Soil Color Charts*, Baltimore 1975. Zu den Einschränkungen bei der Verwendung dieser Tonfarbwertbestimmungstafeln, s. Brandes 1988, S. 37–42, sowie kürzlich Wiederkehr 1990, S. 119–120, die zu recht darauf hinweist, daß primär die Tonbeschaffenheit von Interesse sei, die Tonfarbe hingegen zweitrangig, da sie stark vom Brennvorgang und der Brenntemperatur abhängig ist.

[15] Hiermit entfallen nach subjektiven Kriterien geschaffene Angaben, wie sie etwa Green 1977; *CVA, Philadelphia* 1 [USA 22], für Gnathia-Keramik entwickelt hatte.

[16] In Verwendung u.a. auch bei: Lindros Wohl 1984; Lunsingh Scheurleer 1968; *CVA, Basel, Antikenmuseum* 1 [Schweiz 4]; *CVA, Toronto, Royal Ontario Museum* 1 [Canada 1].

[17] Zur Technik des Herstellungsprozesses, s. Jastrow 1941, ab S. 1; Nicholls 1952; Brandes 1988, S. 55–62.

Provenienz.[18] Ebenso deutet auch die bis auf eine Ausnahme (für das Antefix Kiel B 407) relativ einheitliche Tonfarbwertgebung im Farbbereich von "very pale brown" (=10YR 8/4) auf die Produktion dieser Antefixe in Tarent, da für eine Vielzahl anderer tarentinischer Terrakotten ähnliche Farbwerte mitgeteilt wurden.[19] Farbüberzugsreste finden sich nicht auf den Kieler Antefixen, jedoch Reste weißer Engobe[20] auf Vorder- und Rückseite, so daß antiker Farbauftrag bestanden haben wird.[21]

Die erstmalige Verwendung von plastischen Reliefköpfen auf Antefixplatten sowie der Verlauf ihrer Weiterverbreitung ist bis dato nicht eindeutig geklärt.[22] Aus der bekannten Pliniusstelle[23] über den Koroplasten Butades aus Sikyon läßt sich eine Reliefkopfantefixproduktion nicht eindeutig erschließen, zumal für den erwähnten Produktionsort Korinth direkt bisher keine archäologische Evidenz besteht.[24] Die ersten Nachweise lassen sich im 7. Jh. v. Chr. vielmehr für den Nordwesten Griechenlands, in Thermos, Kalydon, Korfu (Korkyra) sowie im ätolischen Taxiarchos und Sakónina[25] erbringen, der jedoch in dieser Zeit unter korinthischem Einfluß gestanden hat.[26] Schon bald darauf—falls nicht sogar

[18] Vgl. Laviosa 1954; Herdejürgen 1978, S. 84; Kästner 1989, S. 122.
[19] Terrakottaprodukte anderer Herstellungszentren besitzen i.d.R. sowohl eine andere Tonfarbwertgebung als auch eine andere Tonstruktur als die tarentinische, s. hierzu Higgins 1954, S. 9. Da zwar mit einem "Export" von Tonmatrizen gerechnet werden darf, jedoch nicht mit dem Fernhandel von größen Mengen unbearbeiteten Tons bzw. verarbeiteter Terrakotta, ist i.d.R. bei Auffindung von Terrakottaobjekten mit einer Produktion vor Ort oder in der näheren Umgebung zu rechnen. Knoop 1987, S. 208 mit Anm. 536, glaubt hingegen an einen Fernhandel selbst von größeren Tonmengen, auch wenn er keine Nachweise erbringen kann. Der ebda. zitierte Stibbe 1984, S. 138, nennt allerdings keinen naturwissenschaftlichen Beleg für den angeblichen Transport von Ton aus Lakonien nach Lipari. So ein Vorgang ist höchstens bei kleineren Mengen sowie eventuell bei einer "Erstausstattung" von auswandernden Töpfern und Koroplasten vorstellbar, die in tonarme Gegenden migrieren. Ansonsten ist wohl nur der Transport von Modeln, Hohlformen und leichten Hilfsmaterialien wie den Pigmenten vorstellbar. Auch Knoop 1987, S. 208, konzediert "matrix-links with numerous sites." Für die lokale Produktion im Hinterland, die auch "Metapontiner Typen" des späten 6. bzw. 5. Jh. v. C. verwendete, s. z.B. Adamesteanu 1990, S. 146. Bei diesen "Metapontiner Typen" dürfte es sich eher um Antefix-Typen Tarentiner Ursprungs handeln, s. hierzu z.B. Wuilleumier 1939, S. 425 mit Anm. 4; Adamesteanu 1974, S. 254, Taf. 31 und Kästner 1989, S. 123. Der Matrizenhandel—zumindest im 4. Jh. v. Chr.—geht prinzipiell von Tarent in das Umland aus, jedoch nicht zurück, so auch Giuliani 1988, S. 164.
[20] Koch 1912, S. 12. Zur Frage des Engobe-Brandes, s. ebda.; mit Gegenmeinung Steingräber 1980, S. 232.
[21] S. Brandes 1988, S. 46–48; Wuilleumier 1939, S. 425–426; Higgins 1954, S. 7: "The absence of colour... may be explained by the fugitive nature of the pigments employed."
[22] Winter 1974; s. Brandes 1988, S. 21–33.
[23] Pliny, NatHist 35,151–152; vgl. hierzu auch Mertens-Horn 1978, S. 30–31; Winter 1978, S. 29; Torelli 1979, S. 310 und Mertens-Horn und Viola 1990, S. 246.
[24] Corinth IV, i, S. 5–6; s. auch Winter 1978, S. 29; Mertens-Horn 1978, S. 31–36; Torelli 1979, S. 310; Roebuck 1990.
[25] Kalydon: Mertens-Horn 1978, S. 55, Abb. 21; Kästner 1990, S. 258. Korfu: Ervin 1968, Taf. 93, Abb. 41; Mertens-Horn 1978, S. 55–61, Abb. 22, 23. Taxiarchos und Sakónina: Van Buren 1926, S. 59–60 (Sakónina/Konitza: frühes 7. Jh. v. Chr.), S. 62 (Taxiarchos: 7. Jh. v. Chr.), S. 138–144, Taf. 34–38; Winter 1978, S. 28, Abb. 1.
[26] Zur Frage des korinthischen Einflusses in Nordwestgriechenland, s. Mertens-Horn 1978, S. 31, S. 63, die den korinthischen Einfluß für die Erfindung der Dachterrakotten von Thermos und Korfu aus historischen und typologisch-stilistischen Gründen ausschließen will, während D'Andria 1990, S. 285, dieses Gebiet generell im 7. Jh. v. Chr. als "Corinthian colonies with their natural hinterland" sieht. Die stark dominante korinthische Kunstlandschaft dieser Zeit mit prägendem Einfluß auf die nordwestgriechischen Reliefkopfantefixe betont

zeitgleich—erscheinen die Reliefkopfantefixe im etruskisch-kampanischen Raum,[27] und nicht viel später müssen die dädalisierenden Antefixtypen Tarents entstanden sein.[28] Diese frühen tarentinischen Stücke sind allerdings aufgrund der bisher geringen Nachweise und Funddokumentationen mit Vorsicht zu bewerten.[29]

Tarent wird erst im Verlauf der späten Archaik und frühen Klassik unter den verschiedenen griechischen Kunstlandschaften zu dem Hauptproduktionsgebiet für Reliefkopfantefixe, welches es im Gegensatz zu den mutterländischen, ostgriechischen oder sizilischen Werkstätten über die Archaik und Klassik hin bis zum Frühhellenismus durchgehend zu bleiben scheint.[30] Erst im frühen dritten Jahrhundert—eventuell im Zusammenhang mit dem Auftreten der Römer in Unteritalien zu sehen—versiegt die dortige Herstellung von Antefixen, doch scheinen die lokalen koroplastischen Werkstätten durchaus noch auch in der zunehmend römisch dominierten Zeit andere Terrakotta-Objekte weiterproduziert zu haben.[31]

Die nach wie vor neben Herkunft und Verbreitungsverlauf der Reliefkopfantefixe strittige Frage nach der Stimulation für die Verwendung von Kopfprotomen auf Antefixplatten kann hier nicht entschieden werden.[32] Denkbar ist, daß sich die frühen nordwestgriechischen Reliefkopfantefixe von den plastisch gebildeten Köpfen, die an korinthischer Keramik appliziert waren,[33] und die etruskischen Typen eventuell von einheimischen Maskenkulten ableiten lassen, wie Winter das geäußert hatte.[34] Auch sie glaubt aber grundsätzlich an den

---

m.E. zu recht Wallenstein 1971, S. 31, S. 37–40; Winter 1990, S. 23 hält zwar den Einsatz von in Korinth ausgebildeten Arbeitern für möglich, das Konzept und die Ausführungsart seien jedoch "... foreign to ... the pure Corinthian system produced at Corinth," so daß sie im Ätolischen ein "regional roofing system" vermutet. Diese Differenzierung kann sich aber nur auf die allgemeine Anlage der Dachkonstruktion und nicht auf die Besonderheiten der Verwendung von bestimmten Antefixtypen beziehen.

[27] Neils 1976; Winter, 1978, mit Fundkarten; Kästner 1989, S. 115, Anm. 5–6.

[28] Van Buren 1923, S. 80–82, Abb. 66 (6. Jh. v. Chr.), S. 147, Nr. 49; Phillips 1968b; Winter 1978, S. 31, Taf. 8:1, 2, und 4; 9:1; Adamesteanu 1982, S. 311, Abb. 10.

[29] Winter 1978, Taf. 9:1–3. Ähnliches gilt auch für die Reliefköpfe aus Apollonia, Afrati und Ephesos (?) bei Mertens-Horn 1978, S. 63, Abb. 19–26. Es ist schwerlich vorstellbar, daß im 7. Jh. v. Chr. schon eine "dädalische Koiné" für Reliefkopfantefixe vorgelegen haben könnte, welche von Kleinasien (Ephesos) über Kreta (Afrati) und Nordwestgriechenland (Thermos, Kalydon und Korkyra) bzw. Albanien (Apollonia) bis nach Westgriechenland (Etrurien und Unteritalien) reichte. Knoop 1987, S. 204, sieht den Hauptbereich Etruriens mit Murlo und Acquarossa am Ende des 7. Jh. v. Chr. sogar "... almost cut off from Greco-Campanian influences...."

[30] Im Laufe der zweiten Hälfte des 5. Jh. v. Chr. wird Tarent auch im Bereich der Arula-Produktion in Unteritalien führend, deren Wirkung nicht nur dort sondern auch bis über die Adria nachgewiesen werden kann; s. hierzu: van der Mejden 1990, S. 130.

[31] Graepler 1984, S. 88. Coarelli 1970 hatte hierzu noch eine andere Auffassung.

Tarent hat sich kulturell wohl noch bis zum Ausgang der Römischen Republik behaupten können: Metzler 1985, S. 21, und Graepler 1990, S. 90, sowie Steingräber 1990, S. 79. Allgemein zum Einfluß Roms auf tarentinisches Kulturleben bei Pape 1975, S. 8.

[32] Jucker 1961, S. 199, sieht den Ursprung des Motivs der Einzelköpfe der unteritalischen und etruskischen Dekorationskunst in orphischen Unsterblichkeitsvorstellungen. Demnach müßten die orphischen "Heiligen Reden" schon ab der Mitte des 7. Jh. v. Chr. im etruskisch-italischen Raum bekannt gewesen sein, wenn man die frühen Antefixköpfe dieser Landschaften hierdurch stimuliert sähe. Das halte ich für wenig wahrscheinlich.

[33] Wallenstein 1971, S. 31.

[34] Winter 1978 datiert die Antefixe aus Murlo rechts früh schon in die Mitte des 7. Jh. v. Chr.; vgl. z.B. für etruskische Kopfprotomentypen Giglioli 1935, Taf. 161:1; Riis 1981.

korinthischen Impuls aufgrund der inhärenten architektonischen Qualität der plastischen Kopfappliken an korinthischen Vasen, und daß "their adoption into an architectural context was considered a natural transition."[35]

Ob die Übertragung des für Lakonien ebenso nachweisbaren frühen Maskenkultes[36] auf die Pflanzstadt Tarent hinsichtlich der dortigen Anwendung der Kopfprotomen auf Architekturterrakotten ursächlich war, die Anregung aus dem etruskischen oder dem nordwestgriechischen Raum kam, oder ob in Tarent hierfür sogar eine eigene, eventuell aus dem indigenem italiotischen Umfeld beeinflusste Produktion vorliegt, muß vorläufig offenbleiben, da bisher nicht einmal eindeutig zu klären ist, ob die sicherlich zeitlich etwas früher in Etrurien einsetzende Produktion von Reliefkopfantefixen[37] auf externen Anregungen beruht oder wiederum selbst eine Aufnahme heimischer Impulse darstellt.[38] Sowohl zwischen Etrurien und Unteritalien als auch zwischen dem ostadriatischen und dem westadriatischen Küstengebiet sind Beziehungen schon seit früher Zeit nachweisbar, die dem Austausch dieser Reliefköpfe zugrunde liegen könnten.[39]

Antefixe sind zunächst primär funktionale Architekturelemente, da neben dem ästhetisch-schmückenden und einem etwaig deutbaren Chiffre-Charakter der Antefixdekoration die Kalyptere der Traufrandleiste abgedichtet werden.[40] Da sie mit dieser Bestimmung nur im architektonischen Rahmen sinnvoll erscheinen, verwirrt die heutige Art der Aufbewahrung und Präsentation in den Sammlungen als Einzelobjekt durch die Loslösung aus dem Architekturkontext. Antefixe mit Kopfdarstellungen befanden sich an Traufziegeldächern von Gebäuden in Westgriechenland neben dem etrusko-kampanischen[41] vorwiegend im apulisch-lukanischen Raum, besonders in der ehemals von Lakoniern gegen Ende des 8. Jh. v. Chr. gegründeten Kolonie Tarent. Fundvergesellschaftungen an anderen Orten, etwa in Naxos, Himera und Morgantina auf Sizilien oder in Metapont,[42] haben die

[35] Winter 1978, S. 30.
[36] George und Woodward 1929, S. 121–126; Mertens-Horn 1978, S. 64; Kästner 1989, S. 115.
[37] Neils 1976, S. 413; zuletzt zu Murlo mit weiterer Lit. auch Damgaard Andersen 1990 und Phillips 1990.
[38] Während Winter 1978, ein recht frühes, quasi selbständiges Auftreten von Reliefkopfantefixen in Etrurien und dann in Unteritalien andeutet (s. ebda. ihre geographischen Verteilungskarten), sieht Kästner 1982, S. 42–43, nur vereinzelt auftretende Kopfantefixe, die ihre Anregung von den im 7.Jh. v. Ch. entstandenen dädalischen "Gesichterfriesen" der Tempel in Thermos, Kalydon und Korfu erhielten und noch in der Mitte des 6. Jh. v. Chr. in den westlichen Werkstätten in dädalisierender Ikonographie produziert wurden. Wann und wie hier aber die transadriatische Motivwanderung einsetzte bleibt unklar. D'Andria 1990, S. 284, erwähnt für das 7. Jh. v. Chr. die "... migration of small groups coming from the Albanian valleys ... to Italy," und auch Mertens-Horn und Viola 1990, S. 245, vermuten schon sehr früh eine Motivwanderung von Dächern Nordwestgriechenlands nach Unteritalien.
[39] D'Andria 1990 sieht sogar "... a system of relationships polarized by the two Greek colonies of Corcyra and Tarentum and determined by continuous contacts between Greece and the West."
[40] Strong 1914, S. 164: "... they were protective in a double sense, materially against the ravages of the weather, and spiritually against evil spirits..."; vgl. auch Martin 1965, S. 65; Knoop 1987, S. 2. Dieser Wetterschutzcharakter gilt generell für die gesamte Terrakottaverwendung, so Mertens 1990, S. 375: "terracotta revetment is the most suitable protection against weathering...."
[41] Koch 1912; Koch 1915; Van Buren 1921, ab S. 3; Robinson 1923; Stopponi 1979; Rastrelli 1979; Reusser 1980; Riis 1981; Kästner 1984; *Kat. Satricum*, bes. ab S. 73; Knoop 1987; Kästner 1989, S. 115.
[42] Naxos: Van Buren 1923, S. 45–46.
Himera: Marconi 1931, S. 190, der dort Antefixe an kleineren Gebäuden als Tempeln annimmt.

Art der Verwendung von Antefixen an verschiedenen Dachsystemen von Sanktuar- oder Sepulkralgebäuden erwiesen.[43]

Für Tarent selbst ist die archäologische Dokumentation jedoch leider erheblich schlechter, denn es können keine Antefixe mit Sicherheit bestimmten Gebäuden oder Gebäudetypen zugewiesen werden.[44] Auch sind kaum Funde von den übrigen Dachelementen überliefert.[45] Antefixe wurden bei den wenigen geordneten Ausgrabungen in Tarent zu Hunderten gefunden.[46] Diese Funde stammen im wesentlichen aus dem Bereich des auch die Nekropolen umfassenden[47] antiken Tarentiner Stadtgebietes, östlich des heutzutage schiffbaren Kanals, der das sogenannte Mare Grande und das Mare Piccolo verbindet.[48] Über die dortigen Antefixfunde unter der archäologischen Aufsicht L. Violas liegt nur ein sehr

---

Morgantina: Darsow 1938; Orlandini und Griffo 1970, Nr. 62; Kästner 1982, S. 175; Kenfield 1990, berichtet für Morgantina von mehreren "sets" von spätarchaischen Gorgonenantefixen aus den Ruinen eines Naiskos, der nach seinen Aussenmassen wohl eher ein größeres Sanktuar darstellte als ein gewöhlich unter diesem Terminus zu verstehendes Grabmal in Form eines kleinen Tempels; ebenso strittig das bei Bartoccini 1936, S. 200–201, Abb. 105, aufgeführte runde archaische Gorgonenantefix aus dem Ende des 6. Jh. v. Chr. aus einem angeblichen Naiskoskontext; s. hierzu auch: Herdejürgen 1978, S. 85, Anm. 3.

Metapont: Vgl. Mertens 1975; Mertens 1977; Mertens 1979.

[43] In spätklassisch-frühhellenistischer Zeit scheinen bisweilen auch Privatgebäude mit Antefixen geschmückt worden zu sein, s. Brandes 1988, S. 77–79 mit weiterer Lit. Orsi 1933, S. 73, und Herdejürgen 1978, S. 84, Anm. 4, vermuteten das schon für die klassische Zeit; m.E. besteht hier jedoch eine zeitliche Abfolge in der Erweiterung des Gebrauchs von Reliefkopfantefixen in Unteritalien an bestimmten Gebäudetypen, während dagegen Winter 1978, S. 53, meint, daß "(the) employment of the human face as decoration does not seem to be connected with any specific type of building." Für das indigen besiedelte Serra di Vaglio am Basento im 6. und 5. Jh. v. Chr. s. Orlandini 1971, S. 288, Taf. 46:2, sowie Adamesteanu 1990, S. 146: "The main axis was flanked by rectangular buildings of either religious or public character." Damit scheinen aber keine Privatgebäude gemeint zu sein.

[44] Zur Grabungsliteratur, s. Herdejürgen 1982, S. 19, Anm. 2, und Graepler 1984, S. 86, Anm. 3.

[45] Kästner 1982, S. 111. Diese sind eventuell als "wertlose" Objekte nach den Ausgrabungen gar nicht erst mitgesammelt worden, während die Antefixe als zumindest ästhetisch ansprechend für Sammlerzwecke galten. Bartoccini 1936, S. 193–201, Abb. 105, berichtet für eines der früheren Antefixtypen Tarents von Funden im Zusammenhang mit Akroterfiguren und anderen Architekturdetails, die auch auf ein größeres und repräsentativeres Gebäude als einen Grabnaiskos hinweisen könnten, da bisher für das 6./5. Jh. v. Chr. noch kleine glaubhaften Nachweise für Tarentiner Naiskoi erbracht werden konnten; s. hierzu auch Lohmann 1979, S. 7–8, mit Anm. 44–48.

[46] Detaillierte Angaben sind derzeit nicht ermittelbar; s. Laviosa 1954, S. 217, Anm. 1. Dittmers-Herdejürgen 1979, S. 815, Anm. 2, hatte aufgrund der Fundangabe von Bernabò Brea 1940, S. 476, für zahlreiche Antefixe unterschiedlichen Typs und Stils an einem Fundplatz gemeint, "es handelt sich offenbar um eine Art Depot." Hierbei wird es sich allerdings um eine Sekundärverwendung gehandelt haben.

[47] Polybios 8,28.

[48] Drago 1956, S. 32. Eine topographische Übersicht Tarents erstellte der mit archäologischen Sicherungsaufgaben betraute Viola 1881, Taf. 2. Neuere Studien zur Topographie Tarents befinden sich u.a. bei Wuillemier 1939, s. Plan mit Fundort von "Statuettes et antefixes"; Neutsch 1956, S. 198–199; *EAA* VII, 1966, S. 605, *s.v.* Taranto (Degrassi); Herrmann 1966, S. 274–292; Lo Porto 1970, S. 366, Taf. 59–64, sowie zuletzt Graepler 1989, S. 39–46 mit Lit.

knapper Bericht vor, der außer der reinen Tatsache von Funden bestimmter Typen und ihrer Auffindung im Nekropolenbereich Tarents kaum weitere brauchbare Angaben erhält.[49]

Der einzige bisher zeichnerisch erfolgte Rekonstruktionsversuch mit den in Tarent verwendeten Antefixtypen zeigt ein Traufsimadach in Metapont.[50] Es handelt sich in diesem Fall um runde Antefixtypen der archaischen Zeit mit Gorgonengesichtern, wie sie etwa ein Stück im Museum von Brindisi zeigt.[51] Ein von Carter zeichnerisch rekonstruierter Naiskos spätklassischer Zeit nach Funden aus Tarent, Via Umbria, zeigt die Dachkonstruktion nicht im Detail; die hufeisenförmigen Antefixplatten am Traufrand sind nur sehr flüchtig widergegeben, deren Dekor überhaupt nicht zu erkennen.[52] Dennoch kann eigentlich aufgrund von Anzahl, Größe und Fundsituation der Antefixe[53] kaum Zweifel bestehen, daß die zahlreichen Terrakotta-Antefixfunde in Tarent nicht von größeren Repräsentationsbauten wie Tempeln stammen, sondern von den bedauerlicherweise nicht mehr in situ nachweisbaren Naiskoi der Tarentiner Nekropolen.[54] Die von Winter geäußerte Vermutung, daß diese Antefixe als Grabgeschenke, eventuell in Sekundärverwendung, gegolten haben können, läßt sich m.E. nicht aufrecht erhalten, auch wenn Carter Antefixe in hellenistischen Grabanlagen Tarents erwähnte.[55] Hierbei wird es sich jedoch wohl um durch den Einsturz

[49] Viola 1881, S. 543–544: "Si trovano nel terreno, accanto alle tombe, e in tombe gia frugate, et serviranno a decorare la parta superiore degli ipogei"; schon Wolters 1925, S. 10, hatte diese unzureichenden Angaben kritisiert. Möglicherweise bestand der sichtbare Oberbau dieser "ipogei" zumindest zum Teil Holz, dessen Verwendung in der Magna Graecia sogar für Tempelbauten gesichert ist, vgl. Mertens 1990, S. 378, für Cirò. Dieses würde das weitgehende Fehlen von Architekturteilen der Naiskoi erklären. Ebenso auch Lippolis 1987, S. 146, Anm. 24.
[50] Mertens 1979, Abb. 4, vom dortigen Tempel D.
[51] Ohne Inv.-Nr.; s. Brandes 1988, Kat. Nr. II 7.
[52] Carter 1975, S. 194, Taf. 70. Ein neuerer Rekonstruktionsversuch für einen tarentinischen Naiskos bei Lippolis 1987, S. 146, Abb. 32: dieser zeigt an den Längsseiten jedoch keine Antefixe.
[53] Laviosa 1954, S. 220–221, schließt aufgrund der geringen Größe der tarentinischen Antefixe aus, daß diese an großen Tempelbauten angebracht waren (zumal zu bedenken ist, daß der Kalypteransatz auf der Antefixrückseite etliche cm unterhalb der OK des Antefixes ansetzte, wie bei den Kieler Stücken zu beobachten, s.o.); ähnlich argumentieren Orsi 1933, S. 73, für die in Crimisa (Cirò) gefundenen "tarentinischen Typen" sowie Herdejürgen 1978, S. 84. Ebenso sprechen der Fundort sowie die hohe Fundzahl in Tarent gegen eine solche Verwendung, die in starkem Kontrast zu den wenigen Fundresten an Architekturdekoration von Tempelanlagen steht, die außerdem in Westteil der Stadt im Gebiet der antiken Akropolis dokumentiert sind; s. auch Wuilleumier 1939, S. 542, der in bezug auf die Gräber meint: "La plupart des antéfixes doivent avoir la même provenance."
[54] Klumbach 1937, bes. S. 95–99, mit Architekturdetails von Grabbauten, jedoch ohne Antefixfunde. Vermutlich wurden die Reste der Grabnaiskoi als Baumaterial wiederverwendet; s. Graepler 1989, S. 41. Allgemein scheint die Verwendung von Antefixen an Grabbauten aber schon seit archaischer Zeit verbreitet gewesen zu sein, so Manfredini 1969, S. 78; speziell für Tarent wird dieses behauptet in *EAA* VII, 1966, S. 611, *s.v.* Taranto (Degrassi): "Ai naiskoi arcaici possiamo attribuire le antefisse con Gorgoni e Sileni, altri elementi di decorazione fittile..."; Wuilleumier 1939, S. 542, berichtet von drei Gorgonantefixmasken, welche noch *in situ* am Grabbau gefunden worden sein sollen. Bedauerlicherweise gilt aber für Tarent in Hinblick auf die Antefixe das Wort von Coulson 1990, S. 11: "...the presence of architectural terracottas often provides the only evidence for the existence of buildings."
[55] Winter 1978, S. 54, Anm. 95; Carter 1975, S. 103–111; Carter 1973.

der Grabgebäude gestörte Stratigraphien handeln, zumal Graepler für 300 tarentinische Grabkontexte hellenistischer Zeit definitiv keine Antefixe als Grabbeigaben identifizieren konnte.[56] Die von Carter vorgelegten Fundkontexte für Grabbauten schließen auch einige Antefixe mit ein, von denen jedoch nur ein einziges mitabgebildet wurde.[57]

Aufgrund der unsicheren Fundsituation für die Tarentiner Naiskoi lag es nahe, die in zahlreichen Abbildungen vorhandenen Grabbauten in der apulischen Keramik des 4. Jh. v. Chr. auf ihren Realitäts—und Darstellungsgehalt für Rekonstruktions—und Datierungszwecke zu hinterfragen.[58] Erstaunlich ist, daß die aus tarentinischen Werkstätten stammenden Gefäße mit Grabmälerdarstellungen, also dem eigentlichem Zentrum monumentaler Grabmäler, nur außerhalb Tarents gefunden wurden, und dort vermutlich—zumindest zeitweise bis zum Verbringen in die zumeist unterirdisch angelegten Grabkammern[59]—

---

[56] Graepler 1984; vgl. auch D'Amicis 1984. Lunsingh Scheurleer 1986, Nr. 71, hatte bei diesem m.E. singulären Stück ohne Bildplatte an ein Votiv gedacht, doch handelt es sich hierbei um kein Antefix; häufig dienen Antefixe und andere Ziegelfragmente auch als Verschluß im Sepulkralbereich, wie etwa Pagenstecher 1912, S. 18, berichtet, wo ein Gefäß in einem angeblich in das 3. bis 2. Jh. v. Chr. zu datierende Metapontiner Grab von einem "tarentinischen" Stirnziegel bedeckt wurde, vgl. auch Koch 1912, S. 7–8, Abb. 13, Taf. 20, mit einem Firstziegel mit aufgemaltem Medusenhaupt aus einem Kindergrab des 3. Viertel des 6. Jh. v. Chr. (jetzt in Paris, Louvre D 159). Für das archaische Satricum s. Knoop 1987, S. 210, mit Anm. 542, mit einem Fund von zwei Antefixen in einem Votiv unterhalb des ersten Tempels. Es soll hier zwar die Verwendung von Antefixen als Grabbeigabe für sie spätklassische und hellenistische Zeit in Tarent nicht generell ausgeschlossen werden, doch ist aufgrund der bisherigen Befunde weder eine durchgängige noch weitverbreitete derartige Praxis nachweisbar. Die gleiche Vorstellung wie Winter 1978, S. 54, Anm. 95, von einer Verwendung dieser klassischen tarentinischen Antefixtypen als Grabbeigabe, eventuell ebenfalls in Sekundärverwendung, hatte ich anfänglich wegen der teilweise wie abgeschitten wirkenden Kalypteransätze an der Rückseite der Kieler Antefixe (s.o.), doch kann es sich hierbei auch um normale Bruchkanten bzw. durch im Kunsthandel erfolgte "Verschönerungsmaßnahmen" handeln. Außer im Grabkontext fanden sich Antefixe—hier wohl als Füllmaterial—auch in Zisternen: s. Orsi 1933, S. 71 und Foti 1968, S. 154, Taf. 10:1 (aus Reggio Calabria).

[57] Carter 1970, Taf. 31, Abb. 11. Die leider recht unscharfe Aufnahme zeigt ebenso wie bei Kiel B 349 ein längeres Kalypterfragment (es handelt sich bei diesem Antefix um den gleichen Typus wie bei Kiel B 347). Zur Kritik an Carters Fundvergesellschaftungsbeobachtungen und Analysen, s. Dittmer-Herdejürgen 1979, S. 815, sowie Lippolis 1987, S. 142.

[58] Dieses unternahmen u.a. schon früh Holwerda 1899, bes. S. 131; Watzinger 1899; Pagenstecher 1912; und Klumbach 1937, IX und S. 95–99, welcher immerhin aufgrund der Funde von architektonischen Einzelgliedern in Tarent eine Rekonstruktion solcher kleinen Grabtempel für möglich hielt, sie jedoch nicht zeichnerisch durchführte und auch keinerlei Antefixprobleme diskutierte, während Smith 1976, S. 215, die Architekturdetails unvereinbar mit den Naiskosdarstellungen in der apulischen Vasenmalerei des 4. Jh. v. Chr. fand; s. hierzu auch Wuilleumier 1939, S. 553, sowie Lohmann 1979, mit weiterführender Lit. Nach wie vor wird auch in der neueren Lit. der Architekturdarstellung in der unteritalischen Keramik abbildender Charakter zuerkannt, wobei überlieferte tarentinische Architekturfragmente mit diesen Wiedergaben verglichen werden, so z.B. bei Engemann 1973, S. 16; Lippolis 1987, S. 139–154, sowie auch Prange 1989, S. 48. In Vorbreitung ist zu diesen Fragen die Dissertationsarbeit des Verf. über Architekturdarstellungen in der unteritalischen Keramik.

[59] Smith 1976, S. 215, hatte—wohl aufgrund solchartiger Hypogäen in der apulischen Chora sowie des Mangels an oberirdischen Grabbauten in Tarent—sicher zu unrecht vermutet, daß "the development of funerary luxury both at Tarentum and in Apulia was a subterranean affair"; s. für diese Hypogäen z.B. die Abb. 11 bei Langlotz 1957, S. 411, sowie Bartoccini 1936, S. 187, Abb. 100. De Juliis 1989, S. 30, hatte bei den monumentalen Kammergräbern eine Unterbrechung vom Ende des 5. bis zum Ende des 4. Jh. v. Chr.

solche Grabmäler ersetzten.[60] Trotz der großen Anzahl von Abbildungen der Naiskos-Grabbauten ab dem 2. Viertel bis zum Ende des 4. Jh. v. Chr. auf apulischen Vasen läßt sich mit den bisher aufgefunden Teilen von Tarentiner Grabbauten keine detailgenaue Übereinstimmung erkennen. Carter sprach sogar von "striking differences" zwischen den erhaltenen Naiskoselementen und den Darstellungen auf den Vasen,[61] doch hat Lippolis inzwischen für diverse Details der Funerärarchitektur Entsprechungen in der apulischen Keramik nachgewiesen.[62]

Dennoch bleiben Darstellungen von Antefixen auf apulischen Vasen äußerst selten und sind keinesfalls ausreichend für eine Beurteilung der realen Terrakottaobjekte.[63]

---

vermutet. Gerade Tarent jedoch scheint einen kontinuierlichen und parallelen Gebrauch verschiedenster Grabmalstypen in dieser Zeit zu bieten; s. hierzu Steingräber 1990.

[60] Vgl. Orsi 1917, S. 106–108, Abb. 10, und Lohmann 1979, S. 20, sowie jüngst Kaeser 1990, S. 199. Offensichtlich war die Verwendung von aufwendigen Grabbauten außerhalb der Kulturzentren wie Tarent schon aus finanziellen Gründen die Ausnahme, was die große Anzahl von Grabmalvasen im Hinterland erläutern würde. Carter 1990, S. 430 hat für die "rural necropolis" des ländlichen Pantanello, der bisher größten systematisch ausgegrabenen und dokumentierten Nekropole im Gebiet Metapontos, anhand von 255 Gräbern nachgewiesen, daß dort keine Naiskosbauten verwendet wurden, aber alle sonstigen bekannten Grabtypen (s. Carter 1990, S. 435, Abb. 13). Ebenso auch Cerchiai 1982, S. 289 für die Nekropole von Locri Epizefiri des 7. bis 4. Jh. v. Chr., sowie Gualtieri 1982, für Roccagloriosa im lukanischen Hinterland des 4./3. Jh. v. Chr.

[61] Carter 1975, S. 15–16.

[62] Lippolis 1979, Abb. 33–37 und Taf. 16–19.

[63] Zumeist nur in der Form als "Giebelantefix", z.B. im Tympanon der Naiskosdarstellung auf dem Volutenkrater in Tarent. Museum, Inv.-Nr. 9280 (= Trendall and Cambitoglou 1982, S. 771, 24/77); vgl. auch im von der apulischen Vasenmalerei abhängigen Lukanischen auf dem Volutenkrater aus Montesarchio in Salerno (= Trendall 1970 4/556e). Diese "Giebelantefixe" (Antepagmenta) sind wohl von den seit dem frühen 6. Jh. v. Chr. bekannten scheibenförmigen Akroteren mit figürlichen Darstellungen (vgl. Lauter-Bufé 1974, S. 215, Nr. 11, Abb. 2) herzuleiten, wie es z.B. ein westgriechischen Stück aus Salerno bei Neutsch 1956, Abb. 110, zeigt; s. auch Goldberg 1982, und zuletzt Kästner 1990.

Bei den apulischen Darstellungen von Naiskoi sind mir die Volutenkrater Neapel, NM H 2287, Inv.-Nr. 82358 (Trendall and Cambitoglou 1982, S. 784, 24/249, Taf. 290:2, 3) sowie Pavia, Istituto Archeologico, ohne Inv.-Nr. (Lohmann 1979, Kat.-Nr. A586, S. 245, Taf. 51:2 statt 51:3) bekannt, auf denen die Art der Antefixdarstellung über waagerechtem Gebälkstück nicht nur für die Naiskosdarstellung in Apulien äußerst selten ist und eine Vorliebe des Pavia-Malers (Amphoren-Gruppe, ca. 330–310 v. Chr.) zu sein scheint.

Die wenigen weiteren apulischen Beispiele mit Antefixdarstellungen betreffen den Tempel- und Theaterbereich, z.B. der Artemistempel auf dem Volutenkrater Neapel, NM H 3223, Inv.-Nr. 82113 (= Trendall and Cambitoglou 1978, S. 193, 8/3), ca. 370 v. Chr., der Kelchkrater Tarent, NM Inv.-Nr. 52.665 (= Trendall and Cambitoglou 1978, S. 39, 2/24, Taf. 12:1a, b), beide mit sehr stark stilisierten und in Tarent bislang nicht nachgewiesenen Antefixtypen, sowie der apulische Volutenkrater Bari, Museum Inv.-Nr. 3648 (= Trendall and Cambitoglou 1978, S. 210, 8/144), um 350 v. Chr., mit den dreiecksförmigen Antefixen auf der linken Traufseite eines Tempels (eventuell übermalt?), und das bekannte Theater-Fragment in Würzburg, Martin von Wagner-Museum, Inv.-Nr. H 4696 und 4701, ca. Mitte 4. Jh. v. Chr., welches runde archaisch-frühklassische oder archaisierende (wie z.B. in Crimisa im 5./4. Jh. v. Chr., s. Orsi 1933, S. 68 mit Taf. 9) Antefixtypen zeigt; vgl. zu diesem Typus z.B. Herdejürgen 1978, S. 89, Kat. C4 (Anfang 5. Jh. v. Chr.), sowie Herdejürgen 1978, S. 90, Kat. C5 (Mitte 5. Jh. v. Chr.); Adamesteanu 1960, S. 171, Taf. 9:b und Kästner 1982, Abb. 13–17. Vom ionischen Peripteraltempel des frühen 5. Jh. v. Chr. Nachbarstadt Metapont (s. Mertens 1979) stammen die die hiermit vergleichbaren Antefixtypen, die sicher auf tarentinischen Vorgaben beruhen, auch wenn Pagenstecher 1912, S. 15, nicht allzu wörtlich genommen werden dürfte, "alles, was in Metapont zutage

Die Vasenmaler Tarents waren ebenso wie die anderer Landschaften[64] nicht an der Abbildung detailgenauer Realarchitektur–obwohl die handwerklich-künstlerischen Fähigkeiten hierzu vorhanden waren–sondern eher an der Vermittlung einer für den antiken Betrachter geradezu plakativ wirksamen "optischen Botschaft"[65] interessiert, deren exakte Dechiffrierung uns heute ebenso schwerfällt wie die Interpretation der Kopfprotomen auf den Antefixen.[66]

Die Datierungsproblematik für tarentinische Antefixe ergibt sich zum einen aus den bereits erwähnten unklaren Funddokumentationen, zum anderen aus der ebenso unsicheren stilistischen Beurteilung der Reliefköpfe auf den Stirnziegeln. Herdejürgen hat versucht, das umfangreiche Terrakottamaterial Tarents entsprechend der historischen Entwicklung dieser Kunstlandschaft in drei Hauptphasen einzuteilen:[67]

*Phase 1:* Bis in die Mitte des 5. Jh. v. Chr. hinein besaß Tarent als einzige spartanische Kolonie in der Magna Graecia keinen bedeutenden politischen Einfluß. Innergriechische Konflikte, z.B. mit der achäischen Kolonie Metapont, sowie die Auseinandersetzungen mit den Einheimischen hemmten die ungestörte Entwicklung. Die Terrakotten dieser Zeit sind verhältnismäßig bescheiden, das Typenrepertoire ist beschränkt. Die Antefixe dieser Phase zeigen nur Gorgonen- und Silenstypen.

*Phase 2:* Ab der Mitte des 5. Jh. v. Chr. kann sich Tarent behaupten und entwickelt sich zur führenden griechischen Stadt in Unteritalien. Eine kriegerische Auseinandersetzung mit der von Athen mitinitiierten panhellenischen Kolonie Thurioi verläuft für Tarent erfolgreich. Den höchsten Entwicklungsstand erreicht Tarent in der ersten Hälfte des 4. Jh. v. Chr. unter der politischen Führung des berühmten Pythagoreers Archytas. Schon im Verlauf des dritten Viertels des 5. Jh. v. Chr. kommt es zu einer starken Erweiterung des koroplastischen Typenrepertoires, auch im Bereich der Antefixe.[68]

*Phase 3:* Etwa ab der Mitte des 4. Jh. v. Chr. beginnt der politische Abstieg, der mit dem Verlust der Selbständigkeit und der römischen Herrschaft über Tarent endet. In der Koroplastik zeichnet sich ab der Jahrhundertmitte eine Tendenz zur Ausrundung und Vertiefung der Formen ab, was sich auch bei den Antefixen ablesen läßt. Deutlich wird diese Entwicklung an dem Vergleich zwischen dem etwa an das Ende des 5. Jh. v. Chr. zu datierenden Antefixes Kiel B 350 mit dem von mir auf *ca.* 320 datierten Stück B 347.

---

kommt, ist tarentinisch." Zu der von Tarent ausgehenden Verbreitung, s. Orsi 1933, S. 71; Wuilleumier 1939, S. 425; Kingsley 1981, S. 52, sowie Kästner 1982, S. 126. Unklar, ob es sich um stark stilisierte Antefixe handelt, bleibt die Darstellung auf dem apulischen Volutenkrater in der Slg. Marotti, Inv.-Nr. 19; s. De Juliis 1982, Taf. 48:2 (unten).

[64] S. z.B. für die attische Keramik mit Darstellungen von Brunnenbauten bei Glaser 1983, S. 181.

[65] Zu diesem Begriff, vgl. Giuliani 1986, S. 14.

[66] Zur Wirkung und Aussagekraft von Bildinhalten in der Antike, s. Langlotz 1957, S. 398, 405–421; Martini 1986, S. 95, sowie letztens Stähler 1990, S. 206.

[67] Herdejürgen 1982, S. 19. Es ist mit ein entscheidendes Verdienst von Carters Untersuchungen der tarentinischen Plastik, die bis dato geläufigen Vergleiche mit den künstlerischen Entwicklungen anderer Landschaften, insbesondere Attikas, zu relativieren; s. hierzu Dittmers-Herdejürgen 1979, S. 815. Auch Himmelmann 1986, S. 194, mahnte kürzlich erneut zur Vorsicht bei stilistischen Vergleichen zwischen diesen Landschaften.

[68] Vgl. z.B. Brandes 1988, Kat. Nr. II:13, 14, 19, 20.

Die Problematik bei der stilistischen Beurteilung von Terrakotta-Objekten ist allerdings, daß die aus der Matrizentechnik gewonnenen Produkte relativ einheitliche Massengüter sind, und es durch den Gebrauch von Matrizengenerationen über einen längeren Zeitraum hinweg zu Stilretardationen gegenüber anderen Kunstgattungen kommt, die mit der herkömmlichen Stilkritik nur unzureichend analysiert werden können.[69] Die oben in der Tabelle genannten Daten sind demnach nur unter Vorbehalt zu verstehen.[70]

Die Tarentiner Reliefkopfantefix-Typen erscheinen in großer Variationsbreite,[71] von denen nur die archaischen und die früheren klassischen als Gorgonen- und Silensantefixtypen inhaltlich gedeutet werden konnten.[72] Die späteren klassischen sowie die frühhellenistischen Typen entziehen sich bisher einer konkreten Deutung und haben teilweise deutlich voneinander abweichende Benennungen erhalten. Ab dem späten 5. und frühen 4. Jh. v. Chr. treten zunehmend und vor allem im Tarentiner Einflußbereich neue Antefixtypen mit Kopfprotomen auf, die sich von den bisherigen traditionellen Gorgonen- und Silenstypen absetzen und eine Tendenz zur "Humanisierung" des dämonischen Charakters aufweisen.[73]

Die Kieler Antefixgruppe besteht aus sechs Typen und zwei dazugehörigen Varianten.[74] Die Benennung dieser Reliefköpfe auf den Stirnziegeln aus Kiel ist aufgrund des Fehlens eindeutiger Attribute bzw. der bis dahin nicht überlieferten Kombination verschiedener Attribute ungesichert. Herdejürgen hatte für solche Typen die Frage aufgeworfen, ob es sich bei den Kopfantefixtypen dieser Art um die Darstellung bekannter Figuren in variierter Form oder um die Darstellung neuer, im einzelnen nicht bekannter Figuren handelt.[75] Die Typenbezeichnung für Kiel B 346/351 lautet in der archäologischen Literatur gewöhnlicherweise "Artemis-Bendis", die für B 348/408 "Io".[76] Für die anderen Typen existiert keine feste

[69] Zur Terminologie und Technik des Reproduktionsprozesses bei der Terrakottaproduktion mit Hilfe des Matrizeneinsatzes (Hohlformen), s. Brandes 1988, S. 55–62, 91–92; ferner vgl.: Nicholls 1952; Nicholls 1984, S. 24; Olbrich 1979, S. 18. Ein Hilfsmittel in der Beurteilung der relativen Abfolge von Antefixserien aus Matrizen bietet der Trocken- und Brennschwund bzw. die Abnahme der Plastizität: s. hierzu Jastrow 1941; Hitzl 1985, S. 13. Wiederkehr in Schwinzer und Steingräber 1990, S. 118. Zu den Einschränkungen bei diesem Verfahren, s. Giuliani 1988.

[70] Zusätzlich sind typologische Beurteilungen der Kieler Antefixe vorgenommen worden, s. Brandes 1988, S. 80–91. Zur typologischen Entwicklung dieser Gattung zuletzt auch Krauskopf 1990, S. 25–26.

[71] Laviosa 1954, S. 217, Anm. 1, nennt 120 Typen und zeigt davon eine Auswahl von 50 Typen.

[72] S. z.B. bei Herdejürgen 1978, S. 84, 86. Winter 1978, S. 45, versuchte, die inhaltliche Deutung der auf den Antefixen erscheinenden Köpfen über die Zuweisung an bestimmten Gottheiten gewidmete Tempel zu führen, ein Unternehmen, das m.E. bei der häufig unklaren Fundsituation und der fehlenden literarischen Überlieferung in Unteritalien zu keinen eindeutigen Ergebnissen führen kann. Ein ähnlicher Ansatz auch bei von Vacano 1980, S. 470, sowie bei Mertens-Horn 1978, S. 63. Vgl. dagegen Robinson 1923, S. 3. Eher als der Bezug auf eine bestimmte Gottheit scheint mir der apotropäische Schutzcharakter dieser Stücke an einem Gebäude wichtig. Für den Zeitraum unserer Kieler Antefixe entfiele zudem auch diese hermeneutische Möglichkeit, da diese Stücke höchstwahrscheinlich von Sepulkralgebäuden und nicht mehr von Tempeln bestimmbarer Gottheiten stammen; vgl. Brandes 1988, S. 106–107.

[73] Kästner 1982, S. 115. Zur Entwicklung des Gorgoneions, s. Floren 1977, mit weiterführender Lit.

[74] Typusvariationen liegen vor bei Kiel B 346 bzw. B 351 sowie Kiel B 348 bzw. 408.

[75] Herdejürgen 1982, S. 112, und Jucker 1961, S. 200 mit Bedenken, "... ob sich die bildhaft angedeutete Idee für Darsteller und Betrachter jedesmal zu einer benennbaren Gottheit verdichtet haben."

[76] "Artemis-Bendis": Die Bandbreite bisheriger Benennungen allein für diesen Typus zeigt die folgende Auswahl: Viola 1881, S. 544, Nr. 47 ("Omphale"); Dümmler 1883, S. 200–201 ("Artemis"); Walters

Konvention hinsichtlich der Benennung: so kann Kiel B 347 als "Mänaden"-Typus, B 349 als "Pan"-Typus, B 350 als "Gorgo (-Medusa)"-Typus und B 407 als "Hermes"-Typus bezeichnet werden, doch ist keiner dieser Typen ikonographisch eindeutig in dieser Erscheinungsform belegbar.[77] Nur das Antefix des Typus "Gorgo-Medusa" stammt noch aus dem 5. Jh. v. Chr., als die tradierten ikonographischen Schemata erst aufzubrechen beginnen.[78] Die überlieferten Typen gewinnen im Verlauf des 4. Jh. v. Chr. in Unteritalien ein "neues dämonisches Gesicht",[79] dessen Interpretation ähnliche Schwierigkeiten bereitet wie auch die der zahlreich auftretenden Büsten in der unteritalischen Vasenmalerei insbesondere des letzten Drittels des 4. Jh. v. Chr.[80] Eventuell bestehen hier Zusammenhänge in der Verwendung dieser diversen Typen menschlicher und dämonischer Protomen und Gesichter in den verschiedenen Gattungen des spätklassisch-frühhellenistischen Apuliens,[81] die sich nach wie vor einer konkreten akzeptablen Deutung entziehen.[82]

---

1903, D 662 ("Herakles"); Laviosa 1954, S. 241 ("Medusa"); Langlotz 1960, S. 13, Anm. 15 ("Erinys"); Schauenburg 1974, S. 176 (gegen verschiedene Deutungen); Carter 1975, S. 103 ("Perseus"). Die Aussage von Kenfield 1990, S. 272, daß "lion-headed antefixes are rare in the Greek world," gilt hiermit zumindest für Tarent so nicht.

"Io": vgl. Schauenburg 1989, S. 121.

[77] Brandes 1988, S. 116–137. Hierzu kürzlich auch Krauskopf 1990, S. 26.

[78] Winter 1978, S. 57: "... antefixes lost their initial meaning"; Kästner 1982, S. 115, nimmt aufgrund der fortschreitenden Humanisierung des Dämonengesichtes eine Zunahme des dekorativen Charakters an, doch läßt sich diese Überlegung nicht beweisen. Ich sehe eher—wie schon Herdejürgen 1978, S. 84, es andeutete—eine enge Verbindung mit des Jenseitsglaubens, der sich in diesen dämonisch-dionysischen Köpfen ausdrückt.

[79] Herdejürgen 1983, S. 4. Schon Wuilleumier 1939, S. 427, erwähnt, daß "plusieurs types féminins apparaissent à partir de 400 av.C."

[80] Z.B. apulische Loutrophore im Privatbesitz, Slg. Arden, Scottsdale, Arizona, des Meo-Evoli-Malers (= Trendall and Cambitoglou 1982, S. 935, 28/140, Taf. 368:5). Hier erscheint zum einen eine Frauenbüste im Profil in einem Naiskos und zum anderen eine weibliche Büste mit Flügeln oberhalb dieses Grabbaus, was bei diesem Maler auch am Volutenkrater Tarent, Museum Inv.-Nr. 61465, auftritt; apulische Situla in Ruvo, Slg. Jatta 1371 (DAI Inst.-Neg. Nr. 64.1231), mit dem ebenfalls geflügelten jugendlichen Kopf, der aus einer Blüte hervorwächst; Frgt. ehem. Kunsthandel Rom (hier Pl. 93:c nach DAI Inst.-Neg. Nr. 63.482) mit einer am Hals abgeschnittenen Mädchenbüste. Ein durchaus dem Kieler Antefix B 347 vergleichbarer Kopf auf einer apulischen Oinochoe in Bochum, s. Kunisch 1972, S. 138–139, Nr. 119, aus der Mitte des 4. Jh. v. Chr. (wohl eher später), der ebda. als "Erinnye" benannt wird.

[81] S. z.B. auch die Köpfe auf einer tarentinischen Silberschale bei Wuilleumier 1939, Taf. 19:1. Ähnliche Phänomene existieren gleichzeitig auch in anderen Kunstlandschaften, s. z.B. die 24 griechischen Terrakotta-Appliken des späten 4. Jh. v. Chr. "probably the ornament of a wood sarcophagus, ... reportedly from Naukratis/Egypt," Auktionskat. Sotheby's New York, 18.06.1991, Nr. 84. Diese Typen könnten rein formal durchaus auch tarentinischer Provenienz sein; vgl. etwa die Gorgoneionappliken in De Juliis 1985, S. 395, Nr. 37, 38.

[82] Hierzu zählen auch die im 4. Jh. v. Chr. auf den apulischen Volutenkrateren in den Rotellen auftretenden Gorgonen- und sonstigen Masken, s. z.B. Tarent, Privatbesitz Ragusa (DAI Inst.-Neg. Nr. 68.4633), oder *CVA Warschau, Nationalmuseum* 4 [Polen 7] 297 IV Dr, Taf. 18:1–5. Hierzu insbesondere Giuliani 1988, mit Taf. 45–47. Allgemein zu dem Problem der (Ranken-) Köpfe, die laut Trendall 1984, S. 5: "typical of the developed Apulian style" sind: Jucker 1961, bes. S. 197, und jüngst Stähler 1990, S. 204. Mehrfach dazu auch: Schauenburg 1957; Schauenburg 1961, S. 97, und Schauenburg 1989.

Trotz der reich überlieferten Gattung der Tarentiner Terrakotta-Antefixe des späten 5. und 4. Jh. v. Chr., denen hier weitere acht Stücke aus der Kieler Antikensammlung hinzugefügt werden konnten, müssen einige Fragen nach wie vor als ungeklärt gelten.[83]

## BIBLIOGRAPHIE

Adamesteanu, D. 1960. "Gela," *NSc* 14, S. 67–246

———. 1974. "L'attività archeologica in Basilicata," *XIV AttiTaranto*, S. 247–259

———. 1982. "Siris e Metaponto," *ASAtene* 60, n.s. 44, S. 301–313

———. 1990. "Greeks and Natives in Basilicata," in Descoeudres 1990, S. 143–150

Anderson, J. R. 1883. "Antefixes from Tarentum," *JHS* 4, S. 117–121

Andressai, G., A. Alessio, und A. D'Amicas. 1986. *Les ors hellénistique de Tarente* (Kat. Tarent), Tarent, S. 6–65

Andrén, A. 1940. *Architectural Terracottas from Etrusco-Italic Temples* (Acta Instituti Romani Regni Sueciae VI), Lund/Leipzig

*AttiTaranto* = *Atti del Convegno di Studi sulla Magna Graecia*, Tarent/Neapel

Bartoccini, R. 1936. "Taranto," *NSc* 12, S. 107–232

Belli, C. 1970. *Il Tesoro de Taras*, Rom

Bernabò Brea, L. 1940. "Taranto," *NSc* 18, S. 426–505

Brandes, B. 1988. *Eine Gruppe unteritalischer Antefixe in der Kieler Antikensammlung*, Kiel

Brauer, G. C. 1986. *Taras: Its History and Coinage*, New York

Breitenstein, N. 1941. *Catalogue of the Terracottas in the Danish National Museum*, Kopenhagen

Carter, J. C. 1970. "Relief Sculptures from the Necropolis of Taranto," *AJA* 74, S. 125–137

———. 1973. "The Figure in the Naiskos," *OpRom* 9, S. 97–104

———. 1975. *The Sculpture of Taras* (Transactions of the American Philological Association, n.s. 65, no. 79), Philadelphia

———. 1990. "Metapontum–Population and Wealth," in Descoeudres 1990, S. 405–441

Cerchiai, L. 1982. "Sesso e classi di età nelle necropoli greche di Locri Epizefiri," in *La mort, les morts dans les sociétés anciennes* (Kongressbericht Neapel), G. Gnoli und J.-P. Vernant, Hrsg., Neapel 1982, S. 289

Coarelli, F. 1970. "Il dibattito," *X AttiTaranto*, S. 201–203

Cook, R. M. 1974. Rezension, *CR*, n.s. 24, S. 159–161

*Corinth* IV, i = I. Thallon-Hill und L. S. King, *Decorated Architectural Terracottas* (Corinth IV, i), Cambridge, Mass. 1929

Coulson, W. D. E. 1990. Welcoming address, in *Hesperia* 59, S. 11–12

Damgaard Andersen, H. 1990. "The Feline Waterspouts of the Lateral Sima from the Upper Building at Poggio Civitate, Murlo," *OpRom* 18, S. 61–98

D'Amicis, A. 1984. "Taranto," *Taras* 4, S. 47–84

D'Andria, F. 1990. "Greek Influence in the Adriatic," in Descoeudres 1990, S. 281–289

Darsow, W. 1938. *Sizilische Dachterrakotten*, Berlin

De Juliis, E. M. 1982. "L'attività archeologica in Puglia," *XXII AttiTaranto*, S. 503–531

———. 1985. *Gli ori di Taranto in età ellenistica* (Kat. Tarent u.a. Orte), Mailand

———. 1989. "Die tarentinische Goldschmiedekunst," in *Kat. Tarent*, S. 23–27

De Juliis, E. M., und D. Laiacono. 1985. *Taranto. Il Museo Archeologico*, Tarent

Descoeudres, J.-P., Hrsg. 1990. *Greek Colonists and Native Populations: Proceedings of the First International Congress of Classical Archaeology, Sydney 1985*, Sydney

---

[83] Ich danke der American School of Classical Studies at Athens, insbesondere N. A. Winter, für die Gelegenheit zum Vortrag dieses Artikels, der aus meiner unpublizierten Magisterarbeit 1988 an der Universität Kiel hervorgegangen ist (s.u.). Dieser Aufsatz ist Konrad Schauenburg in Dankbarkeit gewidmet.

Abbildungsverzeichnis: Pls. 91–93:b: Kiel, Antikensammlung (Photos J. Raeder); Pl. 93:c: Frgt. Privatbesitz (DAI Rom Inst.-Neg. 63.482). Ich danke B. Schmaltz und J. Raeder von der Antikensammlung der Kunsthalle zu Kiel für die Publikationserlaubnis sowie M. Prange für seine Unterstützung.

Dittmers-Herdejürgen, H. 1979. Rezension zu Carter 1975, *Gnomon* 51, S. 815

Drago, C. 1956. *Il Museo Nazionale di Taranto*, Rom

Dümmler, F. 1883. "Tarenti Repertis," *AdI* 55, S. 192–207

Engemann, J. 1973. *Untersuchungen zur Sepulkralsymbolik der späteren römischen Kaiserzeit*, Münster

Ervin, M. 1968. "News Letter from Greece," *AJA* 72, S. 265–278

Floren, J. 1977. *Studien zur Typologie des Gorgoneion*, Münster

Forti, L., Hrsg., 1966. *Letteratura e arte figurata nella Magna Grecia*, Soprintendenza alle Antichità della Puglia, Hrsg., S. 7–36, Fasano

Foti, G. 1968. "L'attività archeologica in Calabria," *VIII AttiTaranto*, S. 153–162

George, W. S., und A. M. Woodward. 1929. "The Architectural Terracottas," in R. M. Dawkins, Hrsg., *The Sanctuary of Artemis Orthia at Sparta*, London 1929, S. 117–144

Giglioli, G. Q. 1935. *L'arte etrusca*, Mailand

Giuliani, L. 1986. *Bildnis und Botschaft. Hermeneutische Untersuchungen zur Bildniskunst der römischen Republik*, Frankfurt am Main

———. 1988. "Vervielfältigte Lockenköpfe," in *Kanon. Festschrift E. Berger*, M. Schmidt, Hrsg., Basel, S. 159–165

Glaser, F. 1983. *Antike Brunnenbauten in Griechenland*, Wien

Goldberg, M. Y. 1982. "Archaic Greek Akroteria," *AJA* 86, S. 193–217

Graepler, D. 1984. "Untersuchungen zu den hellenistischen Terrakotten aus Tarent," *Taras* 4, S. 85–118

———. 1988. "Die hellenistische Koroplastik von Tarent" (Diss. Maximilians-Universität München 1988)

———. 1989. "Zur Geschichte der archäologischen Forschung in Tarent," in *Kat. Tarent*, S. 39–46

———. 1990. "Neue Forschungen zum hellenistischen Tarent," in Schwinzer und Steingräber 1990, S. 88–96

Green, J. R. 1977. "More Gnathia Pottery in Bonn," *AA [JdI* 92], S. 551–563

Gualtieri, M. 1982. "Cremation among the Lucanians," *AJA* 86, S. 475–479

Guzzo, P., A. Alessio, und A. D'Amicas, 1988. *Il Museo di Taranto*, Tarent

Herdejürgen, H. 1971. *Die tarentinischen Terrakotten des 6. bis 4. Jhs. v. Chr. im Antikenmuseum Basel*, Basel

———. 1978. *Götter, Menschen und Dämonen*, Basel

———. 1982. "Terrakotten und Bronzen," in *Antike Kunstwerke aus der Sammlung Ludwig II*, E. Berger, Hrsg., Basel

———. 1983. "Zur Deutung tarentinischer Terrakotten," *AA [JdI* 98], S. 45–55

Herrmann, W. 1966. "Grabungen und Funde," *AA [JdI* 81], S. 255–367

*Hesperia* 59 = *Proceedings of the First International Conference on Archaic Greek Architectural Terracottas, Athens, December 2–4, 1988* (*Hesperia* 59, 1990), N. A. Winter, Hrsg.

Higgins, R. A. 1954. *Catalogue of the Terracottas in the Department of Greek and Roman Antiquities, British Museum* I, repr. Oxford 1969

Himmelmann, N. 1986. "Ein tarentinisches Kalksteinrelief," in *Festschrift für Konrad Schauenburg*, E. Böhr und W. Martini, Hrsg., Mainz, S. 193–195

Hitzl, K. 1985. "Kretische Schalengriffe," *StädelJb*, N.F. 10, S. 13–26

Holwerda, J. H. 1899. *Die attischen Gräber der Blüthezeit*, Leiden

Jastrow, E. 1941. "Abformung und Typenwandel in der antiken Tonplastik," *OpArch* 2, S. 1–28

Jucker, H. 1961. *Das Bildnis im Blätterkelch*, Olten/Schweiz

Kaeser, B. 1990. "Werte und Sinnbilder," in *Kunst der Schale*, K. Vierneisel und B. Kaeser, Hrsg., München, S. 197–203

Kästner, V. 1982. "Archaische Baukeramik der Westgriechen" (Diss. Humboldt-Universität Berlin-Ost 1982)

———. 1984. "Archaische Frauenkopfantefixe aus Capua," *FuB* 24, S. 66–74

———. 1989. "Gorgoneionantefix aus Süditalien," *FuB* 27, S. 115–128

———. 1990. "Scheibenförmige Akrotere in Griechenland und Italien," in *Hesperia* 59, S. 251–264

*Kat. Satricum* = Nederlands Instituut te Rome, Hrsg., *Satricum—nieuw licht op een oude Stad*, Den Haag 1986

*Kat. Tarent* = Museum für Kunst und Gewerbe Hamburg, Hrsg., *Das Gold von Tarent*, Hamburg 1989

Kenfield, J. F. 1990. "An East Greek Master Coroplast," in *Hesperia* 59, S. 265–274

Kingsley, B. M. 1976. "Tarentine Terracottas in the J. Paul Getty Museum" (Diss. University of California, Berkeley 1976)

———. 1981. "Coroplastic Workshops at Taras," *GettyMusJ* 9, S. 41–52

Klumbach, H. 1937. *Tarentiner Grabkunst*, Reutlingen

Knoop, R. R. 1987. *Antefixa Satricana*, Assen

Koch, H. 1912. *Dachterrakotten aus Campanien*, Berlin

———. 1915. "Studien zu den campanischen Dachterrakotten," *RM* 30, S. 1–115

Krauskopf, I. 1990. "Der Schild der Parthenos und der Typus der Medusa Rondanini," in Schwinzer und Steingräber 1990, S. 22–34

Kunisch, N. 1972. *Katalog Sammlung Funcke in der Ruhr-Universität Bochum*, Bochum

Langlotz, E. 1957. "Vom Sinngehalt attischer Vasenbilder," in *Eine Freundesgabe–Festschrift für Robert Böhringer*, E. Böhringer und W. Hoffmann, Hrsg., Tübingen, S. 397–421

———. 1960. *Der triumphierende Perseus*, Köln

Lauter-Bufé, H. 1974. "Entstehung und Entwicklung des lakonischen Akroters," *AM* 89, S. 205–230

Laviosa, C. 1954. "Le antefisse fittili di Taranto," *ArchCl* 6, S. 217–250

Lenormant, F. 1881–1882. "Notes archéologiques sûr la terre d'Otrante," *GazArch* 7, S. 25–127

Lindros Wohl, B. 1984. "Three Female Head Antefixes from Etruria," *GettyMusJ* 12, S. 111–118

Lippolis, E. 1987. "Organizzazione delle necropoli," in *Römische Gräberstrassen, Kolloquium München 1985*, H. v. Hesberg und P. Zanker, Hrsg., München, S. 139–154

Lohmann, H. 1979. *Grabmäler auf unteritalischen Vasen (Archäologische Forschungen 7)*, Berlin

Lo Porto, F. G. 1970. "Topografia antica di Taranto," *X AttiTaranto*, S. 343–383

Lunsingh Scheurleer, R. A. 1968. *Griek in het klein*, Amsterdam

Manfredini, A. 1969. "Terrecotte archaiche tarentine del Fondo Giovinazzi," *RivStCl* 17, S. 75–89

Marconi, P. 1931. *Himera*, Rom

Martin, R. 1965. *Manuel d'architecture grecque* I, Paris

Martini, W. 1986. "Zwei erotische Vasenbilder," in *Festschrift für Konrad Schauenburg*, E. Böhr und W. Martini, Hrsg., Mainz, S. 95–100

Mertens, D. 1975. "Metaponto," *BdA* 60, S. 26–49

———. 1977. "Der ionische Tempel in Metapont," *Architectura*, S. 152–162

———. 1979. "Der ionische Tempel von Metapont," *RM* 86, S. 103–140

———. 1990. "Some Principal Features of West Greek Colonial Architecture," in Descoeudres 1990, S. 373–382

Mertens-Horn, M. 1978. "Beobachtungen an dädalischen Tondächern," *JdI* 93, S. 30–65

———. 1988. *Die Löwenkopf-Wasserspeier des griechischen Westens im 6. und 5. Jh. v. Chr. (Mitteilungen des Deutschen Archäologischen Instituts, Römische Abteilung. Ergänzungsheft 28)*, Mainz am Rhein

Mertens-Horn, M., und L. Viola. 1990. "Archaische Tondächer westgriechischer Typologie in Delphi und Olympia," in *Hesperia* 59, S. 235–250

Metzler, D. 1985. "Zur Geschichte Apuliens im Altertum," in *Apulien. Kulturberührungen in griechischer Zeit* (Kat. Münster), K. Stähler, Hrsg., Münster, S. 14–24

Neils, J. 1976. "The Terracotta Gorgoneia of Poggio Civitate (Murlo)," *RM* 83, S. 1–29

Neutsch, B. 1956. "Archäologische Grabungen und Funde in Unteritalien," *AA* [*JdI* 71], S. 195–450

Nicholls, R. V. 1952. "Type, Group and Series," *BSA* 47, S. 217–226

———. 1984. "La fabrication des terres cuites," *Histoire et Archéologie* 81, S. 24–31

*Nuovi Quaderni* 1 = *Studi in onore di Filippo Magi*, Istituto di Archeologica di Perugia, Hrsg., Perugia 1979

Olbrich, G. 1979. *Archaische Statuetten eines Metapontiner Heiligtums (Studia Archaeologica 23)*, Rom

Orlandini, P. 1971. "Aspetti dell'arte indigena in Magna Graecia," *XI AttiTaranto*, S. 273–308

Orlandini, P., und P. Griffo. 1970. *Agrigento*, Florent

Orsi, P. 1917. "Locri Epizefiri," *NSc* 14, S. 101–167

———. 1933. *Templum Apollonis Alaei ad Crimisa promontorium*, Rom

Pagenstecher, R. 1912. *Antike Grabdenkmäler in Unteritalien*, Strassburg
Pape, M. 1975. "Griechische Kunstwerke aus Kriegsbeute und ihre öffentliche Aufstellung in Rom" (Diss. Universität Hamburg 1975)
Phillips, K. M., Jr. 1968a. "Perseus and Andromeda," *AJA* 72, S. 1–23
———. 1968b. "Bryn Mawr College Excavations in Tuscany, 1967," *AJA* 72, S. 121–124
———. 1990. "The Lateral Sima from Poggio Civitate (Murlo)," *OpRom* 18, S. 139–157
Prange, M. 1989. "Grabformen und Beigaben der 'Schmuckgräber' von Tarent," in *Kat. Tarent*, S. 47–52
Rastrelli, A. 1979. "Un'antefissa a testa femminile da Orvieto," in *Nuovi Quaderni* 1, S. 149–153
Reusser, C. 1980. "Eine campanische Dachterrakotte," *Hefte des archäologischen Seminares in Bern* 6, S. 5–10
Riis, P. J. 1981. *Etruscan Types of Heads*, Kopenhagen
Robinson, D. M. 1923. "Etruscan-Campanian Antefixes," *AJA* 27, S. 1–22
Roebuck, M. 1990. "Archaic Architectural Terracottas from Corinth," in *Hesperia* 59, S. 47–63
Schauenburg, K. 1957. "Zur Symbolik unteritalischer Rankenmotive," *RM* 64, S. 198–221
———. 1961. "Göttergeliebte auf unteritalischen Vasen," *AuA* 10, S. 77–101
———. 1974. "Bendis in Unteritalien (?)," *JdI* 89, S. 137–186
———. 1989. "Zu einigen Grabkrateren des Malers von Kopenhagen," *NumAntCl* 18, S. 119–149
Schwinzer, E., und S. Steingräber, Hrsg. 1990. *Kunst und Kultur der Magna Graecia* (*Deutscher Archäologen Verband Schriften* XI), Tübingen
Smith, H. R. W. 1976. *Funerary Symbolism in Apulian Vase-Painting*, Berkeley
Stähler, K. 1990. "Der Harmonie entspricht abgeklärtes Wesen," *Boreas* 13, S. 203–212
Steingräber, S. 1980. "Zum Phänomen der etruskisch-italischen Votivköpfe," *RM* 87, S. 215–253
———. 1990. "Traditionelle und innovative Elemente," in Schwinzer und Steingräber 1990, S. 78–87
Stibbe, C. M. 1984. "Reisende lakonische Töpfer, in *Ancient Greek and Related Pottery. Proceedings of the International Vase Symposium in Amsterdam* (Allard Pierson Series 5), H. A. G. Brijder, Hrsg., Amsterdam, S. 135–138
Stopponi, S. 1979. "Terrecotte architettoniche dal sanctuario di Punta della Vipera," in *Nuovo Quaderni* 1, S. 249–270
Strong, S. A. 1914. "The Architectural Decoration in Terracotta from Early Latin Temples in the Museo di Villa Giulia," *JRS* 4, S. 157–181
Todisco, L. 1990. "Eracle," *MEFRA* 102, S. 901–957
Torelli, M. 1979. "Terrecotte architettoniche arcaiche da Gravisca," in *Nuovo Quaderni* 1, S. 305–312
Trendall, A. D. 1967. *The Red-Figured Vases of Lucania, Campania and Sicily*, Oxford
———. 1984. "Medea at Eleusis," *Record of the Art Museum, Princeton University* 43, S. 42–58
Trendall, A. D., und A. Cambitoglou. 1978. *The Red-figured Vases of Apulia*, I, *Early and Middle Apulian*, Oxford
———. 1982. *The Red-figured Vases of Apulia* II, Oxford
Van Buren, E. D. 1921. *Figurative Terra-Cotta Revetments in Etruria and Latium*, London
———. 1923. *Archaic Fictile Revetments in Sicily and Magna Graecia*, London
———. 1926. *Greek Fictile Revetments in the Archaic Period*, London
van der Mejden, E. 1990. "Terrakotta-Arulae," in Schwinzer und Steingräber 1990, S. 127–131
Viola, L. 1881. "Taranto," *NSc* 6, S. 376–436 (= *Memorie. Atti della Accademia nazionale dei Lincei, Classe di scienze morali, storiche e filologiche* 9, S. 487–546)
von Vacano, O.-W. 1980. "Überlegungen zu einer Gruppe von Antefixen aus Pyrgi," in *Forschungen und Funde–Festschrift für B. Neutsch*, F. Krinzinger, B. Otto, und E. Walde-Psenner, Hrsg., Innsbruck, S. 463–475
Wallenstein, K. 1971. *Korinthische Plastik des 7. und 6. Jhs. v. Chr.*, Bonn
Walters, H. B. 1903. *Catalogue of the Terracottas in the British Museum*, London
Watzinger, C. 1899. *De Vasculis Pictis Tarentinis*, Darmstadt
Wiederkehr, E. 1990. "Protomen aus dem Heiligtum der Demeter Malophoros in Selinunt," in Schwinzer und Steingräber 1990, S. 117–126

Winter, N. A. 1974. "Terracotta Representations of Human Heads Used as Architectural Decoration in the Archaic Period" (Diss. Bryn Mawr College 1974)

———. 1978. "Archaic Architectural Terracottas Decorated with Human Heads," *RM* 85, S. 27–58

———. 1990. "Defining Regional Styles in Archaic Greek Architectural Terracottas," in *Hesperia* 59, S. 13–32

Wolters, P. 1925. "Götter oder Heroen?" in *Festschrift für Paul Arndt*, München, S. 9–13

Wuilleumier, P. 1939. *Tarent des origines à la conquête romaine*, Paris

BERND BRANDES-DRUBA

DUEVELSBEKER WEG 4
D-24105 Kiel
Bundesrepublik Deutschland

# A LATE CLASSICAL SIMA FROM HERACLEA IN LUCANIA

(PLATES 94, 95)

IN 1970 the *Soprintendenza Archeologica* of Basilicata excavated the area of the so-called Archaic Temple in the valley to the south of the hill of Policoro (ancient Siris-Heraclea) (Fig. 1).[1] The fragmentary construction that appeared (Fig. 2), until today known only from preliminary reports, was identified as a temple,[2] but its dating remained controversial. The mixed construction technique of the foundation walls and some architectural features of the ground plan (the hypothetical row of columns on the wall in front of the pronaos, the possible buttresses of the naos) appeared to indicate an Archaic construction, but without any certainty.[3] Unfortunately, the reexamination of data from the excavations has not so

---

[1] This ongoing research is extracted from my thesis work on Greek archaeology at the University in Florence. I am grateful to the *Soprintendente* of Basilicata, Dr. Angelo Bottini, and particularly to Prof. Dinu Adamesteanu for permission to study this material. A special thanks to Dr. Madeleine Mertens-Horn for her confidence in me and good advice as always; to Dr. Nancy Winter for her real kindness in allowing my attendance at this conference; not least to Prof. Luigi Beschi, my first teacher, for all that he taught and still gives me and for his patient humanity. Thanks are also due to Nunzia Arcuti Armento for help and advice with photos, and Carmela Petraccone for inking the site and temple plans.

[2] Now, only the foundations of the building, probably a peripteral temple set in the so-called area B (*ca.* 32.80 × 15.20 m.), remain. For the bibliography, see Adamesteanu 1969, pp. 199–200; Adamesteanu 1970/1971, pp. 136–138; Adamesteanu 1970, pp. 483–484, pl. LXXXII; Adamesteanu 1974, p. 97; Mertens 1976, p. 185; Adamesteanu and Dilthey 1978, p. 518; Mertens 1980a, p. 45; Adamesteanu 1980, pp. 87–88; Adamesteanu 1982, p. 307; Gullini 1983, pp. 237–238, pl. XI:1; Adamesteanu 1985a, p. 101; Adamesteanu 1985b, p. 63, fig. 28; Edlund 1987, p. 112; Torelli 1990, p. 11.

[3] Gullini (1983, p. 238) talked about a Proto-Archaic temple, "forse databile anche nel primo quarto del VI secolo," with a wooden peristasis and walls of unfired brick. As far as the mixed building technique is concerned, here documented by the presence of some big blocks of sandstone and conglomerate, approximately squared, and of simple pebbles, its use is commonly acknowledged in the most ancient buildings (cf. Dinsmoor 1950, p. 58) as well as in domestic structures (cf. *Olynthus* VII, pp. 223–224) and in smaller ones generally (cf. Fiorentini 1985, pp. 104–105, buildings I, II, V–VIII; see also Mertens 1980b, pp. 341–343). In any event, it cannot be excluded that in some areas like this, which lack good building stone (cf. Mertens 1981, p. 116; Mertens 1990, p. 374), the use of such a technique continues in some important buildings as well. The hypothetical solution of a row of columns in front of the pronaos seems to recall closely the similar solution adopted for the first phase of Temple B (Heraion) in Metapontum, begun in the second quarter of the 6th century B.C. and unfinished in its original plan (for this temple, see Adamesteanu 1974, pp. 27–28; Mertens 1973, pp. 201–203; Adamesteanu 1976, p. 156; Mertens 1976, pp. 172–174; Mertens 1980b, pp. 329–336; Gullini 1983, p. 240). The incomplete state of the "Archaic Temple" plan, however, requires caution. For the supposed buttresses of the naos, see Mertens 1976, p. 185. The Archaic material recovered from the excavation (mainly some Late Daedalic terracotta statuettes and a few fragments of Ionic bowls) cannot be clearly connected with the architectural structure in question (see note 4 below). For this Archaic material (particularly the statuettes), see Adamesteanu 1981, p. 87, pl. VII:2; Rolley 1980, p. 186, pls. XXXV:2, XXXVII:3; Adamesteanu 1982, p. 307, figs. 5, 6; Orlandini 1983, p. 335, fig. 310.

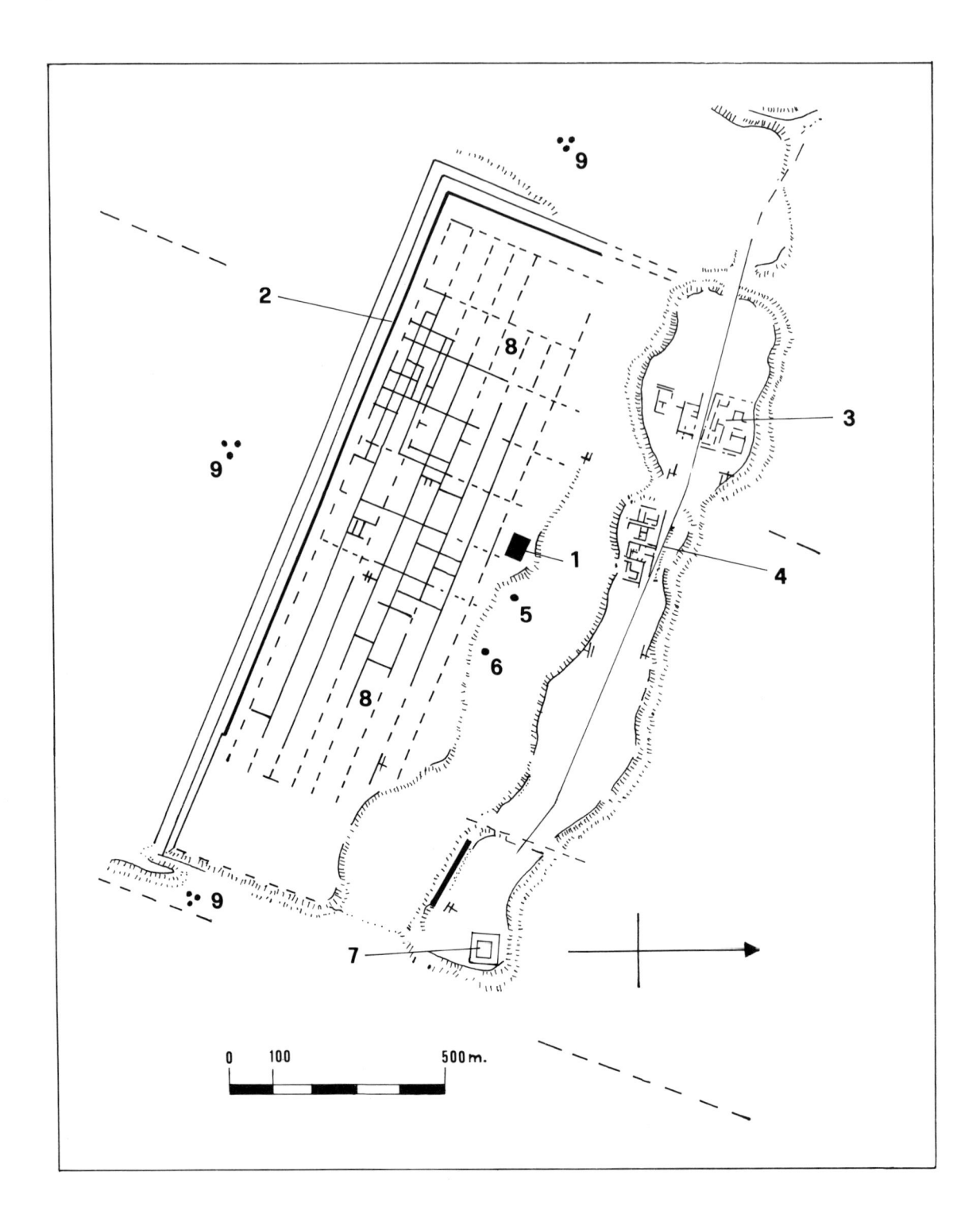

Fig. 1. Policoro, site plan of Heraclea. 1. Museum; 2. City walls; 3. House quarter; 4. Potters' quarter; 5. "Archaic Temple"; 6. Temple of Demetra; 7. so-called Baron's Castle; 8. City area; 9. Necropolis (from Adamesteanu 1985a, fig. 43)

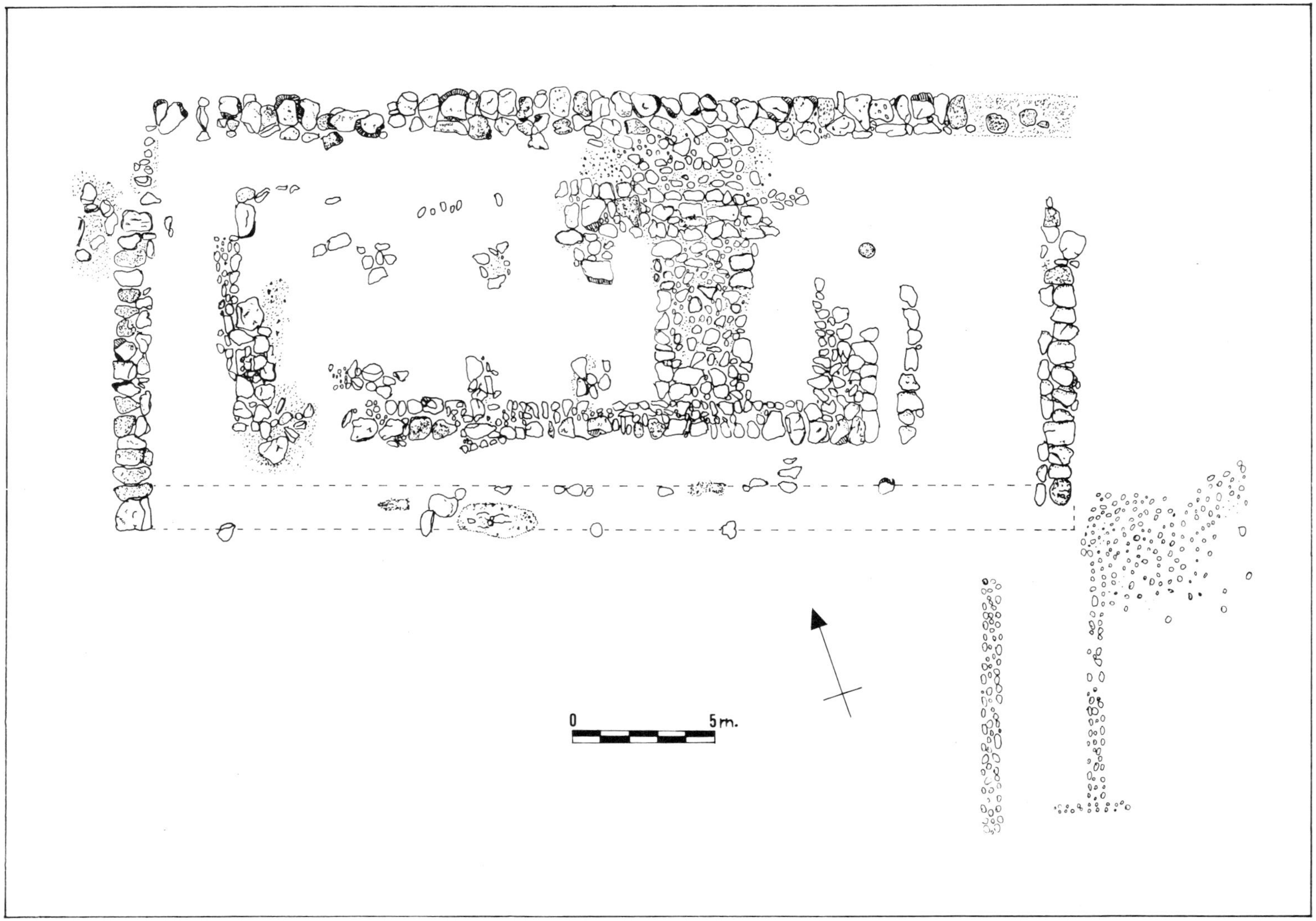

Fig. 2. Policoro, "Archaic Temple", actual-state plan (from Adamesteanu 1985b, fig. 28)

far yielded a clear dating of the monument.[4] A series of trial excavations undertaken in 1980 immediately south of the temple, moreover, revealed the preponderant presence of Late Classical and Hellenistic ceramic and coroplastic material,[5] as previously found in 1970 throughout the area.[6] A dating of the structures in the 4th century B.C. thus becomes more likely.[7]

From the 1970 excavations emerged, but without precise details, 21 small fragments of sima decorated in relief (Pls. 94, 95), today in the Museo della Siritide at Policoro.[8] With all probability, the fragments belong to the same roof.[9] Five of them (**14–18**, Pls. 94:d, e, 95:d, e) are likely part of a lateral sima, whereas a sixth fragment (**19**, Pl. 95:e) appears to belong to a raking sima.[10]

---

[4] For the excavated area, the excavation journal (13 April–26 June 1970) offers no help, lacking plans, drawings, and photographic documentation.

[5] These excavations, carried out to the foundations by Antonio De Siena and Salvatore Bianco, revealed no Archaic material but instead, direct evidence of the Bronze Age. I particularly thank Dr. De Siena for information. For the same excavations, see also, recently, Chiappavento, forthcoming.

[6] Among the non-Archaic material of 1970, it is possible here to mention particularly (with only a few examples cited here for each type): vase fragments in Gnathian style (Inv. 202.004, 202.008, 202.013); fragmentary skyphoi and unguentaria in black paint (Inv. 202.007, 47366); votive terracottas as female heads, with or without polos (Inv. 47427, 47457), or belonging to the so-called Artemis Bendis type (Inv. 47552); children with himation and phiale (Inv. 47432, 47448); a male head of the Dionysos-Hades type (Inv. 47467); pinakes with presumable heroized dead men (Inv. 38765).

[7] At this point the results of the excavations carried out in the same area since 1986 by Perugia University will probably reveal very important information: see Pianu 1991; Pianu, forthcoming.

[8] Photos of the materials on Plates 94 and 95:a, b, d, and e were kindly supplied and authorized by the Archaeological Soprintendenza of Basilicata (photographer N. Arcuti Armento). The numbers for the negatives are as follows: Plate 94:a, Neg. no. 94385; b, Neg. no. 94381; c, Neg. no. 94399; d, Neg. no. 94384; e, Neg. no. 94382; Plate 95:a, Neg. no. 94379; b, Neg. no. 94378; d, Neg. no. 94383; and e, Neg. no. 94380. The photographs on Plates 95:c and f were taken by me.

Besides these fragments, the excavation has produced a greater number of Archaic architectural terracottas (revetment plaques, geison revetments, simas, antefixes) and few Late Classical and Hellenistic antefixes. For some of these terracottas, see Adamesteanu 1980, pp. 87–88, pls. III–VI, VII:1; Rolley 1980, pp. 181, 183, pls. XXVI:1, XXXVI:2; Adamesteanu 1982, p. 307, fig. 7; Orlandini 1983, pp. 336, 335, 402, figs. 324, 332, 422; Rolley 1983, p. 218; Orlandini 1985, p. 109, fig. 58, pl. 47; Olbrich 1986, p. 137, fig. 15; Viola 1990.

[9] The fragments were divided into two different series, one (**1–13**) characterized by the presence of the identical palmette and crown of the vertical plaque, the other (**14–21**) by the presence of the same type of lotus with hanging buds (see below, text). But it is evident that both series belong to the same roof, both for color and quality of clay, which is very similar in all fragments, and for the same measurements registered for the reconstructed decorative motifs (H. palmette and lotus 0.115 m., measurements taken on **1** and **19**). Moreover, only some millimetric variations distinguish, in **3** and **14**, the height of the lower part of the sima, calculated from the top of the horizontal S-motif volutes to the lower plane of the vertical plaque (H. lower part in **3**, 0.048, in **14**, 0.044 m.) At this point, we can add the examination of the same volutes, which below the palmette are always arranged downward, whereas the volutes below the lotus are always disposed upward (see **14, 15, 19, 21**), thus forming a horizontal S-motif as a clear connecting element between the decorative patterns. Finally, it is possible to note that the bead and reel of some fragments of the first series (**1, 2, 4**) are very similar to that of the second series (**18, 20**); on all the fragments in which the profile of the lower part of sima is still visible (**3, 14, 15,** and **19**), the angle between the vertical plaque and the pan tile corresponds closely (see catalogue), on the whole referable to an average of 85 degrees.

[10] That three fragments in particular (**14–16**) belong to a lateral sima is possibly proven by the scale of the acanthus leaf, smaller than in another fragment (**19**), evidence of a device whose aim is to make room

FIG. 3. Policoro, Museo della Siritide, sima reconstruction: (a) profile, (b) decoration

The reconstruction of the profile (Fig. 3:a) suggests a slab *ca.* 0.23 m. high, decorated with an anthemion and bead and reel. The sima is completed at the top by a crowning molding with ovolo, decorated with egg and dart, projecting fillet, small cavetto, and small taenia, from bottom to top. The reconstructed anthemion (Fig. 3:b) shows a palmette with eleven leaves, two of which near the center are bent toward the central leaf (palmette of "exploded" type), and a lotus flower with four petals rising from two acanthus leaves, with a

---

for lion's head waterspouts by reducing the dimensions of the remaining decorative elements (cf. Mertens-Horn 1988, pp. 148–149). Fragment **17** too can belong to a lateral sima because of the clear relationship with **14**, which can be so identified: the execution of the bud stems and their dimensions are exactly the same. For the identification of simas as lateral or raking, the angle between pan tile and vertical plaque is not decisive (on this subject, see also the catalogue). Fragment **18** clearly demonstrates the device for accommodating lion's head spouts mentioned above, since the composition of the lotus flower appears to be deprived of the hanging bud, while the acanthus leaf is raised so that it flanks the entire height of the lion's head waterspout, which was later fixed to the slab. The same expedient is adopted in the raking-sima fragment (**19**), where, however, the elimination of only the bud, not accompanied by the expansion of the acanthus leaf upward (as in **18**), is hypothetically connected with the ornamentation of the final slab on the right of the pediment, probably made for coupling with the following slab belonging to the long sides of the building.

pendant bud on a stem elegantly arranged on each side of the lotus.[11] It is not, however, easy to identify the presumably vegetal motif that flanks the palmette in two fragments (**2** and **5**, Pls. 94:b, e) with three upward "leaves".[12] Lion's head waterspouts, which must have completed the lateral sima, have not survived today but no doubt accompanied the entire slab to the height of the bead and reel (as **18** shows, Pl. 94:e) with a diameter of more than 0.12 m. The slabs, molded with handmade refinishing, were probably joined by means of flanges (as in **5** and **6**, Pl. 94:e), which, however, is not attested in other fragments (as **3** and **11**, Pls. 94:c, 95:c).

Observation of the profile underlines the unusual crowning structure. The presence of the small cavetto, although not very deep, recalls some Western Greek stone simas of a period following the 5th century B.C.[13] The combination of cavetto with ovolo and projecting fillet at the top, however, has no comparisons. In contrast, the superimposition of fillet and cyma decorated with egg and dart recalls some particularly Magna Graecian simas of the 5th century, in which, however, the fillet is a real taenia, higher than here.[14] For a similar fillet, reduced in height and superimposed above the cyma, comparable in some ways is a sima from Vibo Valentia (ancient Hipponium), datable in the second half of the 5th century.[15] The form of the egg and dart has no decisive comparisons. The profile of the ovolo still has a low point of greatest projection, as on some simas of the late 6th century,[16] but it completely lacks a top depth. On the contrary, the shape of the eggs, not very pointed but moderately extended, seems to recall some examples of the first half of the 5th century or even of the end of the preceding century.[17]

[11] The patterns are generally executed regularly. Some slight asymmetries occur, visible, for example, in the drawing of the horizontal S-motif volutes (cf. **3** with **21**) or of the lotus petals (cf. **14** with **18**). On the subject, see Barra Bagnasco 1990, p. 16.

[12] Unlikely is the hypothesis that the apexes of the three "leaves" on each side of the palmette (see **2**) can correspond to the same number of free locks of the mane of two lion's head waterspouts: usually such simas have only one waterspout per slab. When they have two, generally the simas are different in technique and proportion, with a balanced and not so drastically reduced spacing of the spouts, as, on the contrary, in the case of our sima (with only about 0.12 m. distance between the hypothetical spouts): on this point, see some "baldachin simas" from the "Basilica" in Paestum (Mertens-Horn 1988, no. 49, pp. 133–137, 198–199, pls. 59:a, 65:c, d). It is then possible to suggest hypothetically that the three "leaves" can belong to a "centripetal" flame-palmette (cf. for example, Le Roy 1967, series 77, S. 50, p. 152, pl. 58, or Möbius 1968, p. 19 [7:b]). Until some new clarifying fragments of this same sima appear, the connection of such a detail with the already existing palmette and lotus and the eventual new drawing of the anthemion cannot be discussed further here.

[13] Cf. Shoe 1952, pp. 44, 96, pls. V:13, XV:15.

[14] The examples (of terracotta or stone), in particular from Hipponium, Locri Epizephyrii, Croton, and Tarentum, belong mostly to the 5th century B.C., but some of them seem also to belong to the preceding century. See Orsi 1911a, p. 39, fig. 31; Orsi 1911b, p. 109, figs. 88, 89; Orsi 1921, pp. 477–478, fig. 7; Van Buren 1923, pp. 91 (nos. 26–27), 101 (no. 24), 120 (no. 20), figs. 10, 28; Cristofani 1967, pp. 313–314, pl. XCIX; Andreassi 1970, p. 421, pl. LXIX:1; Mertens 1983, pp. 201–202, 206, pls. XXII:a, XXIII:a; Lazzarini 1987 p. 64, fig. on p. 63; Mertens-Horn 1988, pp. 123, 157–158, pls. 53:a, 83:b, 84:b, Encl. 3:r; Barello 1989, pp. 554–556, pl. XXI:2; Barra Bagnasco 1990. The type, in particular those of stone, is also known in Sicily: compare, only as an example, some Selinuntine specimens in Gabrici 1933, cols. 221–222, pls. LIV, LVI, LVII.

[15] Mertens-Horn 1988, no. 79, pp. 160, 206, pl. 81:d; Barello 1989, pp. 551–554, pl. XXI:1.

[16] Cf. Shoe 1952, p. 86.

[17] Compare the eggs of two fragments of Chian fictile basins, datable from the end of the 6th century B.C. to the first half of the 5th century (Simantoni-Bournias 1990, p. 198, pl. 24:b, d). The fragment of a revetment plaque from Histria, datable to about the end of the 6th century, is also somewhat comparable (Zimmermann

The free mixing of the analyzed elements is directly comparable to that free structural composition characteristic of all terracotta roofs of Magna Graecia and particularly connected with a local production area. Confirmation is provided by an unpublished fragment of sima (Pl. 95:f),[18] likewise from the Heraclea area, more precisely from the temenos of a country shrine excavated at the left bank of the Sinni river (Petrulla area),[19] and recently dated between the end of the 5th century and the first half of the 4th century B.C.[20] The fragment reproduces in identical form, although on a smaller scale, the profile and decoration of the observed crown.[21] It can be said, then, that such a structure for a sima is peculiar to the region of Heraclea.

The compositional scheme of the anthemion, with lotus and side buds, appears completely new in the repertory of anthemia represented on Western Greek simas. Vegetal elements of secondary importance (flowers, buds) alongside the lotus are known in some Attic fictile simas and stelai datable from *ca.* 430 B.C., although in none of them are flowers or buds pendant.[22] This last feature is already visible alone on some Attic vases, or vases of Attic style, from the period between the second and third quarter of the 5th century.[23] Thus the anthemion could be a scheme of Attic inspiration since the relations between Heraclea and Attica were active in the last part of the 5th century, after the foundation of the city in 433–432 B.C. by the Panhellenic colony of Thurii, cofounder of Heraclea together with Tarentum.[24] The same scheme is, however, renewed by the presence of some Magna Graecian vegetal motifs such as the palmette, a properly Italiot creation.[25] The type, which appears in ceramics between the end of the 5th and the early 4th century B.C.,[26] is known on some Tarentine and Metapontine antefixes where the motif appears, nevertheless, as a later

---

1990, p. 231, pl. 31:d), as is a fragment of an architectural terracotta from Satyrion, considered to be of the same period (Lo Porto 1964, no. 41, p. 253, fig. 71:5).

[18] Policoro, Museo della Siritide. Inv. no. 43396. H. 0.074 m. L. 0.127 m.; H. eggs 0.023 m., projecting fillet 0.007 m., H. cavetto 0.012–0.018 m., H. taenia 0.006 m. Pinkish orange clay, with composition and slip very similar to that of **1** (see the catalogue). There are a few traces of black on the frames of the egg and dart, and red for the darts.

[19] Bini 1989, pp. 15–16, 19–21, with earlier bibliography.

[20] Bini 1989, p. 20.

[21] It has also the same shape of darts in the egg and dart, a shape that in some fragments (**1, 7–10, 12,** and **13**) can appear more rounded because of the distribution of color. The sima of the fragment from the Petrulla area could probably belong to the pediment of one of the two small aedicules of the temenos.

[22] Compare sima XIX of the Akropolis, datable to about 430 B.C. (Buschor 1929, pp. 40–41, fig. 45, pl. 8), or the later Athenian stele of 394 B.C. (Möbius 1968, pp. 24–25 [9:d]).

[23] I suggest only a few of the numerous possible examples: *CVA, Firenze* 3 [Italy 30], 112:1, 3; 113:1, 3 (460–450 B.C. and 465–460 B.C. respectively); *CVA, Berlin* 3 [Germany 22], 111:5–6 (toward 450 B.C.); *CVA, Altenburg* 2 [Germany 18], 69:5–7 (third quarter of the 5th century). The comparison with the scheme of the sima in question is, however, only good for the manner in which the stems of the vegetal elements are arranged on the cups mentioned.

[24] It is possible to think that the Attic potters' workshop was active in Heraclea between 430 and 420 B.C. and was led by the Policoro Painter. For the Policoro Painter and the grave in Heraclea that took its name from him, see, in particular, Pianu 1989, with earlier bibliography. For the Attic influence on coinage, coroplastics, and ceramics, see briefly Orlandini 1985, p. 109. For the history of Heraclea, see Sartori 1967.

[25] So recognized already by Jacobsthal 1927, p. 178.

[26] Among the earliest representations, see Trendall and Cambitoglou 1978, no. 24, p. 39, pl. 12:1(b), associated with the Painter of the Birth of Dionysos (end of the 5th century B.C.–385 B.C.); Andreassi 1979, no. 43, pp. 91–94, Lecce Painter (between the first and the second quarter of the 4th century B.C.).

creation than the example on the Policoro sima.[27] The same motif, forming a secondary frieze of palmettes only, occurs, moreover, in a later rendition on a revetment plaque in the Museum of Bari dated to the 3rd century B.C.[28]

As far as the lotus flower is concerned, its shape is already enlarged but still vigorous.[29] It is possible to recall a fictile sima from Tarentum or Metapontum, now in the Getty Museum and dated to the last quarter of the 5th century, for the manner in which the four petals are disposed and enlarged, supported by two acanthus leaves, smooth here as well.[30] The relief, however, is more compact here and the indentation of the acanthus leaves simpler.[31] For the shape of the buds, very simple indeed, only general comparisons are possible, still in an Attic sphere of the beginning of the 4th century[32] but more decidedly in some products of Tarentine taste dated from the first half of the same century.[33] Finally, the bead and reel with globular beads at the top of the anthemion can be considered a regular feature from the Classical period.[34]

In conclusion, the sima of Policoro seems to fall within the limits of a typically local production, still marked, if possible, by some Attic influences of the Classical period but more directly by Tarentine influences.[35] The lack of clear stratigraphical data prevents the formulation of a hypothesis of a well-defined date. In light of the analysis presented here, it is possible, however, to suggest a date that can span the whole 4th century. Considering the relationship of the Policoro sima to the sima fragment from the Petrulla area, perhaps as a hypothesis one can suggest a date within the first half of the same century. At the present state of research, it is not possible to attribute the sima to any specific building; its placement on the "Archaic Temple" roof remains to be discussed.[36]

[27] For some different variants, cf. Laviosa 1954, no. 52, p. 249, pl. LXXVIII:4 (Hellenistic period). Among the Metapontine antefixes, unpublished (it was not possible to supply the inventory numbers here), is preserved a variant, probably earlier than the Tarentine type because of its more balanced proportions, the fuller, less tired and stiff shape of the leaves, and the same base slab, now quite semi-elliptical in the model from Taranto.

[28] Rossi 1983, p. 113, pl. 71.

[29] For the development of the lotus on architectural terracottas in the Late Classical period, see Le Roy 1967, p. 166.

[30] Mertens-Horn 1988, no. 74, pp. 154, 205, pl. 80, Encl. 2:m.

[31] On the contrary, it is important to notice on the Policoro sima the sharp projection of the denticles, or thorns, on the rounded end of the acanthus leaves. For the development of the acanthus in the Late Classical period, see Möbius 1968, p. 90.

[32] See the Athenian stele of 394 B.C. previously mentioned (note 22 above).

[33] Compare the vegetal frieze of a fragmentary silver rhyton from Karagodeuašch (South Russia), probably a Tarentine imitation, 370 B.C.–end of the 4th century (Pfrommer 1982, p. 151, fig. 9); or a couple of elix earrings from a Tarentine grave, ca. 350 B.C. (Schojer 1986, no. 103, pp. 178–179); or the more famous golden diadem from Santa Eufemia, ca. 304–289 B.C. (Lippolis 1986, pp. 112–113). Cf. also a sima from Amphipolis, last quarter of the 4th century (Kaltsas 1985, no. 83, pp. 99, 150, pls. XXVIII, IΣT); or, still, some vases of Lucanian production by the Primato Painter, after 350 B.C. (Trendall 1967, nos. 931, 963, pp. 167, 170, pls. 73:4, 75:5). For the development of the bud in the Late Classical period, see Möbius 1968, p. 91.

[34] Among the Western Greek terracotta simas, one of the first examples of a bead and reel with globular beads is on the horizontal gable sima of the Selinuntine Temple C, recently dated by Mertens-Horn to the last quarter of the 6th century B.C. (Wikander 1986, no. 47, pp. 41–42, figs. 3, 12, with earlier bibliography; Mertens-Horn 1988, pp. 81–82, pl. 18, Encl. 1:b).

[35] Concerning the importance and diffusion of Tarentine artistic influence in Magna Graecia and elsewhere in the 4th and 3rd century B.C., see Orlandini 1983, pp. 481–524.

[36] On this subject, see note 7 above.

## CATALOGUE

Descriptions of the individual elements of each fragment (in profile and decoration) have been given from bottom to top. All dimensions are in meters.

**1.** Sima     Pl. 94:a

Inv. no. 38778.
P.H. 0.183, p.L. 0.156, Th. top horizontal plane 0.062.
Adamesteanu 1980, p. 87, pl. IV:2.

Fabric: pinkish orange clay, with few small inclusions of fired brick and stone. Thick light beige slip on front face.

Preserved: entire vertical plaque with top plane, but broken at bottom, missing pan tile and side ends. Colors well preserved only on the palmette.

Profile: vertical plaque tapering toward the height of bead and reel; ovolo (H. 0.028); small projecting fillet (H. 0.028); shallow cavetto (H. 0.033); small taenia (H. 0.007).

Decoration: palmette of exploded type, with black central leaf and side leaves (five on each side), alternating black and red, on a red triangular heart. Below the palmette, downward-curving volutes of two black horizontal S-motifs, here only partially visible. Bead and reel with globular beads (Diam. 0.012, one painted yellow) and lenticular reels. Egg and dart with light beige eggs in a black frame, with central red lance points; red, moderately pointed darts.

**2.** Sima     Pl. 94:b

Inv. no. 47259.
P.H. 0.153, p.L. 0.215, Th. 0.048–0.042.
Unpublished.

Fabric: similar to **1**.

Preserved: only central portion of vertical plaque. Colors badly preserved.

Profile: vertical plaque tapered as **1**.

Decoration: palmette and bead and reel of the same type as preceding; here the bead and reel has alternating red and yellow beads (Diam. 0.012), black reels. On the left of the plaque, near the palmette, a motif not clearly definable: the apexes of three vertical black leaves(?). The same motif probably recurs on the right also.

**3.** Sima     Pl. 94:c

Inv. no. 47258.
P.H. 0.089, p.L. 0.119, Th. vertical plaque 0.056.
Unpublished.

Fabric: clay similar to **1**. Pinkish yellow slip on front face.

Preserved: left-end side and lower part of vertical plaque, with an undamaged edge. Pan tile broken away. Colors badly preserved.

Profile: pan tile and front face of vertical plaque form an angle of 86 degrees. Edge of left-end side completely flat.

Decoration: half-palmette following the left-side edge of the plaque, here only partially visible; its type is very probably the same as on **1**. Below the half-palmette, the same, but here complete, volute (H. 0.035) of the horizontal S-motif as on **1**.

**4.** Sima     Pl. 94:d

Inv. no. 47257.
P.H. 0.109, p.L. 0.096, Th. 0.053–0.042.
Unpublished.

Fabric: similar to **3**.

Preserved: small portion of right-end side of vertical plaque. Traces of yellow on the only entire bead and of red and black on the first and third leaf respectively.

Profile: similar to **2**.

Decoration: half-palmette, here only partially visible, following the right-side edge of plaque; for its type and that of bead and reel (H. beads 0.013), see **1**.

**5.** Sima     Pl. 94:e

Inv. no. 47249.
P.H. 0.082, p.L. 0.078, Th. 0.047–0.041.
Unpublished.

Fabric: similar to **3**.

Preserved: small portion of left-end side of vertical plaque; back side and left edge splintered. Traces of black on fourth leaf from the left.

Profile: a projecting vertical flange on the left-end side, for fitting in a recess of a contiguous slab.

Decoration: half-palmette, here only partially visible, following the left-side edge and probably of the type on **1**. See here also the unclear vegetal (?) motif of **2**, with the apexes of only two leaves (?).

**6.** Sima     Pl. 94:e

Inv. no. 47252.
P.H. 0.033, p.L. 0.047, Th. 0.044–0.042.
Unpublished.

Fabric: similar to **3**.

Preserved: very small portion of left-end side of vertical plaque, with an undamaged edge. Traces of black on third leaf from the left.

Profile: hardly visible tapering of vertical plaque, clearly observed in **1**. A vertical recess, cut as an obtuse angle on the edge of the left-end side, for fitting in of the flange on a contiguous slab.

Decoration: half-palmette, here partially visible, following the left-side edge of plaque; for its type, see **1**.

**7.** Sima                                                      Pl. 95:a

Inv. no. 38766.
P.H. 0.112, p.L. 0.095, Th. 0.039–0.056.
Unpublished.

Fabric: pinkish beige clay, with many small inclusions of fired brick and few of stone. Pale yellow slip on front face.

Preserved: small portion of top part of vertical plaque. Top plane splintered. Colors well preserved.

Profile: molded crown of vertical plaque, as in **1**, with the same bead and reel (Diam. beads 0.014; H. ovolo 0.029, projecting fillet 0.009, cavetto 0.032, taenia 0.008).

Decoration: as **1** (molded crown). The red lance points painted on eggs of the egg and dart are clearly visible here. All the beads of the bead and reel are yellow.

**8.** Sima                                                      Pl. 95:b

Inv. no. 38767.
P.H. 0.097, p.L. 0.081, Th. 0.037–0.068.
Unpublished.

Fabric: reddish orange clay, with small inclusions of fired brick and few of stone. Pinkish yellow slip on front face.

Preserved: small portion of top part of vertical plaque; back side splintered. Few traces of black on frames of egg and dart and red on darts.

Profile: molded crown of vertical plaque, as in **1**, with the same bead and reel (Diam. beads 0.013; H. ovolo 0.028, projecting fillet 0.009, cavetto 0.033, taenia 0.008).

Decoration: as **1** (molded crown).

**9.** Sima                                                      Pl. 95:c

Inv. no. 47244.
P.H. 0.087, p.L. 0.069, Th. top horizontal plane 0.069.
Unpublished.

Fabric: pinkish orange clay, with small inclusions of fired brick and very few of stone. Light beige slip on front face.

Preserved: small portion of top part of vertical plaque. Taenia entirely splintered. Colors well preserved.

Profile: molded crown of vertical plaque, as in **1** (H. ovolo 0.028, projecting fillet 0.010, cavetto 0.032).

Decoration: as **1** (molded crown).

**10.** Sima                                                     Pl. 95:a

Inv. no. 35468.
P.H. 0.104, p.L. 0.127, Th. 0.042–0.057.
Unpublished.

Fabric: similar to **9**.

Preserved: portion of top part of vertical plaque. Taenia entirely splintered. Colors well preserved on egg and dart.

Profile: molded crown of vertical plaque, as in **1**, with the same bead and reel (Diam. beads 0.01; H. ovolo 0.028, projecting fillet 0.011, cavetto 0.032).

Decoration: as **1** (molded crown).

**11.** Sima                                                     Pl. 95:c

Inv. no. 47247.
P.H. 0.082, p.L. 0.058, Th. 0.040–0.057.
Unpublished.

Fabric: similar to **8**.

Preserved: very small portion of left-end side and top part of vertical plaque with an undamaged edge. Cavetto and taenia largely broken away. Colors badly preserved.

Profile: ovolo (H. 0.028), projecting fillet (H. 0.010), and very short part of cavetto; for the type, see **1**. Edge of left-end side completely flat.

Decoration: as **1** (egg and dart).

**12.** Sima                                                     Pl. 95:b

Inv. no. 47255.
P.H. 0.066, p.L. 0.103, Th. 0.039–0.052.
Unpublished.

Fabric: similar to **8**.

Preserved: small portion of top part of vertical plaque. Cavetto and taenia broken away, back side entirely splintered. Colors badly preserved.

Profile: ovolo (H. 0.029), projecting fillet (H. 0.011) and very short part of cavetto; for the type, see **1**.

Decoration: as **1** (egg and dart).

**13.** Sima                                                     Pl. 95:c

Inv. no. 47256.
P.H. 0.047, p.L. 0.049, Th. 0.012.
Unpublished.

Fabric: similar to **9**.

Preserved: very small splinter of top part of vertical plaque. Colors well preserved.

Profile: ovolo (H. 0.029) and projecting fillet (H. 0.010); for the type, see **1**.

Decoration: one egg and two contiguous darts of that egg and dart observed particularly in **1**.

**14.** Lateral sima             Pl. 95:d

Inv. no. 35471.
P.H. 0.104, p.L. 0.132, Th. 0.062–0.041.
Unpublished.

Fabric: similar to **1**.

Preserved: central and lower part of vertical plaque and very small portion of pan tile. Colors badly preserved.

Profile: pan tile and front face of vertical plaque form an angle of 87 degrees.

Decoration: anthemion, only partially visible, formed by (from left): lotus flower (pistil originally painted red and side petals, two on each side, alternating black and red) rising from two smooth, indented acanthus leaves, originally black, on a downward dropping calyx and the upward curving volutes (only one here visible) of two black horizontal S-motifs; palmette likely of the exploded type as in **1** (see here from left, also the red third and black fourth leaf). A pendant bud, on an upright, originally black stem arising from the volute of a lotus, divides the two described motifs.

**15.** Lateral sima             Pl. 95:e

Inv. no. 47245.
P.H. 0.089, p.L. 0.049, Th. 0.063–0.041.
Unpublished.

Fabric: similar to **1**.

Preserved: small portion of lower part of vertical plaque. Pan tile largely broken away. Traces of black on the volute and stem of the bud.

Profile: pan tile and front face of vertical plaque form an angle of 84 degrees.

Decoration: lotus flower, here barely visible, of the same type and scale observed in **14**. Partially recognizable (from left): fourth petal, second acanthus leaf and volute, stem of the right bud.

**16.** Lateral sima             Pl. 94:d

Inv. no. 47254.
P.H. 0.107, p.L. 0.118, Th. 0.058.
Unpublished.

Fabric: clay similar to **1**. Pinkish yellow slip on front face.

Preserved: portion of central part of vertical plaque. Back side broken away. Few traces of black on stem.

Profile: not specifiable at present.

Decoration: decorative scheme observed in **14** and **15**, identical in elements and scale but here recognizable on the left side. Partially visible (from left): bud, stem, first acanthus leaf, and lotus petal; on the right of bud, see the leaf apex of a presumable palmette, very likely as in **14**.

**17.** Lateral sima             Pl. 94:e

Inv. no. 47246.
P.H. 0.071, p.L. 0.069, Th. 0.051.
Unpublished.

Fabric: similar to **16**.

Preserved: small portion of central part of vertical plaque. Back side broken away. Colors badly preserved.

Profile: not specifiable at present.

Decoration: see **16**. Recognizable here: lower part of bud and of stem painted black, and a small part of horizontal S-motif, also black.

**18.** Lateral sima             Pl. 94:e

Inv. no. 47248.
P.H. 0.102, p.L. 0.078, Th. 0.062.
Unpublished.

Fabric: clay similar to **1**. Pale yellow slip on front face.

Preserved: portion of central part of vertical plaque. Back side largely splintered. The hole for the lion's head waterspout is only partially preserved. Traces of black on lotus petal and acanthus leaf.

Profile: not specifiable at present.

Decoration: on the left of the hole (restored Diam. *ca.* 0.082), an acanthus leaf of the type observed on **14–16**, but extended to the bead and reel (Diam. beads 0.013), of the same type on **1**. The apex of the second lotus petal is hardly visible directly below the bead and reel (cf. lotus on **14**).

**19.** Raking sima             Pl. 95:e

Inv. no. 47250.
P.H. 0.096, p.L. 0.072, Th. vertical plaque 0.046–0.041.
Unpublished.

Fabric: similar to **1**.

Preserved: small portion of lower part of vertical plaque. Pan tile broken away. Traces of black on horizontal S-motif and acanthus leaf.

Profile: pan tile and front face of vertical plaque form an angle of 85 degrees.

Decoration: lotus flower, here partially visible, observed on **14**, although on a larger scale. Recognizable (from left): second acanthus leaf and upward-curving complete volute. The absence of the bud has to be noted here, as well as the S-motif, consequently more raised and less distanced from the acanthus leaf than on **14**, **15**, and **17**.

**20.** Sima           Pl. 94:e

Inv. no. 47251.
P.H. 0.045, p.L. 0.054, Th. 0.046.
Unpublished.

Fabric: similar to **1**.

Preserved: very small portion of upper part of vertical plaque. Back side broken away.

Profile: not specifiable at present.

Decoration: lotus flower, here only partially visible but probably of the same type described in detail in **14**. Recognizable (from left): upper part of pistil and third petal, bead and reel (Diam. beads 0.012) of the type observed on **1**.

**21.** Sima           Pl. 95:e

Inv. no. 47253.
P.H. 0.048, p.L. 0.044, Th. 0.023.
Unpublished.

Fabric: similar to **1**.

Preserved: very small splinter of lower part of vertical plaque. Traces of black and red, respectively, on volutes and calyx.

Profile: not specifiable at present.

Decoration: two upward-curving volutes, as in **14**, **15**, and **19**. Only partially visible, divided by a downward-drooping calyx, more visible here than on **14**.

# BIBLIOGRAPHY

Adamesteanu, D. 1969. "Siris-Heraclea," in *Policoro 1959–1969: dieci anni di autonomia comunale*, Matino, pp. 198–215

———. 1970. "L'attività archeologica in Basilicata," *X AttiTaranto*, pp. 467–485

———. 1970/1971. "Origine e sviluppo di centri abitati in Basilicata," *AttiCItRom* 3, 1970/1971, pp. 115–156

———. 1974. *La Basilicata antica. Storia e monumenti*, Cava dei Tirreni

———. 1976. "Santuari metapontini," in *NFGH*, pp. 151–166

———. 1980. "Siris. Il problema topografico," *XX AttiTaranto*, pp. 61–93

———. 1982. "Siris e Metaponto alla luce delle nuove ricerche archeologiche," *ASAtene* 60, pp. 301–313

———. 1985a. "Heraclea," in *Museo*, pp. 93–102

———. 1985b. "Siris," in *Museo*, pp. 57–64

Adamesteanu, D., and H. Dilthey. 1978. "Siris. Nuovi contributi archeologici," *MEFRA* 90, pp. 515–565

Andreassi, G. 1970. Oral contribution, in *X AttiTaranto*, p. 414–422

———. 1979. *Ceramica italiota a figure rosse della Collezione Chini del Museo Civico di Bassano del Grappa*, Rome

AttiCItRom = *Atti. Centro Studi e Documentazione sull'Italia romana*

AttiTaranto = *Convegno di Studi sulla Magna Grecia*, Naples

Barello, F. 1989. "Resti di architettura greca a Hipponion," *AnnPisa* 19, pp. 535–558

Barra Bagnasco, M. 1990. "Gronde in calcare a testa leonina da Locri Epizefiri," *BdA* 60, pp. 1–24

Bini, M. P. 1989. "Il territorio di Eraclea nel IV e III sec. a.C.," in *Studi su Siris-Eraclea*, pp. 15–21

Buschor, E. 1929. *Die Tondächer der Akropolis*, I, *Simen*, Berlin

Chiappavento, L. Forthcoming. "Lo scavo dell'area del 'Tempio Arcaico' di Eraclea Lucana," in *La Siritide ed il Metapontino*

Cristofani, M. 1967. "Le terrecotte architettoniche provenienti dal santuario di Hera Lacinia a Capocolonne," *ArchCl* 19, pp. 313–319

De Juliis, E. M., ed. 1986. *Gli ori di Taranto in età ellenistica*, 4th ed., Milan

Dinsmoor, W. B. 1950. *The Architecture of Ancient Greece*, 3rd ed., London

Edlund, I. E. M. 1987. *The Gods and the Place: Location and Function of Sanctuaries in the Countryside of Etruria and Magna Graecia (700–400 B.C.)*, Stockholm

Fiorentini, G. 1985. "Sacelli sull'acropoli di Gela e a Monte Adranone nella valle del Belice," in *Il tempio greco in Sicilia. Architettura e culti* (*CronCatania* 16, 1977), Istituto di Archeologia dell'Università di Catania, ed., Palermo, pp. 105–114

Gabrici, E. 1933. "Per la storia dell'architettura dorica in Sicilia," *MonAnt* 35, cols. 137–250

Gullini, G. 1983. "Urbanistica e architettura," in *Megale Hellas*, pp. 207–328

*Hesperia* 59 = *Proceedings of the First International Conference on Archaic Greek Architectural Terracottas, Athens, December 2–4, 1988* (*Hesperia* 59, 1990), N. A. Winter, ed.

Jacobsthal, P. 1927. *Ornamente griechischer Vasen*, Berlin

Kaltsas, N. 1985. Πήλινες διακοσμημένες κεραμώσεις από τη Μακεδόνια, Athens

Laviosa, C. 1954. "Le antefisse fittili di Taranto," *ArchCl* 6, pp. 217–250

Lazzarini, M. L. 1987. "I santuari di Atena e di Casa Marafioti," in *Il Museo Nazionale di Reggio Calabria*, E. Lattanzi, ed., Rome/Reggio Calabria, pp. 62–64

Le Roy, Ch. 1967. *Les terres cuites architecturales* (*Fouilles de Delphes* II), Paris

Lippolis, E. 1986. "Diademi," in De Juliis 1986, pp. 111–125

Lo Porto, F. G. 1964. "Satyrion (Taranto). Scavi e ricerche nel luogo del più antico insediamento laconico in Puglia," *NSc* 18, pp. 177–279

*Megale Hellas* = *Megale Hellas. Storia e civiltà della Magna Grecia*, G. Pugliese Carratelli, ed., Milan 1983

Mertens, D. 1973. "L'architettura," *XIII AttiTaranto*, pp. 187–235

———. 1976. "Zur achaischen Architectur der achäischen Kolonien in Unteritalien," in *NFGH*, pp. 167–196

———. 1980a. "Parallelismi strutturali nell'architettura della Magna Grecia e dell'Italia centrale in età arcaica," in *Attività archeologica in Basilicata 1964–1977. Scritti in onore di Dinu Adamesteanu*, E. Lattanzi and M. Padula, eds., Matera, pp. 37–82

———. 1980b. "Rapporto preliminare sui lavori eseguiti dall'Istituto Archeologico Germanico di Roma nell'area del santuario urbano di Metaponto fino all'anno 1972," in *Metaponto* I (*NSc* 29, Supplement), D. Adamesteanu, D. Mertens, and F. D'Andria, eds., Rome 1975 [1980], pp. 313–353

———. 1981. "Per l'urbanistica e l'architettura della Magna Grecia," *XXI AttiTaranto*, pp. 97–135

———. 1983. "Aspetti dell'architettura a Crotone," *XXIII AttiTaranto*, pp. 189–228

———. 1990. "Some Principal Features of West Greek Colonial Architecture," in *Greek Colonists and Native Population. Proceedings of the First Australian Congress of Classical Archaeology (Sydney 1985)*, J.-P. Descoeudres, ed., Oxford 1990, pp. 373–383

Mertens-Horn, M. 1988. *Die Löwenkopf-Wasserspeier des griechischen Westens im 6. und 5. Jahrhunderts v. Chr.* (*Mitteilungen des Deutschen Archäologischen Instituts, Römische Abteilungen. Ergänzungsheft* 28), Mainz am Rhein

Möbius, H. 1968. *Die Ornamente der griechischen Grabstelen, klassicher und nachklassischer Zeit*, 2nd ed., Munich

*Museo* = *Il Museo Nazionale della Siritide di Policoro*, S. Bianco and M. Tagliente, eds., Rome/Bari 1985

*NFGH* = *Neue Forschungen in griechischen Heiligtümern (Olympia 1974)*, U. Jantzen, ed., Tübingen 1976

Olbrich, G. 1986. "Friese und Pinakes aus Magna Graecia," *PP* 41, pp. 122–152

*Olynthus* VII = D. M. Robinson, *The Hellenic House* (*Olynthus* VII), Baltimore 1938

Orlandini, P. 1983. "Le arti figurative in Magna Grecia," in *Megale Hellas*, pp. 331–554

———. 1985. "Le arti a Siris ed Heraclea," in *Museo*, pp. 107–112

Orsi, P. 1911a. "Rapporto preliminaire sulla quinta campagna di scavi nelle Calabrie durante l'anno 1910. I. Locri Epizephyrii" (*NSc* Supplement), pp. 3–76

———. 1911b. "Rapporto preliminaire sulla quinta campagna di scavi nelle Calabrie durante l'anno 1910. II. Croton (Prima campagna di scavi al santuario di Hera Lacinia)" (*NSc* Supplement), pp. 77–124

———. 1921. "Monteleone Calabro. Nuove scoperte," *NSc* 18, pp. 473–485

Pfrommer, M. 1982. "Grossgriechischer und mittelitalischer Einfluss in der Rankenornamentik frühhellenistischer Zeit," *JdI* 97, pp. 119–190

Pianu, G. 1989. "Riflessioni sulla c.d. 'Tomba del Pittore di Policoro'," in *Studi su Siris-Eraclea*, pp. 85–94

———. 1991. "Spazi e riti nell'agorà di Eraclea Lucana," in *L'espace sacrificiel dans les civilisations méditerranéennes de l'antiquité (Lyon 1988)*, R. Étienne and M. T. Le Dinahet, eds., Lyon, pp. 201–204

———. Forthcoming. "Lo scavo nella zona del c.d. Tempio Arcaico," in *La Siritide ed il Metapontino*

Rolley, C. 1980. "Siris: le problème artistique," *XX AttiTaranto*, pp. 175–195

———. 1983. Oral contribution, in *Les Cyclades. Matériaux pour une étude de géographie historique (Table ronde réunie à l'Université de Dijon 1982)*, Dijon University, ed., Paris, p. 218

Rossi, F. 1983. "Le terrecotte architettoniche," in *Il Museo Archeologico di Bari*, E. M. De Juliis, ed., Bari, pp. 101–113

Sartori, F. 1967. "Eraclea di Lucania: profilo storico," in *Herakleiastudien (Mitteilungen des Deutschen Archäologischen Instituts, Römische Abteilungen. Ergänzungsheft* 11), B. Neutsch, ed., Heidelberg, pp. 16–95

Schojer, T. 1986. "Orecchini," in De Juliis 1986, pp. 129–192

Shoe, L. T. 1952. *Profiles of Western Greek Mouldings*, Rome

Simantoni-Bournias, E. 1990. "Chian Relief Pottery and Its Relationship to Chian and East Greek Architectural Terracottas," in *Hesperia* 59, pp. 193–200

*La Siritide ed il Metapontino* = *La Siritide ed il Metapontino: storia di due territori coloniali (Policoro 1991)*, Soprintendenza Archeologica of Basilicata, ed., forthcoming

*Studi su Siris-Eraclea* = *Studi su Siris-Eraclea (Archaeologia perusina 8)*, Istituto di Archeologia dell'Università di Perugia, ed., Rome 1989

Torelli, M. 1990. "Prefazione," in *La necropoli meridionale di Eraclea*, I, *Le tombe di secolo IV e II a.C.*, G. Pianu, Rome, pp. 9–12

Trendall, A. D. 1967. *The Red-figured Vases of Lucania, Campania and Sicily*, Oxford

Trendall, A. D., and A. Cambitoglou. 1978. *The Red-figured Vases of Apulia*, I, *Early and Middle Apulian*, Oxford

Van Buren, E. D. 1923. *Archaic Fictile Revetments in Sicily and Magna Graecia*, London

Viola, L. 1990. "Un tetto fittile arcaico da Siris," in M. Mertens-Horn and L. Viola, "Archaische Töndacher westgriechischer Typologie in Delphi und Olympia," in *Hesperia* 59, pp. 249–250

Wikander, Ch. 1986. *Sicilian Architectural Terracottas. A Reappraisal (Acta Instituti Romani Regni Sueciae, 8°, 15)*, Stockholm

Zimmermann, K. 1990. "Archaische Dachterrakotten aus Histria," in *Hesperia* 59, pp. 223–233

LUISA VIOLA

via F. Baracca, n. 10/A
85013 Genzano di Lucania (Potenza)
Italy

PLATE 1

a. Toronè, sima

b. Musée d'Argos, sima C. 27517

c. Euphronios, Munich, Antiken-
sammlungen 8935, détail

d. Delphes, Temple des Alcméonides, sima de rampant (H. Lacoste)

e. Egine, Temple d'Aphaia, sima de rampant
(C. R. Cockerell)

f. Egine, Temple d'Aphaia, chapiteau d'ante (H. Bankel)

Marie-Françoise Billot: Terres cuites architecturales, peintures et mosaïques

PLATE 2

a. Delphes, Trésor des Athéniens, pronaos, décor de l'épicranitis (P. E. Hoff)

b. Delphes, Trésor des Athéniens, cella, décor de l'épicranitis (A. Tournaire)

c. Euphronios, New York, Met. Mus. of Art 11.140.6, détail

d. Athènes, Acropole, sima d'égout, «Kleine, gemalte Palmettensima»

e. Athènes, Acropole, sima de rampant, «Kleine, gemalte Palmettensima»

f. Athènes, Hécatompédon, sima de rampant, Musée de l'Acropole 3948

MARIE-FRANÇOISE BILLOT: TERRES CUITES ARCHITECTURALES, PEINTURES ET MOSAÏQUES

PLATE 3

a. Acropole, sima X/XI, K. 46

b. Acropole, sima XII, K. 71

c. Acropole, sima XIII, K. 76

d. Acropole, sima XV, K. 84

e. Acropole, sima XIX, K. 91

f. Athènes, rues Apellou, Eupolidos et Lycourgou, sima

g. Acropole, sima XVII, K. 86

h. Acropole, sima XXI, K. 98

i. Acropole, sima XXIII, K. 108

Marie-Françoise Billot: Terres cuites architecturales, peintures et mosaïques

PLATE 4

a. Athènes, Agora, décor d'épicranitis (M. Welker)

b. Athènes, Agora, décor du linteau aux lionnes peintes (Piet de Jong)

c. Athènes, Parthénon, décor de *regula* (A. Paccard)

d. Athènes, Temple de l'Ilissos, décor de l'architrave (J. Stuart)

e. Peintre des Niobides, Musée du Louvre G. 341, détail

f. Parthénon, décor de la sima (A. Paccard)

g. Parthénon, décor de la sima (A. K. Orlandos)

Marie-Françoise Billot: Terres cuites architecturales, peintures et mosaïques

PLATE 5

a. Athènes, Agora, décor de chapiteau d'ante (M. Welker)

b. Delphes, Marmaria, Trésor dorique, assise décorée

c. Athènes, Héphaistéion, décor du geison (A. Paccard)

d. Athènes, Héphaistéion, péristasis, décor du l'épicranitis (E. Schaubert)

e. Sounion, Temple de Poséidon, décor de la sima (A. K. Orlandos)

f. Héraion d'Argos, sima Musée National ΣA 277

g. Athènes, Parthénon, décor de la moulure du larmier rampant (A. Paccard)

Marie-Françoise Billot: Terres cuites architecturales, peintures et mosaïques

PLATE 6

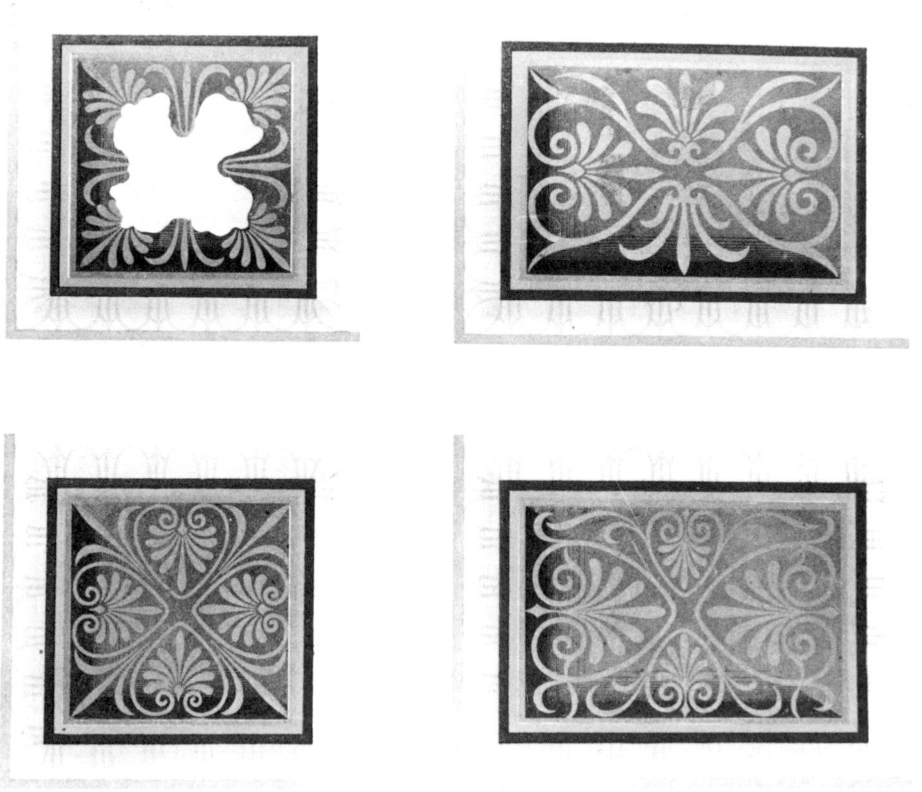

a. Athènes, Propylées, caissons des plafonds (T. I. Willson)

b. Athènes, Parthénon, soffite du geison d'angle Sud-Ouest (A. Paccard)

c. Athènes, Parthénon, décor des caissons A et B (W. B. Dinsmoor, Jr.)

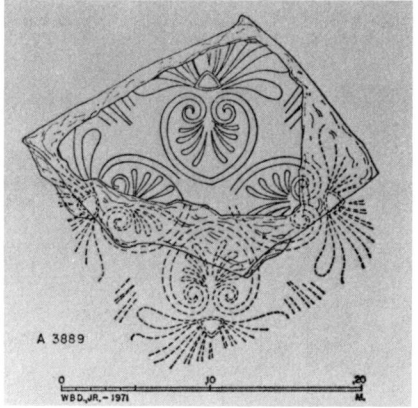

d. Athènes, Parthénon, caisson du pronaos ou de l'opisthodome (W. B. Dinsmoor, Jr.)

Marie-Françoise Billot: Terres cuites architecturales, peintures et mosaïques

PLATE 7

a. Delphes, sima S. 44 (A. Tournaire)

b. Musée d'Argos, sima C. 23719 + C. 23836

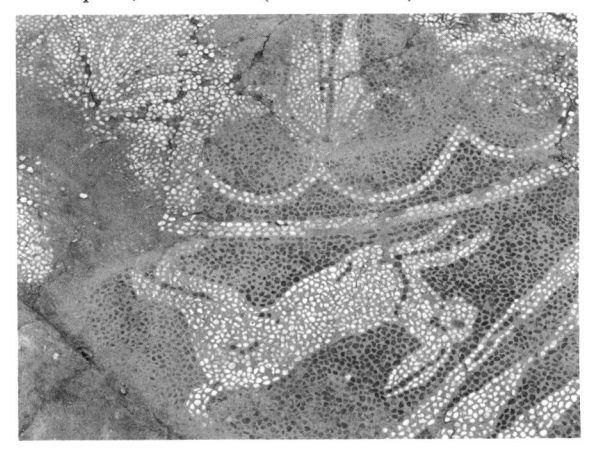

c. Sicyone, mosaïque au gorgonéion, détail

d. Olympie, Temple de Zeus, mosaïque de pronaos, détail d'un angle

e. Corinth, mosaïque du quartier de Théâtre, détail

f. Musée d'Epidaure, sima ME απ 9

g. Sicyone, mosaïque aux centaures, détail d'un angle

MARIE-FRANÇOISE BILLOT: TERRES CUITES ARCHITECTURALES, PEINTURES ET MOSAÏQUES

PLATE 8

a. Olympie, sima d'angle «du Mètrôon», détail

b. Sicyone, mosaïque à décor végétal, détail

c. Sicyone, mosaïque au gorgonéion

d. Corinthe, «Building IV», mosaïque

e. Argos, Théâtre, sima d'égout 73/31.1

Marie-Françoise Billot: Terres cuites architecturales, peintures et mosaïques

PLATE 9

a. FA 125. Combination eaves tile and antefix

b. FA 417. Antefix from kiln wall in Tile Works

c. FS 6. Raking sima

d. FS 428. Raking sima

e. FA 415. Akroterion (?) from kiln wall in Tile Works

f. FA 425. Antefix from cistern in Tile Works

MARY C. ROEBUCK: ARCHITECTURAL TERRACOTTAS FROM CLASSICAL AND HELLENISTIC CORINTH

PLATE 10

a. FA 200. Antefix from Potters' Quarter

b. FS 885. Raking sima from Tile Works

c. FS 900. Raking sima from Asklepieion area

d. FS 876. Raking sima from Tile Works

e. FS 865. Raking sima from kiln wall in Tile Works

MARY C. ROEBUCK: ARCHITECTURAL TERRACOTTAS FROM CLASSICAL AND HELLENISTIC CORINTH

PLATE 11

a. FS 860. Raking sima from Tile Works

b. FS 867. Raking sima from kiln wall in Tile Works

c. FS 877. Raking sima from kiln wall in Tile Works

d. FT 277. Eaves tile from Asklepieion area, showing soffit

MARY C. ROEBUCK: ARCHITECTURAL TERRACOTTAS FROM CLASSICAL AND HELLENISTIC CORINTH

PLATE 12

a. FT 158. Eaves tile from South Stoa area, soffit

b. FT 158. Face

c. FT 168. Eaves tile from Asklepieion area, soffit

d. FT 168. Face

MARY C. ROEBUCK: ARCHITECTURAL TERRACOTTAS FROM CLASSICAL AND HELLENISTIC CORINTH

PLATE 13

c. FT 875. Raking sima from kiln wall in Tile Works

e. FT 170. Eaves tile from kiln wall in Tile Works, showing soffit

d. FS 871. Raking sima from kiln wall in Tile Works

a. FT 156. Eaves tile from Well IV in South Stoa, soffit

b. FT 156. Face

MARY C. ROEBUCK: ARCHITECTURAL TERRACOTTAS FROM CLASSICAL AND HELLENISTIC CORINTH

PLATE 14

a. FA 414. Antefix from kiln wall in Tile Works

b. FS 440. Antefix fragment from Asklepieion area

c. FS 1077. Lateral sima or molding from kiln wall in Tile Works

d. FS 105 + FS 1047. Lateral sima, side section and center spout (right)

e. FS 776. Lateral sima, side section

MARY C. ROEBUCK: ARCHITECTURAL TERRACOTTAS FROM CLASSICAL AND HELLENISTIC CORINTH

PLATE 15

a. FM 38. Finial from kiln wall in Tile Works, side A

b. FM 38. Side B

MARY C. ROEBUCK: ARCHITECTURAL TERRACOTTAS FROM CLASSICAL AND HELLENISTIC CORINTH

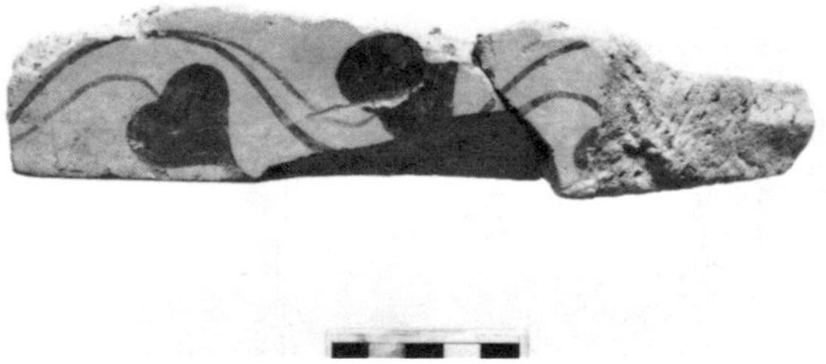

PLATE 16

a. FT 172. Eaves tile from Well A in Tile Works, face

b. FT 172. Soffit

c. FM 27. Corner piece from sima or molding

d. FA 423. Antefix from Tile Works

e. South Stoa raking sima

MARY C. ROEBUCK: ARCHITECTURAL TERRACOTTAS FROM CLASSICAL AND HELLENISTIC CORINTH

PLATE 17

a. South Stoa lateral sima with antefix

b. FR 62 (left), FR 65 (right). South Stoa ridge palmettes from original roof

c. FR 66 (left), FR 68 (right). South Stoa ridge palmettes, Hellenistic replacements

MARY C. ROEBUCK: ARCHITECTURAL TERRACOTTAS FROM CLASSICAL AND HELLENISTIC CORINTH

PLATE 18

a. FS 867b. Raking sima from Tile Works

b. FS 442. Raking sima, probably from Temple of Asklepios

c. FA 184. Lower part of antefix from Temple of Asklepios

d. FA 434. Palmette of antefix from Temple of Asklepios

e. FS 433. Lateral sima, probably from Temple of Asklepios

f. FS 10. Raking sima

MARY C. ROEBUCK: ARCHITECTURAL TERRACOTTAS FROM CLASSICAL AND HELLENISTIC CORINTH

PLATE 19

a. FS 382. Hellenistic corner sima from stoa, showing corner

b. FS 382. View of lateral side of corner sima

c. FS 381. Hellenistic lateral sima from Temple of Apollo

d. FS 50. Hellenistic raking sima used with lateral sima FS 381 (above)

e. FR 41 (left), FR 39 (right). Hellenistic ridge palmettes from Temple of Apollo

MARY C. ROEBUCK: ARCHITECTURAL TERRACOTTAS FROM CLASSICAL AND HELLENISTIC CORINTH

PLATE 20

a. Pentagonal antefix IT 160 (**1**)

b. Pentagonal antefix IT 20 (**3**)

c. Cavetto raking sima IA 663 (**4**)

d. Eaves tile IA 4063 (**6**)

e. Raking sima IA 689 (**7**)

f. Face and soffit of eaves tile IA 687 (**8**)

g. Raking sima IT 173 (**9**)

F. P. Hemans: Greek Architectural Terracottas from the Sanctuary of Poseidon

PLATE 21

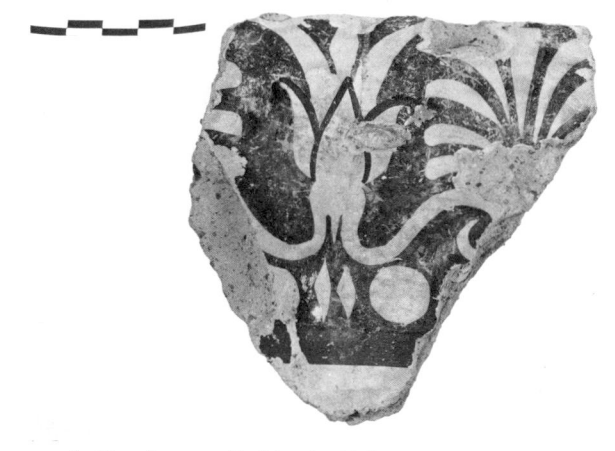

a. Palmette antefix IA 3094 (**12**)

b. Face and soffit of eaves tile IA 704 (**13**)

c. Soffit of eaves tile IA 705 (**14**)

d. Raking sima IA 707 (**15**)

e. Raking sima IA 4040/4041 (**16**)

F. P. Hemans: Greek Architectural Terracottas from the Sanctuary of Poseidon

PLATE 22

a. Palmette antefix IT 168/234 (**17**)

b. Ridge palmette IT 269/278 (**18**)

c. Eaves tile IT 729 (**19**)

d. Palmette antefix IA 4033 (**20**)

e. Eaves tile IA 662 (**21**)

f. Raking sima IA 4071/4080 (**22**)

F. P. Hemans: Greek Architectural Terracottas from the Sanctuary of Poseidon

PLATE 23

a. General view of the *apodyterion* from the west

b. Laconian pan tile, AT 316, upper surface

c. Laconian pan tile, AT 316, lower surface

STEPHEN G. MILLER: SOSIKLES AND THE FOURTH-CENTURY BUILDING PROGRAM

PLATE 24

a. Stamp Type 1a, AT 324

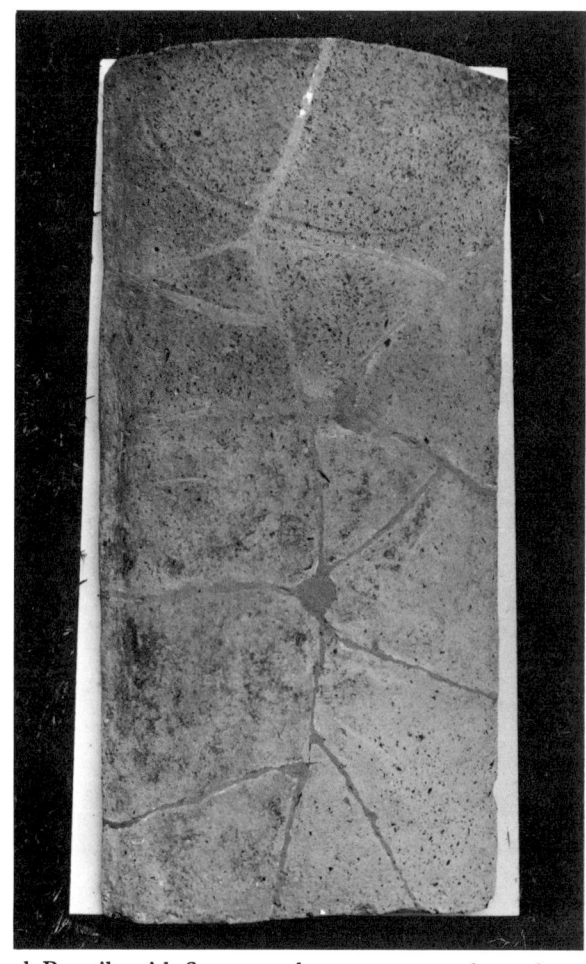

b. Stamp Type 1b, AT 279

c. Stamp Type 2, AT 284

d. Pan tile with finger-made groove on undersurface, AT 314

e. Pan tile with cat's paw imprint, AT 403

STEPHEN G. MILLER: SOSIKLES AND THE FOURTH-CENTURY BUILDING PROGRAM

PLATE 25

a. Fragment of *damosios* stamp, AT 258

b. Fragments of *Nemeiou* stamp, AT 174 and AT 66

c. Fragment of *Nem—* stamp, AT 178

d. Fragment of uninventoried tile from the Argive Heraion, now in the National Archaeological Museum in Athens

STEPHEN G. MILLER: SOSIKLES AND THE FOURTH-CENTURY BUILDING PROGRAM

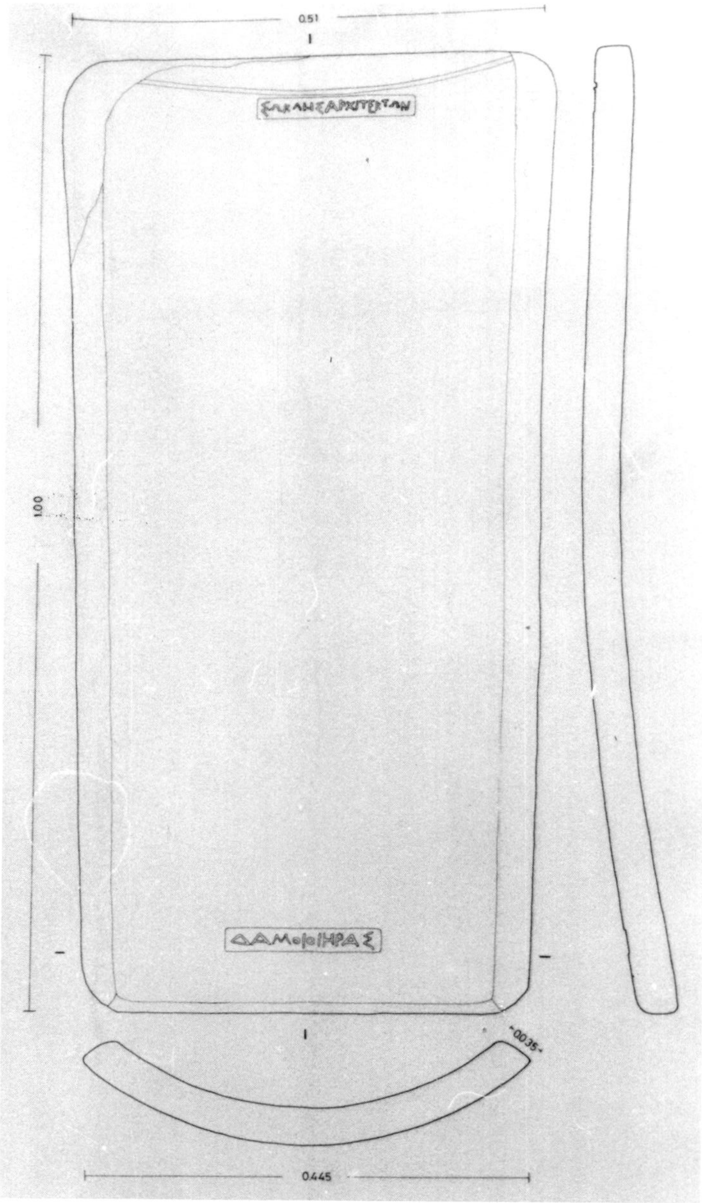

PLATE 26

a. Drawing of NM 10736

b. Photograph of NM 10736

STEPHEN G. MILLER: SOSIKLES AND THE FOURTH-CENTURY BUILDING PROGRAM

PLATE 27

a. Stamps of NM 10736

b. Detail of upper stamp of NM 10736

c. Detail of lower stamp of NM 10736

Stephen G. Miller: Sosikles and the Fourth-Century Building Program

PLATE 28

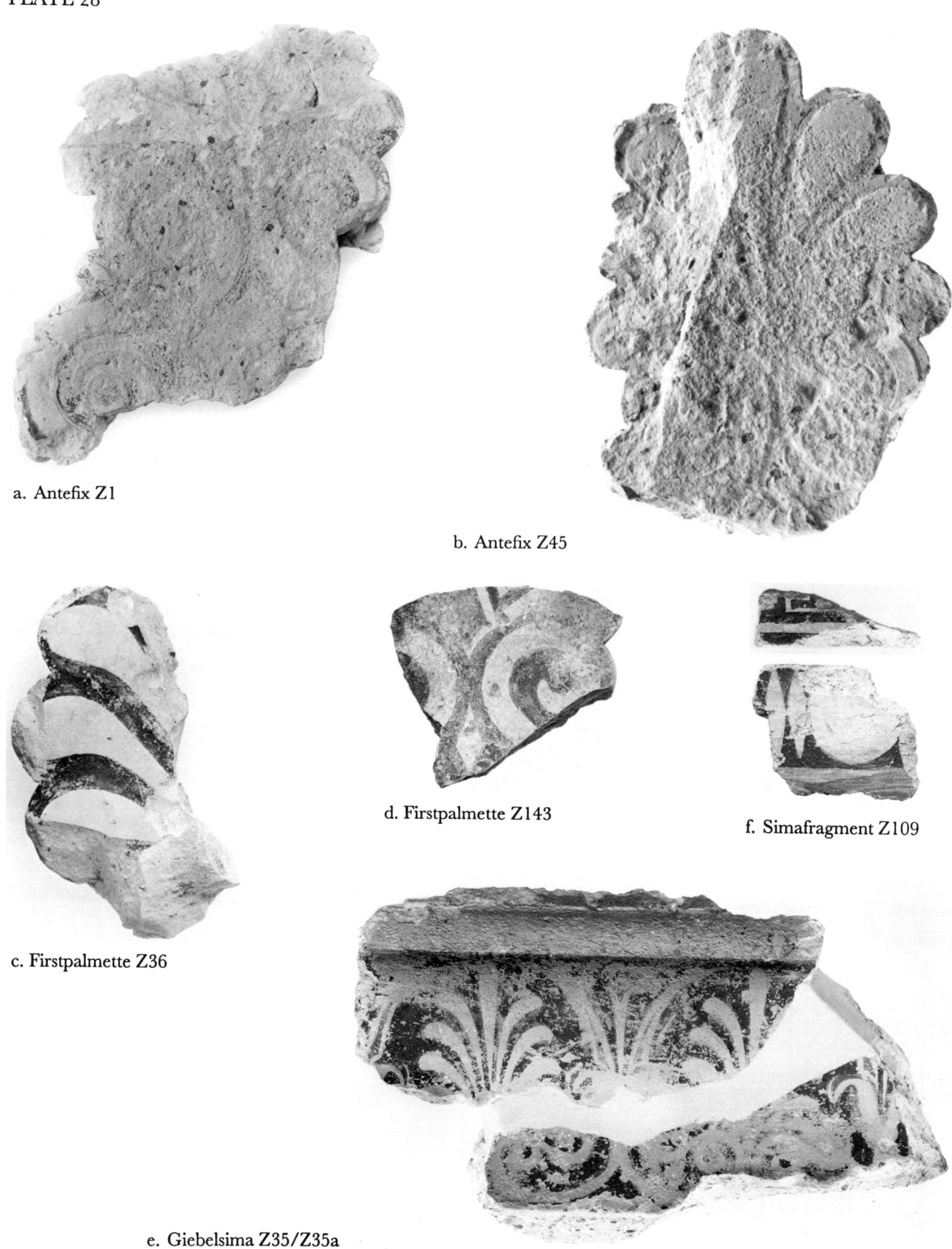

a. Antefix Z1

b. Antefix Z45

c. Firstpalmette Z36

d. Firstpalmette Z143

f. Simafragment Z109

e. Giebelsima Z35/Z35a

KLAUS HOFFELNER: DIE DACHTERRAKOTTEN DES ARTEMISTEMPELS

PLATE 29

a. Giebelsima Z19

b. Giebelsima Z139

c. Traufziegel Z121

d. Antefix Z18

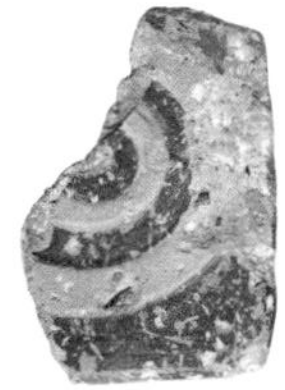

e. Antefix Z29

KLAUS HOFFELNER: DIE DACHTERRAKOTTEN DES ARTEMISTEMPELS

PLATE 30

a. Άνω μισό ακροκεράμου 500 π.Χ.

b. Κάτω μισό ακροκεράμου καλυπτήρα 500 π.Χ.

c. Ακροκέραμος ολόκληρη 500 π.Χ.

CALLIOPI KRYSTALLI-VOTSI: Αρχιτεκτονικές Τερρακότες από την Αρχαία Σικυώνα

PLATE 31

a. Τμήμα αρχαϊκής σίμης

b. Τμήμα σίμης 4ον π.Χ. αιώνα

c. Τμήμα σίμης 4ον π.Χ. αιώνα

d. Τμήμα σίμης 4ον π.Χ. αιώνα

e. Τμήμα σίμης 4ον π.Χ. αιώνα

f. Τμήμα σίμης. Συνανήκει ίσως με το Plate 31:e

CALLIOPI KRYSTALLI-VOTSI: Αρχιτεκτονικές Τερρακότες από την Αρχαία Σικυώνα

PLATE 32

a. Τμήμα σίμης με ανάγλυφη διακόσμηση λεοντοκεφαλή υδρορρόη

b. Το ίδιο από πλάγια γωνία

c. Λεοντοκεφαλή υδρορρόη

d. Τμήμα ωραιότατης λεοντοκεφαλή υδρορρόη (οικόπεδο Καμπάρδη)

CALLIOPI KRYSTALLI-VOTSI: Αρχιτεκτονικές Τερρακότες από την Αρχαία Σικυώνα

PLATE 33

a. Τμήμα σίμης με ανάγλυφη διακόσμηση. Περιοχή ναών

b. Τμήμα σίμης με ανάγλυφη και γραπτή διακόσμηση. Περιοχή ναών

c. Τμήμα σίμης με ανάγλυφη διακόσμηση. Γύρω στο 300–280 π.Χ.

CALLIOPI KRYSTALLI-VOTSI: Αρχιτεκτονικές Τερρακότες από την Αρχαία Σικυώνα

PLATE 34

a. Ακροκέραμος κορυφαία αμφίγραφη

b. Ακροκέραμος κορυφαία αμφίγραφη

c. Ακροκέραμος τύπος Κορίνθου

d. Ακροκέραμος τύπος Επιδαύρου

CALLIOPI KRYSTALLI-VOTSI: Αρχιτεκτονικές Τερρακότες από την Αρχαία Σικυώνα

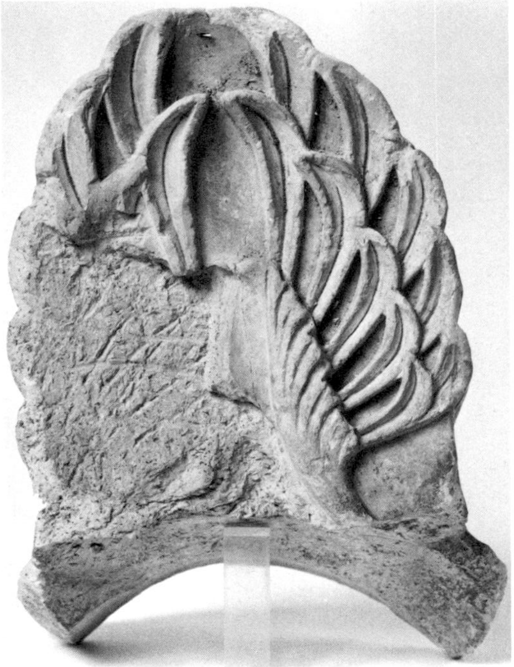

PLATE 35

a. Κορυφαία ακροκέραμος. Θυμίζει επιστέψεις επιτυμβίων στηλών

b. Απλοποιημένος τύπος ακροκεράμου με ανθέμιο

c. Ακροκέραμος με μίσχο έλικες και ανθέμιο που εκφύονται από φύλλα άκανθας

d. Ύστερο τμήμα σίμης

CALLIOPI KRYSTALLI-VOTSI: Αρχιτεκτονικές Τερρακότες από την Αρχαία Σικυώνα

PLATE 36

a. Κάτω επιφάνεια στρωτήρα ηγεμόνα με γραπτή διακόσμηση ανθεμίων

b. Κάτω επιφάνεια στρωτήρα ηγεμόνα

c. Κάτω επιφάνεια στρωτήρα ηγεμόνα

d. Κάτω επιφάνεια στρωτήρα ηγεμόνα φλογωτού ρυθμού

e. Κάτω επιφάνεια στρωτήρα ηγεμόνα φλογωτού ρυθμού

f. Μάζα κακοψημένου πηλού από τον αγρό Χατζηδάκη

CALLIOPI KRYSTALLI-VOTSI: Αρχιτεκτονικές Τερρακότες από την Αρχαία Σικυώνα

PLATE 37

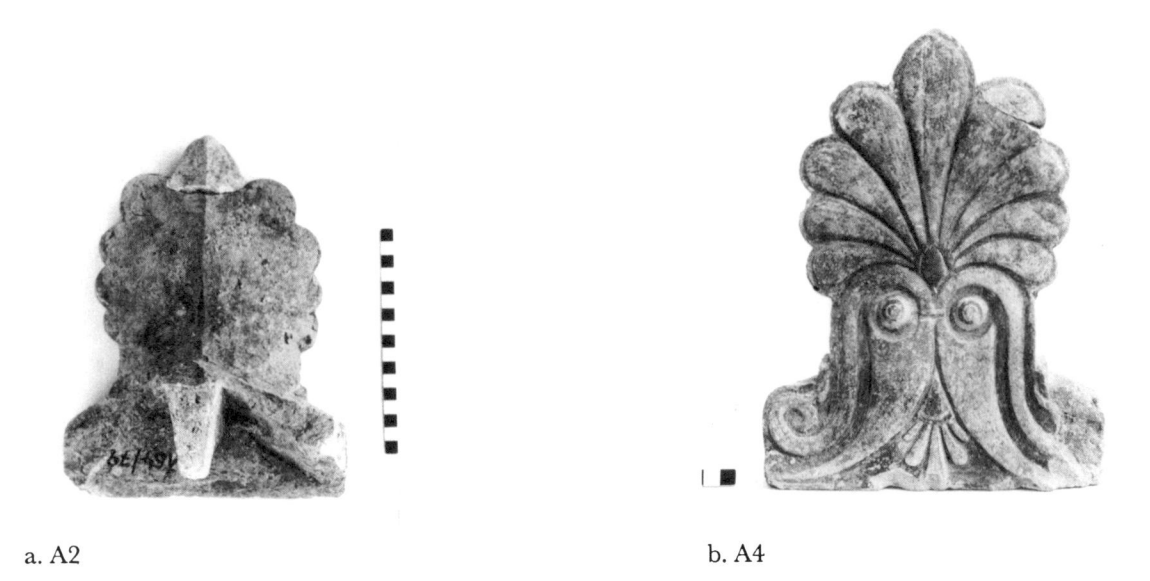

a. A2

b. A4

c. S1

d. A1

e. F1

DORIS GNEISZ: DIE DACHTERRAKOTTEN VON AIGEIRA

PLATE 38

a. A14

b. E 5A

c. E 24/88

d. ATK 21/72

e. ATK 19/72

Doris Gneisz: Die Dachterrakotten von Aigeira

PLATE 39

a. E 6a/88

b. ATK 1988

c. ATK 1986

d. ATK 1987

e. 1/78

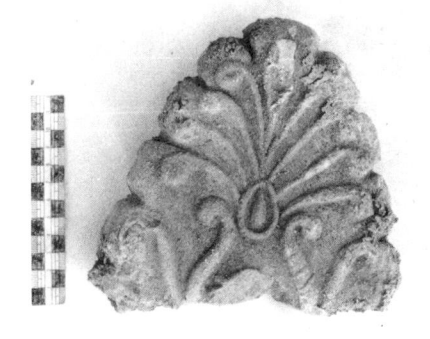

f. ATK 1/72

Doris Gneisz: Die Dachterrakotten von Aigeira

PLATE 40

a. ATK 18/72

b. ATK 11/72

c. ATK 3/77

d. ATK 1985/E

e. Ξ1/81

f. ATK 2/72

Doris Gneisz: Die Dachterrakotten von Aigeira

PLATE 41

a. Giebelsimafragmente SD277 und SD274

b. Traufziegel SD91 und SD103

c. Antefixe SD46 und SD50

Joachim Heiden: Klassische Dächer aus Olympia

PLATE 42

b. Traufziegel 1R8

c. Volute mit Palmette 1R21

a. Rautenziegel SD170

JOACHIM HEIDEN: KLASSISCHE DÄCHER AUS OLYMPIA

PLATE 43

a. Löwenwasserspeier 1R64

b. Gorgo 1R63

c. Giebelsima 10K19

JOACHIM HEIDEN: KLASSISCHE DÄCHER AUS OLYMPIA

PLATE 44

a. Antefix 10K12

b. Antefix 10K5

c. Giebelsima 11K133

JOACHIM HEIDEN: KLASSISCHE DÄCHER AUS OLYMPIA

PLATE 45

a. Traufsima 11K24

b. Traufsima 11K50

JOACHIM HEIDEN: KLASSISCHE DÄCHER AUS OLYMPIA

PLATE 46

a. Tüllenwasserspeier 11K33

b. Rankensima 4R342 und 4R974 und Antefix 4R924

PLATE 47

a. Rankensima 3R3b und 3R3a und Antefix 3R42

b. Rankensima 2R6a und 2R6 und Antefix 2R249

JOACHIM HEIDEN: KLASSISCHE DÄCHER AUS OLYMPIA

PLATE 48

a, b. ΔΑΜΟΣΙΟΣ stamps on Laconian pan and cover tiles (Inv. nos. 155, 156)

c. Circular stamp on Laconian pan tiles (inv. nos. 1481, 1480, 1479)

d. Stone standard of Laconian pan and cover tiles (inv. no. 273)

e. Fragments of Laconian antefix Type 1 with bust of Artemis

PETROS THEMELIS: HELLENISTIC ARCHITECTURAL TERRACOTTAS FROM MESSENE

PLATE 49

a. Laconian antefix Type 2 (inv. no. 1700)

b. East side of the Stadium. Stone seats of the proedria from northwest

c. Fragment of Laconian antefix. Variant of Type 2 (inv. no. 1716)

d. Laconian antefix Type 3 (inv. no. 1721)

e. Laconian antefix Type 4 with Medusa head (inv. no. 96)

f. Fragments of Archaic Laconian acroteria (inv. nos. 1708 [top], 1707 [bottom])

PETROS THEMELIS: HELLENISTIC ARCHITECTURAL TERRACOTTAS FROM MESSENE

PLATE 50

a. Corinthian antefix. Type 1 (inv. no. 3804)

b. Corinthian antefixes Type 2 of Group B (inv. nos. 1412, 3782)

c. Front and underside of sima corresponding to antefix Type 2 (inv. no. 1463)

Petros Themelis: Hellenistic Architectural Terracottas from Messene

PLATE 51

a. Corinthian antefix Type 3 (inv. no. 1612)

b. Fragments of sima Type 3 (inv. nos. 1874, 1872, 1873)

c. Fragments of sima Type 3 (left to right: inv. nos. 1761, 1765, 1447, 1875)

d. Corinthian antefix Type 4 with Artemis bust (inv. no. 1699)

Petros Themelis: Hellenistic Architectural Terracottas from Messene

PLATE 52

a. Two fragments of sima related to antefix Type 4 (inv. nos. 1207, 1832)

b. Fragments of sima related to antefix Type 5 (inv. nos. 3909, 3908)

c. Two Corinthian antefixes of Type 5 (inv. nos. 39, 40)

d. Corinthian antefix Type 6 (inv. no. 1410)

Petros Themelis: Hellenistic Architectural Terracottas from Messene

PLATE 53

a. Antefix Type 7 of Group C and corresponding lateral sima

b. Fragments of raking sima related to antefix Type 7 (inv. nos. 1749, 1746)

c. Fragment of raking sima related to antefix Type 7 (inv. no. 3192)

d. Fragment of raking sima related to antefix Type 7 (inv. no. 1750)

Petros Themelis: Hellenistic Architectural Terracottas from Messene

PLATE 54

a. Corinthian figural capital with winged Eros, detail

b. Corinthian figural capital with winged figure (Nike)

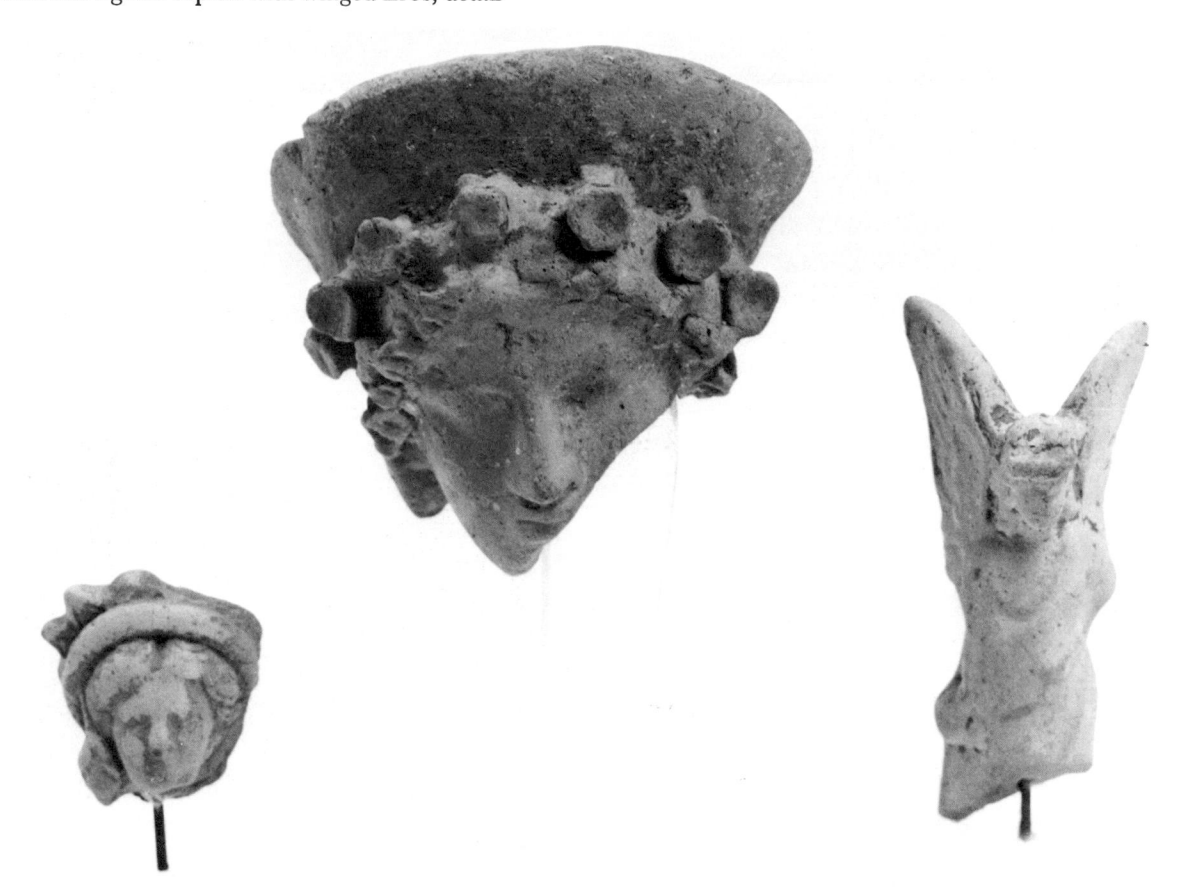

c. Terracotta figurine of winged female figure (lower right) and two heads of Aphrodite

PETROS THEMELIS: HELLENISTIC ARCHITECTURAL TERRACOTTAS FROM MESSENE

PLATE 55

a. Sima fragment (inv. no. 3363) related to antefix Type 8

b. Corinthian antefix Type 8 (inv. no. 1594)

c. Stone antefixes from the temple in the Asklepieion (inv. nos. 635, 634)

Petros Themelis: Hellenistic Architectural Terracottas from Messene

PLATE 56

a. Sima fragments of Group C (inv. nos. 3617, 3618)

b. Sima fragments of Group C (inv. nos. 3008, 1487)

c. Corinthian antefix Type 9, Group D
(inv. no. 1251)

d. Corinthian antefix Type 10 (inv. no. 1723)

Petros Themelis: Hellenistic Architectural Terracottas from Messene

PLATE 57

a. Lorbeerblattziegel (Z 669). Unteransicht und Front

b. Lorbeerblattziegel (Z 669). Unter- und Seitansicht

c. Firstantefixe der beiden klassischen Tempel, links (Z 251) des ersten, rechts (Z 173) des zweiten Daches

GERHILD HÜBNER: DIE KLASSISCHEN TEMPELDÄCHER VON KALAPODI (PHOKIS)

PLATE 58

a. Traufziegel (Z 640, Z 94) des ersten klassischen Temples mit eingesetzten Würfeln. Unteransicht

b. Eingesetzter Würfel (Z 582) mit Resten der Lehmbettung

c. Kalypter (Z 671) des ersten klassischen Daches mit Eisenägel in Bleischalung. Unteransicht

GERHILD HÜBNER: DIE KLASSISCHEN TEMPELDÄCHER VON KALAPODI (PHOKIS)

PLATE 59

a. Fragmente vom Traufrand des zweiten klassischen Daches: links Löwenkopfwasserspeier (Z 260), rechts Standleiste des Hegemon (Z 391), also ohne Volutenplatte

b. Unteransichten der Fragmente (Z 260, Z 391)

c. Kalypter (Z 272) vom First des zweiten klassischen Tempels mit rotem Gittermuster

GERHILD HÜBNER: DIE KLASSISCHEN TEMPELDÄCHER VON KALAPODI (PHOKIS)

PLATE 60

a. Σφράγισμα από την Καστρίτσα Ιωαννίνων

b. Α΄Ι, 1

A. Vlachopoulou-Oikonomou: Τα Σφραγίσματα Κεραμίδων από το Ιερό της Δωδώνης

PLATE 61

a. A′I, 2

b. A′I, 4

A. Vlachopoulou-Oikonomou: Τα Σφραγίσματα Κεραμίδων από το Ιερό της Δωδώνης

PLATE 62

a. A'I, 3

b. B'I, 1

A. Vlachopoulou-Oikonomou: Τα Σφραγίσματα Κεραμίδων από το Ιερό της Δωδώνης

PLATE 63

a. Β΄Ι, 2 (επάνω αριστερά)· Β΄Ι, 4 (επάνω δεξιά)· Β΄Ι, 3 (κάτω αριστερά)· Β΄Ι, 11 (κάτω δεξιά)

b. Β΄Ι, 8 (επάνω αριστερά)· Β΄Ι, 6 (επάνω δεξιά)· Β΄Ι, 7 (κάτω αριστερά)· Β΄Ι, 9 (κάτω δεξιά)

Α. Vlachopoulou-Oikonomou: Τα Σφραγίσματα Κεραμίδων από το Ιερό της Δωδώνης

PLATE 64

a. B′II, 1

b. B′II, 2

A. Vlachopoulou-Oikonomou: Τα Σφραγίσματα Κεραμίδων από το Ιερό της Δωδώνης

PLATE 65

a. Β΄ΙΙΙ, 1 (αριστερά)· Β΄ΙΙΙ, 3 (δεξιά)

b. Β΄ΙΙΙ, 2 (αριστερά)· Β΄ΙΙΙ, 4 (δεξιά)

Α. Vlachopoulou-Oikonomou: Τα Σφραγίσματα Κεραμίδων από το Ιερό της Δωδώνης

PLATE 66

a. B′III, 10

b. B′III, 11

A. Vlachopoulou-Oikonomou: Τα Σφραγίσματα Κεραμίδων από το Ιερό της Δωδώνης

PLATE 67

a. B'III, 13

b. B'III, 18 (αριστερά)· B'III, 19 (δεξιά)

A. Vlachopoulou-Oikonomou: Τα Σφραγίσματα Κεραμίδων από το Ιερό της Δωδώνης

PLATE 68

a. Β΄ΙΙΙ, 24 (αριστερά)· Β΄ΙΙΙ, 27 (μέσον)· Β΄ΙΙΙ, 34 (δεξιά)

b. Β΄ΙΙΙ, 20 (επάνω αριστερά)· Β΄ΙΙΙ, 30 (επάνω δεξιά)· Β΄ΙΙΙ, 37 (κάτω αριστερά)· Β΄ΙΙΙ, 36 (κάτω δεξιά)

Α. Vlachopoulou-Oikonomou: Τα Σφραγίσματα Κεραμίδων από το Ιερό της Δωδώνης

PLATE 69

a. Β΄III, 21 (αριστερά)· Β΄III, 32 (δεξιά)

b. Β΄III, 35 (αριστερά)· Β΄III, 25 (δεξιά)

A. Vlachopoulou-Oikonomou: Τα Σφραγίσματα Κεραμίδων από το Ιερό της Δωδώνης

PLATE 70

a. Γ'I, 1

b. Γ'I, 3

A. Vlachopoulou-Oikonomou: Τα Σφραγίσματα Κεραμίδων από το Ιερό της Δωδώνης

PLATE 71

a. Γ'ΙΙ, 1 (αριστερά)· Γ'ΙΙ, 6 (δεξιά)

b. Γ'ΙΙ, 5

A. Vlachopoulou-Oikonomou: Τα Σφραγίσματα Κεραμίδων από το Ιερό της Δωδώνης

PLATE 72

a. Γ'ΙΙ, 2 (αριστερά)· Γ'ΙΙ, 4 (μέσον)· Γ'ΙΙ, 3 (δεξιά)

b. Γ'ΙΙΙ, 3 (αριστερά)· Γ'ΙΙΙ, 1 (μέσον)· Γ'ΙΙΙ, 2 (δεξιά)

A. Vlachopoulou-Oikonomou: Τα Σφραγίσματα Κεραμίδων από το Ιερό της Δωδώνης

PLATE 73

a. Γ'IV, 1

b. Γ'IV, 3

A. Vlachopoulou-Oikonomou: Τα Σφραγίσματα Κεραμίδων από το Ιερό της Δωδώνης

PLATE 74

a. Γ'V, 12 (επάνω)· Γ'V, 13 (κάτω αριστερά)· Γ'V, 16 (κάτω μέσον)· Γ'V, 22 (κάτω δεξιά)

b. Γ'V, 8 (επάνω)· Γ'V, 10 (κάτω)

A. Vlachopoulou-Oikonomou: Τα Σφραγίσματα Κεραμίδων από το Ιερό της Δωδώνης

PLATE 75

a. Γ'V, 5 (αριστερά)· Γ'V, 15 (δεξιά)

b. Γ'V, 18 (επάνω αριστερά)· Γ'V, 14 (επάνω δεξιά)· Γ'V, 4 (κάτω)

A. Vlachopoulou-Oikonomou: Τα Σφραγίσματα Κεραμίδων από το Ιερό της Δωδώνης

PLATE 76

a. Γ'V, 11 (επάνω αριστερά)· Γ'V, 28 (επάνω δεξιά)· Γ'V, 24 (κάτω αριστερά)· Γ'V, 31 (κάτω δεξιά)

b. Ενσφράγιστη κεραμίδα από την Κασσώπη Πρέβεζας

A. Vlachopoulou-Oikonomou: Τα Σφραγίσματα Κεραμίδων από το Ιερό της Δωδώνης

PLATE 77

Antefixes from Antigoneia: Groups 1 and 2

DHIMOSTEN BUDINA: ARCHITECTURAL TERRACOTTAS FROM THE TOWNS OF KAONIA

PLATE 78

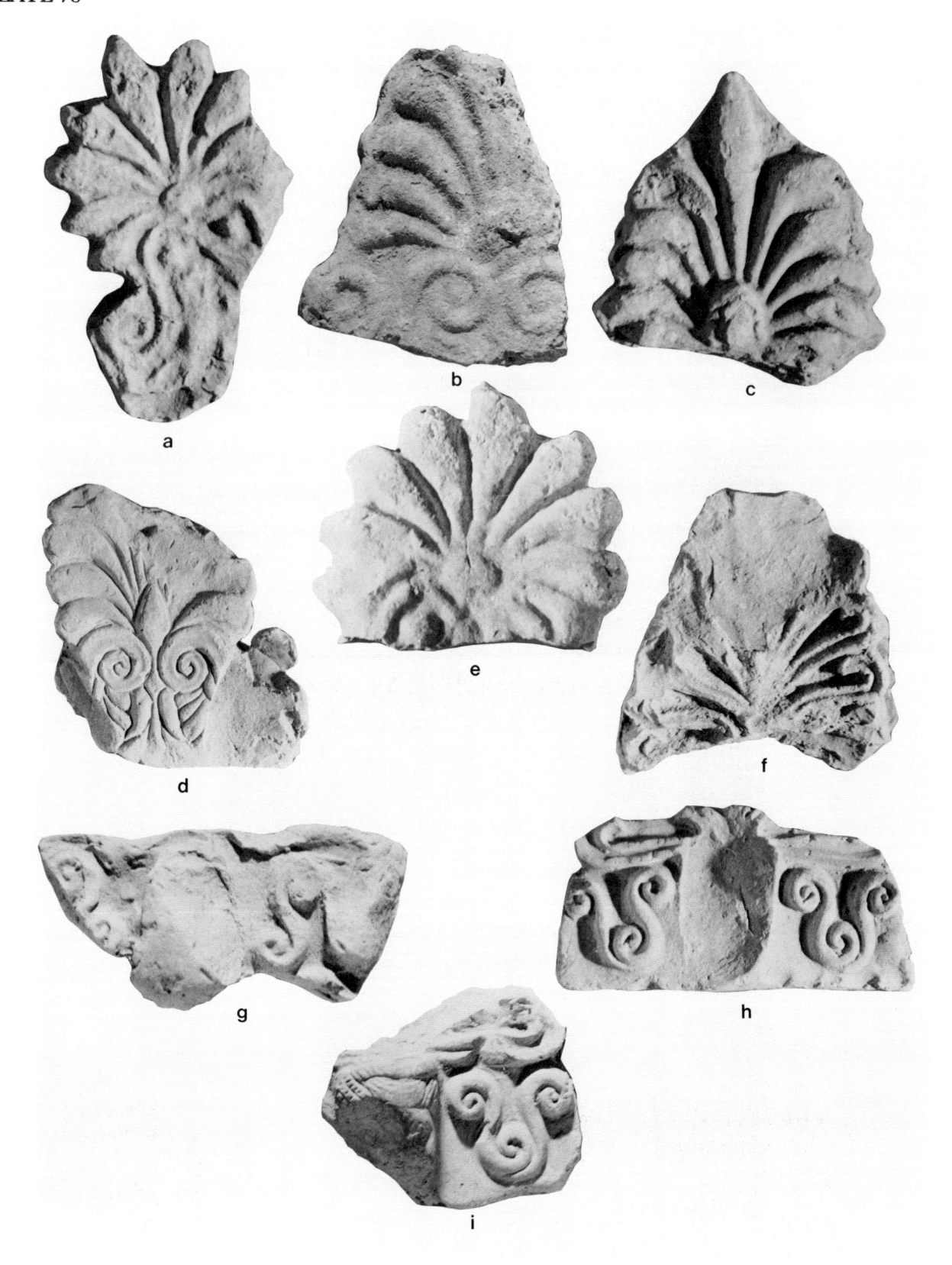

a

b

c

d

e

f

g

h

i

Antefixes from Buthrot

DHIMOSTEN BUDINA: ARCHITECTURAL TERRACOTTAS FROM THE TOWNS OF KAONIA

PLATE 79

a. **15**. Seitenansicht links

b. **15**. Front mit Reliefmäander

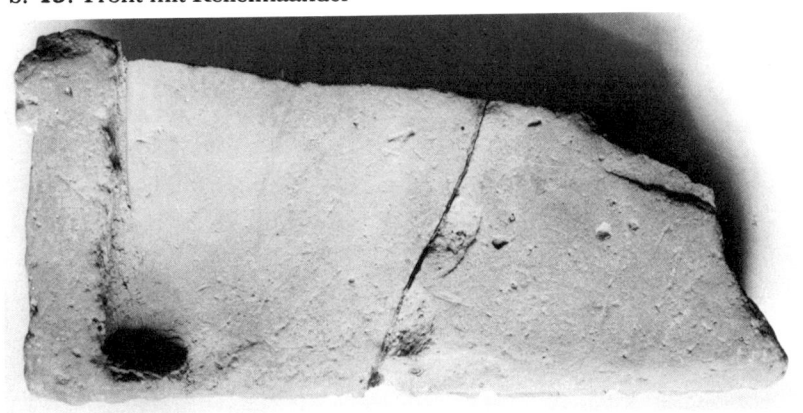

c. **15**. Aufsicht

d. **8**. Front

e. **9**. Front

KONRAD ZIMMERMANN: TRAUFZIEGEL MIT RELIEFMÄANDER AUS DEM SCHWARZMEERGEBIET

PLATE 80

a. Ziegelfragment Inv. P 752

b. Traufziegel Inv. P 717

c. Traufziegel Inv. P 718

VOLKER KÄSTNER: DACHTERRAKOTTEN NACHARCHAISCHER ZEIT AUS PERGAMON

PLATE 81

a. Palmettenantefix Inv. P 712

b. Pentagonalantefix aus dem Asklepieion (ohne Inv. Nr.)

c. Antefix aus Kalkstein

d. Marmorantefix im Marktdepot der Pergamon-Grabung

e. Antefixfragment Inv. P 709

Volker Kästner: Dachterrakotten nacharchaischer Zeit aus Pergamon

PLATE 82

a. Marmorantefix aus dem Asklepieion

b. Antefixfragment Inv. P 710

c. Antefixfragment aus dem Asklepieion (T 59/82)

d. Firstpalmette (nach alter DAI—Aufnahme)

VOLKER KÄSTNER: DACHTERRAKOTTEN NACHARCHAISCHER ZEIT AUS PERGAMON

PLATE 83

a. Antefixfragment aus dem Arsenalbezirk

b. Antefixfragmente Inv. P 711 und P 720

c. Antefixfragment (Antikensammlung ohne Inv. Nr.)

d. Marmorantefix von der Altarterrasse

e. Fragmente von Blütenständen aus dem Fundmaterial von der Altarterrasse

VOLKER KÄSTNER: DACHTERRAKOTTEN NACHARCHAISCHER ZEIT AUS PERGAMON

PLATE 84

a. AT 19

b. AT 30

c. AT 17

d. AT 10 (front view)

e. AT 10 (back view)

f. AT 21

Stella Miller: Architectural Terracottas from Ilion

PLATE 85

a. Classical female-head antefix, inv. no. 82-237

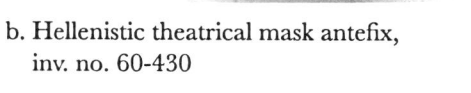

b. Hellenistic theatrical mask antefix, inv. no. 60-430

c. Hellenistic female-head antefix, inv. no. 59-741

d. Classical female-head antefix fragment, inv. no. 60-665

e. Hellenistic Medusa-head antefix, inv. no. 80-401

f. Hellenistic Medusa-head antefix, inv. no. 60-1298

JOHN F. KENFIELD: THE ARCHITECTURAL TERRACOTTAS OF MORGANTINA

PLATE 86

a. Antefissa arcaica a palmetta ritta

b. Antefissa arcaica a palmetta pendula

c. Antefissa classica a testa femminile

d. Antefissa ellenistica a palmetta ritta e bordo lenticolare

GIOVANNA GRECO E MARIA J. STRAZZULLA: LE TERRECOTTE ARCHITETTONICHE DI ELEA-VELIA

PLATE 87

a. Antefissa pentagonale con motivo vegetale

b. Antefissa ad echino con testina e tralci vegetali

GIOVANNA GRECO E MARIA J. STRAZZULLA: LE TERRECOTTE ARCHITETTONICHE DI ELEA-VELIA

PLATE 88

a. Sima con palmette e fiori di loto

b. Sima con palmette alternate tra loro

c. Sima con palmette e tralci di melograno

d. Acroterio con testa di cinghiale

Giovanna Greco e Maria J. Strazzulla: Le terrecotte architettoniche di Elea-Velia

PLATE 89

a. Ansicht von vorne

b. Ansicht von oben

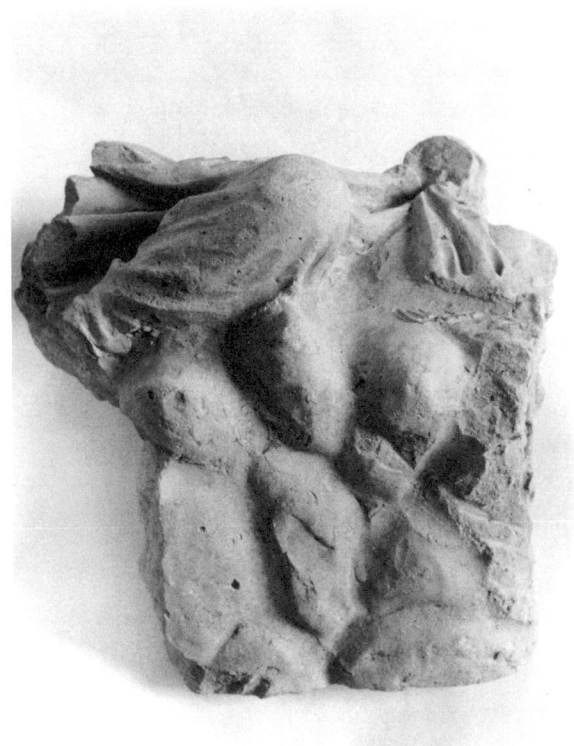

c. Ansicht schräg von unten

d. Ansicht von unten

PETER DANNER: EIN ARCHITEKTONISCHES TERRAKOTTAFRAGMENT AUS REGGIO CALABRIA

PLATE 90

a. Seitenansicht von links

b. Seitenansicht von rechts

c. Schrägansicht von links

d. Schrägansicht von rechts

Peter Danner: Ein architektonisches Terrakottafragment aus Reggio Calabria

PLATE 91

a. B 346

b. B 347

c. B 348

Bernd Brandes-Druba: Einige tarentiner Architekturterrakotten

PLATE 92

a. B 349, Vorderansicht

b. B 349, Rückenansicht

c. B 350

d. B 351

BERND BRANDES-DRUBA: EINIGE TARENTINER ARCHITEKTURTERRAKOTTEN

PLATE 93

a. B 407

b. B 408

c. Fragment. Privatsammlung

BERND BRANDES-DRUBA: EINIGE TARENTINER ARCHITEKTURTERRAKOTTEN

PLATE 94

a. 1

b. 2

c. 3

d. 16, 4

e. 5, 6, 17, 18, 20

Luisa Viola: A Late Classical Sima from Heraclea in Lucania

PLATE 95

c. **9, 11, 13**

f. Policoro, Museo delle Siritide 43396

b. **8, 12**

e. **15, 19, 21**

a. **7, 10**

d. **14**

Luisa Viola: A Late Classical Sima from Heraclea in Lucania